The Scientific Credibility of Freud's Theories and Therapy

THE SCIENTIFIC CREDIBILITY OF FREUD'S THEORIES AND THERAPY

Seymour Fisher
&
Roger P. Greenberg

Basic Books, Inc., Publishers *New York*

To our wives

Rhoda and Vicki

and our children

Eve, Jerid, and Michael

Library of Congress Cataloging in Publication Data

Fisher, Seymour.
The scientific credibility of Freud's theories and therapy.

Bibliography: p. 417
Includes index.
1. Freud, Sigmund, 1856–1939. 2. Psychoanalysis. I. Greenberg, Roger P., joint author. II. Title.
BF173.F85F55 150'.19'52 76-30453
ISBN: 0-465-07385-9

Printed in the United States of America
Designed by Vincent Torre
10 9 8 7 6 5 4 3 2 1

Contents

Acknowledgments

WE HAVE HAD much friendly assistance in the course of writing this book. The requests we made of the library facilities of the Medical School of the State University of New York (Syracuse) have been voracious and unrelenting, but always efficiently handled. A number of our colleagues have read portions of the manuscript and given stimulating advice. We would particularly like to thank Drs. Rhoda Fisher, Marc Hollender, Frank Johnson, Gene Kaplan, and Joseph Masling for their investment of time and energy in our behalf.

Our secretarial assistance has been first-class. We are grateful to Ms. Mary McCargar, Ms. Margaret Snyder, and Ms. Charmaine McKela for their hard work.

Further, we wish to express the good feeling we have about Mr. Erwin Glikes, president and publisher of Basic Books, who was able to see the sense and potential importance of a systematic scientific review of Freud's ideas.

The writing of this book has been an interesting experience to us in terms of our shifting feelings about its main subject, Sigmund Freud. We have, over the last several years, gone through cycles of hostility and admiration—as we have alternately been frustrated by difficulties in translating his ideas into scientific terms, impressed by his wisdom, critical of his defensiveness, and startled by some of his insights. In the end, he has emerged as a very interesting and sharp human being, but like the rest of us not always right.

Preface

SIGMUND FREUD, both as thinker and therapist, has had a remarkable impact on the people of the twentieth century. Aside from the radically new psychotherapeutic procedures that he introduced, he presented a new perspective on human behavior. Freud's concepts have penetrated the very underpinnings of our culture and have become a part of us in far more ways than are usually realized. Not only did he reshape psychiatry, he also set in motion major new currents within formal academic psychology. Furthermore, his ideas have gained an influential hold on historians, sociologists, and political scientists. "Freudian" concepts have also spread with amazing rapidity beyond the formal boundaries of organized disciplines into the thinking of artistic elites around the world. Perhaps most dramatically of all, they are now found firmly implanted in the unexamined beliefs of the average man and woman. Parents have in many cases embarked on radically new ways of raising their children in order to conform to psychoanalytic ideas they have accepted. This has been especially true with reference to toilet training and the transmission of sexual attitudes. Even those who are strongly opposed to psychoanalytic ideas have, in the very forcefulness of their opposition, demonstrated the potency of these ideas. No one can seriously challenge the fact that Freud's theories are now a basic part of our cultural substance. This has all kinds of practical consequences. It influences the ways in which we treat people who develop neurotic and psychotic symptoms. It affects the explanatory models concerning the nature of human behavior that we are offering to our university students. From day to day it regulates the behavior of parents vis-à-vis their children. It even gets into the commercial world, where it offers advertisers seductive new methods for persuading people to buy their products!

Over the years there has been excited debate about the validity of Freud's major formulations. Volumes of dispute are in public records. All conceivable forms of attack have been launched against Freud. He has been accused of everything from immorality to unscientific dilettantism. Much of the disagreement about him has been phrased emotionally. Attempts at factual evaluation are far outweighed by passionate discourses. Strangely, it has been rare to ask whether this or that Freudian model can stand up to the test of what is scientifically known. Freud and his colleagues bear a fair part of the responsibility for this state of affairs. They were shocked by the storm of criticism they initially evoked and were defensively driven to take the position that a true test of psychoanalytic ideas can be made only by those who practice psychoanalysis.[1] One psychologist, who wrote to Freud to cheer him with the news that he had been able to find scientific laboratory support for one of his major ideas, was chagrined to receive in return a hostile letter informing him that psychoanalysis did not need outside validation (Mackinnon and Dukes 1962). Freud had apparently become so fed up with "alien" onslaught that he could not open the door to any "facts" besides those personally under his control. This extreme position on his part was obviously divergent from his own good sense and scientific background. But it could be blamed as much on the vehemence of his opponents as on him.

We think the time has come for a calm, dispassionate look at the validity of Freud's theories. We have written this book in order to evaluate how well these theories stand up to the test of the available scientific literature. In poring over the flow of publications from psychiatry, psychology, anthropology, and other disciplines, it became apparent to us that a large mass of facts that relate to Freud's perspectives was accumulating. We set ourselves the task of gathering these facts and classifying and weighing them. Finally, we tried to integrate them and assess what they had to say about the soundness of various Freudian structures. It was our decision to confine our assessments entirely to Freud's constructs, as he stated them. This was logical, first of all, because most scientific studies have actually focused their hypothesis-testing upon Freud's original models. Secondly, the diversity of the secondary elaborations of Freud's ideas is so Babel-like as to defy the derivation of sensible deductions that can be put to empirical test. Finally, there is no evidence that the secondary elaborations were produced in a fashion that would render them superior to the original forms from which they were derived.

We did not attempt to deal with every theory and idea Freud expressed in his long career. Some are simply too vaguely stated to be objectively evaluated. Others have turned out to be of minor importance. We chose to focus on Freud's major propositions and theories, those that obviously continue to have real impact on the behavioral sciences and our culture in general. However, there is one topic we omitted, namely, Freud's general formulations concerning the existence of the unconscious and the role of unconscious motivation. This omission requires special explanation. It was our feeling that the diverse literature in this area has already been well summarized by others (for example, Solley and Murphy 1960, Stewart 1962, Bevan 1964, Stross and Shevrin 1969, D. Rapaport 1950). Further, the existing scientific documentation is such that little doubt remains that persons' perceptions, attitudes, and responses can be influenced by motivations of which they are not consciously aware and which can therefore, in that sense, be labeled as unconscious. Whether unconscious processes function in the pinpointed ways that Freud depicted them is, in our view, probably best tested in the context of examining individual theories in which he assigned defined properties and functions to unconscious variables.

This book should be of interest to diverse groups. It is directed primarily at the scientific community concerned with psychoanalytic concepts and related personality phenomena. But it is also directed at a host of others who have a stake in the validity of Freud's models: persons who are debating whether to enter psychoanalytic treatment, parents who are wondering whether it is wise to use psychoanalytic principles in rearing their children, novelists who inhabit their stories with characters who function according to psychoanalytic dynamics, and myriads of people who have tried to interpret their own behavior through Freud's eyes.

NOTES

1. Ellenberger (1970) has questioned the actual intensity of the opposition Freud encountered. But there can be little question that Freud felt that his ideas initially met with skepticism and hostility. In his supplementary comments to a later edition of the *Interpretation of Dreams* he rather bitterly declared (1938, p. 186):

> "In most of the literature which has appeared since the publication of my own work, the latter has not been mentioned or discussed; it has, of course, received the least attention from the so-called 'research workers on dreams,' who have thus afforded a brilliant example of the aversion to learning anything new so characteristic of the scientist. . . . If there were such a thing in science as the right of revenge, I, in my turn, should be justified in ignoring the literature which has appeared since the publication of this book. The few reviews which have appeared in the scientific journals are so full of misconceptions and lack of comprehension that my only possible answer to my critics would be a request that they should read the book over again —or perhaps merely that they should read it!"

The Scientific Credibility of Freud's Theories and Therapy

Chapter 1

How Can Freud's Ideas Be Sensibly Tested?

FREUD was a man who was obviously concerned with the validity of his ideas. A glance at any of his works quickly reveals his sensitivity to whether his arguments were sufficiently persuasive. He wove mesh upon mesh of logic to close off all possible loopholes. He vigorously anticipated objections and role-played the skepticism of the reader who might find his statements unconvincing. It was important to him to demonstrate that his formulations did not spring fully formed from his own intuitions but were based, rather, on painstaking observations of real people. His presentations are crowded with innumerable clinical details intended to anchor his theoretical assertions. He was quick to criticize older views that he felt did not square with the facts as he knew them. Incidentally, he was scathing in his criticism of religious dogma for setting itself above scientific evidence. We know that at one stage in his career he was deeply motivated to link and even to translate his theoretical models into the apparently greater scientific solidity of neurological and physiological concepts. It was a disappointment to him that he was not able to achieve this brand of solidity. Despite the self-assurance he usually showed in his essays, it is probably true that he was frustrated about the kinds of proof he could muster to bolster his theorizing. In numerous instances in his writings, he feels called upon to remark that he realizes his statements may strain the reader's credulity but then to add that this would not be true if the reader had had the opportunity to share in the observations available to one who practices psychoanalytic therapy. He was concerned that he had not fully conveyed the apparent sense and "fit" he could see in the behavior of his patients. He feared that those who had not personally witnessed psychoanalytic action would react to the things he described as alien and make-believe.

This concern is obviously not uniquely Freud's. Every psychotherapist who spends his day in the privacy of the clinical situation takes in a lot of events which convince him that certain things are true. But when he airs a conclusion publicly, he really has to ask others to take it on faith, since they are rarely in a position to witness or validate the experiences underlying it. The clinician is really in the same position as the novelist who captures a chunk of life in his writings and tells us that certain things are true of the world, but who ultimately can offer as evidence only the fact that "this is the way I experienced it." It is true that one could render the transaction between a therapist and patient into a more objective medium by means of a sound or video tape recording. Even so, one is confronted by interactions in which the unique attributes of the therapist color, to an unknown extent, what is evoked from the patient. So many uncontrolled forces shape what a therapist and a patient communicate to each other that it is a heroic task to get people to agree on a common version of what took place. In any case, Freud did away with the possibility that others could witness a more objective version of what he experienced in his therapy sessions, by adopting the position that conditions of extreme privacy must prevail. He even recommended against taking notes during the therapy hour, feeling that for record-keeping purposes it was sufficient if the analyst wrote down what he could remember after the patient departed. He incorrectly assumed that the distortions in accuracy introduced by such recall after the fact would not be serious. The validity of Freud's concepts has rested directly on the necessarily imperfect accounts that he and his colleagues presented of what occurred in their interchanges with their patients. It should be repeated again that the imperfection does not lie in Freud's approach, as such, but rather in the scientific fragility of observations made in all clinical settings.

It is a premise of psychoanalysis that men's views and attitudes are often affected by irrational motives beyond conscious control. This premise argues that we should be skeptical of what the lone clinician reports to us. Freud, in his concept of the counter-transference, highlighted the vulnerability of the therapist to distorting his transactions with the patient. The therapist may develop feelings about the patient that interfere with accurate perception of his behavior. Even further, the therapist has a background of training and a loyalty to certain theoretical propositions which motivate him to see the patient's behavior in a particular light. He has a stake in being able to see what the patient says or does as fitting certain theoretical expectations. The stake is often very high, so we must expect sizable biases to appear in how the therapist reports the events of therapy. Such biases are pervasive. They are so powerful that they even affect the outcomes of psychological experiments in which great care has been devoted to guarding against the prejudices of the experimenter. Shakow (1960) takes a hard view of the problems faced by analysts in reporting what they witness. He regards them as "handicapped sensorially, memorically, and expressively . . . Put simply, they are limited in how much they can grasp, in how much they can remember of what they do grasp, and in how much and how well they can report even the slight amount they have grasped and remembered." In a similar vein, one analyst who was concerned with the sloppy methods used by many analysts in reporting therapy transactions stated: "I consider it peculiar that analysts who every day deal with the vagaries of memory should trust their own memories in terms of scientific data."

For years the spectacular mind-expanding nature of Freud's announcements really overshadowed the question of their validity. There was no lack of those who criticized their soundness, but there was an ever-increasing interest in simply considering what they implied concerning the nature of man. It was as if a new psychological world had been discovered; people were fascinated with the novelty of its sights, rather than their reality. In this respect, it is interesting that Freud himself acted like an excited sightseer as he tried his hand at applying his theories of unconscious motivation to a succession of new landmarks—dreams, errors, memories, humor, artistic creativity. People were fascinated with his theories. Their very novelty and the unexpected perspectives they provided armored them with a self-evident power of truth. The viewpoint has been taken by some that all theories are evanescent and that their potency lies primarily in the new vistas for research and thought that they provide. In these terms, Freud's models have already proven themselves spectacularly. It is impossible to look into any major journal dealing with research in the area of personality or disturbed psychological functioning without finding important segments of his thought represented. His concepts relating to repression, unconscious motivation, defense mechanisms, and character development are everywhere imprinted. There are, of course, important "schools" of thought that have maintained impermeability to psychoanalytic thought. Paradoxically, by the very rigidity of their resistance they have registered the impact of Freud's view. Overall, it is reasonable to say that Freudian concepts have already achieved the important objectives of opening up new phenomena for study and introducing additional ways of interpreting old issues.

But the time has come to face up squarely to the scientific sparseness of what has generally been offered as support for Freudian formulations. For a half century the official psychoanalytic establishment has been trying to make its way in the world without openly recognizing its scientific weaknesses. It has boldly taken the position that what it chooses to transmit to outsiders about the events in psychoanalytic therapy transactions is sufficient evidence for believing psychoanalytic propositions.

During the developmental phases of Freud's work, such a position might have been defensible. But times have changed. The avoidance of questions of scientific validity has hurt the psychoanalytic enterprise by encouraging dogmatism. Like the neurotic patient who becomes rigid and defensive because he tries to shut out certain aspects of life, psychoanalytic theory has taken on cast-iron qualities in its attempts to deny that the usual rules of science apply to it. A false certainty is displayed in anticipation of inevitable and basically fair inquiries concerning "Where is your evidence?" The fact that the official psychoanalytic establishment has not admitted to any major faults in its theoretical structure for such a long time is a measure of its defensiveness. This would have amused the inner Freud, who not infrequently pressed himself to the conclusion that important aspects of his theories were incorrect and needed revision.[1] It is true that various analysts (for example, Horney, Erikson) have broken away from the established formulations and offered revisions of their own. But even in these instances the alterations have simply amounted to stating, "I think Freud is wrong about such and such issues. I have some new and better ideas to offer. Let me illustrate the superiority of my revisions by describing some cases that I had in treatment." The revisions do not grow out of any systematic testing of what is valid or invalid in Freud's formulations, but instead represent one individual pitting his judgment against Freud's. Without some kind of systematic testing process in which the rules of evidence are made clear, there is no logical way of knowing whether the revised theories are superior to the originals.[2]

The chief way in which psychoanalysts have hurt themselves in not pursuing the scientific testing of their ideas is that they have not been able to rid themselves of that which is defective and to replace it from the reservoir of new data accumulated by the work of the various behavioral science disciplines. What changes have managed to occur have reflected the power status or persuasive fluency of individuals pleading their special views. There has also been an informal and unspoken attrition of concepts. Some of Freud's ideas (for example, phylogenetic transmission of memories, inherited dispositions, death instinct) have for all practical purposes been ejected by the psychoanalytic establishment. This has occurred without explicit testing of their validity or without a direct statement that they would no longer be given serious weight. In other words, the selection of what is to be considered valid or invalid has been left to a process whose nature is vague and really impossible to specify. The arbitrary and also careless orientation of psychoanalysts toward matters of validity has stimulated neighboring disciplines to be skeptical, it has interfered with the recruitment into the analytic fold of inquiring minds interested in "looking for facts," and it has ultimately imparted a static quality to psychoanalytic writings. Instead of leading in the development of new concepts, as was true during the early part of the century, psychoanalysis has entrenched itself behind concepts that it is largely prepared to defend rather than lay on the line for scholarly scrutiny.

Freud and many other analysts seem to believe sincerely that they have no choice but to reject traditional scientific methodology in approaching psychoanalytic issues. They declare that information pertinent to psychoanalytic concepts can be obtained only by the analyst observing the patient on the couch. They do not see how such information can be meaningfully gathered together in the context of formal experiments or other controlled observational situations. At the same time, it is parenthetically interesting to note that on occasion Freud rather proudly mentioned research findings that supported his views. For example, in *The Interpretation of Dreams* he refers to research work by Schrotter that presumably established the validity of dream symbolism. He says at one point with reference to Schrotter's findings: ". . . the sexual symbolism of dreams has already been directly confirmed *by experiment*" (italics added; 1900, p. 384). Actually, it has been popular among analysts (for example, Kubie 1960, Ramzy,[3] 1962, 1963) to assert that each psychoanalytic hour is a miniature controlled experiment in its own right.[4] That is, since the patient is instructed to respond according to a set of rules, and since the analyst remains relatively detached (and also responds according to a set of rules), the events in the analytic hour can presumably be looked at with a sense of controlled objectivity approaching that found in a laboratory set-up.

This, unfortunately, is not so. It has been shown that psychoanalysts (like all psychotherapists) are not detached observers, and that they influence what the patient says and does in all sorts of uncontrolled and even unknown ways. Psychoanalysts who witness the events of an analytic hour (such as in the form of a typescript) have difficulty agreeing in their interpretations of these events (for example, Marmor 1955, Seitz 1966). The typical analytic hour is so complex and so shaped by unplanned-for influences that it does not even approximate the definition of an experimental situation. This is not to deny that the analytic situation is full of rich and provocative events that may very well provide an astute observer with clues concerning the human psyche. But by no stretch of the imagination can it be equated with a controlled experiment. The idea of an experiment carries with it the concept of predictability. Presumably if the psychoanalyst were conducting miniature experiments, hour by hour, he would size up the patient; make specific interpretations to him on the basis of his evaluations; and then, most crucially, predict how the patient would respond to each. The existing findings in the scientific literature do not provide encouragement that analysts are capable of making such predictions. Interestingly, Freud himself was skeptical that the analyst could predict the behavior or fantasies of patients. He felt that psychoanalysis could *reconstruct* the patient's pattern of defenses from events that had already occurred, but that it was not able to plot them in advance.

The doubts raised by experienced analysts who assert that their complex concepts cannot be adequately studied within experimental guidelines because they force too much artificial simplification deserve careful thought. It has often been declared (for example, D. Rapaport 1960) that Freud's etiological models are unique with reference to the kind of psychological world they portray. For example, Freud's principle of overdetermination argues that behavior is determined simultaneously by many overlapping factors and that it is therefore difficult, if not impossible within such a system, to look for causes in the usual conventional sense. Another example in the same vein that is often cited relates to the complexity of how personality defenses are presumably organized. Freud, in describing such defenses, suggests that a wish may variously express itself in direct pursuit of the goal of the wish, or in outright denial of the wish, or even in the defensive pursuit of goals that are the direct opposite of the wish.[5] How, ask many analysts, can you put this brand of complexity into an experimental design? They point out that the typical experiment involves measuring the way in which altering one variable in a situation affects another. They do not see any room in this simplified context for studying the effects of simultaneous multiple determinants, or for testing motivational models in which either one result or its direct opposite can both have the same significance.

In considering these objections, the first issue that needs to be confronted is whether the phenomena studied by Freud are, in fact, so much more complicated than those dealt with by other theorists and researchers.[6] We would argue that they are not. Look at any psychological problem currently under investigation and you will find a great snarl of difficult questions and relationships that do not confine themselves to simple linearities. Take the classic and unending quest to understand the nature of intelligence. It has turned out that intelligence is a complicated mix of both general and specific classes of abilities. To measure these abilities, it has been necessary to develop a whole new testing technology. The intricacy of the manner in which hereditary and socialization experiences interact in shaping intelligence is documented in a thousand publications. Further, we are only beginning to glimpse the multi-layered interactions between intelligence, personality, and social incentives that determine the effectiveness with which an individual applies his intelligence to real-life problems. We have also learned that the correlation between intelligence and creativity is of a different order than we anticipated. In short, intelligence has turned out to be a puzzling composite, a potentiality mediated by multiple variables that interact in far from simple ways. It is doubtful that the issues which confront the person trying to understand the nature of intelligence are one bit simpler than those dealt with in Freudian models.

In the same vein, consider another convenient example of a problem that has attracted a good deal of research interest but only negligible interest from psychoanalytic quarters. Energetic effort has been devoted to understanding the nature of time perception. What determines how fast or slow time seems to move? As scientific information has accumulated, it has become obvious that this question requires highly sophisticated explanatory models. One finds in the psychological literature that perceived time is simultaneously affected by many variables. There is reasonable evidence that the apparent speed of time is influenced by such multiple factors as what activities an individual is involved in during a particular time period, his body temperature, the strength of his need to push on toward goals, his degree of psychological disturbance, his age, whether he is preoccupied with feelings of failure, and the total amount of change occurring in the immediate situation. Various other influential variables could also be listed; work is actively under way to ascertain their relative importance and the manner in which they interact. But what we would like to underscore is that an understanding of time perception calls for the analysis of an array of factors fully as formidable as those involved in Oedipal relationships or the formation of dreams.

Those who struggle to understand psychological problems outside of the psychoanalytic realm encounter puzzles of the same magnitude as did Freud. They have to cope with multiple determinants, curvilinear relationships, shifts in patterns at different developmental stages, feedback effects, and distortions introduced by the position of the observer himself. They have to be aware of, and account for, such intricacies in order to progress in their investigations. The literature is full of examples of areas of research that have patiently moved through successive empirical studies to the construction of elaborate theoretical models.

The complaint of psychoanalysts—that experimental studies cannot do justice to their concepts—reflects a general dissatisfaction theorists often experience when their ideas are translated into operational experimental terms. Even the best experiment typically captures only a part of the vitality and depth of thought embodied in the theory it is testing. Each experiment can usually sample only one limited aspect of the theory; it often requires many overlapping investigations before justice is done to what is being evaluated. The cosmologist cannot but feel that there is a large disparity between what he has to say about the universe and the limited bits of data that astronomers are able to gather in their observations of outer space. The neurophysiologist who constructs an elaborate theoretical model concerning brain function finds that the experimental methods available for studying the brain are relatively primitive. When Einstein formulated his theories, the techniques available in the physics laboratory for studying them were far short of ideal. What is of crucial import in relation to the present discussion is that Einstein did not take the position that his theories were therefore above investigation. Similarly the neurophysiologist does not declare that his concepts of brain functioning cannot reasonably be evaluated and therefore that he will let them stand on their own immanent validity. In actual fact, experimentalists often chip away at a problem, no matter how formidable the obstacles, and eventually come up with information that helps to clarify matters. As we will show, this has already begun to happen in experimental explorations of psychoanalytic ideas. Intersecting rows of studies now offer markers from which to view objectively a number of important Freudian concepts.

It should be stressed, too, that an empirical approach to testing Freudian theory does not mean that one is confined to the context of a classical experimental design. All that is necessary is that there be clear and repeatable bookkeeping about what is being observed. Theories can be checked not only by predicting in a laboratory situation how altering one variable will affect another, but also by looking at whether certain events in complex situations are correlated with, or have a certain regular sequence with respect to, each other. For example, it may be beyond our present means to test Freud's theory that dreams represent unconscious wish fulfillments by directly manipulating the dreaming process itself. But there is no reason why we cannot look to see if, in a representative sample of persons in therapy, the upsurge of certain wishes in their associations is duplicated by an upsurge of dreams in which analogous wishes are expressed. Or, as has been done by a number of anthropologists (W. N. Stephens 1962), there is no reason why the specific kinds of sexual anxieties occurring in a range of cultures may not, as a means of testing Freud's Oedipal model, be correlated with the styles of parent-child relationships in such cultures. We shall later describe a number of studies in the literature that were not done in a laboratory but that do provide solid information concerning the validity of major Freudian ideas.

Overall, the best argument we can muster for scientifically testing Freud's models is the fact that many competent people have already tried their hand at it and discovered new, interesting things. It should be added that their fairly precise quantitative observations are making it possible to speak in terms of the *degree* to which Freud's ideas are valid or not valid, rather than simply deciding whether to be pro or con. One is provided with the means for graded revision instead of gross acceptance or rejection.

The precedent for using information that is not derived from the events of the psychoanalytic session itself to develop new analytic ideas obviously was set by Freud. His formulations diversely drew upon things he found out about himself, readings in the anthropological literature, and published autobiographical material. His theory concerning the dynamics of paranoia was largely built up from the information provided by Schreber (Freud 1911 *a*) in his autobiographical account of his experiences during a long period of schizophrenic disturbance. Whatever Freud may have said from time to time about the need to confine testing of analytic concepts to data issuing from psychoanalytic therapy transactions, the actual fact is that he repeatedly sought verification of his models outside of such transactions.

Objections to the systematic appraisal of Freud's ideas have paradoxically also come from some scientific quarters. There are those who regard his ideas to be so vaguely and unsystematically stated that they cannot be tested in a reasonable fashion. They argue, first of all, that he revised his concepts in so many scattered places that it is difficult to pull all the pieces together. In other words, they feel there is a problem in saying with assurance exactly what Freud finally concluded about specific issues. Secondly, they consider that many of his hypotheses are expressed in a way that makes it possible for almost any kind of experimental finding to be regarded as supportive. A favorite illustration of this view is the paradigm in which the presence of an unconscious conflict is said to be demonstrated if either a particular behavior or its *opposite* occurs. Thus, the existence of anal conflicts in an individual is presumed to be shown either by his being very messy or very neat. A similar paradigm is encountered when an analyst who makes an interpretation to a patient about an unconscious motive declares that the interpretation has accurately hit the mark if the patient responds by declaring that it is true or even if he does the opposite and declares with affect that it is wrong. Note one version of this approach in Freud's discussion of certain interpretations he made to his well-known patient, Dora (Flowerman 1954, p. 427):

"My expectations were by no means disappointed when this explanation of mine was met by Dora with a most emphatic negative. The 'No' uttered by a patient after a repressed thought has been presented to his conscious perception for the first time does no more than register the existence of a repression and its severity; it acts, as it were, as a gauge of the repression's strength." Again, when Freud discusses Dora's response of "I don't know" to a dream interpretation he made, he states that this response is "the regular formula with which she confessed to anything that had been repressed" (p. 427). It is difficult to ascertain from Freud's account of his work with Dora what signs he would have accepted as proof that he was incorrectly interpreting her productions.

Flowerman has offered some striking examples of how Freud could at times formulate an idea in such a sly way that it was truly impossible to test its validity. He describes in detail the defensive manner in which Freud evolved his theory about the role of fantasies of seduction during childhood in the etiology of adult neurosis. Freud started with the proposition that if a child is seduced by a significant adult, this will lead to neurosis as an adult. He held to it from 1896 to 1900. Then he discovered that his patients had fabricated the stories they told him about being seduced as children. He was at first very discouraged by this setback to his theory, but then arrived at a reformulation to the effect that the patients' fantasies of being seduced, while not literally true, were psychically real and that "in the world of neuroses psychical reality is the determining factor." Flowerman further describes what Freud did with this idea (p. 420):

> Now it can be seen that this kind of hypothesis becomes somewhat more difficult to verify; nevertheless a 'frequency' count could be taken. If every neurotic patient, without pushing by the therapist, reported such fantasies, they would have to be taken seriously as scientific evidence.
>
> The next stage in Freud's thinking process . . . was to question: Why the fantasies of seduction? . . . To this question he supplied at first the answer that in the absence of actual childhood seduction . . . the 'traumatic' fantasy was *invented* 'to cover the childhood period of auto-erotic sexual activity.' He still clung to the idea that 'the neurosis' necessarily *required* such childhood experiences . . . that if the experiences actually did not happen, then the neurotic individual, requiring them for his neurosis, 'would have to invent them as fantasies.'
>
> Having now still further weakened the hypothesis as a scientific assertion, Freud by his next step reduced it to the realm of unscientific and indeterminate speculation.
>
> Freud asked: '. . . Whence comes the necessity for these fantasies . . . . There can be no doubt about the instinctual sources; but how is it to be explained that the same fantasies are always formed with the same content? I have an answer to this which I know will seem to you very daring—I believe that these *primal* fantasies . . . are a phylogenetic possession. It seems to me quite possible that all that today is narrated in analysis in the form of fantasy, seduction in childhood . . . was in prehistoric periods of the human family a reality; and that the child in its fantasy simply fills out the gaps in its true individual experiences with true prehistoric experiences'. . . .
>
> In the end, Freud only *seemed* to have abandoned the hypothesis of sexual trauma which was not verified; in effect, Freud altered the hypothesis and recast it in unverifiable terms. One cannot verify the hypothesis of phylogenetic possession, even with the best of archeological and anthropological data going back several thousand years.

This is an extreme example of the vagueness that does at times obscure Freud's thinking, but it is hardly representative. Many of his important formulations are cast in a form that can be sensibly tested. This is testified to by the fact that numerous researchers have been able to think of practical experiments to appraise various aspects of what he had to say.

Those who criticize psychoanalysis for its subjectivity and lack of rigor forget that it pioneered in attempts to provide objectifying controls for the therapist-patient interaction. Freud was hyperaware of the distortions that a therapist could introduce as he observed and dealt with a patient. He spelled out ground rules for the analytic session that gave maximum freedom for spontaneity to the patient and limited the interventions of the therapist. He wanted the therapist to be sensitive to the fact that his own personality might import irrationalities into the therapy. He did this in terms of his statements dealing with the concept of countertransference. Indeed, he proposed that all psychoanalysts should have a "personal analysis," which would make them aware of their own areas of conflict and immaturity that might lead to misinterpretations of therapy events. He was well ahead of workers in the other behavioral sciences not only in his understanding of how emotional attitudes can shape the observer's interpretations but also in suggesting practical measures for curbing such attitudes. The current fascination in psychology with the fact that experimenter expectancies can affect research results (R. Rosenthal 1966) was well antedated by Freud's shrewd insights about countertransference phenomena. The analyst in training is constantly scrutinized by his supervisors to determine whether he is responding to his patients on the basis of private motives.

Despite this concern, there are certain aspects of the day-to-day practice of psychoanalysis which have an "undoing" effect. The careful concern about objectivity gets seriously diluted once an analyst is certified to practice on his own. He no longer has to expose his work to evaluation by others. More seriously, with respect to psychoanalysis as a scientific enterprise, he is left free to publish his observations and the conclusions he derives from them without any accompanying calibrating data that would make it possible to determine his accuracy and the degree to which he did curb his subjective biases. This state of affairs can be traced to some extent to the fact that psychoanalysis has remained almost entirely a therapeutic procedure practiced in isolation. The demands of clinical practicality have had more weight than scientific ideals. In the heat of the therapy hour there is little place for objective calibration. Freud himself was well aware of the imbalances within psychoanalysis resulting from its overcommitment to clinical practice.

In the course of his own private work each psychoanalyst gradually becomes aware of how often he is making decisions intuitively and impulsively. He learns that formulating interpretations of patients' behaviors is a mixture of knowledge and art. But further, he becomes aware of the fact that many basic Freudian principles are perpetuated by faith and authority. He hears opinions expressed by other analysts and realizes there is no way to put them to the test by means of a generally agreed-upon methodology. As Glover (1952) pointed out, most disputes within psychoanalytic circles are settled by invocation of authority. If an individual analyst develops doubts about Freud's theory of homosexuality or his theory of dream interpretation, he cannot go back and look at a pool of scientific evidence to help him in deciding about the issues. He is limited to looking back at Freud's original statements and case illustrations or other cases that subsequently have been published. We would like to suggest that this state of affairs results in considerably more uncertainty and doubt in the psychoanalytic establishment than is publicly visible. Without scientific anchoring, those who have been trained in, and have grown up in, a milieu of science must periodically look at what they are doing rather skeptically. One must remember that most analysts have been through a long period of college and medical school training in which scientific procedures and data were the core of their everyday activities. They must therefore at least occasionally feel queasy about the scientific fragility of what supports a number of their major propositions. In other words, we are speculating that it is troubling to the average analyst that he cannot cite detailed factual support for his theories and practices. At some level, he must be concerned about how genuine he is. To assemble the existing dependable data concerning the scientific validity of Freud's ideas could potentially do a great deal for the self-feeling of analysts. Even if the data supported some ideas and not others, this would provide a more sustaining platform than not knowing which ideas, if any, can stand the test of empirical appraisal.

When we decided to collect and evaluate all of the existing scientific information bearing on Freud's models, we were confronted with having to set standards concerning the meaning of the term "scientific." We decided to apply the term to any study in which observations had been gathered according to rules more exacting than "This is what I personally witnessed or experienced." We will, in the pages that follow, cite information only when it has been secured through procedures that are repeatable and involve techniques that make it possible to check on the objectivity of the reporting observer. We did not decide in advance to rule out studies that had defects in their experimental designs or that were based on oversimplistic notions concerning Freud's models. It seemed more sensible to make a sweep of the total empirical data, flawed or otherwise, and to draw conclusions from overall trends. It should be specified that we rejected the use of simple case history reports to be found in the literature. While many certainly contain interesting and important information, there is no way to separate the good from the bad. There is no way to gauge which clinical reporters are telling it the way it really happened and which are wishfully seeing things in a way that supports their favorite theoretical stance.

The remainder of this book will be devoted to scrutinizing

what we have been able to draw from the world scientific literature bearing on major sectors of Freud's theories. We will first analyze the findings for each sector and then offer a total view of the scientific status of Freud's models. We have also set ourselves the task of outlining what changes in these models seem to be logical in terms of the accumulated evidence. We are much more interested in exploring potentially sensible revisions than in arriving at approving or disapproving postures. There are those who will interpret our interest in revision as basically antagonistic to Freudian concepts, but our great energy investment in this book is a testimonial to our positive investment in such concepts. Our position is antagonistic only in the sense that we insist that it is time for psychoanalysis to face up to a scientific accounting. We are asking for explicit statements of validity and declarations of what will be accepted as proper evidence.

NOTES

1. But it is, of course, true that Freud was very sensitive to, and resistive of, demands from others that he revise his formulations. Note Bleuler's comments in a letter he sent to Freud concerning the intolerance of psychoanalysis toward dissent or criticism (Alexander and Selesnick, 1965, p. 6): "Scientifically I still do not understand why for you it is so important that the whole edifice [of psychoanalysis] should be accepted. But I remember I told you once that no matter how great your scientific accomplishments are, psychologically you impress me as an artist. From this point of view it is understandable that you do not want your art product to be destroyed. In art we have a unit which cannot be torn apart. In science you made a great discovery which has to stay. How much of what is loosely connected with it will survive is not important."

2. Glover (1952, p. 403) describes a common way in which "new facts" are established in psychoanalytic circles: "An analyst, let us say, of established prestige and seniority, produces a paper advancing some new point of view or alleged discovery in the theoretical or clinical area. Given sufficient enthusiasm and persuasiveness, or even just plain dogmatism on the part of the author, the chances are that without any check, this view or alleged discovery will gain currency, will be quoted and requoted until it attains the status of an accepted conclusion."

3. The extreme view of the research potential of the psychoanalytic therapy hour is presented by Ramzy: "It may be hoped that with more scrutiny of the requirements of logic and scientific method, and of what actually happens in psychoanalytic treatment, it may turn out that, after all, the standard psychoanalytic method will be considered as the best so far suggested. It may turn out that every analyst who merely follows the method he was taught to follow will discover that he has been doing research, just as Moliere's M. Jourdain suddenly discovered that he has been speaking prose for 40 years without knowing it. Psychoanalysts, however, have dire need to learn how to read, write, and correctly spell the prose they have used since the inception of their discipline."

4. Note Glover's (1952, p. 404) view of the qualifications of the analyst to do research: ". . . the general conviction persists in psycho-analytical circles, a legacy from those early days when most students of psychoanalysis were natural investigators, that anyone who is qualified to practice therapeutic analysis is also qualified to conduct research. These times have changed. In fact candidates are seldom chosen because of their suitability for research work . . ."

5. Escalona (1952, p. 16) describes the potential complexity that might be involved

in verifying the existence of Oedipal conflicts (viz., love for mother and hostility toward father) in a young boy: "Thus, if the child gives daddy a good-night hug and insists that he, rather than mummy, tuck him in, this behavior may also confirm our original hypothesis. His desire to have father put him to bed rather than the mother could be the result of a fearful state, i.e., as long as the father is with him the little boy can be sure the father is not doing anything to harm him. On the other hand, or also simultaneously, it may be an act of aggression toward the father in that it separates him from the mother for the time being. Or yet again, it may be because the little boy fears that if mother puts him to bed her seductive powers will prove too much for him . . ."

6. Clinical observers are often credited with modes of analysis that are considered to be ineffably complex. The psychoanalyst has been portrayed in some quarters as arriving at conclusions by putting together infinitely subtle cues. Formal studies of clinical judgments have revealed that a great many involve the application of fixed, stereotyped notions and reasoning based on simple additive formulas.

PART ONE

FREUD'S THEORETICAL VIEWS

Chapter 2

The Dream Theory

What Were Freud's Assumptions?

FREUD took particular pride in the model he constructed to explain the nature of dreaming. He considered his dream theory to be one of his major accomplishments.[1] This theory became the foundation for dream analysis in both formal psychotherapeutic settings and in popular circles. Many Western cultures have enthusiastically embraced Freudian dream principles.

Let us consider what Freud had to say about the dream process. He described the dream as a disguised production that contains beneath its facade a latent meaning, which can be decoded into a "wish" for something the dreamer considers too evil to express openly. He indicated that the dream represents an attempt to vent an unconscious wish, but in a form that conceals from the dreamer himself that he could possibly entertain such urges. He suggested that when an individual enters the sleep state his usual defenses against repressed unconscious impulses become less effective. The repressed impulses become able to exert relatively increased pressure. Further, they take advantage of the regressed mental functioning characteristic of sleep to find expression in the unusually vivid visual (hallucinatory) images of dreaming. However, these images are elaborately disguised "manifest" versions of "latent" meanings. Freud also ascribed considerable importance to the dream as having sleep-preserving power. He reasoned that it permits unconscious impulses to obtain an indirect, substitute, and nonthreatening mode of expression instead of grossly breaching sleep-weakened defensive barriers in a fashion that would alarm and awaken the sleeper.

This brief statement about Freud's dream theory is intended to lead into a more detailed analysis. We would like, at this point, to define the various components of the theory and debate several matters of interpretation regarding what Freud meant in his use of certain terms and concepts. The major components will be reviewed below.

Any description of Freud's dream model must begin with his topographical division of the "psychic apparatus" into *unconscious* and *preconscious*. The unconscious represents, of course, the site of wishes and impulses that are denied, disowned, and repressed. It is depicted as having no access to consciousness except through the contiguous preconscious. That which is in the preconscious "can enter consciousness without further impediment provided that certain other conditions are fulfilled: for instance, that they reach a certain degree of intensity . . ." (Freud 1900, p. 541). The preconscious is also the site that has direct access to the possibility of motoric acting out of impulses. What passes from the unconscious to the preconscious is subject to a censoring or filtering process that excludes material that is too threatening.

Freud (1900) states that the "motive power for producing dreams is furnished by the Ucs. [unconscious]" (p. 541). He indicates that impulses and wishes in the unconscious are constantly pushing to break through to the preconscious but are normally, during the day, held in check. He theorizes that during sleep there is a "lowering of the resistance which guards the frontier between the unconscious and the preconscious . . ." (p. 542). Unconscious impulses (with strong infantile roots) therefore threaten to break through and not only cause distress but also awaken the sleeper. The dream represents a means "of bringing back under control of the preconscious the excitation in the unconscious which has been left free . . ." (p. 579). The dream is described as a compromise mode for controlling the unconscious excitation by giving it partial but safe discharge. It is a nonpainful way of evading the censorship. Freud specifies that the evasion of the censorship requires, first of all, that the unconscious wish attach itself to a nonthreatening idea or "residue" that is left over in the preconscious from past experiences (particularly from the previous day).[2] He notes (1900, pp. 562–563) that: ". . . an unconscious idea is as such quite incapable of entering the preconscious and that it can only exercise any effect there by establishing a connection with an idea which already belongs to the preconscious, by transferring its intensity on to it and by getting itself 'covered' by it."

The unconscious excitation that is thus linked with the "day residue" ideas is said to push for fulfillment of the basic wish it embodies. However, since the possibility for motoric expression (and real gratification) is blocked by the muscular paralysis produced by sleep,[3] the excitation reverses the usual course for an impulse. It instead moves along a "regressive" pathway to the sensory end of the psychic apparatus, where it elicits vivid "hallucinatory," wish-fulfilling visual images. These visual images constitute the dream. The visual imagery of the dream is compared by Freud to what presumably happens during states of primitive functioning when, in the absence of the opportunity to gratify a need, a previous memory of gratification of that need is hallucinatorily conjured up as a substitute. However, Freud theorized that the obvious or "manifest" content of the dream disguises the wish it contains—that it conceals from the dreamer the unconscious urge ("latent" content) he is really expressing, which urge can be uncovered only by obtaining "free associations" to the manifest content.

Presumably, the latent content of the dream is disguised by means of a variety of strategies such as condensation, symbolism, and displacement of emphasis. One figure in a dream may represent a fusion of several others or even its opposite. The apparently least important figure in a dream may actually be the most important. A seemingly neutral object may symbolize something of great emotional intensity. Freud devoted a good part of *The Interpretation of Dreams* to identifying these modes of disguise.[4] He was explicit in his view that the manifest content of the dream is, in its literal sense, a meaningless shell. Overall, he conceptualized the dream as a compromise that partially allows for the gratification of an unconscious wish and yet at the same time fulfills the wish to sleep. He summarized the process in these words (1900, p. 579):

> Dreaming has taken on the task of bringing back under control of the preconscious, the excitation in the unconscious which has been left free; in doing so, it discharges the unconscious excitation, serves it as a safety valve and at the same time preserves the sleep of the preconscious in return for a small expenditure of waking activity.

This overview conveys the two components of Freud's dream theory (namely, wish fulfillment and sleep preservation) which are salient and most often associated with it. Several other subsidiary aspects of his views about dreaming will be considered shortly. But first let us explore what he meant when he specified that dreams were attempts at wish fulfillment. In one area his intent was clear. He said there was a particular class of dreams in which the content could be viewed as direct and undisguised images having to do with obtaining a satisfaction. For example, a hungry child might dream of eating his favorite food. Freud regarded such *direct* wish fulfillment dreams as most likely to occur in young children who had not yet developed well-differentiated distinctions between the unconscious and the preconscious. However, he did cite examples of related kinds of dreams in adults. In fact, at one point he described a dream (1900, p. 123) "that I can produce in myself as often as I like—experimentally, as it were. If I eat anchovies or olives or any other highly salted food in the evening, I develop thirst during the night which wakes me up. But my waking is preceded by a dream; and this always has the same content, namely, that I am drinking. I dream I am swallowing down water in great gulps, and it has the delicious taste that nothing can equal but a cool drink when one is parched with thirst. . . . This simple dream is occasioned by the thirst which I become aware of when I wake. The thirst gives rise to a wish to drink, and the dream shows me that wish fulfilled."[5]

Freud also cites other directly stated "convenience" dreams he has observed in adults (for example, seeing oneself as having already gone to work on a morning when one is particularly resistive to getting up and initiating the day's activities). Here there is no ambiguity in his use of the term "wish fulfilling." But matters become more complicated when he discusses the disguised dream form (in which the wish is hidden in the latent content) that he thinks is by far the most common in adults. One begins to encounter contradictions between what Freud says and does, and also between statements he presents in different contexts. Thus, at one point he makes the definitive statement that the latent content of a dream has to express some version of a "repressed infantile wish." That is, the wish cannot be of contemporary origin but, rather, must be derived from conflicts and frustrations the individual experienced very early in his life. However, as pointed out by Jones (1970), it is difficult to find among the many dreams decoded by Freud in *The Interpretation of Dreams* any that are obviously of the "infantile" wish-fulfilling type. The wishes he repeatedly purports to uncover have to do with the hopes and desires of adult life. They concern such themes as relieving oneself of blame for failure, denying an unwanted pregnancy, removing a competitor, and getting sexual stimulation from someone who catches one's fancy. Whatever Freud may have said *formally* about the adult's dream wish *always* being reducible to an infantile aim, the fact remains that in his published clinical examples he rarely adhered to such a formulation. The concept "wish," *as he applied it* in his published writings, had broad connotations.

The generality of the concept of "wish" as it pertains to dream function was stretched, too, when Freud tried to account for the presence of painful and threatening material in dreams. He had the rather difficult task of explaining why dreams that are presumably dedicated to wish fulfillment could confront the dreamer with disturbing images. His solution involved several speculations. He suggested, first of all, that a repressed wish may somewhat accidentally become linked with a memory of a day experience (day residue) which was itself painful and use this vehicle to gain entrance to the preconscious despite the associated unpleasantness, simply because the pleasure linked with the wish outweighs the pain related to the unpleasant day experience.[6] He suggested further that a painful dream may be "wishful" in the sense that it is a "punishment of the dreamer for a repressed, prohibited wish-impulse." In other words, the unpleasantness of the dream is intended by one sector (for example, the superego) in the individual's personality economy to serve as punishing retaliation for bad intent emanating from another sector.

Freud had to expand his wish fulfillment framework even further in his attempts to account for the repetitious rehearsal of catastrophic incidents that occur at times in the dreams of persons with post-traumatic reactions. That is, he was hard pressed to explain why those who have experienced a severe trauma will endlessly (and at the cost of much suffering) repeat it in their dreams. He concluded that this represents a way of "mastering" the catastrophic stimulus situation "by developing the anxiety whose omission was the cause of the traumatic neurosis." He even went so far as to state that this class of dreams represents "an exception to the proposition that dreams are fulfillments of wishes." He noted, "They arise, rather, in obedience to the compulsion to repeat . . ." (Freud 1920*a,* p. 32). He conjectured that the need to master a disturbing stimulus might be even more basic than the pleasure principle that underlies the dream fulfillment theory.[7] This is one instance in which he explicitly recognized that the dreaming process might have a mastery or problem-solving function.[8] There are other places in which he discusses the fact that solutions to problems may appear in dreams, but he took the position that such solutions had already occurred at unconscious levels prior to the dream and simply popped up in the dream imagery in finished form. He did, however, admit to the possibility that the dream could be the arena in which a solution to a problem would first become evident to an individual. In any case, it is clear that Freud was finally obliged, in at least one area, to break out of the confines of the wish fulfillment theory in order to encompass all of the dream phenomena he encountered.[9]

A similar departure is to be observed in an essay he wrote in which he declared the following (Freud 1922*a*, p. 208):

> Actual experiences of the day are sometimes simply repeated in sleep; reproductions of traumatic scenes in "dreams" have led us only lately to revise the theory of dreams. There are dreams which are to be distinguished from the usual type by certain special qualities, which are, properly speaking, nothing but night-phantasies, not having undergone additions or alterations of any kind and being in all other ways similar to the familiar day-dreams. It would be awkward, no doubt, to exclude these structures from the domain of "dreams." But still they all come from within, are products of our mental life . . .

Here Freud is once again admitting that dream imagery may present itself to the sleeper in a fashion involving no specific wish fulfillment intent. He is also admitting that imagery may present itself to the sleeper with no attempt at camouflage of a secret core.

Even beyond Freud's *operational* stretching of the wish fulfillment theory, we would suggest that, when one penetrates beneath certain aspects of its verbal facade, the theory has always had implications not limited to literal wish fulfillment as such. If one tracks Freud's soliloquies about dream function in *The Interpretation of Dreams,* one finds that he kept questioning what he himself meant when he said that dreams are wish fulfillments. Finally, after much pondering, he comes to the conclusion that dreams are wish fulfilling because all things that emanate from the unconscious represent wishes. Note his comments in this respect (Freud 1900, p. 568):

> But there are reasons for continuing a little with our consideration of wishes as the sole psychical motive force for the construction of dreams. We have accepted the idea that the reason why dreams are invariably wish-fulfillments is that they are products of the system Unconscious, whose activity knows no other aim than the fulfillment of wishes and which has at its command no other forces than wishful impulses.

He then goes on to add that in this sense *all* psychoneurotic symptoms "are to be regarded as fulfillments of unconscious wishes" (p. 569). In still another context he indicates that the motive power behind *all* thought processes is the wish. He states (p. 567):

> Thought is after all nothing but a substitute for a hallucinatory wish; and it is self-evident that dreams must be wish-fulfillments, since nothing

> but a wish can set our mental apparatus at work. Dreams, which fulfill their wishes along the short path of regression, have merely preserved for us in that respect a sample of the psychical apparatus's primary method of working . . .

On the basis of the material just cited, we would propose that when Freud said that dreams are wish fulfilling, he simply meant that they portray impulses that come from the unconscious. They may be regarded as no more *specifically* or uniquely wish fulfilling than a neurotic symptom or a slip of the tongue or any of the other myriad "unconscious manifestations" he scrutinized. What Freud referred to as wishes in many of his dream analyses could just as meaningfully be labeled feelings, attitudes, and conflicts. It is our view that if one examines Freud's *total* writings and operations vis-à-vis dreams, it is reasonable to conclude that he regarded the dream as a vehicle for the *expression* of a variety of unconscious phenomena, such as wishes, attempts to master anxiety-producing stimuli, and registration of vague or subliminal impressions. His preoccupation with the term "wish" in most of his formal statements about the function of the dream strikes us as semantically designed to dramatize the idea that he had made a specific discovery about the nature of dreaming. But it does not adequately embrace his concepts of dreaming as they emerge in the full range of his published observations and decisions about actual dreams.

One should note that although Freud typically ends his analysis of each of the dreams he cites in *The Interpretation of Dreams* with a statement concerning its central wish, he also precedes each with a careful inventory of the various disguised feelings and attitudes it seems to contain. The final wish formulation represents a generalization from a crisscross of themes that have been teased out in this way. The themes that appear in Freud's dream analyses variously concern feelings about other people, warnings to oneself about dangers, beliefs, criticisms of others, and so forth.[10] Freud is *operationally* explicit in his assumption that such themes exist in the latent content of the dream. If so, one may reasonably ask: do they not have as much reality as the final wish formulation to which he reduces them? Indeed, one could argue that the wish aspect of the dream is actually more of an abstraction and less real than the raw manifest themes from which Freud considered he had derived them. We see this as one more reason for approaching Freud's dream theory as a statement about multiple expressions emanating from the unconscious sector of the "psychic apparatus" rather than as a single, narrow category called "wishes." It is a theory about unconscious impulses and tensions being vented in a special form of imagery. This is the version of the dream theory we chose to evaluate in relation to the existing scientific literature concerned with dream phenomena.

Another fundamental aspect of Freud's dream theory that should be considered here is that the theory is inseparably tied to the notion that the material derived from the unconscious, which is presumably contained in the dream, assumes a disguised form. It is a core component of his dream schema that the unconscious content of the dream is elaborately camouflaged. The visible (manifest) content is almost always considered to be a facade that serves defensive purposes only. This would seem to imply that the visible (manifest) dream content does not contain any important information about what is going on in the "unconscious" regions of the individual. But one of the problems with such a conclusion is that Freud *did* describe the manifest dream content as the product of an elaborate sequence of defensive maneuvers, ranging from the use of esoteric symbolism to misleading emphasis or de-emphasis of dream elements. If so, is it not possible that the specific manner in which an individual goes about the business of disguising the unconscious components of his dream reflects important aspects of his personality?[11] His specific mode or style of disguise, if there really is such a thing, might provide information about events in the unconscious sector. In *The Interpretation of Dreams* Freud does periodically point to a particular aspect of the manifest dream content as suggesting something about the nature of what is being concealed in the latent dream content.[12] He goes so far as to say: *"The form of the dream or the form in which it is dreamt is used with quite surprising frequency for representing the concealed subject-matter"* (1900, p. 332). However, even with these facts in mind, it is probably fair to say that *in general* his dream theory does clearly distinguish between manifest and latent content and does conceptualize the latter as containing an overwhelmingly greater amount of information about the unconscious sector than does the former.

One could argue that there really is no alternative within Freudian theory to the proposition that the unconscious impulses presumably expressed in a dream take a concealed or latent form. It would seem to be a logical derivative of Freud's orientation, which asserts that anything emanating from the unconscious will cause unpleasantness and pain if it should break through to conscious awareness. Even so, it has been suggested (for example, French 1954, Spanjaard 1969) that the imprinting of unconscious impulses upon a dream may occur on a continuum embracing both the manifest and latent dream content. That is, the unconscious impulses might fairly openly register in some of the visible imagery, be encoded in a partially concealed fashion in other segments of the visible imagery, and be concealed totally in still other elements of the imagery. The unconscious material is, from this perspective, distributed in a range of forms (from moderately easily detectable to complexly concealed) in the dream structure. What are some possible reasons for even considering that material from the unconscious might be distributed to some degree in the manifest regions of the dream rather than isolated in the so-called latent regions? Several suggest themselves: (1) One might expect that there would be a certain amount of imperfection in the censorship existing between the preconscious and unconscious, so that "leakage" of unconscious material would occur. After all, few psychological functions in the human proceed without error. Unconscious material could gain open representation in the dream imagery as a reflection of error in the system. (2) Secondly, one could point to the diminished intellectual acuity of the individual while in a sleep state and argue that what would appear to be camouflaged during sleep would be less so when subjected to a more alert scrutiny. What seemed to have "manifest" status during sleep would to the awakened observer reveal more "latent" classes of information. That is, an effective form of coding as it confronts the cognitively handicapped sleeper might, in the light of day, prove to have much less real concealment power. (3) There might be marked individual differences in the degree to which persons can "permit" unconscious impulses to gain representation in the open dream imagery. One individual might not be able to face up to even a hint of an unconscious theme in the apparent dream content, while another might be able to tolerate fairly explicit hints and references. The individual with a high tolerance might conceivably be able to "permit" a fair amount of representation of the unconscious impulse into the visible dream imagery.

This matter is not only of theoretical but also of considerable practical import. If Freud is correct in his sharp dichotomy between the manifest and latent content, then one can obtain information about the unconscious impulses expressed in a dream only by use of the complex association techniques he described. In other words, one can find out what is in the dream only by motivating the dreamer to give his private associations to the major elements of the manifest imagery. But if the manifest imagery can for various reasons contain detectable representations of the unconscious impulses, dream interpretation could conceivably, to some degree, proceed on the basis of the manifest imagery.

So we propose looking at the scientific literature to find out the extent to which information about unconscious impulses can be derived from visible dream imagery and, more specifically, the ratio of such information in the manifest as compared to the so-called latent content of the dream.

A third significant component of Freud's dream theory concerns the so-called sleep-preserving function of the dream. Freud argues that when an impulse from the unconscious seeks entry into the preconscious it is potentially sleep-disruptive, insofar as it would produce pain or displeasure should the dreamer become aware of it. That is, if the unconscious impulse were to gain direct access to the sleeper's awareness, it would presumably alarm and therefore rouse him.[13] The dream is considered by Freud to represent a means whereby the unconscious impulse can be given partial outlet but in a form so disguised that it does not disturb the sleeper. He describes the dream as a compromise between the pressure of the unconscious wish and the wish to maintain undisturbed sleep. He states, too, that the dream functions in a sleep-preserving capacity in all those contexts where the sleeper is confronted with stimuli (either from the environment or his own body) that could potentially awaken him. He proposes that the dream assimilates such stimuli and gives them a meaning that diminishes their rousing potential. He comments, "The currently active sensation is woven into a dream *in order to rob it of reality*" (1900, p. 234).[14]

We see this sleep-preserving attribute of the dream as a third basic theoretical notion to be checked out in relation to existing scientific data.

Does the Manifest Content Contain Important Information?

In the process of testing Freud's dream hypothesis, it would be logical to begin with the major one dealing with the role of the dream in expressing or venting tensions from the unconscious sector of the "psychic apparatus." However, it will be necessary to delay evaluation of it in order to explore another that bears on issues seriously complicating the testing of any aspects of Freud's dream theory. This hypothesis has to do with the whole problem of where lies the most important information in the dream. As already noted, Freud was explicit in stating that the apparent or manifest dream content is a meaningless shell, and he insisted that the really significant expressions are contained in the hidden or latent content. This raises a serious dilemma, because many studies in the literature concerned with the nature of the dream process have depended upon analysis of the manifest content. If one simply accepts Freud's view that the manifest content of an individual's dreams reveals little of value about him, all such studies lose their credibility. They cannot be meaningfully included in any tests of validity. We intend, however, to demonstrate that Freud exaggerated the importance of the latent content. Incidentally, many psychoanalysts (for example, Erikson 1954, French 1954) and other students of the dream have already challenged Freud's dismissal of the manifest content as a source of data about the internal psychological economy. They have not only pointed out that Freud himself used cues from the manifest content in a number of his published dream interpretations, they have also cited clinical illustrations in which the manifest dream seemed to reflect significant psychological events.

It also becomes apparent, as one studies the dream literature, that the distinction between what is manifest and latent in a dream is not as crystal clear as one might first assume. Freud indicated that the latent content was deeply concealed and could be decoded only by motivating the person who had dreamed to give his private associations to the various elements of the dream story. But he also said that there were certain widely used symbols in dreams and indicated that one could do a certain amount of dream decoding simply by understanding these symbols. For example, he assumed that an object like a gun or a sword often had phallic significance. A knowledgeable observer who understood such symbols might be able to extract some important data from a dream without ever having secured associations to the dream elements. Thus, Freud was admitting the possibility that the so-called latent content could be at least partially decoded without the formal association procedure. He was really implying that what is concealed behind the manifest content varies in its degree of camouflage, with some chunks becoming fairly visible to an observer equipped with a knowledgeable orientation.

There is an even more important sense in which the distinction between manifest and latent content is hard to maintain. This relates to the fact that the manifest content is not a simple, one-dimensional affair; there are numerous levels at which it can be approached. This has actually been shown by dream investigators. At the simplest level, one can merely attend to the story line in the dream. But one can also more complexly explore a dream by systematically analyzing its "surface" components into categories (based on principles from previous studies of fantasy material) that would not be within the usual awareness of most persons as they look at their own dreams. For example, one can examine how active or passive the central dream figures are. One can ask how much aggression they display. Or one can scan the difference in the nature of interactions portrayed between male figures as compared to those between female figures. One can look at many other variables such as the vividness of the dream imagery, the presence or absence of sexual references, the degree of interest in themes of motility, and so forth. Even though such analyses do not involve obtaining the private associations of the dreamer, they do permit new perspectives with regard to the dream content that would not be apparent to the dreamer unless he were familiar with sophisticated techniques for analyzing fantasy material.

A valid analogy may be drawn in terms of the possible modes of analysis of responses to Rorschach ink blots or to the request to "make up a story." One might argue that the special idiosyncratic meaning of such responses can be determined only by asking the individual to give his private thoughts and associations about them. In fact, it has proved feasible to extract all kinds of basic information from them about an individual's motives and personality by applying a variety of analytical schemes directly to the imagery itself. As testified in a vast literature (for example, Fisher 1967, Molish 1972), by looking for clues in both the formal structure and the content themes of the responses, it is possible to arrive at valid deductions concerning an individual's tensions and conflicts. In other words, the problem of deciding at what level significant data can be extracted from a dream can be viewed as no different from that faced in analyzing any species of fantasy production.

These points and speculations serve to preface a scrutiny of what the scientific literature can tell us about the location of meaning in the dream. A primary question that comes up in the course of such a scrutiny is the nature of the relationship that exists between what Freud called the manifest and latent dream contents. It is striking how willing most persons have been to accept Freud's view about the disparity between manifest and latent without any solid evidence except his strong but only impressionistically based assertions to this effect. For many years not a single attempt was made to test these assertions. There was not even an attempt to find out if different observers using Freud's dream analysis technique can really agree in their interpretations of the same dream material.

In any case, what do we find about the link between what is manifest and latent when we look at the objective data?[15] Let us begin with a study by Reis (1951), which involved twelve male and twelve female college students. First, he secured dreams from each student. Subsequently, he met twice with each and obtained associations and thoughts about the dream material in a fashion analogous to that suggested by Freud as necessary to penetrate to the underlying latent dream meaning. Then, after rapport had been established, each person was asked to lie on a couch and to give associations to, and conjure up meanings for, the individual elements of dream imagery he had previously reported. The dreams were then evaluated by judges who read them repeatedly and rated them with respect to numerous dimensions (for example, aggression, anxiety, psychopathology, attitude toward parents, sexual feelings, narcissism). Some evaluations were based entirely on the dream imagery alone and some on the dream imagery plus the dreamer's associations to the dream. An analysis of the various evaluations resulted in interesting findings. First, it was shown that judges could reliably agree in most of their ratings of the dream imagery. They came to similar conclusions about the dreamer on the basis of the dream material. Secondly, and perhaps more importantly, it was demonstrated that judgments based on the dream imagery alone were largely in agreement with those based on the imagery plus the associations. That is, there was considerable overlap between what could apparently be ascertained from the manifest content as compared to the latent content (defined by the dreamer's associations). Reis felt the free associations added valuable information to what could be derived from the manifest content alone. But it remains true that from a statistical point of view, the two levels of dream material were significantly correlated.

Sheppard and Karon (1964) looked at the comparability of manifest and latent content by studying the dreams of nineteen psychiatric patients (primarily schizophrenics) who were seen individually once a week for eight weeks. Dreams were obtained from each and also associations to the dream material. Independent judges were then asked to rate the dreams alone and the dream associations alone with respect to a series of dimensions (for example, hostile, oral, anal, and genital drives) considered to be meaningful within a psychoanalytic context. Significant relationships were found between ratings based on the dream and those based on the associations for five of the dimensions. There were a few dimensions for which significant relationships could not be established. But the findings indicated clear overlap between the information contained in the manifest and latent dream categories.[16]

Proctor and Briggs (1964) were impressed with the amount of significant information the manifest dream content provided about fourteen children in a psychiatric treatment setting. They asked eight psychiatrists to formulate, on the basis of dream material consisting almost entirely of the manifest content alone, the nature of the conflicts and disturbance characterizing each child. These psychiatrists were successively given other kinds of information (for example, symptoms present and a brief history) to observe how their conclusions changed with such expanded input. It was shown that a major part (57 percent) of the basic conclusions drawn from full background information about a case was deduced from the manifest dream material alone. While this study did not compare the manifest and latent levels, it did demonstrate that the manifest content provides data that fit with formulations based on much more extensive sampling of the individual's behavior.

In still another instance, McReynolds et al. (1966), after securing dreams from thirty college students, asked clinicians to rate them (for hostile and sexual content) in terms of two different approaches. One simply involved the manifest content, but a second encouraged the rater to consider not only the manifest content but also the possible symbolic meanings of the dream material. All of the ratings based on these two approaches proved to be significantly positively correlated. That is, there was a definite similarity between the deductions based purely on the manifest dream imagery and those derived from an attempt to get closer to the latent aspects of the dream.

Finally, mention should be made of a study by Robbins (1966) which did not discern much of a relationship between what can be derived from the manifest as compared to the more latent levels of the dream. He asked twenty-eight college students to think of incidents or events suggested by the various elements of their reported dreams. They wrote descriptions of the incidents and then indicated (from a standard list) what needs or motives seemed to predominate in each. Independent raters were then asked to evaluate the manifest content of the same dreams by indicating (from the same standard list) the presence or absence of various needs. While some agreement between the two modes was observed, the major trend indicated that the manifest and somewhat latent levels were not providing parallel data.

The studies just cited are individually not terribly impressive, and they vary in their direct pertinence to the question whether the manifest and latent contents overlap appreciably. But as a group they initiate a direct challenge to the idea that the manifest content contains little information that is significant.

Other challenges present themselves if one looks at more indirect forms of evidence. There are interesting findings having to do with the relationships between an individual's manifest dream content and the images he produces when responding to projective stimuli like the Rorschach inkblot test. Reasonable data exist indicating that projective tests can detect feelings and impulses in sectors corresponding to what Freud called the unconscious. That is, they are capable of measuring personal drives of which the individual is unaware and which he would probably consciously disavow. Many empirical studies (for example, Megargee 1966, Witkin et al. 1962, Goldfried et al. 1971) may be found in the literature that demonstrate significant correlations between projective test indices and measures that bypass surface defenses (for example, responses to tachistoscopically presented pictures or symbols). If projective tests tap unconscious impulses, one would not, within the context of Freudian theory, expect them to show meaningful ties to measures derived from manifest dream content. As frequently reiterated, Freud regarded the manifest content to be largely a facade that conceals rather than reveals unconscious impulses. What do we find when we look at the studies that have compared an individual's projective images and his manifest dream images?

Bolgar (1954) reported that in a sample made up of psychiatric patients and normal subjects, there are substantial parallels between the affective themes given to Rorschach blots and those present in manifest dream content. She scored the two sets of protocols from each subject for a variety of dimensions, such as hostility, anxiety, dependency, and positive feeling. In her analysis of the scores she found there was significant congruence between the themes an individual indicates occurred in his dreams and those revealed in his inkblot fantasies. Eiduson (1959) noted, in a study of eighteen patients in outpatient psychotherapy, that the greater the rigidity they display in their dream imagery, the greater the rigidity of their Rorschach percepts. Even more impressive is her observation that the amount of rigidity in the manifest dream content is significantly predictive of rigidity in everyday behavior (as rated by each patient's psychotherapist). Krohn (1972) demonstrated that in a sample of psychiatric patients, there was a significant positive correlation between the amount of warmth and solidity of relationships depicted in the Rorschach and the amount present in manifest dream content.

Several researchers have examined correlations between the individual's manifest dream imagery and his imagery when composing imaginative stories to pictures (for example, the Thematic Apperception Test). Brender and Kramer (1967) scored manifest dream and story protocols obtained from normal persons for the presence of themes indicative of such needs as dominance, deference, affiliation, and achievement. They detected a significant trend for the dream and story scores to have a greater than chance association, but they also emphasized that there were a good number of instances in which the correlations were negligible. Foulkes (1969) discovered that in children there were definite links between the amounts of hostility and guilt displayed in their manifest dreams and the amounts in the imaginative stories they created. Gordon (1953–54) observed in a psychiatric sample that there were significant correlations between manifest dreams and stories elicited by Thematic Apperception pictures for such variables as aggression, affiliation, mood, and concern about status. Weingarden (1972) found in a normal sample a significant inverse relationship between aggression in stories based on Thematic Apperception pictures and aggression in manifest dream content. Cartwright (1966b) reported that in a normal sample of individuals, the imaginativeness they showed in their Thematic Apperception Test story productions was positively correlated with that characterizing their manifest dreams. Foulkes and Rechtschaffen (1964) also discerned in a normal group a positive correlation between the imaginativeness shown in Thematic Apperception stories and that shown in dream protocols. But they found no consistent relationships between specific affective themes in the stories and in the dreams.

Urbina (1972) compared the amount of achievement imagery present in the manifest dreams of normal adults with the amount they produced when responding to a semiprojective test, French's Test of Insight, which involves explaining behavior described in a series of sentences. Only chance correlations were found between the two achievement indices.

The weight of the studies[17] just cited is in the direction of indicating that the manifest dream content[18] mirrors attitudes and feelings similar to those that are picked up by projective techniques like the Rorschach inkblots and the Thematic Apperception pictures. If one accepts the assumption that projective tests do not tap superficial defenses but, rather, basic personality vectors, it would seem logical to conclude that the manifest dream content can tap similar vectors.[19]

At this point it would be well to consider still another source of information bearing on the meaning of the manifest dream. A sizable literature has accumulated dealing with the effects of real-life and experimental conditions upon dream imagery. By scanning these effects, it is possible to get a clearer notion of what the manifest imagery expresses. Freud did assume that the dream would reflect an individual's current experiences insofar as "day residues" (memories of life encounters of the previous day) become the vehicles or images upon which unconscious impulses ride, in gaining access to more conscious levels. However, he also assumed that the only function of the day residue imagery is defensive and concealing. It presumably serves only as camouflage and does not directly express anything meaningful about how an individual is feeling or the conflicts with which he is coping.

As will emerge in the material that follows, this is a doubtful view. It will be shown that the manifest content does directly mirror important feelings and tensions. If the manifest content of an individual's dreams demonstrates sensitivity to his immediate life circumstances and feelings, it would seem to be an understatement to describe it as a mere defensive facade. Of course, one could still argue that even if the manifest content reflects meaningful aspects of a person's life experiences, its function is largely defensive. The sensitivity of the manifest content might be explained as a strategy to make its defensive texture more convincing. In other words, one could reason that the dreamer would be less likely to penetrate or be suspicious of the manifest camouflage if it depicts a scenario that makes sense in terms of his current life context. Within a Freudian framework this possibility cannot simply be dismissed. *But it remains true that to the extent one can show that the manifest content parallels dilemmas and problems that have central significance to the dreamer, the less logical it is to interpret it as having only defensive functions.* Even if it has important defensive intent, it might simultaneously serve other expressive or defining purposes. More will be said about this shortly.

In order to provide a richer background for getting at such issues, attention will now be turned to scanning the scientific literature concerned with the sensitivity of manifest dream content to various conditions.

A number of studies have concerned themselves with the sensitivity of the manifest content to significant life experiences. Robbins and Tanck (1969) asked the question whether the manifest content of the dreams of individuals living through a community crisis would register the impact.[20] They obtained dreams from a sample of female college students during a period when there was serious civil disorder in the community, set off by the assassination of Martin Luther King, Jr. They compared the amount of overt hostility in these dreams with the amount in a series of dreams obtained from an equivalent group of college students prior to the civil disorder. It was found that there was significantly *less* hostility in the dreams obtained during the crisis than in those secured during noncrisis. While confronted with community violence, there was inhibition of hostile dream imagery. Robbins and Tanck did not have a real explanation for this phenomenon, but they pointed out that a previous study by Foulkes et al. (1967) had demonstrated that persons exposed to an aggressive film before going to sleep exhibited less overt aggression in their dreams than did persons exposed to a nonaggressive film. It is of special interest that the manifest dream content obtained during the civil disorder did not directly mirror an increase in hostile imagery, but rather the opposite. In other words, the manifest content was clearly sensitive to an important life event, but not in a simple duplicating fashion. Similar complexity of impact is depicted in a study by Newton (1970) in which the dream content of paralyzed (paraplegic and quadraplegic) men was appraised. The question was asked whether the state of being paralyzed would affect the degree to which dream figures were presented as engaged or not engaged in body movement. It was found that the recently paralyzed portrayed more movement and the long-term paralyzed less movement than do normal men. Obviously, one is not dealing here with a simple "day residue" effect. Up to a certain point, body paralysis increases movement in the dream imagery, but with further time duration it has just the opposite result.[21] One can see the possibility, which will become explicit after further presentation of material, that the manner in which the manifest content expresses psychological events may involve rather tricky rules.

Pregnancy provides another naturalistic situation in which the sensitivity of manifest dream content may be examined. Becoming pregnant is obviously a major event in any woman's life, and it is interesting to explore how this event modifies dream imagery. Several investigators (for example, Van De Castle and Kinder 1968, Gillman 1968) have established that pregnant women do exceed nonpregnant women significantly in the frequency with which their dreams explicitly refer to babies and children. It has also been observed that pregnant women show an upsurge of explicit dream imagery concerned with babies pictured in a context of danger and difficulty. Winget and Kapp (1972) have dramatically underscored the meaningfulness of the imagery in pregnant women's dreams. They showed that the greater the anxiety and threat manifestly portrayed in a pregnant woman's dreams, the less protracted was her subsequent delivery. They interpreted this finding within the context of a theory that the function of the dream is to attempt "to master, in fantasy, an anticipated stress in waking life." They presume that the woman who most directly deals with her anxieties about her pregnancy by rehearsing them in her dreams arrives at her delivery with a smaller degree of anxiety capable of adversely affecting the efficiency of her uterine response. Again, what is particularly noteworthy is that the experience of pregnancy reverberates in the manifest dream imagery, and does this so meaningfully that its pattern of occurrence predicts an important physiological event (namely, duration of labor) linked with the pregnancy.

It is of related interest that differences in manifest content have been shown for various phases of the menstrual cycle. There is some evidence that shifts in mood and psychological orientation occur that are related to the cycle. These shifts are presumably tied not only to physiological variables but also to the psychological significance of menstrual events. Swanson and Foulkes (1967) monitored the dreams of young women for eleven consecutive weeks and analyzed them according to phase of the menstrual cycle. They discovered that content referring either to sexuality or hostility was maximal during the menses. Van De Castle (1967) scanned the dreams of a sample of nursing students and found that during menses the dreamer was assigned a relatively more active social role in the dream action, while during ovulation the role assignment was particularly passive. Further, the increased social activity during menses was depicted as being more directed toward males than females.

Porach (1970) analyzed the dream content of masculine as compared to feminine women at different stages of the menstrual cycle and found that significant differences emerged. For example, during the pre-ovulative phase, masculine women exceeded feminine women in the frequency with which they dreamed of friendly interactions with the opposite sex.

An important group of studies indicates that the manifest dream content often reflects key aspects of an individual's role in the culture. To begin with, there are consistently reported differences in the dream imagery of males and females that seem to tie in with their divergent life experiences. For example, Brenneis (1970) presents evidence that (p. 438): "Female dreams more often occur in indoor settings, less often contain certain events which occur beyond the dreamer's control, and more often contain a greater number of people. They also include a greater proportion of familiar people, in particular, parents. On the other hand, the central figure in male dreams is more often in extended motion, while the central figure in female dreams more often opposes a restraining force." He explains these differences by contrasting masculine values, which require establishing one's separateness and ability to accomplish things by active individual effort, and feminine values, which emphasize intimacy and social responsiveness. Also congruent with conventional sex role differences are reports by Paolino (1964), Urbina (1972), and Cohen (1973) that more aggression occurs in the manifest dream content of males than in that of females. Colby (1963) has found analogous sex differences with regard to aggressive motility in dream imagery. It should be added, though, that one study (Fletcher, 1970) could not detect significant differences in amount of aggressive imagery in the manifest content of male and female dreams.

Numerous differences in manifest dream content have been detected in groups differing with respect to where they are in the life cycle. Boys aged six to twelve were observed (Foulkes et al. 1967) to have dreams in which there was greater passivity than found in dreams of young male adults. They were also more likely to depict themes dealing with parents, siblings and male agemates, and less likely to refer to interactions with female agemates. Langs (1967b) determined that a sample of adolescent patients in psychotherapy exceeded adult patients in psychotherapy in the frequency with which their manifest dreams dealt with themes of destructive assertion, intense aggression, and the threat of castration (body damage). They also more often reported dream images of animals and monsters. Langs considered that the pattern of differences underscored fairly well some of the special adjustment problems confronting the adolescent. Barad et al. (1961) described persons in a sample of the aged (sixty-five or older) as dreaming with unusual frequency about manifest themes of loss of resources and strength. Kramer et al. (1970) found a relatively high frequency of death topics in the dreams of the aged.

A correspondence between dream imagery and a life dilemma was described by Goldhirsh (1961). He investigated the dreams of a group of men imprisoned for sex offenses and compared them with dreams of those imprisoned for non-sexual offenses. He found that the sex offenders far exceeded the others in openly portraying sex crime themes (for example, rape).

Extremely interesting are the reports of Winget, et al. (1970) that manifest dreams differ in relation to socio-economic status and race.[22] They noted, among numerous other things, that references to death and misfortune were more common in the lower than upper classes. They found, too, that the dreams of Negroes exceeded those of whites in references to suffering injury, loss, or body damage ("castration anxiety"), but contained fewer accounts in which hostility was expressed toward others in a disguised fashion.

Many other studies could be cited in which the life circumstances and dilemmas of individuals seem to be directly (without serious disguise) represented in their dream imagery. But let us focus now upon experimental studies that have deliberately introduced special conditions into an individual's life in order to ascertain how they find representation in his manifest dream productions.

The "sleep laboratory" has become the major center for the study of dreams. After Aserinsky and Kleitman (1953) discovered that the occurrence of dreams is accompanied by rapid eye movements which can be measured, many installations were established in which dream phenomena could be observed. Typically, subjects were asked to sleep in the laboratory so that they could be periodically awakened and detailed accounts of their dreams obtained when their eye movements indicated the beginning of a dream sequence. In such a context it was possible to study with a new precision the factors affecting the character of dreams. But researchers soon learned of a complication when they brought subjects into the dream laboratory. The dreams of these subjects during the first night they slept in the experimental setting were found to be atypical of their dreams on subsequent nights and permeated with references to the experimenter, his research equipment, and so forth. It has been shown by several investigators (Dement et al. 1965, Hall 1967, Whitman et al. 1962) that the imagery of the "first night" dreams contains many direct and also many only slightly disguised references to how the dreamer is experiencing the sleep laboratory. Note the following two examples of dreams which mirror the laboratory situation (Dement et al. 1965, p. 127):

> "I was dreaming I was here and I was all rigged up to this machine and I got into a position that when I rolled over, I pulled all the lead wires out."
> ". . . I had left the experiment with all the wires still attached to my head. I found myself in the office of one of my professors at the psychological department. Then I realized I had to get back to the experiment."

It has also been reported that the greater the dreamer's personal involvement with the laboratory personnel or the study itself, the more profusely they are referred to in his manifest dreams. Dement et al. (1965) indicate that when male subjects are monitored by male laboratory personnel, their dreams focus on issues of attack and getting hurt, whereas female subjects monitored by males emphasize themes of sexual exploitation. In short, there is decent evidence that the mere fact of an individual participating in a dream experiment not only leaves an obvious imprint on his dreams, it leaves one that specifies feelings and attitudes aroused by the experience.

The degree to which feelings growing out of an experimental situation can color dreams was highlighted in a study by Orr et al. (1968), which looked at the ability of persons to awaken themselves at a specific time after falling asleep—with the incentive of earning a monetary reward for doing so. A significant number were successful in rousing themselves near the specific time; but what is of special interest is that they, in contrast to those who were unsuccessful, consistently had dreams just before awakening in which there was prominent "apprehension and anticipation." That is, the intent to wake up at a specific time was translated into a dream-feeling tone that then perhaps functioned as an "It's time to get up" signal.

Mention should be made of a line of research concerned with the effects of various drugs upon dream imagery. Whitman, et al. (1961) have shown in normal samples that imipramine significantly increases the amount of overt hostility in dreams. Prochlorperazine increases references to heterosexual interaction, and phenobarbital increases imagery dealing with homosexuality. In another project, Whitman et al. (1960) reported that meprobamate produced a significant increase in imagery portraying motility and dependency.

Other studies (Tart 1965, Baekeland et al. 1968, Witkin, 1969, Foulkes and Rechtschaffen 1964) offer evidence that such pre-sleep stimulation as movies, pictures, and word associations may register in dream imagery.[23]

A unique species of responsiveness of the manifest content is pointed up by Stoyva's (1965) demonstration that if persons are hypnotized before going to sleep and given the proper post-hypnotic suggestion that they will later dream about a particular topic (for example, "You are climbing a tree"), they do, actually, tend to do so. Barber et al. (1973) have also demonstrated that pre-sleep suggestion affects dream content. Here one sees a capability of directly translating into the dream imagery an instruction given by another person previous to sleep onset. Freud anticipated this finding when he commented that the psychoanalyst can, by means of the transference, influence his patients to orient their dreams in certain directions.

An individual's dreams exhibit sensitivity not only to what happens to him in the pre-sleep period, but also to stimuli impinging upon him while he is asleep. Freud, of course, minimized the importance of sensory stimuli upon the dreams of someone already asleep and concluded that they could play only a minor role in the total dream structure. The accumulating scientific literature suggests a somewhat different picture. Tart (1965), after reviewing the findings bearing on this matter, concluded that a variety of experimental stimuli, when applied to a dreamer in a laboratory situation, do find perceptible expression in his dreams. For example, raters could distinguish dreams that had occurred while the dreamer had been exposed to hearing the names of persons who were important to him from dreams during which the exposure had been to neutral names. A particularly decisive study by Castaldo and Holzman (1967), relevant to this whole matter, should be cited. They discovered in a sample of normal persons that when a sleeping individual is exposed to a tape recording of his own voice, his dreams under this condition differ from those he produces when exposed to a tape of a voice of another person saying the same words. Under the impact of his own voice, the dreamer has a significantly greater likelihood of experiencing dreams in which the principal figure is active, independent, and assertive. While listening to tapes of someone else's voice, the role of the central dream figure is depicted in passive terms. Castaldo and Holzman suggested that this finding derived from the fact that one's voice serves "as a regulator of voluntary action." Presumably, hearing a stimulus with connotations pertaining to voluntary control was transformed in the manifest dream into a portrayal of the central dream actor as being particularly active and forceful. The degree of activity-passivity of the central dream actor cannot be dismissed as a minor dimension, and one has grounds for regarding the impact of hearing one's own voice during sleep upon one's dream as significant. It is clear from this study and others in the literature that a stimulus experienced by an individual while asleep will effectively get into his dreams if it has some emotional potency. Neutral, noninvolving stimuli will tend not to do so.

Another level at which the meaningfulness of the manifest content can be probed is in terms of its relationships with personality. If the manifest content of an individual's dreams were simply a defensive shell, there would be little reason for expecting it to contain solid information about the sort of person he is. What do we find with respect to this matter when we scan the scientific literature? In fact, many studies have produced correlations between personality indices and measures derived from the manifest dream content. The great majority have found significant relationships. A sample of such findings follows.

Rychlak and Brams (1963) analyzed the major manifest themes in dreams obtained from normal persons and related these themes to a number of personality measures (for example, the Minnesota Multiphasic Personality Inventory and the Edwards Personal Preference Schedule). They observed that persons often reporting dreams in which humans have pleasurable and relaxed interactions were characteristically "socially responsible, orderly, and planful individuals who are somewhat introverted" (p. 232). Interestingly, too, they discovered that persons frequently dreaming of themes of achievement, recognition, and status attainment were portrayed by the personality tests as "rather dominating individuals, who desire leadership responsibility and the attention or admiration of others. They were the more self confident . . . with essentially higher socio-economic value systems . . ." (p. 232).

Meer (1955) examined the correlation, in a normal sample, between manifest dream attributes and authoritarianism. It was predicted, and found, that the greater an individual's authoritarianism, the more likely he was to have dreams in which characters were hostile to strangers (outgroup) but friendly to those classified as close (ingroup). Meer indicated that the findings were congruent with the concept that "authoritarian individuals inhibit the expression of aggression toward family and other ingroup members, and that they project and displace their aggression toward individuals and groups who are socially inferior and those who are perceived as an outgroup" (p. 76). In other words, the manifest dream imagery isomorphically mirrored what has been regarded as a basic dynamic tendency in the personality of the authoritarian individual.

Saul et al. (1954) predicted, on the basis of a psychosomatic formulation concerning the type of personality configuration likely to produce hypertension, that more hostility would appear in the manifest content of dreams of hypertensives than in the dreams of nonhypertensives. This prediction proved to be correct.

King (1971) determined the hypnotic susceptibility (using a standard scale) of persons in a normal sample and demonstrated that it was positively correlated with the vividness and dramatic quality of their manifest dreams.

Foulkes and Rechtschaffen (1964) detected a number of links between personality variables and manifest dream attributes in a normal sample. They observed that the greater an individual's hostility, the more "unpleasant" the tone of his dreams. They found, too, that the greater an individual's tendency to be acting out and to have poor reality testing, the more he portrayed physical aggression in his dreams. A variety of other similar findings emerged.

Framo et al. (1962) developed an hypothesis that psychotic persons who are attempting to cope with their anxiety are likely to behave passively if they feel they are primarily threatened from forces within themselves and actively if they perceive the threat as emanating from others. They tested it, first, by having the manifest dreams of persons in a psychotic sample rated for the presence of threatening forces and then differentiated as to whether these forces are directed toward the self (the dreamer) or others. Secondly, nursing personnel acquainted with the patients evaluated them with respect to how active or passive they typically behave. Analysis of the data indicated that, as predicted, the active patient was characterized by manifest imagery in which threat impinged upon self, with passive patients portraying the threat as directed toward others (presumably from the self).

There is increasing evidence that those who differ in amount of personal "differentiation" (as defined by the Witkin et al. [1962] field dependence-independence dimension) are divergent in their dream constructions. More differentiated persons are described (Witkin 1969) as representing self in their dreams as more active participants in the action than do the less differentiated. Witkin states that they also have an increased likelihood of producing dream imagery that is more imaginative. He reports, too, that when they spend the night in the sleep laboratory, they are less likely to incorporate feelings about their relationships with the experimenter into the manifest dream content.

The examples cited above document the considerable range of personality variables that have proven to be reflected in the manifest dream content. Other examples could have been presented and the future will undoubtedly reveal even more.

An incidental finding should be mentioned that points in still another way to the meaningfulness of manifest content. Several investigators—for example, Dement and Wolpert (1958a, b)—have noted that if one monitors an individual's dreams during a given night, significant consistencies show up in the series. Dement and Wolpert state with respect to quantitative findings based on night-long monitoring of dreams of normal subjects: ". . . the manifest content of nearly every dream exhibited some obvious relationship to one or more dreams occurring on the same night" (1958b, p. 569). They add that such continuities often provide insights concerning an individual's personality. But what we would like to focus on is the phenomenon of continuity itself. We would suggest that if the manifest content were simply a defensive aggregation of disguises, the continuities would not well serve the defensive intent. One can argue that the repeated use of the same or similar disguises would actually increase the possibility that the dreamer could pick up cues that would enable him to decode the so-called latent content. It is, after all, easier to crack any code if a large sample of its applications is available. Further, since the manifest continuities often explicitly concern important life themes and intents, which seem to be relevant to what is known about the personalities of the dreamers, it seems economical to consider that they are more than merely defensive.

The matter of continuity is highlighted in still another way by Verdone (1965). He observed that if dreams (in a normal sample) were followed over the course of the night, there were consistent trends for change in the manifest imagery. The imagery became increasingly vivid and emotional, and the references to time were increasingly to an earlier period in one's life span. It would be particularly difficult, on the basis of a defensive concept of manifest content, to explain why there should be consistent time changes in the dream imagery. One cannot imagine how this would serve defensive functions.

The intent of this section has been to demonstrate that the manifest dream content carries a great deal of meaning. It seems to be sensitive to myriad environmental conditions, it exhibits logical correlations with personality variables, it mirrors dimensions measured by projective tests, it predicts certain aspects of behavior, and it changes over the course of the night in accordance with what appear to be logically consistent patterns. What is even more significant is that ratings of dreams based on manifest content correlate significantly with ratings derived from the so-called latent content. The weight of the evidence argues against viewing the manifest content as a largely meaningless conglomeration of camouflage devices, such as Freud spelled out. This is not to deny that it may conceivably at times function defensively (although this remains to be scientifically verified). But it can be energetically denied that the information it contains is *only* defensive. The manifest content has shown itself to be a reliable source of significant data about the state of the dreamer, his personality, and how he is coping with certain life issues.

After assimilating such findings, we concluded that it would be sensible to include all available research involving the manifest dream content in any thorough analysis of dream function. To omit such information would be equivalent to putting on blinders in the name of theoretical propositions.

Do Dreams Provide an Outlet for Drives and Impulses?

It will be recalled that after reviewing Freud's dream theory, we suggested that the fairest version to test is not one that assigns to dreams the exclusive function of fulfilling wishes. Rather, in the light of Freud's own detailed statements, it seemed more reasonable to regard the theory as asserting that the dream is a vehicle for expressing drives and impulses from the unconscious sector of the "psychic apparatus."

A question that immediately arises in testing this theory relates to how one determines whether a drive or impulse is of unconscious origin. If one can show that a dream does, indeed, express a certain impulse, how is one to be sure the impulse originated in an unconscious sector? This is an extremely difficult question, which could be discussed at length; but ultimately one would have to admit that, operationally, there is no reliable scientific way of defining which dream elements are presumably derived from the unconscious. Freud hypothesized, of course, that the unconscious elements in a dream could be discerned only by a free association technique. However, it is interesting, as reported above, that quite a number of studies have found significant correlations between manifest dream elements and projective test indices often assumed to tap unconscious attitudes or fantasies. Also, significant correlations have been demonstrated between dream indices based on manifest content and others based on the latent content. In any case, one finds that, empirically, the detection of presumed unconscious influences upon dreams becomes a matter of deduction. One has to conjure up alternatives that would seem to flow from the Freudian model and determine which are supported by the actual data. There will follow an analysis of several groups of studies that bear on whether dreams provide a venting outlet for unconscious impulses.

EFFECTS OF REM DEPRIVATION

The first strategy we will adopt in exploring Freud's hypothesis that the dream serves to vent unconscious impulses derives from work showing that dreaming occurs at specific points in the sleep cycle and is signaled by the onset of Rapid Eye Movements (REM). As originally reported by Aserinsky and Kleitman (1953) and subsequently validated by many other investigators, the average person dreams at fairly fixed points during his night of sleep. His periods of dreaming are characterized by specific changes in depth of sleep (defined in terms of electroencephalogram recordings) and the appearance of REM. The correlation between REM and dreaming has been documented by rousing persons when REM occurs and establishing that dreams are more likely to be reported at such times than after awakenings not preceded by REM.[24]

Following this discovery, it was almost inevitable that someone should ponder the question of what would happen if one took advantage of the availability of this indicator of dreaming onset to interfere with dreaming. What if you awoke a person every time he started to dream? How would this affect him? In fact, with further consideration it became obvious that this question may touch directly on Freud's concept of dream function. If, as Freud conjectured, the dream provides a channel for the partial release of unacceptable drives, it should follow that elimination of the channel would produce psychological disequilibrium and disturbance. Being unable to dream should lead to a build-up of tension that would be disquieting and call for special compensatory responses. If significant disturbance did not result from interference with dreaming, this would represent indirect evidence that the venting function Freud ascribed to the dream was either nonexistent or of such minor magnitude as to be inconsequential.

We shall proceed to review the scientific literature dealing with this matter.

A good many investigators have probed the effects of depriving people of the opportunity to dream. They have largely been interested in whether such deprivation leads to disturbance or disequilibrium. Early research reports were unanimous in depicting the impact of dream curtailment as rather serious and at times even catastrophic. The first systematic project was carried out by Dement (1960). He awakened subjects within a minute or two after they began to dream (as signaled by the onset of REM) and managed to achieve 67–75 percent deprivation of dream time (variously from four to seven nights). He observed, first of all, that in a period subsequent to deprivation, subjects spent an extra, compensatory amount of time in the dreaming phase of sleep. He noted, too, that irritability, anxiety, and difficulties in concentration developed during deprivation. One subject manifested "serious anxiety and agitation." Several reported sharp increases in appetite. These symptoms were described as disappearing as soon as the subjects were restored the opportunity to dream. Dement observed, in addition, that when the same subjects were deprived of a phase of sleep that did not interfere with dreaming, no significant signs of disturbance appeared. Subsequent work by Dement and Fisher (1963) and Fisher (1965a,b) was confirmatory of the initial findings. Not only were anxiety, irritability, and increases in appetite again noted, there were also instances in which individuals seemed to become grossly upset. Dement described a few individuals whose disturbance was almost of a borderline psychotic character (for example, paranoid suspiciousness).

In a later study by Hoedemaker et al. (1963) it was reported that ten nights' dream deprivation actually resulted in one subject developing hallucinatory-like experiences. Sampson (1966) could not, by means of psychological tests (for example, word associations, memory for digits, depression scale of MMPI), detect changes in persons exposed to dream deprivation. However, overt behavioral shifts were observed which were congruent with those already cited. Sampson states (p. 316): "Some subjects developed intense hunger and special food cravings; all reported some increase in appetite during one or both deprivation series. . . . Some instances of disturbances in subjects' relationship to reality or feelings of reality were observed and reported. The intensity of reaction to the experimental deprivations was notable, with instances of childish behavior, the emergence of prominent masochistic and even paranoid themes, some injuries to self . . ." One should add that Sampson urged cautious interpretation of his results because he was doubtful of the adequacy of some of his controls. Agnew et al. (1967) could not detect that dream deprivation affected such structured tasks as paced addition and strength of grip, but personality tests (MMPI, Pensacola Z Scale, Taylor Manifest Anxiety Scale, and Cattell's 16 PF) revealed (p. 856): "that subjects became less well integrated and less interpersonally effective." Observations suggested, too, that deprived subjects (p. 856) "tended to show signs of confusion, suspicion, and withdrawal. These subjects seemed anxious, insecure, introspective, and unable to derive support from other people."

Greenberg et al. (1970) found that dream-deprived subjects were not adversely affected, as measured by simple cognitive tasks (for example, vigilance in detecting a signal). But the Rorschach test did register a negative impact.[25] It was possible to demonstrate objectively that specific impulses or feelings that habitually are particularly threatening to an individual are intensified after dream deprivation. Greenberg et al. state (1970, p. 9): "The most striking finding of this study is that, with dream deprivation, *feelings* and *wishes* which have been kept out of consciousness now appear more overtly in the test protocols . . ." Fiss et al. (1968) similarly noted that as dream deprivation proceeds, material pertaining to "repressed conflicts" begins to appear more openly in the manifest content of dreams.[26]

Other, more complex approaches have been adopted in registering the effects of dream deprivation. Greenberg et al. (1972) exposed subjects to an anxiety-provoking film of an autopsy, then dream-deprived them, and finally exposed them to the film for a second time. There was also a control group that went through the same procedure without being dream-deprived. It was shown that if an individual was made anxious (as registered in self-ratings) by the first autopsy film, he adapted less well (registered relatively more anxiety) to the second viewing of the film following dream deprivation than if he was in the control group.[27] Incidentally, it was also noted that the dream-deprived subjects were overtly more anxious than the controls *before* the second film showing.

Grieser et al. (1972) established in a select group of subjects (high in ego strength) that dream deprivation prevented correct recall of threatening material to a greater degree than did control awakenings from non-dream sleep. The dream deprivation was interposed between involvement with threatening material (words linked with a failure experience) and the later task of trying to recall that material. The results suggested that the deprivation produced a disequilibrium that interfered with the cognitive processing of threatening material. One could analogously interpret the findings of Greenberg et al. (1972) just cited above, in which dream deprivation interfered with the assimilation of the disturbance produced by a threatening film.

The apparent venting function of dreaming was interestingly explored by Cartwright and Monroe (1968). They awakened subjects at the onset of dreaming and requested of them, on different occasions, to give two types of responses. In some instances they were simply asked to repeat digits recited to them, but in other instances they were to turn their attention inward and try to recall "What was going on in your mind just before I called you?" They were later observed to determine how much compensatory dream time they needed.[28] Cartwright and Monroe had hypothesized that the task calling for introspective analysis, which therefore provided involvement with, and a chance to rehearse, fantasy material would be followed by less compensatory REM time than would the condition in which the performance of a cognitive task prevented any fantasy activity. The results supported the hypothesis. The fact that an activity involving fantasy could substitute for lost dream time and relieve the pressure for compensatory REM time does seem to buttress the idea that the fantasy aspect of dreaming, as such, serves a special tension-relieving function.

A study by Fiss et al. (1966) is especially pertinent to the findings just described. They asked persons who were awakened from REM sleep to compose stories to Thematic Apperception pictures and to construct other stories when awakened from non-REM sleep. Analysis of the stories indicated that those immediately following the dream deprivation condition were "longer, more complex, visual, bizarre, emotional, and vivid" than those following interruption of non-dream sleep.[29] In other words, the stories following deprivation were particularly intense and emotional. If, as Fiss et al. speculate, it were true that when an individual is roused from REM or non-REM sleep, something of the psychological state characterizing these phases persists briefly, it could be argued that the differences found in Thematic Apperception stories reflect differences in psychological intensity between dream and non-dream states. The greater intensity of the dreaming phase could be viewed as congruent with the idea that it is a time of special psychological release or expression.

A novel exploration by Lerner (1966) adds further weight to this review. Working with the special hypothesis that dreaming serves to protect the integrity of the body image, she examined the impact of dream deprivation upon inkblot responses. She expected, more specifically, that dream deprivation would lead to a disturbance in body image. She obtained results (for example, a compensatory increase in movement responses) which she interpreted as supportive of her hypothesis. Incidentally, Feldstein (1972), in a study of REM deprivation, reported partial confirmation of the finding pertaining to movement responses. Lerner found, too, that dream deprivation led to an increase in fantasies depicting body dissolution. It is a fair interpretation of her findings to say that the deprivation was followed by signs of a psychological need to re-equilibrate.

Against the positive findings just reviewed, one must consider the evidence that does not support the idea that dream deprivation produces psychological disturbance.

Attention should immediately be turned to a paper by Vogel (1968) in which he points out that among the various cases reported by Dement (1960, 1965) and Dement and Fisher (1963) in which sleep deprivation apparently led to psychological disequilibrium, there were also several (involving long periods of deprivation) that manifested no real disturbance. Vogel was led by his own analysis of this data and other studies to the view that the original findings of Dement and Dement and Fisher might be artifacts linked to biased expectations by both the experimenters and the subjects.[30] One study that Vogel cited as most directly challenging Dement's work was carried out by Kales et al. (1964). They deprived two subjects of REM time for up to ten days and were unable to demonstrate adverse effects either in terms of psychological tests (for example, repeating digits, Minnesota Multiphasic Personality Inventory, mood ratings) or observations of overt behavior. Vogel also mentions two cases studied by Snyder (1963) in which the results did not indicate that dream deprivation caused significant disturbance. Vogel certainly raised pertinent criticisms, but it is fair to say that he went too far in his complete dismissal of previous deprivation effects. While he was probably correct in his view that dream deprivation does not produce disturbance of psychotic proportions, a number of findings (already cited above) that have been published since his paper argue that dream deprivation does lead to psychological disequilibrium.

Foulkes et al. (1968) dream-deprived subjects and evaluated their reactions both by means of self-ratings and ratings by objective observers. They could not show that significant psychological disturbance had been provoked. However, it is interesting that when they divided the subjects into those manifesting more compensatory REM time after REM deprivation than after non-REM deprivation and those not manifesting this pattern, the former were rated as showing more disturbance consequent to deprivation. In other words, there were clear individual differences that were tied to how much the deprivation evoked compensatory dream time.

Relatedly, Cartwright et al. (1967) have particularly underscored the great variability persons exhibit in their responses to REM deprivation. They point out that some do not seem to need any compensatory REM time and some require a great deal. They discovered that, in their sample, those most needing compensatory time were the most anxious and most disturbed after ingestion of an hallucinogenic drug. They state (p. 303): "In terms of ego controls and tolerance for changes in usual brain states, these people are weakest." It should be added that other findings they obtained also provided support for the idea that REM compensatory time following deprivation serves the function of providing an additional compensatory *psychological* experience (that is, time for dreaming) rather than merely replacing some kind of lost physiological REM state. They did this by demonstrating that the greater the degree to which an individual reports the presence of dream-like content when he is awakened to deprive him of REM time, the less compensatory REM time he needs in the post-deprivation periods. The more he actually dreams in the brief period before he is awakened, the less he seems to need compensatory REM time. In another study, Cartwright and Ratzel (1972) again reported great variation in how individuals react to dream deprivation. Some of the subjects in their sample did show signs of psychological disequilibrium. But one of the major findings was that persons who are normally somewhat constricted in their use of fantasy actually *benefited* from REM deprivation in the sense that they exhibited increased ability to use fantasy constructively (as measured by Rorschach and intelligence test indices). The deprivation impact was positive rather than negative. It should be emphasized that this finding is unique in the literature and awaits cross-validation.

As one scans the total results that have been laid out, they do suggest that dreaming serves some discharge function. There are inconsistencies and even contradictions in the data, but a major directionality comes through. In various ways it has been shown that if you prevent an individual from dreaming, you upset him psychologically. It is true that the degree of upset was probably exaggerated in earlier reports. One would doubt that disturbance of psychotic proportions is ever really evoked. But in the majority of reported observations at least a small amount of disturbance does appear. One would have to conclude that, at least indirectly, these observations support Freud's hypothesis that the dream helps to maintain psychological equilibrium by providing a partial means for discharging unconscious impulses.

DEEP PERSONAL INVOLVEMENT AND DREAM ATTRIBUTES

There are scattered attempts in the literature to appraise the dream effects of inputs that are deeply personally involving and in some instances even specifically directed at mobilizing unconscious responses. This work is of special import, because it provides an opportunity to ascertain whether conditions that might logically be expected to build up pressures in the unconscious sector actually give rise to signs of disequilibrium in the dream.

Breger et al. (1971) exposed normal subjects to group therapy sessions that were highly emotional and ego involving. During these sessions motives and attitudes were probed and extremely private material was explored. The subjects felt that the most intimate aspects of self had been touched upon. They also showed signs of considerable tension and disturbance. Dreams were obtained from them (in the sleep laboratory) prior to the therapy sessions and immediately subsequent to them. Analysis of the dreams revealed that the effects of the sessions could be spotted in the changes from the pre- to post-dreams. The interactions among dream figures became significantly less pleasant and the dreamer was portrayed in less "adequate" roles. There was a shift such that the dreams displayed greater anxiety, cognitive disturbance, and intensity of personal involvement. Detailed investigation of the individual dreams suggested that the therapy input caused new themes to appear that persisted over a sequence of dreams, as if there were a struggle to cope with tensions that had been aroused.

Breger et al. also considered the impact of being a surgical patient on dreams. There are few life conditions that are more threatening than having to submit to surgery. The dreams were collected from subjects pre- and post-operatively, and they were compared with those of a non-surgical control group. It was found that the pre-surgery dream imagery of the surgical patients was significantly higher in anxiety, cognitive disturbance, implausibility, intensity of involvement, hostility, and castration anxiety than that of the controls. A number of these differences persisted in comparisons of post-surgery with control dreams. The intense stress of facing surgery had a profound effect on dream imagery.

Special attention should be drawn to an unusual research design by Cartwright (1974). For each of a series of subjects she determined the particular psychological area in which he felt deficient or not up to standard. Just before going to sleep he was then instructed to repeat over and over that he wished he had more of the quality or trait with respect to which he felt inferior. Dream reports were obtained that same night during REM periods. Control trials were also run when subjects wished for qualities about which they did not feel deficient. Blind ratings of the collected dreams revealed that the repetitively stated conscious wish was significantly more often detectable in the manifest content when it involved an area of psychological deficiency rather than a control non-tension area. Cartwright analyzed the ways in which wishes about personal deficiency were expressed in the dream content, and noted (p. 392): "The function of these dreams seems not to be one of gratification by carrying out the wish but more often one of reviewing the emotional implications involved." She added (p. 392): "One function of dreaming thought appears to be to explore the emotional components of a tension area which may be different from those available to the waking self."

Freedman et al. (1970) scanned the effects of individual psychoanalytically oriented therapy (twice a week) upon a neurotic woman. She slept in a laboratory on the night intervening between her two therapy sessions, and her amount of REM time was recorded. Whenever she spontaneously awakened, she was asked to describe any dreams that had occurred. Her therapy sessions were tape recorded and clinicians later rated them for a variety of dimensions (for example, oral wishes, anger toward others, heterosexual content). It was hypothesized that "high anxiety and possibly high psychological pressure revealed in psychotherapy sessions would correlate with high dream time" (p. 33). The results obtained did not support the hypothesis. There was, though, an interesting positive correlation between the amount of anxiety expressed in a dream and its length.

In a novel approach, Weingarden (1972) arranged for a group of subjects to fail at a task, then compared their subsequent dreams with those of a group that did not know how well they had performed. He reported that judges found more themes of inadequacy-failure-injury in the dreams of the experimental than in those of the control subjects. The failure experience apparently generated a tension that was depicted in the dream imagery. During a second study Weingarden evaluated the effect of a "decathexis" procedure upon the likelihood of a failure experience gaining representation in dreams. Presumably, the opportunity to "work through" or cope with the failure would diminish its pressure for expression and therefore the probability of appearing in dream form. One sample of subjects was made to fail at a task but then given the opportunity to "work through" the experience by producing associations and focusing on ideas antithetical to failure. Another sample was made to fail, but opportunity to "decathect" the experience was more circuitous and involved considering the possible defects in the "test" that had been used to create the sense of failure. A control group that did not encounter failure was also included. The dreams of all subjects were obtained the night subsequent to the experimental or control procedures, and were analyzed for a number of themes (for example, failure, aggression, achievement). It was found that the "decathecting" procedures did not decrease the likelihood of the failure experiences registering in the dream content. This outcome is obviously not congruent with the notion that the "working through" of an involving, disturbing experience will decrease its pressure for dream outlet.

It should be noted at this point that the dream consequences of exposure to intensely emotionally charged films have been probed by several investigators. Studies have been made of the dream effects of extremely powerful films depicting themes relating to hostility (Foulkes and Rechtschaffen 1964), body mutilation (Witkin 1969), and sex (Cartwright et al. 1969). In all instances the imprint could be detected, although it was somewhat minimal for the aggression theme. The erotic film affected the relationships of figures in the dreams, diminished ability to recall dream content, and increased symbolic sexual material in dream imagery. The body mutilation film increased the number of spontaneous awakenings from REM periods, led to increased anxiety content, and adversely affected dream recall.

Some attention has been devoted to the effects of internal tension states such as thirst and hunger upon dreams. Freud (1900) cited instances in which he observed children who had openly wish-fulfilling dreams involving the consumption of desired or favorite foods. He also reported that when he ate certain foods that made him very thirsty, he subsequently dreamed of thirst-quenching themes. While internal tension states like thirst and hunger are not directly analogous to the kinds of unconscious impulses Freud regarded as basic to dreaming, it is interesting to see what empirical studies have shown concerning such tensions gaining outlet in dream imagery. Dement and Wolpert (1958a) deprived subjects of water for periods of 24 hours or more on several occasions in the sleep laboratory and found little or no evidence that their thirst registered in their dreams. However, Bokert (1968) reported that when he deprived subjects of food and fluids and gave them a salty meal prior to sleep, their dreams reflected more thirst content than did those of nondeprived control subjects. He also found that subjects who had dreams that explicitly gratified thirst or hunger were less thirsty and drank less when they awakened from sleep than subjects who did not experience such gratifying dreams. Relatedly, Domhoff and Kamiya (1964) observed that references to food and drink increased in dreams of subjects over the course of the night. They suggested that this might be a response to the hunger that presumably builds up during sleep. O'Neill (1965) undertook a comparison of the degree to which hunger and thirst imagery appear in the dreams of individuals from cultures differing in how much they habitually deprive persons of food and drink (either because of scarcity or religious rules). As anticipated, hunger and thirst content were particularly prominent in the dreams of those who were from the most deprived cultures. Persons presumably under the greatest tension to find gratification were most likely to exhibit related oral images in their dreams. The findings just outlined obviously represent only a beginning in this area. But they do reveal a trend for internal tensions like hunger and thirst to find expression in dreams.

Wiseman and Reyher (1973) made a direct attempt to manipulate the involvement of the unconscious sector in dreaming. They hypnotized subjects and suggested that they dream about each of the Rorschach inkblots. This was intended to set up a process in which the blots (by virtue of having been incorporated into dreams) would become linked with unconscious elements. It was predicted that when the subjects exposed to this procedure were later asked to respond to the Rorschach blots in a nonhypnotic state, their productions would show more evidence of "primary process thinking" (representatives of unconscious drives) than would those of subjects who had not had the experience of linking the blots to hypnotically induced dreams. The data obtained supported the hypothesis and were viewed as "consistent with Freud's theory of dreaming." Of course, this interpretation is dependent on whether one accepts the idea that "hypnotic dreams" are equivalent to dreams that occur naturally.

There are other interesting reports in the literature that at least tangentially point up the relationship between dream attributes and variables having deep personal significance. For example, Handal and Rychlak (1971) have uncovered a significant link between an individual's anxiety about death and the amount of imagery concerning death in his dreams. Lee (1958) established that Zulu women who are infertile are particularly likely to make references to "baby" in their dreams. This finding takes on significance when one considers that the role adequacy of a Zulu woman is to a major degree defined by her ability to bring forth a child. McReynolds et al. (1966) have reported that the greater the degree to which men feel "unsettled" about particular life themes, the more likely these themes are to appear in their dreams. Kales et al. (1970) observed that when cigarette smokers were deprived of the opportunity to smoke, they manifested more REM time than when not deprived.

The findings we have presented in this section are diverse and really confusing in their multiplicity. What they share is evidence that stimuli that are deeply stressful or involving do result in signs of tension and disequilibrium in dreams that follow.

PSYCHOLOGICAL MALADJUSTMENT AND DREAMING

It has been urged that a good chance to check the venting aspects of Freud's dream theory is provided in the case where psychological maladjustment occurs. Within the context of Freudian theory, such maladjustment presumably signals that unacceptable tensions are building up that are seeking outlet. These tensions might be expected to influence the dreaming process. Note Fisher's analysis of the matter (1967, pp. 102–103):

> If it is true, as Freud proposed, that the dream serves as a safety valve for the discharge of instinctual drives, then in any mental disturbance postulated by psychoanalytic theory to show an increased pressure of drives toward discharge, it would be expected that some change in dreaming process would occur. . . .
>
> For example, it is generally assumed that in acute schizophrenic psychosis there are increased conflict and intensification of the pressure of drives toward discharge in the presence of an ego defect or defects . . . It may be assumed that in any condition in which drive strength increases, total dream time might also increase, in the absence or inadequacy of substitute modes of discharge . . . Leaving aside purely physiological factors, a

> better formulation is that *total dream time on any given night is the resultant of the balance between drive and defense.* There may be an increase of instinctual drive pressure and a weakening of defensive and controlling functions of the ego, a constant drive pressure with a disintegration of defense functions, or increased drive strength with the defenses remaining constant.

Operationally speaking, this means that the dreams of those who are psychologically disturbed should differ from those persons who are not disturbed. The difference should be such as to indicate that the disturbed require either a larger amount of dream time or dream experiences of unusual intensity and vividness (for extra venting).

What do we find when we look at the literature concerned with *amount* of dreaming in relation to psychological disturbance? A few studies should first be mentioned that have analyzed the relationships between signs of disturbance in normal subjects and their REM time.[31] Rechtschaffen and Verdone (1964) reported in one instance that the greater an individual's anxiety level (as measured by the Minnesota Multiphasic Psychological Inventory), the greater his REM time. But they indicate that another investigator (Monroe) was unable to duplicate this result. Cartwright (1972) found that, in a group of "poor sleepers," REM time was positively correlated with a number of indices of personality pathology derived from the Minnesota Multiphasic Psychological Inventory. The equivalent correlations in a "good sleeper" sample were not significant. These results are obviously fragmentary and do not do much to clarify the question under consideration.

What does the literature say about the relationship existing between a more serious form of psychopathology, such as psychosis, and REM time? Generally, the findings have not been encouraging. There were early reports that schizophrenics had augmented REM time. Dement and Fisher (1963) detected a gross increase in a borderline patient who became psychotic while they were observing him in the sleep laboratory.[32] Other scattered reports seemed to point in the same direction (for example, Fisher 1965a,b, Feinberg 1969). However, more and more studies have appeared that challenge their validity (for example, Feinberg et al. 1964, 1965, Koresko et al. 1963, Onheiber et al. 1965, Ornitz et al. 1965—66). After thoroughly analyzing the pertinent literature, Feinberg (1969, p. 747) concluded: "A review of studies of physiological sleep patterns in schizophrenia reveals that basal REM activity is normal in this condition."[33] He adds, too: "While it has been claimed that the response of schizophrenic patients to REM deprivation is abnormal and that this abnormality is linked to the psychopathological mechanism of the illness, the available data seem largely inconsistent with this view."[34] Vogel (1974), in his review of the literature pertinent to this issue, also came to a similar skeptical conclusion. While the last word on the issue of whether psychopathology leads to alterations in REM time is not yet in, the existing findings are not encouraging.

Still another level available for probing the impact of psychological disturbance on dreams involves dream content. If the dreams of persons in a state of psychological equilibrium could be shown to contain themes indicative of a special intensity of discharge, this would support the venting hypothesis.

Two of the most impressive studies in the literature suggest that the greater an individual's psychological disturbance, the more likely are his dreams to be high in fantasy or dreamlike attributes. By way of introduction to these studies, it should be specified that past research has shown that dreams vary along a continuum from bland, matter-of-fact imagery to imagery that is highly imaginative and unreal. This latter imagery comes closer to the state one usually associates with dreaming. As earlier mentioned, it has been shown to be clearly more associated with REM periods in the sleep cycle than with non-REM periods. There is evidence that it is augmented by exposure to stressful experiences. Further, it is most often encountered in the later, longer, and more intense REM periods of the sleep night (Snyder 1967). In short, one can deduce from a network of data that intensified dream activity is signaled by the presence of imagery that is unusually imaginative, unreal, and implausible (dreamlike).

Cartwright (1972) carried out a particularly careful study in which she examined the "bizarreness of the fantasy content" (as defined by objective ratings) of dreams from schizophrenic patients, normal college students with elevated scores on the Schizophrenia scale of the Minnesota Multiphasic Personality Inventory (MMPI), and normal college students without such elevated scores. She found, as predicted, that the schizophrenics' dreams were most "dreamlike." Also, the dreams of the normals who showed signs of disturbance on the MMPI were more dreamlike than the nondisturbed normals. The greater the psychopathology, the more "dreamlike" was the imagery. Relatedly, Foulkes and Rechtschaffen (1964) reported that in a group of normal persons studied, there was a significant positive correlation between how disturbed (as measured by the MMPI) an individual is and how "dreamlike" (vivid, distorted, dramatic) he judges his dreams to be. Foulkes and Rechtschaffen felt these results were (p. 1000): "consistent with the widely held belief . . . that dream experiences serve the function of affect expression and primary process discharge, and that these functions are particularly prominent with an increasing degree of functional pathology."

The two studies just cited are particularly impressive. They indicate that dream intensity (as defined by the criterion of how "dreamlike" the imagery is) varies (even within the restricted range of pathology defined by MMPI scores in normal persons) in a way that is congruent with the concept that the more disturbed individual will have a greater need to vent material in his dreams.[35]

If one turns to the studies that have considered the question whether schizophrenic dreams can be identified, one finds the majority have answered affirmatively. At least ten investigators (for example, Carrington 1972, Kramer 1970, Brenneis 1971) have demonstrated that schizophrenic dreams can be distinguished from those of various control groups. Only a few have come up with contrary findings (for example, Noble 1951, Kant 1942). However, the really important question relates to the nature of the difference between schizophrenic and nonschizophrenic dream imagery. To demonstrate only that the dreams of schizophrenics can be differentiated from neurotics and normals would not in itself constitute support for the venting hypothesis. Schizophrenics are, after all, likely to be disturbed in their ability to communicate and in their mode of relating to anyone collecting dream material from them. This kind of disturbance could easily leave an identifiable mark or aura in their dream accounts.

With this view as a context, one winds up in a dilemma. This is true because the variable that most consistently distinguishes schizophrenic dreams, as indicated by research findings, relates to a dimension embracing terms like "implausibility," "bizarreness," "furthest from daily reality," and "strangeness" (Kramer et al. 1969, Carrington 1972, Langs 1966, Richardson and Moore 1963). Should one interpret this as simply a carryover of psychotic disorganization into the dream, or as an indication that the schizophrenic is more intensely caught up in the dreaming process (and therefore achieving more impulse venting)? This is not an easy question to answer. However, it should be noted that the unrealistic fantasy material in the dreams of schizophrenia is not such that it is blatantly "crazy." There have been studies in which raters had great difficulty in grossly differentiating the dreams of schizophrenics and normals (Brenneis 1971). It is not as though the two classes of dreams were obviously distinguished on the basis of indicators of psychotic thinking. No, the distinction relates more to degrees of implausibility—or, stating it in another way, to the degree to which the dream has the unreal qualities that we typically associate with fantasy. Remember, too, that implausibility has been shown to increase in the dreams of normal persons exposed to various kinds of stress. What is particularly pertinent is that maladjustment in persons who are *in the neurotic rather than psychotic range* has been shown to be accompanied by increased unreality in dream imagery. Thus, one can regard the link between schizophrenia and dream unreality as a more extreme instance of what holds true in other categories. In any case, it would probably be sensible to maintain a cautious attitude about whether the unreal dreams of the schizophrenic individual are more a reflection of his disorganization or his increased need for intense impulse venting.

REVIEW OF VENTING FINDINGS

If we assemble the array of observations concerned with whether venting of impulses occurs in dreams, what can we reasonably declare? There are converging lines of evidence which do reinforce the venting hypothesis. First, if one examines past work concerned with the effects of depriving persons of dream time, it seems fair to say it demonstrates that such deprivation produces psychological disequilibrium. True, the disturbance following dream deprivation is not of the extreme magnitude that the original investigators of this matter thought it to be. It is also true that marked individual differences exist in the mode of adaptation to the deprivation. But there is a discernible average trend for signs of disturbance to appear following limitation of dreaming that fit in with the idea that dreams somehow serve as an outlet or channel for tension reduction.

Another species of support for this view has been provided by studies that have traced the dream impact of stimuli which, because of their stressful and highly involving character, might be presumed to affect the unconscious sectors of the "psychic apparatus." Such stimuli as exposure to group therapy sessions, imminent surgery, and experiencing failure do generate effects that register as augmented tension and concern about specific related themes in the dream imagery.

Still a third source of pertinent information has derived from studies dealing with the relationship between psychopathology and dream characteristics. If one accepts the Freudian notion that personal maladjustment signals the buildup of unacceptable impulses, it should follow that the dreams of those who are psychologically disturbed would exhibit special venting functions. For example, one might expect such individuals to have a need for greater dream time. The empirical data do not support this specific prediction. However, the data do in other ways indicate that the greater an individual's maladjustment, the more his dream imagery is characterized by a heightened intensity. This has been shown within normal samples varying in personal disturbance and also by comparing schizophrenic and nonschizophrenic persons.

A network of scientific results exists compatible with Freud's central concept of dreaming, namely, that it offers an outlet or release for internal (unconscious) tensions. Definitive experiments have yet to be done in which labeled inputs known to arouse specific unconscious tensions are then traced to focal expressive dream imagery. But within the limitations of our present technology for studying the effects of psychological inputs, the results obtained are approximately what one would expect from the Freudian venting model.

Sleep Preservation

A third major aspect of Freud's dream theory relates to the presumed sleep-preserving function of the dream. As earlier described, he hypothesized that the dream helps to maintain sleep in the face of disturbing external or internal stimuli. He proposed that an individual who is asleep and hears the alarm clock go off may preserve his sleep by incorporating the sound of the bell into a dream in which it is given some reassuring, nonarousing significance. Similarly, he suggested that an unconscious impulse pressing for expression which might alarm the dreamer and therefore awaken him is given partial expression in the dream, but in such a disguised fashion that it arouses no overt anxiety with the potential of disrupting sleep.

One can say without hesitation that there is no support in the scientific literature for the "sleep preservation" theory.[36] The accumulated findings from sleep laboratories indicate that dreaming occurs in a regular cyclical fashion (approximately every ninety minutes) that is closer to a fixed biological rhythm than to a pattern indicating adaptation to threatening stimuli from moment to moment (Snyder 1967, Altshuler 1966, Dement and Wolpert 1958b). It is not initiated at scattered or irregular times, such as one might expect if it were a response to stimuli, dangerous to sleep, that appear unpredictably. In other words, dreaming follows a rather rigid schedule relatively independent of the events confronting an individual while asleep. The time allotted to dreaming is held to a biological rhythm that is largely uncorrelated with the impact of individual threats or dangers.[37] Dement and Wolpert (1958a) have even demonstrated that if one tries to interrupt an individual's sleep during nondreaming periods with various stimuli, these stimuli do *not* initiate dreams. The dreamer does not try to protect himself against the invaders of his sleep by incorporating them into dreams. Dement (1964) has commented that if the dream's purpose is to guard sleep, it does a highly inadequate job, since more than half of all REM periods are interrupted by short periods of wakefulness. Freud's assumptions about the sleep-preserving functions of the dream were, of course, made before more recent research had demonstrated the regular cyclic character of the dream process, and it is doubtful he would have held to them if such grossly contradictory data had been available to him.

Appraisal and Revision

A central aspect of Freud's dream theory, which asserts that a dream provides outlet for impulses and tensions, seems to be supported by the scientific evidence that can be mustered. To be more exact, the evidence indicates, first of all, that when people are deprived of dream time they show signs of psychological disturbance. Secondly, it indicates that conditions that produce psychological disequilibrium result in increased signs of tension and concern about specific themes in subsequent dreams. One can say these findings are *congruent* with Freud's venting model. But it should be added that they do not specifically document the model. This will only become feasible when experiments are devised that permit the arousal of focal unconscious drives and the detection of these drives in subsequent dreaming. The data that have been reviewed in this chapter are encouraging but not definitively validating with respect to Freud's venting model. Note, too, that the data imply only that the dream *can* serve a venting function, but not that all dreams do so. It is, of course, possible that dreams serve a number of functions, of which venting is only one. Perhaps dreams do a variety of things, such as defining problems requiring solution, integrating information, providing opportunities for creative fantasy, and so forth. What we can most reasonably say on the basis of the material reviewed is that there is a good probability that one important function of the dream is to provide a framework within which tensions and pent-up feelings may be expressed. However, there is as yet no assurance that Freud was right in declaring that only tensions that are unconscious find expression in this framework. Some of the studies reviewed (for example, the Breger, et al. [1971] observations of surgical patients) suggest that tensions may be in conscious awareness and still be the focus of preoccupation in dreams.

The central truth that has emerged from this critique of the dream literature is that while dreams seem to have a basic expressive or tension-releasing function such as Freud ascribed to them, it is difficult in most other respects to picture the organization of the dream as conforming to the neat, particularized model he formulated. Thus, there is a good deal of evidence that his tight distinction between manifest and latent content is not valid. It is certainly not true that the manifest dream content is a mere camouflaging shell that does not contain significant information about the psychological state and motivational orientation of the dreamer. Past results indicating significant correlations between indices derived from the explicit dream imagery and indices from other fantasy sources (for example, the Rorschach inkblot test and the Thematic Apperception Test) raise the question why dream imagery should be treated as if it were qualitatively different from that produced by an individual in any of a variety of other fantasy states. Dream attributes have been found to be linked not only to the nature of fantasies elicited by projective tests but also to other levels of fantasy production. For example, Cartwright (1966b) has demonstrated that judges can successfully match the dreams produced by individuals with recordings of the contents of their hallucinations elicited by psychotomimetic drugs. The two sets of fantasy materials do share detectable similarities.

Probably one of the reasons why dream imagery has been regarded as unique is because it takes place in a unique state of consciousness. Other forms of fantasy construction, such as daydreaming and responses to inkblots, occur when the individual is awake. But the dream arises in the sleeping organism. Is this a sufficient basis for assuming that the two classes of fantasy cannot be approached in related ways? Giora (1972) has argued persuasively that although the cognitive processes occurring at various levels of consciousness are different, they still represent a unitary system. It is not clear why one should assume that fantasy production during sleep calls into play an entirely different system than does fantasy production when awake. Several of Giora's comments concerning this matter are worth quoting (pp. 1071–1072):

> . . . while indulging in daydreams . . . one is momentarily 'introverted,' and the messages one receives will be assimilated into the ongoing mentation. A fatigued or drowsy man struggles to maintain contact with his sur-

roundings, but he is able to do so only phasically. While sleeping, one will recede from all activity in his relationship with this world. This passivity is the main behavioral characteristic of sleep. But cognition does not cease even in the midst of passivity; we get reports on mental activity from REM as well as from NREM sleep [during which there is an absence of rapid eye movements usually associated with dreaming]; it is only that the level of organization will shift. We may say, therefore, that there are many states of mind, each characterized by a different interaction with the environment and by a specific cognitive organization.

Now, what is the function of the cognition typical of the fatigued? Such a question is as legitimate as the question on the function of cognition while being in REM or NREM sleep. Our answer is hinted at in the question; cognition's function is unitary, but its organization (and effectiveness) is variable. Cognition has many levels, as has wakefulness or consciousness. Actually, the level of cognition is one of the distinctive features of the level of consciousness. They are different aspects of a common essence. . . .

This, then, is the point: the living brain never ceases to process information. One cannot, therefore, ask selectively the function of information processing in certain states of mind, such as dreaming, while taking it for granted at other times. We have much more to learn of the conditions of dreaming, but we should not be bothered by its function. The function of cognition will be the self-same throughout all levels of existence: knowing the world around us and ourselves.

There is little rationale for assuming that continuity does not prevail between processes that occur at different stages of consciousness.[38] It is striking that Fiss et al. (1966) were actually able to show that the characteristic mode of fantasy in the REM state carries over into fantasy obtained directly upon awakening from this state. They report (p. 1069): "Stories produced after interrupted REM sleep were longer, more complex, visual, bizarre, emotional, and vivid than stories produced after interrupted NREM sleep and were more bizarre than stories during control waking periods . . . The results strongly suggest that the distinguishing properties of a sleep stage are not 'switched off' following awakening but may persist into the waking state."

This constitutes a dramatic affirmation of the continuity between the dream and other types of fantasy. One can see in this instance that the dream and another kind of fantasy mirrored the influence of a specific condition in analogous ways.

If one will accept the notion that dreaming is another form of vivid fantasy construction, it becomes possible to apply our considerable stock of knowledge about fantasy in general to understanding the dream. It should be pointed out that the tension-releasing function that Freud ascribed to the dream has been observed to occur for some forms of fantasy in the awake state (for example, Pytkowicz et al. 1967, Feshbach 1955). The fantasy that goes into the construction of an imaginative story can provide an outlet for tensions in the same way dreams apparently do. The tension-releasing role of dreams does not involve a phenomenon that has not already been found to characterize other forms of fantasy. It is true there are various circumstances in which fantasy in the awake state does not relieve tension and even increases it. However, there is also a possibility that some dreams are not tension-reducing and perhaps tension-augmenting.[39]

Systematic and relatively objective procedures have been devised for analyzing various forms of awake fantasy, and there is no reason why they cannot sensibly be applied to dreams. In fact, as indicated, many investigators are already actively analyzing manifest dream content by means of objective scoring schemes that are analogous to a number that have been applied to the fantasies elicited by the Rorschach inkblots and the Thematic Apperception Test. But there is often a note of apology offered for analyzing the manifest rather than the so-called latent content, as if the manifest were only a second-rate substitute for the more valuable latent. Hall and Van De Castle, who have been pioneers in the study of manifest content, boldly challenge this view (Hall and Van De Castle 1966, p. 20): ". . . it could be said that there is no such thing as the latent content of a dream. A dream is a manifest experience, and what is latent lies outside the dream and in the verbal material that the dreamer reports when he is asked to free associate to features of the reported dream. How the psychoanalyst arrives at the 'true meaning' or interpretation of the dream from the verbalized associations is more of an act than a technique."

It is quite possible (although not demonstrated) that the associations offered by a patient in psychoanalytic treatment to the elements of his dreams help to provide useful information about him and even to advance the therapy process. But there is not a shred of empirical or reliable evidence that they provide a unique "true" solution concerning what is contained in the dream.[40] It is interesting, in this respect, that some of the best validated projective tests (for example, the Rorschach or Thematic Apperception Test) are analyzed by means of procedures that do not in any way require knowing the idiosyncratic associations of the individual to the fantasies he has produced. There is no special search for "The Latent Content," such as would be defined by breaking the fantasies down into elements and finding out the specific associations they elicit. There is a search for underlying meaning in the fantasy material, but it is founded on applying various categorizing and scaling dimensions to it.

One could object that such general modes of analysis are meaningful when used in relation to fantasy elicited by a uniform series of stimuli (for example, Rorschach blots), but not when applied in a context where each individual's fantasies represent responses to his own unique internal conditions.[41] However, this objection is negated by the fact that, as already noted, many systems for analyzing manifest dream content in terms of general categories are being fruitfully applied in experimental studies. Such systems scan the dream for attributes like complexity, vividness, patterns of relationship among the dream figures, aggression, passivity, body anxiety, and so forth. They have shown themselves able to detect personality traits (Rychlak and Brams 1963, Foulkes and Rechtschaffen 1964), the impact of exposure to trying or traumatic conditions (Robbins and Tanck 1969), psychological disturbance (Greenberg, Pearlman, and Gampel 1972), and highly personal attitudes toward others (Langs 1967b). They provide a means for understanding how the individual's psychological world is organized.

Freud was well aware of the ambiguities inherent in the search for the meaning of the latent content. He said, in essence, that the search was a matter of hunch and intuition, like solving a crossword puzzle.[42] He indicated, too, there was no definitive way of knowing whether a dream analysis had truly arrived at the essential latent "message." One simply had to judge whether the network of dream associations fell into an apparently meaningful pattern. In other words, within Freud's framework, the analysis of a dream is a highly subjective process. Day (1949) has amusingly shown that dream material, when submitted to various judges for evaluation, can serve as a projective stimulus that elicits interpretations reflecting more of the judge than the dreamer. Freud not only acknowledged the vagaries of validating a specific dream interpretation but also stated that an interpretation of any given dream could proceed at different levels. He indicated that there were multiple perspectives that could be taken in making sense of the latent content "uncovered" by means of the dreamer's associations. This idea is tangentially in tune with modern approaches to decoding fantasy material. Fantasy, like any other sample of psychological behavior, can be looked at manifoldly in relation to such variables as longstanding character attributes, immediate situational tensions or needs, defense patterns, cognitive sets, and so forth. Increasingly, research findings indicate that dream material also provides information about numerous rather than a few particularized aspects of an individual.

What reasonable conclusions about "dream interpretation" can we now offer on the basis of the review unfolded in this chapter?

First, there is no rationale for approaching a dream as if it were a container for a secret wish buried under layers of concealment. It is closer to the facts to regard it as a fantasy produced in a special state of consciousness and containing a spectrum of information about the dreamer.

Secondly, as shown above, one of the major classes of information available in a dream relates to tensions and drives pushing for release. A dream often seems to provide clues as to things an individual wants to do or feelings he is under pressure to vent. However, there is no empirical basis for saying that such is always or even nearly always the case. We do not know what proportion of dreams serves a venting function. We do not know whether there are individual differences in this respect, such that the dreams of some persons rarely act as a venting outlet and the dreams of others almost invariably do so.[43]

Further, it can be said with moderate assurance that extracting meaning from a dream does not *require* that the dreamer give his private associations to the various dream elements.[44] The dream is a fantasy structure in its own right and susceptible to direct forms of inspection and partitioning. It should be cautioned, though, that enough dream data have to be available to enable a reliable sampling. Just as a Rorschach protocol containing only a few responses cannot be reliably analyzed, it is probably also true that a dream that is too brief cannot be inspected with confidence. An important future research task will be to determine what constitutes a reliable sample of dream imagery. It is even possible that reliable analysis is achieved only when several dreams in sequence or from contiguous nights have been obtained. In studying almost any form of human behavior, it has been found that unless a reasonably representative sample of that form is secured, a reliable job cannot be done. There is no reason why dream behavior should be treated as a unique exception to this rule.

The main issue confronting any dream analysis has to do with the categories that will be applied. Since the potential number of categories available is large, one would have to say the choice is dictated by what one is trying to find out. Is the aim to capture a general picture of the dreamer's personality or style of life? Is it to determine what tensions or needs are most pressing for outlet? Is it to detect signs of psychological alarm or anxiety? Is it to ascertain how the dreamer feels about certain prime figures in his current or past life? Is it to evaluate how he feels about himself? Is it simply to uncover his most immediate area of conflict? In each case, the specific question or questions being asked should determine what aspects of the dream imagery are focused upon. The process of focusing can be accomplished by means of formal scales that have been developed by investigators for probing dream imagery. Hall and Van De Castle (1966) describe systematic schemes for looking at such dimensions as the following: regression, achievement, social interaction patterns, sexual orientation, castration anxiety, happiness, confusion. Other researchers have developed scales for depression (Beck 1963), aggression (Saul et al. 1954), masochism (Beck and Hurvich 1959), oral, anal, and genital concern (Sheppard 1963), tension (Rychlak 1960), and so forth. Some of these scoring schemes involve the use of symbolism and also assumptions that the symbols represent statements of unconscious needs or attitudes.

The scoring schemes enumerated have generally shown adequate scoring objectivity. The matter of their validity is more complicated. It is difficult to devise straightforward ways of validating specific dream scales. Similarly, of course, it has been a long and arduous task to validate the primary schemes used in analyzing projective responses, such as are elicited by the Rorschach or Thematic Apperception tests. In any case, a number of them do show promise. Attempts at validation have typically taken such pathways as demonstrating that dream category scores are correlated in logical ways with measured personality traits, psychosomatic symptom patterns, psychiatric symptoms, developmental maturity, peer ratings, and sex differentiation. One could, after reviewing the pertinent literature, object that the demonstrations of the validity of such scales are only in an exploratory stage and that they are not more impressive than the evidence that has accumulated in favor of Freud's mode of dream analysis. However, this is not the case. The truth is that there is little scientific evidence to support the so-called latent content approach to dream analysis. Probably one of the major reasons for this state of affairs is that latent dream analysis remains a hazy process that defies quantification, or even genuine definition. Contrastingly, the empirical dream analysis scales that have been devised not only permit repeatable definition but have demonstrated at least initial promise, as defined by objective data from numerous studies. Even more importantly, they derive from an approach that has proven effective in coping with a range of other forms of fantasy material. That is, they represent an extension of a methodology that has already received a good deal of scientific backing.

We are obviously proposing that dream analysis should not be primarily based on uncovering the dreamer's associations to the elements of his dream. Rather, it should proceed by analyzing the apparent dream content from the vantage point of various well-defined scales. As noted, the choice of scales will depend upon the kind of information one seeks from the dream. We would underscore that such an approach places no limit on possible "depth" interpretations of dream content. There are scales that systematically treat various objects and acts as symbolic representations.[45] These scales, like many which have been successfully applied to projective test responses, assume that an element in a fantasy may have meanings of which the creator of the fantasy may not be immediately aware. They assume, too, that the symbols utilized to carry these meanings are widely shared and therefore do not need to be decoded in terms of the dreamer's private associations. To accept the existence of symbolic material in dreams does not mean that one accepts the notion that the dream is primarily a vehicle for unconscious messages. It no more requires such a position than the observation that as people move their bodies they produce a lot of nonverbal signals to others of which they are unaware requires the conclusion that body movement is primarily devoted to expressing unconscious intents.

The application of an array of scales to analyzing a dream sounds like a laborious job. Undoubtedly it is. But so is the systematic analysis of any fantasy protocol (for example, the Rorschach or Thematic Apperception Tests). If one wants to probe fantasy material in a reliable fashion, one must invest the necessary time and effort. The use of scales in dream analysis has been largely confined to research settings. Their application to clinical contexts will require a period of exploration and trial and error. Clinicians will have to familiarize themselves with the existing scales, learn how to apply them reliably, and decide which are especially useful in dealing with the kinds of problems they most frequently encounter. Thorough familiarity with the scales will make it possible for clinicians to apply them rather informally in diagnostic situations and during psychotherapy sessions. A dream can be quickly sifted through a number of scales that will clarify whether it contains an unusual amount of certain affects or tensions (for example, hostility, anxiety) and also whether it depicts concern with special patterns of relationships. Is there a focus on hostility between males, or on the separation of male and female figures, or on the merging of adult and child figures? Thus, a psychotherapist might be able to extrapolate quickly from the special nature of the dyadic relationships portrayed in a patient's dream in order to clarify the specific tensions existing at that point in the therapy between the patient and himself.

Let us illustrate the application of this kind of dream analysis approach by looking at the famous "Irma Dream" which Freud presented in *The Interpretation of Dreams.* He detailed the dream and his associations to its elements in order to demonstrate his new technique for determining a dream's latent meaning. The dream was as follows (1900, p. 107):

> A great hall—a number of guests, whom we are receiving—among them Irma, whom I immediately take aside, as though to answer her letter, and to reproach her for not yet accepting the 'solution'. I say to her: 'If you still have pains, it is really only your own fault.'—She answers: 'If you only knew what pains I have now in the throat, stomach, and abdomen—I am choked by them.' I am startled, and look at her. She looks pale and puffy. I think that after all I must be overlooking some organic affection. I take her to the window and look into her throat. She offers some resistance to this, like a woman who has a set of false teeth. I think, surely, she doesn't need them.—The mouth then opens wide, and I find a large white spot on the right, and elsewhere I see extensive grayish-white scabs adhering to curiously curled formations, which are evidently shaped like the turbinal bones of the nose.—I quickly call Dr. M., who repeats the examination and confirms it. . . . Dr. M. looks quite unlike his usual self; he is very pale, he limps, and his chin is clean-shaven. . . . Now my friend Otto, too, is standing beside her, and my friend Leopold percusses her covered chest, and says: 'She has a dullness below, on the left,' and also calls attention to an infiltrated portion of skin on the left shoulder (which I can feel, in spite of the dress). . . . M. says: 'There's no doubt that it's an infection, but it doesn't matter; dysentery will follow and the poison will be eliminated.' . . . We know, too, precisely how the infection originated. My friend Otto, not long ago, gave her, when she was feeling unwell, an injection of a preparation of propyl . . . propyls . . . propionic acid . . . trimethylamin (the formula of which I see before me, printed in heavy type) . . . One doesn't give such injections so rashly. . . . Probably, too, the syringe was not clean.

If, according to the logic of the scale approach, one appraises this dream in terms of explicit consistencies and emphasis in its contents, what does one detect? It is immediately apparent that there is an overwhelming focus on the body, particularly as a sick and disabled object. The following is a list of the body references contained in the dream:

If you still have pains
Pains I have now in the throat, stomach, and abdomen
I am choked by them
She looks pale and puffy
I must be overlooking some organic affection
look into her throat
false teeth
The mouth then opens wide, and I find a large white spot . . . and elsewhere . . . extensive, grayish-white scabs
he is very pale, he limps
percusses her covered chest and says: 'She has a dullness below' . . . and also calls attention to an infiltrated portion of the skin

M. says, 'There is no doubt that it's an infection . . . dysentery will follow and the poison will be eliminated.'
infection
injection of a preparation
injections

A word count indicates that over 60 percent of the dream is directly concerned with body themes largely involving illness and poor health. It would seem logical to conclude that a major theme in this dream is concern about health and the vulnerability of the body.[46] In his own interpretation of the dream, presumably based on his associations to its elements, Freud did not ascribe much importance to the body vulnerability theme. He thought the prime message in the dream was a wishful statement that he was not responsible for the difficulties that had arisen in his treatment of a patient named Irma. However, it is interesting that he later makes the following comment (1906, p. 206):

> Still other themes play a part in the dream, and their relation to my non-responsibility for Irma's illness is not so apparent: my daughter's illness, and that of a patient with the same name; the harmfulness of cocaine; the affection of my patient, who was traveling in Egypt; concern about the health of my wife; my brother, and Dr. M.; my own physical troubles, and anxiety concerning my absent friend, who is suffering from suppurative rhinitis. But if I keep all these things in view, they combine into a single train of thought, which might be labelled: concern for the health of myself and others; professional conscientiousness.

He could not escape the prominent role that body disturbance played in the explicit dream content itself. As a matter of fact, there is good evidence that at the point in his life at which he had the "Irma Dream," Freud was confronted by a series of events that did have threatening body implications. His wife had become pregnant for the sixth time, his daughter Anna had been suffering from illness, a number of close friends had had serious episodes of poor health, and, even more importantly, he had developed troublesome physical difficulties of his own. Erikson (1954, p. 9), in commenting on Freud's condition at the time of the "Irma Dream," said that he was "at an age when he seemed to notice with alarm the first signs of aging, and, in fact, of disease." So, the explicit dream theme turns out to be a direct statement of an issue that was central and probably disturbing to Freud.

If one analyzes the personal interactions in the explicit dream content, one finds that they can be differentiated into those involving unfriendly relationships between men and women and those depicting friendly ones between men. Note the following excerpts:

> ... I immediately take (Irma) aside ... and *reproach*[47] her ... I say to her: 'If you still have pains, it is really *your own fault.*' She answers: 'If *you only knew* what pains I have now ....'
> I take her to the window and look into her throat. She offers some *resistance* to this.
> I quickly call Dr. M., who repeats the examination and *confirms* it.
> My *friend* Otto, too, is standing beside her.
> My *friend* Leopold percusses her covered chest.
> *We know,* too, precisely how the infection originated.
> *My friend* Otto ... gave her ... an injection."

The majority of male-female interactions involve hostility and threat. The male-male interactions are, contrastingly, friendly and mutually supportive. If one found such a pattern in a series of Thematic Apperception Test stories, related by an individual, one would conclude that he felt antagonistic toward women and perceived men as more supportive and convivial. To take this view would contradict Freud's own "latent" interpretation of the dream. He felt, on the basis of his private associations, that the dream contained considerable hostility toward significant male figures in his life. There is no convincing way to determine at this late date whether Freud's interpretation or that emerging from the explicit dream content is most valid. It is interesting, however, that Erikson (1954), in his extensive perusal of the "Irma Dream," points out that it occurred at a time when Freud felt hard-pressed by his family responsibilities (for example, his wife's pregnancy) and had (p. 47) "undertaken to find in Fliess, at all costs, a superior friend, an object for idealization ...."[48] Fliess was a physician who became an extremely intimate friend and confidant to Freud. He was unquestionably an important psychological support and a sounding board for his ideas (Jones 1953).

This material from the "Irma Dream" has been presented by way of illustrating how a relatively systematic and objective analysis of the explicit dream content can be undertaken within a general perspective provided by the various dream content scales that have been developed. We have presented only two possible leads that stand out in the explicit dream imagery. These leads strike us as having definite relevance to major problems with which Freud was struggling at the time he had the dream. They do not seem less "deep" or significant than the theme which Freud highlighted in his own interpretation of the dream. We would like to make it clear that we do not believe that analysis of dream material should be restricted to the kinds of scales that currently exist. There is room to devise all forms of new, ingenious approaches. We ask only that these approaches remain congruent with what the scientific literature suggests about the nature of the dream and that they present evidence as to their own validity.

There will be objections that the general approach to dream analysis we have proposed is too broad and diffuse and unguided by a unified theory. This is obviously so, and it will therefore repel persons who are attracted to Freud's dream theories by their apparently neat and focused definition of what a dream represents. While this is unfortunate, the facts cannot be dismissed. The dreaming process simply cannot be contained within the special package Freud put together. It is likewise true that one cannot contain the diverse phenomena associated with other types of fantasy within one unified scheme or package. Fantasy is a highly complex form of behavior, with multiple determinants, goals, and modes of organization.

NOTES

1. Freud (1900, Preface to 3rd English Edition, p. xxxii), said, apropos of his dream discoveries, "Insight such as this falls to one's lot but once in a lifetime." He also said, "During the long years, in which I have been working on the problems of neurosis I have often been in doubt and sometimes been shaken in my convictions. At such times it has always been *The Interpretation of Dreams* that has given me back my certainty" (p. xxxvi).

2. ". . . residues of the previous day have been left over from the activity of waking life and it has not been possible to withdraw the whole cathexis of energy from them . . . The unconscious wish links itself up with the day's residues and affects a transference onto them; this may happen either in the course of the day or not until the state of sleep has been established. A wish now arises which has been transferred onto the recent material. This wish seeks to force its way along the normal path taken by thought processes through the preconscious. But it comes up against the censorship; which is still functioning and to the influence of which it now submits. At this point it takes on the distortion for which the way has already been paved by the transference of the wish onto the recent material" (Freud 1900, p. 573).

Freud's (1900, p. 554) classification of "day residues" is as follows: "(1) what has not been carried to a conclusion during the day owing to some chance hindrance; (2) what has not been dealt with owing to the insufficiency of our intellectual power—what is unsolved; (3) what has been rejected and suppressed during the daytime. To these we must add (4) a powerful group consisting of what has been set in action in our unconscious by the activity of the preconscious in the course of the day; and finally (5) the group of daytime impressions which are indifferent and have for that reason not been dealt with."

3. "Must we not regard it . . . as an act of carelessness on the part of that watchman (the censorship between the unconscious and the preconscious), that it relaxes its activities during the night, allows the suppressed impulses in the unconscious to find expression, and makes it possible for hallucinatory regression to occur once more? I think not. Even though this critical watchman goes to rest—and we have proof that its slumbers are not deep—it also shuts the door upon the power of movement. No matter what impulses from the normally inhibited unconscious may prance upon the stage, we need feel no concern; they remain harmless since they are unable to set in motion the motor apparatus by which alone they might modify the external world. The state of sleep guarantees the security of the citadel that must be guarded" (Freud 1900, pp. 567–568).

4. Freud suggested that disguise of the dream is further accomplished by the "secondary elaboration" that occurs when the dreamer awakens and tries to reconstruct the

dream he earlier experienced. This reconstruction process introduces all kinds of omissions and additions that add another layer of misleading camouflage.

5. Freud (1900) also described a category of "death wish" dreams in which the desire for a loved one to die apparently could escape the "censor" and find direct expression in the image of that person dying.

6. It will be recalled that Freud theorized that a wish in the unconscious could gain entry to the preconscious only by associating (transferring) itself with disguising images derived from the previous day's experiences.

7. "If there is a 'beyond the pleasure principle,' it is only consistent to grant that there was also a time before the purpose of dreams was the fulfillment of wishes. This would imply no denial of their later function. But if once this general rule has been broken, a further question arises. May not dreams which, with a view to the psychical binding of traumatic impressions, obey the compulsion to repeat, may not such dreams occur *outside* analysis as well? And the reply can only be a decided affirmative" (Freud 1920, p. 33).

8. There are differing opinions in the literature as to whether Freud ascribed any problem-solving potential to the dream process (Lipton 1967, Hawkins 1966, Giovacchini 1966).

9. In another context, Freud (1917a) suggests that dreams may be unusually sensitive reflectors of body sensations and states, and may even prognosticate body illnesses before they are evident from other cues. He (1900) notes, too, that a dream may serve to deny the existence of bodily pain that might otherwise awaken the sleeper.

10. In summarizing his analysis of his well-known "Irma's injection" dream, which was basic to illustrating his wish fulfillment hypothesis, Freud (1900, p. 120) said, after concluding that the dream added up to a wish on his part that he not be held responsible for the condition of one of his patients: "Certain *other* themes played a part in the dream, which were not so obviously connected with my exculpation from Irma's illness: my daughter's illness and that of my patient who bore the same name, the injurious effect of cocaine, the disorder of my patient who was travelling in Egypt, my concern about my wife's health and about that of my brother and of Dr. M., my own physical ailments, my anxiety about my absent friend who suffered from suppurative rhinitis. But when I came to consider all of these, they could all be collected into a single group of ideas and labelled, as it were, 'concern about my own and other people's health—professional conscientiousness' " (italics ours). Here one sees that he breaks the dream down into a number of latent elements, some of which are only distantly linked with the ultimate wish that he feels they combine to represent.

His view about the "reality" of the themes in dreams that are uncovered in the course of associating to the dream elements is explicit in the following quotation (1900, pp. 280–281): "In view of the very great number of associations produced in analysis to each individual element of the content of a dream, some readers may be led to doubt whether, as a matter of principle, we are justified in regarding as part of the dream thoughts all the associations that occur to us during the subsequent analysis—whether we are justified, that is, in supposing that all these thoughts were already active during the state of sleep and played a part in the formation of the dream. Is it not more probable that new trains of thought have arisen in the course of the analysis which had no share in forming the dream? I can only give limited assent to this argument. It is no doubt true that some trains of thought arise for the first time during the analysis. But one can convince oneself in all such cases that these new connections are only set up between thoughts which were already linked in loop-lines or short circuits, made possible by the existence of other and deeper-lying connecting paths. It must be allowed that the greater bulk of the thoughts which are revealed in analysis were already active during the process of forming the dream . . ."

11. Note Langs' (1966) comments on this point (p. 641): "Freud's belief . . . that the manifest dream is a compromise similar to a symptom implies that contributions to the manifest dream are made from both sides of psychic conflict, drive, and defense. It would follow from this that the manifest dream is a derivative and disguised expression of the latent content and not an unrelated screen. The manifest content would therefore reflect something of the manner in which a person screens deeper impulses, as well as aspects of what prompts this screening and indications of what is screened."

12. Another complication that is often overlooked with reference to Freud's distinc-

tion between the manifest and latent dream content is that he explicitly admits to the possibility that *some* dreams can openly express a wish. For example, the wish of a child might be manifestly depicted in a dream or the desire of a thirsty man for a drink might be directly reflected in dream imagery. Freud even states (1900, p. 123): "It is easy to prove that dreams *often* reveal themselves without any disguise as fulfillments of wishes" (italics ours). If such be the case, the problem arises of defining when the manifest content is directly representative of the dreamer's intent and when it is only a disguised version. How does one judge *in each specific instance* the degree to which the manifest content has a concealing versus directly expressive function?

13. Freud says (1900, p. 234): "Thus the wish to sleep (which the conscious ego is concentrated upon, and which, together with the dream censorship and the 'secondary revision' . . . constitute the conscious ego's share in dreaming) must in every case be reckoned as one of the motives for the formation of dreams, and every successful dream is a fulfillment of that wish."

14. Freud describes an instance in which he was suffering from a very painful boil at the base of his scrotum and had a dream in which he was riding a horse. He interpreted the dream in the following fashion (1900, p. 230): ". . . precisely the activity in which the dream landed me . . . was the most energetic denial of my illness that could possibly be imagined. . . . But in this dream I was riding as though I had no boil on my perineum—or rather *because I wanted not to have one.* My saddle, to judge from its description, was the poultice which had made it possible for me to fall asleep. Under its assuaging influence I had probably been unaware of my pain during the first hours of sleep. The painful feelings had then announced themselves and sought to wake me; whereupon the dream came and said soothingly: 'No! Go on sleeping! There's no need to wake up. You haven't got a boil; for you're riding on a horse, and it's quite certain that you couldn't ride if you had a boil in that particular place.' "

15. Numerous objective and reliable procedures have been developed for analyzing manifest dream content (for example, Hall and Van De Castle 1966; Hauri, Sawyer, and Rechtschaffen 1967).

16. One rather unfortunately isolated but ingenious attempt to test Freud's ideas about the disguise function of manifest content is to be found in a study by Fancher and Strahan (1971). They indicate that Freud declared: "If the first account given me by a patient of a dream is too hard to follow, I ask him to repeat it. In doing so he rarely uses the same words. But the parts of the dream which he describes in different terms are by that fact revealed to me as the weak spot in the dream's disguise."

That is, Freud offered what he considered to be a specific way in which the defensive strategy of the manifest content facade reveals itself. Fancher and Strahan tried to test the validity of Freud's statement by tape-recording for each of a series of normal subjects an account of a previous dream he had had and simultaneously monitoring him physiologically, by means of the Galvanic Skin Reflex, to determine which sections of the dream were most emotionally arousing. Subsequently, on a second occasion, each individual was tape-recorded as he repeated his account of his dream. It was expected that if Freud's formulation was correct, those elements of the dream associated with affect arousal would for defensive reasons be most likely to be altered upon repetition. The experimental data did not support this expectation. Within the limits of the experimental design employed, this particular aspect of Freud's view of the defensive function of the manifest content was not confirmed.

17. A study by Mann (1955) reported negative results in an attempt to find correlations between a Rorschach index of extraversion-introversion and several dream variables (for example, completeness, detailedness, pleasantness-unpleasantness). However, this study is seriously deficient because there were no apparent or logical reasons why Rorschach extraversion-introversion should be expected to be linked with the manifest dream scores he chose to derive.

18. It is paradoxical that studies that have attempted to demonstrate correlations between the *latent* content of dreams and projective measures have proved to be unsuccessful (for example, Blondel 1958, Hall 1947). Various explanations come to mind. One that we would particularly wonder about is the possible unreliability of latent dream interpretation.

19. Cartwright (1966b) has shown that when a psychotomimetic drug is used to induce hallucinations in normal persons, judges can match each individual's hallucinations with his dreams (manifest content) significantly better than chance. If, as some observers believe, the hallucinatory events induced by drugs represent important areas of unconscious concern, the correlation between dream and hallucinatory imagery is certainly pertinent to the problem under analysis in this section.

20. In all instances where the term "manifest content" is employed, it pertains to quantitative indices that have reasonable scoring reliability. Some of the basic dimensions of the manifest content that have been defined are described by Hauri et al. (1967) and Hall and Van De Castle (1966).

21. Relatedly, Hauri (1967) reported that normal subjects who exercised intensively before going to sleep subsequently dreamed less of physical activity.

22. Some interpretation of symbolism was involved in the scoring systems used to analyze the manifest content, but the major scoring judgments were based on the explicit imagery.

23. Tentative evidence exists that even stimuli that are out of conscious awareness (subliminal) may register in the dream imagery (Paul and Fisher 1959, Shevrin and Luborsky 1958).

24. It should be cautioned that although there is a higher probability that dreams will be reported after REM than non-REM awakenings, evidence exists that some dreaming also occurs during non-REM periods.

25. Clemes and Dement (1967) observed that dream deprivation produced changes in inkblot responses indicative of "elevation of intensity of need and feeling and a depression of certain ego-controls" (p. 491).

26. It is of related interest that Pivik and Foulkes (1966) found that dreams were "intensified" following dream deprivation.

27. Collins (1966) also studied the role of REM deprivation in affecting the responses of subjects to a stressful film, but due to problems that developed during the collection of the data, the results could not be meaningfully interpreted.

28. As earlier mentioned, when persons are deprived of REM time, they subsequently show a compensatory increase in such time.

29. Starker and Goodenough (1970) cross-validated major aspects of these findings.

30. His negative view was reinforced by the fact that he was unable to produce increased disturbance in a schizophrenic sample by means of dream deprivation.

31. It is parenthetically interesting that Cartwright (1966) noted in a normal group that if individuals were given a psychotomimetic drug that produced hallucinations and bizarre fantasy, they had reduced REM time on the following night. One could interpret this as indicating that the opportunity to vent impulses provided by the drug reduced the need for dream venting.

32. This finding was later challenged as possibly reflecting the large dose of "Stelazine" that had been administered to the patient.

33. A study by Greenberg, et al. (1972) demonstrated that patients with a "war neurosis" (that is, within the neurotic rather than psychotic range) do manifest increased pressure for REM time. The dream attributes of neurotic patients have hardly been looked at, and it is conceivable that the venting hypothesis would receive more support in this group than it has in schizophrenic samples.

34. The uncertainties that prevail in this area are illustrated by the fact that several years later, in 1972, Gillin et al. did observe that schizophrenics showed less compensatory REM time after REM deprivation than did normal subjects.

35. Kramer et al. (1968) present evidence suggesting that the therapeutic effects of imipramine are tied in with its power to initiate venting of hostile impulses. They were able to show specifically that imipramine leads to increased hostile imagery in the dreams of the depressed; this, in turn, is often followed by clinical improvement.

36. Hollender (1962, p. 325) comments on some logical inconsistencies in the "sleep preservation" theory: "If we make the assumption that every sleeper wishes to remain asleep, do we then, to be consistent, assume that every person who is awake wishes to remain awake? And then too, how do we explain the relief that is sometimes experienced upon awakening from a dream with the comforting thought, 'It was only a dream?' Whether

or not the dream has failed in 'its function,' the fact still remains that it is less disturbing to be awake than to be asleep."

Note another of his comments (p. 326): "In daydreaming, people not infrequently drift off to sleep. Are daydreams to keep people awake (or perhaps, to help them fall off to sleep)? We would probably state that they are to cope with whatever is 'on one's mind' and that either outcome would be incidental to the primary purpose. Is it not reasonable to assume that the same reasoning might be applied to night dreams?"

37. The fact that dreaming occurs in the context of a relatively fixed schedule apparently based on a biological cycle does not in any way imply that it cannot serve psychological functions. The dream can still be viewed, for example, as a means of venting tensions; but one simply has to be cognizant that the venting is tied to certain time restrictions.

38. Several studies have even suggested that the REM cycle is a manifestation of a biological process that extends into the waking state (Globus 1966, Hartmann 1968a).

39. Such as obviously occurs with nightmares and repetitious dreams saturated with anxiety.

40. We do not even have evidence that experts provided with the same dream data and dream associations can consistently and reliably arrive at the same interpretations as to the meaning of the "latent content."

41. Note the comments of Hall and Van De Castle (1966, pp. 21–211) with respect to this matter: "Dream reports differ from other projective protocols in one important respect . . . they are not given in response to any specifiable stimulus material . . . In dreaming, a person is supposedly projecting something that is entirely within himself; he is not ordinarily responding to the external perceptual field. In the case of the Rorschach, for example, one can analyze the responses made by the subject in relation to the inkblots and ask such questions as how much of the inkblot was used . . . did the subject respond to color, and so forth. This cannot be done with dreams.

"Although there are no identifiable stimuli to which a dream can be referred, one can compare a dream with the external reality represented in the dream and note any discrepancies."

42. Freud's undoubted awareness of the ambiguity of latent dream interpretation is conveyed in the following quotation from his *New Introductory Lectures on Psychoanalysis* (1933c, p. 12) where he says with reference to dream thoughts:

> The latter are contained in the associations like an alkali in the mother-liquor, but yet not quite completely contained in them. On the one hand, the associations give us far more than we need for formulating the latent dream thoughts—namely, all the explanations, transitions, and connections which the patient's intellect is bound to produce in the course of his approach to the dream thoughts. On the other hand, an association often comes to stop precisely before the genuine dream thought: it has only come near to it and has only had contact with it through allusions. At that point we intervene on our own; we fill in the hints, draw undeniable conclusions, and give explicit utterance to what the patient has only touched in his associations. *This sounds as though we allowed our ingenuity and caprice to play with the material . . . Nor is it easy to show the legitimacy of our procedure in an abstract description of it.* But you have only to carry out a dream analysis yourselves or study a good account of one in the literature and you will be convinced of the cogent manner in which interpretative work like this proceeds. (Italics introduced by present writers.)

Just beneath his reassuring bravado, Freud's uncertainties about the dream interpretative procedure come through clearly.

43. The Cartwright et al. work (1967) suggests there may be great individual differences in this respect.

44. We do not mean to imply that private associations may not add valuable data. But it remains for future work to settle this matter.

45. For example, Hall and Van De Castle (1966) present a scheme for detecting the presence of dream imagery that symbolically represents concern about castration. Statements in dreams such as, "I got a haircut," "My leg became paralyzed," and "The crocodiles tried to bite me" are treated as having castration connotations.

46. Hall and Van De Castle (1966) present several formal scales for classifying concern about body disability and attack upon one's body.

47. Italics inserted to call attention to the hostility or friendliness in the interaction.

48. Erikson notes in a related vein (p. 47): "But it furthers an understanding of the Irma Dream to note that only once in all the published correspondence does Freud address Fliess with the lone word *Liebster* ('Dearest'): in the first letter following the Irma Dream (August 8, 1895)."

Jones (1953) quotes from a letter written by Freud to Fliess in 1896 which portrays the depth of Freud's investment in Fliess (p. 298): "People like you should not die out, my dear friend; we others need the like of you too much. How much have I to thank you for in consolation, understanding, stimulation in my loneliness, in the meaning of life you have given me, and lastly in health which no one else could have brought back to me."

Chapter 3

Personality Types: Oral and Anal Characters

FREUD was certainly sensitive to the uncountable ways in which personalities vary. But when it came to classifying this diversity formally, he settled for a limited series of groupings. He considered that adult character structures could be classified within any one of the following types: oral, anal, phallic, genital.[1] These types derive rather logically from his developmental theories.[2] He depicted each child as passing through a fixed sequence of stages in which particular body zones are focused upon, experienced as sources of satisfying gratification, and emphasized as a means for relating to the world. He proposed that during the first year of life the mouth is the major zone in which the child invests. From one to three years it is the anal area. From three to five it is the genitals (and this is also the period during which the "Oedipal" struggle reaches its highest intensity). Five to prepuberty is labeled as the "latency" phase and is considered to be a time of massive repression of genital drives. At puberty a resurgence of the importance of the genitals occurs. During each phase there is an intense urge toward activities that will "satisfy" the dominant erogenous zone.

Freud theorized, too, that there are specific problems and frustrations linked with each phase, growing out of conflicts between what provides erogenous pleasure and rules that forbid such pleasure. For example, during the anal phase, the child would like to maintain his freedom to have the kinds of anal experiences he enjoys but instead is called upon to institute strict control of the anal sphincter and in so doing to cope with the whole issue of submitting to parental standards. He has to learn to renounce important pleasures derived from the anal region. In the course of normal development, indicates Freud, the individual masters the problems of each phase and then moves on to those of the succeeding one. Eventually he renounces the erotogenic sensations of the oral and anal regions and subordinates them to genital primacy. The mature person ("genital character") presumably derives his prime satisfactions from genital arousal and discharge, and sensations from other body zones serve largely to reinforce the genital experience.

Freud's theory of character types assumes that the manner in which a person resolves the problems associated with specific developmental stages determines his personality defenses and style of life. If he cannot cope with the demands of a particular phase, he may become "fixated" at that stage and be unable to move on to the greater maturity represented by the next phase in sequence. Or he may, after moving to a more mature phase, find that he cannot master the new demands it poses and therefore "regress" back to the "easier," preceding one. Failure to master a developmental stage is described as being due either to excessive frustration or excessive gratification with reference to the prime erogenous drive associated with it, or to a combination of the two.

Freud's theory states that a person's behavior will be colored by the phase in which he gets stuck.[3] If, for example, he is fixated at the anal stage, he will develop character traits that reflect his struggles to master the anal sphincter. Thus, his character structure will be shaped by themes relating to self-control, being neat versus being messy, and "nice" retention versus dirty expulsion. Freud specified that the character traits growing out of an individual's efforts to master the problems of a particular phase could involve either reactive or sublimating strategies. The person who is struggling to control anal impulses concerned with defecating and soiling uninhibitedly may anxiously defend against them by a gross reactive denial that results in a style of behavior that emphasizes being rigidly neat and clean. But presumably he might also learn, at a more constructive level, to sublimate anal impulses into artistic or intellectual activities providing symbolic opportunities for "messing" and release of what is pent up within oneself.

What is fundamental to Freud's character scheme is the idea that the individual acquires a cluster of traits that help him to master especially troublesome conflicts traceable to, and associated with, the role that specific zones of his body play in his life.

Freud had relatively little to say about the character types. The only one he described in any detail was the "anal character" (Freud 1908). It was Abraham (1927) and Glover (cited by Abraham, 1927) who constructed the "oral character" on the basis of the general paradigm provided by Freud's developmental theory and the train of logic he invoked in arriving at a picture of the "anal character." It should be noted that Freud (1905d) did indicate his general approval of Abraham's theoretical elaborations. But he had so little to say about the other characters (namely, phallic and genital) that it would be difficult to conjure up versions of these types sufficiently detailed to permit an evaluation of their validity.[4] In fact, the scientific literature dealing with the phallic and genital types is for all practical purposes nonexistent.

This chapter will, of necessity, therefore confine itself to looking at the scientific findings concerned with the oral and anal character types.

The Oral Character Defined

As just mentioned, Freud had little to say directly about the oral character. Abraham (1927) worked out the details of the concept.[5] But we will depart in this section from our originally stated intent to evaluate only those theories that Freud himself developed. We will undertake to review the scientific evidence bearing on the oral character. We feel justified in doing so for two reasons: (1) Abraham derived the oral character by direct analogy with Freud's formulation of the "anal character"; and (2) Freud (1905d) did clearly express approval of Abraham's "oral character" model.[6]

What are some of the major aspects of the oral character concept as Abraham visualized them? First of all, he proposed that one needs to differentiate between those fixated in the early oral stage and those in the late oral stage. The early one is characterized by pleasure in sucking and the later by pleasure in biting. Attributes related to "taking in" will be dominant in the first instance, while more hostile "biting" tendencies will presumably prevail in the second. Abraham (1927) noted with regard to these stages: "The most important differences . . . are those which depend on whether a feature of character has developed on the basis of the earlier or the later oral stage; whether . . . it is the expression of an unconscious tendency to suck or bite. In the latter case we shall find in connection with such a character-trait the most marked symptoms of ambivalence—positive and negative instinctual cravings, hostile and friendly tendencies; while we may assume on the basis of our experience that the character traits derived from the stage of sucking are not as yet subjected to ambivalence" (p. 402). He underscored the pervasive ambivalence of the oral character fixated in the late oral stage. He also pointed up tendencies toward "envy, hostility, and jealousy" and "malice."

Abraham proposed, too, that oral fixation may be traced in some primarily to their early oral needs being "imperfectly gratified"; whereas in others it can be tied to oral overindulgence. He suggested that those who have been highly indulged may develop a world view that "there will always be some kind of person—a representative of the mother, of course—to care for them and to give them everything they need" (1927, p. 399). This may lead to passivity and inactivity.[7] It may also lead to a chronic sense of optimism. Indeed, says Abraham, it can lead to an attitude of generosity, brightness, and sociability.

Abraham (1927), in speaking of the "ungratified" who are "burdened throughout their whole life with the after-effects of an ungratified sucking period" (p. 400), states that they often conduct themselves as if they were asking for something. He refers to their stance as a "sucking" one. He notes that "they are as little to be put off by hard facts as by reasonable arguments, but continue to plead and to insist. One might say that they 'cling like leeches' to other people" (pp. 400–401). He adds that they dislike being alone and that they are impatient people. Interestingly, he theorizes that their longing to receive may be defended against by its opposite, the urge to give. He specifies cases in which the defensive urge to give is converted into a need "to *give* by way of the mouth," which manifests itself in a "constant need to communicate themselves orally to other people." He says of them: "This results in an obstinate urge to talk . . . Persons of this kind have the impression that their fund of thought is inexhaustible, and they ascribe a special power or some unusual value to what they say" (p. 401).

Other general traits that Abraham ascribes here and there to the oral character are as follows:

Being open and accessible to new ideas.
Being curious and interested in observing nature.
Being hasty, restless, and impatient.
Being ambitious.

As indicated by the review just completed, Abraham's portrait of the oral character was rather meandering and vague. He did not systematically specify clusters of traits and their modes of derivation from conditions prevailing in the oral phase. It is difficult to integrate what he presents. At times he seems to ascribe polar opposite traits to the oral character, although the contradictions largely disappear if one carefully notes his qualifications with respect to the early versus late oral stages and the orally overgratified versus nongratified. Actually, Abraham admitted[8] that it was difficult to construct a clearly delineated image of the oral character.[9]

Even so, meaningful patterns can be traced in his ponderings. In order to test the validity of the oral character theory, one has to reduce its diffuse complexity to manageable units. We propose that the major assertions about the oral character can be condensed into a relatively few statements.

1. One primary feature of the theory is that persons with oral character traits develop them as the result of experiences during the first year or "oral phase" of childhood. The specific nature of such experiences has really not been spelled out. Freud and Abraham introduced a good deal of ambiguity into the matter by asserting that "constitutional" factors play an important part in an individual's likelihood of being channeled characterologically.[10] They believed there was a special inherited biological susceptibility to being fixated in a particular developmental phase. This was simply an undocumented belief on their part. It was never clear how much importance was supposed to be assigned to "constitutional" factors as etiological agents. But with regard to nonconstitutional or environmental factors, they were defined pretty much in terms of either too little or too much gratification. Fixation at, or regression to, the oral phase was considered to be caused by either grossly frustrating or overgratifying oral needs. Abraham notes (1927, p. 397): "Whether in this early period of life the child has had to go without pleasure or has been indulged with an excess of it, the effect is the same. It takes leave of the sucking stage under difficulties."

There is, for all practical purposes, no *specification* of the ways in which parents cause their children to fail in coping with the problems of the oral phase and thereby force them to fall back upon an "oral character" adaptation. One is left with only two propositions involving etiology that can be concretely put to the test.

(a) The first asserts that events primarily in the first year or so of life determine the extent to which oral character traits evolve. This proposition can be appraised by determining whether persons fitting the oral character classification did actually have special or unusual experiences during the oral phase.

(b) The second asserts that the probability that parents will cause a child to fix on an oral defense system is a function of their being either extremely frustrating or overgratifying of his oral needs. More particularly, this has to do with the ways in which parents provide opportunities for nourishment, sucking and biting, and general gratification for erogenous sensations arising in the oral zones. It should be noted that it is difficult to find explicit statements by Freud and Abraham concerning how parental behavior, which is not directly linked to feeding and oral stimulation, enters into the picture. There are suggestions here and there that the manner in which parents behave in terms of gratifying a specific body zone is also representative of how they conduct themselves with reference to related issues. For example, those who are unwilling to provide nourishment and satisfaction of oral sensations would presumably also be *generally* reluctant to "give" or provide support. But, as mentioned, this matter remains rather obscure in the actual writings of Freud and Abraham. What presents itself for specific testing is the proposition that the individual who falls into the oral character category must have experienced either too little or too much oral gratification in his relationships with his parents.

2. Another major statement of the oral character theory concerns what is sought of or expected from others. Abraham underscored the salience of taking, getting, and receiving (as equivalents of being fed and nourished) in the oral character's life style. He proposed that those who have been highly gratified during the oral phase are likely to assume that life will be bountiful ("they expect the mother's breast to flow for them eternally"). They are said to have the firm conviction that others will always be willing to give them what they want. A pervasive passivity can arise on this basis: "They make no kind of effort, and in cases they even disdain to undertake a breadwinning occupation" (Abraham 1927, pp. 399–400). But Abraham also assumes that the conviction that others will always be willing to help can, in quite opposite fashion, result in an "energetic conduct in life"—that is, it can also encourage an active striving style of behavior. Further, when he describes persons who had an "ungratified sucking period," he focuses upon their later insatiable expectations that others will give supplies to them. He indicates that whether it be in the form of "aggressive demand" or "modest request", they apply persistent pressure ("cling like leeches") to get others to contribute to them. Clearly, Abraham regards the oral character as centrally preoccupied with the issue of sustenance in all of its ramifications. Whether the preoccupation takes the form of an optimistic expectation of always being fulfilled, a suspicion that scarcity will forever prevail, or a compensatory generosity that conceals

an underlying "avarice," it still focuses on a common theme.

This provides another avenue for testing the oral character theory. It would seem logical to expect that the greater the degree to which an individual fits the oral character classification, the more his behavior and fantasies will indicate preoccupation with issues that have to do with being cared for, supported, and nurtured. This preoccupation could presumably be positive or negative in its tone and direct or compensatory in its form. Another way of translating this formulation would be to say the oral character is unusually caught up with issues relating to dependence-independence and passivity-activity.

Two subsidiary but related testable statements presented by Abraham should also be taken up at this point. One has to do with his view that the oral character's focus upon being in a position to obtain support from others leads him to feel uncomfortable when he is alone. He is motivated to be with the group rather than occupy an isolated position so that potential supplies will be available to him. Operationally, this should mean that the oral character will prefer activities that foster affiliation rather than separation from others.

A second subsidiary statement derives from Abraham's assumption that those who have been well gratified during the oral phase take an optimistic ("I will always be well fed") view of the future; whereas those who have been poorly gratified are pessimistic ("I will never get fed"). If so, one would expect that the oral character would be typified either by an extreme amount of optimism or pessimism, with the additional possibility of a pattern that involves shifting between these two extremes.

3. A good deal is made by Abraham of the existence of unusual *ambivalence* in those oral characters who are fixated in the later "biting" stage of the oral phase. He says (1927, p. 398): "In the child who has been disappointed or over-indulged in the sucking period the pleasure in biting, which is also the most primitive form of sadism, will be especially emphasized. Thus, the formation of character in such a child begins under the influence of an abnormally pronounced ambivalence of feeling." He implies that this ambivalence has to do with a simultaneous urge to incorporate and to destroy by biting. The incorporation and destructive aims are presumably opposed, because if objects are destroyed they cannot also provide sustenance. It is not clear from Abraham's formulation how the "ambivalence of feeling" manifests itself. However, it seems logical to assume that it would take the form of shifting and contradictory attitudes toward significant figures (for example, wife, children, friends).

4. One of Abraham's particularly interesting speculations about the oral character is that he has an openness to novel experiences and ideas that manifests itself in such forms as enhanced curiosity and an interest in understanding nature. He says apropos of this point (1927, pp. 404–405): "The displacement of the infantile pleasure in sucking to the intellectual sphere is of great practical significance. Curiosity and the pleasure in observing receive important reinforcements from this source, and this not only in childhood, but during the subject's whole life. In persons with a special inclination for observing Nature, and for many branches of scientific investigation, psycho-analysis shows a close connection between these impulses and repressed oral desires."

This is certainly a bold statement that should be subject to verification. It would seem to be possible to ascertain whether those identified as oral characters exhibit an unusual amount of interest in new experience, exploration, and understanding of the unknown.

One may appropriately mention, in this context, Abraham's view that the oral character is also typified by "impatient importunity, haste, and restlessness (1924, pp. 403–404)." Impatience and restlessness might be said to overlap with an interest in having new and novel experiences. They could somewhat fancifully be regarded as indirect expressions of the desire to be "fed" a stream of new events.

5. Abraham suggests that unfulfilled oral needs may persist into adulthood in the form of exaggerated modes of oral behavior. He notes (1927, p. 404):

> In many people we find, besides the oral character traits described, other psychological manifestations which we must derive from the same instinctual sources. These are impulses which have escaped any social modification. As examples, a morbidly intense appetite for food and an inclination to various oral perversions are especially to be mentioned.

One may deduce from this statement that those with early oral problems will as adults be more likely to show such behaviors as overeating, smoking, and a preference for oral forms of sexual gratification. Incidentally, Abraham is explicit in saying that the oral character is often heavily invested in oral communication—inclined to an unusual amount of talking and use of words for hostile aims.

6. The most elementary requirement of the oral character type is that it be identifiable as an entity. If there is such a phenomenon as an oral character, one should be able to spell out what it

looks like. As already noted above, many different properties were ascribed by Abraham to those with oral fixations. These properties may be variously summarized in the following terms:

a) Preoccupation with issues of giving-taking (nurturance-succorance, generosity-avarice)
b) Concern about dependence-independence and passivity-activity
c) Special attitudes about closeness and distance to others—being alone versus attachment to the group
d) Extremes of optimism-pessimism
e) Unusual ambivalence
f) An openness to novel experience and ideas, which involves enhanced curiosity and interest in investigating nature
g) A hasty, restless, impatient orientation—wanting to be "fed" with events and things
h) Continued unusual use of oral channels for gratification or compensatory denial of oral needs (for example, overeating, not eating enough, smoking, excessive talking)

If there is an oral character type, it should be possible to demonstrate that these behaviors and attitudes cluster together in more than a chance fashion. Since they are all presumably manifestations of defenses against a common problem, they should be linked together. This is certainly an hypothesis amenable to objective appraisal.

Having reduced the oral character theory to what appears to be a series of manageable statements, we will now turn to an analysis of the scientific literature bearing on these statements.

Is There an Identifiable Oral Character?

The first proposition that will be checked against the existing evidence is whether the major characteristics ascribed to the oral character do actually constitute an identifiable cluster. Do they hang together as an entity?

There are a number of studies that have specifically set out to determine whether there is a perceptible oral dimension. Typically, these studies are based on administering questionnaires that inquire about a wide variety of feelings and ways of dealing with people, and then determining by statistical procedures (usually factor analysis) whether those facets of behavior theoretically ascribed to the oral character are significantly linked to each other. They seek, for example, to determine whether the person who is dependent is also more likely to manifest extremes in optimism-pessimism, to choose oral modes of gratification, and so forth. In scanning such studies, one finds they have differed to some degree in the kinds of behavior they have included in the oral category. But they have also shown fair agreement in terms of their common inquiries concerning dependence, passivity, optimism-pessimism, preference for being alone versus being allied with a group, and interest in use of the mouth for sucking and biting.

A review of these studies reveals that they have generally been able to isolate trait aggregations recognizably resembling the oral character profile. Note the following studies and the clusters they have found (listed roughly in order of their direct bearing on the issues):

Lazare et al. (1966)*
  Passive receptiveness: passivity, suggestibility, dependence
  Pessimism: pessimism, self-doubt
  Withdrawal: egocentricity, rejection of others, fear of sexuality
(Contained in one factor)

Gottheil and Stone (1968)
  Dependency
  Passivity associated with pessimism and an avoidance of responsibility, competition, and leadership
  Demandingness, envy
(Contained in three factors)

Sirota (1957)
  Oral sadism
  Intellectualization
  Business values
  Masculinity
  Verbal interests (negative)
(Contained in one factor defined as follows: "reaction to early oral frustration which is characterized by an active aggressive attempt to secure a steady source of supplies in the outer world, so that the individual does not have to bear a repetition of the oral frustration" [p. 42])

Barnes (1952)
  Pessimism
  Covert aggression
  Dependency
  Self-confidence
  Rigidity
  Biting
(Contained in two factors)

*Substantially cross-validated in a subsequent study (Lazare et al. 1970).

Stagner et al. (1955)[11]
Biting
Collecting things as hobby (males only)
Tolerance for weakness in others (males only)
Buying bargains (females only)
Enjoy playing with mud piles (females only)
(Contained in one separate factor for each sex)

Hubbard (1967)
Conforming oral dependency: dependency, rigidity, submissiveness, severe superego, passivity, avoidance of oral aggression
Withdrawing dependency: pessimism, self-doubt, egocentricity, withdrawn, mistrust, oral aggression
Supply seeking
Oral rejection
Introspection and conscience-ridden submissiveness, passivity, and withdrawal, but aggressive eating preferences
Seclusive and verbally aggressive, with interest in children and need to give affection; passive and oral impulses rejected
Dependent suggestibility
(Multiple factors derived from analysis of Grygier's [1961] Dynamic Personality Inventory, self-ratings, and Blum's [1949] Blacky Test)

Robinson and Hendrix (1966)
Oral eroticism
Oral sadism
Oedipal intensity
Anal retentiveness (negative loading)
(Contained in a factor derived from Blum's [1949] Blacky Test)

Goldman (1948)
Pessimism
Passivity
Aloofness
Oral (verbal) aggression
Endocathexis (withdrawal)
Autonomy
(Contained in one bipolar factor, with the other extreme representing the opposites of the traits listed)

Goldman-Eisler (1951)
Oral pessimism
Impatience
Aggression
Autonomy
(Contained in two factors)

Finney (1961a)
Pessimism
Dependency
Anxiety
Covert passive hostility
(Oral syndrome)

Finney (1961b)
  Demanding
  Exhibitionistic
  Acting out impulsively
(Contained in one factor)

Watson (1952)
  Oral dependency: eager overtures to others
  Oral hostile: much rejection and overt hostility
(Derived from complex cluster analysis involving Blacky Test and multiple measures of behavior in a group)

Comrey (1961, 1962, 1965, 1966)[12]
  Dependency: need for approval, affiliation, lack of self-sufficiency, succorance, deference, conformity
(Contained in one factor)

Mandel (1958)
  Early oral: optimism, generosity, envy
  Late oral: pessimism, ambivalence, possessiveness, defiance

Kagan and Moss (1962)
  Consistent significant intercorrelations among six measures of dependency and passivity in children and adults

Kline (1968a)
  Failed to find an oral factor when analyzed Grygier's (1961) Dynamic Personality Inventory

Stringer (1970)
  Three bipolar oral-anal factors
  Prenatal early oral factor

It would be an exaggeration to declare that the results cited above strongly support the existence of an oral character cluster. But they are moderately supportive. Most of the studies portray an aggregation of traits relating to dependency, passivity, egocentricity, and concern about self-competence in coping with other people. In eight of the studies pessimism is also included in the oral cluster. Further, five of the studies implicate impulses to bite. The clusters deviate from the oral character theory primarily in the sense that they not infrequently include traits that fall outside of the basic paradigm. One finds references to variables such as "fear of sexuality" and "enjoy playing with mud piles," which really do not fit.

At the same time, it should be pointed out that the various studies involved have employed diverse methodologies, both with reference to the content of the questionnaires used and the statistical analyses applied. One could argue that the consistencies that have appeared are remarkable under the circumstances. In any case, it seems fair to conclude that Freud and Abraham were more right than wrong when they stated there are persons who exhibit a group of traits whose nature can be logically derived from difficulties in coping with problems presumably encountered in the oral phase of the developmental sequence.

Can Oral Traits Be Traced to Experiences in the Oral Developmental Phase?

It is a vital part of the oral character theory that oral character attributes arise from experiences during the oral developmental phase, which presumably encompasses the first year or so of life. A surprisingly large number of investigators have examined this proposition. They have, with few exceptions, concerned themselves with early feeding and nurturance conditions provided the child. They have assumed that knowledge of these conditions permits a reasonable assay of how much the child was orally deprived or over-gratified.

Two study paradigms predominate: (1) One is based on asking parents for information about early feeding experiences involving their offspring and then relating such data to various personality measures obtained from these offspring. (2) A second involves direct observation of children during the early years and correlating their nurturance experiences at this time with later childhood and adult behaviors. A large majority of the studies use relatively simple indices to evaluate early feeding experiences. They typically look at the following: breast feeding versus bottle feeding, rigid versus self-demand feeding schedules, time of weaning, and duration (gradualness) of weaning. Some have also appraised such variables as how much parents emphasize that the child learn to be self-sufficient, the amount of anxiety produced by early oral experiences, and the degree of maternal warmth.

It should be reiterated at this point that the oral character theory, as set forth by Abraham, would be supported by evidence that either *under- or overgratification* of oral needs during the oral phase lays the groundwork for certain personality patterns. To consider only undergratification as a significant factor would be to misread the theory.

Table 1 contains brief summaries of the major studies that have looked at the connections between early oral experiences and later behavior. As one scans these studies, they fall roughly into three clusters: (1) those examining the relationship between early

TABLE 1

Summary of Studies Concerned with Relationships Between Early Oral Experiences and Later Behavior

Investigators	Subjects	Indices of Oral Phase Conditions	Major Findings	Comments
Levy (1927–1928)	112 "healthy infants and children."	Breast feeding, feeding schedule, use of pacifier. (Information obtained from interview with mother.)	Children who suck their fingers had "less opportunity for sucking movements." For example, they were more often forced to withdraw from sucking at the "termination of a set period of time." No relation found between use or non-use of breast feeding and finger sucking.	Not really directly pertinent to the oral character hypothesis because involves such young children.
Childers and Hamils (1932)	469 "problem children" (under age of 13).	Whether breast fed and length of breast feeding. (Information obtained from social history based on retrospective recall.)	Number of "undesirable behavior manifestations" increased from points 1 to 4 of following sequence: 1) Breast feeding prolonged beyond 11 months 2) "Normal" amount of breast feeding 3) No breast feeding 4) Weaned between first and sixth months	Difficult to interpret because of lack of tests of statistical significance. Probably not pertinent because the oral character theory does not specify a grossly greater number of symptoms of disturbance in the orally fixated.

TABLE 1 *(continued)*

Investigators	Subjects	Indices of Oral Phase Conditions	Major Findings	Comments
Peterson and Spano (1941–1943)	126 "normal" children in Fels longitudinal study.	Duration of breast feeding. (Information obtained from mother at time of breast feeding)	No relation between length of breast feeding and rated personality traits at nursery school level or adjustment at pre-adolescent stage. Also, no relation between length of breast feeding and ratings of mother's degree of rejection of her child.	A number of the traits rated (for example, "cheerfulness," "jealousy," and "kindness") were clearly pertinent to the oral character concept. The adjustment ratings are not really pertinent to the oral character theory.
Maslow and Szilagyi-Kessler (1946)	418 college students.	Length of breast feeding. (Information obtained by students from their mothers.)	Curvilinear relationship with measure of personal security. Highest security found in those breast fed either less than 3 months or more than 12.	Not directly pertinent to the oral character theory.

Investigators	Subjects	Indices of Oral Phase Conditions	Major Findings	Comments
Holway (1949)	17 nursery school children.	Strictness of feeding schedule, feeling tone of mother about feeding schedule, number of months breast fed. (Information obtained from retrospective interviews with mothers.)	Reality of play positively correlated with degree of self-regulation in feeding and also number of months breast fed. Not correlated with mother's "feeling tone" about the feeding schedule. No relation between aggression in play and oral indices.	No obvious pertinence of the findings to the oral character concept.
Sears and Wise (1950)	80 normal children (ages 2–7).	Age of weaning, reaction to weaning. (Information obtained from retrospective interviews with mothers.)	Late weaned children showed more frustration in response to the weaning than did early weaned. Trend for thumbsucking to be greater in children weaned late than in those weaned early.	Only indirectly pertinent to the oral character theory.
Goldman (1950–1951) Goldman-Eisler (1951)	100 adults.	Whether breast fed and at what age taken off the breast. (Information obtained from mothers retrospectively.)	Those who experienced early frustration in breast feeding show "oral pessimist" traits. Those with "overlong" period of breast feeding develop "oral optimist" traits. Oral traits like impulsion, aggression, and autonomy were not linked to weaning experience.	One of the first methodologically sophisticated studies concerned with the oral character concept.

TABLE 1 *(continued)*

Investigators	Subjects	Indices of Oral Phase Conditions	Major Findings	Comments
Newton (1951)	24 "normal children."	Whether breast fed, rigidity of feeding schedule, age of weaning, responses to feeding and weaning. (Information obtained from mothers retrospectively.)	Newton states (p. 31): "A larger proportion of the early weaned group was friendly toward adults and children, accepted adult suggestions, took responsibility well, and led frequently by giving commands. The late weaned group daydreamed more, and contained all the best and worst adjusted children—" Children fed on flexible schedules exceeded those on non-flexible schedules in "average social adaptability" and were also more popular, less self-conscious with adults, and less likely to show off and act silly.	Formal statistical tests were not done. The results are apparent trends based on percents.

TABLE 1 *(continued)*

Investigators	Subjects	Indices of Oral Phase Conditions	Major Findings	Comments
Thurston and Mussen (1951)	91 male college students.	Length of time breast only source of nourishment, total length of sucking time (breast and bottle), age of weaning from breast. (Information obtained from mothers retrospectively.)	Personality measures derived from Thematic Apperception Test stories which presumably tap oral character traits were largely not correlated with the various measures pertaining to breast feeding.	Although the results were primarily negative, two significant findings are of interest: Subjects with short duration of breast feeding were high on Thematic Apperception measure of "Autonomy." Subjects with short duration of total sucking time were high on a Thematic Apperception measure of attention seeking ("Recognition"). The investigators felt their results "gave no support to the psychoanalytic theory of oral personality."

TABLE 1 *(continued)*

Investigators	Subjects	Indices of Oral Phase Conditions	Major Findings	Comments
Sewell (1952–1953)	162 normal children (ages 5–6).	Whether bottle-fed, self-demand versus fixed feeding schedule, gradualness of weaning. (Information obtained from retrospective interview with mother.)	Largely negative results obtained. The oral indices were generally not correlated with a range of personality ratings and test scores. A few scattered significant relations were observed: Children who were on a self-demand feeding schedule had lower "feelings of belonging." Children who were gradually rather than abruptly weaned had "high feelings of belonging" and also "high social standards."	Many of the personality parameters that were evaluated were not pertinent to the oral character theory.
Sewell and Mussen (1952)	162 normal children (ages 5–6).	Breast fed, bottle fed, fixed feeding schedule, gradualness of weaning. (Information obtained from retrospective interview with mother.)	No consistent relationships of oral indices with measures of adjustment or symptoms indicative of "conflicts around oral-erotic impulses" (for example, nailbiting, eating difficulties).	The relationships involving "adjustment" are not pertinent to the oral character hypothesis.

TABLE 1 *(continued)*

Investigators	Subjects	Indices of Oral Phase Conditions	Major Findings	Comments
Sears et al. (1953)	40 preschool normal children.	The manner in which feeding was scheduled and severity of weaning were evaluated. (Information derived from interviews with mothers.)	Severity of weaning was positively correlated with amount of dependency. Severity of weaning positively correlated with negative attention seeking in boys, but negatively so in girls. Manner in which feeding was scheduled not related to later dependency. The greater the feeding frustrations of children (especially girls), the greater the later dependency.	Carefully designed study.
Whiting and Child (1953)	Numerous cultures studied by anthropologists.	Age and gradualness of weaning, nursing indulgence.	The greater the anxiety associated with oral socialization practices, the more often is illness attributed by the culture to oral ingestion of bad substance or oral forces (for example, incantations). Oral anxiety is not correlated with fear of others.	Especially interesting because tests hypotheses across numerous cultures.

TABLE 1 *(continued)*

Investigators	Subjects	Indices of Oral Phase Conditions	Major Findings	Comments
Stendler (1954)	20 overdependent six-year-olds.	Age of weaning, difficulty of weaning.	There was a trend for the overdependent children to have been weaned later than a comparison control group. No differences with respect to difficulty of weaning.	The data were not analyzed with formal statistical tests.
Bernstein (1955)	50 normal children: about 5 years old.	Length of breast feeding, weaning time and difficulties, scheduled versus flexible feeding. (Information derived from retrospective interviews with mothers.)	Those who suck fingers originally had more sucking reinforcement during early feeding experiences. Those preferring candy which requires sucking had more sucking reinforcement during early feeding. Those with symptoms of constipation had more sucking reinforcement. Those inclined to "collect objects" had less sucking reinforcement.	Looked at feeding behavior primarily in terms of opportunity provided for reinforcing sucking behavior.

TABLE 1 *(continued)*

Investigators	Subjects	Indices of Oral Phase Conditions	Major Findings	Comments
Straus (1957)	73 children in third grade in Ceylon.	Scheduled versus flexible feeding, when feeding of solids began, weaning time, how sudden weaning was. (Information derived from retrospective interviews with mothers.)	No consistent relationships between index of oral frustration and insecurity or various dimensions derived from California Test of Personality (for example, sense of personal worth, self-reliance, feeling of belonging).	Analyzed data in terms of a single total Oral Frustration index
Sears et al. (1957)	379 normal kindergarten children.	Whether breast fed, scheduling of feeding, age and gradualness of weaning, amount of emotional upset in relation to feeding practices. (Information obtained from retrospective interviews with mothers.)	Largely negative results. No relationship between severity of weaning and dependency.	Unusually careful and well designed study.

TABLE 1 *(continued)*

Investigators	Subjects	Indices of Oral Phase Conditions	Major Findings	Comments
McArthur et al. (1958)	252 Harvard alumni.	Number of months breast fed. (Information obtained by questionnaire from parents.)	The longer an individual was breast fed the more easily he was able to stop smoking.	
Stein (1958)	77 psychotic males. 112 normal adolescent boys.	Age of completion of weaning. Coerciveness of weaning process. (Information obtained from retrospective interviews with mothers.)	Coerciveness of weaning was significantly correlated in complex fashion with manner in which moral "transgression" themes were handled in projective stories.	
Lambert et al. (1959)	31 cultures.	Ratings by anthropologists of how infant treated (for example, overall indulgence, immediacy of drive reduction, constancy of presence of nurturing agent).	"Societies with beliefs in aggressive supernaturals were significantly more likely than those with beliefs in benevolent gods and spirits to be described as having generally punitive or hurtful practices in treating infants" (p. 168).	

TABLE 1 *(continued)*

Investigators	Subjects	Indices of Oral Phase Conditions	Major Findings	Comments
Finney (1961b)	31 children (boys) in child guidance clinic.	Interviews with mothers about how nurturant and encouraging of dependency they are in their child-rearing practices.	"A child who is pessimistic, dependent, anxious, and passively resentful (hurt feelings or sulking) is most likely to be produced by an overprotective mother who is lacking in real warmth or affection" (p. 263). "The findings presented here confirm the influence of maternal nurturance on the 'oral' qualities in the child" (p. 264).	This study does not specifically attempt to trace the effect of mother's nurturant behavior during the early "oral phase" years. Rather, it largely considers mother's attributes as she manifested them at the time of the study. It is possible that a mother's degree of nurturance is rather consistent over the years, but this is not an established fact.
Murphy (1962)	32 normal children in Menninger longitudinal study.	Detailed observation of mother's style of relating to child in a variety of situations. Observations of child's "oral" behavior during infancy.	In boys, "infancy oral gratification" was positively and significantly correlated with: sense of self-worth autonomy positive self-appraisal ability to control the impact of the environment	Data for girls not presented. Only a small part of the quantitative data is cited.

TABLE 1 *(continued)*

Investigators	Subjects	Indices of Oral Phase Conditions	Major Findings	Comments
Kagan and Moss (1962)	89 persons in Fels longitudinal study.	Frequent observation of mother's nurturance behavior in the home as she related to her child.	The more a mother treated her infant male child in a strongly nurturant and protective fashion, the more dependent his behavior was for the first 10 years of life, but not during adolescence or adulthood. When mother treated the infant female in a highly nurturant and protective fashion, the result was a pattern of "adult withdrawal behavior" and diminished independence during the 10–14 age period.	While the results for boys show some consistency, those for girls are fragmentary.
Heinstein (1963)	94 persons evaluated over course of 18 years in a longitudinal study.	Length of breast feeding, length of nursing, warmth of mother as determined from actual observations and ratings during individual's infancy	Boys breast fed as children were later more likely to display the following: enunciation difficulties; feelings of frustration regarding dependency needs, and "controlled" aggression (as revealed in projective stories).	Well designed. Important study

TABLE 1 *(continued)*

Investigators	Subjects	Indices of Oral Phase Conditions	Major Findings	Comments
			Girls who were breast fed showed a trend toward high jealousy, excess reserve in relationships, strong strivings for independence, and more "controlled" but less "primitive" aggression. Long nursed boys were especially finicky about food, low in demanding excess attention, quite "reserved," inclined to a good deal of nailbiting, and showing a high frequency of enunciation defects. Long nursed girls did not differ from short nursed ones for a variety of personality parameters.	

TABLE 1 *(continued)*

Investigators	Subjects	Indices of Oral Phase Conditions	Major Findings	Comments
			Boys with "warm" mothers had few appetite problems, little food finickiness, limited imagery (in projective stories) about giving up independence. Girls with "warm" mothers displayed few "behavior problems," were not food finicky, had few enunciation defects, were low in personal "reserve," seemed well adjusted in Rorschach terms. But were high on nailbiting.	
Davis and Ruiz (1965)	80 adolescent boys and girls.	Mode of infant feeding: breast, bottle, cup, mixed. (Information obtained retrospectively from parents.)	No consistent relations of oral indices to various scores derived from the Minnesota Multiphasic Personality Inventory.	The findings, which primarily concern degree of maladjustment, are not directly pertinent to the oral character theory.

TABLE 1 *(continued)*

Investigators	Subjects	Indices of Oral Phase Conditions	Major Findings	Comments
Bacon et al. (1965)	110 cultures studied anthropologically.	Indulgence of dependency in infancy.	High frequency of drunkenness associated with low dependency indulgence. High general consumption of alcohol correlated with low indulgence of dependency.	
Rosenblatt (1966)	21 cultures studied anthropologically.	Modes of oral and dependency socialization.	Early frustration of oral needs was positively correlated with the importance placed on romantic love (close affection) as a basis for choice of marital partner. Early frustration of dependency needs was not correlated with emphasis placed on romantic love.	

TABLE 1 *(continued)*

Investigators	Subjects	Indices of Oral Phase Conditions	Major Findings	Comments
Sears, Rau, and Alpert (1965)	40 nursery school children.	Whether breast fed, duration of breast feeding, severity of weaning, rigidity of feeding schedule, severity of early separation from mother and father. (Information obtained retrospectively from mother and father.)	Severity of early separation from parents not correlated with dependency. Duration of breast feeding is positively correlated with negative attention seeking in boys, but has a chance relation with measures of dependency. It is also not correlated with dependency in girls. In boys, severity of weaning is positively correlated with dependency and negative attention seeking. In girls, severity of weaning and dependency tend to be negatively related.	A large proportion of the findings were not significant.

TABLE 1 *(continued)*

Investigators	Subjects	Indices of Oral Phase Conditions	Major Findings	Comments
Miller and Swanson (1966)	Several hundred male junior high and college students.	Severity of weaning. (Information obtained retrospectively from mothers.)	Early weaning correlated with presence of medium rather than high or low guilt. Early weaning correlated with low severity of guilt about theft and disobedience in projective stories. Weaning severity not linked with use of denial or other mechanisms of defense.	Carefully designed and thoughtful study.
Benfari (1969)	20 cultures studied anthropologically.	Degree to which culture fosters childhood dependence.	Societies fostering childhood dependence are those in which the patient-healer relationship is particularly likely to be defined as one in which there is support and care-giving provided.	

feeding practices and later behavior; (2) those concerned with the influence of early maternal behavior, as defined by such variables as "warmth" and "attitude toward dependence" (rather than feeding practices), upon later behavior; and (3) those with an anthropological perspective that consider the link between the oral socialization practices of whole cultures and their modal behavior styles.

The studies concerned with the link between feeding practices and later behavior are vulnerable to criticism because of their rather simplistic assumption that the manner in which a mother feeds her child is a valid index of how much she and the child's father *generally* gratify or do not gratify his wants. There is actually an absence of scientific data pertinent to this issue, and one's skepticism is encouraged when confronted by studies like that of Peterson and Spano (1941), in which the length of time mothers breast-fed their children proved not to be correlated with ratings of how rejecting they were of these children.

Even so, among the studies cited in Table 1 that concern the link between feeding indices and later behavior, about 60 to 70 percent report convincing significant correlations. There are studies that describe significant correlations between length of breast feeding and optimism-pessimism[13] (Goldman 1950–1951, Goldman-Eisler 1951), age of weaning and acceptance of responsibility (Newton 1951), severity of weaning and dependency (Sears et al. 1953, Sears et al. 1965), opportunity for sucking in early feeding and later preference for candy requiring sucking (Bernstein 1955), length of breast feeding and amount of smoking (McArthur et al. 1958), severity of weaning and guilt about theft (taking?) and disobedience (behaving autonomously?), and lengthy nursing and being finicky about food (but low in demanding "excess attention" [Heinstein, 1963]).

There are also studies that failed to detect relationships between the following: duration of breast feeding and traits like "cheerfulness" and "jealousy" (Peterson and Spano 1941), weaning procedure and traits pertinent to dependency (Thurston and Mussen 1950–1951, Sears et al. 1957), various indices of feeding (for example, whether breast-fed, how weaned), and symptoms indicative of "oral conflict" (for example, nailbiting, eating difficulties) (Sewell and Mussen 1952).

One finds about an equal representation of good and poor research designs in the supportive and nonsupportive studies. Indeed, after intensive analysis we have not been able to ascertain what distinguishes the two groups of studies. They do not differ systematically with reference to the samples investigated, methods used, or hypotheses tested.[14] Perhaps one should not really be surprised that differences in results are encountered, in view of the fact that most of the studies had to rely on extremely gross evaluative procedures. For example, retrospective reports of mothers were the most frequent source of information about early feeding practices, and they are notoriously unreliable and subject to error. Actually, what is remarkable is that so many of the studies did identify tangible ties between early feeding practices and later (often many years so) attitudes and traits falling within the oral character paradigm. While one has every right to remain skeptical about these studies in view of their attenuated logic and gross methods, it is fair to acknowledge their positive implications.[15]

There are several studies in Table 1 that represent a cluster insofar as they probed the relationship between the mother's warmth and nurturance in her early contacts with her child and the subsequent personality attributes of that child. They have largely come up with results favoring the oral character formulation. Thus, Finney (1961b) found that an "overprotective mother who is lacking in real warmth or affection" tends to raise a child who is "pessimistic, dependent, anxious, and passively resentful." Murphy (1962) reported (in rather abbreviated fashion) that boys who during infancy had been dealt with by their mothers in a "gratifying" fashion, were in later years likely to display nondependent traits. Kagan and Moss (1962) observed that mothers who treated infant male sons in a strongly nurturant and protective manner were likely to shape them in the direction of unusual dependency. Similar patterns were found to apply to mothers' treatment of daughters. However, such ties held primarily for behavior up to adolescence and not beyond that point. Heinstein (1963) noted that boys raised by "warm" mothers later had few appetite problems, little food finickiness, and limited imagery about being passive. He stated, too, that girls reared by "warm" mothers turned out later not to be food-finicky and had few enunciation defects but were high on nailbiting. The overall trend of these studies is fairly consistent. They indicate that early patterns of maternal nurturance and warmth register in the child's later inclinations toward passive fantasy and behavior and also toward indirect forms of oral gratification. The results are not unidirectional. In one study, high maternal nurturance leads to passivity; in another, it produces independence. But once again, it needs to be repeated that the oral character theory proposes that both under- and overgratification can have similar consequences for a developing child.

A third cluster of studies in Table 1 embraces a number of anthropological investigations that have traced relationships between the ways in which various cultures impose standards of oral gratification upon children and subsequent aspects of adult behavior. Briefly, the following findings have emerged. Whiting and Child (1953) demonstrated that the greater the anxiety associated with oral socialization in a range of cultures, the more likely was illness to be attributed to oral ingestion of bad substances or the influence of bad oral forces (for example, incantations). Lambert et al. (1959) presented evidence that (p. 168) "Societies with beliefs in aggressive supernaturals were significantly more likely than those with beliefs in benevolent gods and spirits to be described as having generally punitive or hurtful practices in treating infants." Bacon et al. (1965) noted across 110 cultures that the likelihood of drunkenness and high alcohol consumption occurring was maximized by not indulging the child's dependence in early years. Rosenblatt (1966) demonstrated that the need for close affection in adults (as defined by an emphasis on romantic love as a basis for choice of marital partner) in twenty-one different cultures was positively correlated with the amount of early oral frustration encountered. Benfari (1969) reported that societies fostering childhood dependence are those in which the relationship between the sick individual and the healer is particularly likely to be defined as one in which much support and care-giving are provided.

A few of these studies are a bit tangential to the original oral character formulation, but they are still pertinent in the sense that they support the idea that early nurturance experiences can have an impact that extends into adulthood. Actually, the five studies just enumerated are quite impressive in their unanimous presentation of significant ties between childhood and adult variables with oral meaning.

The ideal approach to exploring the question whether an oral orientation can be traced back to early experiences would be to follow children longitudinally and examine the impact of what happens in the first year or so of life (oral phase) upon the probability of later developing oral character traits. There have been a few longitudinal studies that could potentially lend themselves to such a plan, but in only one instance do the measures employed actually make this possible. Kagan and Moss (1962) analyzed passive and dependent behavior in samples of males and females from birth through adulthood. Multiple ratings by observers and interviewers at various ages made possible objective and reliable evaluation of each child over a significant segment of his life span. Each child was rated with respect to variables like passivity, dependency, independence, and anxiety about loss of nurturance. As adults, each was rated with respect to such variables as dependency on love objects, dependency on parents, and seeking dependent gratification in vocational choice. It should be said at this point, in anticipation of an analysis that will be elaborated later, that there is good evidence that passivity and dependence are core attributes of the oral character. Thus, the elaborate ratings of passivity and dependence in the Kagan and Moss study are directly pertinent. It is immediately striking that they reported that the amount of passivity manifested during the first two years of life by girls was significantly predictive of their passivity in later phases of childhood and of general dependency in adulthood. Their reports about males indicate much less consistency. Passivity during the first two years of life was predictive of passivity at ages three to six, but not at later age periods in childhood. Further, while it was also significantly correlated with the amount of dependence on love objects during adulthood, it had only chance relationships with a number of other indices of adult dependency.

One is left with the impression that in females there may be a real continuity between early childhood and adulthood with respect to a core trait in the oral character syndrome. This would, of course, fit well with the theory that oral character attitudes can be traced back to conditions encountered in the oral phase of development. On the other hand, the findings involving men are, at best, only weakly suggestive of such a continuity process. This, of course, raises a possibility that Abraham did not explicitly consider, namely, that the processes involved in oral character development may not be the same in the two sexes. Kagan and Moss suggested the following explanation for the difference they found between males and females (p. 58): "The primary reason for this lack of continuity in males is the development of conflict over passive and dependent behavior. A passive orientation to problems is inappropriate for the male role. As boys approach school age, the important figures in their lives begin to manipulate rewards and punishments in an attempt to encourage independence and autonomy . . . Moreover, the boy begins to model his behavior after heroes who symbolize dominance, retaliation, and independence, and who regard passivity as synonymous with infancy, senility, and femininity. Some boys, therefore, become conflicted over a passive orientation. This conflict, which does not swell to such strong proportions in middle-class girls, leads to minimal continuity between childhood and adult dependency for males."

It is possible that in males the impact of oral-phase experiences upon later oral character behavior is much more modified by intervening life experiences than is true for females.

Overall, the material that has been skimmed in this section is fairly persuasive in pointing to a link between pertinent oral experiences in infancy and later adult attributes. It is also persuasive in the more specific sense of documenting a connection between pertinent oral infancy experiences and later adult behaviors (for example, dependence, optimism-pessimism) that have a defined significance within the oral character paradigm. However, that is about all one can say on the positive side. There is not enough consistency to weigh the relative contributions of under- as compared with over-oral gratification to oral character development. There is little information about how specific maternal (not to mention paternal) behaviors lay the foundation for later oral character traits. We have no empirical data to help us conceptualize why early maternal nurturance may in one instance be antecedent to strong dependency but in another promote the opposite. In short, we are in the simplistic state of merely being able to declare the existence of a correlation that is roughly congruent with a theory.

Do Oral Characters Behave in Predictable Ways?

The next matter we will consider is whether people who are defined as oral characters behave in ways that are predictable from the oral character theory. As pointed out earlier, it was hypothesized by Abraham (and affirmed by Freud) that a person caught up in the problems of the oral period would relate to people in particular ways and be preoccupied with certain issues. Diverse studies have been launched to find out if this is so. They are diverse not only with respect to their methods for defining who should be labeled as an oral character but also with respect to the extrapolations they make about how this type of character should behave. What we will focus upon primarily in this section are experiments that have exposed oral characters to specific conditions and tried to predict how they would respond. But attention will also be devoted to related studies that are less experimental and more correlational.

Let us first contemplate a cluster of reports having to do with passivity and dependency. Priority is given to appraising this cluster because the concepts of dependency and attachment are, as spelled out by Abraham, central to defining oral character traits. Typically, in the course of studies pertinent to this area, persons designated by some criterion as oral characters have been evaluated to determine how passively they will conduct themselves when they are called upon to cope with certain instructions or demands. Paradoxically, several of the most impressive and carefully planned studies have involved conditioning procedures derived from a tradition rather alien to psychoanalysis: Timmons and Noblin (1963) used an ingenious experimental design based on comparing the behavior of the oral character with that of the anal character. A good deal will be said about the anal character in a later portion of this chapter, but for present purposes it should be noted that this concept was developed by Freud to depict the type of individual who continues to struggle with anal impulses to besmirch and dirty that were originally linked with the toilet training period. Presumably the anal character is particularly concerned with sensations of being controlled and "forced," and defensively adopts resistive stubborn strategies. Timmons and Noblin contrast such an orientation with that of the oral character, whom they portray as "being dependent . . . highly susceptible to suggestion from authority figures" (p. 383).

Their experiment was based on the prediction that the dependent oral character and the stubborn anal character would respond in opposite fashion to a procedure designed to produce a conditioned response. Representatives of the oral and anal character categories were chosen by administering the Blacky Test (Blum, 1949) to college students and identifying those with special oral or anal orientations. The Blacky Test consists of a series of pictures of a dog (Blacky) who is depicted in various situations that have direct or symbolic significance from a psychoanalytic perspective. For example, an Oral Sadism picture shows Blacky biting his mother's collar, and an Anal Eroticism picture shows Blacky defecating. Responses to such pictures are obtained by asking subjects to compose stories about them and to pick multiple choice interpretations of them. When fifteen orals and fifteen anals had been identified by means of Blacky responses, they were individually exposed to the following conditioning paradigm. Each was asked to look at a series of cards on which there were incomplete sentences preceded either by a third person or first person pronoun, and in each instance to compose any kind of sentence he wished. Baseline trials were obtained to ascertain the frequency with which his sentences were phrased in the first as compared to the third person. Then, in a second conditioning set of trials the experimenter gave a mild affirmatory response (for example, "That's fine") whenever the individual used the first person pronoun to compose each sentence. Finally, there was an extinction series during which the experimenter no longer voiced evaluative reactions to the choices of pronouns. It was predicted that the orals would condition better than the anals (that is, use the first-person pronoun more frequently), because their dependent orientation would make them more susceptible to "mild, affirmatory words from an authority figure . . . used as reinforcing stimuli" (p. 383). The results were clearly supportive of the hypothesis. The orals did respond more compliantly than the anals, and their patterns of behavior during the task were quite contrasting.

In another related study Noblin et al. (1966) explored in more detail the differences between the ways orals and anals respond to conditioning. Twenty-four of each category were chosen in terms of their responses to the Blacky Test. Once again it was predicted that orals would condition better than the anals when reinforced by positive approval. However, the additional hypothesis was tested that negative (disapproving) reinforcement would result in better conditioning for the anals than the orals. The hypothesis concerning anals was based on the psychoanalytic formulation that anal characters are "negative, hostile, and resistant to suggestions from authority figures" (p. 225). The conditioning paradigm, concerned with producing changes in use of personal pronouns in constructing sentences, was the same as that described immediately above with reference to the Timmons and Noblin study. However, part of the sample was conditioned not by positive reinforcement but rather by the experimenter expressing disapproval (for example, "You can do better") of pronoun usages that he intended to discourage. Analysis of the overall results indicated again that the orals conditioned better than the anals when provided with positive reinforcement. Actually, the anals, in contrast to the orals, decreased their use of the target pronouns during the affirmative conditions. When exposed to negative reinforcement, the orals showed a decrease in their use of the target pronouns, but the anals showed an increase! It was noted, "The verbal behavior of the oral group appeared to be contingent on the approval of the experimenter while anals demonstrated an apparent resistance to the suggestions of the experimenter" (p. 227). The conclusion was drawn: "These results strengthen the psychoanalytic assertions that orals are dependent, compliant, and submissive to suggestions from authority figures . . ." (p. 228).

In a third related study, Noblin (1962) selected thirty orals and thirty anals from a hospitalized male psychiatric population. Classification was based not only on responses to the Blacky Test but also on ward behavior (for example, amount of impatience to eat at lunchtime) and diagnosis (for example, as suggested by psychoanalytic formulations, a manic-depressive classification was considered to be linked with orality and a paranoid one with anality). The same conditioning paradigm concerned with use of personal pronouns, as described above, was used. However, the means of reinforcement were different. In some groups the reinforcement was provided by giving the subjects gumballs and in others by giving pennies. It was hypothesized that gumballs would be particularly effective with orals and pennies especially effective with anals. The reasoning behind the use of the gumballs is obvious, but that related to the use of pennies needs at least brief clarification. Noblin simply theorized that since money is considered by Freud to have important symbolic associations with dirt and feces and for that reason to be particularly attractive to the anal character, it should be highly potent as a reward to anals. The results of the experiment were nicely congruent with expectation. Orals conditioned relatively better when reinforced with gumballs and anals conditioned relatively better when presented with pennies.

The three studies just reviewed that made use of the conditioning paradigm are impressive in their clearcut directionality. They indicate that persons identified by a particular technique as oral characters are unusually influenced not only by communications that define one as having a positive, dependent relationship with an authority figure, but also by oral rewards.

The consistency of the effects described in the three studies just reviewed has been called into question by Cooperman and Child (1971). They selected extreme oral (N = 16) and anal (N = 16) male subjects by means of the Blacky Test and exposed them to a verbal conditioning paradigm very similar to that employed in the three studies. Half were exposed to positive reinforcement and half to negative reinforcement. But contrary to previous reports, oral and anal subjects did not respond differentially to the conditioning procedures. Cooperman and Child, in speculating about the reason for their failure to support previous related work, did note that the reinforcement in their study was administered by an undergraduate student, whereas in the previous studies it was administered by a faculty member. The difference in the prestige of the student versus faculty member might well be a significant confounding factor. One is left in the position of perhaps being a bit more skeptical about the conditioning studies, but still not being able to dismiss the fact that the Cooperman and Child results represent an isolated contradiction of three other mutually confirming sets of observations.

Lish (1969) looked at the impact of success and failure experiences upon 134 male college students differing in their degree of orality (as defined by Grygier's [1961] Dynamic Personality Inventory). The success and failure experiences were induced by telling subjects they had done well or poorly on certain tests. It was found that under the success condition, high orals felt more approved of than low orals. Relatedly, high orals felt more "respected" during success than failure, whereas low orals did not differ with reference to these two conditions. There was no support for a formal hypothesis that was tested to the effect that high orals would be particularly likely to suffer loss of self-esteem and to feel depressed during failure. It is difficult to provide a capsule summary of what this study demonstrated. As defined by measures of self-esteem and depression, orality was not linked to modes of response to success and failure. But in terms of other criteria, high orals did seem to feel relatively better under conditions in which they were approved and dealt with positively. These results are rather supportive of the findings of the conditioning studies just cited.

One of the early ambitious attempts to evaluate the oral character theory empirically was made by Blum and Miller (1952). They checked out a series of hypotheses by studying a group of eighteen boys and girls (eight-year-olds) in the same school class. Their method for determining each child's degree of "orality" was to observe him for brief periods over several weeks and to tabulate the number of times he exhibited "nonpurposive mouth activities" (for example, thumb-sucking, licking the lips). Several of their hypotheses directly or indirectly touched on the theme of dependency and will now be briefly enumerated. They asked whether "orality" was correlated with the following:

1. Child's need to be liked and approved.

This was measured by asking teachers who knew the children to designate those particularly eager to get teachers and other children to like them. Also, observations were made of how often the children actually approached teachers and other children for approval.

2. Child's dependency.

Evaluation was undertaken by asking the teachers of the children to indicate which "are most able to take care of themselves without the help of adults or other children."

3. Child's need to be ingratiating.

Measurement was based on asking teachers to indicate "which children seem to be always eager to help even when they are inconvenienced" and also by actual observation of how often each child went out of his way to do favors for others.

4. Child's social isolation as a result of "his passivity, his

excessive demands for attention, and his hostility when these demands are not gratified."

Evaluation was derived by asking members of the class to indicate whom they liked and disliked.

5. Child's inability to divide loyalties between two friends because they "both represent potential sources of supply" (that is, potential dependency attachments).

Determination was made by asking each child to choose in several ways between his two best friends and also his two best-liked teachers, and then observing his behavior, comments, and expressive movements at the time.

6. Child's suggestibility, which presumably can be traced to his degree of need for love and approval.

Measurement was undertaken both by asking teachers which children accept suggestions uncritically and also by observing which children accepted certain illusions (for example, smelling a nonexistent perfume) suggested to them.

The orality measure proved to be convincingly correlated in predicted directions with measures of the child's need for liking and approval, his dependency, and his social isolation.[16] It was not meaningfully related to his need to be ingratiating, his inability to divide loyalties, and his suggestibility. In other words, about half of the hypotheses relevant to dependency and the need for support were reasonably borne out by the data.

The question whether oral characters have a need to attach themselves (dependently) to others has been approached, too, in the context of appraising how they conduct themselves when their anxiety is whipped up. Consider the results of the following studies.

Rapaport (1963) fashioned an inquiry involving forty males defined as oral characters because they were drug addicts, "diagnosed as having oral-dependent neurotic characteristics" in hospital records, and also high in orality as measured by the Grygier (1961) Dynamic Personality Inventory. Another forty males (nonpsychotic hospitalized patients) were selected as anal characters on the basis of their anal scores on the Dynamic Personality Inventory and also of evaluations by hospital personnel. Half of the oral subjects were exposed (under guise of a physiological study) to a condition designed to arouse oral anxiety by creating the expectation that they were going to have to place various objects (for example, nipple, pacifier) in their mouths and suck them. The other half were exposed to an anal anxiety condition in which they were given the impression that in the name of "research in proctology" they would have to insert suppositories in themselves anally. The anal character sample was analogously split into those exposed to the oral anxiety condition and those exposed to the anal anxiety condition. At the height of the anxiety-provoking procedures, each subject was told that there would be a delay in the experimental sequence. He was given the choice of waiting alone or with others until time for resumption. The amount of anxiety evoked was also measured by means of a semiprojective technique. It was found, as predicted, that the oral characters exposed to the oral anxiety condition were more likely to want to "affiliate" with others when offered the choice than to be alone. The opposite was true for the anal characters exposed to the anal anxiety condition. There were numerous other findings, but they are not pertinent to our central concern: whether oral characters have a special need for affiliative bonds. Rapaport concluded with regard to this matter (p. 60): " . . . the two character groups . . . can be distinguished in terms of their social responses in anxiety arousing situations. Anal characters chose to isolate themselves and oral characters chose to affiliate."

The need of the oral character to maintain positive or dependent ties with others is pointed up in three studies involving yielding behavior. Masling et al. (1968) measured degree of oral orientation in forty-four college students by counting the number of references to oral themes in their Rorschach protocols. The students were then exposed to a conformity experiment in which they were asked to estimate the number of clicks they heard while wearing headphones. But previous to each estimate they heard statements by four other persons presumably attending to the same clicks, and the statements were deliberately erroneous. A "yielding score" was determined for each subject in terms of how often he agreed with the erroneous statements. The final results indicated that the greater an individual's orality score, the more likely he was to "yield." Weiss (1969) proposed, in a similar vein, that persons with an oral orientation would, if they participated in a psychological experiment, be particularly prone to conform to the expectations of the experimenter. Thirty-six male and thirty-six female college students who obtained high orality scores on the Blacky Test participated. Also, thirty-six male and thirty-six female college students with high Blacky anality scores were included. Subjects were asked to estimate the numbers of dots briefly exposed during trials on a tachistoscope. Just before viewing the dot stimuli, various subsamples were given different instructions designed to create special expectations: namely, that the dots could be best perceived by underestimating the number that *appeared* to be present or, contrastingly, by overestimating. Other conditions of the experiment were also manipulated, but they are not pertinent to our immediate concern. The total results indicated that for the women there was a significant trend for those most orally oriented to comply the most. But in the male group such an effect could not be shown.

Tribich and Messer (1974) expected that male college students with high orality scores, as defined by the Blacky Test, would be more suggestible than males with high anal scores or those low on both orality and anality. These subjects were asked to judge the distance that a light appeared to move in a dark room (autokinetic phenomenon). Half in each group (numbering twenty each) were paired with an authority figure and half with a low authority figure. In order to influence the judgments of the subjects, the confederates of the experimenters expressed fake opinions, at fixed points in the procedure, about the amount of movement that had occurred. It was found that the orals were significantly more influenced than the subjects in the other two groups by both the authority and nonauthority figures. They were, as hypothesized, particularly susceptible to suggestion and influence.

Johnson (1973) employed the Rorschach orality index developed by Masling, described above, to determine if it would predict "asking for help" behavior in college students (forty male, forty female) when confronted by a puzzle task. She found a significant positive correlation between the orality index and dependent behavior when the subject and the experimenter were of the same sex. But there were unexpected shifts in the results when subject and experimenter were of unlike sex. For example, high oral females with a male experimenter asked for very little help.

Beller (1957) explored the relationship between orality and dependency in a group of twenty-five problem boys and twenty-seven girls (ages twenty-eight to seventy-four months) in a therapeutic nursery. Orality was defined in terms of how frequently teachers observed the presence of such behaviors as the following: biting, nailbiting, sucking, overeating, spitting, talking nonsense. Dependency was evaluated on the basis of teacher ratings of nursery behavior. The collected data indicated that there was a significant positive correlation between orality and dependency.

A complex technique employed by Blatt (1964) demonstrated that conflict about orality is accompanied by special tension with regard to issues of autonomy. Expert raters rank-ordered twenty needs in terms of how well they depict "optimal personality integration." Each of a sample of 116 male research scientists was then asked to rank-order the same needs as they apply to himself. One of the needs pertained to being autonomous or independent as contrasted to dependent. The deviation of each subject's need rank from the ideal (good mental health) rank assigned to that need by the group of experts was computed. All subjects had responded to the Blacky Test, and an index was available of their amount of oral conflict. Blatt found a consistent trend for those most orally conflicted to show the greatest tension about the autonomy need (as defined by the deviation of self-ranking for autonomy from the ideal ranking).

Interesting attempts have been made to pinpoint the effects of arousing oral anxieties. In accordance with the oral character formulation, it has been assumed that intensifying an individual's oral anxiety will push him in the direction of being more dependent and affiliative. Sarnoff and Zimbardo (1961), while working with seventy-two male college students, created expectations in one sample that they would have to participate in a procedure that involved sucking objects like nipples and pacifiers. Another sample was led to believe they would have to respond to a variety of stimuli applied to the skin of the hand and arm. While under the influence of such expectations, subjects were told there would be a delay in the procedure and were given the choice of waiting either alone or in a group. The data analysis revealed that those instilled with anxious oral expectations were significantly more likely to want to be with others than those in the other group. They preferred the affiliative context rather than aloneness.

It is perhaps congruent with this finding that Podolnick and Field (1970), in their work with forty-eight college students, demonstrated that those exposed to an oral anxiety situation equivalent to that in the Sarnoff and Zimbardo study just described proved to be more hypnotizable than those not exposed to such a situation. They offered as one explanation for their results the possibility that hypnosis, because it permits dependence upon the hypnotist and escape into a "passive sleepy relaxation," resolved the oral conflict and anxiety created by the experimental condition. That is, the dependence available through being hypnotized presumably provided a channel for resolving the pressure of oral impulses that had been stirred up.

However, this report must be set against the observation of Dawson et al. (1965) that persons (sixteen female college students) classified as to degree of orality and anality by means of the Blacky Test did not differ in their degree of hypnotizability. The orally oriented individual was not, contrary to expectation, a particularly good hypnotic subject.

The idea that the oral character is drawn to others (presumably for purposes of attachment) has also been looked at from some rather tangential perspectives. Masling et al. (1974) reasoned that if oral characters seek dependency and external support, "it would be important for them to develop skills in assessing the motives of others in order to get others to do for him what they cannot do for themselves." They studied thirty-two male and thirty-four female college students whose degree of orality was defined in terms of the number of oral images they produced when responding to an inkblot series. They evaluated their skill in assessing the attitudes and characteristics of others by having each spend 15 minutes becoming acquainted with another individual and then trying to predict how that individual would respond to a detailed questionnaire about his own attributes and values (for example, whether the person has a boyfriend or girlfriend, and his or her personal likes and dislikes). The results indicated that high oral males were significantly better at such prediction in relation to other males (but not females) than low oral males. But the hypothesis did not hold up at all in the female sample. Masling et al. repeated the study with thirty-three male and fourteen female college students who were in a Peace Corps program. The design of this second study was the same as the first, except that subjects were asked to predict the responses of roommates whom they knew well. The results obtained were precisely the same as those for the first study. No good explanation could be provided for the greater predictive value of orality in the males than in females. Also, there was no obvious rationale as to why orality was positively correlated with men making successful predictions about other men, but not correlated with their adequacy in predicting the attributes of women. So one would have to say that it was clearly shown that the male oral character was particularly skillful in assessing the attitudes and motives of other men (presumably to facilitate influencing them). But he was not especially skillful in "reading" the female, and the female oral character was not typified by enhanced ability to assess either males or other females.[17]

Gottschalk (1968) reasoned that the presence of oral imagery in psychiatric patients' spontaneous verbalizations (obtained under standardized conditions) should be predictive of how well they would respond to psychotherapy. He conjectured that references to oral-dependent and oral-receptive themes would be predictive "because of the likelihood that such references suggest that the speaker maintains hope that human relations will provide relief, help, sustenance" (p. 612). A total Human Relations Score, based to a significant extent on orality themes, successfully predicted who would benefit most from brief psychotherapy in two different samples, one containing ten and the other twenty-two subjects.

Spence, et al. (1966) describe an unusual experiment that tried to demonstrate a direct link between orality and concern about being rejected by others. They aroused feelings of rejection in one segment of several classes of college students and feelings of acceptance in other segments. They did this by asking each class member to rate the others as to how much he would like to have them as friends, but then arbitrarily (and without really using the ratings) informed half of each group they were in the rejected category and the other half that they were in a popular category. Each individual was subsequently exposed (tachistoscopically) to the subliminal visual stimulus word "milk," then to a clearly visible list of thirty words (sixteen of which had oral connotations), and was finally asked to recall as many of the words in the list as possible. In one control group the procedure was exactly the same, except that a blank slide was substituted for the subliminal stimulus. All of the subjects responded to a questionnaire designed to evaluate their degree of orality as defined by their inclination to use food as a substitute for affection. It called for responses to such statements as, "When I am feeling blue I try to find something to eat." Rather complex findings emerged, but in essence they indicated that the greater an individual's investment in orality, the more likely was the experience of being rejected—when combined with the subliminal oral stimulus—to have an impact upon him (as defined by the manner in which he learned the word list). Thus, he was particularly likely to recall words as having been on the list that were not originally included. These "importations" were to a significant degree characterized by their "regressive oral" quality (for example, milk, bottle, nipple). It was considered that the findings supported the view that the experimental conditions were most likely to produce compensatory fantasies of being fed in those who felt rejected and who were high in orality.

The array of studies that has just been examined bearing on the relationship between degree of oral orientation and the need to be affiliative (to hold on to others) is largely supportive of what Abraham had to say about this issue in his oral character formulation. Those with oral inclinations have diversely shown themselves to be especially sensitive to conditioning procedures that provide affiliative reassurance or oral supplies, to be invested in seeking approval, to prefer affiliative contact rather than aloneness when exposed to stresses that activate oral anxieties, to yield easily, and to conform to experimenter expectations (as a way of maintaining positive bonds). It is true that there have also been scattered negative findings, but the bulk of the formal studies has sounded a confirmatory note in this sector.

The passivity ascribed to the oral character has been carefully appraised in the context of two studies concerned with learning behavior. King (1970) hypothesized that if the oral character is, indeed, passive, this should become evident when he is asked to learn something. The passivity should interfere with effective learning. He measured orality in a sample of eighty female college students by means of two methods: (1) counting the number of oral images given in response to inkblots, and (2) ascertaining the frequency of mouth movements while performing a routine task. Further, he appraised learning ability, and he defined it in terms both of effectiveness in learning nonsense syllables presented on a memory drum and recall of a meaningful passage. He was able to show on the basis of his data that the greater the subject's orality (as indicated either by oral images or mouth movements), the less well she tended to perform on the nonsense-syllable learning task. Orality did not straightforwardly predict ability to recall a meaningful passage that had been learned, but when intelligence was partialled out, the inkblot orality measure (but not the mouth movement index) was significantly and negatively correlated with recall. Those with an oral orientation did evidence reduced efficiency in their learning.

Marcus (1965) had earlier undertaken a related study with forty-four boys and forty-eight girls in the fourth grade. She hypothesized that while the "orally fixated" will not be deficient in learning material that requires a "minimal amount of effort," they will do relatively poorly on a learning task demanding active output. She also predicted that the orally fixated would not do well on tasks that called for sustained effort (persistence). Orality was evaluated in terms of number of mouth movements manifested by each child during a set period of time. It was further measured by means of a revised orality scale taken from Grygier's (1961) Dynamic Personality Inventory. Learning efficiency was appraised with several techniques: (1) ability to recognize information contained in a story that was presented (as indicated by responses to multiple choice items), (2) ability to reproduce a story that was read, (3) memory for words presented on a tachistoscope (in one context the task made the learning of the word incidental and in another intentional), and (4) persistence in mastering a maze. The findings of the study indicated (as predicted) that those most orally oriented performed poorly on the active recall test, but their performance was not (as predicted) significantly inferior on the easier or more passive learning recognition test. No further significant results emerged with reference to the relationships between orality and the other learning and persistence tasks that were used. Marcus concluded that the results provided only partial support for the hypothesis she had tested.

If one considers the Marcus results in tandem with those of King (1970) just reviewed above, there does seem to be moderate evidence that the orally oriented are less efficient in coping with learning tasks that call for an active rather than passive approach.

It will be recalled that one of the novel aspects of Abraham's formulations is the assumption that the oral character has a special openness to novel ideas—enhanced curiosity and an interest in understanding nature. There are several empirical studies in the literature that bear on this issue. Shorr (1971) reviewed a number of them and also investigated the problem herself. She focused specifically on the relationship between how orally oriented an individual is and his degree of originality (openness to new ideas and concepts). She pointed out a few positive leads in this respect: Von Holt et al. (1960) reported a significant positive correlation between the number of inkblot images with oral content produced and the ability to solve a sorting task; and Holt (1966) obtained evidence that "less socialized oral responses" were positively correlated with enjoyment of sensuous experiences, cognitive flexibility, and enjoyment of visual pleasures. Encouraged by such findings, she looked at the relationship between inkblot oral images and measures of originality in twenty males and thirty females. She was surprised to find rather different results in the male and female samples. The greater the number of oral images produced by the men, the more original they tended to be. An opposite tendency was observed for the women. She states (p. 74): "Generally, it appears then that direct oral receptivity is a concomitant of low creativity in women, and that more socialized oral receptivity is related to high flexibility in men." It should be underscored that the results indicated only weak to moderate trends.

Feirstein (1967) could not, in a sample of twenty male college students, find any relationship between the degree to which they liked paintings with oral themes and their ability to perceive and accept unrealistic experiences induced in various ways (for example, aniseikonic lenses that provide images of unequal size to each eye or reversible figures).

Cooperman and Child (1968) investigated the link between orality and esthetic sensitivity. Orality was measured with two different techniques: (1) a Food Preference Inventory developed by Wolowitz (1964) that evaluates relative preferences for active versus passive food choices (for example, hard versus soft food, salty versus nonsalty food); and (2) ratings of pleasantness of certain chewing experiences (for example, gnawing on a steak bone). Esthetic sensitivity was determined by asking each individual to indicate his preferences among various slides depicting works of art and then comparing his judgments with those of experts. This variable could be interpreted as having to do with how understanding and perceptive an individual is with respect to esthetic stimuli. The subjects consisted of 172 male college students. Good evidence emerged that the greater the number of active food preferences expressed by an individual, the more esthetically sensitive he was. Also, the more subjects rated various gnawing and biting activities as unpleasant, the lower were their esthetic sensitivity scores.

Child et al. (1969) reported, on the basis of data from 105 male college students, that preference for active foods and esthetic sensitivity were, indeed, positively correlated. They also found that preference for active foods was linked with a general inclination toward active modes (such as a desire for sensory and intellectual challenge, or a liking for vigorous work). The findings of these studies concerned with esthetic sensitivity are not easily interpretable. They do not demonstrate that orality, as such, and a particular species of sensitivity to stimuli are tied together. Rather, they suggest that one kind of positive oral investment versus another kind plays a role in the sensitivity. Wolowitz (1964) associated preference for active foods with involvement with the oral sadistic —the later biting—phase of the oral period, and preference for passive foods with the earlier oral receptive phase. In these terms, an oral sadistic orientation would be the one most likely to be accompanied by esthetic sensitivity and, by implication, by a more general sensitivity to stimuli. Abraham did not suggest this specific possibility in his theoretical statements.

One can see that the findings pertaining to the relationship between orality and openness to novelty are somewhat fragmentary. But again, the trend is congruent with expectations from theory.

Do Oral Characters Seek Special Oral Gratifications?

Freud and Abraham both suggested that the oral character would manifest an unusual use of oral channels for gratification or compensatory denial of oral needs. Freud mentioned thumbsucking as an example of a mode of oral gratification to relieve the pressure of unsatisfied oral needs. Abraham referred to a "morbidly intense appetite for food" as having analogous significance. The question we shall consider in this section is whether the empirical literature indicates a link between an oral orientation and unusual or special investments in such oral modes of gratification as eating, drinking alcohol, and smoking.

The obese, who obviously overeat, represent a logical point to initiate our inquiry. A number of investigators have published pertinent findings. Masling et al. (1967) compared the amount of oral imagery present in the Rorschach and Thematic Apperception protocols of twenty obese persons to that present in suitable controls. For both of the measures of oral imagery employed, scores were significantly higher in the obese sample. In another study, Weiss and Masling (1970) reported that thirteen obese patients who were psychiatric outpatients produced significantly more oral imagery in response to inkblots than did appropriate controls. McCully et al. (1968) also found elevated oral imagery in the inkblot protocols of six hospitalized, "severely obese" patients. It is noteworthy that these patients did not show a change in amount of oral imagery after they lost weight (even when the loss returned them to normal weight for their age and height). Such findings would tend to argue against the idea that the high orality scores of the obese simply reflected their awareness of their overweight state.

Further, Migdole (1967) used several methods to compare orality in a group of twenty-five obese adolescent girls with that in a control group of twenty-six non-obese girls. Orality was measured by means of inkblots, the Blacky Test, and a sentence completion test. The inkblot and Blacky orality indices did not differentiate the groups. But the orality index derived from the sentence completion test resulted in significantly higher scores for the obese than the controls. Still another study, by Orbach (1960), compared fifteen obese patients, twenty-five ulcer patients, and a control group of twenty-five with reference to orality scores based on two different procedures (the Blacky Test, and an orality questionnaire that inquired concerning such attributes as autonomy and oral aggression). The Blacky Test was administered not only in its usual format but also in a novel fashion that involved presenting the Blacky pictures in groups at high speed—that is, tachistoscopically—to determine how well they could be identified. Results from the Blacky completely failed to support the hypothesis that the obese and ulcer patients were more orally oriented than the controls. However, the orality questionnaire did indicate that the obese group had significantly more oral character attributes than the controls.[18]

Friedman (1959) reported that overweight female college students produced significantly more oral-sadistic responses (as defined by the Blacky Test) than did controls, but not more oral-erotic responses. Zechowy (1969) conducted an elaborate study of obese and control subjects in working-class and middle-class samples and found that they did not differ in the amount of oral imagery produced when responding to inkblots. Within the limitations of the methods employed, the results of all the above-cited studies do indicate a trend for an oral orientation and obesity to be linked.[19]

Let us now probe what is known about the relationship between orality and alcoholism. Story (1968) asked thirty male alcoholics and thirty male controls to respond with free associations to oral and non-oral words. He also asked them to interpret oral and non-oral proverbs. As predicted, he found that the alcoholics showed greater involvement, conflict, and response inhibition in relation to the oral as compared to non-oral stimuli; furthermore, they exceeded the controls in this respect. Bertrand and Masling (1969) reported that twenty male alcoholics gave significantly more oral imagery in response to inkblots than did twenty non-alcoholic psychiatric controls. Wiener (1956) had earlier reported that twenty-seven alcoholics gave more oral inkblot percepts than fifteen non-alcoholic depressed patients. In still another study involving inkblots, Weiss and Masling (1970) discerned higher orality scores in a diagnosed "alcoholic" sample of nine subjects than in a control sample. But members of a "heavy drinking" group (not diagnosed as "alcoholic") were not typified by high orality scores. All of the studies enumerated largely support the notion of a link between oral fantasy and alcoholism.[20]

Taking up the next issue, a scattering of studies have successfully detected oral motivations in smoking.

Veldman and Bown (1969) used a sentence completion technique to explore the occurrence of orality (as defined by references to food, eating, drinking, and smoking) in 401 smokers and 1,820 nonsmokers. They found a significantly greater frequency of orality in the smokers.

The work of Jacobs et al. (1965) and Jacobs et al. (1966) represents a series of studies in which heavy cigarette smokers were appraised to determine whether they manifested trait clusters expected to occur in the oral character. In their 1965 project they looked at two successive male samples, one involving 97 and the other 136 subjects. Questionnaires were administered that inquired concerning orality (preoccupation with non-nutritional oral intake), traits presumably linked to the oral character pattern (for example, impetuousness, emotional lability, danger seeking), and maternal characteristics. In the first sample, heavy smokers did indicate greater preoccupation with orality than did moderate, mild, or former smokers (and nonsmokers), but the difference was not statistically significant. The results in the second sample were in the same direction and statistically significant. Findings from a second study (1966) that involved a third sample also turned out significantly in this same direction. In both samples of the first study, the heavy smokers were particularly typified by oral character personality traits such as impetuousness and lability. Further, in this first study it turned out, as predicted, that heavy smokers were especially likely to perceive their mothers as controlling, cold, and harsh (that is, fitting the role of the orally depriving mother figure). In the second study a similar result pertaining to the mother was obtained, but it did not quite attain statistical significance. Jacobs et al. (1965) state at one point (p. 167): "The results . . . support the hypothesis that factors identified as associated with difficulties at the oral level of development are more intensely present in cigarette smokers engaging in the habit to extremes than they are in nonsmokers or mild smokers."

Jacobs and Spilken (1971) measured oral attributes in a sample of 42 male heavy smokers and 108 nonsmokers. Oral preoccupation was probed with a questionnaire that inquired concerning oral modes. For example, subjects were asked to respond to statements such as "I bit my fingernails as a child." They also responded to a cluster of items relevant to various oral traits that were described with reference to the Jacobs et al. (1965, 1966) papers. It was established that the smokers were characterized by a high degree of oral preoccupation and also attitudes (impulsivity, danger seeking, perceiving mother as cold) presumably representative of oral conflicts and a personality strategy directed at denying dependency.

Kimeldorf and Geiwitz (1966) demonstrated, in a sample of twenty-two male college students, that heavy smokers were higher on "oral craving" (as measured by the Blacky Test) than nonsmokers. They concluded (p. 168): "Thus, the overall picture of the heavy smoker, as drawn by Blacky Test responses, is of an individual with relatively intense oral desires who tends to avoid overt exhibition of animosity in interpersonal relations, perhaps to avoid offending a possible source of oral supplies."

Finally, it should be mentioned that in a complex experiment Spence and Ehrenberg (1964) observed that the impact of a subliminal oral stimulus upon learning was mediated by the amount an individual smokes. Presumably, this was due to the difference between smokers and nonsmokers in their general oral orientation.

Overview

We have pursued logical derivatives of the oral character theory to determine how well they stand up to scrutiny. One of the first issues we confronted is whether there are traits and attitudes that hang together in accordance with the oral model. The various traits assigned by Abraham to the oral character, such as extremes of optimism-pessimism and need to affiliate with others, might, because of their presumed related significance, be expected to occur simultaneously in the same individual with unusual frequency. There proved to be many studies in the literature concerned with this matter, and they were largely corroborative of expectation. What Abraham and Freud labeled as oral traits do frequently cluster together. The empirical studies do not as yet tell us in any decipherable fashion about the patterning of these traits (for example, whether they form typical hierarchies in which some are dominant over others). We can only say that there are trends for certain traits to show up more frequently in the clusters. Dependency is in the forefront, and pessimism is a close second. Among the others most often identified are passivity, egocentricity, tendencies to be either unusually affiliative or withdrawing in one's relationship with people, and the inclination toward various brands of hostile expression (for example, "covert hostility" or "sadism"). Apropos of the hostility findings just mentioned, it will be recalled that Abraham emphasized both the role of frustration in oral character formation and the special significance of biting in the later phases of the oral period.

In reviewing the studies concerned with the oral character, it is somewhat bewildering to discover what an exotic array of procedures has been used to measure degree of oral orientation. Consider the following list of measurement techniques we compiled from the literature:

Questionnaires that systematically inquire about oral interests and attitudes
Number of oral images given in response to inkblots
References to oral themes when completing incomplete sentences
Relative preference for pictures with oral themes

Number of "mouth movements" manifested
Food preferences
Pattern of behavior in a psychiatric setting (for example, whether acts dependently on the ward)
Responses to pictures depicting a dog (Blacky) involved in oral activities (for example, biting, sucking)
Frequency with which engages in activities like nail-biting and pencil chewing
Diagnosis (for example, alcoholic, stomach ulcer)

Obviously, every conceivable approach has been tried. But there is really no solid information available concerning the validity of the various orality measures; and it is not known whether they are consistently correlated with each other. Each investigator has been inclined to evolve his own methods for identifying the oral character. It should be noted that at a conceptual level most of them do have in common the evaluation of how important mouth sensations and experiences are to the individual. We would, of course, be better off if we had studies that examined the extent to which such methods are tapping a common dimension. At the same time one must acknowledge that despite the diversity of the methodologies they have often come up with similar results, and so in that sense one would anticipate that they would eventually prove to have significant overlap with each other.

At this point it would be well to review formally the major hypotheses we extracted from Abraham's description of the oral character, and to offer an appraisal of how each has fared vis-à-vis existing scientific observation.

One major hypothesis that was deduced was that the oral character is particularly preoccupied with issues of giving and taking (nurturance-succorance, generosity-avarice). However, as one undertakes concretely to evaluate this hypothesis, one can see that it cannot be clearly separated from another major one which asserts that the oral character is caught up with issues of dependence-independence and passivity-activity. These enumerated dimensions, namely, nurturance-succorance, dependence-independence, and passivity-activity, really refer to whether the individual seeks to obtain gratification through his own efforts or is motivated to get others to care for and comfort him. Further, one could argue that a third hypothesis derived from Abraham's statements—that the oral character has special attitudes about closeness-distance to others—is part of the same cluster. Attitudes concerning closeness-distance (being alone versus attached) obviously have a good deal to do with whether one is interested in operating on one's own or getting support from others.

The empirical research findings are quite convincing in their support of this cluster of hypotheses. First of all, persons identified as orally oriented have shown themselves to be unusually susceptible to the effects of being approved by those they consider significant. They seek experiences that assure them they are in the good graces of persons who have power and are in a position to provide support and help. They will behave submissively and passively in their efforts to maintain positive contact with potential supporters. For example, they will distort their own judgments in order to conform to unreasonable judgments made by significant others. There are even suggestions that they cultivate skills enabling them to be especially sensitive to the motives and intents of others, presumably so that they can maintain ties and contacts. Also, there is adequate evidence that under stress they are particularly anxious to be *with people* rather than apart from them. When threatened in an experimental context and given the choice of being alone or part of a group, they choose the latter alternative. It should be added, though, that in one study (Blum and Miller 1952) orally oriented children were paradoxically found to occupy rejected and isolated roles in the group because their demandingness apparently made them unpopular with their peers. The oral character has also been observed to prefer passivity when confronted with certain situations. Thus, two studies (King 1970, Marcus 1965) have pointed up a tendency for the orally inclined to respond in an inefficient manner (which can be construed as a manifestation of passivity) when asked to learn new material. Overall, one can say there are converging lines of verification concerning the tie between an oral orientation and motivation to be close to others in order to persuade them to provide support.

The hypothesis that those who are orally oriented will manifest extremes of optimism-pessimism has been affirmed primarily in the sense that such individuals seem to be particularly pessimistic. Quite a number of studies have been cited in which orality and a pessimistic view of the world have been linked together. The fact that optimism, as such, does not appear more prominently in the orality cluster is not congruent with Abraham's formulations.[21] The prominence of pessimism suggests that the orally oriented do not expect to get what they want. Their persistent interest in attachment to others may be one means of reassuring themselves they will have available future supplies, and therefore that things won't turn out as badly as they fear.

Particularly good support has emerged from empirical studies for the hypothesis that the orally oriented continue to make unusual use of oral channels of gratification. From diverse perspectives it has been shown that the oral character is inclined to such behaviors as overeating, consuming large amounts of alcohol, and smoking. It is interesting that one study (Noblin 1962) demonstrated that oral characters respond to an unusual degree to oral (food) rewards.

Some effort has been made to investigate the hypothesis that the oral character exhibits an above-average openness to novel experiences and ideas. While the initial findings have been mildly encouraging, they are still too sparse and in some instances contradictory to permit a reliable evaluation of the hypothesis. This is obviously an area particularly in need of further systematic probing.

Two remaining hypotheses, one proposing that the oral character is typified by unusual ambivalence and the other that he has a hasty, restless, impatient orientation, have not, in actuality, been tested. So little has been done to evaluate these propositions that they remain unknown quantities. They, too, await empirical exploration.

Major parts of the oral character concept do seem to have substance. Abraham and Freud apparently spotted a constellation of traits that can be identified by others. Persons who are unusually preoccupied with oral imagery or who exhibit a special focus on mouth activities are to a significant degree motivated to set up relationships that will assure them of support and sustenance. Abraham and Freud did quite accurately detect this oral syndrome in the patients they treated. One of the most original aspects of their formulation was the idea that the oral syndrome could be traced back to conditions that produced and fixated a specific kind of psychological disequilibrium during early childhood (oral phase). But this was largely an assumption on their part. They did not, in fact, have any direct evidence involving observation of young children during the so-called oral phase that would permit tracing the impact of events during this phase upon later oral attitudes. The etiological aspect of the oral character theory is the vaguest and least verified.

Abraham was really quite indefinite about the specific elements that go into oral fixation. In a somewhat confusing fashion he mentioned constitutional disposition, deprivation, and also over-indulgence. One does not emerge from his presentation with a knowledgeable picture of just what has to happen to a child to give him a lifelong oral orientation. Presumably a prime element is a disturbance in the eating and nurturance relationships with one's parents, especially the mother. But this is a broad, rather non-operational level of explanation and would not help much in predicting whether individual children were likely to become oral characters. We lack a list of clear definitions of just what parental attitudes and environmental conditions will elicit a long-term oral adaptation. In the face of this, it is remarkable, as described earlier, that some tangential support for the etiological theory has appeared in the literature. The support is meager and based on extremely crude indices (for example, whether the subject was breast-fed, and how abruptly the subject was weaned). But even in its attenuated form it cannot be denied; and it should encourage further, more precise evaluation. Obviously, what are needed are good longitudinal projects in which the consequences of particular early modes of child-parent interaction can be followed into adulthood.

One project by Kagan and Moss (1962) was cited earlier because it did indeed provide an opportunity to trace continuities between passive-dependent behavior in the first two years of life, and later phases of both childhood and adulthood. For females, the continuity between the oral phase and later time periods was rather consistently significant, and therefore supportive of Freud's and Abraham's oral character theory. While there was also some continuity found for males, it was of barely borderline magnitude. This suggests that oral character development may proceed differently in the two sexes—which should really not be surprising, in view of the accumulating data (Fisher 1973) that indicate male and female personalities often evolve divergently. Kagan and Moss conjectured that there may be less continuity in passive dependent behavior for males than females, because the male encounters more conditions, as he grows up, that motivate him to deny passivity and cultivate its opposite. It is more permissable to the female than the male to persist in a passive pattern that she may have evolved early in life. If so, one would expect the oral character pattern to be generally more "covered over" and camouflaged by compensatory denial in males than in females. This possibility is obviously open to empirical checking. The idea that the oral character pattern may have unlike implications in men and women is also supported by a few other scattered findings previously cited. It will be recalled that Shorr (1971) reported that men displaying originality were characterized by high orality, but original women showed an *opposite* tendency. Relatedly, Masling et al. (1974) discovered that while men with a strong oral orientation were particularly skillful in assessing the motives of others in certain contexts, the same skill was not present in oral women. This difference is probably a reliable one, because it held up in two studies.

Surprisingly, tucked away in the scientific studies we have reviewed is a novel fact that may have major implications for the oral character theory. With minor exceptions, these studies have shown that the greater an individual's orality, the more likely he is to be dependent and affiliative and invested in establishing relationships guaranteeing support and comfort. Thus the link between orality and dependent behavior appears to be a *direct* one. There are few signs of compensation or reaction formation. Yet it is often presumed that the oral personality evolves complexly, with layer upon layer of defensive denial. Presumably, not only do the persistent oral wishes often get blocked and contained, they also result in the build-up of a peripheral facade that camouflages oral intent. Few, if any, patterns of this sort are visible in the empirical literature. It is probable that most investigators of the oral character have looked at their data with an eye to detecting defensive patterns (for example, curvilinear relationships between orality and dependence), but nothing substantial of this sort has appeared.

We would propose, on the basis of such material, that the defensive aspects of oral character development have been exaggerated. Actually, Abraham acknowledged that oral wishes can secure numerous acceptable outlets and may not require as much concealment as drives with anal or sexual connotations. This is not to deny the possibility that some individuals—for example, men with unusually intense needs to deny weakness—may fashion elaborate compensatory strategies, but one cannot say that such has generally been true in the largely normal samples that have been studied. We may need to revise our perspectives concerning how unacceptable oral wishes are and the degree to which they can find fairly direct outlet.

A final matter that needs mention relates to the earlier-described distinction between the so-called oral-receptive and oral-sadistic stages. Abraham made a good deal of this distinction. He depicted the individual who is fixated in the oral-sadistic phase as likely to exhibit "the most marked symptoms of ambivalence—positive and negative instinctual cravings, hostile and friendly tendencies." He also ascribed such traits as envy, hostility, and jealousy and "malice" to such an individual. On the other hand, he viewed the individual fixated in the earlier oral-receptive stage as primarily invested in setting up relationships that will satisfy his succorant needs. One way of differentiating the two "types" would seem to be in terms of the degree to which ambivalence, hostility, and competitive jealousy characterize their overt behavior and perhaps also their fantasies. There are scattered findings in the scientific literature that bear on the issue of distinguishing the oral-receptive and the oral-sadistic. Thus, several studies that factor-analyzed a range of orality measures have isolated separate factors (Lazare et al. 1966, Watson 1952) with "receptive" as contrasted to "sadistic" elements. It is also important that several investigators have found that oral-receptive fantasies, such as derived from inkblot responses, predict different aspects of behavior than do oral-sadistic fantasies. For example, Masling et al. (1967) noted that Rorschach oral-receptive images occurred with unusual frequency in obese persons, but oral-sadistic images did not. Weiss and Masling (1970) discovered that oral-receptive images elicited by inkblots distinguished alcoholics and others with presumed oral symptoms, but oral-sadistic images did not. Masling, et al. (1968) found Rorschach oral-receptive responses significantly elevated in those who yield to suggestions, but oral-sadistic responses were not. Rosen (1971) observed that oral-receptive and oral-sadistic imagery were each correlated with *different* aspects of creativity. Wolowitz (1964) constructed a questionnaire that evaluates in part the degree to which one prefers soft, easily ingested (passive) foods versus those that are hard and chewy (active), and has successfully differentiated a number of groups (for example, alcoholics) on the basis of this preference difference. On the other hand, after a complex study involving numerous orality measures, Hubbard (1967) concluded that it was impossible to divide "the configurations of character traits resulting from oral deprivation into the categories of oral aggressive and oral receptive" (p. 70).

A sufficient number of persuasive clues have been uncovered to warrant our considering with further interest the oral-receptive versus oral-sadistic as a meaningful dimension.[22] It remains to be seen whether, as Abraham speculated, this distinction has anything to do with whether the individual is primarily caught up with the problems of an early versus late oral stage.

The Anal Character

As noted earlier, Freud's concept of the anal character provided the prototype for Abraham and others to design the oral character. He suggested (1908) in his essay, "Character and Anal Erotism," that there were persons with a functional cluster of traits that had evolved in the course of their attempts to master anal sensations and impulses. He stated (p. 169):

> The people I am about to describe are noteworthy for a regular combination of the three following characteristics. They are especially *orderly, parsimonious* and *obstinate.* Each of these words actually covers a small group or series of interrelated character-traits. "Orderly" covers the notion of bodily cleanliness, as well as of conscientiousness in carrying out small duties and trustworthiness. Its opposite would be "untidy" and "neglectful." Parsimony may appear in the exaggerated form of avarice; and obstinacy can go over into defiance, to which rage and revengefulness are easily joined.

He further proposed that such traits represented defenses against unusually intense "erotogenicity of the anal zone." He remarked with reference to this point (p. 170):

> It is easy to gather from these people's early childhood history that they took a comparatively long time to overcome their infantile faecal incontinence, and that even in later childhood they suffered from isolated failures of this function. As infants, they seem to have belonged to the class who refuse to empty their bowels when they are put on the pot because they derive a subsidiary pleasure from defaecating; for they tell us that even in somewhat later years they enjoyed holding back their stool . . . From these indications we infer that such people are born with a sexual constitution in which the erotogenicity of the anal zone is exceptionally strong. But since none of these weaknesses and idiosyncracies are to be found in them once their childhood has been passed, we must conclude that the anal zone had lost its erotogenic significance in the course of development; and it is to be suspected that the regularity with which this triad of properties is present in their character may be brought into relation with the disappearance of their anal erotism.

In other words, he theorized that some persons are born with unusually intense anal sensitivity, which leads them in early childhood to maximize anal experiences. But as they grow up such anal experiences become unacceptable, and they need to deny and repress them. Freud reasoned that a build-up of "shame" and "disgust" occurs, which serves as a "dam" against anal impulses. The anal impulses have as their aim uninhibited and unregulated defecation and free impulsive expression of besmirching impulses. The impulses are repressed, "sublimated," and redirected into "orderliness, parsimony, and obstinacy."[23] Presumably, orderliness provides reassurance against the dirty aspects of anal impulses.

As for obstinacy, Freud implicated it in the following manner (p. 173): "To relate obstinacy to an interest in defaecation would seem no easy task; but it should be remembered that even babies can show self-will about parting with their stool . . . and that it is a general practice in children's upbringing to administer painful stimuli to the skin of the buttocks—which is linked up with the erotogenic anal zone—in order to break their obstinacy and make them submissive." Note that in this analysis Freud did not portray obstinacy as a sublimation but rather as the persistence of a response that developed in reaction to frustration of anal impulses.

The trait of parsimony Freud ascribed to the anal character was elaborately traced by him to the symbolic meaning of money. He noted, first of all, that practical experience in doing psychoanalysis has demonstrated that it is possible to cure "long-standing cases of what is described as habitual constipation in neurotics" only "if one deals with the patient's money complex and induces them to bring it into consciousness with all its connections." He considered that constipation and fantasies about money are linked, and that this represents an obvious link between money and anality. But further, he stated that there is a basic "archaic" equation between money and feces. He remarked (p. 174):

> In reality, whenever archaic modes of thought have predominated or persist—in the ancient civilizations, in myths, fairy tales and superstition, in unconscious thinking, in dreams and in neuroses—money is brought into the most intimate relationship with dirt. We know that the gold which the devil gives his paramours turns into excrement after his departure, and the devil is certainly nothing else than the personification of the repressed unconscious instinctual life. We also know about the superstition which connects the finding of treasure with defaecation . . .
>
> It is possible that the contrast between the most precious substance known to men and the most worthless, which they reject as waste matter ("refuse"), has led to this specific identification of gold with faeces.

Freud also somewhat clumsily suggested that the equation is facilitated by the fact that the "original erotic interest in defaecation" is "extinguished in later years," which are the very years in which the "interest in money makes its appearance as a new interest." He concluded (p. 175), "This makes it easier for the earlier impulsion, which is in process of losing its aim, to be carried over to the newly emerging aim." It is difficult to follow his train of logic with respect to this point.

But, in any case, he conjectured that the trait of parsimony, with its goal of saving and hoarding money, represented in the anal character a sublimated means for maintaining contact with a substance having secret fecal or anal significance. At the end of his essay, "Character and Anal Erotism," he summed up his perspective about the formation of the anal character as follows (p. 175): "We can at any rate lay down a formula for the way in which character in its final shape is formed out of the constituent instincts: the permanent character traits are either unchanged prolongations of the original instincts, or sublimations of these instincts, or reaction-formations against them."

He assumed, too, that early anal experiences and unconscious attitudes about feces carry over and affect later genital attitudes. He suggested (1917b) that feces are unconsciously equated with baby and penis; and also that anus and vagina are associated.[24] Such equations can presumably affect later, more genitally based behavior, in that attitudes that have evolved during the anal phase may be transposed to the process of experiencing the penis, the vagina, and the whole sequence of procreation. For example, the boy's concern about castration, which is said to be aroused when he discovers that women lack a penis, may be reinforced because he draws an analogy between the penis and "faeces, the first piece of bodily substance the child has to part with" (p. 133). By way of another example of the role of such an equation, Freud cited the link between feces and baby, with both presumably analogous in the sense that the child originally perceives them as "something which becomes detached from the body by passing through the bowel" (p. 130). He indicated that when a baby "appears on the scene," an individual consequently may react to it not only in terms of its intrinsic qualities but also as an object with "powerful anal-erotic interest."

It would seem to be a logical deduction from Freud's formulations that such anal equations would occur with particular intensity in the fantasies of the anal character.

In other contexts, Freud (1909b, 1913b, 1918) conceptualized anally fixated persons to be particularly susceptible to the development of obsessive-compulsive neurotic symptomatology.[25] He presented detailed case histories of obsessives in which he felt he demonstrated an unusual degree of early childhood preoccupation with anal matters. In these case histories he also indicated that those intensely caught up with anal eroticism have special difficulties about expressing hostility, which are reflected in conflicts involving the dimension of sadism-masochism. At one point he referred to the "extraordinary part played by impulses of hatred and anal erotism in the symptomatology of obsessional neurosis" (1913b, p. 321). The problems of the anal character that are said to revolve so prominently about submitting to controls over one's body presumably maximize frustration and deep anger.[26] Freud further indicated that anal characters have heightened anxiety over being motorically spontaneous or impulsive, with the implication of loss of body control, and they develop a variety of defenses (for example, intellectualization, doubt, pairing of opposites) directed at attenuating and blocking direct motor expression.

What testable hypotheses can be derived from Freud's statements about the anal character? The following seem reasonable:

1. It is true that Freud (1909b) referred to the anal character as someone "with a sexual constitution in which the erotogenicity of the anal zone is exceptionally strong" (p. 170) and in that sense indicated that constitutional factors are important in the development of the anal defense system. But even so, one finds in his published clinical cases that he described patients as evolving anal character attributes at least to some degree as the result of specific interactions with important figures (especially parents and parent substitutes). Within the context of his theoretical system, one would have to say that persons who fit the anal character classification should have had special experiences, during the anal phase, of an unusually frustrating or disturbing quality. This is not to deny the importance Freud placed upon those disturbing experiences subsequent to the anal phase which, he said, make it untenable to maintain a genital organization and force regression to an anal orientation. But he did, at the same time, consider that vulnerability to regression to a particular phase was the result of predisposing experiences that had occurred during that phase.

2. A second obvious hypothesis is that the anal character will be inclined toward a neat, orderly style of life. Presumably, he will have a special need to defend against loss of control, being dirty, and the general appearance of unkempt looseness. In other words, he needs to avoid any implications that he does not have secure control of his anal functions. This is accomplished, said Freud, by exaggerated efforts to represent oneself as always putting things in the right place, preventing dirt in the environment from contaminating one's personal world, and being predictable, precise, and trustworthy.

3. Freud also hypothesized that the anal character would be unusually "parsimonious." He assumed that this character type would save things, hoard, and generally hold on to money. This would presumably reflect not only the anal character's careful controlled orientation but, more importantly, the fact that money is unconsciously equated with feces. Freud theorized that by holding on to money, the anal character provides himself with an acceptable channel for indulging his secret wishes to touch and be involved with anal material.

4. Still another major trait Freud ascribed to the anal character was obstinacy. He reasoned that it was a reaction to being forced to control anal functions ("show self-will about parting with their stool"). That is, the anal character's sense of being controlled would make him want to resist and drag his feet whenever people

expect him to behave in a certain way. The anal character would be expected to be stubborn, oppositional, and defiant in various camouflaged ways.

5. Relatedly, Freud viewed the anal character as full of anger that could emerge in both sadistic and masochistic ways. He portrayed this type of individual as having serious problems with reference to how to control hostile impulses and often using unusual tangential strategies for venting such impulses (for example, cutting oneself, hurting animals). This may be put in the form of the hypothesis that the anal character will be found to have particularly intense hostile *fantasies* and will also be marked by patterns of hostility expression that are atypical of other people in their masochistic or sadistic extremeness.

6. With regard to the area of psychopathology, Freud proposed that the anal character has a predisposition to the development of obsessive-compulsive symptomatology. He should presumably display a more than average incidence of obsessive thinking, compulsive acts and rituals, and other features of the obsessive-compulsive syndrome as Freud portrayed them (for example, doubt, magical thinking, ascribing omnipotence to thought).

7. It is implied in a number of Freud's works (1908, 1909b, 1913b) that the anal character is especially susceptible to symptoms involving the lower gastro-intestinal tract. He repeatedly cites instances in which an anal-erotic orientation is accompanied both in childhood and adulthood by symptoms such as constipation and other anal irregularities.

8. Once again, it would be expected that if the anal character concept is a reality, so-called anal attributes would relate to each other with significant consistency. Traits such as parsimony, obstinacy, and orderliness should be meaningfully intercorrelated. A real live anal character should exhibit a more than chance clustering of those qualities that have been ascribed to the anally fixated.

Is There an Anal Trait Constellation?

Let us first inquire whether there are recognizable clusters of traits conforming to the anal character framework. A conglomerate of researchers has administered multiple tests to subjects and factor-analyzed them to ascertain whether there are definable anal groupings. With few exceptions, the tests have consisted of questionnaires that ask the individual to indicate how he relates to others, the kinds of things he prefers to do, and his general style of behavior. A brief overview of the results of these factor analytic studies follows.

Sears (1943)
Found significant intercorrelations among ratings of orderliness, stinginess, and stubbornness

Barnes (1952)
Anal: orderliness, meticulousness, reliability, cleanliness, law abidance
(Contained in one factor; other presumed anal traits such as sadism, defiance, and concern about money do not fall within this factor)

Stagner et al. (1955)
Early anal: giving things away, doing things for others, collecting stamps (male factor)
Late anal: being on time, biting and chewing, winning a race (male factor)
Early anal and late anal: buying bargains, preserving things, chewing, playing with mudpies, painting in oil (female factor)

Rapaport (1955)
Significant but low intercorrelations among orderliness, parsimony, and obstinacy

Beloff (1957)
Anality: feels he is often in position to say,
"I told you so"; active and "bossy" in family affairs; feels unpunctuality is a vice; agrees that it is necessary for a housewife to have everything "just so"; does not find it difficult to see a job through to the end; admits revenge is sweet; dislikes lending books and other possessions
(Contained in one factor)

Sirota (1957)
No distinct anal factor could be identified

Mandel (1958)
Early anal: generosity, concern with dirt, smelly behavior
Late anal: cleanliness, collects things, parsimony

Sandler and Hazari (1960)
Anal-reactive (reactive-narcissistic): systematic, methodical, punctual, interest in details, aversion to dirt
(Contained in one factor)

Finney (1961a)
Anal compulsive: orderly, stingy, stubborn, rigid
(Contained in one factor)

Hetherington and Brackbill (1963)
Significant intercorrelations among composite measures of orderliness, obstinacy, and parsimony in girls, but not in boys

Schlesinger (1963)
Multiple anal factors rather than one general factor:
responsibility, regularity and meticulousness, retentiveness, obstinacy,

rigidity, frugality, concern about dirt, orderliness, self-righteous hostility, anxiety over loss of control, sensitivity to smells, retentiveness in relation to possessions

Gottheil (1965a,b)
Significant intercorrelation among diverse questionnaire items concerning presumed modes of anal behavior (as derived from various psychoanalytic writings)

Comrey (1965)
Compulsion: need for order, love of routine, drive to finish, meticulousness, cautiousness, impulsivity (negative)
(Contained in one factor)

Pichot and Perse (cited in Kline, 1972)
Anal character: anality, obsessional, repression, not psychopathic
(Contained in one factor)

Gottheil and Stone (1968)
Anal traits: carefulness, parsimony, orderliness
(Contained in one factor)

Lazare et al. (1966)*
Obsessive traits: orderly, severe superego, perseverance, obstinacy, rigidity, rejection of others, parsimony, emotional constriction
(Contained in one factor)

Hubbard (1967)
Obsessive-compulsive (based on self-ratings): parsimony, rigidity, orderliness, severe superego, emotional constriction, obstinacy, perseverance, self-doubt
(Contained in one factor; other data derived from Blacky Test and peer ratings did not produce an anal factor)

Kline (1968a)
Anal factor:[27] hypocrisy, submission to authority, conservatism, attention to detail, hoarding, anal sadism
(Contained in one factor)

Brooks (1969)
Obsessional trait: intense application, perseverance, orderliness, cleanliness, diminished self-satisfaction
(Contained in two factors)

There is no question but that past studies have almost unanimously found it possible to isolate recognizable clusters of anal traits and attitudes.[28] Repeatedly, these studies depict trait patterns quite reminiscent of Freud's anal character.

Orderly and parsimonious traits are, indeed, among the most frequently cited in the anal clusters. While the third member of Freud's anal triad, stubbornness, is relatively infrequently directly mentioned, there are parallel qualities such as perseverance and

*Cross-validated in a subsequent study (Lazare et al., 1970).

rigidity that often appear. Traits related to being clean and avoiding dirt are also referred to relatively often. It is rare to find qualities included in the anal clusters that are totally alien to the spirit of Freud's formulation.

The Role of Events in the Anal Period

What do empirical findings tell us about the determinants of the anal character syndrome?

Freud was not very definitive about the major variables that he felt contributed to an anal orientation. As mentioned earlier, his developmental theory implied that one major variable is the occurrence of events during the anal phase (largely equivalent to the formal toilet training period) that are frustrating and disturbing and therefore likely to result in anal "fixations." He also explicitly assigned considerable weight to "constitutional" influences, which he said result in a special sensitivity to anal sensations and therefore render the toilet training experience unusually frustrating. In commenting upon the events during the toilet training period that presumably interact with constitutional predisposition and affect anal fixation, Freud noted (as cited by Fenichel, 1945, p. 305):

> The anal-erotic drives meet in infancy with the training for cleanliness, and the way in which this training is carried out determines whether or not anal fixations result. The training may be too early, too late, too strict, too libidinous. If it is done too early, the typical result is a repression of anal eroticism, characterized by a superficial fear and obedience and a deep tendency toward rebellion; if it is done too late, rebellion and stubbornness are to be expected; strictness causes fixations because of the frustration involved; a libidinous behavior on the part of the mother causes fixation because of gratification . . .

He is actually saying that any kind of *extreme* management of the toilet training process may lead to anal fixation. If toilet training is too early, too late, too frustrating, or too gratifying, it may establish an anal orientation.[29]

A number of studies have tried to establish a tie between toilet training practices and anal attributes: Huschka (1942), Holway (1949), Whiting and Child (1953), Sewell (1952–1953), Prugh (1953–1954), Alper et al. (1955), Bernstein (1955), Sears et al. (1953), Beloff (1957), Sears et al. (1957), Straus (1957), Stein (1958), Durrett (1959), Hetherington and Brackbill (1963), Finney

(1963), Sears et al. (1965), Miller and Swanson (1966), Kline (1969a). These studies have primarily looked at two toilet training indices: the age toilet training started, and the age toilet training completed. The usual intent has been to establish whether the training was extreme in its laxness or severity. A few projects have also examined the mother's feelings about toilet training and the child's emotional responses to such training. With rare exceptions, the basic design of the studies has been to interview the mother about the toilet training period (which was sometimes years previous) and to relate her recall (of when and how the training proceeded) to her offspring's degree of anal orientation. The offspring was usually, at the time of the study, still in early or middle childhood, although in a few instances of college age. Measurement of his predilection to anal traits has been diversely undertaken in terms of his responses to anality questionnaires, parental and teacher ratings, and his performance on both standard and improvised personality tests.

Sifting through the disparate findings, one is forced to conclude there is little support for the hypothesis that a child's toilet training determines whether he will manifest the three traits (orderliness, obstinacy, parsimony) Freud linked with anality. A number of carefully executed projects have failed to discern correlations between toilet training indices and anal traits. Beloff (1957) interviewed the mothers of a sample of post-graduate college students to determine how coercively they had conducted toilet training. She also asked each student to rate himself with respect to a range of anal traits. The same ratings of the student were made by acquaintances. Such ratings proved to have only chance relationships with the toilet training information. Hetherington and Brackbill (1963) administered a battery of behavioral tests to a sample of kindergarten-level children. These tests sampled such traits as neatness, persistence, stubbornness, stinginess, and interest in hoarding. Further, the mothers of the children provided data concerning their toilet training timing and procedures. No correlations of significance emerged between the personality measures and the toilet training modes. Finney (1963) had clinicians and teachers rate a sample of children with respect to traits like stubbornness, messiness, hoarding, and hostility. He secured from the mothers of these children data concerning strictness of toilet training. Once again the toilet training and personality parameters were unrelated. Sears et al. (1965) similarly reported that toilet training procedures, as described by mothers of young children, were unrelated to various ratings of these children, directly and indirectly, having to do with an anal orientation.

Still further, on the negative side, there are several reports indicating a lack of relationship between toilet training practices and various modes of expressing aggression (Straus, 1957; Durrett, 1959; Holway, 1949; Miller and Swanson, 1966).[30] This is important because Freud clearly involved aggression (as defined by terms such as sadism and masochism) in the anal trait cluster.

There are a few studies that do, although somewhat obliquely, trace a connection between toilet training and anal attributes. Alper et al. (1955) reasoned, on the basis of reports in the literature, that it is logical to assume middle-class children experience more severe toilet training than do lower-class children. They then hypothesized that the former would react more negatively to getting dirty (because anal characters find dirt too suggestive of the anal impulses they repress) than the latter. Using a finger-painting task, which involved smearing, they were able to find significant support (in a sample of young children) for their hypothesis. Kline (1969a) found that college students from Ghana obtain higher scores on an anality questionnaire than do English college students. He somewhat skeptically suggested that this might be due to the fact that only those with strong anal traits such as persistence and orderliness could attain college in Ghana.

But note, on the negative side again, that Straus (1957) discerned no relationship between toilet training in Singhalese children and a number of traits, of which some were pertinent to the anal syndrome (for example, sense of personal freedom, self-reliance). In a related negative vein, Whiting and Child (1953) discovered, after analysis of numerous cultures, that the nature of toilet training in each was not meaningfully correlated with diverse variables they theorized might be shaped by anal attributes (for example, the importance ascribed by the culture to anal factors in producing illness). It is interesting that they were much more successful, as described earlier, in demonstrating that *oral* socialization practices leave their stamp on various cultural beliefs about illness and also on specific kinds of anxieties. The apparent limited effect of toilet training, as such, upon the individual's degree of anal orientation contrasts at times with its apparent strong impact upon other aspects of behavior not usually included in the anal syndrome. For example, Sears et al. (1965) reported that severe toilet training results in enhanced femininity in girls and diminished masculinity in boys.[31]

While the search for a simple connection between an individual's anality and his toilet training experiences does not seem promising, there are observations in the literature suggesting a connection between his anality and the existence of anal traits in his mother.[32] Three studies are particularly impressive with respect to this point. Beloff (1957) measured anal orientation in a sample of male and female college students by means of a questionnaire concerned with anal traits. She administered the same questionnaire to their mothers. She found that the more anal the mother's orientation, the greater the anality of her offspring. Similarly, Hetherington and Brackbill (1963) administered a questionnaire measuring the anal triad (obstinacy, orderliness, and parsimony) to a sample of mothers and fathers of male and female children whose anality had been evaluated by means of a series of tasks measuring such behaviors as persistence, stubbornness, and parsimony. Significant positive correlations were obtained between a mother's degree of anality and her daughter's, but not between a mother's and her son's. Only chance correlations occurred between a father's anality and that of either his son or daughter. Finney (1963), taking a cue from the work of Sears et al. (1953), which suggested that strict toilet training is only one manifestation of a mother's *general* rigidity, predicted that a child's anality would be positively correlated with his mother's degree of rigidity.[33] He obtained clinicians' ratings of general rigidity in a sample of mothers. He also secured ratings of their children with respect to a number of anal attributes. His results demonstrated fairly convincingly that the greater the mother's rigidity, the more her child was characterized by anal traits.

The material presented does not, of course, rule out the possibility that the way a child *experiences* toilet training plays a significant role in his likelihood of developing an anal orientation. Simple indices such as when toilet training was started or when it was completed may provide quite incomplete information about the real nature of the child's subjective experience. Such indices also tell little about the mother's toilet training style (for example, the strictness or fervor she invests in enforcing her demands). The mother with an anal orientation may pursue toilet training with an exaggerated intensity devastating to her child, even though she does not begin toilet training unusually early or late. Another point to ponder is that since there are indications that a mother with an anal orientation is often rigid about other training procedures beside those having to do with anal sphincter control, it may be that her impact on her child will also register importantly during non-anal developmental phases. Perhaps what happens during toilet training interacts complexly with the strictness patterns she has already imposed on the child during an earlier phase. The potential complexity of such interactions is pointed up by the findings of Sears et al. (1957) that severe toilet training is particularly upsetting to a child when it is administered by a mother who is "relatively cold and undemonstrative." Relatedly, Miller and Swanson (1966) have, in the process of measuring the effects of toilet training on child behavior, uncovered interesting interactions between harshness of toilet training and social class. For example, middle-class boys subjected to severe toilet training were more repressive and defensive about their inability to complete (persevere at) a task than were severely trained lower-class boys. Such complexities render it less probable that any gross index based solely on what a mother does during the toilet training period will predict anal trait development.

The Experimental Exploration of Anal Traits

The traits Freud ascribed to the anal character were sufficiently explicit to encourage fairly precise investigation of them. Multiple pathways have been taken to find out if people defined as anal characters behave as Freud said they should. In the sections that follow, the findings relevant to each component of the anal triad will be evaluated.[34]

ORDERLINESS

The need to maintain order as a defense against bad, sloppy anal impulses was one of the salient traits ascribed by Freud to the anal profile. Let us examine a number of studies concerned with this trait.

Rosenwald (1972b) looked at the issue by measuring intensity of anal orientation of forty male college students and then relating this measure to their behavior when asked to cope with a messy situation. Anal attitudes were tapped in three ways: (1) efficiency in solving a problem that involved putting one's hands into a dirty, messy substance with obvious anal connotations; (2) responses to a questionnaire directly inquiring about one's anxieties in dealing with dirt (for example, "When I have been in a dirty place, I feel contaminated"); and (3) responses to a questionnaire concerned with anxieties about issues with presumed (indirect) anal connotations (for example, "I frequently get upset because my routines are interfered with"). In order to appraise orderliness behavior, a situation was contrived such that when the subject first arrived to participate in the experiment, he was ushered into a room by the experimenter, who, looking distracted and hurried, casually asked him if he would straighten out a pile of magazines scattered on one table and move them to another. The amount of time (and presumed care) the subject devoted to this straightening out was ascertained with a concealed stopwatch. Analysis of the various measures obtained indicated that those subjects scoring high on the questionnaire dealing with indirect anal anxieties devoted significantly more time to putting the magazines in order than did those scoring low. But the magazine orderliness measure was not related to the efficiency with which the subject coped with the task requiring him to put his hands in an "anal" substance or the questionnaire measure of anxiety about dirt.

One finds in the work of Blatt (1964) a complex approach to the tie between anality and orderliness. He asked raters (advanced graduate students in clinical psychology) to put in rank order the degree to which twenty different needs were descriptive of "optimal personality integration" (that is, good "mental health"), and found rather high agreement in their rankings. He then asked each of a sample of 116 male research scientists to rank the twenty needs in terms of how descriptive they were of himself. One of the needs had to do with orderliness. The deviation of the self rank for each need from the ideal (optimal personality integration) rank of that need previously determined by a group of raters was computed. All subjects were also administered the Blacky Test, and the amount of conflict with respect to the retentive anality dimension (among others) was scored. A consistent trend was observed for the degree of deviation from the ideal of an individual's self-description for orderliness to be positively correlated with his degree of anal retentive conflict. Tension about anality as expressed in responses to the Blacky pictures was mirrored by a sign of deviance or tension with respect to the issue of being orderly.

The orderliness issue has also been approached by comparing the anality of persons in occupations that seem to differ in how much they require one to be careful, systematic, and compulsive. Segal (1961) contrasted a sample of fifteen accounting students with a sample of fifteen creative writing students. He assumed, of course, that accountants have to be more orderly and methodical than creative writers. He equated anal orientation with the degree to which the individual accepts social norms, tries to be emotionally controlled, maintains compulsive defenses, restrains hostile impulses, avoids ambiguity, and shows signs of a "rigid, fearful identification." His measures of such variables were derived (through quantitative indices) from the Rorschach inkblot test and the Bender-Gestalt test (copying geometric figures). He did find that the accountant group differed from the creative writing group in being more emotionally controlled, less open in expressing hostile imagery, less tolerant of ambiguity, and more rigid in their identifications. But the two groups did not differ with respect to compulsiveness or conformity to social norms.

Relatedly, Schlesinger (1963) compared anality in accountants, chemical engineers, and educational psychologists. She expected accountants to be strongly anally oriented because their work "requires care and precision about details" and also because they are much concerned with money—which they "accumulate, store and carefully spend (albeit on paper, not in actuality)" (pp. 27–28). She classified chemical engineers as less anal than the accountants, but more so than the psychologists. She cited, as evidence of their anality, the fact that they are required to "make precise observations and to classify in an orderly way," and also that they are involved with chemical substances that "flow" and "must be contained and controlled through various receptacles." The psychologists were classed as lowest in anality because their work seems to require less methodical behavior and to be focused on service to people and communication of feelings.

The actual measure of anality employed was a questionnaire containing items from several other anality inventories. The items had been factor-analyzed and were differentiated into twelve factor scores. Schlesinger summarized her overall findings as follows (pp. 81–82): " . . . the accounting students tend most consistently to respond in terms of the variety of anal compulsive attitudes . . . A liking for cleanliness, orderliness, regularity, accumulation and retention of possessions, friendly relations with other people, as well as a distaste for direct expressions of aggression except in fantasy, and for wastefulness of any kind all characterize this group. Engineers proved to be very like the accountants in this study . . . Psychologists' attitudes are mainly defined negatively, that is, in terms of lacking the attitudes the others endorse. They seem unworried about order and all it implies."

This study and that of Segal (1961) just cited both appear to affirm the notion that those who prefer an occupation such as accounting, which calls for careful, systematic, and orderly procedures, are anal in their orientation.

Rosenberg (1953) explored the perceptual correlates of compulsiveness. He began with the assumption that the compulsive has a predilection for "exactness, order, uniformity, familiarity, and congruity" (p. 507). He chose persons in psychiatric treatment who manifested strong "obsessive-compulsive" tendencies to represent a compulsive extreme, and compared them with a normal control group. The obsessive-compulsive syndrome has been shown to have significant anal character components (Ingram 1961, Kline 1972). Rosenberg reasoned that the obsessive-compulsive would be inclined, because of his need for order and uniformity, to impose symmetry upon ambiguous stimuli that are not symmetrical. Subjects were tachistoscopically shown a series of designs and asked, after each exposure, to identify the one they had just seen from a multiple-choice list. The choices in the list varied with respect to how symmetrical they were. It was found that the obsessive-compulsives significantly exceeded the controls in how often they favored the symmetrical alternatives. They apparently had a greater need to impose this kind of order on their perceptual experiences.

The concept of orderliness as applied to the anal character has been extended by Adelson and Redmond (1958) in a somewhat tangential fashion. They proposed that the "retentive" anal character, when compared to the "expulsive" character, would be found to be superior in verbal recall.[35] Their rationale for this prediction was that the retentive anal character has learned more efficient ways to sublimate anal impulses and is able to mobilize a more "systematic and orderly" cognitive style. They presumed the superiority in processing intellectual information would result in a superiority in recall of verbal material. They added that the anal retentive's cognitive efficiency derived also from his use of defenses that permit a "heightening of attention to external stimuli" and a tendency to "hypercathect words." But the core of their explanation involves the idea that the anal retentive had orderly and systematic ways of coping with material that result in focused intellectual effectiveness. Sixty-one college women who, on the basis of their responses to the Blacky Test, had been selected as representing either the anal retentive, anal expulsive, or neutral (in-between) positions were asked to learn a disturbing and a neutral prose passage. It was possible to demonstrate that the retentives recalled significantly more of both passages than did the expulsives (with the neutrals falling in between these two groups). Adelson and Redmond reported further that Nahin (1953) replicated these findings in terms of recall of a "disturbing" prose passage.

Attempts by still other investigators to cross-validate these findings have produced inconsistent results.

Marcus (1963) used the Blacky Test to obtain a sample of sixty-four female college students containing anal retentives, expulsives, and neutrals. These subjects were asked to learn neutral and hostile English words, Turkish words, and Chinese characters. It was found that the retentives were superior to the expulsives in delayed, but not immediate, recall of words. There were suggestions that the expulsives had more difficulty than the retentives in learning the hostile as compared to neutral words. Marcus considered that she had replicated a significant part of the Adelson and Redmond findings. One of the chief discrepancies was that Adelson and Redmond had observed the retentives to be superior with respect to both immediate and delayed recall, whereas Marcus found the superiority to apply only to delayed recall.

Pedersen and Marlowe (1950), using a design quite similar to Adelson and Redmond (except that they studied seventy males rather than females), were unable to duplicate their results. In fact, there were even a few trends opposite to expectation.

Fisher and Keen (1972) employed the Blacky Test to select extreme retentives and expulsives and also a neutral group. Their total sample consisted of thirty-three U.S. Army enlisted men. They evaluated recall ability with an elaborate array of procedures that included recall for a paragraph, paired-associate learning, and memory for sexual material they heard during a group discussion. No significant relationships were found between the anality measures and the recall indices.

The diverse results from the five studies are not very reassuring. However, it is noteworthy that the three studies (Adelson and Redmond; Nahin; Marcus) with positive findings used female subjects, while the two with negative findings used males. There may be an important sex difference in this area. A few more better designed studies could give us an answer concerning this possibility. Despite the negative findings cited, one cannot dismiss the more positive ones. There is real justification for keeping alive the hypothesis that initiated the work dealing with the relationship between anal attitudes and the ability to recall learned material.

Overall, the studies presented in this section concerning orderliness are like vague lines of a sketch not yet sufficiently articulated to be recognizable. There have been few direct attempts to establish a link between anality and orderliness. The study by Rosenwald (1972b) demonstrating a positive correlation between a measure of anality and the time devoted to straightening up some magazines is probably the most straightforward and ingenious to date. The partially positive results emerging from this study are encouraging, but only a beginning. The other encouraging leads involve apparent relationships between anality and such variables as self-investment in "orderly" kinds of occupations, a need to perceive things symmetrically, and an efficiency in processing information that suggests a special knack for organized, orderly cognition.

OBSTINACY

Another major trait Freud ascribed to the anal character is obstinacy. He indicated that the demands of parents that the child "part with" his stool and limit his anal impulses arouse intense frustration and a consequent desire to resist control. The anal character is presumably one who was intensely frustrated by demands that he discipline his anal functions and who therefore chronically and resentfully prepares to resist whatever is expected of him. It is said that negativism, in various guises, becomes a dominant theme in his style of life. Freud (1908, p. 170) noted the anal character's obstinacy "can go over into defiance, to which rage and revengefulness are easily joined." He underscored the prominence of anger and the urge to get even. However, in his descriptions of clinical cases he also indicated that the anally oriented individual is uneasy about his hostile fantasies and concerned about keeping them under control.

Researchers who have evaluated the anal character model have probed issues of anger and resentment in some depth.

Let us return to the above-mentioned study of Rosenwald (1972b) in which he related measures of anality to a number of behavioral evaluations of trait qualities in a male college sample consisting of forty subjects. Several of the traits he appraised are pertinent to obstinacy and hostility; the methods he used in his appraisals will now be described.

Aggression. Four procedures were applied to measuring aggression. (1) The Buss-Durkee Aggression Inventory (a questionnaire about frequency and mode of expression of angry feelings) was administered. (2) Subjects were asked to complete the beginning of a violent story and their completions were rated by judges as to degree of violence. (3) Subjects were given a doll and a knife and told to demolish the doll in the way a small boy in a temper tantrum might. Their aggressive vigor and amount of damage inflicted on the doll were recorded. (4) Subjects were asked to sort a series of cartoons into those they liked, disliked, or reacted to indifferently. The cartoons had been selected so that an equal number were aggressive and neutral, and note was taken of how many of the aggressive ones were accepted or rejected. Rosenwald predicted that those with the most anal anxiety would have the greatest difficulty in expressing or admitting to overt hostile impulses. He felt that while angry fantasies are prominent in the anally oriented, they arouse unusual anxiety and are carefully held in check.

Autonomy and persistence. An insoluble jigsaw puzzle was presented to subjects, and they were told that it was so difficult few persons could solve it without help. They were further informed that during the five-minute period given to solve it, they would periodically be offered helpful cues. A score was computed on the basis of how many times the subject was willing to accept help. Rosenwald suggested that "rigid insistence on self-determination" would be expected to typify the anal character.

Criticalness. Subjects were shown two lights and told that the experimenter wanted them to be of exactly equal brightness, but that it had been difficult to equate them. They were to observe the two lights flashing for a series of trials and to report any instances in which they did not look exactly alike. The lights were, in fact, of equal intensity; and subjects' perceptions of them as unequal were treated as indicators of a "critical" orientation. This form of criticalness would presumably be elevated in the anally oriented.

Obstinacy. Subjects were asked to indicate on quantitative scales their attitudes about brushing one's teeth after each meal and also undergoing periodic medical examinations. Later they were exposed to fictitious authoritative information about the hazards of excessive tooth brushing and also the limited value of health examinations. Then they were told to fill out again the attitude scales to which they had initially responded. Obstinacy was measured in terms of how much attitude change occurred. It was anticipated, of course, that anality and obstinacy would be positively related.

It will be recalled that Rosenwald employed several measures of anality. One was based on how much decrement in performance is produced when an individual is asked to identify certain geometrical forms with his hands while they are immersed in a smelly fecal-like substance, as compared to performance when his hands are immersed only in water. Two questionnaire measures were also secured: Responses to questions directly inquiring about one's anxieties in dealing with dirt, and responses to questions concerned with issues with presumed (indirect) anal connotations.

Mixed results were obtained in relating the anality measures to the hostility indices. Those performing most efficiently in the fecal-like medium also used a significantly greater variety of methods for destroying the doll and described themselves as significantly more assaultive in expressing hostility (as measured by the Buss-Durkee Aggression Inventory). Those scoring high on the direct anal anxiety scale were significantly elevated in their dislike of aggressive cartoons. The subjects high on the derived anal anxiety state showed significantly elevated signs of anxious rigidity and slowness of performance during destruction of the doll. Also, those high on the direct anal anxiety scale showed significantly slower performance during the doll destruction task. The trend of these results suggests that inhibition of direct aggression and anxiety about being blatantly hostile are positively tied to an anal orientation or anal anxiety.

No relationships of significance were observed between the anality measures and either the measure of autonomy or criticality. However, obstinacy (as defined by resistance to change in attitude) was shown to be significantly higher in subjects who performed poorly as compared to those performing efficiently in the fecal-like medium. It was not related to any of the other anality measures. While there were gaps in the results and inconsistencies in the relationships of the three major anality indices with each of the hostility and obstinacy measures, the observed patterns are interestingly suggestive. This is especially true with reference to the positive link between anal anxiety and obstinacy.

Multiple overlapping data from other sources support the notion that the anal character behaves in an oppositional, "You can't make me do that" fashion. Consider the following. Couch and Keniston (1960) demonstrated that persons who are inclined to be non-acquiescent, who lean toward saying "no" when asked something, are typified by traits that fit the "anal retentive" category. They showed that persons with the negative stance have probably internalized strong parental demands for self-control and are particularly anxious about anal themes and impulses (as measured by various anality questionnaires). Bishop (1967), proceeding on the assumption that anal characters (as defined by questionnaire) have an "oppositional personality," predicted that under conditions of high privation and forced compliance they would express intense dislike for a disagreeable task. That is, they would respond with special negative intensity. This hypothesis was supported by results from a complex experiment. Rapaport (1963), in a study previously described in detail in the section dealing with orality, mustered evidence that when anal characters (as defined both by questionnaire and clinical behavior) are exposed to threatening anal stimuli (for example, the possibility of having to insert something anally), they prefer isolating themselves from people. He attributed this reaction to several factors, including the impact of hostility aroused by the *imposed* conditions of the experiment. He theorized that the hostility was projected and then aroused anxiety about the potential danger of being with people, thus resulting in a defensive need to isolate self.

A series of experiments dealing with the responses of the anally versus the orally oriented to verbal conditioning (Noblin 1962, Timmons and Noblin 1963, Noblin, et al., 1966) is pertinent to the matter under discussion. These experiments were outlined in the previous section concerned with orality. They evaluated the effects of positive and negative rewards upon persons classified as orals and anals on the basis of the Blacky Test. In brief, they disclosed that the anal character behaves negativistically, in the sense that he is poorly motivated by positive rewards. He resists the intent of the experimenter to influence him by means of the bestowal of praise. One could even say he behaves obstinately in the context of an attempt to control him through his need for approval. But interestingly, it was also shown that the anal character's behavior during conditioning is more influenced than is the oral character's, when disapproval is used as a motivating agent.

Obstinacy in anal characters was appraised in an investigation by Tribich and Messer (1974) that was described in the section dealing with orality. Briefly, the design of this investigation was such that the Blacky Test was used to select oral, anal, and neutral (low on orality and anality) male character types who were then asked to judge the distance an autokinetic stimulus had moved. At the same time, confederates of the experimenters tried to influence their judgments. The results showed, as predicted, that the anals moved in a direction opposite to that suggested by the confederates. The orals, however, moved in the same direction as suggested. The neutrals responded more like the anals than the orals.

Further, with regard to the matter of responding resistively, a study by Dawson et al. (1965) found that orals and anals (as defined by the Blacky Test) did not differ in their hypnotizability. The anals were no more resistive to the hypnotic procedures than were the orals.

The presumed pent-up resistive and cantankerous feelings of the anal character suggested to one investigator (Farber 1955) that such a person should be especially invested in expressing negative feelings through political attitudes. He stated (p. 488): "The political area offers him an opportunity for such indirect expressions [of hostility] in a conformist framework.[36] He will hold rigidly conventional views, but with aggressive passion . . . it might be hypothesized that aggressive conventionality is the dominant political style of the anal character."

In pursuing his hypothesis, he administered an anality scale and a questionnaire measure of "political aggression" (as applied to one's views about communism) to a sample of 130 male and female college students. He was able to report that the greater the anality (for example, favoring orderliness and parsimony), the more power and violence were advocated as solutions to problems associated with communism. Centers (1969) was able to demonstrate an analogous phenomenon. He administered an anality scale and a measure of attitudes toward teenagers and social recipients to 562 non-student adults. He predicted that the anal character (p. 502) "would take a 'hard line' rather than a permissive and lenient position, and manifest . . . *social severity of attitude.*" The results significantly supported his prediction.

Rabinowitz (1957) reported that he could not confirm Farber's original results when he looked at the relationship of measures of anality and political aggression in a sample of 143 college students. He emphasized the fact that, contrary to the state of affairs in Farber's study, he had constructed the items in the two questionnaires so that they were free of the bias of an "acquiescent set" (that is, high scores could be obtained by answering "yes" to some and "no" to others). Farber (1958) responded that the special scales constructed by Rabinowitz did not measure the same dimensions as his scales had. Also, he argued that the Rabinowitz scales were an unknown quantity in that the discriminatory powers of the individual items had not been tested.

One cannot easily resolve this disagreement. However, in view of the fact that Centers (1969) affirmed Farber's idea of a link between anality and severity of political attitudes in a large-scale study, Farber's formulation continues to retain credibility.[37]

It can be said, too, that the evidence generally favors Freud's proposition that the anal character is obstinate and set to resist. We have reviewed a range of studies indicating that the anal character is quick to say "no," slow to change his opinion when persuasion is tried on him, difficult to influence in a verbal conditioning context that relies on approval as a reward, and likely to isolate himself (in a defensive way) when exposed to certain stresses.

PARSIMONY

The third basic trait Freud assigned to the anal triad was parsimony. As earlier noted, he theorized that feces and money are unconsciously equated. It was his view that the anal character attaches importance to hoarding and saving money (or anything of value) because it provides a sublimated way of continuing contact with a substance having secret fecal or anal meaning.[38]

Noblin (1962) has presented direct cogent information about the importance of money in the motivational system of the anal character. He studied, as earlier described, sixty hospitalized male psychiatric patients. Thirty were extreme anals and thirty were extreme orals, as defined by complex criteria involving ward behavior, diagnosis, and response to the Blacky Test. Noblin exposed each subject to a conditioning paradigm designed to increase his use of specific pronouns while constructing sentences from words presented on a screen. Subjects were variously rewarded for the right answer (that is, using a specific pronoun) by giving them gumballs or pennies. Rather complex results were obtained, but they can be reduced to the general statement that anals were best motivated by giving them pennies and the orals by offering them gumballs. Noblin had predicted the selective facilitating effect of pennies for the anals on the basis of Freud's theory that the anal character attaches augmented value to money because of its symbolic fecal implications.

The desire to collect and hoard things presumably represents a sublimation of the wish to retain feces. It is regarded as another form of parsimony. Working with this perspective, Lerner (1961) hypothesized that persons highly invested in stamp collecting would show more exaggerated or deviant responses to words with anal meaning than to neutral words. He stated further that in a control group of noncollectors, such a difference in response to anal as compared to neutral words would not occur. His study involved fifteen boys who were serious stamp collectors and fifteen boys who were not interested in any kind of collecting activity. Their average age was about fifteen, and they were equated for intelligence and reading level. Their ability to correctly perceive anal versus neutral words was evaluated in two ways: (1) they were asked to identify a series of words typed with increasing heaviness on a sequence of sheets of paper, and their thresholds for correct identification were ascertained. (2) They were similarly asked to identify anal and neutral words presented with increasing intensity on a tape recorder. The results obtained by means of these methods indicated that the stamp collectors did differ significantly in their perception of anal as compared to neutral words when the words were presented auditorally. In some instances there was unusually great sensitivity to the anal words and in others there was selective insensitivity. No difference was found when the words were presented visually. In the noncollector sample, perception of anal versus neutral words did not differ, either for the auditory or visual presentations. Generally, Lerner felt, on the basis of his findings, that (p. 95): "The data lend credence to the existence of differences between stamp collectors and noncollectors, with regard to sensitivity to anal stimuli."

Another direct test of the parsimony concept was undertaken in the previously described study of Rosenwald (1972b). He arranged for forty male college students to participate in a betting situation that involved letting them win a small amount of money and then determining how much of that money they were willing to wager on a second possibility. Each subject's anal orientation was measured both by means of questionnaires and by efficiency shown during a task that required him to immerse his hands in a fecal-like substance. The results indicated a significant trend, as predicted, for those who displayed high anal anxiety, as defined by an anal questionnaire (containing such items as "I frequently get upset because my routines are interfered with") to wager less than those with low anal anxiety. One can interpret this as indicating a more parsimonious attitude on the part of those with the high anal anxiety scores. But to emphasize the limitations of these results, it must be specified that the amount wagered was not related to the other two indices of anality employed.

Rapaport (1955) came up with negative results when he compared thirty-two high anal subjects with thirty-two control (moderate and low anal) subjects in relation to how much concern with money they displayed in their Thematic Apperception Test stories. He noted that the differences were in the predicted direction, but not significantly so. Incidentally, he evaluated several other hypotheses concerning the anal character; but they will not be described because they were inappropriate, either methodologically or in terms of their content.

Some investigators have reasoned that if the anal character is truly parsimonious, he should display this trait when dealing with time. That is, he should save and "retain" time in a fashion analogous to his treatment of money. Taking this view, Campos (1966) measured retentive personality traits (by means of a questionnaire) in 100 male college students and also had them estimate how long it took them to complete the questionnaire. He was able to show that the greater the anal orientation, the greater the tendency to overestimate the time interval. Presumably the overestimation is the result of regarding time as something of unusual value (to be saved and hoarded). Campos reported that in a previous study he had analogously found that the greater an individual's anality, the more he described himself as using time in a careful, parsimonious fashion. In another instance, Pettit (1969) provided corroborative data in the same direction. He administered two anality scales and a questionnaire concerning time attitudes to ninety-one college students. The time questionnaire contained such statements as "Time as money" and "I often don't know what the date is." The results indicated significant positive correlations between the inclination to attach great importance to time and degree of anality as defined by both of the anality scales. At this point, one would have to conclude that the anal character does, indeed, treat time in a somewhat miserly fashion.

OTHER CHARACTERISTICS

Aside from the anal triad, there are other subsidiary qualities that Freud ascribed to the anal character. Thus, Freud (1909b) portrayed the obsessive-compulsive (who is a variety of the anal character) as plagued by ambivalence and indecision. He also described him as unusually invested in words and an intellectual approach to things. The ambivalence and the intellectuality presumably represent defenses against impulsive, messy, out-of-control behavior. Apropos of this formulation, Rosenwald et al. (1966) looked at the relationship of "indecisiveness" and "narrow intellectualism" to anal anxiety. As described earlier, the measurement of anal anxiety in this study was based on asking forty-eight male college students to identify certain geometric forms with their hands, which were immersed in a fecal-like substance, and then comparing their performance under such conditions with that in which the forms were simply immersed in water. Indecisiveness was evaluated in terms of how much time the subjects judged they needed to make a series of simple perceptual estimates. Ability to respond with flexibility to an intellectual task was probed by means of a standard "remote associates" task, which calls for the subject to grasp the basic similarity among various words that superficially appear not to be related. Some of the words (for example, cookies, sixteen, heart) were neutral. Others specifically pertained to anal themes. The results indicated that the more difficulty a subject had in coping with the task involving exposure to the fecal-like material, the more indecisive he was. However, there was only a chance relationship between the performance in the fecal-like medium and intellectual flexibility in relation to neutral words. Surprisingly, those who had the most difficulty in the fecal-like medium were the *better* performers on the "remote associates" task when it pertained to words with anal connotations. By way of explanation of this last finding, Rosenwald et al. suggested that those with anal anxieties may have a "readiness for the expression of anal symbols and themes," which would give them an advantage when asked to cope with anal words. Incidentally, it was also observed that those performing poorly in the fecal-like medium obtained high scores on an anal anxiety questionnaire that was administered, but nondistinguishing scores on a questionnaire measure of anal character traits and another of general anxiety.

The presumed indecisive attitudes of the anal character have been put to the test by Gordon (1966, 1967) in two separate studies. In both she asked clinical psychologists and trainees to evaluate information about a hypothetical psychiatric patient. They were to arrive at conclusions and also indicate their degree of confidence in these conclusions. The anality attitudes of all the subjects were evaluated by means of a questionnaire. In both studies, the findings indicated, as predicted, that the more anal the orientation of an individual, the more likely he was to indicate low confidence (indecisiveness) in his clinical judgments, to make fewer specific predictions about the patient, and, interestingly, to identify a low amount of pathology in the patient. In one of the studies (1967), the possibility was tested that the indecisiveness of the anally oriented clinician would be intensified if he was asked to evaluate a patient with definite anal traits. But this expectation was not supported. The results of the Gordon studies, when considered in conjunction with the Rosenwald et al. findings just reviewed above, do lend weight to the idea that the anal character is indecisive.

Freud explicitly declared that the anal character is inclined to have defectatory difficulties (for example, constipation). The empirical findings with regard to this matter are scattered and inconclusive. Note the following. Gottheil and Stone (1968) found no relationship between anal traits and "bowel habits" in males. But Sandler and Pollock (1954) reported that men with "defaecatory difficulty" were typified by a number of salient anal character attributes. Waxenberg (1955) could not discern a correlation between amount of anal imagery in inkblot responses and the presence of colitis symptoms. To complicate matters more, there are some studies that have found constipation to be positively related to orality (for example, Bernstein 1955). There is simply not enough consistent information available concerning this whole matter to arrive at a reasonable evaluation.

It is apropos of this general matter to point out that Fisher (1970) has established that the adult person with anal traits focuses an unusual amount of attention on the back of his body. Since the anus is associated with the back, this represents indirect support for Freud's view that anal traits trace back defensively to some kind of fundamental concern about anal sensations.

Various other correlations between anality and modes of behavior have been reported in the literature which do not seem to have real relevance for the anal character theory as Freud stated it. For example, Cooperman and Child (1968) reported that esthetic sensitivity goes along with tolerance for activities that result in dirtying. Allen (1967) could detect no relationship between early anal training in a range of cultures and the "ego strength" of adults in those cultures. Barron (1955) has shown that anal-retentive attitudes are lower in original (creative) than nonoriginal individuals. Other such studies could be cited, but they are not pertinent to the objective of this chapter.

Overview

We would declare with simple directness that the scientific evidence gathered up to this point favors a good part of what Freud said about the anal character. There does seem to be an aggregation of traits and attitudes corresponding to the anal character image. An impressive tally of studies carried out by investigators with different theoretical perspectives has affirmed that the three major qualities (orderliness, obstinacy, parsimony) that Freud ascribed to the anally oriented do hang together understandably.

It is also true that various general measures of anality have proven to be significantly correlated with specific behavioral indices of orderliness, obstinacy, and parsimony that have been devised. The anality measures have consisted largely of questionnaires that call for self-evaluation with regard to a range of feelings and behaviors directly or indirectly falling within the province of the anal triad. To a lesser extent, other anality indices, such as the Blacky Test, ratings of ward behavior, and response to fecal-like substances have also been applied.

Little is known at present about the comparability of these diverse techniques. So it is striking that the majority of studies have obtained predicted results when correlating anality measures with specific performance measures of traits Freud presumed to be linked with them. One cannot help but be impressed by a study like Rosenwald's (1972b), which found that the amount of anxiety expressed by persons about anal matters predicted how carefully they arranged magazines that were in disarray. This same study dramatically showed that difficulty in coping with a fecal-like substance predicted obstinacy in shifting one's opinions. This last-mentioned result would not make sense in any other current theoretical schema except the psychoanalytic. One cannot but be impressed, too, with studies such as those of Noblin (1962), Timmons and Noblin 1963, and Noblin et al. (1966), which have demonstrated that anal attitudes affect, in predictable ways, the individual's reaction to different kinds of rewards (for example, negative response to praise but positive response to pennies). Further, one cannot easily dismiss a study such as Lerner's (1961), which points up a relationship between being a stamp collector and a selective response to words with anal connotations. These and other studies have begun to weave a containing network of some strength. As each study is added to the stockpile, it becomes more and more difficult to order them sensibly in any but within the anal character paradigm.

The most ambiguous and uncertain part of Freud's theory about anality relates to his concept of how anal traits evolve. The ambiguity derives to a considerable extent from his own vagueness about the relative importance of constitutional and environmental factors. Even in his attempts to be specific about the sorts of parental behaviors displayed during the toilet training period that are likely to induce anal fixation, he diversely blames (as cited by Fenichel 1945, p. 305) training that is "too early, too late, too strict, too libidinous." One is left with the rather poorly defined message that any kind of unusual or extreme parental behavior may have a fixating impact. Unfortunately, the studies that have looked at extreme toilet training procedures, as defined by such indices as the age toilet training was initiated, the severity of training, and the age training was completed, have largely failed to establish that they are correlated with the existence of anal character traits.

However, it is important to point out that several investigators have identified significant positive relationships between the anality of individuals and the intensity of anal attitudes present in their mothers. This obviously suggests that anal traits derive from associating with a parent who treats you in certain ways or provides you with models of how the world is to be interpreted. One should add that since a mother's anal traits are probably a permanent part of her personality repertoire, it would be reasonable to assume they would continue to affect her offspring not only during the toilet-training period but also throughout her contacts with him. This does not rule out the theoretical possibility that the effect of her anal traits would be maximal during the toilet training period, when she was confronted by so many experiences that vividly highlight anal themes, thus stirring up anxiety and eliciting extreme forms of response from her. But one can also ask why her anal attitudes might not be profoundly mobilized during the pre-toilet training period, when she was confronted by a child with no control over its anal sphincter and also no immediate prospect of gaining such control. One could really argue that in some ways the pre-toilet training phase would be more threatening to an anally oriented mother than the toilet training phase itself, because she would have less capability in the first instance of exerting control over the "dirty" behavior of her child. Without solid facts, we are left with all sorts of speculative possibilities. Overall, it would be fair to say that the historical part of Freud's anal character formulation is most in need of investigation. The only thing we can state with even moderate assurance is that a mother with anal character traits will tend to raise an offspring with analogous traits.

Looking at the combined results pertaining to both the oral and the anal characters reviewed in this chapter, we are impressed with Freud's underlying idea that it is meaningful to analyze personality traits in the context of how they are related to body zones that are important loci in the child's interactions with the world. It is a convincing fact that so many studies demonstrate significant correlations between attitudes toward activities linked to organs such as the mouth and the anus, and certain logically related forms of behavior. There would seem to be real profit in pursuing Freud's basic concept by determining whether attitudes toward other body activities are linked with specific trait clusters. For example, Freud has referred to the "phallic" character, but there has been almost a complete failure to investigate empirically whether persons with special attitudes toward the phallus and phallic activities manifest the kinds of traits Freud ascribed to the phallic orientation.

The potentialities of extending Freud's body-based paradigm for interpreting personality phenomena have been documented by Fisher (1970). He carried out a series of studies in which he measured the amount of attention persons direct to major sectors of their bodies, and he demonstrated that the tendency to focus upon specific sectors was associated with certain attitudes and conflicts. Thus, men who focused upon the back of the body were found to have anal character traits. Women who focused upon the head were discovered to be unusually inhibited about dealing with sexual impulses. Personality correlates have also been shown with respect to focusing attention upon other body regions such as the heart, the stomach, and the right as compared to the left side of the body. Perhaps Freud oversimplified things in his analysis of the body zones that play a part in personality development. Other body areas besides the mouth and stomach, anus, and genital organs may be of import. Significant personality traits may accrete as the result of the individual's experiences with such body areas as his eyes or his heart or his legs. There may even be particular developmental phases when experiences with these regions have heightened impact. For example, at the time the child begins to become aware of the power of his eyes to gather information and to make contact with others at a distance, he may encounter resistance from his parents to this enlarged activity on his part. They may not accept the change in his degree of passivity and his enhanced facility in reaching out into the world. Conflicts and traits relevant to incorporation, achievement, and motility might well be mobilized within such a context.

Most contemporary personality theories pay only lip service to drives and body needs as playing a role in character development. They do not give us an account of how a specific need, manifesting itself in the sensations occurring in a real live body, interacts over time with life events and thereby results in certain personality dispositions. Freud highlighted the existence of needs as *personal* body experiences. He particularly portrayed the impact of such experiences in childhood upon those who care for children or have intimate contact with them. He explicitly noted that body experiences can produce diverse responses such as disgust, anger, enhanced narcissism, and sensual pleasure in both self and others. Many of the most frequently cited personality variables in the current scientific literature have an abstract quality that divorces them from the body realm. Variables such as achievement drive, external versus internal orientation, guilt, authoritarianism, and so forth are presented as if they were neat cognitive forces tucked away in some brain center. We are given little or no hint that they involve a massive framework of body experiences and perhaps have been crucially shaped by parent-child *body* transactions.

A core message contained in Freud's statements about character types is that personality develops, in an important sense, around problems of satisfying and inhibiting body needs as they are personally experienced in specific body areas that have social connotations. As we have seen, there is now a good deal of scientific evidence to support Freud's message. Incidentally, there has been a trend for contemporary psychoanalytic theorists to draw away from Freud's body-oriented formulations and to turn to "cultural" concepts of a less earthy sort. More will be said at a later point about the implications of Freud's character formulations for other aspects of his theoretical structure and also for personality theory in general.

NOTES

1. Freud (1916) also briefly sketched a personality typology based upon the relative dominance of ego, id, and superego forces, but he did not pursue it, and there have been no attempts to examine it scientifically.

2. However, it is interesting that in one of Freud's first detailed formulations concerning the existence of a character type ("anal character"), he explicitly noted that the formulation derived not from theory but from clinical observation (Freud, 1908, p. 169): "Among those whom we try to help by our psycho-analytic efforts we often come across

a type of person who is marked by the possession of a certain set of character-traits, while at the same time our attention is drawn to the behavior in his childhood of one of his bodily functions and the organ concerned in it. I cannot say at this date what particular occasions began to give me an impression that there was some organic connection between this type of character and the behavior of an organ, but *I can assure the reader that no theoretical expectation played any part* in that impression" (italics ours).

3. Freud was explicit in stating that an individual rarely becomes fixated completely in one phase. He assumed that while one phase may dominate, evidence of the overlapping influence of other phases can usually be discerned.

4. See Fenichel (1945) for a detailed consideration of these character "types."

5. Glover (cited by Abraham, 1927) also contributed importantly to the concept, but Abraham's formulation was fundamental and also explicitly supported by Freud.

6. It should be added that Freud did explicitly indicate his belief that early oral experiences affect orally related behaviors in later life. Note the following (Freud, 1905d, p. 182): "It is not every child who sucks in this way. . . . these same children when they are grown up will become epicures in kissing, will be inclined to perverse kissing, or, if males, will have a powerful motive for drinking and smoking. If, however, repression ensues, they will feel disgust at food and will produce hysterical vomiting."

7. "They make no kind of effort, and in some cases even disdain to undertake a breadwinning occupation" (Abraham, 1927, pp. 399–400).

8. He said (1927): "What I shall be able to say about character-traits of oral origin will perhaps be disappointing in some respects, because I cannot offer a picture comparable in completeness to that of the anal character." He indicated that the relative ambiguity of the oral character concept as compared to the anal character concept was due to the fact that "of the pleasurable tendencies that are connected with intestinal processes only a small part can come to form part of normal erotism in an unrepressed form; whereas an incomparably greater part of the libidinal cathexis of the mouth which characterizes infancy can still be employed in later life. Thus, the oral elements of infantile sexuality do not need to be changed into character-formation or sublimated to the same extent as the anal ones" (p. 394).

9. Lazare et al. (1966) have nicely summarized the complexities of the oral character formulation:

". . . oral traits are contradictory and may be subdivided many ways, such as sucking versus biting, active versus passive, gratified versus ungratified, fixation due to shortening versus fixation due to prolongation of sucking" (p. 629).

10. Abraham (1927) states: "Clinical experience has led Freud to the view that in many people the particular libidinal emphasis that attaches to the intestinal process is a constitutional factor. There can be no doubt that this is so. We need only call to mind how in certain families positive phenomena of anal erotism as well as anal character-traits are everywhere observable in the most different families" (p. 395).

11. In a later study, Stagner and Moffitt (1956), working with similar questionnaire items, could not discern the presence of clusters that would fit Freud's idea of character "typologies." They state: "The data are interpreted as casting doubt on the appropriateness of using typological formulations as proposed by Freud and some of his followers. A concept of independent traits corresponding to the various alleged 'types' seemed to be more defensible" (p. 74).

12. Kline (1972) has also looked at the extensive factor-analytic work of Cattell (1957), Eysenck (1964), and Guilford (1959), who were not specifically concerned with testing the existence of the Freudian character types, to see if any of their findings were congruent with the "oral character" concept. Only in Cattell's data did he observe clusters with significant oral meaning.

13. The findings cited are those specifically pertinent to traits and attitudes that presumably characterize the oral character.

14. It is interesting in this respect that the magnitude of correlations involving early oral experiences versus later oral behavior was not affected by the length of time that had elapsed between the two sets of measures. That is, correlations were no higher in samples of children that in samples of adults.

15. A considerable literature should be mentioned which concerns itself with the role

of early oral experience on later thumbsucking behavior. Reviews of these studies have been offered by Caldwell (1964), Yarrow (1954), and Ross et al. (1957). The results relevant to this matter remain difficult to formulate in any clearcut, meaningful way, because of the complexity and contradictory nature of the data issuing from various studies.

16. Miller and Stine (1951) also found that high oral children (as defined by the Blacky Test) were more often rejected by their peers (presumably because their need to "hold on" antagonizes others).

17. It is, incidentally, interesting that for both the males and females of the second sample, orality was positively correlated with an independent evaluation of how "fit" each individual was for his Peace Corps assignment. This result is noted because it underscores that an oral orientation does not necessarily mean that one will behave weakly or ineffectively.

18. There are several other studies pertinent to the obesity issue insofar as they demonstrate that measures of oral character attributes are correlated with special interest in, and sensitivity to, food and stimuli with food connotations. For example, Blum and Miller (1952) observed that orally oriented children ate an unusually large amount of ice cream when given access to an unlimited supply. Jacobs (1957) reported that oral characters attend selectively to briefly exposed pictures of food objects (for example, an apple or an ice cream cone).

19. Interestingly, King (1970) reported that within a sample of persons of *normal weight,* the number of oral responses given to inkblots was *negatively* correlated with weight. No obvious explanation for this finding presents itself.

20. It is an interesting sidelight that Wolowitz (1964) and Barker (1968) have found that alcoholics are particularly likely to prefer foods that have passive receptive as compared to oral sadistic connotations. However, Kish (1970) was not able to support such findings.

21. Note, though, that one study has found support for Abraham's formulation concerning the differential basis for the presence of optimism as compared to pessimism in the oral character. Goldman-Eisler (1951) reported that early weaning was correlated with the presence of pessimism and late weaning with optimism.

It is also interesting that Finney (1961b) observed a highly significant positive correlation between pessimism in children and the degree of hostility of their mothers.

22. The ambivalence that Abraham considered to be specifically associated with the oral sadistic orientation has not been detected in empirical studies. However, it is also true that effective methods for measuring ambivalence do not really exist.

23. Freud theorized that the pregenital zones become subordinated to the genital zone and, when genital primacy is attained, make "Important contributions to 'sexual excitement.'" But presumably only a portion of the excitation from the pregenital zones is "made use of in sex life" and the remaining portion is "deflected" into "sublimation."

24. (p. 562) "'Faeces', 'child', and 'penis' thus form a unity, an unconscious concept . . . the concept, namely, of a little thing that can become separated from one's body."

25. Freud also proposed that an anal-erotic fixation played a role in homosexual attitudes and conflicts. More will be said about this at a later point.

26. Body excretions are viewed as having a besmirching and depreciating significance that uniquely associates them with hostility and attack. The core of oppositional anger that Freud attributed to the anal orientation was particularly well spelled out in the following observation (1913b, pp. 323–324): "It is a well-known fact, and one that has given much ground for complaint, that after women have lost their genital function their character often undergoes a peculiar alteration. They become quarrelsome, vexatious, and overbearing, petty and stingy; that is to say, they exhibit typically sadistic and anal-erotic traits which they did not possess earlier, during their period of womanliness. Writers of comedy and satirists have in all ages directed their invectives against the 'old dragon' into which the charming girl, the loving wife and the tender mother have been transformed. We can see that this alteration of character corresponds to a regression of sexual life to the pregenital sadistic and anal-erotic stage . . ."

27. Stringer (1970), upon re-analyzing Kline's data, also established the existence of an anal factor.

28. It should be added that Cattell (1957) concluded, on the basis of certain traits

he isolated through his factor-analytic studies, that the concept of an anal syndrome is meaningful.

29. Freud indicated, too, that anal fixation is affected by other factors such as difficulties in coping with Oedipal problems and conflicts about activity-passivity.

30. Only one solid positive correlation between toilet training severity and aggression (negativism) could be found in the literature (Bernstein, 1955).

31. It is true that one could conceivably argue that these findings are congruent with Freud's constructs, because he did suggest that enhanced anal eroticism, by highlighting the anal opening, reinforces passive-feminine aims.

32. This is not to deny that severe toilet training is often disturbing and disruptive. Both Huschka (1942) and Prugh (1953–1954) have documented not only the development of "anxiety, rage, negativism, excessive cleanliness, guilt" in children exposed to harsh toilet training, but also colonic symptoms such as constipation.

33. Data collected by Wittenborn (1956), Hetherington and Brackbill (1963), and Sears et al. (1957) point in the same direction. It should be added, though, that Kagan and Moss (1962), in their longitudinal study, could not find a relationship between maternal restrictiveness and the later degree of compulsiveness of offspring.

34. While little space will be devoted to the matter, one should note that a number of experiments have shown that anal attitudes may in various ways affect cognitive and perceptual processes (for example, Smock 1956, Carpenter 1965, Lerner 1961, Gordon 1967).

35. The "retentive anal character" corresponds to the "anal character" as the term has generally been used in this chapter. It presumably refers to the defense system linked with fixation in the "late anal" stage, when anal impulses are repressed and defended against. It is sometimes (see Fenichel 1945) contrasted with the "expulsive anal character" who is presumably fixated in the early part of the anal phase and responds not with inhibitions to his anal impulses but, rather, by being messy, rebellious, and impulsive.

36. As previously stated, Cooperman and Child (1971) were not able to corroborate the results of the studies just reviewed. However, there were significant differences in the design of the Cooperman and Child study, which might explain the disparity.

37. Watson (1952) has also found significant correlations between anality and social attitudes, but in contexts only peripherally pertinent to Farber's formulation.

38. The negative and dirty meanings assigned to money are well documented in a study by Wernimont and Fitzpatrick (1972). They asked a variety of subjects to rate the concept of money on multiple scales. When they factor-analyzed these ratings, the following factors emerged: *shameful failure, social acceptability, pooh-pooh attitude, moral evil, comfortable security, social unacceptability,* and *conservative business values.* A number of these factors clearly relate to a perception of money as bad, evil, and a source of shame.

Chapter 4

Oedipal Dynamics and Consequences

Introduction

ONE OF FREUD'S most expansive statements about human affairs is contained in his Oedipal theory. The Oedipal theory presents us with a series of generalizations about how parents and children perceive each other, the process whereby sexual identity evolves, the origins of conscience, and the forces shaping heterosexual object choice. It also touches on such other phenomena as homosexuality, separation anxiety, and psychopathology. Over the years, as Freud pondered Oedipal issues, he was increasingly convinced that they affected every component of man's behavior. Let us assemble Freud's Oedipal formulations and analyze their implications.

He theorized that in every family a complex mixture of love and competition characterizes the interactions between parents and their children. He was particularly novel in postulating the existence of powerful sexual attractions between young children and their parents of the opposite sex and also of jealous rivalry with their parents of the same sex. He stated that at the age of four or five, the child could have sexual aims with regard to the opposite sex parent quite analogous to those an adult would entertain toward a heterosexual love object. Presumably, these aims and the forces opposing them create a dilemma (the Oedipal complex) of crisis proportions; the way in which the dilemma is resolved shapes major facets of personality development. In actuality, Freud depicted the Oedipal process as being radically different for males as contrasted to females. He proposed the following male paradigm.

In the first few years of life the little boy takes his mother as a prime object of attachment and affection. This derives from the fact of her nurturant and intimate closeness. Her ministrations to his body are often pleasant and arouse sensations in erogenous zones. By the time he reaches what Freud calls the phallic stage (age four or five) of development, his interest in mother takes on a clear sexual coloring and he has fantasies in which he uses his penis to have intercourse with her. Mother becomes the focus for his surging phallic sensations. Also, he becomes concerned about gaining exclusive possession of her and getting rid of father, his obvious rival for her love.[1] Thus, a potentially intense and disruptive conflict situation builds up. However, added Freud, certain counter forces accumulate, which normally lead to a rather constructive resolution of the situation. These forces derive primarily from the boy's anxiety about provoking his father into castrating him if he does not cease to be a rival for possession of mother. His "castration anxiety" is said to be incited in several ways. First, he observes that girls lack a penis and he concludes that they have been castrated. This, in turn, implies that the same thing could happen to him. Secondly, he receives direct or indirect threats of castration from his parents when they catch him masturbating. Third, he gets many cues from father that he is angry about their rivalry and motivated to get revenge. Finally, he has a variety of basic experiences, which convince him that one can, indeed, lose cherished parts of one's body. For example, he has to give up the breast when he is weaned; and at that age, when he is so fused with mother, he may interpret the loss as if it were a part of his own body. Relatedly, says Freud, he probably perceives the discharge of feces as a constant reminder that part of his own substance may be separated from him. When confronted by the stark fact that his Oedipal stance may result in the loss of his penis, he concludes (unconsciously) that he must give up his sexual intent toward mother.[2] Instead, he shifts toward a close identification with father, his rival, and redirects his sexual interests to other non-mother feminine objects.

At the same time, the anlage for the superego (conscience) is laid down because, in the process of rejecting his bad impulses toward mother and identifying with father, he "introjects" father's prohibitions and proscriptions.[3] This is the crucial period in which an outside evaluative attitude about self is taken in and made a part of that self. Following this resolution of the Oedipal struggle, the child then is said to move into the latency phase during which there is massive repression of sexual impulses. Only later, at puberty, is there a resurgence of heterosexual interest, which eventually culminates in an adult heterosexual relationship. Freud indicated that the nature of this relationship would be strongly influenced by the manner in which the original Oedipal conflict was resolved. Thus, a man may emerge from the Oedipal situation with a drive to find someone closely resembling his mother, or very much different from her—or even with the conviction that he had better not get sexually involved with a woman at all.

The Oedipal paradigm Freud outlined for the female is as follows.

She, too, starts out life with her mother as the prime object of her interest and love.[4] However, when she discovers that the male possesses a penis, she concludes that she has been castrated and therefore has an inferior body.[5] She develops a deep sense of disappointment and blames her dilemma on her mother. Her disappointment gains intensity from previous frustrations encountered in her relationships with mother. Freud suggests that she had earlier blamed mother for such offenses as not feeding her sufficiently, giving what seemed to be an unfair amount of attention to other members of the family, and frustrating her sexual wishes (for example, punishing masturbation). Within this context, the discovery that she lacks a penis becomes the trigger that turns her finally against mother and causes her to take father as a love object. Presumably, up to this point her clitoris was her main source (through masturbation) of erotic pleasure. With her discovery that she has an inferior organ, she gives up her investment in the phallic clitoris and moves toward a more passive orientation. Further, she constructs the fantasy that father will impregnate her and that she will bear him a child. This potential child has important compensatory value because unconsciously she equates it with the penis.[6] To have a child by father is to regain a version of her lost penis. A more passive, feminine attitude is said to evolve at this time, and the vagina takes on new significance for her. She has renounced mother and turned, in fantasy, to father for a sexual relationship that will provide her with a compensatory baby.

It is less clear in the case of the female than the male, says Freud, as to how the Oedipal dilemma is resolved. He vaguely refers in several instances to the role of "constitutional factors" in how the female copes with her complicated position. He also indicates that the female settles Oedipal matters in a less definite and more gradual fashion than does the male. He conjectures that she introjects parental prohibitions against her Oedipal aims less clearly and therefore develops a less well-formed and less stringent superego.[7] Presumably because she is already castrated, she does not have the same peremptory motivation for resolving the

Oedipal conflict as the male who expects immediate castration if he does not change his ways. Freud suggests that the "setting up of a superego" and the "breaking off of the infantile genital organization" in the girl is more the "result of upbringing and of intimidation from outside which threatens her with a loss of love" (Freud 1924, p. 178).[8] At the core of the Oedipal resolution is identifying with mother's sexual potential and perceiving men as sex objects who can help to compensate for her lack of a penis by impregnating her and permitting her to produce a baby that has a symbolic penis equation.

Subsequent to the Oedipal phase the girl, too, is said to progress to a latency phase in which there is massive repression of sexual aims. Finally, at puberty, a revival of sexual aims occurs, and these aims are thought to be significantly influenced by her Oedipal experiences. Freud emphasized the continuing role of disappointment about penis loss in the woman's sexual behavior. He theorized that "penis envy" intruded into multiple levels of behavior of most women.[9]

Freud pointed out that his basic description of the Oedipal process was an oversimplification. He indicated there were many shades of variation in patterns of child-parent interaction and the modes whereby parent-child conflicts are resolved. Note his following statement (Freud, 1923, p. 33):

"For one gets the impression that the simple Oedipus complex is by no means its commonest form, but rather represents a simplification or schematization . . . that is to say, a boy has not merely an ambivalent attitude toward his father and an affectionate object-choice toward his mother, but at the same time he also behaves like a girl and displays an affectionate feminine attitude to his father and a corresponding jealousy and hostility toward his mother."

It is well to keep in mind Freud's awareness of such complexity, even as we proceed to analyze how well his basic Oedipal schema stands up to the facts.

Oedipal Propositions

The detailed nature of the Oedipal theory permits probing its validity at a number of fairly crucial points. Let us consider the specific hypotheses one can reasonably derive from Freud's Oedipal statements.

1. One of the primary Oedipal constructs has to do with the

process of identification. Freud detailed a series of steps each child presumably goes through as it focuses positive or negative feelings first on one parent and then another, ultimately equating self more with the same-sex than the opposite-sex parent and perceiving the opposite one as a potential sex object. Several aspects of this developmental formulation offer themselves for evaluation.

a. First, there is the clear implication that prior to the Oedipal period, children of both sexes regard mother more positively and as psychologically closer than they do father.

b. Secondly, it is specified that with the onset of the Oedipal phase the child feels more hostile to the same-sex than opposite-sex parent.

c. Thirdly, during the Oedipal period the child feels more sexual attraction to the parent of the opposite sex than to the parent of the same sex.

d. Finally, as described by Freud, the sequence of the identification process is more complex for the female than the male. That is, the male is depicted as taking mother as his love object early in life and therefore not having to make a radical shift when he ultimately settles upon her and other women as heterosexual love objects. But the female is described as having to shift from mother as her original love object to father and other men as heterosexual love objects.

2. Another major proposal Freud made was that the male child experiences more castration anxiety than the female. He indicated that fear of castration plays a decisive part in the male child's decision to resolve his rivalry with father in relation to mother. He stated that castration anxiety could be only a minimal factor in the girl's Oedipal development because she already lacked a phallus. Presumably she could not fear the loss of something she does not possess.

3. Fear of loss of love was regarded by Freud as a more prominent motivating element in the girl's Oedipal sequence than in the boy's. He suggested that in the case of the female one of the prominent elements in initiating superego formation and resolution of the Oedipal dilemma was concern about losing the love of important figures, rather than anxiety about castration.

4. Penis envy was ascribed by Freud more to the female than the male. He theorized that after the girl discovers she lacks a penis, she seeks to compensate for this by constructing a relationship with father that will eventuate in his impregnating her and thus permitting her to produce a baby that can symbolically and compensatorily be equated with a penis. Presumably, this can only partially compensate her. Freud consid-

ered that most women continue to suffer from a sense of body inferiority and to entertain jealous fantasies toward the penis possessed by the male.

5. Freud was explicit in his assumption that the Oedipal situation results in the male developing a more severe superego than the female. He viewed the male as having to introject prohibitions from the father in a definite and decisive fashion in order to cope with his acute castration anxiety.[10] But he regarded the female, since she was not under the pressure of castration anxiety, as being able to cope with her Oedipal dilemma in a more gradual fashion not requiring forceful introjection of standards of conduct. Therefore, he concluded that the male governs himself by a stricter set of do's and don'ts than the female. If he was correct, one should be able to demonstrate that men do, indeed, hold to stricter values and rules than do women.

6. Still another logical derivative of the Oedipus schema would be that those who fail to achieve Oedipal resolution by solidly identifying with the same-sex parent would have special difficulty in their heterosexual adjustment. That is, they would show particular signs of strain and discomfort in their attempts to establish intimacy with heterosexual love objects. Their failure to resolve their antagonisms with the same-sex parent would lead to guilt and inhibition in heterosexual contacts.

7. Prominent in Freud's description of the Oedipal sequence was the idea that inability to master the problems linked with that sequence will result in serious persistent conflicts that will increase vulnerability to psychopathology. Many of Freud's clinical presentations focus on unresolved Oedipal conflicts as a source of disturbance and symptomatology. He highlighted Oedipal-derived anxiety as responsible for the repression of sexual wishes, which he regarded as basic to most forms of psychological disturbance.

8. Tangential to the Oedipal theory, but still tied to it, was Freud's view that the average woman shifts from clitoral to vaginal dominance as she gives up her phallic orientation and moves toward the more passive, feminine, receptive attitude that presumably accompanies identifying with mother and converting her desire for a penis into a desire for a child. He regarded orgasm produced by direct clitoral stimulation to be less mature than orgasm resulting from penile stimulation of the vagina. It would follow from his formulation that the greater the preference of a woman for vaginal as compared to clitoral stimulation, the more mature she would be. There would also be the implication that she had adapted to the Oedipal crisis relatively more effectively.

9. Also tangential to the Oedipal theory was Freud's proposal that the resolution of the acute Oedipal crisis is followed by a latency period in which massive repression of sexual impulses occurs. If so, one should find that in latency-aged children there is a significant decrease in sexual wishes, fantasies, and behavior.

The evaluation of these hypotheses is fraught with difficulties and complications. As will become evident, there are instances in which we simply do not have enough information upon which we can count. In other instances, the research results are contradictory. Still another nagging problem relates to whether one must tap into unconscious levels of response in order to look at certain of the Oedipal formulations meaningfully. More will be said about this last issue in the context of specific problems to be considered shortly.

Identification Pattern

As already noted, the core of the Oedipal theory consists of a group of propositions about the shifting identifications of the child as it moves toward sexual maturity. Freud conjectured that during the pre-Oedipal period (ages one through three), the male and female child both take the mother as their first intimate object of attachment. He depicted them as feeling closer to her than to father. Incidentally, he was really quite vague about the nature of their attitudes toward father during this period. But during the phallic period, which is said to begin around the age of four, the Oedipal struggle crests. After going through a stormy period in which he has strong erotic feelings for mother and very hostile ones against father, the male child is said to make peace with father by identifying with him. Relatedly, the female child is portrayed as getting into conflict with mother as a presumed rival for the erotic favors of father, and then moving on to a resolution that involves identifying with mother's sexual potential (rather than perceiving her simply as a love attachment or object). Operating within this framework, one would expect to find the following to be true:

1. Both boys and girls are psychologically closer to mother than father during the pre-Oedipal period.

2. Both boys and girls feel relatively more hostile to the parent of the same than the opposite sex during the Oedipal phase, and

the obverse is true with respect to feelings of sexual attraction.

3. Both boys and girls emerge from the Oedipal period more identified with the parent of the same than the opposite sex.

4. Finally, since the girl has to shift from mother as her pre-Oedipal object to father as her object during the Oedipal phase, while the boy presumably can continue to relate consistently to mother as a love object throughout his development, there should be signs that the female pattern of identification and object relationships is more complex (and therefore probably more difficult) than the male's.

Pre-Oedipal Closeness to Mother

Since the pre-Oedipal period involves an age range (roughly one through three) in which the child has limited verbal capacity to respond to tests or inquiries, it has proved technically difficult to investigate his attitudes toward his parents. However, what little objective data exist do suggest that both male and female children in this age range feel closer and more attached to mother than to father. Schaffer and Emerson (1964) found that, as defined by reactions to separation, male and female infants were generally more attached to the mother than the father. Ainsworth et al. (1972) observed (in terms of crying and seeking maternal contact in the home environment) that boy and girl infants became extremely attached to mother in the first year of life. Hagman (1932) reported that when he interviewed mothers of children (boys and girls) between the ages of twenty-three and seventy months, there was a trend for mothers' fears and those of their children to be positively related. However, there were no findings with regard to possible similarities of the children's fears to those of their fathers. Lynn (1969) cites, in support of the intense intimacy between the baby and its maternal caretaker, a report by Escalona that each baby in a nursery she studied showed a preference for orange juice versus tomato juice in accordance with whether the particular nurse caring for it liked orange or tomato juice. Rabban (1950) noted, on the basis of his own data and a review of the literature, that children of both sexes "prefer" mother as early as age three.

In general, the scattered results just cited do suggest that both boys and girls in the pre-Oedipal phase have a relatively special psychological closeness to mother.[11]

Attitudes Toward Same-Sex Versus Opposite-Sex Parent

Exploring the Oedipal hypotheses further, do we find, as Freud would predict, that during the Oedipal phase each sex feels relatively positive toward the opposite-sex parent and negative toward the same-sex parent? Unfortunately, we will not be able to give a real answer to this crucial question. We could not find more than a few studies that have even tackled the issue peripherally. Ammons and Ammons (1949) used both direct questions and a doll play procedure to evaluate attitudes toward father and mother in a sample of fifty-eight children ages three to five. They found a general trend for the children to "prefer the same-sex parent" and concluded that the finding contradicted what would be expected in terms of an Oedipal paradigm. It is pertinent, too, that they observed that three-year-old girls (who would be considered pre-Oedipal) expressed significantly greater father preference than four- or five-year-old girls (who are presumably more in the Oedipal phase).[12] Obviously, the Oedipal hypothesis would lead one to expect just the opposite outcome. Since the results outlined for the Ammons and Ammons study involved the use of a projective technique (doll play), which within a psychoanalytic framework would be regarded as tapping a somewhat unconscious level of response, one cannot easily dismiss their implications by labeling them as superficial or merely representative of defensive response bias.

In another study, Kagan and Lemkin (1960) evaluated children's attitudes toward their parents. Sixty-seven boys and girls in the age range three to eight were studied by means of both direct questioning and responses to projective "family pictures." Interestingly, the direct and projective approaches produced largely parallel results. There was a significant trend for girls to indicate more hostility toward father than mother; but for boys, no difference in father-versus-mother answers occurred. Since the majority of the girls were approximately of Oedipal age (median = five and a half years for the total sample), one might have expected them to express more hostility toward mother than father. The converse might have been anticipated for the boys. Neither of these expectations was fulfilled. However, the vagueness of the definitions offered by Freud with reference to the age boundaries for the various pre-Oedipal, post-Oedipal, and Oedipal phases makes precise interpretation of such data rather hazardous.

Simpson (1935) had 500 boys and girls in the five to nine age range respond to a series of pictures designed to elicit indirectly their preferences for one of the two parents. An example of one of the pictures was a scene involving a man and a woman, both smiling pleasantly; the child was asked which of the two figures he "liked better." Tabulation of responses by separate ages indicated that the boys consistently expressed preference for the mother figure. This would seem to conform generally to the Oedipal paradigm. The results for the girls indicated a significant preference for father as compared to mother in the five-year-old group, but then at six and for all succeeding ages a preference for mother was expressed. The preference for father at age five is interesting and congruent with Oedipal theory. However, the results for age six are contradictory. Indeed, what one sees in the results obtained in this study is simply an overall preference for mother.

Friedman (1952) used ingenious techniques to probe attraction-repulsion with respect to same- versus opposite-sex parents in children ranging in age from five to sixteen. One of the particularly interesting things he did was to compare results based on responses presumably derived from a conscious level with those unconsciously based. First, to tap a largely conscious mode of response, he showed each child a picture depicting a child and the back view of two parents looking at him. He then asked, "Which parent does the child love best?" and "Which parent loves the child the best?" He was unable to demonstrate any consistent attitudes of like-dislike with respect to same- versus opposite-sex parents. At this level he discerned no support for Freud's formulations. But then, in order to involve more unconscious response levels, he used two other procedures. One called for the child to complete two "Oedipal fables" that had to do with engaging in a pleasurable activity alone with a parent and then meeting the other parent. The second procedure called upon the child to make up stories about two pictures, one portraying a child and a "father-surrogate" and the other a child and a "mother-surrogate." It was predicted and significantly affirmed that the children would give more negative endings to the "Oedipal fables" in which they were initially alone with the opposite-sex parent and subsequently met the same-sex parent. It was also predicted and significantly affirmed that when making up stories about interactions with mother and father surrogates, the boys would produce a greater proportion of conflict themes than girls when the stimulus was a father-figure, and girls would produce a greater proportion of conflict themes than boys when the stimulus was a mother-figure.[13] Friedman considered these findings to be strongly supportive of Freud's Oedipal theory; and he also highlighted the fact that significant results emerged only when a methodology was employed that tapped an unconscious level of response.[14]

Friedman's results are impressive. But their import is at times hazy because of the age categories of the subjects studied. The data concerning the "Oedipal fables" were based only on children in the fifteen to sixteen age range. As far as they go, they are congruent with the idea of a resurgence of Oedipal wishes and concerns at the time of adolescence. The data derived from stories about father and mother surrogate pictures spanned three age groups: five to six, seven to eight, and fifteen to sixteen. The five to six and fifteen to sixteen groups would logically be expected to be particularly concerned with Oedipal matters. However, the seven to eight group fits Freud's latency phase, when Oedipal conflicts are presumably strongly repressed and quiescent. Friedman found no consistent shifts in Oedipal themes over the three age phases for the boys. He did find that in the female sample there was decreasing conflict with father and increasing conflict with mother over the three age phases. Neither of these patterns fits the Oedipal paradigm so far as development sequence is concerned. One would have expected highest Oedipal concern in the five to six age group, least concern in the seven to eight group, and perhaps an in-between amount in the fifteen to sixteen group. However, it remains important that Friedman was able to demonstrate the existence of a core Oedipal pattern, namely, relatively more positive feelings toward the opposite-sex parent than toward the same-sex parent, in both boys and girls.

Assorted other attempts can be found in the literature to determine whether adults entertain feelings toward parents that are logically linked to Oedipal concepts. Consider the following.

A. R. Miller (1969) asked forty female college students to rate a series of pictured physiques (for example, mesomorph, ectomorph) of males with respect to how well they resemble their fathers and also a number of other persons and concepts. Later they were asked to choose the one pictured physique they would most like to have in a lover. A significant trend was found for the picture chosen as lover to be the one designated either as most like or most unlike father. The association of the lover picture with extreme acceptance or rejection of it as representative of father could be seen as tangentially supportive of Freud's view that the female develops strong eroticized attitudes toward father—attitudes that may require defensive denial and continue to exert an influence even in adulthood.

Schill (1966) exposed thirty-eight male and sixty female college students to a picture from Blum's (1949) Blacky Test that depicts a dog with a knife poised over its tail as if about to cut it off. He asked the students to fantasize which member of the dog's imaginary family had arranged for this to happen. As predicted, there was a significant trend for the males to see father as the "castrating" agent, whereas the females blamed mother. In other words, the same-sex parent was cast in the more hostile role.

C.S. Hall (1963) made use of dream imagery to support the idea that males experience the father as more hostile than do females.[15] He speculated that father is often perceived as a hostile intruder and that, if so, he would be represented in dreams by the image of the "male stranger." In a study of a large number of males and females (primarily adults) he was able to show that the males did cast more "male strangers" in their dreams than did the females.

Imber (1969) employed an unusually clever design to investigate feelings about mother and father as they relate to Oedipal conflict. He hypothesized that (p. 9) "males who show indications of unresolved Oedipal involvement have retained an excessively strong attachment to their mothers coupled with feelings of rivalry and hostility toward their fathers." He determined intensity of Oedipal conflict in 144 male college students by scoring their responses to two pictures in the Blacky Test (Blum, 1949)—for example, one depicting a dog named Blacky in a rivalry situation with his father vis-à-vis mother. In one phase of the study he had high Oedipal anxiety subjects and low Oedipal anxiety subjects learn to discriminate a series of "benevolent" from "threatening" words by administering a mild shock to them each time they pressed a signal button indicating they had not properly classified the word presented to them. When proper discriminatory power had been demonstrated, the subject was shown the word *mother* or *father* and asked to signal whether it was benevolent or threatening. An appropriate control word was also introduced. It was found, as predicted, that subjects with high Oedipal anxiety had more difficulty in responding to the word *father* than did subjects with low anxiety. But no difference occurred for the word *mother.* In another phase of the study, subjects were exposed to the same basic procedure, except that they were given verbal rather than shock feedback when they made the wrong discrimination between "benevolent" and "threatening" words. Also, while they were responding, measures were taken of heart rate. A significant trend was observed for high Oedipal anxiety subjects to exceed the lows for heart-rate variability when exposed to the word *mother*, but not when exposed to *father.* In general, one can say that the results of the study indicated a definite tendency for Oedipally conflicted subjects to exhibit the sort of anxiety about father and mother representations that Freud presumed to exist.

Apropos of the matter of attitudes toward one's parents, Rabin (1958) investigated the effects upon Oedipal anxiety of being raised in an Israeli kibbutz. Children in the kibbutz are raised with a group of other children in the "children's house" and are visited by their parents for relatively limited periods of time. Most of the time they are supervised by a parent surrogate (nurse). Rabin hypothesized that because children reared in this way have a much less intense pattern of interaction with their parents than do children reared in conventional families, the former would have less Oedipal anxiety than the latter. He had twenty-seven fourth grade boys reared in a kibbutz and twenty-seven fourth grade boys from conventional families respond to the Blacky pictures (portraying the dog Blacky in a variety of situations, such as rivalry with father for mother). An analysis of the responses indicated, as predicted, that the kibbutz boys had significantly less Oedipal anxiety than the boys in the control group.

A rather heterogeneous group of research reports has been perused in this section. The studies that involve young children have not delineated the kinds of shifts in attitude toward same- versus opposite-sex parents that Freud suggested would occur in the vicinity of the Oedipal period. However, other studies, primarily involving adults, have shown a trend for persons to entertain more positive feelings toward the opposite-sex than the same-sex parent. Still other studies have presented suggestive evidence that Oedipal parameters do logically predict selective feelings of anxiety or disturbance about one's parents. The studies involving adults have produced results that seem to make sense within Freud's Oedipal frame of reference.

Identification with Same-Sex Parent

Another aspect of parental identification predicted by the Oedipal theory is that resolution of the Oedipal crisis will be paralleled by increased identification with the same-sex parent. One should therefore be able to show that by the end of the Oedipal period (approximately the late part of age five and the early part of age six), such an intensified identification takes place. It should also be true that in subsequent ages the average individual will display his prime identification with the same-sex parent.

Only a few studies qualify to throw light on the question of increased identification with the same-sex parent at the end of the Oedipal phase. We looked for research reports in which reasonably sophisticated techniques for measuring identification had been applied to children in the age ranges pertinent to the Oedipal formulation. Several were found, and they will now be briefly reviewed.

Ward (1969) evaluated relative degree of identification with father versus mother in thirty-two boys and girls selected from kindergarten, first, and second grades.[16] Identification was determined by asking each child to decide which of a series of adjectives should be associated with three different cards labeled "mother," "father," and "self." A score was derived based on the frequency with which the adjectives applied to "self" overlapped with those applied to "mother" and "father." When the younger half of the boys in the sample were compared to the older half (roughly five and a half versus seven and a half years of age), it was found that they did not differ significantly in their relative mother versus father identification. For the male group as a whole there was a slight trend to be more identified with mother than father. The age distribution in the female sample made it impossible to evaluate it meaningfully with reference to the Oedipal time phases. However, one can say that the results for the boys seemed not to match theoretical expectation.

In another study Hartup (1962) used a doll play technique to appraise relative mother-versus-father identification in a sample of sixty-three boys and girls ranging in age from three and a half through five and a half. He presented each child with a series of situations in which a father doll and a mother doll moved in certain ways or rendered specific judgments, but in all instances the behavior of the father and mother dolls was in conflict. The child was asked to perform an analogous series of behaviors with a doll of his own sex, but he was confronted with the task of imitating either what the father or mother doll had done. Overall, the boys were found to imitate the father doll significantly more than did the girls, and the girls imitated mother significantly more than did the boys. However, when the sample was split into younger and older halves (roughly age four versus age five), it was found that the older boys did not imitate the father doll significantly more than the younger ones. Relatedly, older girls did not imitate the mother doll significantly more than the younger ones. The Oedipal paradigm might have led one to anticipate that the older boys, being closer to Oedipal resolution, would express their relatively closer identification with father by imitating the father doll more than the younger boys did. Analogously, one might have expected the older girls to indicate closer identification with mother than did the younger. However, there is once again a serious problem of interpretation because of the difficulty in specifying the exact age at which Oedipal conflict is typically at its maximum and the age at which it is presumably significantly reduced.

A third pertinent study was carried out by Kohlberg and Zigler (1966). It involved an examination of sex-role attitudes in sixty-four boys and girls of average and above-average intelligence who varied in age from four to eight. A variety of experimental techniques was applied, but we will concern ourselves only with those techniques specifically concerned with relative identification with father versus mother. One procedure was a duplicate of that just described above for the Hartup study. A second was similar and involved the child deciding whether a doll of his own sex preferred a mother or father doll to relate to and assist him in a range of situations. When the results for the various age levels in children of average intelligence were plotted, it was observed that in the male sample there was a clear trend to show greater identification with the father than the mother doll by age four. There was also a trend (although with some irregularity) for the identification to increase from ages four through six. These results seem to fit the Freudian model. In the case of the females, the findings indicated that in the age range four through six there was greater overall identification with mother than father. However, what does not seem to fit the Oedipal paradigm is the fact that there was also a definite trend to show increased *identification* with father over the age sequence from four through six.[17] Interestingly, too, intelligence was found to play a role in identification patterns. More will be said later about the import of this observation.

An investigation should be mentioned that is a bit tangential to the issue under consideration, but pertinent to the question of whether there are age-sequence changes in coping with Oedipal wishes and attitudes. Scheffler (1971) pinpointed the period from age five through age six as the one in which a considerable resolution of Oedipal conflicts occurs. She therefore obtained a variety of fantasy material (spontaneous stories and responses to projective stimuli) from children (boys and girls) when they were five and then a year later. She was impressed with the vivid and almost obvious nature of the Oedipal situations that occurred in the stories of the five-year-olds. Analysis of the fantasy material with quantitative techniques revealed that, as predicted, there was a significant decrease in tension about Oedipal themes from age five to six. While this finding is impressive, one would feel more secure about its implications if a control group involving shifts from age four to five had been employed to demonstrate the particular uniqueness of the shifts at ages five to six. If the latter were indeed unique, it would support Freud's concept of the Oedipal period being followed by a latency period in which sexual fantasies are repressed.

Apropos of this same issue, we call attention to a study by Cameron (1967). He examined the Oedipal stages in terms of children's reactions to designs with supposed symbolic masculine or feminine connotations. Phallic designs were equated with the masculine, and rounded, enclosing ones with the feminine. A total of 2,336 children of both sexes over the age range three to seventeen were studied. They were asked to choose, from a series of paired designs, which design of each pair they liked the best. It was expected that the preferences would reflect attitudes toward masculine and feminine objects. More specifically, and on the basis of deductions from the Oedipal paradigm, it was predicted that under the age of four there would be no difference in preference for male versus female designs; that for ages four to six (Oedipal period), children would prefer shapes representative of the opposite sex; that for ages seven to eleven or twelve, they would prefer shapes of the same sex, presumably because sexual wishes are strongly repressed during this latency period; and that for ages over twelve, when there is a resurgence of sexuality, shape preference would once again be for the opposite sex. The results obtained from the study significantly supported this network of hypotheses. It is not clear why Cameron predicted that boys and girls would not have differentiated preferences before the age of four. After all, Freud did suggest that both sexes take mother as their object during this age phase. But, in general, one is struck by the coincidence of the shifts in masculine-feminine symbol preference with the crucial Oedipal age shifts Freud spelled out.

The studies scanned above that specifically concern identification are too few and contradictory to add up to anything meaningful. However, the two studies (Scheffler 1971, Cameron 1967) that successfully predicted changes in children's reactions to stimuli with sexual or Oedipal connotations as a function of their relative age (on the continuum of Oedipal development) are quite impressive.

Let us address ourselves to the matter of whether, in the years following Oedipal resolution, each sex identifies primarily with the like-sex parent. Quite a number of studies relating to this may be found in the literature. The typical design of such studies involves the individual responding first to a questionnaire concerning his beliefs, modes of conduct, and traits. He is then asked to respond to the questionnaire twice more, as he visualizes each of his parents would. The discrepancies between his perception of himself and his perception of each parent can be quantitatively expressed; and the further determination can be made as to whether he regards himself as more like father or mother. By and large, studies of this design have shown a greater "identification" with the parent of the same sex than with that of the opposite sex (for example, Gray and Klaus 1956, Beier and Ratzenburg 1953, Sopchak 1952). Similar results have been obtained with diverse other techniques and with various age groups (Pishkin 1960, Ryle and Lunghi 1972, Byrne 1965). It is true that a number of studies have not found evidence for identification with the same-sex parent, and in some instances the results have been significant for one sex and not the other (Krieger and Worchel 1959, Lynn 1969, Kohlberg 1966). But it is still fair to say that the majority of the evidence indicates that same-sex identification is the most prevalent pattern. At the same time there are other reports in the literature that suggest that the process of same-sex identification may be more circuitous and complex than envisioned by Freud.

More will be said about this later, but a few examples of the complexity are in order. Thus, several investigators have mustered evidence that when a boy seems to be identifying with his father, he may to a noteworthy extent be simply identifying with widely accepted masculine values. That is, a part of the similarity between father and himself may reflect coincidental aspects of the culturally current masculine stereotype they have both adopted. The apparent similarity between the boy and his father would not be merely a direct introjection by the boy of the father's qualities (Kohlberg 1966, Lynn 1969). Another illustration of the complexity involved is provided by reports that femininity in girls beyond adolescence may be positively correlated with the intensity of their father identification (for example, Sopchak 1952). While Freudian theory would predict a partial link between femininity and love attachment to father, it would not predict a link between femininity and *identification* with him.

At an attenuated level, one can conclude that the empirical findings concerning identification with the like-sex parent in the post-Oedipal phase are consistent with Freud's views. However, as already intimated, there are also data indicating that his views were somewhat simplistic with respect to the multiple factors that contribute to identification with the same-sex parent.[18]

Complexity of Identification for Males and Females[19]

The next point we will take up is whether the sequence of the identification process is, as Freud stated, more complex for the female than the male. Freud was convinced that the girl's sex-identification task is more difficult than the boy's. He felt that this was true because he assumed that since boys and girls both start out with the mother as their first love object, the boy can continue, even as he matures, to hold to an opposite-sex love object, whereas the girl must, as she develops, shift from mother to a male object (father). Presumably, the need for the girl to shift from the mother to a male object introduces an extra step and an extra complication into the process of her learning her sex role. Others (especially Mowrer 1950) proposed, in opposition to Freud's formulation, that the child's original relationship with the mother is more in the nature of identifying with her rather than taking her as a love object. From this view, it would be the boy who must shift when he turns to father and identifies with his masculinity. The girl, on the other hand, would continue, throughout her development, to adhere to the same feminine figure for her identification. The identification task would, therefore, be more difficult for the male than for the female.

Lynn (1969) has been particularly prominent among those who argue for the Mowrer perspective. Actually, he takes a complex position. Lynn proposes that girls have an easier time in arriving at a like-sex identification than boys do, but that with increasing age both sexes come to live in a world in which the male and his values are considered to be superior to that which is female —with the consequence that the female becomes less secure and the male more secure about sexual identity. He notes (p. 66), "When the girl leaves infancy she goes from a woman's world of mother care to a man's world. Being feminine, she thus moves from a same-sex to an opposite-sex-oriented world, whereas the boy moves from an opposite-sex to a same-sex-oriented world . . . the girl . . . is, in a sense, punished simply for being born female, whereas the boy is rewarded simply for being born male." In discussing the differential problems of the female and male in learning the sex role, Lynn suggests that their tasks are almost qualitatively different. He compares the identification task of the girl to that of following a map containing much detail, whereas the task for the boy is that of trying to grasp a map in which there are only sketchy outlines of main features. He points out that when the girl is acquiring sex-role information, it is continuously available to her in great detail because she is almost always with her mother, whom she can observe and imitate. This he contrasts with the situation of the boy whose identification model, father, is away at work most of the day and who, even when he arrives home, is not as intimately and easily available for interaction as is mother. Little empirical support has been offered for this concept that the tasks of the girl and boy in learning sex role are radically different. It is based largely upon the observation that the mother is more consistently and perhaps intimately available as an object of identification than is the father.

There are alternative pathways and criteria that can be considered in the course of judging comparability of sex-role identification problems for girls and boys. One may ask which of the two sexes more quickly arrives at a concept of sex role. One may ask which experiences more difficulty and anxiety during the identification process. One may ask which is able to construct the most definite and consistent definition of its sex role. And there are still other alternative questions pertinent to this issue that could be raised. It is difficult to find research data that consistently answer such questions in a unidirectional way.

Let us explore the matter of which sex is the first to arrive at a definition of sex role. One approach to the issue has involved studying the relative frequencies with which girls and boys sketch a same-sex figure, rather than one of the opposite sex, when asked to draw a picture of a person. The assumption has been made (without solid empirical support) that an individual with minimal conflict about his sex role has a set or readiness to produce a like-sex figure when the instructions leave him a choice as to which of the two sexes to draw. Several investigators have actually examined the relative frequencies with which females and males depict their own sex first in their drawings. Bieliauskas (1965), Brown and Tolor (1957), and others have reviewed findings that indicate that at younger age levels (five to eleven), girls draw same-sex figures more often than boys. But, interestingly, this trend shifts with increasing age, and there are data indicating that college-age males draw same-sex figures more often than females. This pattern of results is, of course, nicely congruent with the theories of Lynn (1969) and others, who theorize that girls have an easier task than boys in initially arriving at a sex-role definition because they can, from the very beginning, remain identified with their mothers, whereas boys have to shift from mothers (their first models) to fathers in order to adopt male models. These investigators have proposed, congruently with the figure-drawing findings, that as individuals advance to adulthood, they increasingly encounter a world in which masculinity has higher prestige than femininity; thus the male's sex identity is bolstered and the female's is attenuated. This is paralleled by the fact that in the figure-drawing data a shift occurs so that adult males draw same-sex figures more often than adult females, rather than less often.

Numerous studies have considered how early and how consistently girls and boys show preferences for female versus male toys and activities. As indicated by various papers (Slote 1962, Hall and Keith 1964, Rabban 1959), there is fairly good consensus that boys adhere earlier and more definitely to same-sex preferences than do girls. Girls typically indicate relatively more preferences for masculine activities than do boys for feminine activities.[20] Some have interpreted this fact to signify that boys more quickly evolve a clear concept of their sex role. However, others (Brown 1958, Minuchin 1965) have argued that it indicates that girls have more freedom than boys in defining their sex roles. Brown refers (p. 235) to the "*greater latitude* of the girls compared to the boys in sex-role development. It appears somewhat paradoxical that, although restricted much more in practically all other respects, girls are allowed more freedom than boys in sex-role learning . . . For a girl to be a tomboy does not involve the censure that results when a boy is a sissy. With little, if any, embarrassment or threat, girls may show strong preference for the masculine role; this is not true in the case of boys." Brown points out that, behaviorally, girls may without real criticism wear masculine articles of clothing, have masculine names, and play with masculine toys, but boys would receive severe disapproval for equivalent kinds of feminine behavior. The findings pertaining to feminine versus masculine preferences are obviously open to divergent interpretations. It is interesting, though, that there have been a few studies that, upon examining aspects of sex role in terms of actual performance measures (rather than mere preference), found girls to be more knowledgeable (or "expert") about sex differences than boys. Katcher and Levin (1955) reported that when young children were asked to make size judgments concerning miniature child and adult representations, the girls seemed to be more realistically aware of their femininity (as defined in size terms) than the boys were of their masculinity. Similarly, as noted, Katcher (1955) found that young girls could, more realistically than boys, identify the difference between female and male genitals.

Kagan and Lemkin (1960) and others have been impressed with the potential conflict that confronts the girl as she attempts to identify with her mother who, in terms of cultural stereotypes, may be regarded as the less competent sex and also as less capable than her father. She is told by the culture to model herself after a woman called mother, but she is simultaneously informed, state Kagan and Lemkin, that being a woman implies inferiority. They add that this is reflected in the fact that surveys find more females who state they would prefer to be males than males who would prefer to be females. Although there is probably some validity in the point made by Kagan and Lemkin, the identification dilemma faced by the female child may not be as great as they visualize it to be. Hartley et al. (1962) studied attitudes about female and male children in a group of 132 children (ages eight to eleven). The subjects were asked to complete a story about a couple who wanted to adopt a child and had to choose between a girl and a boy. They were also asked direct questions about whether they would prefer to have female or male children when they grew up and got married. The findings indicated that they were most likely to assume that adults prefer to have children the same sex as themselves. Fathers were seen as wanting boys and mothers as wanting girls. A majority of the directly expressed preferences of the subjects followed an analogous pattern. Girls wanted to have female children, and boys, male children. These results imply that although there is a broad cultural stereotype about female inferiority, girls somehow learn to regard their own sex as "preferred" by mothers and themselves.

Similarly, Kohlberg (1966) comments that despite the general assumption that females are less competent than males, the concept of "woman" still retains many other positive connotations that makes it attractive to a young girl. For example, it is attractive as a model even on the basis of the simple fact that an adult woman is superior in power to a child of either sex. Adult femininity represents to the little girl a certain measure of power and competence. In addition, there are positive connotations linked with femininity that contrast with certain negative connotations of masculinity. Femininity is associated with being nurturant and "nice," which have positive significance, whereas the aggressiveness of masculinity has "bad" implications. Kohlberg also points out that women are often perceived as superior to men in terms of their attractiveness and physical beauty. Outside of the realm of power, there are important qualities associated with femininity that could make a girl feel that identifying with mother is a positive and advantageous thing to do.

The work of Douvan and Adelson (1966) is appropriate to introduce into the discussion at this point, because it bears on the matter of how clearly girls structure their sex identity. They studied a large sample of female adolescents and found that it was common for such girls to postpone a crystallization of their values and attitudes in anticipation of the time when they will meet a future husband and better be able to judge what style of behavior on their own part would be most harmonious with his attributes. If their findings are valid, this would mean that the feminine sex role requires, as a normative process, the maintenance of a certain degree of ambiguity in self-definition. Paradoxically, then, any vagueness in the girl's sex-role definition might represent a standardized ambiguity with adaptive value in terms of the kinds of demands made upon women. Apropos this point, Tryon (1939) reported that the values of girls change much more than boys between the ages of twelve through fifteen. She remarked (p. 79), "There is much greater demand upon these girls . . . as compared to the boys for flexibility, for capacity to readjust their ideals, for ability to reorient themselves to new goals."

In spite of the "ambiguity" that may be built into the feminine role, there is evidence that females are probably as consistent and integrated as men in their sex-role attributes. For example, Sears et al. (1965) administered a battery of measures of gender role to male and female nursery school samples and found much more consistent intercorrelation among the girls' scores than the boys'. The median correlation for the girls was .36 and that for the boys .15. Sears et al. were so impressed with this difference that they concluded that the girls at this age had a more stable gender role structure than the boys. One can also cite the work of Zuk (1958), who reviewed the stability of measures of "sex appropriate" behavior during adolescence in girls and boys who were studied longitudinally (in the California Adolescent Growth Study) for several years. He found that (p. 30) "Boys did not match girls in increase in sex-appropriateness of behavior during the period of adolescence studied; nor did they demonstrate in their behavior the year-to-year consistency or stability of girls." Another interesting pertinent study was carried out by DeLucia (1960), who evaluated the differential effects upon girls and boys (ages five to six) of being praised or censured for their choices of pictures depicting either "masculine" or "feminine" toys. He demonstrated that the sex-appropriate choices of the boys were more unstable and more easily manipulated by the experimental procedure than were those of the girls. The results were seen as indicating that the girls had less difficulty than the boys in structuring a same-sex identification.

Kagan and Moss (1962) were able to look at the stability of sex-related behaviors in girls and boys who were followed in a longitudinal study from the beginning of childhood into adulthood. Elaborate observational and test data were available at many time points in the developmental sequence. It was found that in both girls and boys the amount of interest displayed during adolescence in activities that were not traditional for their own sex could be significantly predicted from the amount displayed very early in childhood. As Kagan and Moss state (p. 159), "The boys who preferred music and reading to team athletics and mechanical interests— the girls who preferred climbing trees to baking cookies—retained this orientation from school entrance to adolescence." One particularly interesting aspect of these findings was the fact that failure in boys to adopt masculine interests during ages three to ten was predictive of high sex anxiety as an adult, but for girls the amount of interest invested in masculine (nonfeminine) activities did not predict an adult level of sex anxiety. This was interpreted by Kagan and Moss to mean that girls have more freedom than boys to indulge in opposite-sex activities without violating their definitions of proper sex role. However, it should be added that they also found that whereas the amount of interest in opposite sex activities during childhood predicted the nature of such interests for males during adulthood, similar predictions could not be made for females; the female pattern was less consistent. One possible way of interpreting these findings is to assert that women are less stable than men in sex-role-related interests.

If one reviews the information presented in this section concerning the differential problems and difficulties of females and males in structuring sex roles, it is apparent that our present stage of knowledge does not permit simple generalizations. It would be premature to say that one sex has more difficulty than the other in this structuring process. The emphasis that Freud put upon the idea that the girl's sex-role identification problem is more complex than that of the boy's has not been empirically corroborated. Indeed, one might be able to argue persuasively from the known facts for a view that would be the opposite of the analytic position.

Castration Anxiety, Loss of Love, and Identification with the Potentially Punishing Same-Sex Parent

A key theme in Freud's Oedipal theory, as it applies to the male, concerns the role of the threatening father and castration anxiety. One of the most explicit statements in the theory is that the male child resolves his Oedipal dilemma under the pressure of his fear of massive retaliation from father (which is visualized as castration). The theory also specifies that the mode of resolution involves identifying with the threatening father. In other words, the identification with him is a way of coping with his threatening attributes. Fear is then presumably a major variable in this identification process. Freud further specified that, contrastingly, castration anxiety plays a minor role in the female Oedipal adaptation.[21] But it will be recalled that he gave considerable weight to fear of loss of love (primarily mother's) as a motivator that gets the Oedipal-age girl moving toward relieving some of the Oedipal tension by identifying with her mother (as a sexual person), who presumably confronts her as a threatening competitor for father. Identification with her at this point is portrayed as arising to an important degree out of fear. However, Freud also underscored the importance in the girl's identification with her mother of pre-Oedipal *positive* feelings. As will be indicated shortly, this introduces greater complexity into Freud's notion of the feminine identification process, which makes it difficult to evaluate straightforwardly.

If Freud's thinking is valid, we should find, first of all, that males have more castration anxiety than females and, conversely, that females have more anxiety about loss of love.[22] In addition, we should find that the intensity and completeness of the male child's identification with father in the Oedipal period are positively correlated with how threatening and potentially punitive (namely, castrating) that parent is. But, as already indicated, the fact that Freud emphasized the contribution of both positive and negative mother attitudes in the girl's identification process renders evaluations of his statements in this area extremely difficult.

CASTRATION ANXIETY

The differences between males and females with regard to castration anxiety and fear of loss of love have been extensively investigated. Let us first consider the issue of castration anxiety. While castration anxiety literally refers to concern about genital mutilation, it has been regarded by Freud and others as including a wide range of concerns about body vulnerability. Castration anxiety has been equated with anxiety that one's body will be hurt or damaged. With this perspective, let us review what is known about sex differences in body anxiety.

Are men more concerned than women with the possibility of their bodies being hurt?[23] The available evidence suggests a positive answer. The accumulating data indicate that males have more anxiety about body damage than do females. Consider the following. Pitcher and Prelinger (1963) found that when young children were asked to make up spontaneous stories, the boys introduced significantly more themes than the females pertaining to getting physically injured. Gottschalk et al. (1963) reported that when males and females were asked to speak spontaneously for a brief period of time and their verbalizations were objectively analyzed, the males produced significantly more themes pertaining to "mutilation" and "death." Blum (1949) observed a sex difference in castration anxiety when he applied the Blacky Test to college students. This test requires subjects to describe and make judgments about a series of pictures portraying a dog in typical crisis situations as they are spelled out by psychoanalytic theory. For example, there is a castration picture in which a dog is threatened with the loss of his tail. In his analysis of responses to the pictures, Blum discovered that the males displayed more "castration anxiety" than the females. Friedman (1952) had children complete a story that concerned a monkey involved in adventures in which he might or might not lose his tail. Scoring the stories for castration anxiety, he found that, at ages five to seven, the boys seemed to be more disturbed by the potential body loss than the girls. However, he also noted that at ages eleven to twelve the trend was significantly reversed, whereas at ages eight to nine the two sexes did not differ. Friedman suggested that the difference in results for the five to six versus the eleven to twelve age periods reflected the fact that, at the earlier age, girls had already resolved their Oedipal conflicts and boys were still struggling with them, therefore experiencing more castration anxiety; but at the later age, girls were entering adolescence, with its attendant anxieties about body changes, earlier than the boys, who had not yet developed as far. Hall and Van de Castle (1965) observed that a greater percentage of women than men evidenced no castration anxiety in the manifest content of their dreams. Schwartz (1956) devised a measure of castration anxiety that could be derived from Thematic Apperception stories.[24] In a college population, males turned out to have higher castration scores than did females. It should be added, though, that Bradford (1968) could not distinguish between the sexes in terms of a Thematic Apperception Test castration index. Lane (1966) objectively evaluated the dreams of patients before and after surgery in an unusually intensive fashion, and discovered that those of men contained much more castration material than those of women. Relatedly, Schneider (1960), who used the Thematic Apperception Test, Figure Drawings, and Story Completions to study children awaiting surgery, found that boys are more concerned with castration themes than are girls. Lewis (1969) was able to demonstrate that when males and females are exposed to a film containing castration material (subincision rites), the males evidence a significantly greater amount of direct castration imagery in their Thematic Apperception Test stories than do the females.

These overall findings, while not conclusive, may be sensibly interpreted as indicating that males are probably characterized by more anxiety about, and preoccupation with, body damage (castration) than are females. Freud's theory concerning this matter is moderately well affirmed.

It is pertinent to the concept of castration anxiety to look for a moment at several studies that have inquired concerning conditions that incite castration concern. More specifically, a number of experimental designs have been applied to exploring whether castration anxiety in the male is reinforced by sexual fantasy. It has been suggested that although castration anxiety is originally related to entertaining forbidden sexual fantasies about mother, it becomes linked to the arousal of sexual fantasy in general. Note the remarks of Sarnoff and Corwin (1959) with regard to this point (p. 376):

> When the child attains adulthood, he should experience no anxiety when his heterosexual desires are aroused by any woman other than his mother, for he has learned to anticipate castration only when his mother is the object of his sexual desire. In actuality, however, children are exposed to varying degrees of castration threat; and if the amount of threat has been excessive, the individual may be led to repress his sexual feelings not only for his mother in particular, but also for women in general. In such cases the arousal of his repressed sexuality by *any* female may elicit the anxiety which has become associated with the incipient manifestation of a highly punishable motive. For a man who has suffered excessive threats of castration in childhood, therefore, sexual arousal, even by a female who is not his mother, is likely to evoke the anticipation of castration.

Freud similarly expressed the view that Oedipal resolution is often imperfect and confused and results in non-mother sexual stimuli arousing the same kind of anxiety that mother-linked sexual stimuli originally evoked. With this perspective, the Oedipal theory would predict that arousal of sexual fantasy in the average man would result in an increase in castration anxiety.[25] Respectable support for this deduction has emerged. Sarnoff and Corwin exposed one sample of twenty-nine male college students to a sexually arousing condition that involved viewing pictures of nude women and another sample of twenty-seven to a low sexually arousing condition that involved looking at pictures of clothed women. Well before the experimental condition, each subject was asked to fill out a questionnaire measuring his degree of fear of death. Furthermore, he responded to a picture from the Blacky Test (Blum, 1949) depicting a castration theme (Blacky, the dog, standing blindfolded, with a knife apparently ready to cut his tail). Subsequent to exposure to the erotic stimuli, the subject responded a second time to the fear-of-death questionnaire. Sarnoff and Corwin constructed this experiment with the assumption that fear of death ("fear of the most extreme consequence of injury") is a basic manifestation of castration anxiety, and that changes in the fear-of-death scores would mirror the amount of castration anxiety aroused by the erotic stimuli. Analysis of the data indicated that, as predicted, the greater the individual's initial castration anxiety, the more likely he was to show an increase in fear of death when exposed to the nude pictures. Further, as predicted, no relationship between initial castration score and shift in fear of death occurred in the control condition.

Brener (1969), who operated with the same theoretical perspective as Sarnoff and Corwin, administered the Rorschach inkblots and Thematic Apperception Test (TAT) pictures to forty male college students. An experimental group was then asked to read passages describing sexual intercourse. Immediately afterwards the Rorschach and TAT were administered again. A control group followed exactly the same procedure, except that the passage they read contained no sexual material. It was expected that the subjects exposed to the sexual material would show a greater increase in castration themes in their Rorschach and TAT protocols than would the controls. This did not prove to be true. However, since all subjects had been asked to rate how aroused they were by the sexual passages, it was possible to analyze the data further with reference to this dimension. When the control and non-aroused subjects were compared with those clearly aroused, there were significant trends for the latter to evidence a greater increase in castration imagery.

Relatedly, Bromberg (1967) established in the course of an extremely complex experiment involving 216 male college students that exposure to sexually arousing stimuli evoked more anxiety in persons with high castration anxiety (as measured by a questionnaire) than those low in this respect.

Saltzstein (1971) examined the effects of three different conditions (exposure to a story with an Oedipal sexual theme, a story with a non-Oedipal sexual theme, a neutral story) upon castration anxiety (as measured by the Blacky Test). A sample of 376 boys of high school age were studied. Each third of the sample was exposed to one of the three conditions. Saltzstein did not find castration anxiety to differ significantly among the conditions. However, when she applied information she had collected about traumatic experiences in the earlier childhood of the subjects, she discovered that castration anxiety was maximized in those who had had a trauma (for example, loss of father) during the Oedipal period (ages three to six) and were exposed to the Oedipal theme. She interpreted her findings as follows (p. 78):

> The findings are consistent with Freudian psychosexual theory. If a boy in the throes of love-hate rivalry toward his father and wish for his mother experiences powerful related events (such as death or separation from the father, trauma to his own body), he will have difficulty with resolution of those feelings. Theory indicates that this resolution is accomplished via castration feelings . . . which serve to repress the Oedipal strivings. That the boy who has experienced relevant trauma in the midst of those Oedipal events would develop a greater sense of punishment or castration anxiety is reasonable. If this set of events is re-aroused later via stress of an Oedipal sort, feelings of castration would be expected.[26]

Despite discrepancies and irregularities, the cumulative impact of the findings just reviewed is positive.[27] When adult males are exposed to sexual stimuli they do, among other things, tend to respond with concerns about sustaining body damage ("castration"); and there may be a special proclivity to do so in terms of the preexisting level of castration anxiety.[28] The predictions in the experiments cited are impressive. We cannot visualize any other existing theory that would similarly hypothesize that males would respond to sexual arousal with imagery relating to getting hurt and damaged and to a degree greater than that observed in females.

One parenthetical negative note should be mentioned at this point. Freud assumed that an important factor in the initiation of castration anxiety in the boy was the discovery that the female lacks a penis. Supposedly, this discovery signifies to the boy that girls are castrated and that the same thing could happen to him. In outlining the role of discovery of the existence of such "castration," Freud stated that until the age of five or so, the boy assumes the penis is the universal natural genital organ. Thus, his shock is triggered when the absence of the penis first comes to his attention. But Kreitler and Shulamith (1966) have challenged Freud's assumptions about what young children actually know about genital differences. They demonstrated, on the basis of controlled interview procedures, that children as young as four and five do have rather clear concepts of such differences and that they do not assume the penis is the universal organ. They regarded their observations as a direct challenge to Freud's views not only because they contradict his explicit statements but also because their methodology, namely, direct questioning of children, was endorsed by

Freud as one applicable to children. Freud considered direct reports by young children about their sexual beliefs as "the most unequivocal and fertile source" of data.

LOSS OF LOVE

Having ascertained that males display more castration anxiety than females, let us look at Freud's parallel formulation that females should be characterized by more concern about loss of love than are males. The following provides a quick overview of the relevant literature.[29]

Manosevitz and Lanyon (1965) reported that in their questionnaire study concerned with the fears of women and men, women obtained their highest scores in responding to questions about "Being rejected by others." Of twelve questions that evoked the greatest admission of fear from the women, seven pertained to interpersonal issues. Gleser, Gottschalk, and Springer (1961) analyzed five-minute samples of spontaneous speech of male and female psychiatric patients and demonstrated that concern with fears about being separated from others was significantly higher in the females than in the males. Bradford (1968) devised a reliable scoring system for evaluating anxiety about loss of love, as expressed in Thematic Apperception Test stories, and affirmed the hypothesis that women would manifest more such anxiety than men. In discussing the possible origin of "loss of love" anxiety in women, Bradford conjectures (p. 88): "It might be argued that from infancy on, females are encouraged to be people and home oriented; that parents tend to use withdrawal of love rather than physical punishment in disciplining girls and thus their extreme sensitivity to this threat . . ."

Lewis (1969) exposed females and males to a film containing a loss-of-love theme and found that the former were made more anxious by it (as defined by their Thematic Apperception Test stories) than were the latter.

Lowery (1965) has even found that the woman's concept of death conforms to her special investment in interpersonal contact and avoiding loss of love. He concluded on the basis of an empirical analysis of imaginative productions that (p. 183): ". . . females tend to see death as a force which threatens to rob them of love or . . . to put them out of communion with the objects of their love." By way of contrast, he noted that males tend to see death as a form of failure or mutilation ("castration").

It is rare to find such complete consistency in experimental outcomes. Freud seems to have been precisely on the mark when he concluded women have more concern about loss of love than do men. If one further considers that Freud was quite accurate in his conclusion that men experience more castration anxiety than do women, an important part of the Oedipal theory jigsaw becomes reliably articulated. One is inspired to feel reasonable confidence in Freud's differentiation between the kinds of anxieties preoccupying males as compared to females during their Oedipal interactions with their parents. More will be said about the meaning of the findings just outlined in the context of a final integration of material presented at the end of this chapter.

PENIS ENVY

In the immediate context of appraising the issues of castration anxiety and concern about loss of love, it would seem sensible to include a consideration of "penis envy." Freud stated that when the female discovers the male possesses a penis, she experiences deep disappointment about her own lack in this respect. He gave considerable weight to this disappointment as a factor which initiated her alienation from mother and her turning toward father. As earlier described, she is presumably inclined to blame mother for the lack; and she evolves complex fantasies about recouping her "lost organ" by getting father to impregnate her and thus provide her with a baby that symbolically represents "penis." Freud theorized that the female never fully accepts her lack of a penis.[30] He consequently portrayed her as unable to shake a chronic sense of body inferiority, envious of those who do possess a penis, and motivated to find substitutes.[31]

It can be immediately declared that Freud was wrong in his assumption that the average woman perceives her body in more negative and depreciated terms than the average man. Fisher (1970, 1973) has elsewhere analyzed the existing literature bearing on this matter at considerable length and concluded that, if anything, women are more comfortable with their body experiences than are men. The details of this extensive analysis will not be repeated here. Suffice it to say that consistent evidence exists that the female exceeds the male in general body awareness, sense of body security, adaptability to changes in body sensations and appearance, and the ability to integrate body experiences in a fashion meaningfully consistent with life role. The male is clearly less accepting of, and less comfortable with, his body than is the female.[32]

Straightforward efforts to examine scientifically the existence of penis-envy attitudes in women are sparse. However, there are several carefully designed studies that are informative.

Consider first the work of Levin (1966). She explored the question whether women who, because of their occupational and marriage history, could be classified as having invested in a compensatory "masculine social role" with phallic connotations, would be characterized by a special degree of concern about not possessing a penis. She compared twenty-six career women (unmarried and employed in masculine occupations) with twenty-five "homemakers" (married, mothers of two or more children, not gainfully employed outside the home). The comparison was based on an analysis of their responses to the Rorschach Inkblot Test. Levin developed a scoring system designed to detect concern about penis loss. It was based on such criteria as the kinds of responses given to blot areas with genital connotations, confusion in assigning sex identity to figures, and the use of phallic symbolism.[33] The total derived penis-loss score proved, as predicted, to be significantly higher in the "career" than the "homemaker" group. A specific subscore concerned with "envious, hostile, and/or fearful reactions to the male genitals" was significantly higher in the first than the second group. The results could be interpreted as indicating that women who pursue masculine goals have a special underlying preoccupation with penis loss and inadequacy.

An extremely complex experimental design was employed by Ellman (1970) to determine if women differing in concern about penis loss could be distinguished in a number of other ways. She used the same inkblot measure as devised by Levin to evaluate the "penis envy" variable. From a larger college student population she selected forty women high on the Levin index and forty low in this respect. She compared them with reference to amount of achievement imagery, depression, hypomania, hostility, and concern about being defective in their Thematic Apperception Test stories. She also compared them with reference to depression, hypomania, and hostility as defined by adjectives they chose as being self-descriptive. It was found that the group with high penis envy exceeded the other group in terms of amount of depression, general hostility, and hostility toward men expressed in their Thematic Apperception stories. No differences occurred for achievement imagery. Also, no differences were detected for any of the measures based on choice of self-descriptive adjectives.

The subjects in this study were also evaluated before and after exposure to a tachistoscopically presented subliminal message (namely, the phrase "woman menstruating"), which was intended to stir up fantasies relating to female anatomy (especially as something damaged and lacking). Thematic Apperception stories and self-ratings based on adjective choices were obtained before and after the subliminal stimulus. Control subjects went through the same procedure, except the subliminal stimulus was neutral in quality. Ellman predicted that women high in penis-envy concern would respond differently than those low in this respect under the impact of the threatening "woman menstruating" message. She expected the former to show a defensive increase in achievement imagery, changes in feelings of loss, and an increase in hostility (particularly toward men). But generally, her predictions did not hold up. She did find an overall significant trend for those with the high penis-envy scores to respond to the subliminal threat with an increase in "denial" defenses. It was as if they were particularly disturbed by exposure to the phrase with genital-loss implications and had to adopt a special defensive stance. The defensiveness aroused was interestingly expressed, too, in an unusual number of mistakes in the sex-labeling of figures in the Thematic Apperception pictures, in a fashion suggesting a desire to minimize differences between the sexes. Basically, what this study tells us is that women who are unusually concerned with themes interpretatively linked to penis envy are inclined to depressive affect, hostility (especially toward men), and a heightened defensive response to a stimulus presumed to stir up ideation about genital damage. Another perspective one can take is that it affirms that some women are preoccupied with "penis envy" themes, and that this preoccupation affects their reactions to stimuli that conjure up images of penis loss or phallic competitiveness.

Still another study specifically concerned with penis envy was carried out by Bombard (1969). He was primarily interested in determining the impact of exposure to pictures of male and female nudes (with the genitals explicitly shown) upon ninety-three women high and low in masculinity (as measured by the projective Franck-Rosen drawing test). He reasoned that the sight of the genitals would activate penis-envy conflicts, and that women high in masculinity would adapt differently because their initial differences in masculinity represented long-term contrasts in modes of coping with penis-envy problems. Presumably the high masculine woman has sought in a "wish fulfillment" fashion to act as if she possesses a penis, whereas the low masculine woman has "given up all masculine proclivities, and seeks to gain revenge as her only compensation." Following exposure to the nudes with genitals showing, the subjects were asked to compose Thematic Apperception Test stories and also to draw male and female human figures. The Thematic Apperception Test stories were scored for such variables as fear of being exposed, intrusiveness, and compensation for defect. The figure drawings were scored for such variables as degree of phallic protrusiveness and overall size. A control group was exposed to pictures of nudes in which the genitals were concealed. Bombard found that his various predictions about the differences in the ways women high versus low in masculinity would react to the sight of genitals were not supported. For example, he had expected the high masculine woman to respond to the sight of genitals by producing more Thematic Apperception stories than the low masculine woman in which there would be themes of intrusion, being "found out" (linked to the fear that others will discover she really lacks a penis), and compensation for defect. No such differences emerged. Similarly, the high masculine woman did not sketch more phallic-looking human figures than did the low masculine woman after viewing the nudes with explicit genitals. The concept of penis envy, as operationalized by Bombard, proved to have little predictive power.

The three studies reviewed above are the major ones we have located dealing with penis envy.[34] It will take more than the several reports just perused to answer the question of whether Freud's concept of penis envy in women is sound. But one is struck with the fact that both the Levin and the Ellman studies, each of which utilized the Levin scheme for scoring penis-envy fantasies in inkblot responses, came up with significant results. Women who are, as defined by Levin scores, caught up with penis-envy concern do display masculinized attitudes and behaviors. This is especially true in Levin's data where one observes that women who have evolved a life style based on not marrying and on pursuing occupations usually regarded as masculine are characterized by an unusual amount of what Levin conceptualizes as penis-envy imagery. Freud would have predicted precisely such a relationship. What we need now are more studies that will attack the following sorts of questions:

Do women generally have more penis-envy fantasies than men? A positive answer to this question is demanded by Freud's theory, and it would be a telling negative finding if such proved not to be the case.

Do women who display what appears to be blatantly compensatory phallic behavior evidence a high degree of penis-envy preoccupation? For example, what do we find with reference to professional women athletes, or women who choose to join the Army, or who engage in police work?

Do women who typically direct an extreme quantity of jealous hostility and derogation toward men exhibit unusually intense penis-envy imagery?

Fear-Inspired Identification

We come now to a consideration of a crucial feature of the Oedipal theory. As Freud envisioned it, the Oedipal confrontation is resolved for the boy when his fear of being hurt by the threatening, castrating father opponent motivates him to identify with that opponent. He identifies with him in order to cope with his fear of him—to escape an untenable confrontation. In a more gradual fashion, the girl presumably goes about resolving her Oedipal rivalry with mother, which threatens traumatic loss of love, by identifying with her (especially her power to become pregnant and produce a child that has a symbolically compensatory value). However, it is simultaneously true that Freud considered identification of the girl with her mother to derive also from feelings of positive warmth. He theorized that the close dependent relationship the girl establishes with her mother in the pre-Oedipal period is basic to her later identification with her. Note the following statement by Freud with regard to this point (1933b, p. 134):

> A woman's identification with her mother allows us to distinguish two strata: the pre-Oedipus one which rests on her affectionate attachment to her mother and takes her as a model, and the later one from the Oedipus complex which seeks to get rid of her mother and take her place with her father. . . . But the phase of the affectionate pre-Oedipus attachment is the decisive one for a woman's future: during it preparations are made for the acquisition of the characteristics with which she will later fulfill her role in the sexual function and perform her invaluable social tasks.

Because of Freud's assignment of considerable import to both nurturant and hostile aspects of the girl's relationship with her mother in the process of evolving identification, it becomes almost impossible to test his identification theory in a really decisive way with reference to women. Only with respect to males is the theory of identification sufficiently definite to permit clear testing. A number of observers (for example, Bronfenbrenner, 1960) have pointed out that Freud's description of the Oedipal process in males conceptualizes the individual's identification with the same-sex parent (and the acquisition of sex role self-definition) as the outcome of fear and as a maneuver largely motivated by threat.[35] Freud's emphasis on threat as the prime force in the identification process was his own unique invention and represents a feature of salient originality in the Oedipal theory. The specificity of his views in this area with regard to males makes it quite attractive as a testing ground.

Fortunately, a good deal of solid work has been done concerning the conditions affecting identification of the male with his father. A reading of this literature argues persuasively against Freud's position. The male's identification is not primarily triggered by threat and anxiety. Rather, most studies have shown that friendly and nurturant attitudes on the part of the father are most likely to cause his son to become like him. These studies have been quite heterogeneous. They usually involve measuring how similar a father and his son are (or how similar a son perceives himself to be to his father). Such a measure is then related to information concerning the amount of threat, as contrasted to nurturance, that the father has displayed in his behavior toward his son. This information is diversely obtained from recollections of the child, reports of spouses, and expressed attitudes of the parent about child rearing.

As mentioned, the studies that have found a nurturant father attitude underlying close identification of the son have been numerous. Let us quickly scan them. Seven studies (Bronson 1959, Mussen and Distler 1960, Distler 1964, Mussen 1961, Mussen and Rutherford 1963, Payne and Mussen 1956, Mussen et al. 1963) have taken masculinity as an index of how much the boy has identified with his father and, in turn, related this index to information concerning the father's degree of nurturance.[36] In all instances, masculinity and father nurturance proved to be positively linked. Thus, in both the Mussen and Distler and Mussen and Rutherford studies just cited, a projective measure of sex role preference was employed with young children and was shown to be positively correlated with their feelings about the father, as ascertained from observations of their doll play. Analogously, the Mussen et al. study just cited demonstrated in a cross-cultural sample that the boys who least identified with their fathers regarded them as low in nurturance. In the Bronson study mentioned above, there was a positive correlation between boys producing masculine play constructions and the masculinity of their fathers (based on interview ratings), but only in the subsample where fathers were observed to be warm and affectionate. In the subsample where father was critical and frustrating, the relationship between the father's and the son's masculinity did not occur. The Mussen study cited above detected a positive correlation between a boy's masculinity (measured by the Strong Vocational Interest Blank) and the degree to which rewarding and positive attitudes were attributed to father figures in their interactions with sons in Thematic Apperception stories. The Payne and Mussen study disclosed that the more boys responded to a personality inventory in the same fashion as their fathers, the more they described them as rewarding and affectionate on a story completion task. The Distler study indicated that men who were most masculine (in terms of the adjectives they applied to themselves) perceived their fathers as most nurturant.

Consider also other related publications. Sears (1953) noted that preschool boys with warm, friendly fathers were particularly likely to take on the father role in their doll play. In another instance, while Sears et al. (1965) did not detect a significant relationship between father's nurturance and son's masculinity, they did report a pattern of data suggesting that the son's masculinity was indirectly tied to how much father participated in the infant care of his son. Bandura et al. (1963a) examined behavior of children in a laboratory setting where they were given the opportunity to imitate adults playing various kinds of parental roles. They concluded (p. 533): "To the extent that the imitative behavior elicited in the present experiment may be considered an elementary prototype of identification within a nuclear family group, the data fail to support the interpretations of identificatory learning as the outcome of a rivalrous interaction between the child and the adult who occupies an envied status in respect to the consumption of highly desired resources." Jourard (1957) found evidence that the male's perception of self as similar to the father was positively related to how favorably (friendly) father was regarded. Still other findings could be enumerated that tie the male's identification to a friendly rather than threatening mode of interaction. But the general consistency of the material just reviewed speaks sufficiently for itself.

There are a few studies in the literature that might suggest a positive link between degree of identification with father and fear of him. For example, Cava and Rausch (1952) reported that in a sample of high school boys, there was a positive correlation between castration anxiety (measured by Blacky Test) and an index of similarity to father (as defined by the similarities between the boy's responses to a vocational interest questionnaire and the responses he imagined his father would give to that same questionnaire). However, it is important to point out that the measure of castration anxiety employed was a general one and in no way specified that the anxiety need be traced to feelings about father. A few studies (Altucher 1957, Moulton et al. 1966) have shown that young men who perceive their fathers as limit setters and rule makers are inclined to be especially masculine in their orientation. But two studies concerned with this very issue failed to reveal analogous significant relationships (Distler 1964, Mussen

1961). Two studies should also be mentioned that have found that masculinity in boys is positively correlated with the amount of dominance behavior displayed by father (Biller 1969, Hetherington 1967).

In general, the empirical results contained in the literature weigh in favor of a boy's identification being facilitated by a nurturant rather than fear-inspiring stance on the part of father. Others who have carefully reviewed the evidence pertaining to this issue have come to a similar conclusion. Biller and Borstelmann (1967) remark (pp. 272–273): " . . . father's nurturance appears to facilitate masculine development more than father's punitiveness. . . ." Kohlberg (1963) observes (p. 304): " . . . there is almost no evidence that variations in parental power influence . . . strength of identification with parents."[37] Biller (1971) explicitly concludes (p. 31): "Paternal nurturance facilitates masculine development to a greater degree than does paternal punitiveness."[38]

In poring over the rapidly expanding literature dealing with identification, one cannot but be impressed with the fact that it has revealed a complexity considerably greater than Freud suspected.[39] Although he was in his time not only original in the sense that he coined the concept of identification and pointed out factors contributing to the process that few had discerned, the subsequent years have established a variety of facts beyond his awareness. Illustratively, it has now been demonstrated that superior intelligence may hasten phases of the identification sequence (Kohlberg and Zigler 1966). Relatedly, there may be other cognitive variables defined within Piaget's system that affect the child's ability to establish identification (Kohlberg 1966, Hartley 1964). Social class factors may significantly interact with the kinds of parental behavior that contribute to identification. Thus, the use of physical punishment versus psychological modes of discipline may differentially affect identification as a function of whether employed by lower- or middle-class parents (Hoffman 1963). The role of siblings may affect identification to a considerably greater degree than previously judged (Kohlberg 1966). Peer attitudes and cultural stereotypes may compete strongly with family variables in shaping identification (Kohlberg 1966). Each of the variables just enumerated may be important not only in its own right, but also as a member of a cumulative group of influences that go beyond the nuclear family interactions central to Freud's identification paradigm. In other words, Freud's concept of identification may deal with only a restricted portion of what goes into the whole process.

If one takes seriously the empirical information presented in this section with regard to identification, it is inescapable that Freud's theory of identification is in serious error. More will be said about the implications of this error at a later point.

The Oedipal Influence Upon Superego Formation

Freud assumed that the moralizing, rule-oriented part of the psychic structure which he labled the "superego" springs in a major sense from the Oedipal crisis. In the case of the male, he said the superego represents an introjection of father's superego values at the time that castration anxiety forces the boy to give up his competitive stance vis-à-vis father and to identify with him.[40] The superego is in this sense forced upon the boy as part of an identificatory process designed to evade overwhelming punishment. In other words, just as identification was visualized by Freud to be largely motivated by fear, he regarded the acceptance of superego rules to be powered by the same fear.[41]

Freud offered a less decipherable template with regard to the presumed source of the woman's superego. His superego formulation for the female was really vague and at times difficult to follow logically. First, he portrayed the girl in the Oedipal phase as less likely than the boy to end the Oedipal confrontation in a sharp, decisive manner (because her fear of loss of love is not as decisive and threatening as is fear of castration). One result of this, he said, was that the female has less motivation to introject a complete and definitive set of superego standards. While this explanation is often accepted at face value, it is actually true that a variety of experimental studies (Kohlberg 1966, Hoffman and Hoffman 1964) has shown that fear of loss of love is one of the most powerful motivators that can be aroused. In any case, Freud further conjectured that the female introjects superego standards from father and to a lesser extent from mother. The idea that father's superego becomes a prominent source of the girl's superego does not logically follow the paradigm provided by Freud's assumption, in the case of the male, that the introjected superego represents a coming to terms with the parent who is the major threat or frustrator. By this token, it is the mother's superego that should dominate the girl's superego formation. But Freud felt that the dominant role of the father in the patriarchal family gave him a special power that rendered his standards preeminent. He was also unclear as to exactly how the girl made father's superego standards part of herself. Freud's account of superego formation in the female (particularly as it relates to Oedipal events) is so vague and at times confused that one cannot really reduce it to testable propositions. The one testable proposition that does present itself relates to Freud's view that the female superego is less strict or severe than the male's.

Fortunately, the statements he makes about superego formation in the male with respect to Oedipal dynamics do largely lend themselves to fairly direct appraisal. His concept of the derivation of the male superego leads one to expect that the strength or severity of the superego will be positively related to the punitive qualities of father.[42] As earlier mentioned, Freud stated that it was the boy's extreme fear of being castrated by father during the Oedipal phase that motivated him to identify with him and also to incorporate his superego values. It was the supposition that the male has greater fear than the female about the consequences of not settling the Oedipal dilemma that played a key role in Freud's depiction of the male superego as more harsh than the female superego. What do we find in the empirical literature concerning the relationship between superego harshness and father's degree of punitiveness?

An immediate question that needs to be faced in looking at any issue involving the superego is whether it can be treated as a unified entity. Freud typically conceptualizes the superego as if it were an internally consistent system. When referring to an individual with a "strict superego," he conveys the idea that strictness permeates all of the moral decisions and attitudes of that individual. However, those who have examined the moral decisions and behavior of persons in a variety of situations find only a low order of consistency (Miller and Swanson 1966, Hartshorne and May 1929, Minkowich 1959, Sears 1960, Burton et al. 1961, Hoffman 1963). Numerous studies have shown only limited interrelationships among measures of moral behavior in the same person. The person who is severely inhibited about impulse expression in the area of hostility may be extremely free in his sexual standards and at the same time about average in his standards with regard to cheating when money is involved. Irregular rather than consistent patterns seem to predominate. It is important to keep in mind, then, that the term superego as used by Freud was oversimplified in its connotations of unity. Researchers (shortly to be cited) who have explored superego (conscience) phenomena have found it necessary to use composite average scores based on behavior or attitudes pertinent to a range of moral behaviors to represent The Superego.

Many different techniques have been pressed into service to measure moral (conscience) behavior. Consider the following diversity:

Observing subjects in situations where they would be tempted to cheat and where they were unaware that their cheating could be detected.

Eliciting projective stories about moral themes (for example, someone who has to decide whether to transgress) that can be scored for moral attitudes.

Administering questionnaires that inquire concerning strength of moral convictions in a number of areas (for example, aggression, sex).

Analyzing specific types of imagery in Thematic Apperception Test stories and Rorschach Inkblot responses.

Observing real life transgression behavior (for example, delinquency).

Measuring the inclination to confess or to experience guilt after moral transgression.

Various studies have correlated indices derived from such techniques with child-rearing practices. That is, they have examined the question whether tendencies toward a high or low moralistic orientation can be traced to specific parental behaviors. Actually, because of Freud's speculation apropos the Oedipal theory, that superego harshness in the male derives from father's punitive stance, a good many of the empirical studies have been directed at determining whether severity of the male's moral standards is linked to how punitively his father behaves. Analysis of these studies indicates quite unequivocally that the fathers of males with strong moral standards are not typified by strictness (for example, Bandura and Walters 1959, Minkowich 1959, Sears et al. 1957). It is difficult to find a single well-designed and convincing study in which the strictness of the male's conscience has been shown to be positively and significantly correlated with how punishing or tough father has been. On the contrary, punitive behavior on father's part is more frequently linked with the son manifesting weak moral standards. For example, Bandura and Walters reported that the fathers of delinquent-acting boys were significantly more often punitive in their child-rearing practices than were fathers of matched nondelinquent boys. Relatedly, Sears et al. (1957) reported that 11 percent of father-rejected boys had a "high conscience," whereas 22 percent of the nonrejected had "high conscience." This difference was statistically significant.

As findings of this tenor have accumulated, they have been viewed as indicating that it is difficult for an individual to acquire standards from someone he fears or dislikes (notwithstanding the popularity of the concept of identification with the aggressor that Anna Freud did so much to popularize).[43] In fact, it has been explicitly proposed by a number of investigators (for example, Kohlberg 1963, 1966, Hoffman 1963) who have minutely considered the literature in this area that strictness of moral standards is likely to be greater in boys whose fathers have been friendly and nurturant than in those whose fathers have adopted a threatening role. There are a fair number of findings that support this position (Hoffman 1963, Moulton et al. 1966, Unger 1962, Kohlberg 1966). But there are also contradictory reports (LaVoie et al. 1973, Grinder 1962, Heinecke 1953). The matter is still unsettled and open to debate.[44] There are additional reports that suggest the relationship between conscience formation in the boy and the degree of nurturance shown by his father may be more complex than that conceptualized by a simple plus-minus continuum. Illustratively, Bronfenbrenner (1960) and Burton et al. (1961) indicated that maximum conscience is displayed not by children whose parents have been highly nurturant but by those who have been modally nurturant. Further, Moulton et al. (1966) discovered that father's nurturance was positively correlated with his child's strictness of conscience only when he was the dominant parent in the family.

One would have to conclude from the available scientific evidence that a punitive paternal stance does not facilitate the development of strict superego standards. In actuality, there are solid hints that a nurturant and friendly father is likely to encourage a strong moral structure in his son.[45] This does not fit well with the picture of superego formation Freud gave us in his Oedipal theory. Incidentally, another fact that has emerged in the research literature that Freud did not take much account of relates to the importance of mother in shaping the boy's superego. Reports by Hoffman and Saltzstein (1967), Yarrow et al. (1968), Sears et al. (1965), and Miller and Swanson (1966), just to mention a few, present interesting data demonstrating that a boy's superego may be as much influenced by his mother's relationship with him as his father's. Although Freud considered the boy's pre-Oedipal relationship with his mother to be an important influence in his life, the fact remains that he conceived of the boy's superego as *primarily* the product of a defensive fusion with father.

One final issue remains to be scrutinized that bears on the superego as a derivative of the Oedipal phase. As already described, Freud asserted—without any qualifying disclaimers—that the male has a much more severe superego than the female, presumably because the male is forced by his castration anxiety to make a decisive end to the Oedipal conflict by identifying with father and introjecting his superego, whereas the female, who is said to have a much less powerful motive (fear of loss of love) for resolving the Oedipal crisis, does not decisively introject superego values. Investigators have tried to check out this hypothesis; disparate, often confusing conclusions have been offered.

One of the problems encountered has revolved about the fact that the modal socialization for the female emphasizes obedience and limited aggressiveness. Should conforming nonaggressiveness be regarded as a sign of a strong superego? This is a debatable question. It can be argued that timidity is a sign of anxiety rather than representing a style of behavior based on well-defined standards of what is good or moral. If one simply counts up the number of studies that have concluded either that the male (for example, Douvan and Adelson 1966, Lansky et al. 1961, Kohlberg 1963, 1966) or the female (for example, Rempel and Signori 1964, Blum 1949, Sears et al. 1957) has the stronger moral standards, the box score is about even for each side, with perhaps a slight edge for the males. Some investigators explicitly report they can detect no differences between the sexes (Grinder 1962). The contrasting methods and levels of approach employed in various studies make consistent interpretations almost impossible. Thus, one study (Rempel and Signori 1964) reports that females rate themselves as higher on conscience than males, whereas another declares (Hall 1964) that, in terms of symbolic dream material, males have a more strict superego than females. One of the most thorough and systematic investigations of sex differences in conscience to be found in the entire literature (Sears et al. 1965) reported shifting difference patterns as a function of the particular morality measure considered, but did conclude that young girls have a stronger conscience than boys. However, Kohlberg (1966), after examining the sex difference literature, concluded (p. 123): "Where sex differences are found in measures of resistance to temptation, or in measures of guilt under conditions of apparent nonsurveillance, the differences are in the direction of a stronger conscience in boys." Aronfreed (1968), who also systematically sifted the sex difference literature, indicated that (p. 330) "Boys are more honest than girls in their overt conduct in private temptation situations, and in the accuracy of report of their own social behavior . . ." But he also pointed out (p. 330) that "girls are more prone than are boys to confess their transgressions . . ." Generally, though, he was persuaded that boys rely more than girls do on internalized (superego?) standards to guide their conduct.

We are inclined to urge caution about a final decision with respect to this issue. Not only are there conflicting experimental findings, but even when sex differences are isolated they are of small magnitude. True, there is a trend favoring Freud's hypothesis. But even if the trend receives further substantiation, it is hardly of such proportions as to support the rather dramatic distinction that Freud sought to make between the male and female superego.

Clitoral-Vaginal Response

A theoretically minor, but practically important, part of Freud's Oedipal story is his view that one expression of an adequate Oedipal resolution in the case of the female is a shift from clitoral to vaginal erotogenicity. Supposedly, the female who masters her Oedipal problems gives up her phallic aspirations, adapts a more passive orientation, and invests in the passive-receptive vagina as the prime sexual organ. The sexually mature woman is therefore pictured as capable of achieving orgasm primarily by means of penile stimulation of the vagina. But the immature woman is said either not to be able to reach orgasm at all or to rely primarily on stimulation delivered to the clitoral area. It is striking how widely this theory has been accepted. But we have been unable to find any solid empirical support for it. The only published scientific investigation pertinent to this matter has contradicted it. Fisher (1973) obtained ratings from several different samples of married women with regard to the degree to which they prefer clitoral as compared to vaginal stimulation in the process of attaining orgasm. He found no indications that women with a clitoral orientation were especially inferior in their psychological adaptation. Surprisingly, there were consistent significant trends indicating a *positive* correlation between degree of vaginal preference and anxiety (measured in multiple ways). It was not the clitorally-oriented woman who was most anxious, as would be expected within the Freudian framework, but rather the vaginally-oriented one. Further, the more vaginally oriented were found to experience their bodies in a depersonalized fashion and to have an exaggerated need to mute the intensity of the experiences to which they expose themselves. The more vaginally oriented also recalled their fathers as having been unusually reluctant to communicate love and warmth. These findings were replicated with sufficient consistency to suggest they are reliable, although they await cross-validation by other investigators. In their present form they do stand apparently opposed to Freud's assertions.

Maladjustment

Satisfactory resolution of Oedipal problems was regarded by Freud as fundamental to adequate life adjustment. It was his view that if serious Oedipal conflicts persisted, an individual was likely to develop significant disturbance. The disturbance could take manifold forms, ranging from neurotic symptomatology to gross sexual dysfunction. In essence, Freud regarded effective adaptation to the Oedipal crisis as the fulcrum for lifting oneself to successful psychological adjustment. No empirical studies have tested this formulation directly. However, there are a number that indirectly have pertinence.

One cluster of studies has looked at the impact of losing a parent upon adjustment.[46] The typical rationale of such studies is that if a parent is lost early in life (especially during the Oedipal period), this will seriously interfere with the kinds of transactions between parent and child necessary to work through Oedipal conflicts. The parent-deprived individual will therefore manifest an unusual amount of psychological disturbance. Probably one of the best-designed investigations concerned with the effects of parent loss was undertaken by Grayson (1967). He compared samples of 123 female high school and college students who had lost a parent (primarily the father) through death at different points in childhood: during the Oedipal phase (ages two and a half to six), pre-Oedipal (birth to two and a half), during latency (seven to eleven), and early adolescence (twelve to fourteen). There was also a control group that had not suffered parent loss. Projective tests were administered and quantitatively scored to detect the presence of "psychosexual conflict," "sex role disturbance," and related kinds of difficulties in role definition in the subjects. They included the Rorschach Inkblot Test, Thematic Apperception Test, Draw-A-Person Test and Coles Animal Test.[47] It was predicted that, from highest to lowest, the samples would show disturbance in the following order: Oedipal loss, pre-Oedipal, early adolescence, latency, and controls. Analysis of the material provided surprisingly good support for the hypothesis. There was an overall significant trend for disturbance (as defined by all of the tests except the Rorschach) to be greatest in those who had lost a parent during the Oedipal phase; and scores for the other groups fell into the expected sequence. This is a telling study because of the specificity of the prediction that was upheld. What theoretical scheme, besides Freud's, would have correctly pinpointed loss during the two and a half to six age period (because it embraces the Oedipal phase) as most damaging to the individual?

Another study by Leichty (1959–60) is indirectly corroborative of Grayson's results. She administered the Blacky Test (Blum, 1949), which evaluates responses to pictures of a dog involved in situations depicting psychoanalytic themes, to thirty-three male college students whose fathers were separated from them (because they were away on Army service) during the Oedipal phase. She also administered the test to a control group of twenty-nine male college students whose fathers had not been absent when they were growing up. Scoring of the Blacky Test responses revealed, as predicted, that those who suffered absence of father during the Oedipal period had more defensive tension about attachment to mother than did the controls. The father-absent subjects did not show an expected elevated level of castration anxiety. But they did manifest significant disturbance in their identification with father. Of these results, the one demonstrating more defensive tension among the father-absent subjects about attachment to mother is especially noteworthy. It is again difficult to envision any other existing theory that would so neatly conceptualize absence of father as creating negative tensions between son and mother (presumably because the enhanced closeness to mother would intensify forbidden incestuous fantasies).

Quite a number of other reports have appeared that indicate loss of a parent early in life results in the child being more vulnerable to later psychological disturbance (Biller 1971). Difficulties in sexual adjustment have been prominently mentioned (Jacobson and Ryder 1969). Some writers have interpreted such findings as support for the Oedipal theory, in the sense that they indicate adjustment difficulties for those who have not had both parents around to help them work through and settle Oedipal conflicts. However, such a line of interpretation seems unwarranted in view of the fact that the studies in question have not controlled for age of parental loss. Unless consequences of loss in the Oedipal phase can be differentiated from those at other points in the developmental sequence, they merely demonstrate that loss, as such, is harmful to adaptation.

It is apropos to mention here a sequence of observations by

Winch (1943, 1946, 1949, 1950, 1951), who was, among other things, interested in the relationship of parent loss to heterosexual maturity. He secured information from a large sample of male and female college students concerning loss of parents during childhood and also roughly evaluated their heterosexual maturity in terms of their courtship behavior. A limited amount of dating was equated with immaturity. Intense courtship, as represented by being married or formally engaged, was regarded as a sign of heterosexual maturity. Winch demonstrated that males who had lost their father were less mature heterosexually, and he regarded this as support for the Oedipal theory. He interpreted this to mean that in the absence of the opportunity to identify with father, immature ties to mother would persist and interfere with investment in other women. But it should be added that he found no relationship in female samples between mother loss and courtship behavior. In related studies, involving other large college student samples, he explored the question of whether degree of attachment to the opposite-sex parent had an apparent effect on courtship behavior. He was able to establish with some consistency that the greater the male's "love" (attachment) to his mother (as defined by self-ratings), the less active he was in his heterosexual behavior.[48] Liking for father had only a chance link with such behavior. Winch interpreted his findings within the framework of Oedipal theory as indicating that heterosexual inhibition reflects the effect of overcloseness or attachment to mother, which is itself presumably the result of an unresolved Oedipal problem. However, he was not able to show consistent relationships in women between heterosexual inhibition and liking for father or mother.

Oedipal theory has stimulated a good deal of research into the effects of closeness between mother and son. It has been typically hypothesized, in line with Freud's perspective, that if a boy is too closely attached to his mother (especially during the Oedipal phase), this indicates inadequate resolution of the Oedipal struggle, and will result in disturbance of his sexuality. One of the most ambitious investigations of this issue was carried out by Stephens (1962) and is presented in detail in a book titled *The Oedipus Complex: Cross Cultural Evidence.* Essentially, what Stephens did was to evaluate objectively a range of cultures (more than sixty) with respect to how much they encourage intimate closeness between mother and son during childhood and then to predict that the greater the closeness, the more there will be signs, in any given culture, of male anxiety about sexuality. His raw data consisted of coded judgments derived from the observations of anthropologists who had studied different cultures around the world. He focused particularly upon the *post partum* sex taboo as a means for testing his hypothesis. Cultures differ with respect to how long parents delay resuming sexual intercourse after the birth of a child. The taboo about resuming intercourse may extend for many months in some cultures and only a short period in others. Stephens reasoned that in the case where the mother and father cannot have intercourse for an extended time, the mother will turn to her male child for compensation and will establish an unusually intense tie with him that has sexually seductive connotations.[49] Such a tie will presumably interfere with the boy's ability to achieve normal resolution of his Oedipal relations and result in his developing compensatory defenses.

Stephens puts it in these terms (p. 40): "(1) the long post partum sex taboo intensifies the mother's interest in her child; (2) this intensifies the child's sexual interest in her; (3) this in turn intensifies . . . the *effects* of the Oedipus complex." He theorized that the longer the *post partum* taboo period in a culture, the more likely were the following direct and indirect signs of disturbed sexual adaptation in males to appear:

1. Fear of menstruation, because it symbolizes the bleeding genital, which in turn symbolizes the castration fear aroused in the Oedipal situation.[50]

2. Sexual anxiety, as defined by such variables as severe rules about premarital intercourse, sexual explanations of illness, and themes of punishment for sexual intercourse in folklore themes.

3. Unusual concern about incestuous fantasies, as represented by severe kin-avoidance rules (for example, tight restriction on permissible relationships between a man and his mother-in-law).

4. Occurrence of special punishing initiatory rites for the boy, which apparently reflect rivalry between son and father.[51]

Stephen's quantitative analysis of a vast amount of anthropological data available to him was largely supportive of the propositions just listed.[52] The results did fit the complex theoretical paradigm he derived from Freud and translated into anthropological terms. If one accepts his initial assumption that the length of the *post partum* sex intercourse taboo is an index of the degree of intimacy of the mother-son relationship, his findings come across as convincing. Incidentally, he assiduously enumerated a variety of statistical relationships in his data apparently supportive of that initial assumption.

It is important to cite at this point an ingenious study by Peskin (1973), which directly bears on the effects of mother closeness upon the adaptation of her son. The study involved families that were observed and evaluated longitudinally for many years.

Peskin reasoned that if Freud's Oedipal theory has validity, it should follow that boys who are exposed to an excessive amount of mother closeness or love during early childhood should have particular difficulty in coping with the maturational changes associated with adolescence that so prominently involve the emergence of sexual drives and wishes. He designated one group of eleven boys as Strong Oedipal who, when they were in the thirty-six to forty-eight month age period, had been judged by raters to be receiving more love from mother than she directed to her spouse. A second group of sixteen boys was labeled as Normal Oedipal, who had been rated as receiving no more love from mother than she gave to her spouse. The findings supported Peskin's hypothesis. The Strong Oedipals were found to be significantly more socially withdrawn and also more repressive toward inner feelings than the Normal Oedipals. Such data represent an indirect replication in an American setting of one of Stephen's important hypotheses.

It has been reasoned by some that if Oedipal difficulties are etiologically significant for psychopathology, signs of unresolved Oedipal conflicts should typify persons with neurotic symptomatology. Kokonis (1972) explicitly examined this proposition by using sex-role identification as an index of how well Oedipal difficulties have been solved. He said it would follow from Freudian theory (p. 52) "that the neurotic's sex-role identification development is impaired inasmuch as sex-role identification is dependent upon normally going through and resolving the Oedipal conflict. . . ." He measured sex role identification in sixty adult males by means of several techniques (for example, masculinity-femininity questionnaire). Half of the sample consisted of normal subjects and the other half of patients in treatment for psychological problems. Kokonis' results indicated that neurotics score significantly lower than normally functioning subjects in relation to masculinity. He interpreted them to mean that "Evidently, the neurotic falls short of the normally functioning subject in sex-role identification development owing to unresolved Oedipal conflicts and consequent developmental fixation" (p. 55).

Other investigators have similarly reported that male neurotics have poor identification with father or the masculine role (Kayton and Biller 1972, Biller and Barry 1971, Mussen 1961, Sopchak 1952, Lazowick 1955, Kline 1969b). While such findings regarding a link between sex role and psychopathology are interesting and suggestive, they are quite tangential in their pertinence to the Oedipal theory. One could conjure up all kinds of other factors besides poor Oedipal resolution to explain why male neurotics have a poor sense of masculinity. Furthermore, it should be pointed out that there has been little success in demonstrating an equivalent pattern of findings for females (Heilbrun 1968). If the hypothesis has any validity for males, it does not extend to females.

Looking back at the information compiled in this section, it seems reasonable to say that acceptable tests of the possible role of Oedipal factors in *psychopathology* have not yet been designed. True, a few indirect bits of evidence have turned up favorable to Freud's view. For example, male neurotics (but not female neurotics) do seem to have a less satisfactory identification with the like-sex parent than do normal controls. Also, women who have lost a parent during the Oedipal phase show more signs of psychosexual confusion and disturbance than do those who lost a parent during non-Oedipal phases. But there are no studies in which one can trace even a moderately direct connection between measures of disturbed Oedipal relationships and neurotic symptomatology in later life. More substantial is the intricate network of predictions and confirmations presented by Stephens (1962) with regard to how a boy's degree of intimacy with his mother during the early childhood years (across multiple cultures) finds expression in his later phobic, defensive responses to sexual situations. By the way, a bit of support for Stephen's results was provided by the earlier mentioned findings of Winch that males who are inhibited about heterosexual courtship feel unusually attracted to their mothers. In any case, Stephens' pinpointed and often validated hypotheses suggest the complex usefulness of Freud's Oedipal concepts in generating novel approaches to accumulated observational material.

Overview

Our probing of the Oedipus concept has documented its layered, aggregate structure. The so-called Oedipus theory is obviously a collection of theories about a number of major socialization events. It tries to explain such diverse things as how the child learns to focus his sex drives, the manner in which he puts on his sex role, and the process whereby he makes moral rules part of himself. In addition, it offers a different theoretical account for the male as compared to the female. What aspects of the theory can we declare are reasonably supported by the scientific findings?

First of all, one can say that the findings mildly affirm parts of the identification sequence pictured by Freud. Both sexes do apparently begin life with a closer attachment to mother than to father. But what about the reality of the shift Freud predicted around age four with regard to the child developing positive sexual feelings toward the parent of the opposite sex and antagonism toward the parent of the same sex? The data directly bearing on this point that were derived from studies of children have been too limited in scope and design to permit sound conclusions. However, there have been other studies (Miller 1969, Schill 1966, Hall 1963, Imber 1969, Rabin 1958) more tangential in approach that have suggested the existence of attitudes toward father and mother that might be expected if there were the love-hate involvement with them Freud conceptualized. For example, it will be recalled that Imber found that men characterized by high "Oedipal conflict" responded with special anxiety to references to father. Miller presented evidence that women have erotized attitudes toward father which register in the form of defensive reactions. Hall was able to demonstrate in terms of dream imagery that men perceive father figures as more hostile than do women. Such studies are only suggestive, because they often involve elaborate assumptions and fifth-order deductions. At the same time they cannot, as a group, be dismissed, because they do give results in accord with Freud's theorizing. They fit the notion that the individual has to learn to cope with both erotized and hostile feelings vis-à-vis his parents. However, whether, as Freud said, the crest of such feelings occurs in the age period four through six or seven remains to be seen. Looking further at the identification sequence, one can say the evidence is mixed as to whether the Oedipal phase is clearly followed by intensified identification with the parent of the same sex. Little of substance has emerged to indicate that there is a surge of closer identification with the same-sex parent in the immediate post-Oedipal period. There is a fairly well validated normal trend, though, for each sex beyond the age of nine or ten to identify more with the same than the opposite-sex parent.

The information bearing on Oedipal identification sequences is plainly of patchwork quality. What we really know can be reduced to the following:

1. Both males and females are probably closer to mother than father in the pre-Oedipal period.

2. At some later point each sex identifies more with the same than the opposite-sex parent.

3. There are defensive attitudes detectable in persons beyond the Oedipal phase which suggest they have had to cope with erotic

feelings toward the opposite-sex parent and hostility toward the same-sex parent.

One of the most telling clusters of studies bearing on this pattern of erotic-hostile involvement with one's parents relates to castration anxiety. Just as conjectured by Freud, castration anxiety (fear of body harm or attack) is a common occurrence in men. But what is remarkable is that castration anxiety has been shown to be intensified by exposure to heterosexual stimuli (Sarnoff and Corwin 1959, Brener 1969, Bromberg 1967, Saltzstein 1971). Such findings touch the core of the Oedipal formulation as it applies to men. They fit Freud's basic idea that the conditions of the Oedipal encounter build the expectation that experiencing erotic impulses will lead to being hurt and attacked. While these studies vary a good deal individually with regard to the statistical significance of their results, they are persuasive as a group. Freud was upheld, too, in his assumption that castration anxiety is greater in men than women and that the obverse is true for fear of loss of love. This adds construct validity to his model concerning the nature of castration anxiety. It will be recalled that he argued that castration anxiety is rather specific to the male because he possesses a penis which might potentially be removed as an act of punishment (for his Oedipal wishes), while the female lacks a penis and therefore cannot be made to fear loss of what is already gone.

However, it would be well to specify at this point that most of the other predictions Freud made about Oedipally linked sex differences have simply not held up to empirical scrutiny. There is no evidence that women, because they have a vagina instead of a penis, experience their body as inferior to that of men. This is generally true even though signs of penis envy may be detected in some women who have identified more with masculine than feminine aims. Another of Freud's sex difference theories that has not held up concerns the idea that the female has a more complex and difficult course to follow in attaining a definition of sex role than does the male. He derived this proposition from the view that both boys and girls start out with mother as their first love object, but that later the girl has to shift to the male as an opposite-sex love object, whereas the boy can continue to take the female as his object. This presumably introduces an extra step into the girl's heterosexual adaptation that could potentially result in more difficulties for her. But the empirical literature suggested that, if anything, the female has less difficulty than the male in the process of evolving a sex role.

Still a third sex difference hypothesis, namely, that the female has a less severe superego than the male, was only partially supported by the research literature. Indeed, the literature clearly did not confirm the existence of a superego difference as great or dramatic in magnitude as Freud visualized. Most of the distinctions Freud attributed to the male and female in the context of the Oedipal process do not appear to be valid. Only his parallel propositions regarding differences in castration anxiety and fear of loss of love were verified. In addition, a number of his Oedipal formulations with regard to the female have proven to be so vague or contradictory they cannot be reasonably evaluated. This was earlier pointed out in relation to his theory of identification and also his theory of superego formation as they apply to the female. Really, we are left with little of substance when we try to put together the major elements in Freud's account of Oedipal development in women. To begin with, he did not have a clear working model in mind.[53] Further, some of the key elements he did detail were in a sense defined in terms of how they differ from the equivalent elements in the male; and as we have seen, these supposed differences have turned out to be largely fictional.

The Oedipal theory, as it applies to the male, seems to be reasonable in its assertion of a sequence that begins with attachment to mother, tense rivalry with father and fantasies of sexual closeness with mother, and ultimately identification with father and his sex role. A drastic defect in the theory that our empirical analysis has revealed concerns the motivating force behind the resolution of the Oedipal rivalry and identification with the father. Freud insisted that castration anxiety was the force. It is true that experimental studies have shown not only that castration anxiety is common in males but also that it is incited by sexual fantasy. That much conforms to theoretical expectation. But the evidence is quite convincing that what motivates the boy to identify with father and his masculinity is not fear, but rather father's nurturant friendliness. The boy apparently gives up his competitive struggle with father because his positive, friendly attitude invites one to become like him.

Apropos of this issue, it should be noted that Freud was also distinctly wrong when he speculated that the formation of the boy's superego is energized by the same castration fear that drives him to identify with father. Experimental data from diverse sources indicate that conscience severity is probably positively correlated with nurturant rather than severe or fear-provoking attitudes on the part of one's parent. Within the context of the two defects in Freud's theory just mentioned, it becomes necessary to consider a radical alteration in the theory. A formal revision seems in order that would conceptualize the resolution of the Oedipal crisis in the male as occurring not primarily out of anxiety but rather on the basis of trust.

The research findings suggest that the boy does go through a phase when he feels strongly in competition with father and does entertain castration fantasies that are probably linked in some way to unacceptable erotic wishes (which we will assume are directed at mother). But it would appear that he gives up his acute competitive stance vis-à-vis father because father transmits friendly positive messages inviting him to join up rather than fight. That is, father reassures him there is no reason for the competition and also convinces him that he has no intention of being the vengeful castrator. He invites his son to draw close, to form an alliance, to adopt his identity, and to accept his values. He makes it clear that he does not intend to attack (castrate) him catastrophically. At another level, one might say that he tells his son that it would be more profitable to give up his aim of achieving an eroticized relationship with mother and to form a masculine alliance with him. Apparently, the son finds such communications convincing. He does model himself after father and he adopts his father's moral values. In these terms, the resolution of the Oedipus crisis would be based primarily on warmth and trust rather than fear. This does not, of course, rule out the possibility that one factor in the Oedipal resolution might be the boy's perception that father is a good deal more powerful than he is and that he could do a lot of damage if persistently opposed. But the empirical findings indicate that it is, at best, a secondary rather than major factor. If Oedipal tension between father and son is actually dissipated as the result of a friendly rather than frightening transaction, this would give the Oedipal phase a meaning quite different from that usually ascribed to it in psychoanalytic circles. It would be a time of father-son reconciliation rather than of the son's submission to paternal power.

Of course, the possibility exists that in different cultures threat and nurturance may enter in varying proportions into the Oedipal resolution. Perhaps Freud's male patients who were reared near the end of the last century in an Austrian setting were primarily motivated by fear of the tough patriarchal father in their resolution of Oedipal competition. The more contemporary male in the United States, who has been the subject of the empirical studies of Oedipal phenomena, may have had available a more nurturantly based resolution. One cannot dismiss such a possibility. Even so, a reading of the modern research literature makes it difficult to jettison the idea that paternal intimidation and hostility would produce counter-hostility that leads not to resolution of antagonism or to the son's identification with the father's values, but rather to alienation and intensified conflict.

The structuring of the superego would, within the framework of the theory revision proposed, consist of the acceptance of father's moral system as part of a process of forming an alliance with him. This, by the way, would be more congruent with the guilt-inducing role assigned to the superego by Freud than is the concept of superego as a product of fearful identification. There is a considerable literature indicating that guilt is more commonly evoked by deviating from expectations of those who have been nurturant and loving than of those who have been hostile (Aronfreed, 1968). The taking over of a set of superego values from someone with positive valence would in all likelihood create a greater sense of obligation than would acquisition of such values from someone who is punitive. As mentioned earlier, it has been shown that delinquent boys who flaunt rules with little apparent guilt more often have severe threatening fathers than boys who are law abiding. We would underscore that we do not agree with Freud's notion that the boy's superego is acquired in package form as part of the Oedipal resolution. While important moral values may very well be made part of oneself at that time, Kohlberg (1963, 1966) has reviewed a considerable pool of studies indicating that children may learn basic moral standards both before and well after the Oedipal phase. They also take over such standards not only from father but from mother, peers, and other sources. No factual rationale exists for picturing the superego as a glob that is grossly introjected at a focused point in time.

Freud's perception of Oedipal dynamics as basic to whether an individual will develop later psychopathology and sexual difficulties has not yet been evaluated adequately. A few well-designed studies do favor Freud's view. It will be recalled that Grayson (1967) found that loss of a parent during the Oedipal period produced more "psychosexual conflict" than loss of a parent at any other phase of childhood. Winch (1943, 1946, 1949, 1950, 1951) demonstrated interesting relationships in males between inhibited heterosexual behavior and unusually close involvement with mother. Stephens (1962) successfully traced, in cross-cultural data, a series of hypotheses indicating that prolonged intimacy between mother and child results in a variety of disturbed and phobic sexual attitudes. Studies of this sort are promising, but obviously far from definitive.

Freud's persuasive sweep in presenting the Oedipal theory creates the impression that it is a unified entity. However, as already noted, it embraces a number of large behavioral areas. It covers almost every major aspect of the entire socialization process beyond the age of three. There is no one experiment or even series of experiments that can check out the validity of such a theory *as a totality.* One must necessarily investigate it in manageable chunks. This means that when one assembles the pertinent empirical findings, they fall into clumps; the grand design of the original theory is not brightly visible. The empirical bits and pieces lack the glamour of the theory as an apparently unified structure. What we have found in our search is that parts of the Oedipal theory are directly or indirectly well affirmed and others distinctly contradicted. We take this to mean not that the overall theory is invalid, but that parts of it need serious restatement. Replacements are needed for some of the mini-theories that make up the full Oedipal string. Dropping certain of the mini-theories does not necessarily detract from the validity of others. There is no reason why the mini-theory about the boy's competition with father for mother cannot be true, while at the same time the mini-theory about how this competition is resolved is false. Or the mini-theory about the arousal of castration anxiety in the male as he competes with father may be true, while the mini-theory about his superego development may be fallacious. It is quite feasible to make new insertions at specific nodal points. We have, on the basis of our analysis, proposed three major Oedipal theory revisions: (1) to redefine the prime factor that resolves the Oedipal crisis as father friendliness rather than father threat, (2) to reformulate superego development in the boy as the acceptance of a morality system (less completely formed than Freud envisioned) more on the basis of warm than of punitive communication with father, and (3) to accept the fact that most of the formulations concerning the Oedipal process in the female are either uselessly vague or empirically contradicted and therefore need complete rethinking.

NOTES

1. (Freud 1923b, pp. 31–32): "At a very early age the little boy develops an object-cathexis for his mother, which originally related to the mother's breast . . . the boy deals with his father by identifying himself with him. For a time these two relationships proceed side by side, until the boy's sexual wishes in regard to his mother become more intense and his father is perceived as an obstacle to him; from this the Oedipus complex originates. His identification with his father then takes on a hostile colouring and changes into a wish to get rid of his father in order to take his place with his mother."

2. (Freud 1924, p. 176): "If the satisfaction of love in the field of the Oedipus complex is to cost the child his penis, a conflict is bound to arise between his narcissistic interest in that part of his body and the libidinal cathexis of his parental objects. In this

conflict the first of these forces normally triumphs: the child's ego turns away from the Oedipus complex."

3. (Freud 1924, pp. 176–177): "The authority of the father or the parents is introjected into the ego, and there it forms the nucleus of the super-ego, which takes over the severity of the father and perpetuates his prohibition against incest, and so secures the ego from the return of the libidinal object-cathexis. The libidinal trends belonging to the Oedipus complex are in part desexualized and sublimated . . . The whole process has . . . preserved the genital organ—has averted the danger of its loss . . . This process ushers in the latency period, which now interrupts the child's sexual development."

4. Mother is simultaneously a love object and an object of primary identification. This would also be true for the boy.

5. (Freud 1933, pp. 126–127): "Her self-love is mortified by the comparison with the boy's far superior equipment and in consequence she renounces her masturbatory satisfaction from her clitoris, repudiates her love for her mother and at the same time not infrequently represses a good part of her sexual trends in general. . . . Her love was directed to her *phallic* mother; with the discovery that her mother is castrated it becomes possible to drop her as an object, so that the motives for hostility, which have long been accumulating, gain the upper hand."

6. (Freud 1933, p. 128): "The wish with which the girl turns to her father is no doubt originally the wish for a penis which her mother has refused her and which she now expects from her father. The feminine situation is only established, however, if the wish for a penis is replaced by one for a baby, if, that is, a baby takes the place of a penis."

(Freud 1933, p. 129): "With the transference of the wish for a penis-baby on to the father, the girl has entered the situation of the Oedipus complex. Her hostility to her mother, which did not need to be freshly created, is now greatly intensified, for she becomes the girl's rival, who receives from her father everything that she desires from him."

7. (Freud 1933, p. 129): "In the absence of fear of castration the chief motive is lacking which leads boys to surmount the Oedipus complex. Girls remain in it for an indeterminate length of time; they demolish it late and, even so, incompletely. In these circumstances the formation of the super-ego must suffer; it cannot attain the strength and independence which give it its cultural significance . . . ."

8. Freud's view about the special importance for the female of fear of loss of love is expressed in the following (1933b, p. 121): "Fear of castration is naturally not the only motive for repression; to start with, it has no place in the psychology of women; they have, of course, a castration complex, but they cannot have any fear of castration. In its place, for the other sex, is found fear of the loss of love, obviously a continuation of the fear of the infant at the breast when it misses its mother."

9. Freud (1925, p. 253): "After a woman has become aware of the wound to her narcissism, she develops, like a scar, a sense of inferiority. When she has passed beyond her first attempts at explaining her lack of a penis as being a punishment personal to herself and has realized that that sexual character is a universal one, she begins to share the contempt felt by men for a sex which is the lesser in so important a respect, and, at least in holding that opinion, insists on being like a man."

(Freud, 1932, p. 125): "The girl's recognition of the fact of her being without a penis does not by any means imply that she submits to the fact easily. . . . she continues to hold on for a long time to the wish to get something like it herself and she believes in that possibility for improbably long years . . .

"One cannot very well doubt the importance of envy for the penis. . . . envy and jealousy play an even greater part in the mental life of women than of men."

10. Freud did ponder the possible role of an "identification of an affectionate sort" with father by the male child, but it is accurate to say that he regarded the defensive identification with the punitive father as the major factor in resolving the Oedipal dilemma.

11. In the case of the boy this closeness does not necessarily mean that he is identified with mother or feminine values. Kohlberg (1966) cited evidence that by age three or four, boys already demonstrate considerable preferential male sex-typing. Note, too, that by three or four, girls show preferential female sex-typing. The boy's closeness to mother does not mean that father's influence upon him is not important. Biller (1971) has summarized

a considerable literature indicating that the loss of father in the first few years of life may "have a particularly profound effect on masculine development" in the boy.

12. This result would appear to contradict the previously stated idea that children in the pre-Oedipal phase feel closer to mother than father.

13. Friedman also analyzed responses to certain elements in the pictures he regarded as having special symbolic erotic or Oedipal meaning. For example, he speculated that a toy shown in the father-surrogate picture would lend itself particularly well to equation with the "baby-penis" Freud theorized girls fantasy getting from the father. From this premise, he predicted that girls would exceed boys in the frequency with which they described the father in the picture as picking up, repairing, or buying a new toy for the child in the picture. This prediction was significantly supported. It was also successfully predicted that when girls reacted to the father-surrogate picture, they would more frequently than boys portray the father surrogate as climbing some stairs shown in that particular picture, because climbing stairs symbolically represents "the sexual act"—a wishful element of the girl's Oedipal fantasies about father. Still another successful prediction was made with regard to boys reacting to the mother-surrogate picture, depicting the child as moving *toward* the mother figure (that is, positively) with greater frequency than would the girls.

14. Bernick (1966) also found a difference in children between their verbally stated preferences for mother and father representations and their preferences as defined by their pupillary responses (increased pupil size) to pictures depicting mother and father figures. Bernick often observed the verbal and pupillary indicators going in opposite directions and concluded that the verbal response was usually shaped by social desirability factors. Such data suggest that the level of response is, indeed, a basic parameter in judging the meaningfulness of information concerned with children's like-dislike feelings toward parents. It should be added that the parental preferences of boys and girls, as defined by the pupillary index, did not change over the age range five to eighteen in a fashion consistent with Freud's Oedipal paradigm.

15. He also investigated a number of other hypotheses that are not directly pertinent to the issue under consideration.

16. Other measures concerned with masculinity-femininity but not specifically with father-mother identification were also applied. They are not considered pertinent to the issue under discussion.

17. Note that Kohlberg (1966) did *not* feel that this pattern of results contradicted Freud's views. He states (p. 145): "Freud's description of feminine heterosexual love as narcissistic-identificatory rather than anaclitic implies this . . . ."

18. Apropos of this general matter, it is an interesting bit of information that Kagan and Moss (1962) found that sex-role behavior displayed by boys as early as ages three to six was significantly predictive of adult sex-role interests. Since this age period falls roughly in what Freud defines as the Oedipal phase, this reinforces the theoretical possibility that sex role behavior in adulthood can be significantly shaped by experiences during the Oedipal period. However, it is also true that Kagan and Moss did not find an equivalent kind of relationship in a female group, and they were really not able to explain why such a difference should occur.

19. The material in this section is taken from *The Female Orgasm* (Fisher 1973).

20. An exception to this trend is reported by Sears et al. (1957). They observed that during doll play, five-year-old girls more consistently used the mother doll than boys of the same age used father dolls. They interpreted the difference as indicating that boys have greater difficulty than girls in arriving at identification with the same-sex parent.

21. Freud said that castration anxiety is minimal in the female because she does not have a penis and therefore has nothing to lose. That is, she cannot fear losing what she has already lost. It is apropos of this view that Block and Ventur (1963) indirectly evaluated the impact of having suffered a major kind of castration experience upon later castration anxiety. They studied twenty male amputees whom they compared with twenty males without amputations. They anticipated (p. 522): "Since amputees have already experienced symbolically what they once feared, castration, they should show significantly lower (castration anxiety)." The Blacky Test was used to measure castration anxiety and the results significantly supported the hypothesis. This empirical finding lends some sup-

port to Freud's assumption about the reason for diminished castration anxiety in the female.

22. A pertinent question that can be raised is whether one should expect to find such differences in persons who are beyond the Oedipal age phase. If there is satisfactory resolution of Oedipal tensions in the four to six age period, would not castration anxiety and fear of loss of love wane and disappear as significant forces in the psychological economy? It is difficult to answer this question on the basis of a definitive statement made by Freud. However, he did indicate in his clinical essays and elsewhere that resolution of the Oedipal dilemma was rarely perfect and that most persons continue to be faced throughout their life span with tensions and conflicts radiating from inadequate and incomplete Oedipal adaptations.

23. The review that follows is taken from *The Female Orgasm* (Fisher 1973).

24. In an earlier study Schwartz (1955) demonstrated that this measure was sensitive to conditions designed to increase castration concern.

25. Parenthetically, it should be noted that Leichty (1959–60) obtained negative results when she tested the hypothesis that castration anxiety would be lower in boys from families where father was absent than from those where father was present. She reasoned (p. 213): "The mother is said to be renounced as a love object because of threatened castration. If there is no father to act as a threat, the boy will not develop castration anxiety in relation to his Oedipal wishes." But castration anxiety, as measured by the Blacky Test (Blum 1949), did not differentiate father-absent from father-present boys.

26. It is apropos to note a study by Wilkinson and Cargill (1955), who asked male and female college students to read an Oedipal story with a strong theme of erotic involvement of a boy with his mother and another control story involving intimate contact of a boy with his brother. After reading each passage, the subject tried to recall as much of it as he could. The males had significantly greater difficulty in recalling the Oedipal story than the control one. The Oedipal theme presumably aroused a relatively high degree of anxiety that resulted in defensive repression. The females tended to have more difficulty with the story portraying contact between the boy and his brother.

27. An interesting series of studies by Stephens (1962), which examined the construct validity of the concept of castration anxiety in the context of attitudes toward menstruation in various cultures, came up with interesting and positive findings. These studies will be reviewed at a later point in this chapter because they are embedded in material pertinent to another topic.

28. Kamil (1970), starting with the notion that fear of snakes in males is a symbolic expression of castration anxiety, examined the effects of a snake desensitization therapy upon castration imagery in the Rorschach and Thematic Apperception tests. He found that those exposed to desensitization revealed significantly less castration concern in their Thematic Apperception stories than a control group. But there was no difference in castration anxiety as measured by the Rorschach.

29. This section is taken from *The Female Orgasm* (Fisher 1973).

30. Freud stated that women find it difficult to give up the masculine aspects of self because problems of bisexuality are particularly prominent for them. He felt their bisexual conflicts were heightened by the fact that they possess two sexual organs rather than one, like the man. That is, they have a vagina and a clitoris (analogous to a small penis). Freud conjectured that early development is dominated by the masculine clitoris and later developmental phases by what he considered to be the more feminine vagina.

31. Freud specified in detail the various ways in which women may adapt to their penis envy problems (Freud 1933, p. 285): ". . . she may follow one of three lines of development. The first leads to her turning back on sexuality altogether. The budding woman, frightened by the comparison of herself with boys, becomes dissatisfied with her clitoris and gives up her phallic activity and therewith her sexuality in general and a considerable part of her masculine proclivities in other fields. If she pursues the second line, she clings in obstinate self-assertion to her threatened masculinity; the hope of getting a penis sometime is cherished to an incredibly late age and becomes the aim of her life, whilst the phantasy of really being a man, in spite of everything, often dominates long periods of her life. This 'masculinity complex' may also result in a manifestly homosexual object choice. Only if her development follows the third, very circuitous path does she arrive at

the ultimate normal feminine attitude in which she takes her father as love-object, and thus arrives at the Oedipus complex in its feminine form."

32. The idea that women have an inferior body concept was given considerable impetus by the work of Witkin and his associates (Witkin et al. 1954). As is well known, they found that if persons are asked to adjust a luminous rod to the correct position of vertical in a darkened room, while experiencing conflicting cues (for example, a tilted luminous frame around the rod) that interfere with the perception of verticality, men consistently show greater skill at this task than do women. Witkin et al. theorized that men do better than women in this test because they are better able, in an unstructured spatial context, to use kinesthetic cues from their bodies to define the spatial coordinates. This, in turn, was interpreted as evidence that men have a "better" or more efficiently functional body concept than do women. Indeed, Witkin et al., in one of their publications (Witkin et al. 1954), speculated that Freud's theory about the female's chronic sense of body inferiority might help to explain why the female's spatial judgments were less accurate than the male's. This perspective regarding the "inferiority" of the woman's body experiences has grossly pervaded thinking in the behavioral sciences.

The truth is that Witkin's data indicated only that women were not as effective as men in using kinesthetic cues to make spatial judgments when they also were confronted with visual cues that could be used for the same purpose. When women were permitted to make spatial judgments entirely on the basis of kinesthetic input, they did as well as men. They were as capable as men of utilizing their bodies as a guiding judgmental framework.

33. Mention should be made at this point of a study by Lansky et al. (1961) that demonstrated that adolescent girls who are inhibited about responding to inkblot areas resembling female genitalia are unusually critical of their mothers, achievement-oriented, and low in guilt about being aggressive toward authority figures. The fact that a species of anxiety about a genital representation was tied in with an aggressive behavior syndrome has obvious penis envy implications.

34. There are a few other research efforts that might have been cited that are pertinent to the penis envy theme, but we chose not to either because they were so poorly controlled or minor in their implications (for example, Johnson 1966, Landy 1967, Levy 1940).

35. Freud did mention positive, affectionate factors that motivate the boy's identification with father, but his major emphasis was upon the hostile, threatening ones.

36. There is a fair amount of evidence that masculinity and degree of identification with father are positively correlated (Kohlberg 1966).

37. The methodologies employed in a good many of the studies of identification have avoided superficial response levels based on simply asking for "conscious" judgments. Projective and semiprojective measures have been widely applied. They diversely include producing stories about pictures, doll play behavior, and ascribing attributes to vaguely defined figures. It is important to call attention to this fact in order to head off objections that the studies cited are unfair insofar as they dealt with behavior at a "superficial" rather than more unconscious level.

38. Biller does emphasize the idea that not only must father be nurturant in order to facilitate his son's masculine development, he must also demonstrate that he is a competent person with a significant share of the power in the family.

39. Kohlberg (1966), after analyzing the literature concerned with loss or absence of the father from the family, concluded that such loss seemed to have relatively little impact on the development of masculine identity in the male child. He speculated on this basis that father *as an individual* may play a less important role in male identity development than suggested by psychoanalytic theory. However, Biller (1971), after a literature review, takes a quite obverse view about the disturbing effects of father loss on the son's development.

40. Freud actually said that the superego of the child was based on the superego of the parents. He said (1933c, p. 67): "As a rule parents and authorities analogous to them follow the percepts of their own super-egos in educating children. Whatever understanding their ego may have come to with their super-ego, they are severe and exacting in educating children. They have forgotten the difficulties of their own childhood and they are glad to be able now to identify themselves fully with their own parents who in the past laid such

severe restrictions upon them. Thus a child's super-ego is in fact constructed on the model not of its parents but of its parents' super-ego . . . ."

41. Freud did in various contexts acknowledge that other factors besides Oedipal ones (for example, toilet training experiences, cultural norms, pre-Oedipal learning from father) influenced superego formation; but he clearly gave major weight to the Oedipal experience. He also acknowledged that inputs from both parents gained representation in the superego (Sandler, 1960); but in the case of the male, his central emphasis was upon what is taken over from father. Further, it should be acknowledged that Freud explicitly theorized that the character of the superego is affected by the id ("the ego forms the superego out of the id"); and so the nature of id impulses pressing for expression may have a significant influence on the superego (for example, modifying its strictness and harshness).

42. Freud (1928) explicitly concluded that the severity of the boy's superego is a direct function of the degree to which "the father was hard, violent, and cruel."

43. Pertinent to this same issue is the fact that it is now well established that psychological forms of control on the part of parents rather than direct punitive ones such as spanking result in greater conscience development in children (Mackinnon 1938, Minkowich 1959, Grinder 1962, Aronfreed 1961).

44. Aronfreed (1968), after reviewing the literature bearing on this issue, concluded (p. 313): "In summary, then, a substantial positive attachment to nurturant socializing agents . . . appears to be required for the effectiveness of all of the forms of learning through which children acquire internalized control over their behavior. The nurturance of socializing agents is a crucial and general determinant of internalization . . . ."

45. There are data suggesting that the more the son identifies with his father, the higher are his scores on various moral standard measures (Kohlberg 1963). Also, Hoffman (1971) and Biller (1971) cite material indicating that boys who have grown up in father-absent families score lower on "moral indexes" than do boys who consistently had father available.

46. Freud (1915a) commented that early loss of one parent could have powerful effects on sexual identification and result in "permanent inversion." Anna Freud (Freud and Burlingham, 1943) observed phenomena among children who had suffered parent loss due to war that she felt substantially reaffirmed the impact of such loss on Oedipal mechanisms and ultimately on ability to cope with problems.

47. The Draw-A-Person Test involves the subject drawing a full-length picture of a person and then one of the opposite sex. The Cole Animal Test requests subjects to indicate what kind of animal they would most prefer and not prefer to be.

48. There was also a significant positive correlation between courtship intensity and intensity of feeling about mother (based on extremeness of like-dislike ratings of mother, irrespective of their direction).

49. Stephens did not consider the impact of the *post partum* taboo upon the female child.

50. Stephens sought to support his view (that severity of menstrual taboos reflects castration anxiety) by exploring the correlations between menstrual taboos and various phenomena he logically linked with castration anxiety (for example, sex anxiety, severity of punishment for masturbation, strictness of father's obedience demands). By and large, the data confirmed his expectations. Incidentally, he reported a significant curvilinear relationship between extensiveness of menstrual taboos and number of references to physical injury in folklore themes.

51. Exaggerated closeness to mother has been viewed not only as a cause of rivalry with father but also as a factor in depriving the male child of the opportunity to identify with father. This deprivation, in turn, is said to lead to a sense of inferiority about one's masculinity and to motivate a good deal of compensatory masculine aggression (for example, stealing, delinquency) (Bacon, Barry, Child 1963). One study (Ritz 1969) has specifically shown that boys who manifest unusually aggressive behavior (with "I am a man" connotations) in the latency period are unusually confused about sexual identity and experience intensified castration anxiety (as measured by projective tests).

52. Stephens' analysis of the effects of the intimacy between mother and male child resulting from the *post partum* sex taboo does potentially suffer from one serious logical

defect insofar as it is considered to be specifically pertinent to the Oedipal hypothesis. This relates to the fact that the *post partum* sex taboo period includes a time span prior to the Oedipal phase. Of course, one could argue that the intimacy established pre-Oedipally continues to exert a significant impact during the Oedipal period.

53. This is paradoxical when one recalls that a majority of Freud's early patients were women. One would have thought that he would have acquired considerably more information about psychological processes in women than in men. The discrepancy adds support to those who feel that many of Freud's major formulations were derived from introspection and self-analysis.

Chapter 5

The Origins of Homosexuality

Concepts of Male Homosexuality

SCATTERED throughout Freud's writings are attempts to understand why some people choose homosexual love objects. He considered homosexuality to be not a form of "degeneracy" but, rather, an expression of conflicts and polarities qualitatively similar to those faced by the average person. As was so often true, he found it easier to visualize a meaningful explanation for men than for women. Although he had a good deal to say about homosexuality, the disparate parts of his theoretical statements are sometimes difficult to assemble. Let us begin by scanning his ideas concerning how the male becomes homosexually oriented.

Freud consistently highlighted the importance of constitutional bisexuality as a factor in both male and female homosexuality. He presumed, on the basis of biological information available to him, that each sex retains basic anatomic elements of the other sex. He asserted that a certain amount of "anatomical hermaphroditism" is inherent in the structure of the normal male and female sex organs. For example, the female clitoris can be regarded as a miniature penis. Freud assumed that bisexual tendencies are also present in each person at a psychological level, and one repeatedly gets the impression that the strength of such tendencies (as derived from "constitutional" factors) played a salient part in his thinking about the etiology of homosexuality. He often appealed to the strength of "bisexual dispositions" of supposedly innate origin as a factor that could enter into whether an individual became homosexual. He also assumed there were inherent inclinations toward activity and passivity that mediate the possibility of homosexual development. When he came to analyze the psychological factors contributing to homosexuality, it was always within the context that they were limited by, and interacted with, innate predispositions.

Central to his psychological explanation of male homosexuality was the Oedipal dilemma. He theorized that homosexuals were people who could not adequately master the conflicts of the Oedipal period. More specifically, he stated that they form an unusually intense "erotic attachment" to mother, which was "favored by too much love from the mother herself" and furthered by the "retirement or absence of the father during the childhood period." He emphasized that they were inordinately under "feminine influence." Presumably, one result of this exaggerated closeness to mother is to intensify the boy's Oedipal conflict with father and thereby to maximize his castration anxiety. He is said to become unusually concerned about penis loss. Freud argued that this concern was one important reason why such an individual could not take a woman as a love object. The homosexual was depicted as not being able to tolerate the sight of the female genitals because they lack a penis and thus vividly conjure up an image of what could happen to him. Also, he was said to unconsciously equate any female love object with his forbidden, overly intense erotic relationship with mother, and therefore to re-experience in every heterosexual contact the guilt and forbidden quality associated with his Oedipal tie to mother.

Freud speculated that when the male who is to become homosexual discovers that he cannot safely love mother, he copes with the dilemma by means of a special adaptive maneuver.[1] He "identifies himself with her" and chooses to love others as he assumes she would. He defensively shifts so that he plays her role instead of relating to her as a love object. In fact, said Freud, the homosexual unconsciously takes himself as a model of the kind of object mother would prefer, and so he sexually favors males who resemble himself (narcissistic equivalents). The sex object he seeks, then, is himself, but transposed from a "mother loves me" paradigm. It is especially important that the sex object possess a penis whose presence helps him to quiet his castration fears. Freud underscored the over-evaluation the homosexual places upon the penis. In a sense the homosexual seeks as a love object a "girl with a penis." Incidentally, Freud was impressed with the fact that the homosexual remains true to his mother. He observed that the "homosexual . . . remains fixed in his unconscious on the memory picture of his mother" (Freud, 1910b, p. 62). Presumably by repressing his love for his mother, he "conserves" it in his unconscious and "remains faithful" to her. When in the role of the lover he apparently seeks other males, he really "runs away" from women who could "cause him to become disloyal to his mother."

A final variable that Freud referred to as playing a part in becoming homosexual was anal eroticism.[2] He considered that anal stimulation is often important in homosexual relationships, and proposed that experiences producing fixation during the anal period encourage homosexual trends. Anal fixation was said to increase interest in passive experiences ("The passive trend is fed from anal erotism"), especially those involving penetration of the anal opening. Anal eroticism was linked by Freud with both constitutional predisposition and parental behavior during the anal phase.

What are the essential testable propositions contained in Freud's theory of homosexuality? We would propose the following:

1. The homosexual male has had an unusually close and intense involvement with his mother. In his relationship with her, particularly during the Oedipal phase, there was an extreme erotic attachment. But the erotic attachment is subsequently replaced by a defensive identification with her. It is pertinent to these two points just cited that Freud also theorized that once a defensive identification with mother has been established, there is a tendency to chose male love objects that particularly resemble oneself. It should be possible to demonstrate that the love object of the male homosexual does in some way (in addition to sex) bear a special similarity to him.

2. The homosexual's relationship with father has been characterized by distance, coldness, and conflict. He perceives father, to an unusual degree, as a hostile competitor.

3. As the result of such intense conflict with father, he has been particularly fearful of attack and castration. His castration anxiety is highly augmented. Relatedly, he is very disturbed by the sight of female genitals, because they remind him of the possibility that a genital may exist that does not include the penis.

4. One would further hypothesize that the homosexual male is characterized by a more than average degree of anal fixation. Freud speculated that what he regarded as the enhanced anal sensitivity of the male homosexual was due partially to innate or constitutional factors. But one can logically deduce from his gen-

eral theoretical position about anal sensitivity that he would also trace it to fixating experiences during the anal phase.

PERCEPTION OF PARENTS

Numerous attempts have been made to clarify the question whether the male homosexual has had experiences with his parents analogous to those Freud theorized to be of etiological importance. Does the accumulated evidence indicate that the male homosexual had, as Freud stated, an unusually close and intimate involvement with his mother? Does it also indicate that his relationship with his father has been distant and antagonistic? The pertinent studies have been based largely on retrospective material. Typically, they involve asking the homosexual to describe his feelings and attitudes toward his parents and to recall how they treated him. The responses elicited are then compared with the responses of nonhomosexual males who have usually been matched for age, education, degree of psychopathology, and other control variables. One may roughly differentiate the studies in the literature into those based on interview and clinical appraisal versus those using a more controlled, questionnaire-type methodology.[3]

Let us first review those based on interview material. What we will do is to summarize the salient perceptions of mother and father that emerge in each study and also provide a brief description of the observational procedures involved. First we will consider those studies that are partially or wholly supportive of Freud's hypotheses and then we will take up the negative ones.

Terman and Miles (1936) compiled case-history evaluations of the most feminine of a larger sample of 125 homosexuals and concluded that the homosexual's mother is characterized by being affectionately demonstrative and emotional. They depicted the homosexual's father as unsympathetic, autocratic, brutal, and often absent from home.

Jonas (1944) interviewed fifty homosexual and fifty nonhomosexual psychiatric patients by means of a set series of questions with regard to their parents. He reported that a preponderant number of the homosexuals favored mother over father. They were inclined to display a suitor relationship to mother, to bring her gifts and treat her as a girlfriend.

West (1959–60) compared case history data (coded in terms of blind ratings) of fifty neurotic homosexual and fifty neurotic heterosexual males. He particularly focused on the "intensity" of the mother-son relationship and concluded that it was significantly more intense in the homosexuals than the controls. He also reported that the homosexual's relationship with his father was often rated as "unsatisfactory."

Edwards (1963) conducted a study that involved comparing sixteen homosexual prisoners with an equal number of nonhomosexual prisoners in terms of ratings of interview material systematically obtained from them. The interview material focused on recall of mothers' and fathers' behaviors. Mothers were found to be depicted by the homosexuals as "excessively controlling," but not particularly "nurturant" or "rewarding." Fathers were portrayed by the homosexual as especially low in "nurturance" and showing a trend toward "exercising more restraints" and "administering more punishment."

O'Connor (1964) examined parental attitudes, as revealed by case history material, in fifty homosexually inclined neurotics and fifty nonhomosexual neurotics. He found a definite trend for the homosexuals to be "more attached to their mothers than to father," and he generally considered that "overattachment to mother typified them." Further, he observed a clear trend for the homosexuals to have had a relatively poorer relationship with father than did the nonhomosexuals.

Whitener and Nikelly (1964) obtained evaluations by a "diagnostic team" (in a psychiatric setting) of a largely male group of thirty-nine homosexuals. Subjective reports from the patients, interview observations, and psychological test results provided the basis for evaluation. It was stated that the homosexual has a "considerably closer tie to his mother" than to father (p. 490). He was also depicted as having a father who was "more passive and rejecting."

Braaten and Darling (1965) studied thirty-four homosexuals and control samples of college students in a psychiatric setting. They used not only case history data but also several formal questionnaires and the Minnesota Multiphasic Personality Inventory. They discovered that the mothers of homosexuals had maintained a "close-binding-intimate" relationship with their sons. As for the fathers, they were described as typically "detached" and "indifferent."

Next come those studies, supportive of Freud, that are based on the use of systematic questionnaires or psychological tests.

An investigation by Thomas (1951) will be mentioned, although it did not directly deal with parental attitudes. It involved forty hospitalized homosexual men, some of whom had neuropsychiatric diagnoses, and a control group of nonhomosexuals hospitalized with physical symptoms. The differential psychiatric status of the two groups is obviously a serious defect in the design of the study. The Blacky Test (Blum 1949) was administered to the subjects and revealed, as predicted, that the homosexuals showed significantly more disturbance about an Oedipal theme (a picture of mother, son, father interaction) than did the controls. This difference would be logically expected in terms of Freud's assumption that the homosexual male is unusually attached to mother and antagonistic to father. Active and passive homosexuals did not differ in degree of Oedipal disturbance.

Ullman (1960) reported that when homosexual prisoners were compared with nonhomosexual prisoners in terms of their ratings of their mothers and fathers, there were clear differences. The homosexuals rated their mothers as giving *"too much"* love, affection, punishment, and "bawling out"; and portrayed their fathers as giving *"too little"* attention, love, affection, and "bawling out." While this result roughly conforms to Freud's formulation, the description of mother as giving "too much" and the father "too little" punishment does not fit.

Chang and Block (1960) asked twenty homosexuals and twenty nonhomosexual controls to describe (by choice of a series of adjectives) their ideal self, mother, father, and self. They demonstrated, as expected, that the homosexuals were relatively more "identified" with mother and "disidentified" with father.

McCord et al. (1961–1962) analyzed extensive rating and observational data accumulated on a sample of 650 lower-class boys. It was found that a small subgroup with "latent or overt" homosexual tendencies came from a "repressive, disordered familial atmosphere," and the choice of a "feminine, passive role seems to have been encouraged by their fathers' absence, brutality, and rejection" (p. 171). The mother was depicted rather vaguely as "authoritarian" and having high "sexual anxiety." In this instance the father pattern fits with Freud's theoretical notions, but that of the mother does not.

One of the most influential studies in the literature derives from the efforts of Bieber et al. (1962). They asked a sample of psychoanalysts to fill out an extensive questionnaire about a large sample of homosexual men they had treated. The analysts also provided information about a control group of nonhomosexual men in treatment. Many of the items in the questionnaires concerned relationships with parents. Bieber et al. obtained significant differences between the homosexuals and the controls, of the following character:

1. The mother of the homosexual was particularly likely to have a relationship of "extraordinary intimacy" with him. She "exerted a binding influence on her son through preferential treat-

ment and seductiveness on the one hand, and inhibiting, overcontrolling attitudes on the other. In many instances, the son was the most significant individual in her life and the husband was usually replaced by the son as her love object" (p. 47). Bieber et al. added that she "sexually overstimulated" her son "through seductiveness . . . or through sexual overstimulation implicit in overclose intimacy" (p. 79).

2. The father of the homosexual was typified by the poor quality of his ties with his son. Bieber et al. noted that "profound interpersonal disturbance is unremitting" in this father-son relation. They found significant trends for the father to be "detached, hostile, minimizing, and openly rejecting" (p. 114). They remarked that "the outstanding attitudes of homosexuals toward their fathers were hatred and fear" (p. 114). In a summary they stated (p. 316):

"By the time the (homosexual) son has reached the preadolescent period, he has suffered a diffuse personality disorder. Maternal over-anxiety about health and injury—demasculinizing attitudes, and interference with sexuality—interpenetrating with paternal rejection, hostility, and lack of support—produce an excessively fearful child, pathologically dependent upon his mother and beset by feelings of inadequacy, impotence, and self-contempt."

Paitich (1964) compared, among other groups, thirty-four male homosexuals (self- or court-referred to a psychiatric clinic) and a normal (nonpsychiatric) sample. The subjects were asked to respond to scaled questionnaires concerning their parents. No differences between homosexuals and nonhomosexuals could be detected with reference to feelings about mother. However, the homosexuals did manifest significantly less favorable attitudes toward father. Further, a combination of highly unfavorable attitudes toward *both* father and mother was found to typify the homosexuals. There are obvious problems in interpreting the findings, because the homosexuals and normal controls were not matched for psychiatric status.

Bene (1965b) administered a standardized, semiprojective test (Bene-Anthony Family Relations Test) to a sample of eighty-three nonpsychiatric male homosexuals and a normal heterosexual (married) sample. The test involved each subject sorting a series of statements in terms of whether their content "fit" various important figures in his childhood (who were literally depicted in the test situation by miniature cutout representations). Bene concluded after analysis of the data that (p. 805): " . . . the homosexuals expressed far more hostility and far less affection both going toward and coming from their fathers than did the married men; but . . . they also expressed somewhat more hostility and less affection with regard to their mothers." She specifically pointed out that there was no evidence that the homosexuals had been more strongly attached to mother than was true of the controls.

Evans (1969), too, set out to check the solidity of the earlier-reported findings by Bieber et al. (1962) concerning the close-binding mother and hostile father of the male homosexual. He asked forty-three male homosexuals, recruited on a volunteer basis, and an equal number of normal heterosexual subjects to answer a series of questions about their family background analogous to those in the Bieber et al. study. His results were strongly supportive of the report. He found that mothers of homosexuals were more often described as insisting on being the "center of the son's attention," making him a confidant, acting seductively toward him, and allying with him against father. Also, he determined that fathers of homosexuals were more often depicted as spending little time with the son, eliciting feelings of hate from him, making him feel that he might be physically harmed, and showing him little affection and respect.

Apperson and McAdoo, Jr. (1968) also focused on checking some of the findings previously reported by Bieber et al. (1962). They compared twenty-two homosexual (nonpsychiatric) males with normal heterosexual controls. Their measurement technique involved asking subjects to choose, from a list of various behaviors, twenty-five that would have "bothered" father and twenty-five that would have "bothered" mother when the subjects were children. The results were complex, but one clear finding was that the homosexuals perceived father as "cold and impatient" and apparently had a "poorer relationship" with him. It was stated that (p. 206): " . . . the homosexual subjects (showed) marked differences from controls in perceiving the father more as critical, impatient, and rejecting, and less as the socializing agent." In addition, the mother was portrayed by the homosexuals as "being less concerned with training the child in socialization" (p. 206). Apperson and McAdoo, Jr. indicated that she was "less restrictive" (or "overpermissive") as compared to the typical mother of the heterosexual controls, and they considered this to contradict the Bieber et al. (1962) findings concerning mothers of homosexuals.

Snortum et al. (1969) represent still another effort to evaluate the reliability of the original Bieber et al. (1962) data. They studied forty-six homosexual men being separated from military service because of homosexual behavior, and two normal nonhomosexual control samples. Subjects were asked to respond to an inventory that elicited reactions to clusters of items dealing with mother-son, father-son and other relationships. The results rather completely supported the Bieber et al. observations. The same "close-binding-intimate" mother emerged as characteristic of the homosexual's background. Similarly, the same "rejecting" and "detached" father was identified for the homosexual. Snortum et al. emphasized that their results helped to extend the generality of the Bieber et al. results, because their homosexual sample came from a lower socio-economic class than was true of the Bieber et al. sample (which consisted entirely of patients in psychoanalytic treatment).

Gigi (1970) sent a questionnaire to 2,400 male (nonpsychiatric) homosexuals and received back 887 that were usable. One of the tasks set by the questionnaire was to describe one's father and mother. A tabulation of the descriptions indicated that mother was predominantly depicted in positive terms. Thus, the adjectives "caring" and "affectionate" were the two most frequently used. Father, however, was predominantly depicted negatively. The two most frequently used adjectives were "domineering" and "unaffectionate." Gigi concluded (p. 58): "When the data regarding favored parent is coupled with the respondent's descriptions of both mother and father, we come close to Bieber's descriptions of the classical homosexual family pattern." It should be underscored here, too, that the absence of a control group in this study prevents straightforward acceptance of its apparent findings.

Pritt (1971) measured a number of variables in a male homosexual sample (twenty-one who had been in psychotherapy and twenty-one never in therapy) and also a normal heterosexual sample. Questionnaires and a standardized parental attitude scale were used to obtain data concerning perception of parents. Few differences were found between homosexuals and heterosexuals in attitudes toward mother, although significantly more of the former than the latter indicated they respected mother to a greater degree than father. As for father, the homosexuals registered significantly more dislike than the heterosexuals for him and also more often designated him as "unimportant."

Stephan (1973) secured responses to an extensive questionnaire dealing with many aspects of early upbringing from eighty-eight male (nonpsychiatric) homosexuals and a control normal heterosexual sample. The homosexuals described mother as more often dominant and "making family decisions" than did the heterosexuals, whereas the latter more often felt they were "respected" by mother. In relation to these findings, Stephan remarked (p. 510): "The data from the present sample concerning the relatively unaffectionate mother-son relationships among the homosexuals differ from the conclusions of Bieber et al. (1962)," who emphasized the "close, binding, intimate" relationships between mother and son. However, with respect to father, the results paralleled the Bieber et al. observations. Thus, the homosexuals more often perceived him as absent, rigid, fearful, insecure, not affectionate or likable, and not deserving of or giving respect.

Thompson et al. (1973) pretty well supported the Bieber et al. (1962) findings in the data they obtained by means of questionnaires and measures of masculinity-femininity from 127 male (nonpsychiatric) homosexuals and 123 normal male heterosexual controls. They reported with respect to the homosexuals as follows (p. 14): " . . . we have the picture of a modal seductive mother working against maleness in her son, and a weak and/or hostile and rejecting father who discourages modeling on himself and who is also very likely to be consistently undercut by his wife as his son moves through childhood."

Freund et al. (1974) looked at views of parents in a sample of 206 nonpsychiatric male homosexuals and a normal control sample of 193. The homosexuals reported in their questionnaire responses that they had had a significantly poorer relationship with father and greater closeness to mother than was true of the heterosexuals.

At least passing mention should be made of an unusual investigation by Silverman et al. (1973), which sought to demonstrate that a group of thirty-six male homosexuals would be more influenced by a subliminal stimulus with Oedipal, incestuous meaning than would nonhomosexual controls. Presumably this should be so because, as defined by Freudian theory, the homosexual is to an unusual extent conflicted by incestuous urges to attach himself to his mother. Under the impact of a subliminal visual stimulus (which consisted of the phrase "Fuck Mommy"), the homosexuals showed a defensive increase in homosexual sex-object preference. The heterosexuals did not register an analogous response.[4]

There are several studies in the literature that to a large extent have not matched Freud's concept of the male homosexual's experiences with his parents.

Greenstein (1966) systematically interviewed the parents of twenty-five delinquent boys from homes in which the father was largely absent, and fifty delinquent boys from father-present homes. The average age of the boys was about fifteen. It was found that homosexuality no more characterized one group than the other. Actually, only a small proportion of the boys in each category were found to be overt homosexuals. The interviews with the parents were used mainly to provide data for rating the ways in which warm versus cold fathers behaved vis-à-vis their sons. Contrary to expectation, there was a significant positive correlation between "father closeness" and the frequency of overt homosexuality in the boys. Freudian theory would have predicted just the opposite. The limited number of overt homosexuals involved in this study detracts seriously from its significance.

DeLuca (1967), after administering the Blacky Test, which evaluates responses to pictures depicting psychoanalytic themes, could find no real differences between a male (nonpsychiatric) sample of twenty homosexuals and a normal heterosexual group. It is particularly pertinent that no difference emerged for the Oedipal theme. This is not supportive of the previously mentioned Thomas (1951) report that male homosexuals display relatively great disturbance in coping with Oedipal material.

Kendrick and Clarke (1967) asked twenty male homosexuals seen in a psychiatric setting and twenty control heterosexuals (nonpsychiatric) to rate their parents, among other concepts, on a series of Osgood et al. (1957) Semantic Differential scales. There was really no difference between the two groups in their parental attitudes. One significant difference that did emerge indicated that the homosexuals perceived their mothers less favorably than did the heterosexuals. This study must be regarded with skepticism not only because the homosexuals and heterosexuals differed in psychiatric status but also because of the seriously biasing fact that of the twenty controls "twelve were acquaintances of the writer."

Lewis and Schoenfeldt (1973) administered a very detailed biographical questionnaire to forty male (nonpsychiatric) homosexuals and normal heterosexual controls. One level of analysis undertaken concerned parental behavior (for example, warmth, control). No significant differences could be detected between the homosexuals and controls in their views of mother or father.

Greenblatt (1966) compared thirty male homosexuals (nonpsychiatric) and thirty normal heterosexuals with respect to ratings of mother, father, and the nature of son-parent interactions. He found, contrary to his prediction, that the homosexuals did not perceive mother as close and binding and did not characterize father as negative and distant.

Siegelman (1974) completed an unusually sophisticated study concerned with variables that increase or decrease the apparent differences between homosexuals and heterosexuals in their perceptions of their parents. He compared a sample of 307 male (nonpsychiatric) homosexuals with a normal heterosexual one. A standardized parent-child attitudes scale, a biographical inventory, and other tests were administered to the subjects. Overall, the results indicated that homosexuals "described their fathers and mothers as more rejecting and less loving and that they were less close to their fathers than heterosexuals . . ." (p. 3). These results were congruent with the Bieber et al. (1962) portrayal of the homosexual's father, but not of his mother. However, to clarify the variables contributing to these results, Siegelman undertook another analysis in which he compared homosexuals and controls who had the lowest scores on an inventory measuring neuroticism. In these controlled samples he found that all differences in perception of parents disappeared. On the basis of such data he concluded that (p. 16) "The present findings, in fact, seriously question the existence of *any* association between family relations and homosexuality *vs.* heterosexuality." He suggested that all past studies that have discerned special attitudes toward parents in homosexuals have been biased by their failure to control carefully for differences in psychopathology between the homosexuals and comparison samples.

Obviously, one basic reason Siegelman obtained the pattern of results he did was because his original homosexual and heterosexual samples differed in degree of neuroticism, with the homosexuals higher in this respect. Siegelman explicitly declared that a similar difference probably existed in all previous studies that differentiated parental perception in homosexuals and heterosexuals. However, this was only an assumption on his part. In fact, quite a number of past studies that did find a characteristic familial pattern for homosexuals tried hard to control for psychopathology in their contrasting samples (for example, Chang and Block 1960, Braaten and Darling 1965).[5] Siegelman's argument is worth keeping in mind, but it cannot, as a single study, cancel out the impressive array of other studies that have been reviewed above.

What kind of a summary statement can we make concerning the material just reviewed? First, the reports concerning the male homosexual's view of his father are overwhelmingly supportive of Freud's hypothesis. With only a few exceptions, the male homosexual declares that father has been a negative influence in his life. He refers to him with such adjectives as cold, unfriendly, punishing, brutal, distant, detached. There is not a single even moderately well controlled study that we have been able to locate in which male homosexuals refer to father positively or affectionately. On the contrary, they consistently regard him as an antagonist. He easily fills the unusually intense, competitive, Oedipal role Freud ascribed to him.

The results with regard to the male homosexual's mother are

more debatable. Numerically, about half of the studies in the literature favor Freud's description of her as a person unusually close and intimately (seductively) involved with her son. The other half either portray her as not different from the mothers of heterosexual men or use such descriptive terms as "authoritarian," "dominant," "have high sex anxiety," or "hostile." After pondering these studies in detail, we would give the edge to those supportive of Freud. We would do so primarily on the basis of a bloc of investigations initiated by Bieber et al. (1962) and subsequently continued by others (Braaten and Darling 1965, Evans 1969, Snortum et al. 1969, Thompson et al. 1973, Gigi 1970). These studies, as outlined above, have analyzed the responses of homosexuals (who were not psychiatric patients) to a similar core of questions about mother and father. They have quite consistently obtained results that identify mother as close, binding, and intimate in her relationships with her homosexual son. The major challenge to these studies has come from Siegelman (1974), who considers that they have not controlled adequately for presumably greater psychopathology in the homosexuals as compared to heterosexual controls. However, as already pointed out, this criticism can be countered by the fact that, first of all, a number of the studies have used, as subjects, homosexuals who were adjusting very adequately and felt no need for psychiatric treatment. Secondly, Braaten and Darling (1965) obtained results similar to those of Bieber et al. (1962), even when they psychometrically equated psychological disturbance in their homosexual and heterosexual samples by means of the Minnesota Multiphasic Personality Inventory.

IDENTIFICATION WITH MOTHER

Does the male homosexual identity with mother, as Freud suggested? Presumably, when the male child who is to become a homosexual finds it too threatening, for various reasons (for example, castration anxiety), to take mother and other women as heterosexual objects, he defensively shifts and identifies with mother. In this role he then takes male love objects. The empirical evidence concerning this hypothesis is slim.

In an early study by Chang and Block (1960), there did seem to be confirmation of the hypothesis. Twenty male homosexuals who were not psychiatric patients were compared with normal heterosexual controls in terms of the adjectives they chose to describe a series of concepts: "ideal self," "mother," "father," and "self." It was found that the homosexual perceived himself as more similar to his mother than to his father.

However, in a later study Thompson et al. (1973) did not find such an identification pattern. They asked 127 male homosexuals who were not psychiatric patients, and also normal heterosexual controls, to rate a series of concepts that included "my mother," "my father," and "myself." The pattern of ratings indicated that the homosexuals were not more identified with mother than the controls.

Matters become even more confusing when we consider two studies that dealt with the responses of homosexual men when they were asked directly whether they were more like mother than father. Thus, Bieber et al. (1962), in their earlier-described study, reported, at a significant level, a sense of greater resemblance to mother than father in a male homosexual sample (as compared to controls). But Bene (1965b) could find no such difference between eighty-three male (nonpsychiatric) homosexuals and an equal number of normal heterosexuals.

Another approach to the identification issue is possible in terms of the dimension of masculinity-femininity. One could reason that the greater an individual's equation of self with mother, the more feminine would be his orientation. If one accepts this debatable perspective, the evidence is overwhelmingly in favor of the male homosexual being mother-identified. Numerous studies, involving diverse homosexual samples, have found that homosexuals respond in a more feminine fashion than do controls to formal measures of masculinity-femininity (Thompson et al. 1973, Oliver and Mosher 1968, Doidge and Holtzman 1960, Siegelman 1972, Dean and Richardson 1964, Greenblatt 1966, Singer 1970, Grygier 1958, Carstairs and Grygier 1957, Aaronson and Grumpelt 1961). The Masculinity-Femininity scale of the Minnesota Multiphasic Personality Inventory has been the formal measure most frequently employed. There have been a few studies (for example, Lewis and Schoenfeldt 1973) that have not shown the male homosexual to be more feminine than heterosexuals, but they are far outweighed by others that have been able to demonstrate this point.

We would hesitate to draw any definite conclusions from the material we have just presented concerning the identification process. One of the interpretative problems relates simply to the fact that our technology for measuring identification is rather weak. There is little agreement in the literature concerning the "best way" to measure identification patterns. In a way it is appealing to accept the proposition that a man's degree of femininity can be taken as an index of how much he has adopted mother as his model. In these terms, the experimental literature could be interpreted as strongly supportive of Freud's hypothesis. However, there are complicating issues which make it necessary to maintain a cautious attitude. It is conceivable that the male homosexual attains a more feminine score than the heterosexual control on formal measures of masculinity-femininity because his father was more feminine than the heterosexual's father. The homosexual could possibly sense and identify with the stronger feminine elements in his father. His femininity would derive, then, from his father rather than his mother. Of course, one could counter this argument by pointing to the fact, as demonstrated above, that male homosexuals do tend to feel closer to mother than father and to be more intimately "joined" to her. This would suggest that it is more logical to regard his femininity as derived from his interactions with her than with father. We will conclude our discussion of the identification issue by stating that it is too soon to offer a final decision. We must acknowledge, though, that the data relating to masculinity-femininity are quite supportive of Freud.

CASTRATION ANXIETY AND FEAR OF FEMALE GENITALS

The findings are sparse bearing on Freud's assumption that the homosexual male avoids female love objects not only because they incite castration anxiety in relation to their Oedipal meaning but also because their genitals represent a threatening image of the potential for castration.

Schwartz (1956) attempted a direct test of this proposition by administering the Thematic Apperception Test to twenty male homosexuals who were college students without apparent psychopathology and to twenty normal heterosexual controls. An analysis was made of the stories obtained in terms of the number of references to castration themes (for example, loss of body parts, personal inadequacy). It was found, as predicted, that the homosexuals obtained significantly higher castration scores than the heterosexuals.

Pertinent information has also come from the Bieber et al. (1962) investigation in which psychoanalysts treating male homosexuals were asked to provide detailed information concerning their attitudes and behavior. This information was compared with analysts' reports about heterosexual males in treatment. While the evidence was negative with regard to the homosexuals being more concerned that their fathers would hurt (castrate them), there were significant trends for them to be more anxious about the possibility of being physically hurt. Bieber et al. note (p. 204): "Excessive fear of physical injury in childhood was noted among three quarters of the (homosexual) patients, and most avoided fights. An elevated number of homosexuals considered themselves to have been "frail" during childhood (despite no indications of an unusual amount of actual physical illness in this group). Bieber et al. also reported a significant tendency for the homosexuals to exceed the heterosexuals in their "fear/aversion" toward female genitalia. Interestingly, there was a significant positive link in both the homosexual and heterosexual samples between fearing injury to one's own genitals and feeling aversion to female genitals. The sense of body fragility and concern about getting hurt that Bieber et al. observed to characterize the homosexual male as he is growing up have also been reported by others (for example, Evans 1969, Snortum et al. 1969, Saghir and Robins 1971). One can reasonably interpret such findings as paralleling the dimension of castration anxiety. They constitute a fairly firm bloc of evidence on this point.

More on the negative side, it should be indicated that two investigators (Thomas, 1951; DeLuca, 1967) have not been able to demonstrate greater castration anxiety in male homosexuals than heterosexual controls in terms of their responses to a castration theme picture in the Blacky Test (Blum, 1949).

Manosevitz (1970) indicated that he could not verify the fear of female genitalia said by Bieber et al. to typify the male homosexual. He compared twenty-eight male (nonpsychiatric) homosexuals with normal male heterosexual controls in their responses to direct questions about their reactions to the sight of female genitalia. He found that only one of the homosexuals stated that he experienced anxiety with respect to such genitalia.

In another study pertinent to this matter, Gibbins and Walters (1960) exposed sixteen male homosexuals (who had been arrested for homosexual behavior but were not psychiatric patients) to a series of paired representations (varying in degree of disguise or explicit structure) of male and female genitalia and asked them to decide for each pair which they found most attractive. A normal heterosexual and an alcoholic heterosexual sample responded to the same stimuli. The results indicated that the homosexuals preferred the male representations to a significantly greater degree than did the normal heterosexuals. But the difference between the homosexuals and alcoholics was not significant. Incidentally, the alcoholics significantly exceeded the normal heterosexuals in their preference for the male representations. Gibbins and Walters had assumed that preference for the male versus female representations would indicate relative preference for male versus female objects, and they interpreted the results as giving some support to the idea that alcoholics have a latent tendency toward homosexuality. One can also regard the task that was set for the subjects as a measure of how negatively they reacted to the sight of male versus female genitalia, and with this perspective one could say that the homosexuals were more negative toward the female genitalia than the normal heterosexuals. Why no difference emerged when homosexuals were compared with alcoholics is unclear, unless one wishes to accept the idea that alcoholics have strong latent homosexual inclinations (as has been suggested by a number of psychoanalysts).

We are once again confronted with mixed positive and negative findings. A definite conclusion about whether male homosexuals have an unusual amount of castration anxiety and fear of female genitalia would go beyond the facts. However, we feel that there is a trend favoring Freud's views. The most substantial part of this trend are the several studies that have depicted the homosexual as being unusually concerned about getting hurt as he is growing up. A number of observers have detected in the young potential homosexual an exaggerated sense of fragility and of needing to avoid the possibility of physical trauma.

OTHER HYPOTHESES

It will be recalled that several other hypotheses were derived for testing from Freud's statements about male homosexuality: namely, those relating to choice of a narcissistic love object and the influence of anal eroticism. A review of the existing literature has convinced us that the data do not yet exist for a reasonable evaluation of such hypotheses. There are a few scattered pertinent findings. For example, Exner (1969) did show that narcissism was significantly elevated, as defined by Rorschach responses, in homosexuals. It is also true that Thomas (1951) found tendencies for male homosexuals to be more disturbed by anal themes in the Blacky Test (Blum 1949) than heterosexual controls. At the same time, DeLuca (1967) and Lindner (1953) failed to observe such tendencies in their comparison of homosexuals and controls. Obviously these meager findings do not begin to offer reasonable grounds for judgment.

OVERVIEW

Freud's ideas about male homosexuality have been only partially tested. But it is true that the available empirical data support his core concept about the kind of parents who are likely to shape a homosexual son. Just as he theorized, the father of the homosexual is likely to be an unfriendly, threatening person who would presumably be an unusually intense Oedipal competitor. Some additional affirmation for this concept of father as threatening also comes from studies, cited above, that indicate the male homosexual has an elevated concern, while he is growing up, about getting hurt. This concern could be regarded as an indicator of castration anxiety, which in the Freudian framework would be primarily traced to relationships with father. There is also moderate support for the view that the mother of the homosexual is particularly close, intimate, and restrictive in her relationship with her son. She fits well the stereotype of the seductive mother. It is pertinent to this issue that some evidence has been uncovered that the male homosexual identifies (defensively) with mother, or at least with her feminine values.

We do not have adequate empirical readings on other aspects of Freud's theory: namely, that the homosexual chooses narcissistic love objects and that he is characterized by strong anal eroticism. We can only recommend that future investigations of the male homosexual focus on these issues.

Theoretical Constructs Concerning Female Homosexuality

Freud (1920b, 1922b) regarded constitutional bisexual factors to be just as important in the etiology of female homosexuality as he did in the instance of male homosexuality. But he was equally vague about the nature of these constitutional factors.

With reference to developmental influences in the shaping of the female homosexual, Freud sketched a theory that is in some ways a mirror image of the one he presented for the male homosexual. In essence, he offered the following picture, which begins with the Oedipal dilemma he specified had to be faced by all girls. He indicated that around the time of the Oedipal period, after years of close attachment to mother, the girl becomes disillusioned with and angry at her for various reasons. One reason he particularly emphasized was her discovery that she lacks a penis, which she blames on mother. He portrayed her as feeling deeply disappointed over this lack and perceiving herself as inferior to the male. By way of reparation she supposedly turns to father as a love object and fantasies that she will regain her lost phallus by bearing him a child who is symbolically a penis equivalent. Freud felt that the potential homosexual girl was one who encountered an unusual amount of frustration and disappointment at the point when she turned to father as a love object. He indicated that such disappointment caused her defensively to identify with him and thereby to return (regressively) to taking mother (and other feminine figures) as love objects. His view of this process was spelled out in his paper (1920b) titled "The Psychogenesis of A Case of Homosexuality in A Woman." He described a young women he had treated who was absorbed in an homosexual attachment to a woman older than herself. He attributed her homosexual orientation to the fact that around the time of puberty, when she was "just experiencing the revival of the infantile Oedipus-complex," her mother gave birth to a child which directly contradicted her own unconscious fantasies about presenting father with a child (". . . it was not *she* who bore the child, but her unconsciously hated rival, her mother"). He theorized that she was so deeply traumatized by this experience that she "turned away" from father and "from men altogether," and defensively substituted mother as a love object. Freud states (p. 158), "She changed into a man and took her mother in place of her father as the object of her love." He remarks that this is a regressive process in which the girl returns to a previous relationship, namely, her attachment to mother.[6] Taking mother as a love-object appeared to him also as a way for the homosexual girl to overcompensate for her current hostility toward mother and to offer her reassurance that she intended no competition for the available male love objects. The presumed defensive identification of the female homosexual with father, as the result of her disappointments with him, parallels the defensive identification with mother that Freud attributed to the male homosexual. It is important to add that he felt a contributing factor to the homosexuality of the girl he described in his essay on female homosexuality was a long persistent "masculinity complex" based on a "pronounced envy of the penis." Actually, Freud suggested in various ways that attitudes toward the penis are significant in the female homosexual orientation. He indicated that the penis has negative implications to the female homosexual in terms of the envy it stirs. He also indicated that it was threatening to her insofar as it is an instrument that can produce pregnancy, which in turn can result in body damage and mutilation (Freud 1920b).[7]

What are the potentially testable propositions that can be extracted from Freud's statements about the female homosexual?

1. One salient proposition would be that she had a frustrating or disturbing relationship with her father. This would be expected if Freud were correct in assuming that her retreat from heterosexuality and her defensive identification with father derive from disappointing interactions with him. But, paradoxically, one should also

find her to be more *identified* with father than are heterosexual women.

2. It is not readily apparent what traits or qualities Freud would ascribe to the mother of the female homosexual. He implies a special quality in the pre-Oedipal relationship between mother and her daughter (who is to become homosexual) that results in the daughter being susceptible to regressing to that relationship later in life when frustrations are encountered. The nature of the special quality cannot be specified. One can only hypothesize that the homosexual woman would have had an atypical attachment to her mother that encouraged dependency on her and perhaps also encouraged a less than average tolerance for threat or disappointment. Unfortunately, such a vaguely stated hypothesis does not provide much of an operational target upon which to focus.

3. Another possible derivative from Freud's statements relates to feelings about the genitals. Parallel with his idea that the male homosexual fears the sight of the "castrated" female genital, one would expect the female homosexual, because of her presumed penis envy, to be threatened by the sight of the male genital.

ATTITUDES TOWARD PARENTS

Much less research has been devoted to the female than the male homosexual. However, there is a consistent train of findings supportive of Freud's view that the father of the female homosexual dealt with her in a frustrating, disappointing fashion. Note the descriptive phrases used in the following studies to characterize the female homosexual's father.

Bene (1965a) compared thirty-seven lesbians who were not psychiatric patients with an equal number of normal female heterosexuals in their responses to the Bene-Anthony Family Relations Test ("a device that facilitates the recollection of childhood family feelings"). She found (p. 821) "The lesbians were more often hostile toward and afraid of their fathers than were the married women and they felt more often that their fathers were weak and incompetent."

Kaye et al. (1967) investigated differences between female homosexual and female nonhomosexual samples of twenty-four each. The women in both samples were in psychoanalytic treatment and their therapists were asked to fill out extensive questionnaires concerning their behavior and attitudes. The following was concluded concerning the fathers of the female homosexuals (p. 634): "They tend to be puritanical, exploitive, and feared by their daughters, although the fear is not that of being physically abused. He is overly possessive, and is subtly interested in his daughter physically, yet tends to discourage her development as an adult."

Kenyon (1968a,b) sent 150 questionnaires dealing with family history and related variables to members of several lesbian organizations and received back 123. These responses were compared to those of normal heterosexual women. There was a significant trend for more lesbians than heterosexuals to state they had had poor relationships with father.

Kremer and Rifkin (1969) conducted an impressionistic survey of twenty-five young lesbians in a school who were referred for psychiatric evaluation. There was no control group. It was concluded that the fathers of the lesbians were (p. 95) "hostile, exploitative, detached, and absent."

In an unusually carefully designed study, Thompson et al. (1973) contrasted eighty-four female (nonpsychiatric) homosexuals with an equal number of normal female heterosexuals. Among various measures administered was a questionnaire that dealt with parent-child interactions. The homosexuals were nonaccepting of father significantly more often than the heterosexuals. But, paradoxically, they significantly more often felt that father "openly preferred" them to mother. Overall, Thompson et al. considered that the female homosexuals had had more negative relations with their fathers in childhood than was true of the female controls.

Loney (1973) studied eleven (nonpsychiatric) lesbians and eleven normal female heterosexuals. A projective questionnaire was used to elicit information about attitudes toward parents and other socialization variables. Significant trends were observed for the lesbians to describe father as (p. 348) "neglecting, moody, disappointing, unloving, mean, selfish, and untrustworthy."

Without exception, these studies indicate that the female homosexual thinks of her father as an unfriendly, unpleasant person who had little to offer by way of a relationship. It is just such lack of reward in relating to father that Freud considered fundamental in turning the potential female homosexual away from male love objects.

No dependable information could be assembled from the literature that would permit testing the hypothesis that the female homosexual exceeds the heterosexual woman in her degree of identification with her father.

As indicated earlier, it is difficult to derive from Freud's statements the pattern of interaction he envisioned the female homosexual having with her mother. But this turns out not to be of immediate consequence when one reviews the findings in the empirical literature concerning the attitudes of female homosexuals toward their mothers. One can only say that these findings are highly inconsistent. The female homosexual's mother is variously characterized as close, distant, friendly, unfriendly—and, in some instances, not at all different from the mothers of heterosexual women (for example, Bene 1965a, Kaye et al. 1967, Thompson et al. 1973, Loney 1973). At this point the probability seems low that it will be possible to isolate a typical relationship pattern for the homosexual woman and her mother.

ANXIETY ABOUT THE PENIS

Is there any evidence that the female homosexual, because of her presumed penis envy problem, feels unusually disturbed when she encounters the penis? Only two studies could be found that seemed pertinent to this question, but in both instances the results were congruent with Freud's views. Kaye et al. (1967) obtained a variety of information (by means of questionnaire) from psychoanalysts concerning twenty-four female homosexuals and also nonhomosexual women they were treating. There was a significant trend for the homosexuals to be described as having more "fear and/or aversion to the penis" than the nonhomosexuals. Goldberg and Milstein (1965) reported that ten normal women with "High-Latent" homosexual tendencies (defined by the Minnesota Multiphasic Personality Inventory) showed, as predicted, more disturbance in response to a picture of a nude male with genitals exposed than did normal women classified as "Low-Latent" with respect to homosexuality.[8] Of course, it will take more than these two studies to permit a really confident conclusion concerning this hypothesis.

OVERVIEW

A major aspect of Freud's formulation concerning female homosexuality did receive empirical reinforcement. As he theorized, the female homosexual seems to have the kind of negative and disappointing relationship with her father that could turn her away from him and other male love objects. We do not, however, have any dependable information about whether she identifies with father in the defensive fashion Freud visualized. We have also discovered that not only was Freud vague about the nature of the interaction pattern between the homosexual woman and her mother, but also that the empirical studies of this matter have been unable to demonstrate any consistent results. Finally, it should be noted that there are hints in the literature that the homosexual woman may have, as Freud suggested, an unusual amount of anxiety about the penis.

It is difficult to make a summary statement about the extent to which the scientific literature is in agreement with Freud's views about female homosexuality. This difficulty stems from such factors as Freud's relatively vague description of the etiology of homosexuality in women and the real sparseness of empirical studies in this area. Also, one does not know how to weigh the significance of affirming results in specific areas. To what degree is the overall theory supported by the finding that homosexual women do, as anticipated by the theory, perceive father as a frustrating and unpleasant person or experience an unusual amount of anxiety when confronted by the penis? We are inclined to take the position that the findings that have emerged are more supportive of, than opposed to, Freud's formulation. We would also point out that there is a cumulative impact in the fact that the empirical findings for both male and female homosexuals tend to be in accord with Freud.

NOTES

1. In commenting on this maneuver, Fenichel (1945) states (p. 331): "Following the loss of an object or disappointment in an object, everyone tends to regress from the level of object love to that of identification; he becomes the object which he cannot possess. Thus, the homosexual individual identifies himself with the object, after having been disappointed by its genitals . . . The homosexual man identifies himself with his frustrating mother in one particular respect: like her, he loves men." He notes further (p. 332): "Having identified himself with his mother, he behaves as he previously had wished his mother to behave toward him. He chooses as love objects young men or boys who, for him, are similar to himself, and he loves them and treats them with the tenderness he had desired from his mother."

2. Freud acknowledged that situational factors (for example, being confined in prison without women) could provoke homosexual behavior. He also detailed other events (such as a traumatic perception of parental intercourse or accidental homosexual seduction by another individual) that could have an impact that encouraged a homosexual pattern.

Note the following particularly good summary that Freud (1922b, pp. 230–231) offered concerning the core components of his homosexuality formulation: "The typical process . . . is that a few years after the termination of puberty, a young man, who until this time has been strongly fixated to his mother, changes his attitude; he identifies himself with his mother, and looks about for love objects in whom he can re-discover himself, and whom he might love as his mother loved him. . . . We have come to know of various factors contributing to this result . . . First, there is the fixation on the mother, which makes it difficult to pass on to another woman. Identification with the mother is an outcome of this attachment, and at the same time . . . it enables the son to keep true to her . . . Then there is the inclination toward a narcissistic object-choice . . . Behind this latter factor lies concealed another . . . the high value set upon the male organ and the inability to tolerate its absence in a love-object . . . another powerful motive urging toward homosexual object-choice (is) regard for the father or fear of him; for the renunciation of women means that all rivalry with him . . . is avoided."

3. Only those clinical studies will be considered in which some attempt was made to control for observer bias and to quantify observations.

4. Two clinically oriented studies that used quantitative analyses (Brown 1963, Miller 1958) have also stated that the male homosexual has a close, binding relationship with mother and a hostile, negative one with father. However, neither made use of control groups, and so the results are essentially uninterpretable.

5. Braaten and Darling (1965) found differences in parental attitudes between homosexuals and heterosexuals (several in the same direction as Bieber et al. [1962] reported), despite the fact that the two samples were equated for psychopathology in terms of Minnesota Multiphasic Personality Inventory scores. Thompson et al. (1971) demonstrated that it is possible to recruit a nonpsychiatric sample of homosexuals who do not differ from heterosexual controls in amount of psychopathology (as defined by a formal measure of adjustment).

6. Freud (1933c) commented that the interactions between homosexual men often seem to reproduce the relations between mother and baby.

7. Fenichel (1945), by way of summary of the Freudian position concerning the etiology of female homosexuality, pinpoints the following: "(a) the repulsion from heterosexuality originated in the castration complex, and (b) the attraction through early fixations on the mother" (p. 338).

8. A study by Armon (1960) should be mentioned that is tangential to the issue under discussion. She scored Rorschach protocols of homosexual and heterosexual women to evaluate attitudes toward phallic symbols and male representations. Her results were complex and difficult to interpret. But there were a few significant differences between the groups, such that the homosexuals were more "castrating" in their remarks about male representations.

Chapter 6

Paranoia: Defensive Projection of Homosexual Impulses

FREUD can certainly not be accused of ambiguity in his conception of how paranoid delusions evolve. He straightforwardly defined such delusions as defensive attempts to deny and contain unacceptable homosexual impulses. Surprisingly, too, he assumed that the same explanation for paranoid symptoms can be offered for both sexes.

As is well known, his ideas concerning paranoia crystallized around the published account of a German jurist, Daniel Paul Schreber, who described his experiences during a schizophrenic breakdown. Schreber revealed in minute detail his feelings and delusions, which were often strongly paranoid. One of the ideas prominent in his delusional system was that a psychiatrist (Dr. Flechsig), who had earlier treated him and helped him to recover from a severe neurotic episode in which hypochondriacal feelings predominated, had launched a campaign of persecution against him. He accused this psychiatrist of being a "soulmurderer" who intended by devious means to transform him into a woman. Freud (1911a) quotes Schreber's version of this persecution as follows (p. 19): " 'In this way a conspiracy against me was brought to a head . . . Its object was to contrive that, when once my nervous complaint had been recognized as incurable or assumed to be so, I should be handed over to a certain person in a particular manner: my soul was to be delivered up to him; but my body . . . was to be transformed into a female body . . . with a view to sexual abuse.' " Freud pointed out that ideas of being emasculated had appeared in Schreber's fantasies before his acute psychosis. One morning, prior to the break (p. 13), "in a state between sleeping and waking, the idea occurred to him 'that after all it really must be very nice to be a woman submitting to the act of copulation.' " Freud concluded, after a detailed analysis of Schreber's psychotic fantasies and the available details concerning his family background, that the psychosis had been precipitated by an upsurge of homosexual feelings directed to his psychiatrist. Further, he interpreted Schreber's presumed homosexual attraction to his psychiatrist as a "transference" of feelings he had long unconsciously entertained toward his father.[1] He concluded that in essence Schreber's "illness" represented a "means of warding off a homosexual wishful phantasy" (p. 59).

Freud stated that in his review of other cases of paranoia involving "both men and women, and varied in race, occupations, and social standing . . . the very centre of the conflict which underlay the disease" was a "homosexual wish" (p. 59).[2] He considered that the male paranoid was an individual who had had a disturbed relationship with his father (growing out of the Oedipal confrontation and fear of castration), which fixated him at a level where he was strongly attracted to a role involving sexual submission to father. That is, the paranoid was fearful of the consequences of relating sexually to a woman and defensively retreated to father as a love object. Presumably, his sexual attraction to father was unacceptable and he strongly repressed it. But later circumstances, such as a particularly frustrating experience with a heterosexual love object or serious blows to self-esteem,[3] could cause regression to the fantasied homosexual relationship with father[4]—which has such alarming connotations that it must be denied, even to the extreme of a psychotic reconstruction of the world. Analogously, the paranoid woman was depicted by Freud as having had a pattern of experiences that made heterosexual object-choice difficult and fostered a susceptibility to homosexual attachment to mother, which had to be repressed and controlled and, ultimately, to be defensively translated into a paranoid system. Freud theorized that the paranoid delusion was a translation of an "I love" fantasy into an "I hate" version. His specific formulation concerning this matter can be best conveyed in his own words (p. 63):

"... it is a remarkable fact that the familiar principal forms of paranoia can all be represented as contradictions of the single proposition: 'I (a man) *love him*[5] (a man)'. . . .

"The proposition 'I (a man) love him' is contradicted by:

"(a) Delusions of *persecution;* for they loudly assert

" 'I do not *love* him—I *hate* him.' This contradiction . . . cannot . . . become conscious to a paranoic in this form. The mechanism of symptom-formation in paranoia requires that internal perceptions—feelings—shall be replaced by external perceptions. Consequently, the proposition 'I hate him' becomes transformed by *projection* into another one: *'He hates* (persecutes) *me,* which will justify me in hating him.' "[6]

Freud was definite in asserting that the persecutor in the paranoid's delusional system is a concealed representation of a homosexual love object. Therefore, it would be expected that the persecutor would typically be of the same sex as the persecuted one. Freud declared (1915a, p. 265): ". . . patients suffering from paranoia *are struggling* against an intensification of their homosexual trends. And . . . the persecutor is at bottom someone whom the patient loves or has loved in the past. A synthesis of the two propositions would lead us to the necessary conclusion that the persecutor must be of the same sex as the person persecuted."

In trying to specify the unique conditions that result in the defense against homosexual impulses taking a paranoid form, Freud suggested the existence of a heightened narcissistic propensity. He conjectured that the paranoid person has been particularly fixated at the narcissistic stage of development. He stated (p. 72):

"In paranoia the clinical evidence goes to show that the libido . . . is put to a special use . . . the majority of cases of paranoia exhibit traces of megalomania . . . From this it may be concluded that in paranoia the liberated libido becomes attached to the ego, and is used for the aggrandizement of the ego. A return is then made to the stage of narcissism . . . in which a person's only sexual object is his own ego. On the basis of this clinical evidence we can suppose that paranoics have brought along with them a *fixation at the stage of narcissism . . .*"

There are a variety of tangential hypotheses that one might derive for testing from Freud's concepts about paranoia. But, in actuality, only a few emerge that meaningfully reflect his theorizing.[7]

1. Foremost is the simple statement that the paranoid delusion represents a defensive attempt to control and repress unacceptable homosexual wishes by projecting them.[8]

2. At a more secondary level, it would be expected, as Freud

specifically suggested, that the persecutor in the paranoid's delusion would (in terms of its homosexual equation) be of the same sex as the paranoid.[9]

Clinical Studies

The attempts by investigators to check out Freud's formulations about paranoia range from impressionistic clinical surveys to carefully controlled experiments. The clinical surveys are interesting to trace. They begin with Freud's own analysis (1915a) of a case of a paranoid woman that seemed initially to run counter to his theory, but which he felt upon further study did support his views. Various psychoanalysts in the same period published case descriptions of paranoids that they considered to be congruent with Freud's repressed-homosexuality paradigm.

However, beginning in the 1930s and 1940s, one finds the first attempts to appraise the paradigm with some semblance of objectivity. Concern began to appear about such variables as observer bias and proper control groups. One of the major difficulties that immediately confronted studies that were undertaken was how to define whether homosexual conflict was present in a paranoid patient. Various approaches to this issue were adopted. Some observers gave weight to the overt homosexual involvements of the patient, as determined from his own reports and outside sources. Others ascertained the presence of explicit homosexual material in the delusional system. Still others considered the amount of symbolic preoccupation with homosexual themes in both the patient's therapy verbalizations and delusional system.

Obviously, questions can be raised about the logic of some of these approaches. For example, does evidence that a paranoid individual engaged in overt homosexual contacts indicate that he is unconsciously conflicted about homosexual impulses? Within the context of Freud's usual perspective about unconscious conflict, this definitely does not make sense. Unconscious impulses that are disturbing are presumably repressed and contained to prevent their overt expression. One would expect an inverse relationship between the probability of acting out an impulse and its conflict-arousal potential. In several instances it has been argued that the presence of explicit homosexual imagery in the delusional productions of a paranoid psychotic represents a "breakthrough" of repressed material due to the collapse of ego defenses. Presumably, what was repressed becomes visible because the repressive mechanism has been disabled. However, this view also lacks logic if positioned within the framework of Freud's assertion that the paranoid delusion itself is designed to maintain denial and control of homosexual wishes. If the delusion is a means of sealing off threatening material, it would seem to be incongruous that, at the very same time the delusion is verbalized, other imagery should be present that reveals what is being concealed. We would therefore take the position that the appearance of overt homosexual imagery or acting out in the paranoid would represent a contradiction rather than affirmation of Freud's theory of paranoia.

In reviewing past clinical studies pertaining to the paranoia theory that have gone beyond looking impressionistically at a few cases, we discovered only a handful (Gardner 1931, Miller 1941, Norman 1948, Klein and Horwitz 1949, Klaf and Davis 1960, Klaf 1961, Moore and Selzer 1963, Planansky and Johnston 1962, Friberg 1965). In these papers we found investigators looking at sizable samples of paranoid schizophrenics (for example, as many as 120) and comparing them with nonparanoid schizophrenics and other diagnostic categories. Data were typically derived from case records or interviews. In one study (Norman 1948) the interviews were conducted while the patient was under the influence of sodium amytal. Attention was often focused on the degree to which homosexual behavior or ideation was present. Control procedures were sparse and inadequate. Thus, judgments about the patients were made with full knowledge of their diagnostic classification and the investigators' prejudices could reign unhindered. Overall, the results of these studies were variable. Some concluded that a fair number of paranoid patients are troubled by homosexual concerns, while others focused on the large number who seem not to have such homosexual anxieties. As mentioned earlier, interpretation of these studies is a confusing matter, because some consider the appearance of overt homosexual imagery and behavior to indicate the presence of unusual homosexual conflict. We have already defined our objections to such an interpretation. In any case, it would be fair to say that the clinical studies have been plagued by so many methodological problems and are so divergent in their findings that they throw no real light on the validity of Freud's paranoia theory.

Several of the clinical studies specifically dealt with the matter of the sex of the persecutor. Klein and Horwitz (1949) analyzed the frequency with which the paranoid's persecutor was male or female and found that for both male and female patients the majority pictured the persecutor as male. In the instance of the males this supports Freud's statement about the sex of the persecutor, but with reference to the females it clearly contradicts him. Klaf and Davis (1960) reported that in a sample of male paranoid schizophrenics, about 85 percent depicted the persecutor as being of the same sex as themselves. But Klaf (1961) observed in a sample of female paranoids that 61 percent conceived of the persecutor as the opposite of their own sex. Relatedly, Friberg (1965) noted in a male schizophrenic group that there was no consistency in the sex of the chief persecutor. Greenspan (1963) found for fifteen female paranoid schizophrenics that the great majority pictured the persecutor as being of their own sex. The results just reviewed are obviously mixed and inconclusive and do not represent consistent support for the deduction that the persecutor should be of the same sex as the individual who constructs the paranoid system.

Experimental Studies

A number of the most ingenious efforts to appraise Freud's formulation have been based on the idea that it should be possible to demonstrate that the presumed homosexual conflicts of the paranoid render him selectively responsive to stimuli with homosexual connotations. The typical experiment conducted within this framework has involved exposing paranoid schizophrenics and appropriate control subjects to homosexual stimuli and showing that the two differ significantly in their reactions.

One of the earliest and most successful experiments was conducted by Zamansky (1958). He hypothesized that if Freud's theory concerning paranoia is correct, "Men with paranoid delusions when compared to men without these delusions will manifest a greater attraction to males than to females" (p. 412). He indicated that this attraction would occur at an unconscious level. Further, he predicted that the paranoid male would particularly avoid "homosexually threatening stimuli," and, in the same vein, would defensively express a greater preference for women than for men in a setting where it was obvious that his attitudes toward male and female love objects were being evaluated. These hypotheses were tested by means of an apparatus that permitted exposing pairs of pictures and monitoring the amount of time the subject looked at each while performing a task (defined as deciding "which picture had the greater overall surface area") that camouflaged the true intent of the procedure. In actuality, the paired pictures consisted of various combinations of male and female figures, and also scenes with and without homosexually threatening themes. It was assumed that the amount of time the subject spent looking at one type of picture versus another would be a function of feelings of attraction versus repulsion with respect to the themes presented. The subjects consisted of twenty male paranoid and twenty male nonparanoid schizophrenics. It was found, as predicted from Freud's formulation, that the paranoids looked longer at the males than the females of the pictured pairs, and the nonparanoids looked longer at the females. The overall difference was statistically significant. Zamansky considered that the paranoid's focus of attention on the male figures was an indicator of his unconscious homosexual attraction to men. But, interestingly, when the paranoids and nonparanoids were asked to indicate for each of a series of male-female paired pictures "Which do you prefer?" they did not differ. That is, as predicted, the paranoids defensively concealed their attraction to the male figures that had been evident when their distribution of attention to male versus female pictures was monitored without their knowledge. However, when the responses of the paranoids and nonparanoids to pictures with obvious, straightforward homosexual content were compared, differences could not be detected. The paranoids did not in this instance defensively spend less time looking at the homosexual themes. Generally, Zamansky interpreted the pattern of findings to mean (p. 419): "The present experiment has corroborated the hypothesis that men with paranoid delusions are characterized by stronger homosexual needs than men who do not suffer from these delusions." He added that although the findings fit Freud's theory, they did not necessarily prove that fear of homosexuality causes delusions. Thus, he considered it possible that there could be a more basic etiology, with the homosexual anxiety representing only a secondary manifestation.

Let us turn to a complex study by Sternlof (1964). It involved twenty male paranoid schizophrenics and twenty male patients classified as having prominent depressive symptomatology (for example, manic depressive, schizophrenic depressive). It was anticipated, on the basis of theory, that the paranoids would have a "strong affective investment" in men and the depressives a special investment in women (protective mother figures). Further controls for anxiety, as such, were provided by twenty normal males and twenty males classified as chronic brain syndrome. All subjects were asked to view a series of paired pictures presented in a stereoscope. One series consisted of male-female pairs; when the subject described what he saw in the stereoscope (which presented one picture to the right eye and the second to the left eye), note was made of whether the male or female dominated in his perception. The paranoids significantly exceeded the other subjects in the frequency with which they reported seeing the male rather than the female. In terms of previous research concerned with the determinants of what produces dominance of disparate stimuli presented stereoscopically, this finding was interpreted as supportive of the hypothesis that the paranoids have an especially intense emotional investment in male figures. Interestingly, when a similar series of male-female pictures was stereoscopically exposed and the subjects were told explicitly that both male and female representations were included, the paranoids no longer evidenced the greater tendency to investment in the males than the females. Sternlof had predicted this on the basis of the assumption that telling the paranoid explicitly that the stereoscope contained male and female pictures would put him on his guard and elicit a compensatory defensive stance. It will be recalled that Zamansky observed a similar defensive phenomenon when he asked paranoids to react to male and female pictures in a context where they knew they were being evaluated.

Sternlof also asked the subjects in his study to look at stereoscopically presented pairs of pictures of symbolic male and female representations (for example, banana versus apple) and found that, as predicted, the paranoids significantly more often perceived the male representation (as compared to the female) than did the normals and chronic brain syndrome controls; but while they also exceeded the nonparanoids in this respect, the difference did not attain significance. Still another phase of the study involved asking the subjects simply to look (nonstereoscopically) at a number of male and female pictures and to tell "what kind of a person you think he or she is." While a given subject examined the pictures, a record was kept of how long he looked at each before responding. The results indicated that the paranoids delayed significantly longer in responding to the male pictures than did the other groups. But there were no differences in the amount of delay in dealing with the female pictures. These results were attributed to the paranoid's intense ambivalent attitudes toward men (attraction and repulsion), which presumably rendered judgments of the male pictures particularly difficult. Other measures and procedures were obtained by Sternlof, but they will not be described because they were of minor import. In general, it would be fair to say that the various findings added up to a substantial confirmation of Freud's notions about the paranoid's attraction to the male and his defensive warding off of awareness of this attraction.

McLaughlin (1972) used a physiological index to measure the responses of twelve male paranoid and twelve male nonparanoid schizophrenics to a series of slides involving the following categories: physically strong men, men holding positions of authority, physically attractive men, and men rated low on each of the categories just enumerated. The index was the total no-alpha-time (derived from electroencephalographic recordings) during an interval following the presentation of each slide. It represented an evaluation of how alertly the subject attended to the stimulus. Analysis of the data indicated that with minor exceptions the paranoids could not be distinguished from the nonparanoids in their patterns of response to the various types of pictures. As defined by the alpha measures, the paranoids did not manifest an unusual amount of investment in the themes with homosexual connotations.

Similarly, when Sheflin (1969) measured the pupillary responses of twenty male paranoid and twenty male nonparanoid schizophrenics to a series of neutral, nude female and nude male pictures, he did not find a significant difference. The paranoids did not exhibit a selective reaction to the male nudes. This study and the McLaughlin (1972) study seem to indicate that physiological measures are not sensitive to whatever differences may exist between paranoids and nonparanoids in their reactions to homosexual stimuli.

Wolowitz (1965) attempted to check out Freud's paranoia theory by studying thirty-five paranoid and twenty-four nonparanoid male schizophrenics. He asked each subject to move each of a sequence of photographs along a tunnel toward himself until he found the place where "it looked best." The assumption was made that the closer he placed a picture to himself, the more he was interested in approaching it; the farther away he placed it, the more he wanted to avoid it. There were twenty-four photographs of male faces, nineteen of female faces, and five of neutral inanimate objects. Each of the photos of persons had been previously rated in terms of the three Osgood et al. (1957) Semantic Differential dimensions (potency, activity, evaluation). Wolowitz was primarily interested in testing his own hypothesis that paranoids are fearful of power in men (but not in women), and that therefore the greater the potency of a male picture, the farther they would place it from themselves. This hypothesis was significantly supported by the data obtained.[10]

Wolowitz also examined Freud's hypothesis by analyzing the relative placements of the photos of the male, female, and inanimate objects. He reasoned that if Freud's hypothesis were correct, the male photos should be placed closer to themselves by the paranoids (because of their homosexual attraction) than by the non-paranoids. The findings bearing on this point did not give much support to Freud, as operationally defined by Wolowitz. The paranoids, when compared to the nonparanoids, placed the male photos significantly *farther* from themselves than the pictures of the neutral objects. Also, the paranoids, when compared to the nonparanoids, put the pictures of the females significantly farther away than those of the inanimate objects. There was a trend for the paranoids, as contrasted with the nonparanoids, to place the male photos farther away than the female photos (p. 20). Although Wolowitz declared that such findings contradict Freud, one cannot but be impressed with the fact that the paranoids and nonparanoids tended to differ with respect to how they dealt with the male as compared to the other photos. There was a trend for the paranoids to put the male photos farther away from self. Wolowitz reasoned that this indicates a lesser degree of attraction to men by the paranoids. But this may be an oversimplification. As shown by Zamansky (1958) and also Sternlof (1964), paranoids will *defensively* retreat from male or homosexual stimuli if there is any hint in the experimental context that their attitudes toward men are being evaluated. Therefore, it is not farfetched to speculate that the design of the Wolowitz study (which called for the subject to judge where, on an obvious continuum of closeness-distance, pictures of males and females "look best") would have threatening significance to the paranoid and alert him to the possibility of revealing homosexual interests. Wolowitz' results may have reflected defensiveness triggered in the paranoid.

An approach similar to that of Wolowitz was used by Slavin (1970) to explore response differences between twenty-seven female paranoid and twenty-seven nonparanoid schizophrenics to female and male photographs that had been previously rated and also to several photos of inanimate objects. The ratings included not only the Semantic Differential categories obtained by Wolowitz but also judgments concerning the attractiveness of the female photos. Responses to the photos were obtained with the same apparatus used by Wolowitz, which involved determining how far the subject placed each photo from herself. A record was kept of how much time the subject spent dealing with each photo. Slavin tested several hypotheses about paranoids that were linked to Wolowitz' original work, but he was also interested in evaluating

Freud's theory. He considered that Freud's theory would be supported if the paranoid women (who were presumably homosexually attracted to the photos of the women) placed the female photos so that the greater their rated attractiveness, the closer they were to themselves. He reasoned, too, that support for Freud would be shown if the amount of time the paranoids spent with each female picture were positively correlated with its attractiveness. Within this theoretical perspective, the nonparanoids should not show either of the two response patterns just stated, because presumably they would not be homosexually invested in the female photos. No differences were found between the paranoids and nonparanoids in the degree to which they placed the more attractive female photos close to themselves. But the paranoids were significantly more likely to spend *less* time with each female photo as a function of its greater attractiveness.[11] That is, a significant finding opposite to Slavin's expectation on this point was obtained. It will be recalled that Wolowitz' results were characterized by an analogous type of reversal. The same question can be raised as to whether the present reversal reflects a defensive response of the paranoids to the homosexual implications of the judgments they were asked to make.[12]

Quite a different experimental approach was adopted by Daston (1956). He studied the responses of twenty-five paranoid schizophrenics, twenty-five nonparanoid schizophrenics, and twenty-five normals (all male) to words tachistoscopically exposed for very brief intervals.[13] The words included those with explicit homosexual and heterosexual meanings, and those with nonsexual meanings. These words were matched for length, familiarity, and affective quality. Determination was made of how much difficulty subjects had in recognizing each word when it was presented (typically for intervals of less than one second). The groups did not differ in their ability to perceive the heterosexual words. However, it was shown, as predicted, that the paranoids were significantly *faster* than either the nonparanoid schizophrenics or the normals in correctly identifying the homosexual words. Daston predicted this result on the basis of the assumption that concern about a theme sensitizes an individual to stimuli pertinent to that theme. Of course, one could raise the question of whether the paranoid's presumed anxiety about homosexuality might not interfere with his perception of homosexual words. In this sense, a prediction opposite to that of Daston's might have been just as logical. Indeed, it is now well known that concern about an issue can result in either sensitization or inhibition with respect to perceptions relevant to that issue. Thus, one is led back to the matter that arose in interpreting the Wolowitz (1965) and Slavin (1970) data cited above. There seems to be little justification for insisting that the paranoid's presumed concern about homosexuality will produce a specific *unidirectional* response to homosexual stimuli. The existence of such concern can register either in enhancement or denial of the stimuli. We would argue that it is the fact that the paranoid responds *differently* from the nonparanoid that is important, rather than the direction of the difference.

A particularly good demonstration of the effects of defensiveness upon the reactions of paranoids to homosexual stimuli has been provided by Watson (1965). He appraised twenty-three paranoid and twenty-three nonparanoid male schizophrenics. When he administered to them a "Homosexuality Awareness" scale, which called for responses to such statements as "I guess I am more attracted to men than most people" and "I once was in love with another man," the paranoids described themselves as significantly less homosexually oriented than the nonparanoids. Further, when the subjects were asked to create stories about a picture with an implicit homosexual theme and another without such a theme (both equated for amount of *general* anxiety they elicit), it was found, as predicted, that the paranoids took significantly longer than the nonparanoids to respond to the homosexual as compared to the neutral picture. Watson considered this finding to mean that the paranoids were made more anxious than the nonparanoids by the homosexual as compared to the neutral picture.

One finds a cluster of studies in the literature concerned with Freud's theory that have focused on comparing paranoids and nonparanoids in relation to how much sexual confusion and homosexual fantasy they reveal in their responses to projective stimuli. Let us quickly scan them. Musiker (1952) compared twenty-eight paranoid and twenty-five nonparanoid male schizophrenics with reference to the number of "homosexual signs" present in their Rorschach inkblot protocols. The scoring of homosexual signs was based on criteria ("Wheeler signs") that have proved to possess moderately good validity. As predicted, the paranoids projected a greater number of these signs into the blots than did the nonparanoids. Musiker also examined "unconscious" femininity and sex role conflict as expressed in Thematic Apperception Test stories, drawings of the human figure (Draw-A-Person Test), and the Franck-Rosen test (1949), which is based on whether subjects complete a series of drawings with masculine or feminine configurations. He reported that for all three of these procedures the results indicated, as predicted, that the paranoids were more conflicted about sexual identity (less clearly masculine in orientation) than the nonparanoids.[14] However, Higdon (1972) compared ten female paranoid schizophrenics, ten female nonparanoid schizophrenics, and ten female nonschizophrenics in terms of how much sexual confusion and overt concern about homosexual themes appeared in their story responses to Thematic Apperception pictures. The paranoids could not be distinguished from the other groups.

Aronson[15] (1952), Kapotas[16] (1955), and Meketon et al. (1962) have presented data supporting Musiker in the sense that they found Wheeler "homosexual signs" to be significantly more predominant in the inkblot responses of paranoids than nonparanoids. Grauer (1954) was not able to find more such homosexual signs in a collected sample of thirty-one paranoid schizophrenics than had been reported for nonparanoid schizophrenics in the Aronson (1952) study just cited above. Note, though, that he did not collect his own nonparanoid controls, but instead used as a comparison sample the one obtained by Aronson under different conditions. The possible noncomparability of the two samples raises some question about how to interpret the fact that his study disagrees with the other related studies that have been enumerated.

Zeichner (1955) examined inkblot and Thematic Apperception differences between fifteen male paranoid and fifteen nonparanoid schizophrenics. There was also a normal control group of males hospitalized for physical symptoms. Elaborate, fairly objective quantitative scoring systems were applied to determine the presence of signs of femininity, psychosexual confusion, and homosexual preoccupation. The nonparanoids turned out, contrary to prediction, to display more signs of psychosexual confusion than the paranoids, but the paranoids did exceed the normal controls in such confusion. There was, in addition, a significant trend for the paranoids to exceed the nonparanoids and normals in signs of femininity. Finally, with respect to stories with homosexual connotations elicited by the Thematic Apperception Test, there was a borderline significant tendency for paranoids to produce more involving male figures, while the nonparanoids produced more focused on female figures. Paranoids did not give a greater total number of themes with homosexual implications than did the nonparanoids. These results are obviously of a mixed variety, but one does note that the paranoids were high on projective test signs of femininity and also with respect to indicators of homosexual concern in the context of stories about males.

Overview

The experimental literature dealing with Freud's theory of the etiology of the paranoid delusion is a record of valiant attempts to objectify and quantify an exceedingly complex variable. When Freud theorized that the paranoid delusion arises out of the denial and projection of homosexual wishes, he was simultaneously suggesting the existence of homosexual urges of unusual intensity and also counter-defenses of unusual strength. Obviously, if an individual is set to deny certain feelings within himself, this will make it difficult to obtain evidence of the existence of such feelings. One cannot simply ask the paranoid if he has homosexual wishes. One has to find ways of sampling his ideation by circumventing his presumed set to conceal. Practically every technique in the armamentarium of procedures that has been experimentally developed to examine fantasies and wishes has been pressed into service by those interested in testing Freud's theory. The tachistoscope, stereoscope, measures of attention, inkblots, and story productions—just to mention several representative examples—have been variously utilized.

As one reviews the results of the studies that have typically applied such diverse techniques to comparing paranoid and nonparanoid schizophrenics, one cannot but be impressed with the convergence that has emerged from the diversity. In numerous ways it has been shown that paranoids and nonparanoids respond significantly differently to stimuli with homosexual connotations. It is a fact that the majority of the experimental studies have demonstrated that the paranoid has a unique pattern of reaction to anything that has the potential for conjuring up homosexual images. Since most of the studies have devoted care to equating the paranoids and nonparanoids for variables such as age, chronicity, cooperativeness, and socioeconomic status, there is persuasive reason to conclude that the two classes of schizophrenics do differ in their orientation toward homosexual themes. As already detailed at an earlier point, a number of the studies where the results have not fallen in the predicted direction can reasonably be reinterpreted as reflecting the defensive maneuver of the paranoid when he feels threatened with the potential exposure of his underlying homosexual orientation. It should be noted at this point that the clinical studies in the literature that have concerned themselves with testing Freud's theory have proven to be so methodologically weak and inconsistent in their statements of hypotheses that they have contributed little but confusion to the debate about the validity of Freud's views. However, they did provide evidence that Freud's assumption that the sex of the persecutor in the paranoid's delusion is always the same as that of the paranoid is probably not tenable.

Several investigators have pointed out that even though Freud's theory about the role of repressed homosexuality in paranoia has received rather good experimental verification, this does not mean that Freud was correct in assigning prime etiological significance to the homosexual factor. Presumably, the homosexuality could be a minor etiological variable, with some other variable being of much greater importance. Or the concern about homosexuality in the paranoid might be a by-product of a larger process that is basic to the development of a paranoid orientation. This may very well be true, and only future studies will bring clarification. But at the same time it cannot be too greatly emphasized that Freud's formulation about paranoia was not only highly novel in its time, it also represented the outcome of a step-by-step analysis of a series of facts that were available concerning the Schreber case. Indeed, so far as we know, there is no other theoretical model that would logically predict the existence of a difference in response to homosexual themes in paranoid as compared to nonparanoid schizophrenics. At this point in time, we are impressed that the existing facts do fall into line with a core aspect of Freud's theory of paranoid delusion formulation. One final word of caution should be added. With minor exceptions, the experimental work dealing with paranoids has involved male subjects. It is therefore questionable whether the findings should be generalized to include women.

NOTES

1. With reference to the role of Schreber's relationship with his father in the breakdown, Freud noted (p. 55): "Thus in the case of Schreber we find ourselves once again on the familiar ground of the father-complex. The patient's struggle with Flechsig became revealed to him as a conflict with God, and we must therefore construe it as an infantile conflict with the father whom he loved; the details of that conflict (of which we know nothing) are what determined the content of his delusions." Freud added in relation to this same point (p. 50): "The feminine phantasy, which aroused such violent opposition in the patient, thus had its root in a longing, intensified to an erotic pitch, for his father and brother."

2. Klein and Iker (1974) concluded, after an elaborate computer analysis of the word content of Schreber's description of his psychotic experiences, that Schreber evidenced poor differentiation in his use of the terms "male" and "female."

3. Freud suggested that one factor that may have triggered Schreber's breakdown was the inability of he and his wife to have any children. Freud speculated that this was a disappointment not only in terms of not being able to perpetuate the Schreber line but also

because it meant that Schreber had "no son who might have consoled him for the loss of his father and brother and upon whom he might have drained off his unsatisfied homosexual affections" (p. 57).

4. Fenichel (1945, p. 89) comments on this pattern of relationship to father as follows: "In general, boys with a special development of the negative Oedipus complex have repressed phallic strivings toward the mother and mobilized pregenital passive aims toward the father instead. Analysis of pregenitally oriented compulsive characters or of certain homosexuals sometimes shows that an infantile phallic period has not disappeared with the repression of an Oedipus complex directed at the mother, but that the repressed impulse connected with the penis has been directed toward the father."

5. In the case of the female paranoid the masculine references would, of course, be replaced by feminine ones.

6. Freud (1923b,c) also speculated that an original tendency to have *ambivalent* relationships (for example, with father or brother) prepares the individual for defensive shifts between love and hate and vice versa.

7. For example, one might predict on the basis of a number of Freud's statements that the paranoid would be unusually narcissistic; and there is, in fact, support for such an hypothesis (Havener and Izard 1962, Feldman 1965). Or it might even be possible to tease out a series of hypotheses concerning the special nature of the paranoid's relationship with his father. However, such hypotheses would really not be specific to the paranoid syndrome, and would in their general form apply about equally well to the homosexual.

8. The existence of defensive maneuvers equivalent to Freud's concept of projection has been well documented in a variety of studies (for example, Cohen 1956, Sears 1936).

9. Although Freud specified this point, it is not clear why, for purposes of disguise, the homosexual significance of the persecutor might not be represented by a figure of the opposite sex to that of the individual entertaining the paranoid delusion.

10. Wolowitz and Shorkey (1966, 1969) have mustered other evidence that male paranoid schizophrenics are particularly concerned about, and influenced by, power themes.

11. This finding emerged particularly with an analysis of the cases that were considered to be most reliably diagnosed.

12. Slavin actually discussed the ambiguity of the measure concerned with amount of time spent with each photo and considered the possibility that it had a meaning opposite to that which he had assigned to it.

13. A tachistoscopic study by Eriksen (1951) dealing with the response of paranoid schizophrenics to homosexual stimuli has not been reviewed because its design does not permit a meaningful test of Freud's hypothesis.

14. A measure of masculinity-femininity based on conscious reports of attitudes and interests largely failed to discriminate the paranoids and nonparanoids. Numerous other studies have similarly failed to detect the presence of feminine attitudes in paranoids when the measuring instrument has been the standard masculinity-femininity scale whose intent is rather obvious to most intelligent individuals (Scagnelli 1971, Coslett 1965, Butler and Bieliauskas 1972, Watson 1965).

15. Aronson (1953) also administered the Blacky Test to these samples and found, among other things, that the paranoids had more anxiety than the nonparanoids about anal retentive themes, castration anxiety, and several themes concerned with sexual identity.

16. Kapotas also administered a sentence completion test and the Blacky Test to the male paranoid (N = 30) and nonparanoid (N = 30) schizophrenic samples he studied. No significant differences were detected in "sexual attitudes" between the samples as defined by the rather vague sentence completion criteria. The Blacky Test demonstrated the paranoids to be significantly higher than the nonparanoids for Oral Sadism, Anal Retentiveness, and Oedipal Intensity, and to be higher at a borderline level for Anal Expulsiveness.

PART TWO

FREUD'S THERAPY

Chapter 7

Freud's Psychoanalytic Therapy and the Realities of Current Analytic Practices

AMONG the general population the term "psychoanalysis" has come to be vaguely equated with all theories and practices having to do with psychotherapy. By some it tends to be breathlessly regarded as a mystical, all-powerful technique for revealing one's inner thoughts and motives, while others regard the practice as a frivolous and foolish waste of time. This dichotomy seems well reflected by the media, which widely portray analysts and analysis as subjects either for comedy or drama. Within the comedic category the analyst is usually portrayed as an insensitive, odd character who is, if anything, madder than his patients. He rarely listens and constantly displays bizarre behavior, and his patients are not helped. The dramatic version of the analyst tends to show a flawless therapist with uncanny sensitivity and insight into his patients' problems. He exudes empathy, delivers masterful interpretations of the causes of his patients' difficulties, and achieves miraculous results with complete remission of symptoms tending to occur within the one or two hours allotted to the production. Professionals within the mental health field are also drawn by their training and predilection to view psychoanalytic practice in an extremely positive or negative fashion. Therefore, in attempting to present a picture of what has been empirically learned about psychoanalysis as a therapy, we run the risk of strong criticism from both sides, since it is our expectation that psychoanalysis will not prove to be either all good or all bad. Nevertheless, we feel it is important that the attempt be made to dispassionately present the experimental evidence that has accumulated in the literature, in order to promote opinions based on reasoned judgment rather than on emotional generalizations.

Over the course of Freud's career the term "psychoanalysis" came to have many meanings. In 1923 Freud wrote: "Psychoanalysis is the name (1) of a procedure for the investigation of mental processes which are almost inaccessible in any other way, (2) of a method (based upon that investigation) for the treatment of neurotic disorders, and (3) of a collection of psychological information obtained along those lines, which is gradually being accumulated into a new scientific discipline" (Freud, 1923d, p. 235).

The aim of this chapter and the two that follow is to present what is empirically known about psychoanalysis as a method of psychotherapy. Specifically, within this chapter we will try to present an overview description of what psychoanalytic therapy is, where it came from, and who is involved in it. In so doing we will take a look at Freud's data and the activities of those currently involved in the practice of psychoanalysis. The chapters that follow will focus on the nature of the results obtained with this method of therapy and what goes into obtaining those results. Within the jargon of psychotherapy research, the aim is to look at psychoanalysis both in terms of its outcome and its process. A word should be said about our biases. We started our search of the literature with the notion, based on our clinical experience, that a dynamic understanding of the causes of a patient's difficulties and a therapy based on that understanding is meaningful and useful. However, we were well aware of the disagreements and diversity of viewpoints in the literature and have attempted to shape our judgments on the basis of empirically collected data rather than on the basis of personalities or prestige of various authors. Freud also seems to have affirmed such a position in his essay on Leonardo, where he approvingly said of Leonardo: "He dared to utter the bold assertion which contains within itself the justification for all independent research . . . (that) 'he who appeals to authority when there is a difference of opinion works with his memory rather than with his reason' " (Freud, 1910b, p. 122).

While it may seem paradoxical to quote Freud on this point, we do so not to legitimize this approach but to point out that his own work paralleled this quest for answers based on observation rather than on blind acceptance of what had come before. Indeed, this is what made his contribution so unique and stimulating. In contrast, many of Freud's followers have chosen to accept the early theories and observations with relatively little questioning. This is reflected to some degree by a recent survey of psychoanalysts conducted by Hofling and Meyers (1972). Of the ninety analysts who responded, the majority conveyed in one way or another misgivings about the value and originality of work over the past thirty years. We suggest that the reader ask himself whether any data could be sufficient to alter his opinions, either pro or con, as to the nature and validity of psychoanalysis. It is doubtful that this or any other presentation of research could be seen as having much value if the reader cannot conceive of any potential data that would cause a change of opinion. This issue has in the past caused many philosophers to question the scientific validity of psychoanalysis. For example, Nagel, writing in a volume edited by Hook (1959), pointed out that psychoanalysis falls short of the scientific tenet which holds that "a credible theory must not only be confirmed by observational evidence but must also be capable of being negated by such evidence" (p. 40).

We should also point out that we do not feel the success or lack of success of the therapy should be taken to validate or invalidate psychoanalytic theory. It seems tenable to assume that the "causes" of an individual's behavior might correctly be understood without therapeutic movement, or that positive changes could occur without any understanding of what caused the behavior in the first place. The validity of these assumptions is subject, of course, to empirical test. What we are pointing out is that psychoanalysis represents a theory of therapy as well as a theory of personality and that these two domains, although related, are not the same and must be evaluated on their own merits. Glover (1972) has also argued for independent evaluation of the theory and therapy. His 1938 questionnaire survey of the British Psychoanalytical Society (Glover 1958) revealed that there was a "marked division" among the twenty-four surveyed analysts as to whether the theory was related to their practice. While several analysts felt unable to reply to this issue, one half of the sample denied that they approached analysis with a theoretical outline in mind. A similar point is raised by a survey of mental health professionals in Chicago (Henry, Sims, and Spray 1968) which included 61.3 percent of the psychoanalysts in practice in the area. Of that group, 11 percent were classified as not psychoanalytic in theoretical orientation. For the moment we will not raise the question of whether those in agreement with the theory put it into practice in a similar way.

Traditionally, psychoanalysts have followed Freud in using the case presentation as evidence for therapeutic validity rather than data obtained from large groups of patients under controlled conditions. The implicit assumption has been that the uniqueness of each case may be lost and the applicability may be tenuous if you examine large groups of patients with regard to any particular question. Freud (1933c) exemplifies this viewpoint in his comment on the Berlin Psychoanalytic Institute's report of treatment results over the first ten years of its existence:

"Its therapeutic successes give grounds neither for boasting nor for being ashamed. But statistics of that kind are in general uninstructive; the material worked upon is so heterogeneous that only very large numbers would show anything. It is wiser to examine one's individual experiences" (p. 152).

Clearly, generalization must be at the basis of any attempt to apply a consistent set of hypotheses to an observation. Freud continually stated generalizations in subsuming the behavior of his patients under theoretical classifications (such as Oedipal problems and oral problems). While the need for generalization is inevitable, we cannot agree that Freud's case study method is the only or the best way to arrive at generalizations, since the individual observer is so prone to censor and distort his observations because of his own needs and expectations. Freud's formulation of counter-transference and the therapist's subsequent distortion of the therapeutic encounter suggest that he was well aware of this problem. The empirical literature of social psychology has demonstrated over and over again the potential for experimenter or observer distortion. For example, Chapman and Chapman (1967, 1969) have shown in their studies of illusory correlations that theoretical biases tend to lead clinicians to observe significant relationships in their data even when the relationships are absent in the material presented. Research has also demonstrated that when an observer enters into transaction with the object of his observations, as in psychotherapy, he is likely to create the behavior he is looking for in a manner analogous to a self-fulfilling prophecy. This concept has been extensively documented by Rosenthal (1966) in his delineation of experimenter bias effects.

Probable sources for the distortion of data in analytic case histories are succinctly summarized by Sherwood (1969), who writes: "In such records the dangers of distortion have been compounded. First, there is the analyst's influence upon the patient's own statements, which remains a completely unassessable factor since verbatim records are not available. Second, there is the selective nature of the analyst's recollections of the case and the possibility of his reconstructing earlier material in the light of later observations. Thus, the psychoanalyst's theoretical commitment can influence both the patient's utterances themselves and the manner in which they are organized, written up, and interpreted. Finally, almost all psychoanalytic case histories, in contrast to those standard for physical medicine, do not differentiate between exposition of the case—including chief complaint, present illness, and personal history—and diagnosis, etiology, pathogenesis, and prognosis" (p. 71).

It would seem to us extremely questionable to assess the validity of ideas solely on the basis of one man's uncorroborated, nonstandardized observations, no matter how persuasive that one man's arguments may appear.

Another potential difficulty in making generalizations is linked to the similarity between the originally observed patients and the future patients about whom predictions will be made. The more dissimilar these two groups are on relevant dimensions, the less likely it is that observations of one group will lead to general statements of theory applicable to the second group. Freud's original observations and theories have become widely generalized, with a resultant application of his theory of personality to all humans and his theory of therapy to a somewhat more select group. We must ask if Freud's original sample of patients is representative of the patient population as a whole. If Freud's observations have been based on a select sample, his conclusions would be most applicable to similar patients seen under similar conditions. In any case, both the extension of his theories to other types of patients and the validation of these hypotheses through similar types of patients require precise definition of the expected results and independent corroboration by objective, nonbiased investigators.

Freud's Data

In tracing the history of Freud's therapy, one can note a shift in emphasis from the treatment of symptoms to the gaining of knowledge concerning underlying causes and their role in symptom formation. This shift is paralleled by changes in treatment techniques. Originally, Freud followed Breuer's lead in helping patients to overcome hysterical symptoms through hypnotically reexperiencing painful feelings and memories that had been forgotten. This process of forgetting was labeled "repression," and the therapeutic procedure was described as "cathartic." Two basic conclusions were drawn from these early cases: ". . . first that hysterical symptoms have sense and meaning, being substitutes for normal mental acts; and secondly, that the uncovering of this unknown meaning is accompanied by the removal of the symptoms" (Freud 1923d, p. 236).

With time Freud found that he could not hypnotize all of his patients, so he altered his technique by forcefully suggesting to patients in the waking state that they had forgotten something and could remember. The patients often resisted these suggestions and became unproductive. As a result Freud again changed his technique, finding that resistance could be lessened if he asked patients to follow what has come to be known as the "fundamental technical rule" of psychoanalysis: free association. In this procedure, the patient is asked to become a dispassionate self-observer and report any and all ideas that come into his awareness. It was hypothesized that the material thus produced by the patient has hidden meanings that can be discovered with the help of the analyst. The analyst, by suspending preconceptions and following the themes and symbolism of the associations, helps the patient to understand the underlying meaning of his communications and behavior through interpretation. It was also hypothesized that during this therapeutic self-exploration, patients inevitably begin to have intense feelings about the therapist. These feelings are reproductions of earlier erotic attitudes that the patient had toward his parents (transference). The job of patient and therapist becomes that of working through resistance to recognizing these early feelings and memories. Theoretically, over the course of therapy these feelings are increasingly expressed in the patient's relationship to his therapist (transference neurosis). It was conjectured that intensive and repeated exploration of the many roots of the symptoms provides the patient with insight into how his past feelings are inappropriately operating in the present. As the patient gains insight into the motives for his behavior and into the repetition of neurotic childhood patterns evidenced in his relationship with the therapist, he should show change through decreased symptomatology, along with increased feelings of mastery and control over internal and external problems.

Freud's main support for the theory of therapy briefly outlined above came from examples drawn from cases. In trying to put together a brief overview of Freud's data, we are struck by the inconsistency in the type of data reported on various cases and the tendency to pick out only that material that lends support to a particular idea. We are struck by how few cases Freud reported in any detail, and by the obvious biases that must have been built into the sample of patients he worked with. In addition, it should be noted that there have been relatively few attempts to organize, either empirically or semi-empirically, the data from which Freud's conclusions were drawn. Our focus here will be on the patients Freud actually worked with, although many of his observations and hypotheses were based on nonclinical observations, colleagues' case material, self-observation, and armchair analyses of literary and historical figures. We cannot of course know anything about patient contacts that Freud had but did not write about.

Perhaps the most detailed analysis of Freud's case load appears in a paper by Brody (1970), who reviewed Freud's complete works in categorizing all of the patients Freud ever reported working with. Major and minor cases were categorized from a search of 114 papers, and all of Freud's twenty-two books were examined for major cases. The major category included all cases where there were several pages of discussion and some statement of the patient's life circumstances that could serve as the vehicle for theoretical discussion. The minor cases included all other cases mentioned by Freud. This analysis revealed that Freud supported his theory and therapy through an extensive discussion of only twelve cases and mention of 133 minor cases that he had actually seen. Therefore, although we know Freud saw many patients, he presented only minimal data except in a handful of select cases. It is perhaps a tribute to Freud's persuasiveness that in spite of the selectivity of his presentations, his conclusions have been so widely adopted and advocated by others.

A demographic examination of Freud's cases is also quite revealing. For example, women composed about two thirds of all of Freud's published cases; only four out of his twelve major cases were male. In view of this it is surprising that he seemed relatively more assured with his formulation of male than female psychology. In discussing the psychosexual development of girls, he stated: "At this point our material—for some incomprehensible reason—becomes far more obscure and full of gaps" (Freud 1924, p. 177). We might speculate that Freud had a harder time theorizing about his female data because of the larger sample size and thus presumably greater heterogeneity of the female patients he was working with. There is also the obvious fact that he was male and possibly felt more assured of the hypotheses he had come to on the basis of self-observation.

The age of Freud's patients also places a limitation on the generality of the conclusions that can be drawn. Only two patients in his entire reported case load were over the age of forty-five. About 90 percent of the total patient group falls between ages twenty and forty-four. He saw very few adolescents and practically no children. Of the twelve major cases, nine were between eighteen and twenty, two were older than thirty, and one was a child. Interestingly, a look at the ages of Freud's four major male cases reveals both the general unrepresentativeness of his sample and his amazing ability to draw hypotheses from highly nonuniform data. Freud's major male cases were described in age as "youngish," about twenty-three, thirty-eight, and five years old!

Social class is another area in which Freud's patients appear to be highly select. Attempts to classify Freud's patients result in the conclusion that his cases predominantly came from the upper class. This idea is supported by both Brody's (1970) classification based on the Warner Scale of Social Status and Wassermann's (1958) cruder and less complete analysis based on the statements in Freud's writings. Others have attempted to link Freud's theory and practice to his value system which seemed quite autocratic in its concern with the maintenance of status and power (Ansbacher 1959, Riesman 1955).

Freud's diagnosis of the great majority of his patients as neurotic is another area for concern in terms of generalizability. Brody's (1970) analysis of Freud's reported cases indicated that more than 95 percent were given some type of neurotic diagnosis (hysteria, obsessional neurosis, phobia, anxiety neurosis). This has led to the implication that the theory is most applicable to "neurotic" patients and that the therapy works best with neurotic patients. Assuming diagnostic categories can be consistently applied, recent investigations using Freud's original patient descriptions as data have raised questions as to whether his patients would be labeled neurotic today. Freud (1905b) himself states in an early paper that he had only been able to test his therapeutic method on the "severest cases," patients who had tried everything else without success and who had spent many years in sanatoria. Goshen (1952) presents character sketches of eight of Freud's major cases in Freud's and Breuer's own words. The descriptions consistently indicate that the patients were quite disturbed, with bizarre symptoms, hallucinations, delusions, and instances of irrational, disorganized thinking. Goshen concludes that Freud's patients would probably be diagnosed as schizophrenic today. A report of the Annual Meeting of the American Psychoanalytic Association (Pfeffer 1963a,b) has also pointed out that many analysts and psychiatrists would not agree that most of Freud's case studies would fall into the category of psychoneuroses. Similarly, a report from a scientific workshop of the Institute for Psychoanalysis states that "we would now refer to some of the early patients Freud was studying as 'borderline characters' or 'severe ego disturbances' " (Sadow et al. 1968). At the least, such observations indicate that there may be a marked difference between the patients Freud originally observed and those to whom psychoanalytic therapy is applied today.

In his paper "On Psychotherapy," Freud (1905b) presented a series of tentative criteria defining patient suitability for psychoanalysis. He stated that the most suitable patient would be a young adult, past adolescence, but still in the prime of adulthood (that is, under fifty years of age), of good intelligence, reasonably educated, "educable," and of reliable character. He felt that "psychoses, states of confusion and deeply rooted depression" were not suitable for the therapy as he practiced it. He also stressed that the patient be motivated, seek treatment voluntarily, and not require speedy removal of dangerous symptoms, such as in the case of "hysterical anorexia." It appears from the above description that Freud's known cases for the most part display the attributes he considered important for positive therapeutic outcome, although as a group they seem much more disturbed than his description of the ideal analytic candidate. Nonetheless, we must question how he knew his method was most appropriate with this type of patient, since he did not report treating other types.

It might be argued that Freud is done an injustice by viewing his treatment in this way, since he did not describe all of his cases or present most cases in sufficient detail to make appropriate judgments possible. In other words, the data from which the conclusions are drawn may be "fragmentary and unreliable" (Gutheil 1958). If this is the case, our concerns become even more pronounced, since it suggests that Freud's reports are not accurate representations of his practice and that he has presented only the data that would support his ideas.[1] In fairness to Freud it should be noted that he stressed the tentative nature of conclusions and the limitations in the scope of the activities within his practice (Freud 1905b, 1937a). Still, many of Freud's statements and practices have become rigidly institutionalized by others; as, for example, the tendency to exclude many types of patients from consideration as good candidates for intensive uncovering psychotherapy. Freud's initial statements seem to be reflected in Schofield's (1964) survey of large representative samples of psychotherapists, which found that there is a general systematic selection of patients for psychotherapy who present the "Yavis" syndrome—Young, Attractive, Verbal, Intelligent, and Successful. We do not mean to imply that Freud's statements concerning the most amenable candidates for psychoanalysis are wrong, but merely that one cannot draw any conclusions about the validity of these hypotheses on the basis of the data presented by Freud.

In a similar fashion we are struck by the fact that many of Freud's conclusions regarding therapy have been widely accepted without individuals even questioning whether Freud himself achieved good results with his therapy. Nowhere in Freud's writings do we get an overview of his practice which would enable us to come to some objective conclusions about whether the therapy Freud was practicing achieved better results than other approaches or no therapy at all. Freud himself, over the course of his career, seemed to become more circumspect in evaluating the results of his therapy. Some may choose to label Freud's caution as pessimism, while others may see him becoming more realistic in his assessment of treatment possibilities. Probably Freud's most complete statement regarding his conclusions about the therapy are contained in his essay "Analysis Terminable and Interminable" (Freud 1937a). Within this paper Freud begins to erase the notion that analysis is all-powerful and magical in its treatment results. As he remarks, "One has the impression that one ought not to be surprised if it should turn out in the end that the difference between a person who has not been analysed and the behaviour of a person after he has been analysed is not so thoroughgoing as we aim at making it and as we expect and maintain it to be. . . . I really cannot commit myself to a decision on this point, nor do I know whether a decision is possible at the present time" (p. 228). A similar reserved conclusion is revealed by Freud in commenting, "I do not think our cures can compete with those of Lourdes. There are so many more people who believe in the miracles of the Blessed Virgin than in the existence of the unconscious" (Freud, 1933c, p. 152).

We should point out that Freud did consider his treatment to be the best and most thorough available at the time in spite of his growing awareness of its possible limitations. In his earlier writings Freud seemed more enthusiastic about psychoanalysis as a therapy than as a theory. For example, he stated in his discussion of the case of Little Hans: "Psychoanalysis is not an impartial scientific investigation, but a therapeutic measure. Its essence is not to prove anything, but merely to alter something" (Freud, 1909a, p. 104). In his later evaluations his emphasis shifted. He seemed to place more confidence in the theory than in the therapy, as in his statement that "analysis, in claiming to cure neuroses by ensuring control over instinct, is always right in theory but not always right in practice" (Freud, 1937a, p. 229). This view is further amplified in another paper: "I have told you that psychoanalysis began as a method of treatment, but I did not want to commend it to your interest as a method of treatment but on account of the truths it contains, on account of the information it gives us about what concerns human beings most of all—their own nature—and on account of the connections it discloses between the most different of their activities" (Freud, 1933c, pp. 156–157).

A reading of Freud's major cases reveals the general incomparability of data presented as a result of the numerous differences in format of case presentation, treatment technique, and treatment situations. Despite Freud's tendency to dogmatically present his conclusions, a reading of these cases is also a testimony to the nondogmatic way in which Freud went about applying his techniques. It is noteworthy that there is relatively little stress placed on description of outcome in Freud's major case descriptions. The aim seems much more to describe and explain theoretical points. Further, the cases Freud described came from a relatively early period in his career when his theories were undergoing significant changes (Brody 1970, Sherwood 1969). On the whole, Freud's statements about the outcome of individual cases he saw were not exceedingly positive.

In *Studies in Hysteria* (Breuer and Freud, 1893–95), Freud described four cases he had seen (Emmy Von N., Lucie R., Katharina and Elisabeth V.R.). It could be argued that because of the nature of the therapeutic techniques employed, these cases have little to do with psychoanalysis as a therapy. Freud variously described treatment procedures as consisting of hypnosis, pressing on the head combined with suggestions, and "conversation." In treating Elisabeth V.R., Freud prepared her for verbal therapy by conducting four weeks of "sham treatment" during which he treated the patient's painful legs with strong "Franklin sparks." Clearly Freud revealed in these cases a strong desire to help patients overcome their symptoms by a variety of treatment techniques. In addition, the treatment settings for each of these cases was significantly different (Emmy Von N., sanatorium; Lucie R., office; Katharina, Alpine Inn; Elisabeth V.R., patient's house) and the length of treatment tended to be short and variable (respectively, seven weeks, nine weeks, one session, less than one year). In general, Freud reported fairly positive changes in two of these patients (Lucie R. and Elisabeth V.R.), who each demonstrated amelioration of symptoms at treatment termination and follow-up two to four months later. Results with the other two patients were, respectively, unknown and negative. Katharina was seen for only one session in an Alpine Inn in a situation Freud described more as conversation and "guessing" than psychotherapy and analysis. Freud never saw her again. Emmy Von N. was the first case Freud saw using Breuer's hypnotic method, and he pointed out that the case could not be used for strong proof of the efficacy of the cathartic method. While there was some initial symptom improvement, the patient relapsed, and the "tendency to become sick in the same manner from new traumatic occurrences was not removed" (Breuer and Freud 1895, p. 73).

As noted, many would not consider the above cases as adequate examples of psychoanalysis in terms of either techniques employed or theoretical explanations of behavior using standard psychoanalytic principles. Thus, when Sherwood (1969) attempted to systematically examine Freud's case histories as a group, he was impressed by the fact that in all there were only six extended accounts of individual patients. Further, the accounts had basic shortcomings. Two of the cases were not really examples of Freud's therapy at all, since he had no real firsthand contact with either patient. The Schreber (1911) case was reconstructed entirely from the patient's published memoirs. The case of Little Hans (1909) was conducted by the patient's father, who served as an intermediary between Freud and the patient. The cases of Dora (1905) and the female homosexual (1920) both were terminated in a relatively short period of time. As Sherwood (1969) points out, neither of these two cases provides a complete history or the chance to watch development and change over the course of therapy.

We might add that the case of Dora could be classified as negative treatment outcome, since she was described as being in a "muddle" for four or five weeks after prematurely terminating the three months of treatment. In addition, her symptoms were noted to appear and disappear spontaneously over time. Within nine months of her treatment she experienced a reoccurrence of an attack of aphonia that lasted for six weeks. There is no strong evidence that the treatment had much effect in this case. Similarly, the female homosexual showed no evidence of treatment effects. The patient did not regard homosexuality as a problem and sought treatment only on the urging of her parents. Treatment did not proceed beyond the evaluation of the problem stage. In his description of this case Freud remarked that psychoanalysis is not a very successful treatment for homosexual problems.

Of the two remaining cases (Wolf Man, 1914; Rat Man, 1909), the Wolf Man was described by Freud as not a particularly favorable case and is generally presented as being an interminable analysis. The patient was seen for many years by different analysts and eventually broke down into a paranoid state. We are therefore left with the case of Paul Lorenz (the Rat Man). This case represents Freud's *only* record of a complete and successful analysis. The case appears to have had a very successful outcome at the end of the eleven months of treatment, with the patient experiencing total and lasting improvement. Freud described the treatment as leading to the "complete restoration of the patient's personality and to the removal of his inhibitions" (Freud 1909b, p. 155).

In sum, Freud described in detail only four cases he had seen using psychoanalytic treatment (Dora, female homosexual, Wolf Man, Rat Man). Of these cases only one shows any evidence of significant improvement (Rat Man). It is both curious and striking that Freud chose to demonstrate the utility of psychoanalysis through descriptions of largely unsuccessful cases. Indeed, we must conclude that Freud never presented any data, in statistical or case study form, that demonstrated that his treatment was of benefit to a significant number of the patients he himself saw.

The Nonexistence of Psychoanalysis As an Agreed-upon Therapy

In seeking to review empirical studies of psychoanalysis, one is suddenly confronted with the fact that a unified and consistent treatment approach called "psychoanalysis" does *not* exist. As Kubie observes, the term "psychoanalysis" does not stand for any single or unitary procedure; different individuals can and have used the same label for procedures that vary significantly along many dimensions (Oberndorf et al. 1949). Perhaps one of the most basic and broadest definitions of psychoanalytic therapy is given by Freud (1914b, p. 16):

> It may thus be said that the theory of psychoanalysis is an attempt to account for two striking and unexpected facts of observation which emerge whenever an attempt is made to trace the symptoms of a neurotic back to their sources in his past life: the facts of transference and resistance. Any line of investigation [therapy] which recognizes these two facts and takes

> them as the starting-point of its work has a right to call itself psychoanalysis, even though it arrives at results other than my own. But anyone who takes up other sides of the problem while avoiding these two hypotheses will hardly escape a charge of misappropriation of property by attempted impersonation, if he persists in calling himself a psychoanalyst.

While this definition at least sets psychoanalysis within a framework, studies have shown considerable disagreement among analytic practitioners as to exactly what this form of therapy is. Oberndorf in 1941 sent a questionnaire to twenty-four leading analysts, all of whom had more than twenty years of experience. Eighteen replies were received, and the data were extremely disconcerting. "There was nothing upon which they agreed, not on the type of case best suited for analysis, nor the method of approach, nor the method of termination, nor results, nor how many patients were helped through analysis to avoid serious mental illnesses" (Oberndorf et al 1949, p. 11). Similarly Glover (1958), in his survey of British analysts, noted that except for the analysis of the transference, considerable variations in practice existed with little overall consensus on treatment techniques. Szasz and Nemiroff (1963), in a large-scale survey of 519 analysts in the American, British, and Canadian Psychoanalytic societies, also concluded that psychoanalysts are not a homogeneous group in their practices. In contrast to Hollingshead and Redlich's (1958) prediction, analysts as a group were not consistently analytic and psychological in orientation, rather than directive and organic. Szasz and Nemiroff found that there were very few analysts who did not perform "non-analytic" activities such as physical examinations, treating and communicating with patients' families and others about patients, and prescribing drugs. These authors judged that the difference in practices between analysts and other psychiatrists has become "blurred." Hayman (1967), in a survey of Southern California analysts, also concluded that analysts use drugs with patients they are analyzing considerably more than they freely admit or realize.

Seward (1962–63) reported a study in which sixty-five analysts representing the theoretical schools of Freud, Jung, Horney, and Sullivan were questioned about their goals and anticipated therapy results. While the other schools were found to favor some therapeutic goals and anticipated changes, the nineteen Freudian analysts surveyed did not evidence any agreed upon goals or expected changes. The majority of Freudians did *not* set as a goal conformity to external conditions, better relationships with people, or self-realization and expression. They were about equally divided as to whether insight into personal dynamics was a goal of analysis. With regard to changes they expected as a result of analysis, the large majority of Freudian analysts did *not* expect their therapy would result in symptom relief, self-acceptance and expression, or increases in personal responsibility. They were about equally divided in expecting analysis to lead to improved social adjustment. In short, the study revealed some agreement among the Freudians as to what they were not doing. However, there was no clear consensus between Freudians on either treatment goals or anticipated outcomes.

Vagueness in definition is shown by the experience of the Committee on Evaluation of Psychoanalytic Therapy, set up within the American Psychoanalytic Association in 1947. This committee was not able to attain any widespread agreement as to exactly what constitutes psychoanalysis or psychoanalytic psychotherapy (Rangell 1954). The committee even concluded that there was a strong resistance to investigation of this problem by the members of the American Psychoanalytic Association. Rangell highlights the fact that while some analysts would restrict the definition of psychoanalysis, others feel it should include all treatments utilizing the basic psychoanalytic psychodynamic concepts in an uncovering-insight type of psychotherapy. A number of other authors have also underlined the increasing tendency to obliterate any differences between psychoanalysis and "dynamic" psychotherapy, so that in practice they may be indistinguishable (for example, Alexander 1954, Alexander 1956, Murphy 1958, Strupp and Bergin 1969, Strupp 1973a,b).

Kiesler (1966), in his discussion of some myths of psychotherapy research, calls attention to the "therapist uniformity assumption." This assumption leads researchers toward grouping all analysts together in a research design suggesting they are more alike than different and that whatever they do with their patients may be called "psychoanalysis." In short, the assumptions are that psychoanalysis is whatever psychoanalysts do and that they do the same things. The surveys reviewed above, however, combined with the many studies of therapist behavior and personality, clearly suggest that psychoanalysts may vary widely in terms of what they are calling psychoanalysis. We make this point only to call attention to the fact that studies purporting to look at psychoanalytic therapy may in fact be looking at therapies and therapists differing significantly along many dimensions. It is crucial that researchers adequately describe within their studies the essential ingredients of the therapy they are calling psychoanalysis, and then measure to ensure that those ingredients have been present in the treatment groups. Unfortunately, very few outcome studies describe in detail what they are calling psychoanalysis and even fewer take any measurements to ensure that the patients actually received the ingredients of the described treatment.

The intent of this book is to present the evidence concerning the hypotheses posited by Freud. Yet, as can be seen, this becomes a problem in the area of psychotherapy outcome research, since Freud adopted a relatively broad view as to what constituted the psychoanalytic process. In fact, he was quite hesitant to detail the technique of psychoanalysis.[2] Freud (1913a) concluded, using an analogy between chess and psychotherapy, that we know only some of the opening and closing moves, having nothing but intuitively applied guidelines for the rest. Thus psychoanalytic outcome research is a test more of the therapies labeled analysis by various analysts than it is a direct test of therapy the way Freud might have done it.

Related to the question of whether psychoanalysis exists as a finite therapy is the research investigating the relationship between professed orientation and therapist attitudes and behaviors. Studies show both a considerable degree of heterogeneity in the analytically oriented group and areas in which analysts may be indistinguishable from other therapists. For example, Fiedler (1950a,b) found considerable agreement in the description of the ideal therapeutic relationship, in small and unrepresentative samples of therapists espousing psychoanalytic, nondirective, Adlerian, and eclectic viewpoints. Similarly, Raskin (1965), using much larger samples, obtained results suggesting that Freudian, client-centered, and eclectic therapists show high agreement on what they consider to be characteristics of the ideal therapist.

This is not to deny that differences between analysts and nonanalysts are also clearly detectable. Strupp has been able to show differences between analytically oriented and Rogerian therapists in their responses to a series of patient statements extracted from actual therapeutic interviews (Strupp 1955b) and in their responses to a filmed patient (Strupp 1958b). In the former study, using Bales' system of interaction process analysis,[3] Strupp found that analytically oriented therapists differed significantly in all categories from Rogerians. They showed a marked predilection for exploratory responses, but they also displayed a greater and more even distribution over a variety of other techniques such as passive acceptance, structuring, interpretation, reassurance, direct factual questions, and passive rejection. The Rogerians relied heavily on reflective techniques as opposed to all other categories. Most of the differences between the two groups might well have been due to the Rogerians leaning predominantly on one technique (reflection of feelings), while the analytically oriented therapists displayed a variety of techniques, leaning most heavily on exploratory questions. It should be noted that the many techniques used by analytically oriented therapists suggest the multidimensionality of the label.

In a later investigation, Strupp (1958b) asked groups of analytically oriented psychologists and client-centered therapists to assume they were interviewing a patient presented on film and to write down their responses to the patient at each point where the film sequence was interrupted for thirty seconds. The therapists were free to respond or to remain "silent." Following the film, all therapists filled out a comprehensive questionnaire encompassing their views about the presented patient and his treatment. As in the previous study, Rogerians strongly favored the reflection of feeling technique, while the analytic sample preferred exploratory questions. Analytic therapists responded with significantly more silence and with responses showing a higher degree of inference or initiative. The groups did not differ with regard to diagnoses offered or evaluations of the patient's degree of ego strength, anxiety, insight, social adjustment, and disturbance. However, analytic therapists were significantly less favorable in their prognostic judgments, and they professed a more negative attitude toward the patient.[4] Analysts were also more inclined to make treatment plans and to set up therapeutic goals. In addition, analytic therapists tended to advocate procedures in which the therapist actively attempts to induce patient change in attitudes and feelings (interpretations, reassurance, firmness). Notable in this study was the finding that psychoanalysts in the sample (members of the American Psychoanalytic Association), whose training might be assumed to be relatively homogeneous, varied more widely in their responses than client-centered therapists.

Fey (1958) used a questionnaire (composed of issues commonly arising in the conduct of psychotherapy) to study differences between thirty-four therapists who identified their orientation as Rogerian, analytic, or eclectic. Consistent with the previous studies, correlations between therapists showed greatest homogeneity among Rogerians and greatest heterogeneity among analysts with regard to how they would behave with patients. The notion that analysts are more variable in approach than client-centered therapists is also supported by Strupp's (1957) analysis of two psychotherapy protocols respectively reflecting client-centered therapy and "insight therapy with reeducative goals based on psychoanalytic principles." Over the course of the therapy sessions examined, the therapists' activity in analytically oriented therapy varied in terms of type of therapeutic activity, degree of inference, dynamic focus, and initiative. In contrast, the client-centered therapists' activity consisted principally of reflections of feeling.

Sloane et al. (1975b) were able to compare three experienced behavior therapists with three experienced analysts in terms of how they interacted with patients. Analysts placed much more emphasis on the therapeutic relationship and were much less directive. They spoke less, offered fewer suggestions, gave less information, and were less revealing of their own values. Although both groups showed similar levels of warmth and acceptance, analysts showed lower levels of accurate empathy, depth of interpersonal contact, and therapist genuineness. Some of the obtained differences between the two groups of therapists may have been due to one of the analysts being consistently rated lower than all the other therapists on the measures of acceptance, empathy, interpersonal contact, and genuineness. Overall, patients viewed the analysts as less authoritarian and believed that they encouraged greater independence than did the behavior therapists.

Other studies have used factor-analytic statistical techniques to try to arrive at basic dimensions that might differentiate therapists ascribing to different orientations. Sundland and Barker (1962), on the basis of their data, took issue with Fiedler's (1950a, 1950b) general conclusion that experienced therapists of different orientations are more similar than experienced and inexperienced therapists of the same orientation. They concluded that experienced therapists of different schools are alike in their stress on some factors, such as the importance of empathy, but significantly different on other dimensions. They found one general factor that seemed to differentiate Freudians, Sullivanians, and Rogerians irrespective of the level of therapist experience. The two poles of this general factor were labeled "analytic" and "experiential." Freudians and Rogerians fell toward the extremes of the analytic and experiential poles, respectively, with Sullivanians falling in the middle. "The analytic pole stresses conceptualizing, the training of the therapist, planning of therapy, unconscious processes, and a restriction of therapist spontaneity. The experiential pole deemphasizes conceptualizing, stresses the personality of the therapist, an unplanned approach to therapy, and accepts therapist spontaneity" (Sundland and Barker 1962, p. 205).

McNair and Lorr (1964) postulated three dimensions to adequately characterize therapeutic technique. Factor analysis of a constructed inventory revealed the following three hypothesized technique dimensions: psychoanalytic, impersonal versus personal, and directive techniques. Psychoanalytic techniques referred to such things as analysis of resistance and transference;

free association; interpretation of dreams, mannerisms, and slips of the tongue; the unconscious; discussion of childhood events; and the notion that change depends on understanding childhood. Impersonal versus personal techniques were hypothesized to represent therapists' affective responses to patients in terms of distance and objectivity versus warmth and spontaneity. Directiveness was hypothesized to represent a directive, active approach to treatment. High scores on this dimension represented such things as therapists setting the goals for treatment, being active during the hour, leading the interview, having an overall treatment plan, and aiming at improving the patient's social adjustment. The measures were developed on a sample of 265 psychiatrists, psychologists, and social workers. The therapists were not compared in terms of their stated orientation, and there were no psychoanalysts in the sample. Nonetheless, the relative independence of the three factors indicates that therapists ascribing to "psychoanalytic techniques" may vary significantly in the degree to which they control the course of therapy and the degree to which they maintain personal-affective relationships with their patients. Differences among therapists ascribing to different orientations were also found by Wallach and Strupp (1964) in a questionnaire study based on samples of orthodox Freudians, Sullivanians, Rogerians, and general psychoanalytic therapists. Orthodox Freudians were highest in maintaining personal distance and keeping verbal interventions at a minimum. They were lowest in considering therapy as an artistic activity. The client-centered group was distinct in their lack of preference for intensive psychotherapy and their considering therapy as an art.

The studies outlined above all seem to be consistent with the idea that therapists ascribing to Freudian ideas may differ in some gross ways from therapists ascribing to other theories. However, from our perspective, one of the most striking features of these studies is the extreme variability as to what analytic therapy may mean. In fact, it may well be that therapists identifying themselves as analysts represent a greater diversity of techniques and treatment behaviors than therapists identifying themselves with other schools of thought. Interestingly, research using Rogerian therapists, who appear to be a relatively homogeneous group in the studies just cited, has suggested that these therapists are quite variable in the degree to which they reflect qualities considered necessary for successful therapy: warmth, empathy, and genuineness (Truax and Carkhuff 1967; Truax and Mitchell 1971). The general conclusion drawn from much of this work has been that therapy can be for better or for worse, and that it is significantly dependent on the therapeutic conditions the therapist is able to provide. Consequently, if it is true that analytic therapists as a group are at least as variable in approach as therapists espousing other orientations, we would expect the overall results of treatment to be variable. The data reviewed thus far suggests that analysts may be even more variable as a group than other clinicians.

The variability of analysts in obtaining treatment results is illustrated by Klein's (1965) study of analysts in training. Part of this study involved re-interviewing a sample of patients one to seven years after they had been treated by student analysts. A global score of therapeutic change for each patient was then compared with the faculties' overall average rating of each analyst at the end of training. Of the patients treated by "superior" students, 63 percent showed substantial changes, while only 39 percent treated by "average" students and 28 percent treated by "below average" students evidenced comparable changes. A similar finding is reported by Cartwright (1956) in his re-analysis of data collected by Barron and Leary (1955) comparing Minnesota Multiphasic Personality Inventory profile changes in psychoneurotic patients with and without psychotherapy. While the psychiatrist, psychologist, and social-worker therapists in the study were not psychoanalysts, they all had at least three years of postdoctoral or postgraduate training and experience, and their therapy was conducted from a "psychoanalytic" theoretical orientation. The original data analysis revealed that the therapy patients did not improve significantly more than did the nontreated, waiting-list control patients. Cartwright's re-analysis of the data demonstrated that being in therapy led to significantly more *variable* results than being on the waiting list. While some patients in therapy deteriorated to a greater extent than did the waiting-list patients, others improved significantly more. Comparing the mean changes in both groups deceptively covered the fact that therapy either led to patients getting better or getting worse! The variability of results in other studies to be cited may similarly be indicative of differences in therapists, techniques, or even patients selected as suitable for treatment.

In many of the studies presented above, those identified as being analytic in orientation were not necessarily trained analysts and were thus potentially more heterogeneous in training background. Further, it is possible that analysts might be in basic agreement in their understanding of a case but choose alternative pathways in their attempts to reach a common goal. However, studies in which trained psychoanalysts have attempted to formulate and make judgments concerning case material have also suggested discrepancies between analysts in their definition and use of psychoanalytic concepts. Seitz (1966) reports a study in which six analysts at the Chicago Institute of Psychoanalysis met for three years in an attempt to see whether they could eventually develop a method that would yield a relatively high consensus between analysts in their independent formulations of the same case material. The group eventually disbanded unable to make progress in developing a reliable interpretive technique.

The forthrightness of Seitz's paper and the openness concerning the nature of the difficulties in reaching consensus reveal some of the problems surrounding the appraisal of analytic case material. The six analysts gave independent interpretive formulations of both dreams and an ongoing single continuous case. The material to be interpreted consisted of interview notes written by the treatment analyst during and after each interview. The analysts' task was to interpret what they considered to be the "focal" conflict in each interview. They were also to identify the factors and events giving rise to the conflict (precipitating stimuli), and the principle defenses against and attempted solutions of the focal conflict. It is possible that the difficulties the analysts had in reaching agreement reflects the ambiguity of the interview notes as well as the vagueness of the concepts being used. The chief defect in the judgments, according to Seitz, was an excessive reliance on intuitive impressions and insufficient attention to systematic and critical checking of interpretations. The analysts showed greatest agreement in identifying the focal conflict and least agreement in identifying principal defenses and attempted solutions. Meetings between the analysts to resolve disagreements resulted in an overall modification of the interpretation 30 percent of the time. The notion of large differences between analysts is supported by the fairly wide range in how often each analyst modified his interpretations. One analyst changed his formulations 54 percent of the time, while another made modifications only 8 percent of the time.

Seitz points out that judgments by analysts may lack consensus because of the concept of "overdetermination." That is, observed behavior may be determined by more than one cause. The lack of consensus could therefore mean that various interpretations are all partially right rather than that some are wholly right while others are all wrong. In addition, Seitz suggests that analysts may be able to obtain better consensus with material obtained toward the end of a successful analysis than at the beginning, since the meaning of the material produced at that point should theoretically be less disguised and obscure. If this is so, it could also mean that successful patients learn to produce material that analysts can agree on, or that successful treatment is defined in terms of the production of material that analysts tend to interpret in the same way. In any event, Seitz's study demonstrates that there is a consensus problem, that analysts vary as to what they select as important, and that it is possible that some analysts are much more accurate in their interpretations than others.

Weber et al. (1966) arrived at very similar findings in an examination of the reliability attained by nine psychoanalysts in rating ego strength on nine specific five-point scales or balances. Clinic records at the Columbia Psychoanalytic Clinic were coded by the analysts at the beginning and end of treatment in terms of the degree to which the patients rated were either overly active or overly inhibited on each of the dimensions of "ego strength" being rated: dependency, pleasure, sex, affect, defense, emergency emotions, guilt, pathology, and social relations. Coding took place over a period of approximately two years. As in the Seitz study, the analysts were highly variable in their ratings at the beginning of therapy, with a tendency toward greater reliability at therapy termination. In general, however, while each coder demonstrated a consistent and characteristic style in assessing ego strength, there was no overall consistency among the different analysts.

A study by Sklansky et al. (1966) focused on verbal interaction, therapist interventions, and levels of meaning in psychotherapy. Data for the study were obtained from ratings made on transcripts of six psychotherapy cases. Five of the six therapists were psychoanalysts. Again the findings highlighted analyst variability. The authors wrote: "Our therapists were highly idiosyncratic in the nature of their interventions, and each one had preferred response tendencies. For instance, while one therapist used direct intervention at the manifest level almost half the time, another preferred the indirect approach at all levels of meaning for almost half of his activity. More than a quarter of the interventions of two of our therapists were scored as not relevant to the meaning of the immediate segment. Even the amount of verbalization varied tremendously among the therapists. Clearly, a standardized technique of psychotherapeutic intervention is not revealed in this study" (pp. 167–168).

Another pertinent study is reported by Lakin and Lebovits (1958), who were interested in investigating the influence of theoretical orientation upon a therapist's conceptualization of a patient. Minimal identifying information concerning a patient in the initial phase of therapy was provided to seventeen psychotherapists (nine psychoanalytically trained psychiatrists, five eclectic psychiatrists, and three client-centered therapists). After presentation of the information, the therapists were asked to "free associate" to the question: "As a psychotherapist, how would you think about this person?" Responses were compared in terms of the mode of speculation and selective emphasis. Findings paralleled the results of Seitz's study. Analysts were found to produce many more associations than the other two therapist groups; they speculated much more freely, were less concerned about the possibility of being grossly in error, and even seemed to tolerate mutually contradictory associations. Analysts were also more concerned with the etiology of the patient's difficulties than the other therapists. The variation in analyst speculations was highlighted by the considerable differences shown in their assessments of the patient's diagnosis, which included obsessive personality, character neurosis, reactive depression, psychosis, and phobic reaction. Most of the therapists in the other groups did not feel there was enough evidence to venture a diagnosis. This study again clearly reveals extensive analyst heterogeneity as well as the tendency to speculate on minimal data.

A similar conclusion is drawn by Cutler et al. (1958) in a study of therapist ability to rate depth of interpretation from both typescript and tape-recorded interviews. Ratings were obtained from a group of clinical psychologists and compared with ratings obtained from four psychoanalysts and four psychiatrists who had completed their personal analysis and were undergoing control training in psychoanalysis ("fledglings"). The expectation was that there would be progressively greater sensitivity and hence reliability in rating depth of interpretation with increasing analytic training. While the differences were small, the results proved to be just the opposite of the hypothesis. Psychologists consistently showed the highest reliability and analysts the greatest variability. The authors noted—as have others faced with the same type of results—that perhaps analytic training makes it possible to entertain a greater number of alternative possibilities and thus decreases reliability. Isaacs and Haggard (1966) report another investigation showing reliability ratings obtained by various professional therapist groups. As part of a larger project, samples of experienced psychologists, social workers, and psychoanalysts rated patient statements on a five-point scale for "meaningfulness." While there was a significant correlation within each professional group, both the psychologist and social worker groups showed higher agreement among themselves than the psychoanalyst group.

Studies of analysts' abilities to make consistent judgments and predictions about patient behavior have also raised questions concerning the vagueness and variety of definitions used by analysts for the same concepts (Bellak 1958, 1961, Bellak and Smith 1956, Benjamin 1959, Knapp 1963).[5] As Bellak and Smith (1956) write in a study of analysts' judgments of recorded analytic sessions:

> There was great divergence in the conception and definition of variables among the participants. Though clinically each seemed to know what he was doing and talking about, it became strikingly clear that analytic concepts are poorly defined and not so useful for communication as they might be. This state of affairs results doubtless from the fact that Freud, a pioneer, formulated hypotheses that helped him at a particular time to understand, predict, and analyze. As he advanced in clinical understanding, he reformulated his hypotheses to achieve progressively more fitting models of what he observed. Sometimes he remembered his earlier formulations and integrated them with later ones, sometimes not. The result is that at best one can use a concept by stating its date, but even then there are divergences. We suggest that a team of psychoanalysts and social scientists be formed for attempts at definition of the basic vocabulary (pp. 411–412).

This discussion should not be taken to mean that precise, agreed-upon definitions of analytic concepts cannot be arrived at. Indeed the hundreds of studies cited throughout this book attest to the fact that analytic variables can be operationally defined. Even in Bellak and Smith's (1956) judgment study, analysts were shown to be in significant agreement with each other as to the amount of a variable present once they agreed it was present in the first place. For example, analysts' ratings of the intensity of transference, resistance, and insight were significantly correlated if they first identified these variables as being present in the session they were rating. Analysts were also in significant agreement in picking the central themes of sessions from a presented series of equally plausible choices. The many studies of psychoanalytic hypotheses suggest that it is quite possible for analysts to arrive at consistent judgments, provided they start out with the same operational definitions for the concepts they are judging. It seems plausible that the day-to-day therapeutic practice of analysts may be based on less consistent and precise definitions than are found in research studies where analysts or others are asked to make thoughtful judgments in highly defined and often artificial situations. It is probable that merely asking analysts to focus on their operations and thought processes, as in a research project, may foster greater clarity, precision, and consistency in the definitions used.

Again, these points suggest even greater variability in actual therapeutic practice than in structured research tasks. Viewing analyst judgment and activities from the vantage point of research projects raises the idea that there are significant differences between analysts in approach to patients. However, research studies often leave out the intricacies of therapist-patient interaction. It is possible that therapy may be a self-corrective process and that different analysts might move toward similar interactions with the same patients over time. While differential skill and sensitivity might result in some therapists reaching an optimal level of therapeutic efficiency long before others, most analysts might eventually arrive at the same conclusions, given enough time and therapist flexibility.

Further, it is an open question as to how consistent or valid a therapist's operations or hypotheses have to be to either keep patients coming to therapy or produce changes in them. Certainly the fact that typical analyses are expected to take hundreds of sessions and possibly years of time allows for analysts becoming more like one another with a given case as a result of feedback. While this is consistent with Freud's (1913a) point of knowing only the opening and closing moves of an analysis, it is only speculation at this point that most analysts would eventually arrive on the same conceptual or technique path if they were to work with the same patient.

Uniformities in the Psychoanalytic Appearance

In spite of the strong evidence that psychoanalysts are extremely variable with regard to how they practice analysis and the concepts they emphasize in understanding the causes of a patient's difficulties, there seems to be a push toward viewing analytic therapy as a single, uniform procedure. Such a view leads people toward being for or against a totality called "analysis" without raising questions as to whether individual aspects of the therapy should stand or fall on their individual merits. We find ourselves asking why this blindness to differences and nuances in analytic practice should exist. Perhaps one answer lies in the deceptive surface similarities between analysts, analytic patients, and the settings in which analytic therapy takes place. It is our conjecture that these similarities lend themselves to a stereotyping of the analytic appearance and the false generalization that all analytic therapy is the same, since there tends to be some consistency in the general analytic appearance.

The fact that similarities in appearance exist is demonstrated by demographic studies of American psychoanalysts and their patients. Representative of these studies is a large-scale survey by Henry et al. (1971) of the majority of therapists in New York, Chicago, and Los Angeles. They found psychoanalysts, clinical psychologists, and psychiatric social workers to be startlingly similar in a number of ways (see also Holt and Luborsky 1958, Hollingshead and Redlich 1958). Further, their findings of background similarity tended to show even higher levels of homogeneity for psychoanalysts than for the other groups of therapist practitioners and tended to support some of the popular stereotypes concerning analyst background. In brief, analysts were predominantly upwardly mobile, politically liberal Jewish men who traced their origins to eastern European countries and who grew up in large metropolitan areas. They also tended to be either second generation Americans or foreign born (25 percent of the analysts indicated they were born in other countries). By examining age in relation to other factors, it was discovered that rather than broadening their base, analysts are becoming increasingly recruited from the ranks of Jews with eastern European ethnic ties. In short, psychoanalysis is becoming even more homogeneous with regard to the cultural identities of its practitioners. Henry et al. point to the values of the eastern European Jewish cultural tradition as a factor producing an affinity between psychoanalysis and individuals with this background. In particular, they note an emphasis on ritual, a strong accent on intellectual knowledge, and a nontranscendental approach to understanding human behavior. The tendency for analytic therapists to have similar backgrounds has probably reinforced the notion that their in-treatment behavior is also similar. However, as we have pointed out, the weight of the evidence suggests that this conclusion is false.

In like manner, surveys of patients in psychoanalysis have highlighted some general similarities in the patients accepted for this form of treatment (Aronson and Weintraub 1968a, Bieber et al. 1962, Hamburg et al. 1967, Kadushin 1969, Klee and Warthen 1968, Siegel 1962, Srole et al. 1962, Weintraub and Aronson 1968). We underline the term "accepted," as analytic patients tend to be a highly select group of individuals who represent a small minority of the number of people who actually apply for psychoanalytic treatment. More will be said about this point in our discussion of the problems in evaluating current outcome data in psychoanalysis. Representative of the data gathered on analytic patients in America are Weintraub and Aronson's demographic survey of the complete case loads (144 patients) of thirty East Coast analysts (Aronson and Weintraub 1968a, Weintraub and Aronson 1968). This survey revealed that typical private analytic patients are almost all native Americans, white, relatively young (between the ages of thirty and fifty), and predominantly of Jewish or Protestant background. While Jews are greatly overrepresented in the patient population, Catholics are greatly underrepresented. This finding is paralleled in the data on analyst religion described above. In addition, patients tend to be well educated, with only a small minority not having at least some training beyond the high school level.

Another finding of the survey was that over half the patients were either active as practitioners within the mental health field or closely related to a mental health practitioner. The majority of patients were psychiatrists, psychologists, psychiatric social workers, psychiatric nurses, or married to a member of the mental health profession. Knapp and his co-workers (1960) have also reported that "approximately half" of a sample of 100 cases applying for analysis with candidates in analytic training were workers in mental health fields. The high number of mental health workers seeking analysis raises the question whether analysis is practiced primarily as a form of treatment or as a form of education (gaining self-knowledge). As we have suggested earlier, Freud himself seemed to move in the direction of viewing the value of analysis more in terms of educational than therapeutic gains. This view has since been re-echoed many times (Menninger 1958, Szasz 1963). Aronson and Weintraub's findings indicate that the more senior and experienced the analyst, the more his practice is devoted to treating professionals and mental health workers. They write: "Analysis is openly considered an educational process as well as a therapeutic technique for candidates in analytic training. The same can undoubtedly be said for other patients/students who may use their analytic discoveries in their work. To a great extent, therefore, the analytic session is a tutorial encounter. The senior faculty teaches 'graduates' while the candidates carry much of the 'undergraduate' load" (Aronson and Weintraub 1968a, p. 96).

The relatively high level of educational and professional success of most analytic patients also suggests that as a group they may give fewer indications of gross psychological disturbance than patients being treated by other forms of therapy. Indeed, it would seem, from most of the studies reporting on the selection of patients for different forms of treatment, that analytic candidates are typically chosen from patients displaying a greater number of assets and less impaired functioning (Feldman 1968, Kernberg et al. 1972, Knapp et al. 1960, Weber et al. 1967). Luborsky (1962) utilized a 100-point "Health-Sickness Rating Scale" in showing that analytic patients at the Menninger Foundation begin treatment at significantly "healthier" points than patients being treated by either expressive or supportive psychotherapy.

Obviously, seeking private treatment for three to five sessions a week is an expensive proposition. Thus, it is not surprising to find that private analytic patients tend to earn significantly more money than the average citizen. This general conclusion, drawn from the cited studies of analytic patients, is underlined by Aronson and Weintraub's (1968a) finding that 32 percent of the analytic patients in their sample obtained all or part of their income from inherited wealth or personal investment. As these researchers note, the need to get away for a number of appointments each week also increases the probability that analytic patients would be either high-ranking executives, self-employed professionals, or housewives. One might expect that analytic patients being seen in clinic facilities would be less affluent than those seen privately. Still, there are indications that current or future financial position, even in analytic clinics, may play some role in whether a patient is accepted for treatment. Feldman (1968) reports that one of the difficulties for student analysts is trying to select patients who may be able to pay their own way after 200 or 300 hours of analysis. It is also true that many patients are seen in clinics when they can no longer afford private treatment.

A possible problem arises in evaluating the meaning of results obtained in clinic research if we assume differences in economic and professional status between clinic and private patients. If significant differences in patient populations exist, it is questionable whether the conclusions drawn about outcome from clinic treatment are generalizable to private treatment. An obviously related fact is that clinic patients tend to be seen by less experienced and presumably less skillful analysts, raising again the question of comparability of results. Luborsky et al. (1971), in an extensive review of factors influencing the outcome of psychotherapy, found that eight of thirteen studies dealing with therapist experience showed that more experienced therapists achieved better results with patients than inexperienced therapists. Additionally, three of five studies showed a positive relationship between a therapist's skill and treatment outcome.

In terms of the comparability of clinic and private analysands, there is evidence that patients being seen in analytic clinics may be quite similar to their private practice counterparts. Kadushin (1969) reports an extensive study of patient motivation for seeking treatment at ten psychiatric clinics in New York City. The clinics represented three different major treatment approaches: analytic, medical, and religio-psychiatric. The psychoanalytic clinics used in the study were those oriented toward training new psychoanalysts while perpetuating and developing psychoanalytic theory. The obtained data support the idea that analytic clinic patients tend to be drawn from the same pool of individuals as analytic private patients, with one qualification. Again, the patients were found to be almost all white and predominantly Jewish, as Jews represented 60 percent of all applicants to the psychoanalytic clinics.[6] In addition, the patients' level of sophistication, educational attainments, and occupational characteristics were all similar to those of private patients.[7] In general, the more closely affiliated a clinic was with the orthodox psychoanalytic movement, the higher was the patient applicants' social class in terms of education and occupation. Most of the patients at the analytic clinics had at least some college education, and the clinic populations evidenced a large number of college and postgraduate students. Most patients had already seen at least one therapist. Perhaps the chief differentiating characteristic between clinic and private analytic patients was that clinic analysands were somewhat younger and relatedly lacked the funds for private treatment. In most other ways the two groups of patients appeared to be members of the same social groups that make up the mass of analytic patients.

Kadushin (1969), in his study and review of the literature, develops the idea that a major segment of the applicants to psychotherapy clinics and, most notably, applicants to analytic clinics represent a fairly homogeneous and definable group: "The Friends and Supporters of Psychotherapy." This group tends to be quite identified with and knowledgeable about psychotherapy. Generally, they know others with similar problems, have friends who are seeing psychotherapists, and have done some reading about therapy. Culturally sophisticated, they are likely to have attended plays, concerts, museums, art galleries, and cocktail parties several times a year. Additionally, this group is more likely to come from professions in the arts, communication, teaching, and medicine rather than from engineering, law, or business. Kadushin's study also supports the idea that patients accepted at analytic clinics tend to match their therapist in expectations about psychoanalysis. Through discussions, previous therapy experiences, and reading books about psychotherapy, the analytic patients surveyed expected to do most of the therapeutic work themselves and expected that treatment would last for at least one year. They also evidenced a desire for changes in their sexual lives and their basic values.

In line with the question whether analysis is basically educational or therapeutic was the typical analytic patient's expressed hope for "greater self-understanding." Goldstein (1962, 1973) concludes from his review of the empirical literature on therapist expectations that dynamic therapists typically anticipate being reflective rather than active, personality-oriented rather than problem-oriented, largely abstract rather than concrete, and catalytic or interpretive rather than directive. Investigations of analytic patients thus clearly suggest that they are in high expectational tune with their potential analysts. The careful selection of analytic patients from the large pool of patient applicants would tend to further increase the probability of a high expectational match between therapist and patient.

Interestingly, despite this apparent surface similarity, there is evidence that analysts may be quite heterogeneous in their values. Welkowitz et al. (1967) report a study in which they measured the values of thirty-eight therapists from psychoanalytic training institutes in New York City. Values were measured by means of the Ways to Live scale and the Strong Vocational Interest Blank.[8] Both of these measures provide scales over a wide range of dimensions and different preferences. One finding of this study was that the analysts did not share a general set of values. Consistent with all the other studies cited in this chapter, there was considerable heterogeneity with regard to personal preferences and desirable ways to live. We should note, however, that according to the classical analytic position, differences in analyst personality should not affect the therapy process. Seward (1962–63), in his study of analysts from different schools of therapy, did indeed find that in direct opposition to the data from other analytic schools, Freudians significantly denied the influence of their values on treatment. The studies reviewed thus far, as well as those to be reviewed in later sections, are not in agreement with this belief in analyst interchangeability.

Aside from the similarities between analysts and their patients that we have discussed, there are other uniformities in treatment appearance that would tend to foster the notion of analysis as a uniform procedure. These include the fact that analysis as a therapy usually requires a number of fifty-minute to one-hour sessions per week over a period of time that can be calculated in years and a significant financial investment if the therapy is to be undertaken privately. The sessions tend to revolve around a patient talking about himself and the relationship of his past to his present. The fact that therapists share the same title "psychoanalyst" and maybe even use the same theoretical vocabulary also fosters the notion that they are doing the same thing.

Overview and Comment

Within this chapter we have sketched the evolution of Freud's therapy and the data he used to justify his conclusions. In general, the therapy shifted from an initial concern with the treatment of symptoms into a search for the underlying motivations of a patient's conflicts. Implicit in this shift from therapeutic focus to theoretical understanding was the untested idea that a patient would feel better if he understood the causes of his conflicts. From this assumption, most readers appear to translate the substantiation of theoretical points to mean therapeutic successes. However, we do not believe the potential validity of the theory can be taken as a measure of therapeutic success. Hence any presentation focusing primarily on the substantiation of Freud's personality theory does not tell us whether the therapy helps people to overcome their conflicts and discomforts.

Freud's data consisted principally of theoretically focused case descriptions drawn from a select population of patients, with very few cases being presented in any detail. There was little emphasis placed on therapeutic outcome, and Freud presents virtually no evidence that his therapy was of value to a significant number of the patients he himself saw. In spite of this, Freud's persuasive discussions of his theory have apparently left the impression that his therapy was successful. Further, although Freud gave no indications of having tried his therapy on very diverse groups of patients and presented little evidence of therapeutic success, his explicit and implicit list of positive pretherapy patient attributes have come to be broadly used as indicators of psychoanalytic therapy potential: youth, education, intelligence, motivation, time, money, and a relative lack of profound personality disturbance. Current practitioners of analytic therapy seem to have followed Freud's lead in selecting patients with the general attributes he outlined. They seem to have used his admittedly incomplete presentations of analytic therapy as a guide for their speculations and actions. Therefore, a cursory look at psychoanalysis may give the impression that analysts are involved in the same procedure. The experimental literature argues against this conclusion in demonstrating that analytic therapy can be an extremely variable phenomenon. Freud's writings have provided analysts with an impetus for speculation that has led toward multiple, sometimes inconsistent hypotheses often based on minimal data. The lack of reliability between analysts in the speculation process suggests that analysts as a group are not rigorous enough in their examination of the evidence for and against the hypotheses raised during their interactions with patients. Again we must note that analysis may be ineffective in helping a patient feel better, even if all the hypotheses concerning that patient's personality are correct.

The validity of psychoanalysis as a therapy has been greatly clouded by the controversy as to whether the eventual goal is symptom reduction or solely the acquisition of self-knowledge.[9] This presents no problem if self-knowledge (insight) results directly in symptom reduction, an issue we will explore more thoroughly in our section on insight. However, if insight and symptom reduction are not highly correlated, we are left with the possibility of a valid personality theory and a therapy of dubious value, unless the primary goal of the "treatment" is educational. Interestingly, as we have noted, many practitioners do emphasize the educational aspects of analysis over the treatment aspects. Our review also suggests that patients typically selected for analysis are those who might value a goal of knowledge acquisition in and of itself. The basic issue of whether symptom improvement is a primary goal of psychoanalysis is complicated even more by Freud's warning of the danger in analysts displaying too great an interest in patient change.[10] The experimental literature seems most supportive of viewing psychoanalysis, as currently practiced, more in terms of a framework of conceptual and technique possibilities than as a single, unified, monolithic approach to patients that is applied in a consistent manner by different therapists. Nonetheless, since a considerable amount of work has been published, we will devote the next chapter to a review of the studies attempting to evaluate whether a therapy labeled "psychoanalysis" is of help to patients seeking treatment. This review will focus on both the problems and results found in these studies. In viewing these global evaluations, we caution that the lack of consistency in the therapies being called "psychoanalysis" may obscure the potential validity of specific analytic techniques and explanations.

NOTES

1. Sherwood (1969) has called attention to discrepancies between Freud's notes and his published account of the Lorenz case. Sherwood makes the point that such transpositions and omissions of material exemplify a tendency toward differential recollection and emphasis that is presumably dependent upon the analyst's interests and theoretical presuppositions.

2. Strachey concludes that Freud was reluctant to publish material on his technique for a number of reasons. He was hesitant to allow his patients to know too many of the details of his approach, felt that new analysts in training should not be given hard and fast rules, and thought that the proper mastery of the subject could best be acquired from

clinical experiences and the analyst's own analysis rather than books (Strachey 1958, p. 87).

3. Bales' (1950) interaction process analysis is a rating system for classifying the interaction process into twelve categories representing the positive and negative aspects of orientation, evaluation, decision making, control over others, tension management, and integration. The unit of observation is the simple sentence and typically specific classes of nonverbal behavior are scored at one-minute intervals. The principal scores derived are the number of acts of a given kind in each category and the ratios of such scores.

4. In contrast, Weiss (1972) reports a study in which students with an analytic orientation displayed a significant bias toward judging therapeutic outcome more positively than students with a behavioristic orientation.

5. Freud appeared somewhat pessimistic about using psychoanalytic theory to predict future behavior. He stated:

> So long as we trace the development from its final outcome backwards, the chain of events appears continuous, and we feel we have gained an insight which is completely satisfactory or even exhaustive. But if we proceed the reverse way, if we start from the premises inferred from the analysis and try to follow these up to the final result, then we no longer get the impression of an inevitable sequence of events which could not have been otherwise determined. We notice at once that there might have been another result, and that we might have been just as well able to understand and explain the latter. The synthesis is thus not so satisfactory as the analysis; in other words, from a knowledge of the premises we could not have foretold the nature of the result . . . we never know beforehand which of the determining factors will prove the weaker or the stronger. We only say at the end that those which succeeded must have been the stronger. Hence the chain of causation can always be recognized with certainty if we follow the line of analysis, whereas to predict it along the line of synthesis is impossible. (Freud 1920b, pp. 167–168)

6. Srole et al. (1962), in a study of mental health in midtown Manhattan, found that in proportion to their representation in the population, Jews are about four times as likely to attend psychiatric outpatient clinics as are Catholics or Protestants. In the Manhattan population identified as having psychiatric impairment, Jews were also ten times as likely as Catholics and two and one half times as likely as Protestants to be psychiatric outpatients. In contrast to these psychiatric figures are Suckman's (1964) results on physical illness obtained from a sample of patients in a Manhattan neighborhood. These results support the idea that the Jewish tendency to seek psychiatric treatment does not reflect a general hypochondriasis, in that Jews are not more likely to consult a physician for physical problems than other ethnic groups.

7. Results paralleling the finding of psychiatric outpatients being better educated and of higher social class than the general population are reported for outpatient clinics by Avnet (1952), Gurin et al. (1960), Srole et al. (1962), and for the private patients of a sample of New York psychoanalysts by Bieber et al. (1962).

8. The Ways to Live scale (Morris 1956) is an instrument which aims at measuring basic human values. It is composed of thirteen different paragraphs, each describing a way of life, which the respondent rates on a seven-point scale for the degree to which he personally would like to lead that way of life. The Strong Vocational Interest Blank (Strong 1943) consists of 400 items concerned with the subject's preferences in occupations, school subjects, amusements, miscellaneous activities, and peculiarities of people.

9. We have designated insight and/or symptom reduction as major goals of analysis, since we believe this is where Freud placed the emphasis in his writings. Insight acquisition is stressed in Freud's famous statement regarding the aims of psychoanalytic therapeutic efforts: "Its intention is, indeed, to strengthen the ego, to make it more independent of the superego, to widen its field of perception and enlarge its organization, so that it can appropriate fresh portions of the id. Where id was, there shall ego be. It is a work of culture —not unlike the draining of the Zuider Zee (Freud 1933c, p. 80)." Nunberg at the Marienbad symposium on the therapeutic results of psychoanalysis restated this major emphasis in Freud's writing: "Wherever Freud speaks about therapy, he ascribes the main share in healing to the *process* of bringing into consciousness that which is unconscious. All we know about therapy is actually comprised in this single sentence (Nunberg 1937, p. 161)."

Freud also gave indications in his writings of a desire for symptom reduction and positive behavioral changes. His simplest and most famous statement of this aim is the goal of being able to love and to work (Erikson 1950, p. 141). Both behavioral and insight goals are stressed in Freud's statement concerning what is meant by "the end of an analysis." He wrote:

> From a practical standpoint it is easy to answer. An analysis is ended when the analyst and the patient cease to meet each other for the analytic session. This happens when two conditions have been approximately fulfilled: first, that the patient shall no longer be suffering from his symptoms and shall have overcome his anxieties and inhibitions; and secondly, that the analyst shall judge that so much repressed material has been made conscious, so much that was unintelligible has been explained, and so much internal resistance conquered, that there is no need to fear a repetition of the pathological processes concerned. If one is prevented by external difficulties from reaching this goal, it is better to speak of an *incomplete* analysis rather than of an *unfinished* one. (Freud 1937a, p. 219)

It should not need repetition at this point that analysts currently practicing are not in total agreement with a goal of either insight and/or symptom reduction.

10. Greenacre has documented that this warning against "furor therapeuticus" appears in numerous places in Freud's writings (Oberndorf et al. 1949). Wallerstein (1965) also comments at length on the seeming paradox between goallessness as a technical tool marking the proper analytic therapeutic stance and the analyst's ambitious goal of fundamental personality change. Freud seemed to feel that marked therapeutic zeal on the part of the analyst could be a reflection of underlying sadism and could result in the distortion of case material. This concern is a possible indication of Freud's desire to obtain nondistorted data for his personality theory even if the data are obtained at the expense of positive therapeutic effect.

Chapter 8

The Outcome of Psychoanalytic Treatment

INDICATIONS are that Freud would not have accepted empirical studies based on statistical techniques as suitable evidence for evaluating the effectiveness of his therapy. He seemed to feel that individual differences between cases precluded their being statistically combined in a globally meaningful way. He felt that one's individual experience with patients was the most convincing proof of the efficacy of psychoanalysis. Clinical perception clearly was given supremacy over gross statistical evaluation. Further, Freud dismissed the possible impact of research studies with the feeling that attitudes toward therapeutic validity are largely based on biases that allow little room for reasonable, open-minded viewing of data. Freud stated in a 1917 lecture:

> Friends of analysis have advised us to meet the threatened publication of our failures with statistics of our successes drawn up by ourselves. I did not agree to this. I pointed out that statistics are worthless if the items assembled in them are too heterogeneous; and the cases of neurotic illness which we had taken into treatment were in fact incomparable in a great variety of respects. Moreover, the period of time that could be covered was too short to make it possible to judge the durability of the cures. And it was altogether impossible to report on many of the cases; they concerned people who had kept both their illness and its treatment secret, and their recovery had equally to be kept secret. But the strongest reason for holding back lay in the realization that in matters of therapy people behave highly irrationally, so that one has no prospect of accomplishing anything with them by rational means. (Freud 1917c, p. 461)[1]

It would appear that Freud's reservations are mirrored in the general approach that has been taken in many of the studies dealing with the outcome of psychoanalytic therapy. There is a strong concern that the natural clinical process not be distorted for the sake of "objective" investigation or increased experimental control of the therapy. The analyst as clinician has hindered controlled research by emphasizing the primacy and confidentiality of the therapist-patient relationship. At the same time, analysts have eschewed the meaningfulness of attempts to draw generalizations about analytic therapy from contrived analogue studies or research making use of student therapists who are presumably therapizing from an analytic framework. There is a general sense that the nuances in behavior and the sensitivities of clinical observation may be lost in the attempt to categorize statistically that which seems so meaningful to the clinician experientially. The clinician's bias is in the direction of accepting only the data supporting what he believes to be the case on the basis of his experience. If research conclusions run counter to vested expectations, the tendency is to look for the defects in the research and not in the therapy. One gets the uneasy feeling that at times the research may be acceptable to the investigator only if it succeeds in translating clinical preconceptions into numerical findings. Opposed to this bias is the researcher's tendency to follow the data blindly, without questioning their fit with the reality of the experiences and observations of clinicians and their patients.

In reviewing research on psychoanalytic outcome, we attempted to limit ourselves to studies indicating the therapists had or were receiving training in psychoanalysis. We also tried to focus only on therapies that were being described and conceptualized as psychoanalysis. In practice we found this very difficult to do because of the vagueness in definition employed by most studies, the lack of universally accepted criteria for psychoanalysis among studies, and a common absence of reporting concerning the therapists and the nature of the therapy. The end result is that we have selected studies where the author labels the treatment as psychoanalysis and where there is enough adherence to experimental methodology to at least warrant speculation about the meaning of the results. The concern for clinical purity gives some of this research the quality of a series of pilot studies, where the testing of hypotheses may be clouded by uncontrolled variables, and the search for answers is often mingled with the search for meaningful questions and valid measures.[2] The variability in experimental rigor and methodology demonstrated within the analytic-therapy empirical literature also suggests that care needs to be taken in drawing any generalizations from the findings of individual studies. Nonetheless, we feel the weight of the network of data collected permits a number of observations and tentative conclusions about the outcome of psychoanalytic therapy. The aim of this chapter is to explore the conclusions and issues raised by the available evidence.

The Question of Spontaneous Remission

In general, studies of psychoanalytic therapy can be broken down into those that simply attempt to assess what percentage of patients is benefited by psychoanalysis and those geared toward assessing what kinds of changes take place and which factors are associated with positive therapeutic outcome.

Focusing simply on what percentage of patients improves as a result of therapy has led to a good deal of controversy and at times an illusory search for an improvement rate that could statistically demonstrate that analysis, or any other therapy for that matter, is better than no treatment at all. Within the therapy literature, Eysenck (1952, 1961a), Landis (1937), and others have described the concept of spontaneous remission, which holds that there is a general tendency for nonpsychotic psychiatric patients to improve with the passage of time and without benefit of treatment. Further, they have pointed to improvement data on relatively untreated patients to assert that the results of analytic therapy, as well as other therapies, are at best equivalent to no treatment at all and at worst harmful to the patients treated. The Eysenck (1952) argument is principally based on two uncontrolled surveys of large samples of cases (Landis 1937, Denker 1947). Landis (1937) reported that approximately two thirds of the patients diagnosed as psychoneurotic in New York State hospitals in 1914 and in United States hospitals in 1933 were discharged as recovered or improved within one year. Landis noted that since improvement rates from psychotherapy studies did not significantly exceed this figure, there was little evidence that therapy added anything to no treatment. Subsequently, Eysenck pointed to the Denker report as indicating a similar finding. Denker (1947) did a tabulation of the decrease in life-insurance disability claims from patients diagnosed psychoneurotic and treated by their general practitioners. Over a two-year period, 72 percent of these patients withdrew their insurance claims. Using the two thirds figure derived from the Landis and Denker studies as the base rate for nontreated improvement, Eysenck then went on to examine the data on psychotherapy outcome. Combining the improvement rates from the available therapy studies, he pessimistically concluded that only 44 percent of the patients treated by means of psychoanalysis improve, whereas 64 percent of the patients treated eclectically improve.

As might be expected, Eysenck's arguments against the efficacy of analysis and psychotherapy produced a flood of critical responses aimed at demonstrating the defects both in Eysenck's arguments and the data he based them on (DeCharms, Levy, and Wertheimer 1954, Luborsky 1954, Rosenzweig 1954, Cartwright 1955b, Strupp 1963–64a, 1963–64b, Kiesler 1966, Meltzoff and Kornreich 1970, Bergin 1971, Subotnik 1972a,b). Eysenck vehemently pressed his views in replying to the criticisms (Eysenck 1954, 1955, 1964, 1966).

Overall, the consensus of Eysenck's critics has been that the studies used to establish a base line for nontreated improvement are not suitable in a number of ways for comparison with treatment results. As both Kiesler (1966) and Subotnik (1972b) point out and substantiate in their overview articles, the arguments against the use of the Landis and Denker data as a control for therapy results can be grouped into three general categories: (1) the improvement criteria are not consistent with or comparable to those used by psychotherapists; (2) the patient groups are not comparable to those seen in psychotherapy; and (3) the patient groups in both studies were not no-treatment groups and actually received some form of therapy.[3]

In addition, Bergin (1971) has demonstrated that if Eysenck had used the same method for calculating improvement in the Landis study as he used in calculating improvement in the therapy studies, the Landis spontaneous remission rate would have been 52 percent, not 72 percent. Bergin's (1971) review of fourteen nontreated patient samples reported in thirteen different studies also was at great variance with a two thirds spontaneous remission base rate. The studies reviewed by Bergin were highly variable in the percent rated improved, with a range of 0 to 46 percent improvement without treatment.[4] The median no-treatment improvement rate derived from these thirteen studies is approximately 30 percent, although Bergin rightfully cautions against combining results from these many disparate and heterogeneous studies to arrive at a new mythical base line for nontreated improvement. However, the results do suggest that spontaneous improvement across a "general" group of nonpsychotic patients may be considerably less than the two thirds figure.

Typically, studies measuring improvement rates in either treated or nontreated patient groups depend on global clinical judgment of patient improvement, with minimal evidence that the judgments would be reliable across different clinicians. Subotnik (1972b) makes the interesting point that if judgments were made in a completely random fashion with a sorting of patients into the three categories commonly used (much improved, somewhat improved, and unimproved or worse), we would arrive at the conclusion of two thirds improvement just as Eysenck has proposed.

Another cogent point relates to the implication of the spontaneous remission hypothesis that improvement of untreated patients should increase as a function of time (Eysenck 1961a). Subotnik (1972a,b) has noted that no studies have shown that merely the passage of time leads to an increase in the improvement rate and few studies have even attended to this issue (Wallace and Whyte 1959, Schorer et al. 1968). Two studies by Subotnik have focused specifically on this question. In one he gathered test-retest data on fifty-nine patients of general practitioners who initially scored above a cutting point indicating emotional disturbance on the Cornell Medical Index Health Questionnaire. None of the patients had received treatment by a professional psychotherapist. Five groups of subjects were compared in terms of the elapsed time between test and retest, with times ranging from less than one year to more than four years. There was no significant relationship between the amount of time elapsed and improvement (Subotnik 1969). In a later study Subotnik (1972a), using deviant Minnesota Multiphasic Personality Inventories (a questionnaire calling for self-description) as a measure of disturbance, again found no relationship between nontreated improvement and the amount of time elapsed, with elapsed times ranging from nine to thirty-three months.

It would seem that the only logical conclusion that one can draw from the many arguments and studies that have found their way into the debate is that no one figure can be used as the standard against which all studies of psychotherapy outcome can be compared. Variability between studies with regard to treatment settings, patient characteristics, severity of disturbance, and outcome criteria would seem to preclude a meaningful combining of data between studies to arrive at one figure that can be used as *the* standard nontreated improvement rate.

In spite of this conclusion, however, the basic point of the spontaneous remission argument is still pivotal in any discussion of psychotherapy outcome. In order for treatment to be deemed "successful," it must be reasonably demonstrated that the result would not have occurred without treatment or that the results of treatment can be predicted from a knowledge of different levels of the treatment variables. For this reason we feel it is meaningless to evaluate therapeutic results by utilizing therapy outcome surveys offering no bases for comparison. Unfortunately, many of the outcome studies of both psychotherapy and psychoanalysis are based solely on this type of global survey data.

Meltzoff and Kornreich (1970), in their review of research in psychotherapy, highlight the difficulties encountered in trying to interpret survey results. They write:

> More often than not, surveys have been retrospective in nature. They consist of tabulations of judgments of success and failure, either dichotomized or scaled to reflect the degree of improvement, and are summarized in a percentage of improvement. In most surveys, there is no way of knowing what such terms as 'recovered,' 'much improved,' and 'slightly improved' mean. There is little constancy in the meaning of these terms from survey to survey. The original data is poor because it usually relies exclusively on the subjective judgment of the therapist or that of the researcher, who depends on case records written by the therapist. The errors are compounded by a reviewer . . . who takes the improvement percentages (which may be grossly inaccurate to start with) from diverse sources and averages them to arrive at a total estimate of outcome regarded as authoritative because it is based upon so many thousands of cases. The size of the N in such an amalgamation is bound to be impressive but contributes not at all to the validity of the information. (pp. 64–65)

Large-scale surveys of the results of psychoanalysis are permeated with the problems alluded to above (Fenichel 1930, Kessel and Hyman 1933, Hyman 1936, Jones 1936, Alexander 1937, Knight 1941, Hamburg et al. 1967, Feldman 1968). Many of the investigators are quite open in revealing the vagueness and inconsistency in their measures. For example, Fenichel (1930), in reporting on the results obtained by analysts in training at the Berlin Psychoanalytic Institute, noted that it soon "became apparent that there was, by no means, uniformity in the use of either diagnostic or success criteria in reporting individual cases by the analysts" (p. 3).

Similarly, Hamburg et al. (1967) state, in their report on a questionnaire survey of the analytic results obtained by members of the American Psychoanalytic Association, "The bare phrases employed in the questionnaire meant different things to different analysts, and for this reason rendered it difficult to make meaningful comparisons" (p. 843).

Feldman (1968) provides another example of the nonobjective nature of many of the survey measures, in his report on the results obtained at the Clinic of the Southern California Psychoanalytic Institute. One indicator of improvement in this study was based on the author's rating (without a reliability check) of patient records. In this case the evaluation may have been more a measure of the analysts' writing ability than patient improvement, because of the variability in therapist reports. Feldman points out the subjectivity involved in making judgments of improvement due to the fact that the student analyst reports varied greatly in "length, detail, and language" (p. 281).

A major problem of measurement in much of the survey data relates to the general question of whether relatively inexperienced analysts are able to reliably report the status of cases and render judgments about their patients in an objective, nonbiased way. The suspicion is that they cannot, since there are a number of studies indicating that the reports of student therapists contain significant distortions and omissions (Matarazzo 1971). Further, studies by Knapp et al. (1960), Feldman (1968), and Lower et al. (1972) show that student analyst judgment of case material may differ significantly from group judgments made by experienced analysts. Specifically, Lower et al. (1972) concluded that student analysts tended to judge patient suitability for analysis on less objective criteria than a committee of experienced analysts. Knapp et al. (1960) and Feldman (1968) found groups of experienced analysts superior to their students in selecting patients most likely to benefit from treatment.[5] Other questions about the objectivity of analyst judgment have been raised by investigators comparing biased perceptions in analytic clinicians and behaviorists. For example, Weiss (1972), in a study utilizing two ambiguous taped therapy excerpts alternately labeled "early" and "late" therapy sessions, found that analytic therapists were more likely than behaviorists to perceive positive changes where none existed. Langer and Abelson (1974) showed a similar biasing tendency in the finding that analytic clinicians, as opposed to behaviorists, were more likely to describe an interviewee as significantly more disturbed when he was described as a "patient" than when he was labeled "job applicant."

Even if we could accept the idea that the ratings made in each study are based on comparable dimensions, a reading of the surveys quickly reveals that they are incomparable in other important ways. To illustrate this point, we have but to look at the differences between psychoanalytic clinics in their willingness to accept a patient for treatment. It seems probable that different criteria for patient selection would lead to different improvement rates. A sample of reports from the London Clinic of Psychoanalysis (Jones

1936), the Berlin Psychoanalytic Institute (Fenichel 1930), and the Southern California Psychoanalytic Institute (Feldman 1968) indicates just such differences, with respective acceptance rates of 80 percent, 37 percent, and 12 percent. Kadushin (1969), in his survey of New York City clinics, reports on a University Psychoanalytic Clinic that seems to use even more stringent criteria in that only 4 percent of the patients applying for treatment are judged to be suitable cases!

With such variability both within and between studies, it is not surprising to find that the judgment of successful outcome varies widely from study to study. In addition, as Bergin (1971) has demonstrated, the statistical results of the survey studies change dramatically, depending on whether premature dropouts are excluded from the sample and whether improvement is defined as a rating of "moderately improved or better" or "much improved." This is concretely demonstrated by three different reviews for the same six major psychoanalytic surveys (Fenichel 1930, Kessel and Hyman 1933, Hyman 1936, Jones 1936, Alexander 1937, Knight 1941), using different criteria for outcome (Knight 1941, Eysenck 1952, Bergin 1971). Knight excluded premature dropouts and defined improvement as only a rating of "much improved." He thus found improvement rates of 47 to 89 percent, with an average of 62 percent. Eysenck, looking at the same studies, included premature dropouts and defined improvement in the same manner as Knight. He found improvement rates of 39 to 67 percent, with an average of 44 percent. In contrast to both these reviews, Bergin (1971) excluded dropouts and defined improvement as a rating of "moderately improved or better." He found improvement rates of 60 to 91 percent, with an average of 83 percent. The study showing the most improvement for Bergin (Fenichel 1930, 91 percent) was the same study showing the least improvement for Eysenck (39 percent). Similarly, Bergin's review of Knight's data revealed that the sampled clinics obtained very different results with patients given the same diagnosis.

The point to be made from this brief discussion is that individual global surveys are highly variable in results as well as methodology. They offer little in the way of generalizable findings without the inclusion of a control group or some way of estimating what the results would have been either with different levels of the treatment variables or without treatment at all. In view of the variability evidenced, it seems wise to evaluate studies individually before seeking generalizations, rather than pooling the statistical data from a number of sources to reach a conclusion. If the bulk of studies in an area demonstrate the same general findings, despite their inherent differences, we may be able to place more confidence in the robustness of the conclusions drawn.

Psychoanalysis Versus No-Treatment

Since it does not appear meaningful to compare the results of separate studies with a hypothetical rate of nontreated improvement, we are left with the question whether there are any studies in the literature that offer evidence about the effects of analysis as compared to no-treatment. Our search revealed six studies bearing on this specific issue (Schjelderup 1955, Orgel 1958, Barendregt et al. 1961, Cappon 1964, O'Connor et al. 1964, Duhrssen and Jorswieck 1965).[6] As will be seen, these investigations have a number of drawbacks or methodological flaws that raise questions about the significance of the results. Yet all of the studies are consistent with each other in indicating analysis as producing results different from no-treatment.

Orgel (1958) reports on the treatment of fifteen ulcer patients seen in his psychoanalytic practice over the course of twenty-five years. Of these cases, five were not considered to have completed the analysis, since three had little or no analysis with respectively one, seven, and twenty-one sessions, and two stopped treatment abruptly when their symptoms disappeared (seventy-seven and 138 sessions). The remaining ten cases were terminated by the mutual decision of therapist and patient after three to five years of treatment (592 to 942 sessions). Therapy was conducted in fifty-minute sessions, five times a week, with the use of the couch and free association. A deep transference relationship was allowed to develop. Of the ten patients completing treatment, *all* were symptom-free at termination and at a follow-up interview eleven to twenty-two years after the therapy terminated. It would be difficult to attribute the complete remission of symptoms in all of these patients to anything other than the therapy, since symptoms had occurred and persisted in all cases for five to fifteen years before treatment began. From termination to follow-up these patients did not require any medications or restrictions in their diets, and none developed any new symptoms.

Cappon (1964) reports on the analytic results obtained on a sample of 201 consecutive private patients that he had seen in his practice. The therapy was described as a "personal modification of analytic technique" with an influence of Jungian theory. The patients had had their presenting or main problem for an average of fifteen years before treatment. The mean treatment duration was six and one half months. The results were measured at both termination and a follow-up point an average of 19.9 months following treatment. Cappon found the percentage of patients changing for the better varied from 21 percent to 76 percent, depending upon the method of measurement. The three most optimistic measures of improvement were the therapist's or patient's ratings at termination of marked improvement and the loss of at least one symptom. These three indices were reported to be significantly correlated and indications of "very evident" improvement. These measures indicated that three quarters of the patients significantly improved with treatment. The other measures produced lower ratings of change: the loss of all symptoms (21 percent); the loss of the presenting or main symptom (40 percent); a marked change in ratings of the patients' dreams (51 percent). At follow-up the relapse rate across both optimistic and pessimistic measures was about 10 percent, although this figure is biased by the fact that the sample of patients who returned follow-up questionnaires had done twice as well at treatment termination as those who did not return questionnaires.

Cappon argues that it would be difficult to ascribe the changes to anything other than the treatment, since the patients had experienced their main problem for an average of fifteen years before therapy. Further, the patients showed twice as much improvement, on most measures, during the period of active psychotherapy as they did during the inactive time span of twenty months following therapy. Conversely, depending on which measure is used, four to fifteen times as many patients changed for the worse during the follow-up no-treatment period as compared to the therapy period. These findings argue against a spontaneous remission phenomena in that significantly more change for the better occurred during therapy versus no-therapy periods, and more change for the worse occurred in the no-therapy versus therapy times.

Schjelderup (1955) did a follow-up investigation of twenty-eight cases that he had analyzed over a seventeen-year period. The cases represented all of his patients with neuroses of a definitely chronic nature, that he was able to trace and follow up at the time of the study, eight to 24 years after the therapy. The average patient had been experiencing symptoms for more than eleven years before analysis.[7] Treatment lasted one to five years with a frequency of two to six hours per week (the average being four sessions a week for two years three months). The therapy was simply described as psychoanalysis without further amplification. The data for the study were based on questionnaires filled out by the patients concerning their condition before analysis, immediately after the analysis, and subsequently. The therapist was able to compare the patients' retrospective accounts with information obtained at the time of treatment. This revealed a general tendency to minimize rather than magnify changes that occurred.

Within a few months of filling out the questionnaire, the patients were interviewed by Schjelderup and in many cases by a second analyst. Observations were also supplemented wherever possible by information obtained from relatives, close friends of the patients, and other treating doctors or hospitals where the patient had been. In short, the investigation represented a global uncontrolled attempt to try to find out by all means possible whether the patients had benefited in a lasting way as a result of the therapy. Gains were judged on a number of subjective dimensions, with patients who had changed in a positive way rated as *not* improving if it was felt that the changes could not readily be attributed to the therapy. Like Cappon, Schjelderup found that the degree of improvement varied according to the measure used, with three quarters of the cases being rated as either "very satisfactory" or "satisfactory outcome"[8] by the therapist as compared to 89 percent of the cases being rated as least "satisfactory outcome" by the patients. Other measures of change were the following: symptom improvement (75 percent); patient reports of positive changes in interpersonal relationships (89 percent); improved ability and enjoyment of work (79 percent); decided improvement in the ability to enjoy life (50 percent); improved sex life (54 percent); changes in the perception of reality (43 percent).

Duhrssen and Jorswieck (1965) stressed the need for an appropriate nontreated control group in a study of the outcome of psychoanalytic treatment at the Institute for Psychogenic Disease in Berlin. Typically, at this clinic, an initial judgment was made as to the likelihood that each patient would improve as a result of therapy. The authors found in a previous investigation of over 1,000 patients that there was a high correlation between initial prognosis and a rating of improvement five years later. It was decided in the present study that treatment and control groups should be matched on the variable of prognosis for improvement in order to minimize potential differences in spontaneous remission rates between groups. The hypothesis put forth in this study was that analytically treated chronic neurotic patients would require fewer days of hospitalization, *for any reason,* during the five years after therapy, as compared to a nontreated control group matched on initial prognosis for improvement.

The treatment group consisted of 125 patients who had completed their psychoanalytic therapy in 1958. Another 100 patients matched for prognosis were chosen at random from the waiting list to serve as nontreated controls. These patients had had an initial screening interview. A third group of 100 people who had never come in contact with the clinic were selected at random from the records of the Berlin Department of Social Medicine. There was no reason to believe that any of the individuals in the third group had experienced psychiatric symptoms. This group was set up to serve as a control for changes in hospitalization rates within the general population. Data obtained from the Berlin Department of Social Health were used to compare the number of days of hospitalization between groups.

There was no significant difference between the treated and waiting list patients on the average number of days of hospitalization per year for the five years preceding the initiation of therapy or the screening interview. However, both patient groups, treated and untreated, had a significantly higher average number of hospitalization days during the five years prior to clinic contact than the group of individuals from the general population of Berlin. Thus, the patient groups had a history of greater hospitalization than the general population.

Following treatment, the analytic group showed a significant decrease in the number of days of hospitalization during a five-year period. Neither the patients on the waiting list nor the group from the general population showed any changes in hospitalization rates during comparable five-year periods. Further data analysis revealed that the analytic group spent significantly fewer days in hospitals following treatment than *either* of the other groups. The waiting list neurotics still spent more time in hospitals than the general population subjects.

Duhrssen and Jorswieck (1965) conclude that their results show clear support for the hypothesis that chronically neurotic patients are significantly improved with long-term psychoanalytic therapy, on the objective criteria of days of hospitalization. The authors feel that at least some of the patients on the waiting list must have received superficial treatments of various kinds during the five years following their screening interview. However, even if other treatments did occur, they apparently proved ineffective in terms of the health status of the patients. The hypothesis that neurotic patients heal spontaneously or that minor psychotherapy by a general practitioner is sufficient to produce change is not supported by these findings. This study offers no description of the therapy, the therapists, or the patients, leaving the question of how the treatment compares with other approaches unanswerable.

O'Connor et al. (1964) offer another report bearing on the issue of how analytic treatment compares with no-treatment. In this study fifty-seven ulcerative colitis patients treated in psychotherapy *or* psychoanalysis were compared with a no-psychotherapy control group of fifty-seven colitis patients matched on the variables of sex of patient, severity of illness, age at disease onset, and use of steroids. The control group was not matched in terms of psychopathology, and in fact the experimental group had been specifically referred for therapy because of greater evidence of disturbance. One third of the treated group was diagnosed schizophrenic, as compared to only 5 percent of the controls. The average duration of illness in the treated group was fifteen years. No detailed description of the therapy or the therapists is presented, and no rationale is given for assigning patients to different types of psychotherapy. In later papers these same authors attempt to associate pretreatment and treatment factors with response to therapy in colitis patients (Karush et al. 1968, Karush et al. 1969).

Results of the treatment were measured periodically by independent raters who were not involved in the therapy. However, the report does not state that the raters were unaware of the therapy status of patients they were examining. Measures for the treated and control groups centered on proctoscopic findings recording inflammatory changes observed in the rectum and symptom ratings based on the severity of bowel symptoms. Both proctoscopic and symptom ratings indicated an improvement in the treated group, beginning about the third year after treatment initiation and continuing throughout the eight years of measurement. In general, over the time period sampled, the treated group showed a marked and sustained improvement, while the control group evidenced relatively little change. The differences between the groups are heightened if the schizophrenic patients are eliminated, with the nonschizophrenic treated patients showing almost complete remission of symptoms at the last year of measurement and the controls showing no change.

Conclusions that can be drawn from these findings are limited by the fact that no analyses of the data for statistical significance are reported. In addition, there is no breakdown given comparing the nontreated group with the different types of therapies used (short term psychotherapy, analytically oriented psychotherapy, and reconstructive analysis). The authors do report that the *type* of psychotherapy treatment did not correlate with physiological improvement. The implication is left that psychoanalysis led to more physiological changes than no-treatment but was not superior to other psychotherapies in achieving physical symptom relief. There were no differences in surgical or mortality rates between the treated and control groups; but this finding is contaminated by the fact that there were many more schizophrenic patients in the treated group, and two thirds of the deaths as well as approximately half of the surgery occurred among the schizophrenic cases.

Barendregt et al. (1961) describe another study concerned in part with comparing the results of psychoanalysis with no-treatment at the Institute for Psychoanalysis in Amsterdam. The comparisons of interest are between forty-seven patients receiving psychoanalysis and a control group of seventy-four patients who were either placed on a waiting list or not advised to go into therapy. The control group consisted of those patients who did not get treatment and were still waiting two and one half years later at the completion of the study. The appropriateness of the control group as a suitable comparison can be questioned, as patients were assigned to treatment or no-treatment on a selective rather than random basis. Patients were considered to have had psychoanalysis if they received a form of treatment their therapist considered to be analysis. Yet almost all the therapists had very little experience, and many of the patients were only first or second cases for the therapists.

Change was appraised by a series of eight measures given to each patient on application to the clinic and after approximately two and one half years of treatment, although most of the analytic cases continued in therapy beyond this point. Measurements included the patients' rating of their sense of well-being on a ten-point scale as well as a retrospective rating of how they felt two and one half years earlier; the Wechsler-Bellevue Verbal IQ; measures derived from personality scales of neuroticism, introversion-extroversion, and lie score (an indication of how much a patient is defending himself by exaggerating the social desirability of his behavior); Thematic Apperception Test (TAT) changes (scores attained from patients telling stories about ambiguous pictures); and Rorschach changes based on a composite of 12 signs that presumably reflect changes for the better.

Data analysis comparing controls with psychoanalytic patients revealed only one significant finding: a greater drop in the lie score for two samples of analyzed patients. This was interpreted to mean a decrease in rigidity and lessened defensiveness. Barendregt et al. (1961) also point to a trend within the TAT data as indicating possible decreased defensiveness in the analytic group: analyzed patients increased in their expression of fears of frustration with respect to various needs. In sum, despite the use of a number of measures, this study revealed only the possibility of decreased defensiveness as a result of analysis. The conclusions can be questioned, however, on the basis of the incomparability of the control group, the inexperience of the therapists, the incompleteness of the therapy, and the possible insensitivity of the measures to therapeutic effects.

One can question whether some of the measures could have been reasonably expected to yield changes. For example, the mean Verbal IQ score for the patients seen in analysis was already in the superior range—at the 95th percentile—before treatment even began, and therefore change could have been limited by a ceiling effect. In contrast to these results, Appelbaum et al. (1969) found a significant increase in Wechsler-Bellevue IQ over a course of psychoanalysis lasting an average of almost five years (twice as long as Barendregt et al.). Changes were greatest in the Performance IQ (only the Verbal IQ was measured by Barendregt et al.). The finding of Performance IQ change after psychotherapy makes some theoretical sense in view of the fact that all of the performance subtests are timed. Therefore, the psychomotor retardation and inability to concentrate that is associated with depression and anxiety should lead to slower performance and lower test scores (Wechsler 1958). Based on this rationale, therapy that leads to decreases in depression or anxiety would tend to be reflected more by increases in Performance IQ than Verbal IQ scores. The Rorschach results are also puzzling, in that Barendregt et al. point out somewhat vaguely that the Rorschach differences were found in the predicted direction but the prediction was not "confirmed in a convincing way." There was also no report of individual results for each of the twelve Rorschach signs. It is possible that some signs changed significantly while others did not.

In general, the six studies reviewed all offer evidence indicating that psychoanalysis produces change over and above no-treatment. Yet the reports present obvious methodological flaws or deficiencies. Three of the studies are questionable as tests of the efficacy of psychoanalysis, since they are each based on the cases of one therapist (Schjelderup, 1955; Orgel, 1958; Cappon, 1964). Therefore, the results obtained in these investigations could be as easily attributed to specific therapist characteristics as to the analytic treatment method employed. There is no way of determining the comparability of the treatments of these three practitioners or knowing how control groups of nontreated patients would have progressed in the same time period. The conclusion that these studies provide evidence of change is largely based on the fact that the patients treated were chronic cases who had experienced many years of symptoms without relief from either previous treatments or "spontaneous" improvement. Parenthetically, in view of the careful selection of patients by clinics, some might be surprised to find analysts reviewing case loads indicating extensive treatment of chronic and extremely difficult cases.

It could be argued that some of the outcome measures are of dubious validity insofar as they depend on therapist and patient ratings of unknown reliability. The ratings are also potentially affected by the vested need of therapists and patients to perceive improvement. Nonetheless, the studies do offer a series of compelling observations from a number of viewpoints and methodologies indicating positive and lasting changes in patients who had previously exhibited many years of unremitting symptomatology. Of particular note are the decided physical changes in chronic nonpsychotic ulcer patients (Orgel, 1958) and colitis patients (O'Connor et al. 1964), as well as the decreased hospitalization rates (Duhrssen and Jorswieck 1965) following periods of analytic therapy. In the global analytic surveys previously reviewed, two studies included groups of psychosomatic patients in assessing improvement with psychoanalysis as a function of diagnosis. In both of these studies, although the numbers of patients were relatively small, the highest rate of improvement occurred in the psychosomatic groups (Fenichel 1930, Alexander 1937).

While we cannot conclude that the studies offer unequivocal evidence that analysis is more effective than no-treatment, they do indicate with consistency that this seems probable with regard to a number of analysts and their nonpsychotic, chronic patients. Interestingly, as we noted in the previous chapter, Freud convinced himself of the efficacy of analytic therapy largely on the basis of his experiences with very disturbed, chronic cases. It should also be noted that aside from the Barendregt et al. study, the other investigations made use of relatively experienced therapists; this factor may partially account for the positive results.

We found no studies in the literature indicating that the absence of treatment was uniformly equivalent to or superior to analysis. The question of whether analysis is superior to no-treatment with acute neurotic cases is largely unrepresented in the experimental literature. Perhaps the one study of the six reviewed that has the most bearing on this issue is the one by Barendregt et al. (1961), which offered the least indication that analysis was superior in effects to the absence of treatment. Obviously the area could greatly benefit from a number of future studies offering more controlled tests of the effects of intensive analysis by experienced and inexperienced analysts on neurotic patients with both chronic and acute disturbances.

Psychoanalysis Versus Alternative Treatments

The question of concern in this section is whether the results of psychoanalysis are significantly different from the results obtained by other treatment approaches. In seeking to find what is experimentally known about this question, we reviewed a number of studies that offer some data on this issue. These studies highlight all of the vagueness in definition and practice described in the last chapter. The myth that psychoanalysis represents a uniform approach is strikingly challenged by a reading of the investigations in this area. We hope that our accounts of some of the experimental reports will serve to capture the heterogeneous, poorly controlled nature of much of the literature we encountered.

The studies in the last section represented relatively clear alternatives in comparing psychoanalysis to no-treatment. The differences become much less clear when one begins to speak of alternative treatments. There is a real question in many cases as to whether the alternatives are really different on significant dimensions or whether the potential differences in approach are consistently different between groups. Studies presenting comparative data have used groups of patients treated with analysis and patients treated either with some form of "analytically oriented" therapy or a therapy presumably based on a different theory of personality. The distinctions made between analysis and analytically oriented therapy are somewhat vague but have primarily focused on analysis being a more intensive treatment lasting for a longer period of time, with a less active therapist and a greater focus on the transference aspects of the relationship. Distinctions between the effects of analysis and significantly different treatment approaches also turn out to be problematic in that the treatment groups labeled "analytic" often represent a conglomeration of diverse approaches.

Perhaps the major contaminating factor in studies offering the potential for comparative data is the implicit assumption that analysis is *the* superior form of treatment and that patients judged suitable for analysis would be done a disservice in being assigned to other types of therapy. As a consequence of this assumption, patients have not been assigned to different treatments in a random fashion. It has been the general practice to accept different types of patients for the different types of treatment. The typical procedure is to accept for psychoanalysis those patients clinically judged to have greater emotional and intellectual assets, while providing alternative therapies for the remaining, less prognostically "desirable" cases. Therefore, any differences obtained in outcome might be as easily attributed to initial patient differences as to treatment differences. Major questions that can be asked of each study are whether the treatments described are actually different, whether the therapists have training and background in the techniques they are applying, and whether sufficient treatment time has elapsed for evaluating the results.

Our general conclusion, in reviewing the data, is that there is very little evidence in the experimental literature even suggesting that the results of therapies called "psychoanalysis" are in any way different from the results obtained by treatments given other labels. This finding is in marked contrast to our conclusion that psychoanalysis appears to achieve results significantly different from no-treatment. Before discussing our general conclusions, we will present a brief overview of the studies offering comparative data. This review will be divided into a group of investigations comparing psychoanalysis with approaches that appear to be significantly different and a group of studies comparing psychoanalysis with analytically oriented therapies. Hopefully, these brief study descriptions will convey the flavor of the work that has been done and provide a representative sampling of the experimental weaknesses that have been so common in this area of research.

PSYCHOANALYSIS VERSUS THEORETICALLY DIFFERENT TREATMENTS

Cartwright (1966a) reports what is probably one of the most well-controlled studies in the literature comparing psychoanalytic therapy with another approach to treatment: client-centered therapy, a treatment facilitating patient self-exploration through therapist acceptance, empathy, and warmth. Even this study, however, has a number of methodological drawbacks. The investigation utilized only four therapists and four patients: one analyst and one client-centered therapist with extensive experience, and one therapist of each type with moderate experience. Therapists were also matched in terms of sex and reputation for expertness. There was one male and one female patient in each of the two modes of therapy and the patients were matched on age, sex, presenting problems, and total number of interviews. Patients were studied over the course of only thirty to forty sessions and cases differed in both duration and frequency. For example, one case was seen five times a week for eight weeks, while another was seen twice a week for twenty weeks. Even the two psychoanalytic cases were seen under different conditions, with one having face-to-face therapy once a week and the other having treatment five times a week lying on the couch. Changes were compared on three different measures: one derived from client-centered theory, one derived from psychoanalytic theory, and one independent of the two theoretical approaches.[9] The study found that while therapists of the different orientations did tend to use different techniques consistent with their theoretical biases, the obtained levels of self-observation and expression of feelings were similar for the two types of treatment. There were no indications that one form of treatment was superior to the other or different in treatment results.

Heine (1953) comes to a very similar conclusion in a study of twenty-four patients, of whom eight had been treated in each of three schools of psychotherapy: psychoanalytic, client-centered, and Adlerian. There was no further description of the therapies or the therapists. Each patient was presented with a list of 120 prepared statements describing possible changes resulting from therapy and asked to sort the statements into changes that applied to him and those that did not. Patients also sorted another group of statements so as to indicate the extent to which each "factor" described was responsible for the changes they had experienced. Heine found that patients reported similar changes regardless of the type of psychotherapy they had experienced. However, patients did attribute the changes to different factors depending on the orientation of their therapist. Analytic patients tended to attribute their changes to favorable therapy techniques, while client-centered patients put more emphasis on the therapeutic atmosphere. Adlerian patients fell between the two other groups. The type of therapy thus affected the patient's conception of how change came about, but not the degree or nature of the change.

Cremerius (1962) presents (in German) an outcome study, with follow-up, comparing a large number of chronic neurotic patients treated with analysis to four other groups of patients treated with verbal discussion, hypnotic and narcohypnotic therapy, autogenic training (learning to self-regulate and control body processes), and a combination of treatments. The study is badly controlled, in that patients seen in analytic treatment were quite different from patients seen with the other approaches. Nearly all patients receiving analysis had psychosomatic symptoms, while almost none of the patients treated in the hypnotic group had such symptoms. In addition, there was a decided bias to select for analytic therapy those asking for it and those judged to be responsive to an insight type of relationship. Patients in the analytic group also were of higher social class than patients selected for other treatments. There is no indication in the report that the therapists were either experienced or highly trained in the techniques they were applying. There is also no indication as to whether the different treatments were being conducted by different therapists. Evaluation of outcome was made after a relatively brief treatment period compared to usual analytic standards. The average treatment duration for the analytic group was seventy sessions, with a high of ninety. Nonanalytic patients were seen on an average of forty sessions. Patients were also followed up eight to ten years after treatment.

Outcome was measured primarily in terms of ratings of symptom abolition, symptom improvement, symptom worsening, and symptom substitution.[10] At the end of the treatment period, hypnosis showed the best results for symptom cure or improvement (85 percent) and combined treatments the worst (58 percent). Analytic psychotherapy occupied an intermediate position, with 70 percent symptom cure or improvement. The figures for analytic outcome, in terms of symptom improvement, may well be an underestimate of treatment success, as the analytic group had a much higher proportion of premature terminating patients than the other groups, and these patients were counted as treatment failures.[11] Not counting patients who dropped out leads to the conclusion that analytic therapy, verbal discussion, and hypnosis all produced the most change, with a symptom improvement and cure rate of about 90 percent. It should also be noted that the comparison of symptom outcome at "termination" was based on less than half the total number of patients in the analytic sample, since most of the cases in the analytic group were continuing treatment at the time the ratings were made and hence were not included. The analytic results may *not* therefore be representative of the group as a whole, as they are based on a select part of the patient sample: those who terminated treatment in relatively few sessions. The data for all other groups were based on the total number of cases treated.

A follow-up was done on the patients who could be traced eight to ten years following the treatment (86 percent of the total sample). Results at that time showed the analytic patients to have retained significantly greater symptom improvement and cure and to have a lower rate of judged symptom substitution. The percentage of symptom cure and improvement for each of the treatment groups at follow-up was: analytic, 54; verbal discussion, 35; hypnosis, 17; autogenic training, 29; combined methods, 21.

Eysenck (1969), in a review of this study, is rightfully cautious about concluding that the follow-up data indicate patients treated with psychoanalytic methods have less of a tendency to relapse. Obviously, there were major differences between the patient groups to begin with. In addition, however, we do not feel the initial data of this study can be used to meaningfully argue either that analysis is inferior to the other treatments or that it is inferior to the results obtained for no-treatment (spontaneous remission) under the conditions of other studies. Further, there is no way of telling what constituted the therapy labeled "analytic" in this report.

Ellis (1957) presents an investigation focusing on results he achieved during three separate phases of his practice when he employed three different therapeutic methods: orthodox psychoanalysis, psychoanalytically oriented therapy, and rational-emotive therapy (a treatment aimed at helping the patient to see the illogical ideas he repeats to himself). After the completion of seven years of training and a personal analysis, Ellis began to do "orthodox psychoanalysis" under supervision. Therapy used the couch, free association, dream analysis, and resolution of the transference neurosis. Three years later he abandoned this approach in favor of a face-to-face, highly active and interpretative psychoanalytically oriented technique. After another three years he began treating patients with an approach he developed and called rational therapy. This study compared improvement ratings made at the time of termination by Ellis on a number of patients treated by the various approaches. The groups were fairly well matched in terms of sex, age, education, and diagnosis. They differed in treatment duration, with the sixteen analyzed patients being seen for an average of ninety-three sessions, the seventy-eight analytically oriented patients being seen for an average of thirty-five sessions, and the seventy-eight rational therapy patients treated for an average of twenty-six sessions. Distinct or considerable improvement was rated in 90 percent of the patients treated with rational therapy, 63 percent of the patients treated with analytically oriented therapy, and 50 percent of those treated with psychoanalysis. Statistical analysis revealed that the rational approach was significantly superior to the other two treatments.

Ellis himself points to the possible bias in the findings due to potential prejudices in his outcome ratings and to differential energy and zeal being devoted to the different treatments. The use of only one therapist further limits generalizability. Interpretation of the results is also clouded by the fact that both the therapy and the judgments regarding improvement occurred under three different levels of therapist experience. Therefore, increases in experience may account for the differences rather than change in treatment approach. In sum, it is difficult to draw any reasonable general conclusions regarding comparative therapies on the basis of this study.

Two other reported studies have attempted to compare analysis with distinctly different approaches, using psychological test data as the measures of change and outcome. Dudek (1970) analyzed pre- and post-therapy Rorschach records of patients voluntarily hospitalized and treated at a psychiatric institute in Montreal. About 9 percent of the sample was drawn from patients treated privately. All cases having pre- and post-therapy records and not diagnosed organic were included in the study. In this way it was possible to compare changes in groups treated by three different methods: a group of twenty-six in psychoanalytic therapy, thirty-three in medical therapy, and twenty-nine in maintenance therapy. This study has the common problem of nonrandom assignment to groups, with the patients seen in psychoanalytic therapy tending to be younger and to have an earlier age of problem onset, problems of lesser severity, and fewer psychotic diagnoses. The data are also contaminated by the fact that about one third of the psychoanalytic group were seen privately, as opposed to none of the patients in the other two groups. Another contaminating factor is that the time between pre- and post-testing varied between the groups, with the medical therapy cases having an average of twenty months and the maintenance group having an average time of nine and one half years. Another difficulty, for our purposes, is that there is no indication that the therapists in the analytic group had been trained to do analytic therapy, and that only five of the patients in this group were described as receiving "orthodox psychoanalysis." The remaining twenty-one cases in the analytic group received "psychoanalytically oriented" therapy relying partially on the techniques of free association and dream analysis. The medical therapy patients were treated by drugs and massive electroconvulsive therapy (ECT). The maintenance patients were treated with supportive therapy, occasional drugs or ECT, and little if any formal therapy focusing on insight or uncovering of underlying causes for the problems.

Changes on eleven Rorschach factors were calculated as measures of outcome, although initial differences between groups on some of the factors suggest these comparisons are of dubious validity. The general findings, consistent with the initial hypotheses, were that the psychoanalytic group evidenced significant changes in the direction of greater energy, fantasy, and flexibility,[12] while the medical group changed in the direction of greater constriction, lessened productivity, and increased stereotypic, conventional thinking. The maintenance group as a whole showed a trend in the same direction as the medical cases, with slightly less marked constriction. The major conclusion suggested by this study was that different types of therapy have different personality effects. While both analytic therapy and medical therapy resulted in improved reality adjustment, this occurred in the context of increased energy and flexibility in the former treatment and at the price of marked personality constriction in the latter approach. Needless to say, the many methodological problems with this study categorize the findings more as suggestions for future hypotheses than as firm conclusions.

The other study using psychological testing data is by Barendregt et al. (1961). It was partially reviewed and discussed in the previous section. Comparisons between groups of patients receiving psychoanalysis, psychotherapy (of an unspecified type), and no-treatment were made on eight test measures given before treatment and after two and one half years. Treatment was conducted by very inexperienced therapists. Of interest here are the differences obtained between patients treated with analysis and those treated with the unspecified psychotherapy. In general, while most of the measures revealed no differences, two significant findings pointed in the same direction as the findings of the Dudek study described above. The analytic patients showed a greater drop in the lie score than the unspecified psychotherapy patients, and the psychotherapy group showed indications of increased defensiveness on the TAT as compared to the analytic group. Barendregt et al. note that these two findings could be taken as indications that analysis reduces defenses and increases flexibility, while nonanalytic psychotherapy increases defenses and personality constriction.

PSYCHOANALYSIS VERSUS ANALYTICALLY ORIENTED THERAPY

Weber et al. (1966, 1967) have presented a vast array of data based on the case records of patients seen at Columbia University's Psychoanalytic Clinic for Training and Research. Patients were seen by analysts in training either in psychoanalysis on the "Reconstructive Service" or in analytically oriented therapy on the "Reparative" and "Psychosomatic Services." As with other investigations, these studies do not provide comparable groups, in that patients for psychoanalysis were selected by a more rigorous set of criteria. Patients selected for psychoanalysis were those judged to be well motivated and better integrated, with less evidence of severe pathology. In general, analytically oriented therapy was offered on the Reparative Service when there was an acute or circumscribed situational problem, when practical considerations or motivation ruled out an analytic schedule, or when there was some doubt regarding the patient's motivation or potential for change. Patients with at least one physical complaint considered psychosomatic were seen in analytically oriented therapy on the Psychosomatic Service. Aside from differences in the patient groups treated, this project is flawed by the possibility of major differences in the quantity and quality of the case notes recorded for the different types of treatment, and all of the findings are based on ratings of the case notes. It is also probable that coders were not blind to the treatment differences in the cases they were coding. Further bias is introduced by the fact that coders were not blind as to whether they were rating records of the beginning or end of treatment. The authors of this study point out the deficiencies in the methodology and, as is common in these reports, emphasize the investigation's exploratory nature.

The general findings were that both those patients treated with analysis and those treated with analytically oriented approaches showed comparable improvement in areas of largest net change (Work Performance, Physical Symptoms, and Neurotic Symptoms). A relatively greater proportion of patients in analysis tended to show improvements in the areas of Personal Relations, Sex, and Dissatisfaction with Personal Behavior, while patients seen in analytically oriented therapy (excluding psychosomatic cases) improved most in the areas of General Attitude and Feeling and Nervous System Symptoms. In both types of treatment there was a general shift over time away from structured symptoms to emphasis on disturbance in interpersonal relations.

In another report, Weber et al. (1966) compared the patients treated with analysis to those treated with analytically oriented therapy, using nine ratings of ego strength coded from clinic records (dependency, pleasure, sex, affect, defense, emergency emotions, guilt, pathology, and social relations). This study is beset by all of the methodological problems alluded to above, as well as the question of unreliability in the ego strength ratings. The overall finding was that differences in treatment results were related to time in treatment. For patients in therapy up to one year, the analytically oriented cases showed a larger net improvement on all nine ratings than the analysis cases. Results for cases seen between one and two years were equal on most measures, with analyzed patients showing greater improvements in the areas of sex, defensiveness, and pathology. For cases seen beyond two years, the analyzed patients showed greater improvement on all scales. The authors interpret the results as showing a differential relationship between improvement and time in treatment. The analytically oriented cases reached a maximum improvement in six months to one year; the analysis cases showed a slower rate of improvement, but one that generally surpassed the analytically oriented cases if treatment went beyond a period of two to three years. The difficulty with this reasoning is that the majority of analytically oriented cases were terminated in less than one year. Therefore, we would assume that comparisons beyond that point were made between the most difficult analytically oriented cases and the typical cases in analysis. Again, the noncomparability of groups makes the drawing of conclusions extremely suspect.

In the section on psychoanalysis versus no-treatment, we reported on the study by O'Connor et al. (1964) investigating the results of therapy on chronic ulcerative colitis patients. Patients in this study were treated by either short-term psychotherapy, or psychoanalytically oriented psychotherapy, or psychoanalysis, although no detailed differences among the treatments are described. The study found no relationship between the type of treatment and the degree of physiological improvement. Duration and intensity of treatment, however, were significantly correlated with the degree of psychological improvement, as measured by ratings of adjustment in the following areas: work, sex and marriage, family, and self-esteem. While no specific data are presented, the authors state that the psychoanalyzed patients showed a greater improvement in their life adjustment than those who had short-term therapy. Of course this difference in favor of psychoanalysis need not be attributed to the treatment, as there was a possibility of bias in the ratings, and it is likely the patients selected for analysis had a more favorable prognosis with regard to future adjustment.

An eighteen-year research investigation of twenty-one cases seen in psychoanalysis and twenty-one cases seen in psychoanalytically oriented therapy at the Menninger Clinic has been summarized by Kernberg et al. (1972). A number of earlier papers and progress reports have been published on this project (for example, Robbins and Wallerstein 1962, Wallerstein 1966, Wallerstein 1968b). The method of the study was "naturalistic" in that therapists and patients were not made aware that they were part of the investigation while therapy was in progress. The research was built around the therapy as it naturally occurred, leaving a number of variables contaminated or without the conventional experimental controls. The testing of dozens of hypotheses was seen as exploratory and suggestive for future research.

The data for the study were based primarily on judgments of case material made by clinicians at three points in time: at the beginning of treatment, at treatment termination, and at a follow-up point approximately two years later. Judgments focused mainly on comparisons between patients: which patient of a given pair had more of a particular variable? Principal measures of outcome included ratings of global change, ego strength, transference resolution, achievement of therapists' goals, and changes in Health-Sickness Scale scores. The broad aim of the project involved generating hypotheses about the associations between outcome and what had occurred in the treatment (process).

The therapists were described as predominantly psychoanalysts who were at least three to five years beyond their residency training. Psychotherapy was the primary treatment modality for the patients, although approximately half of the cases were hospitalized during the course of treatment (Wallerstein 1966). The study was not designed to compare the two treatments and, as in other projects, it is likely that patients for the two groups were selected on the basis of different implicit criteria. This contention is supported by Luborsky's (1962) finding that patients in analysis at the Menninger Clinic attained "healthier" initial scores on the Health-Sickness rating scale than patients treated by analytically oriented therapy. Differences between the groups in the nature of their case records—a major source of data—are also probable, with much more detailed process notes available for the cases seen in analysis (Robbins and Wallerstein 1962).

In spite of the methodological weaknesses and a statement in an early report that the study was not designed to compare treatments, the authors do make comparisons between treatments in the final summary. They report that the general statistical results found no evidence for "qualitative" differences in the improvement of patients treated with psychoanalysis or psychoanalytically oriented therapy.[13] A major finding was that patients with high Ego Strength (operationally defined in terms of severity of symptoms, quality of interpersonal relationships, patterning of defenses, and anxiety tolerance) improved regardless of the treatment modality or the skill of the therapist. Patients judged as being high in Ego Strength improved the most with each type of therapy; those judged to be low in Ego Strength improved the least. Interestingly, therapists judged as being relatively more skillful did well with their patients no matter what form the treatment took. Therapists judged less skillful did better when the treatment was analysis than when it was analytically oriented therapy. The authors explain this finding primarily in terms of psychoanalysis requiring less interpersonal involvement and a more "neutral" stance on the therapist's part. Variants of psychoanalysis seem to require additional therapist skill, due to the increased possibility of the therapist's personality and counter-transference reactions playing a part in the treatment process (Kernberg et al. 1972, p. 189). Overall, this highly complex study does not statistically support the idea that psychoanalysis is *the* superior form of treatment or that it requires greater therapist skill than analytically oriented therapy.

Heilbrunn (1963, 1966), in two surveys of his analytic practice, also concludes that the results he obtained with psychoanalysis and briefer analytic approaches were more or less comparable. These reports suffer from all the common methodological difficulties and problems in generalization associated with one therapist reviewing his own work. For the purposes of this study, Heilbrunn, guided by the standards of the American Psychoanalytic Association, defined psychoanalysis as a procedure exceeding 300 therapeutic hours at a frequency of at least three sessions per week, with the analyst following a predominantly passive and observing role. Therapy where the therapist took a more active role and where the duration was less than 300 hours or less than three sessions per week, or both, was labeled psychoanalytically oriented. Heilbrunn compared the improvement rates of more than 241 patients in five major diagnostic categories treated under four different levels of treatment duration: psychoanalysis (exceeding 300 tri-weekly sessions), extended psychotherapy (101 to 300 hours), and brief psychotherapy (one to twenty, and twenty-one to 100 hours). Treatment outcome was rated at termination as improved (greatly or moderately improved) or unimproved (slightly improved and unimproved). These ratings represented the sum of symptom improvement and personality change derived from separate four-point rating scales. Personality change was evaluated primarily in terms of impulse control and recognition and the ability to love and work at an "optimal psychoeconomic level." Again, the type of treatment was not determined randomly. Heilbrunn states that the approach was dictated by the chronicity of the patient's problems and in many instances by time factors, the patient's economic situation, or by other circumstances.

Heilbrunn found no significant differences in outcome for patients treated by the various methods. His general conclusion was that psychoanalysis did not emerge as a general treatment of choice, since at best it did not produce results superior to briefer treatments and at worst it required an unnecessary expenditure of money, time, and energy. We must repeat, however, that the non-comparability of treatment groups makes this study a poor test of the comparative effects of treatments of various durations. It should also be noted that the treatment called psychoanalysis in many other studies would be called psychoanalytically oriented or brief psychotherapy by this author, if outcome measures were taken before the 300-session mark.

Overview, Comments, and Conclusions

Within the last section we have reviewed ten studies dealing with the question of how the results of psychoanalysis compare with the results obtained by other treatments. The weight of the evidence to date suggests no major differences in outcome between therapies labeled psychoanalysis and other approaches. However, the studies as a group possess glaring deficiencies in methodology that make it impossible to draw firm conclusions. The major deficiency is the fact that most studies do not use a random assignment of patients to the various forms of treatment. This makes it possible to attribute differences in outcome to dissimilarities in the patients or other factors rather than the treatment differences. Weaknesses are readily apparent in the few studies even suggesting differences in outcome. For example, in the Cremerius (1962) study, initial comparisons revealed equivalent treatment outcomes among the five treatments, while an eight-to-ten-year follow-up showed analysis patients as retaining significantly greater symptom improvement than patients treated by other methods. Yet these findings can be explained either in terms of differences in prognosis of patients assigned to the various groups or in terms of greater duration of treatment for patients in analysis.

As we expected, based on the discussion in the previous chapter, there is considerable diversity and vagueness concerning what is labeled psychoanalysis by various investigators. The therapy called psychoanalysis in one report may fit the definition given for psychoanalytically oriented therapy in another investigation. Often there is no explicit description of the therapy, and almost always there is no attempt to measure whether the therapy taking place actually matches the description.

A review of the general therapy research literature by Luborsky and his co-workers (1971) strongly supports the idea that longer treatment leads to more positive outcome. Similarly, a number of studies of psychoanalysis have reported a significant relationship between duration and positive outcome (Bieber et al. 1962, O'Connor et al. 1964, Weber et al. 1966, Aronson and Weintraub 1968b). Therefore, since duration of treatment appears to be a major factor used to differentiate psychoanalysis from psychoanalytically oriented therapies, it seems curious that the studies do not show clear differences favoring the outcome of psychoanalysis. The results of the investigation by Weber et al. (1966) partially suggest that change is related to duration with *both* psychoanalysis and analytically oriented approaches, but that the rate of change may be slower with psychoanalysis. Aronson and Weintraub (1968b) also found a tendency to report very modest improvements over the first few years of analytic treatment, in a study of 127 cases retrospectively rated by twenty-eight analysts for improvement in symptoms, vocational functioning, object relations, and pleasure capacity. The percentage of patients rated as showing changes increased dramatically when treatment surpassed three or four years of duration. A slowing of the reported rate of change could result from analysts' expectations that therapy should be "long" in order to be meaningful. In meeting this expectation, therapists may either overestimate changes in patients treated for longer periods of time or assume that real change cannot occur before a specified number of sessions has passed (Luborsky et al. 1971).[14] The studies reviewed indicate a strong possibility that outcome ratings could have been biased by the rater knowing how long the patient had been in treatment and having the expectation that longer is better.

One of the questions raised by a reading of the studies is, how long does long-term psychotherapy have to last to be maximally effective? Heilbrunn's (1963, 1966) studies suggest, at least for him, that relatively little was added to observable improvement by continuing therapy with most of the cases he saw beyond the 300-session mark. In general, while the comparative data collected to this point are certainly weak, lengthening therapy for the majority of patients into many years of treatment does not appear to be justified on the grounds of superior therapeutic outcome. The studies by Weber et al. (1966), Aronson and Weintraub (1968b), and O'Connor et al. (1964) do suggest that future comparisons of analysis to alternative approaches or no-treatment on *comparable patients* should involve a time span of at least three to four years, following the initiation of therapy, to insure maximum effects.

Despite the lack of objective evidence substantiating the value of unlimited treatment duration, there are indications in the literature that analysts over time have tended toward expecting and obtaining longer analyses. It is of interest to repeat that Freud's reported cases were seen for relatively brief periods compared to the more recent standards of hundreds of sessions and many years in treatment. Grinker (1974), recalling his experiences as one of Freud's patients, has stated that Freud would not have favored today's beliefs that analysis must be lengthy to be effective or that the more weekly treatment hours the better. Other evidence that analysis used to be considered a much briefer treatment is contained in probably the earliest survey of an analyst's practice, where Coriat (1917) indicated that treating severe neurotics often required intensive prolonged treatment lasting for as long as four to six months! Malan (1963) cited statistics based on the German psychoanalytic journals in coming to the conclusion that the course of analysis has been lengthening. He found that between 1909 and 1920 there was a significant drop to zero in the published number of case histories reflecting successful brief psychoanalytic treatment. Malan went on to summarize a number of theoretical and technique factors in trying to account for the movement in the direction of longer analyses: resistance, over-determination, necessity for working through, roots of neurosis in early childhood, transference, dependency, negative transference connected with termination, the transference neurosis, a tendency toward passivity and the willingness to follow where the patient leads, a sense of timelessness conveyed to the patient, therapeutic perfectionism, and an increasing preoccupation with ever deeper and earlier experiences (p. 9). Interestingly, Malan quotes others such as Balint, Glover, and Watterson, who suggest that the early analysts (and even current analysts beginning their careers) may achieve results in a relatively brief period of time because of their heightened excitement and high level of enthusiasm.[15]

In sum, while we are well aware that measuring increments of change may become more and more difficult as therapy lengthens into years, we read the current data as indicating no justification for claiming that lengthy psychoanalysis with acute neurotic cases is superior in outcome to shorter term therapies labeled psychoanalytically oriented. The strength of this conclusion is limited by a literature sorely lacking well-controlled studies comparing psychoanalysis with other approaches. We could not find, for example, any controlled studies comparing the effects of psychoanalysis with behavior therapy.[16, 17]

In the initial section of this chapter we concluded that the available evidence suggests that psychoanalysis as a therapy is superior to no-treatment. We find ourselves asking why studies do not similarly show that analysis is superior to other treatments. There are a number of possible reasons for not finding differences. The simplest reason, of course, is that no differences exist. Alternatively, typical measures may not be sensitive enough or may not be focused on the areas most likely to reveal differences. Another possible reason relates to vagueness in the definition and practice of analysis. It may well be that much of the comparative data is not based on treatments that are really different in any essential ways.

A fourth explanation is suggested by looking at the differences in the cited studies comparing psychoanalysis to no-treatment and those comparing psychoanalysis to alternative approaches. The former group of studies found analysis superior to the absence of treatment in predominantly severe, chronic neurotic cases. In contrast, studies offering comparative data have tended to focus on more acute cases of lesser severity. One could argue that the less severe the disturbance, the more likely it is that any treatment will result in change. In fact, it seems tenable that patients possessing the greatest number of strengths and assets would be the ones most likely to improve without benefit of any formal treatment at all. Interestingly, Luborsky and Spence (1971) conclude in their review of quantitative research on psychoanalytic therapy, that the patients with the best general personality functioning attain the best treatment outcomes. This conclusion is consistent with the Menninger Project findings on psychoanalysis (Kernberg et al. 1972) and the findings based on other therapeutic approaches (Luborsky et al. 1971). Our contention is, however, that studies gathering data on the most prognostically desirable cases may be minimizing the possibility of finding significant differences between treatments or between a treatment and no therapy. For "good" patients, any treatment or no-treatment may lead to an equally high percentage of improvement. Whereas for difficult cases, even though the absolute percentage of patients improving with treatment would probably be smaller, the differences between treated and nontreated groups may be greater. This idea is consonant with Freud's early stated views on the development of psychoanalytic therapy. He wrote:

> Actually, I have been able to elaborate and to test my therapeutic method only on severe, indeed on the severest cases; at first my material consisted entirely of patients who had tried everything else without success, and had spent long years in sanatoria. I have scarcely been able to bring together sufficient material to enable me to say how my method works with those slighter, episodic cases which we see recovering under all kinds of influences and even spontaneously. Psychoanalytic therapy was created through and

> for the treatment of patients permanently unfit for existence, and its triumph has been that it has made a satisfactorily large number of these permanently fit for existence. (Freud 1905a, p. 263)

While we are suggesting that differences between outcomes of alternative treatments may be maximized if more severe and difficult neurotic cases are utilized, we do not wish to imply that psychoanalysis is the treatment of choice for patients with psychotic diagnoses. Our reading of the literature revealed a number of indications that the therapist passivity and encouragement of patient regression associated with orthodox analytic technique, may, in the hands of relatively inexperienced therapists, be harmful to patients with tenuous personality defenses. Klein (1960), in a study at the Columbia Psychoanalytic Clinic of thirty analyzed cases originally diagnosed psychoneurotic, found that while no patients were hospitalized, 23 percent (seven) were diagnosed "schizotypal" disorder at a follow-up interview by experienced analysts. This raises the possibility that approximately one quarter of the patients deteriorated in their functioning as a result of treatment. Weber et al. (1966) also presented data gathered at the Columbia Psychoanalytic Clinic suggesting that analysis is not the treatment of choice for borderline patients. They found indications of positive changes on ego-strength rating scales following analytically oriented therapy for patients diagnosed psychotic or psychotic personality. Patients with the same diagnosis treated by psychoanalysis showed virtually no changes on the ego strength scales. Further, of the patients seen in analysis and diagnosed as psychotic personalities of relatively less severity, 2 percent improved while 44.4 percent were rated as becoming worse. In a later report Weber et al. (1967) investigated changes in diagnoses over the course of treatment. They found that even though there was a tendency toward increasing psychotic diagnoses with the various treatments, this change was most striking among analyzed patients, where psychosis was diagnosed three times more often at treatment termination than at treatment initiation. Rather than attributing a move in the direction of more impaired functioning to the treatment, the authors chose to conclude that change in diagnosis was reflective of new information available from the therapy. Why new information should become more available with analysis than with analytically oriented therapy is left unexplained.

Kernberg et al. (1972), on the basis of the data gathered by the Menninger Research Project, also conclude that orthodox psychoanalysis is not the treatment of choice for patients diagnosed as borderline personalities. They attributed the borderline patients' relatively poor outcome with psychoanalysis to a lack of tolerance for regression and a proneness to develop a transference psychosis. They found that borderline patients did relatively better in a treatment characterized by greater therapist activity, higher therapist skill, and high focus on the transference relationship.

Grinspoon et al. (1968) found phenothiazine therapy superior to analytic therapy in the treatment of a group of chronic schizophrenic patients. Therapists in this study were all senior staff psychiatrists who were either psychoanalysts or psychoanalytically oriented. All had considerable experience in therapy with schizophrenic patients. While all patients were seen at least twice a week for a two-year period, there is no description or measurement of the nature of the therapy, raising questions about whether the treatment can be given the analytic label. Overall, the findings revealed no changes on various behavioral ratings and scales for patients receiving placebos plus analytic therapy, whereas patients receiving phenothiazines plus therapy evidenced significant changes on all measures. We should note that Karon and VandenBos (1972, 1973) have presented empirical evidence indicating that a psychoanalytic therapy can achieve results superior to phenothiazines with *acute* schizophrenic patients. However, although the conceptualization of the cases in these studies was based on psychoanalytic theory, the treatment technique would probably not be called psychoanalysis by most practitioners. Treatment was generally quite active and focused on the transference, in a fashion similar to the Menninger Project's recommendations for the treatment of borderline cases (Karon, 1963).

Weintraub and Aronson (1969b), in a survey investigation of thirty analysts' reports on 126 patients in classical psychoanalysis, came to a conclusion somewhat at variance with the results of the studies reviewed above. They concluded that classical psychoanalysis need not be a dangerous procedure. Patients within their sample were all seen on the couch predominantly three to five sessions per week. Indications were that all therapists attempted to adhere to their notion of classical techniques as closely as possible. Results revealed little evidence of any regression, self-destructive behavior, or decompensation in patients. Only one patient was hospitalized and only one developed psychotic symptoms. There were no suicides, although there were three attempts. No explanation was given for three patients being switched from analysis to psychotherapy.

Weintraub and Aronson felt their data indicated that the dangers of serious decompensation with analysis are minimal if the analysts are well trained and careful in their selection of patients.

They conjectured that the precipitation of borderline patients into psychosis may be the result of poor technique and "wild" analysis rather than the result of competent therapists applying classical methods. In explaining the results of their study they pointed to the high quality of training for the analysts in their sample, along with their analysts' tendency to be very conservative in judging patients suitable for analysis and avoiding nonclassical techniques. It should be noted that there were only fifteen patients diagnosed as borderline psychotic in this study. Although these patients were not reported to have manifested serious psychotic regression or dangerous self-destructive behavior, another investigation of the same patients revealed that the proportion of borderline cases becoming worse with psychoanalysis was greater than the deterioration in either neurotic or character disorder groups on ratings of symptom status, vocational adjustment, object relations, and capacity to experience pleasure. There were not enough cases, however, to establish the difference statistically (Aronson and Weintraub 1968b).

The effects of the experience and expertise of the therapist are issues requiring more attention in studies of psychoanalysis. Luborsky et al. (1971), in their review of the general therapy research literature, substantiated that the majority of studies addressing these issues found a significant positive relationship between patient improvement and therapist level of experience and skill. It was our feeling that the studies we reviewed comparing the outcome of psychoanalysis with no-treatment may have utilized more experienced analysts than the studies focusing on comparative treatments. We cannot validate this impression because of the general lack of detailed therapist descriptions presented by most studies. It is quite possible that studies of alternative therapies performed by highly experienced therapists with chronic patients drawn randomly from the same source might be more revealing of treatment differences. Such studies have not yet been done.

Perhaps one of the most interesting hypotheses suggested by the studies of various therapies is that psychoanalysis may result in greater patient flexibility and lower defensiveness than other therapeutic approaches (Barendregt et al. 1961, Dudek 1970). The validity of this hypothesis might be tested in the future by outcome measures geared toward patients' creativity, cognitive complexity, or simple ability to generate alternative explanations for events. The data we reviewed in the last chapter certainly suggest that analysts as a group seem to generate more alternative explanations for their observations than other therapist groups. In any event, the increased flexibility hypothesis certainly appears to warrant future study under more controlled conditions.

Our review of studies of the outcome of psychoanalysis seems to come down to two general conclusions: (1) psychoanalysis has been shown to be consistently more effective than no-treatment with chronic neurotic patients, and (2) psychoanalysis has not been shown to be significantly more effective than *other* forms of psychotherapy with any type of patient. The research on patient qualities desirable in analytic patients is in line with the idea of minimal differences between various forms of psychotherapy. It has been found that the attributes generally associated with positive changes in analytic patients are the same patient attributes associated with positive changes in other therapies (Luborsky et al. 1971). These attributes, as reviewed by Luborsky and Spence (1971), would include better general personality functioning, stronger anxiety, and a higher educational level. Luborsky and Spence also include "younger age," but the findings on this variable have been equivocal in the studies they cite, with Hamburg et al. (1967) finding younger patients doing better and Knapp et al. (1960) finding that older patients improve more (although the ages ranged only from twenty to forty-one years).

In practical terms the literature suggests that a patient suffering from chronic neurotic symptoms would do better with psychoanalysis than without it. However, there is at present no justification for a patient to assume that he will achieve a greater degree of improvement in a therapy called psychoanalysis than in a therapy given another label such as analytically oriented, client-centered, or behavioral. There is virtually no evidence that psychoanalysis generally results in more long-lasting or profound patient change than other therapies. Freud (1937a,b) himself stated that there was no way of predicting what would happen later to a patient who had been cured by analysis. Indeed, both Pfeffer (1959) and Deutsch (1959) have found evidence of unresolved neurotic conflicts in successfully analyzed patients years after their treatment. This does not mean that differences in outcome between therapies may not exist, but simply that they have not been clearly or consistently demonstrated. As in Freud's statement that therapists should examine their own experiences in evaluating the effectiveness of their therapy, patients should also not be blinded by labels in evaluating whether their treatment with their therapist is beneficial to them.

We have tried to suggest some future research questions and methods that might be more revealing of treatment differences. For the present we must conclude that there is nothing magical about psychoanalysis and that future improvements in therapeutic effectiveness will be more dependent on identifying the active therapeutic ingredients in theories, therapies, and therapists than in trying to demonstrate that one mythical treatment label is superior to another.

NOTES

1. A similar point is made by Freud in a later paper:

> At one time a complaint was made against analysis that it was not to be taken seriously as a treatment since it did not dare to issue any statistics of its successes. Since then, the Psycho-Analytic Institute in Berlin, which was founded by Dr. Max Eddington, has published a statement of its results during its first ten years. Its therapeutic successes give grounds neither for boasting nor for being ashamed. But statistics of that kind are in general uninstructive; the material worked upon is so heterogeneous that only very large numbers would show anything. It is wiser to examine one's individual experiences. (Freud 1933e, p. 152)

2. Kernberg et al. (1972) provide an example of this research flavor in their final report on the eighteen-year research project on psychoanalysis and psychotherapy at the Menninger Clinic. They write:

> To an experimentalist, probably the most severe limitation of this study would be its naturalistic character and concomitant lack of a formal experimental design. This study is not one in which conceptualization and methodology had progressed to the point where at the beginning of the study it was possible (1) to list the variables needed to test the theory; (2) to have methods of quantification for these variables, preferably existing scales which would yield adequate reliability and validity; (3) to be able to choose and provide control conditions which could rule out alternative explanations for results (or even to be able to list all the possible conditions that needed to be controlled for); (4) to state the hypotheses to be tested; or, finally (5) to conduct the research according to this design. At the time of the inception of this Project conceptualization in the field as a whole had not progressed to the point where it would have been possible to set up such an experimental design for any such proposed research. We also feel that our Project and others of a similar nature have made it more possible to plan for such formal research today with a likelihood of being able to obtain meaningful results. (p. 76)

3. Malan et al. (1968, 1975), in studying symptomatic and psychodynamic changes in a group of "non-treated" neurotic patients, found evidence of mechanisms in everyday life that led to therapeutic changes and unexpected evidence that even a single dynamic therapy interview appeared to lead toward significant and lasting changes for a number of patients.

4. The studies cited by Bergin and the reported percentage of spontaneous improvement rates for neuroses are as follows: Friess and Nelson (1942), 29; Friess and Nelson (1942), 35; Shore and Massimo (1966), 30; Orgel (1958), 0; Materson (1967), 38; Vorster (1966), 34; Hastings (1958), 46; Graham (1960), 37; O'Connor et al. (1964), 0; Cappon (1964), 0; Endicott and Endicott (1963), 52 (inflated by the inclusion of "slightly improved"); Koegler and Brill (1967), 0; Paul (1967), 18; and Kringlen (1965), 25.

5. The superiority of experienced analysts in judging patient suitability for treatment may have had more to do with the fact that judgments were made by a group than the fact that the analysts were experienced. In addition, a group putting patients through a very elaborate intake interviewing procedure, as described by Feldman (1968), might in itself increase positive outcome by raising a patient's attraction to the therapy through a mecha-

nism akin to cognitive dissonance (Aronson 1961, Aronson and Mills 1959)—the general principle being: the more difficult it is to get into the therapy, the more attractive and desirable it may become. Indeed, the general difficulty in being accepted as an analytic patient may increase its attractiveness and thereby indirectly enhance the patients' responsivity to therapist interpretation.

6. Another study that we considered as potentially offering data on how psychoanalysis compares with no-treatment is reported by Jersild et al. (1962). This study sought to compare a group of teachers who had undergone "psychoanalysis or intensive therapy" with a group who had not. The data for this study consisted entirely of retrospective answers to a twenty-page questionnaire concerning problems and changes that had occurred. The control group appears totally inadequate and incomparable to the therapy group, as they were not patients and had not sought therapy. They were simply asked about problems that had arisen prior to or during the past four-year period and changes that had occurred during that time. Not surprisingly, the major "finding" of this study was that the therapy group was more prone to report they had had problems and that they had experienced "great improvement" in many more areas than had the control group.

The sole reliance on retrospective reports of unknown reliability and validity, the incomparability of the control group, and the huge number of questions asked, combined with the lack of reported statistical tests of significance, are all major reasons why we have discounted this study as offering even meaningful suggestive evidence on the question of psychoanalysis versus no-treatment.

7. Schjelderup (1955) points out that the greatest number of these patients were referred by a physician named Saethre, who said of them:

> The patient material is quite out of the common. These are patients who weigh like a nightmare upon the doctor who must try to treat them. The burden of the one, out of perhaps a hundred patients seen in a week, before whom he stands utterly helpless, and who comes again and again—he has been to all the other nerve specialists already!—the burden of this one patient is unspeakable. And the relief is correspondingly great when, after all his own attempts have proved abortive, he can resort to the possibilities that analysis holds out, at any rate for some of these wretched neurotics. This must not be left out of the final therapeutic balance sheet. It is our 'worst' cases that we send to the analysts—the most impossible material in a nerve specialist's practice and in the psychiatric clinics. (p. 121)

8. For Schjelderup (1955) a rating of very satisfactory indicated symptom cure and, in addition, personality changes making possible a definitely better social adjustment (with regard to work, interpersonal relations, and sex). The patient should be able to undergo severe strain without a relapse and should not have the desire or need for further treatment.

A rating of satisfactory indicated a lasting and decided positive change with regard to both symptoms and adjustment since the therapy. The cure is not complete in that temporary relapses may occur under stress. The sense that more might be accomplished may foster a desire for further treatment.

9. The measures used by Cartwright (1966a) were, respectively, the Rogers-Rablen Process Scale (which codifies the degree to which feelings are experienced in a flexible and personal way), a Self-Observation Scale, and the Bales Interaction Process Analysis.

10. Cremerius (1962) also collected data regarding the percentage of patients working at the beginning and end of treatment. These data are of interest, since Eysenck bases his argument for spontaneous remission in part on the percentage of patients who drop their worker's disability claims. Cremerius found that by the end of treatment almost all of the patients seen were employed (an increase from 63 percent to 92 percent). Therefore, if one chose to regard changes in disability claims as a valid indicator of therapy outcome, this study shows evidence of change greater than the "spontaneous remission" rate.

11. Aronson and Weintraub (1968b), in a study of 127 patients in psychoanalysis, found that the early dropout group was not generally made up of patients who had not improved. In fact, patients who dropped out earliest showed greater symptomatic improvement than did nonterminators at the same level of treatment duration.

12. Dudek's (1970) conclusions were based on the following significant Rorschach changes in the analytic groups: Increases in productivity (more verbal production and a

higher number of responses), enriched fantasy life (higher M), increase in affect (more color), heightened sensitivity (more shading), and increased awareness of norms (more P). Increases were also noted in sexual imagery and FM responsiveness.

13. An analysis of the data from the Menninger project utilizing Multidimensional Scalogram Analysis and Guttman's facet theory suggested that patients with high initial Ego Strength showed greatest improvement with psychoanalysis. This finding, however, cannot be tested for statistical significance or stated in probability terms, due to the fact that Multidimensional Scalogram Analysis, like factor analysis, is a mathematical rather than a statistical approach (Kernberg et al. 1972, p. 96).

14. Freud's statements at times reflect the assumption that real and lasting change cannot come about too quickly. For example, he wrote:

> You will remember that it was a *frustration* that made the patient ill, and that his symptoms serve him as substitutive satisfactions. It is possible to observe during the treatment that every improvement in his condition reduces the rate at which he recovers and diminishes the instinctual force impelling him towards recovery. But this instinctual force is indispensible; reduction of it endangers our aim—the patient's restoration to health. What, then, is the conclusion that forces itself inevitably upon us? Cruel though it may sound, we must see to it that the patient's suffering, to a degree that is in some way or other effective, does not come to an end prematurely. If, owing to the symptoms having been taken apart and lost their value, his suffering becomes mitigated, we must re-instate it elsewhere in the form of some appreciable privation; otherwise we run the danger of never achieving any improvements except quite insignificant and transitory ones. (Freud 1919b, pp. 162–163)

15. The increasing of positive therapeutic results as a function of the therapist's expectations or enthusiasm is independent of the therapist's professed orientation and has been discussed in detail within the therapy literature under topics such as therapist-patient expectancies (Goldstein 1962), faith healing (Frank 1961), and placebos (Shapiro 1971).

16. A paper by Meyer (1966) does attempt to provide comparative data on the treatment of homosexuals by psychoanalysis and behavior therapy. It is highly questionable, however, whether the data are really comparable, as they are drawn from two separate studies with differences in patient characteristics (education, marital status, effeminacy), patient selection, treatment settings, treatment duration, and source of data. The psychoanalytically treated sample results were obtained from a study by Bieber et al. (1962) and the results with behaviorally treated homosexuals were obtained from reports by Freund (1960, 1963).

The behaviorally treated patients were all seen personally by Freund, whose treatment is described as a combination of aversion conditioning and positive conditioning. Aversion was produced by exposing patients to slides of male nudes while they were experiencing drug-induced nausea. Positive conditioning was defined as showing patients motion pictures of nude and seminude women seven hours after the patients had received 10 mg of testosteronum propionicum.

Data on the psychoanalytically treated group were obtained from questionnaires returned by fifty-eight out of 100 members of the Society of Medical Psychoanalysts. Obviously, those who returned questionnaires may not be representative of the group as a whole. Another possible bias is raised by the fact that the analysts each reported on homosexual patients *they* selected from their private practices. There was no measurement of what actually occurred in therapy.

Outcome measured in terms of either a shift toward greater heterosexual behavior or exclusive heterosexual behavior revealed that the results of psychoanalysis were significantly superior to the behavior therapy results. Overall, psychoanalysis resulted in a shift to exclusive heterosexuality in 27 percent of the 106 cases and behavior therapy resulted in 12 percent of the 67 patients shifting in the direction of greater heterosexuality, with only one patient becoming exclusively heterosexual.

As noted, the numerous differences between studies would seem to preclude a valid comparison of results. We might add in passing that Bieber et al. reported a number of favorable prognostic indicators that were associated, in their sample, with homosexuals becoming exclusively heterosexual: (1) patient was bisexual at the beginning of analysis; (2)

analysis begun before age thirty-five; (3) analysis continued for at least 150 hours; (4) patient wanted to become heterosexual; (5) patient's father was at least ambivalent; (6) patient's father respected and/or admitted the patient, was affectionate, was more intimate with patient than with other male siblings, and liked women; (7) patient idolized women; (8) patient had tried heterosexual activity; and (9) patient had heterosexual activity in manifest dream content.

17. Sloane et al. (1975a,b) compared short-term analytically oriented psychotherapy to behavior therapy in the treatment of outpatients with a diagnosis of neurosis or personality disorder. Patients were randomly assigned to one of the two treatment groups or a waiting list control group. Therapists were experienced psychoanalysts and experienced, formerly trained behavior therapists. Comparisons after four months of treatment (an average of only thirteen to fourteen sessions) revealed that the target symptoms of all three groups had significantly improved. However, the two treatment groups had improved to an equal degree and significantly more than patients on the waiting list. The behavior therapy patients were rated most improved on a global measure of improvement, while there were no differences among groups on scaled measures of work and social adjustment. One- and two-year follow-up measures were also taken, but the results are confounded by the fact that different amounts of further treatment were given in the three groups after the initial four-month study period. The authors conclude that there is no clear evidence for the superiority of either form of treatment to the other, although both are superior to no-treatment. This conclusion is quite similar to our overall findings regarding the comparative effectiveness of "psychoanalysis" and other approaches.

Chapter 9

The Mechanisms of Psychoanalytic Therapy: The Search for Insight

The Testing of Freud's Changing Concept of Insight

THROUGHOUT Freud's writings, one is continually reminded that the central task of psychoanalytic therapy is to make the patient aware of the motivations for his actions and the repressed impulses or forgotten traumatic events that theoretically underlie his symptoms. The aim of the therapy would seem to revolve around the gaining of insight and the overcoming of resistances to "making the unconscious conscious" (for example, Freud 1914c, 1919b). Over the course of the development of psychoanalytic therapy the technique shifted from having the patient recall hypnotically and affectively the pathogenic traumatic events thought to underlie his neurosis, to recovering significant forgotten memories and accurately reconstructing the past through free associations and analyses of dreams and slips of the tongue. Emphasis gradually changed from the mere recall of memories to a demonstration of how the past unnecessarily repeated itself in the patient's relationship to others and to the analyst (transference). The analyst used verbal interpretations in helping the patient overcome resistances and in revealing the links between past and present. The implicit idea in the approach was that the patient would be benefited by knowing, understanding, and experiencing his "deepest" thoughts and motivations. Further, it was deemed important that change come about not through therapist suggestion or persuasion but through the patient's learning the "truth" about himself and his feelings. It was conjectured that attacking only the patient's symptoms without revealing their "true" cause would result in short-lived cures and the probability of new symptoms developing from the same unresolved conflicts (symptom substitution). To increase self-disclosure and to reduce the probability of the analyst suggesting or distorting the patient's communications, the patient was placed on a couch and instructed to free associate to an unseen, ambiguous therapist. Therapist ambiguity theoretically served to facilitate the patient's projecting his past reactions to parental figures onto the analyst. It was hypothesized that therapist distortion of the patient material (countertransference) could be reduced through the analyst's own analysis.

The major thrust of Freud's writings on treatment would seem to rest on the idea that a therapy facilitating insight and understanding of the causes of one's behavior is superior in outcome and durability to treatments concerned with more "superficial" alleviation of symptoms. The idea of a significant relationship between depth of exploration and curative potential is strongly implied, particularly in Freud's earlier works (for example, Freud 1905b,c). The more thoroughly the patient understands the historical roots of his current behavior and the "deeper" the roots go into the past, presumably the more likely it is that he will experience lasting changes in behavior, attitudes, and symptoms. While self-education and self-understanding can be seen as therapy goals in and of themselves, Freud's early hypothesis suggested that these attainments would lead directly and automatically to other changes. The idea that insight leads to change has become the hallmark of dynamic "treatment" approaches, even though Freud himself expressed doubts at the end of his career about the possibility of promoting profound and lasting changes through psychoanalytic therapy (Freud 1937a). Freud's early statements associating insight with change are apparently so persuasive that some analysts have assumed that significant change can come about only as a function of insight. This has sometimes resulted in the circular argument that changes occurring without insight are not "real" or are only apparently lacking in insight (Abroms 1968). Conversely, apparent insights not resulting in change have been labeled false, incomplete, or intellectual (London 1964, Brady 1967).

Freud's later writing on therapy indicated that he was placing a greater and greater distance between the gaining of self-understanding and the automatic remission of symptoms. The change in emphasis from the uncovering of repressed memories to the overcoming of patient resistances moved the therapy away from the earlier simple association between increased self-awareness and decreased symptomatology. Insight alone was no longer considered sufficient for producing patient change. Indeed, many of the factors that eventuated in the lengthening of psychoanalytic treatment, such as the necessity for transference interpretations and the notion that symptoms are over-determined, can be seen as indications of Freud backing away from the idea that change automatically and simply follows insight. In his discussion of 'wild' psychoanalysis, Freud was careful to point out the limited role of insight as well as the dangers and contraindications to prematurely and nondiscriminately forcing insights upon patients. He wrote:

> It is a long superseded idea, and one derived from superficial appearances, that the patient suffers from a sort of ignorance, and that if one removes his ignorance by giving him information . . . he is bound to recover. The pathological factor is not his ignorance in itself, but the root of his ignorance in his *inner resistances* . . . The task of the treatment is in combating these resistances. Informing the patient of what he does not know because he has repressed it is only one of the necessary preliminaries to the treatment . . . for informing the patient of his unconscious regularly results in an intensification of the conflict in him and an exacerbation of his troubles . . . Since, however psycho-analysis cannot dispense with giving this information, it lays down that this shall not be done before two conditions have been fulfilled. First the patient must, through preparation, himself have reached the neighborhood of what he has repressed, and secondly, he must have formed a sufficient attachment (transference) to the physician for his emotional relationship to him to make a fresh flight impossible. (Freud, 1910d, pp. 225–226)

Freud further reduced the direct role of insight in producing change with the formal incorporation into his theory of therapy of the notion that change requires time, during which time the patient is provided with the opportunity to "work through" his resistances to the newly acquired perceptions and ideas. The patient is faced again and again with illustrations of how perceptions and feelings from the past unnecessarily repeat themselves in influencing present relationships to the therapist and "real life" outside of therapy. The concept of "working through," so important for Freud's conception of change, is largely ignored in research dealing with therapy given the "insight" label. The tendency on the part of researchers, as well as many therapists, is to follow Freud's earlier and simpler implication that behavior change evolves directly from insight. Yet, as Freud's later position clearly held:

> One must allow the patient time to become more conversant with this resistance with which he has now become acquainted, to *work through* it, to overcome it, by continuing, in defiance of it, the analytic work according to

> the fundamental rule of analysis . . . This working-through of the resistances may in practice turn out to be an arduous task for the subject of the analysis and a trial of patience for the analyst. Nevertheless, it is a part of the work which effects the greatest changes in the patient and which distinguishes analytic treatment from any kind of treatment by suggestion. (Freud 1914c, pp. 155–156)

The question of whether insight gained through therapy leads to superior therapeutic results has been examined in comparative studies of the outcomes of insight- versus non-insight-oriented therapies. Most of these studies seem to implicitly equate interpretations with insight. If interpretations have been given, it is assumed insight has been produced. Obviously, however, the fact that interpretations have been given is no guarantee that patients feel any more insightful about their problems. Therefore, to be more accurate, these therapies should be labeled "interpretive" rather than "insight-oriented."

Aside from this partly semantic issue, there are a number of other problems in regarding these studies as having any direct bearing on Freud's hypotheses. For example, most of the reports appear to assume that insights alone should lead directly and automatically to change, an idea which we feel Freud himself abandoned in later elaborations of his theory. As a consequence of the assumed direct relationship between insight and change, most studies utilize interpretive treatments lasting for only a very limited number of sessions. The idea that insight treatment, in the Freudian sense, could be conducted within a few hours is highly inconsistent with Freud's already discussed statements on "working through" and the dangers of prematurely forcing insights upon patients (Freud 1910d, 1914c). Further, in these studies, the patients, therapists, type of therapy (group versus individual treatment), and conditions of therapy (treatment techniques, frequency) are for the most part at variance with Freud's general descriptions. For instance, the patients in the large majority of all the reports we reviewed were either chronic hospitalized schizophrenics or college students recruited for a psychological study. Freud was not an advocate of psychoanalytic therapy for schizophrenic patients and, as we have previously indicated, he did not develop or selectively endorse his approach for the treatment of acute circumscribed disorders. The questionable practice of evaluating a treatment approach with relatively untrained, inexperienced therapists should require no further comment.

Perhaps the biggest impediment to generalizing from most studies to Freud's linkage of insight with change lies in deficiencies in experimental methodology and differences in the way the concept of "insight" has been defined. It appears unreasonable to draw conclusions about the association between the development of insight and various measures of change if it has not first been *independently* demonstrated that insight has increased. Yet, as Roback (1974) has summarized, many of the studies do not define what they are calling insight; do not employ a measure of the amount and kind of insight produced; do not describe the specific therapist operations designed to produce insight; do not validate that the therapist employed the specific operations; and, most importantly, do not measure to ensure that the patients receiving "insight therapy" actually evidence greater gains in insight than those who do not. While few studies have even attempted to provide insight measures, those that do have employed operational definitions that bear only a superficial and tangential relationship to Freud's statements. For Freud, insight seems to require an increasing sense of awareness of the relationship between early conflicts and current neurotic problems, a sense of being able to explain present behavior and feelings on the basis of past events. The measures of insight that have been utilized offer a significant contrast to this definition: the ability to respond to a test as another individual (empathic insight), congruence between a person's self-perceptions and the perceptions others have of him, the ability to understand the underlying motivation of others, and the awareness of an individual that his intellectual or emotional functioning is impaired (Roback 1974).

In order to provide a sampling of the type of work that has been done, we will briefly review a number of interpretive therapy outcome studies that do not measure changes in insight and a number that do measure such changes. We feel that more than anything else, these investigations are a demonstration of the lack of specificity in the concepts and their application. We caution the reader to recognize both the methodological problems we have outlined and the numerous ways in which the reports do not coincide with Freud's conceptions of psychoanalytic therapy.

Comparative Studies of Insight Therapy Not Measuring Insight Change

A number of studies have purported to assess the comparative effects of insight- and non-insight-oriented treatments on schizophrenic patients. Outcome is typically measured in these reports by an assessment of whether the patient's hospital adjustment has improved. The usual finding is that insight-oriented treatments are inferior or no different from other approaches in improving the hospital adjustment of schizophrenic patients.

Hartlage (1970) compared the outcome for chronic female hospitalized schizophrenic patients seen in either traditional therapy or reinforcement therapy by student nurses. The mean length of hospitalization was seventeen years, and the length of therapy training for the student nurses was ten hours. Traditional therapy was described as time spent interpreting statements, fostering transference, and encouraging insight. The reinforcement therapy approach consisted of rewarding patients for responses defined as adaptive with social reinforcers (smiles and approval), material reinforcers (cigarettes or coffee), and privilege reinforcers (favors and time off from work assignments). Patients and therapists met one hour per day for seven weeks. Patients in the two groups were matched on the Hospital Adjustment Scale (HAS) before treatment. Results following treatment indicated the reinforcement group improved to a significantly greater degree on total HAS scores and on the communication and interpersonal relations subscales. Therapists' global ratings of improvement also favored the reinforcement group. No differences between groups were found on the self-care or activity-participation subscales of the HAS. Similarly, no differences were obtained between groups on a patient-rated self-concept measure, although both groups showed positive changes over therapy. At best, this study seems to show that long-term chronic schizophrenic female patients show better adaptation to the hospital when inexperienced, untrained therapists treat them with reinforcement techniques rather than a vague therapy labeled "traditional." However, as Roback (1974) points out, the study offers no definition of insight, no measures to insure insight was produced, and no assessment of whether the therapists carried out the specified techniques. To make matters even more confusing, Hartlage states that it was very difficult to keep the two therapeutic methods totally separate.

Related to Hartlage's investigation of the relationship of developing insight to schizophrenic prognosis is an earlier report by Rennie and Fowler (1941) concerned with the analysis of 100 "recovered" schizophrenic cases. The report is based on 100 cases selected from clinic files where recovery was maintained for five to twenty-five years and considered unequivocal.[1] A major aim of the paper was to look at how various factors were associated, if at all, with the recoveries. No specific treatments were described, although it was noted that the most striking factor for recovery appeared to be a long-term contact with a physician or clinic. With regard to insight, the report found that the majority of patients did not have insight into their "illness" at the time of discharge. This led to the conclusion that insight is presumably not very important for recovery. Again no definition is given for insight and no attempts at measurement are described. Further, there is no control group of nonremitted schizophrenics, making it impossible to ascertain whether the development of insight is more frequently associated with recovery.

Semon and Goldstein (1957) report a study dealing with the hospital adaptation of chronic schizophrenic patients receiving either no therapy or else fifty hours of group therapy characterized by one of two contrasting styles of leadership roles: active-participant or active-interpretive. In the active-participant role the leader functioned as a quasi-group member in his attempts to promote group interaction, support, and sharing of feelings. Investigation of personality dynamics was minimized. The aim of the active-interpretive role was to facilitate the understanding of underlying motivations through investigation and interpretation. Blind judgments of the therapy tapes by psychiatric residents revealed that the group leaders were indeed assuming the prescribed roles. Outcome as measured by a scale of hospital adjustment and a subscale measure of interpersonal functioning revealed no significant differences between the two group methods, although both therapy groups produced greater improvements than the control group. The fact that no measure of insight was used makes it impossible to assess whether gaining insights was related in any way to the results.

The differential effects of insight and interaction group psychotherapy techniques on hospitalized psychiatric patients (mainly diagnosed schizophrenics) were also examined in a study by Coons (1957). The group treatments consisted of three one-hour sessions per week, with a range of eight to eighty-seven sessions. Outcomes for the two types of therapy groups and a control group receiving the usual hospital treatment were compared by means of pre- and post-treatment measures of intelligence using the Wechsler Bellevue Adult Intelligence Scale, and by blind global judgments of adjustment based on the Rorschach Technique of Personality Diagnosis. The insight group techniques were geared toward cognitive understanding of personal difficulties. The focus was on problem origins, manifestations, and solutions. The therapeutic climate was described as "benignly authoritarian," and interaction was limited to that between patient and therapist. The interaction group techniques stressed interpersonal interactions between group members in a warm, accepting, and permissive atmosphere. There were no therapist attempts at facilitating insights or focusing on difficulties. An analysis of the therapy transcripts demonstrated that there had been more patient-to-patient interaction in the interaction groups. Outcomes on both the measures of adjustment and intelligence revealed that the interaction group improved significantly more than either the insight or control groups. Coons concludes that his study shows that interaction, rather than insight, appears to be the essential condition for therapeutic change. However, the study did not measure to ensure that insight change had occurred in any of the groups. In addition, it can be conjectured that the "therapeutic climates" (benign authoritarian versus warm, accepting, permissive), rather than the techniques, may have played a substantial role in the obtained outcome. Other studies with schizophrenic patients have also indicated that activity groups of various kinds are superior to insight-oriented groups in promoting behavioral adjustment to the hospital (Anker and Walsh 1961, DiGiovanni 1958). In fact, one study even raised the possibility of insight-oriented groups hindering the patients' adjustment to hospital routine (MacDonald et al. 1964).

A series of investigations, using either recruited college students or severely phobic chronic psychiatric patients, has pitted behavior therapy techniques against interpretive techniques. As with the studies of schizophrenic patients, the results broadly tend to show that the interpretive approach is not the treatment of choice for dealing with circumscribed symptomatology. Again, however, insight development is not measured, and in many cases the interpretive techniques are only vaguely specified, as compared to detailed and specific accounts of the behavioral techniques used.

Paul (1966) compared the effects of three types of treatment techniques on the reduction of speech anxiety in a group of selected college students enrolled in a public speaking course. It is important to note that the criteria for selection and the results of administered psychological tests are consistent in indicating that these students were essentially "normal" and not classifiable as neurotic. Students were randomly assigned to one of five experienced therapists and "treatments" were limited to five hours over a six-week period. Physiological, cognitive, and behavioral measures revealed the group of subjects treated with a systematic relaxation and desensitization procedure evidenced significantly greater anxiety reduction than subjects treated with either insight-oriented psychotherapy or an attention-placebo treatment administered by the same therapists. Anxiety reduction in the relaxation-desensitization subjects was also superior to the outcome for an untreated "wait-list" control group and an untreated "no-contact" control group. A follow-up study showed that the relative gains and superiority of the desensitization treatment were maintained over a two-year period (Paul 1967). In another investigation (Paul and Shannon 1966), some of the previously untreated control subjects were seen for a nine-session group application of systematic desensitization plus "intensive group discussion with re-educative goals." Results indicated that this treatment was also consistently superior to the previously administered insight and placebo treatments and equally as effective as individual desensitization for reducing anxiety. Aside from the subjects not really being patients and the dubious possibility of gaining profound insights within only a few hours, these studies have been criticized for offering only a vague definition of insight, no operational description of the insight techniques, and, of course, no measurement of insight development (Roback 1974; Meichenbaum et al. 1971). Again, the amorphous nature of treatments labeled "insight-oriented" is evident.

An investigation by Meichenbaum et al. (1971) attempted to be more precise in operationally defining and comparing the effects of a specific insight-group treatment and a specific group desensitization therapy on the reduction of speech anxiety. The subjects were university students recruited through a campus newspaper advertisement. The insight-group treatment in this study was patterned after Ellis' rational-emotive therapy, not Freud's psychoanalysis. It emphasized making subjects aware of both their anxiety-producing self-verbalizations and ways they might counter such verbalizations. The group desensitization and relaxation procedure was patterned after the descriptions by Paul and Shannon (1966). Subjects received one of five possible treatments: group desensitization, group "insight," combined group desensitization plus insight, group discussion, or a waiting list control. All groups were run by the same two therapists for eight weekly sessions of one hour each. Despite the authors' care in describing the different treatments and holding regular therapist discussions, no attempt was made at systematically measuring differences in the treatments or the development of insight.

Both the specified insight therapy and the desensitization therapy were significantly superior to the other conditions in reducing speech anxiety as measured by behavioral, cognitive, and self-report measures at treatment termination and at a three-month follow-up. Perhaps of greater interest, however, was the finding that different types of patients benefited from the desensitization and insight treatments. When speech anxiety was a problem only in public-speaking situations, desensitization produced superior results. In contrast, those subjects who manifested social anxiety across a variety of interpersonal situations were most benefited by the insight approach. Other studies have also suggested that desensitization works best with phobias limited to one area rather than with more pervasive anxiety states (Clark 1963, Gelder et al. 1967, Lang and Lazovik 1963, Lazarus 1963, Marks and Gelder 1965, Wolpe 1964).

Investigations of the treatment of severely incapacitating phobias have similarly compared interpretive techniques with behavioral approaches. The outcomes have uniformly not supported interpretive techniques as being the treatment of choice although, with very severe chronic cases, differences in treatment outcomes have tended to be less striking and at times nonexistent. On the whole, the superiority of the behavioral desensitization techniques has appeared most evident when the number of sessions has been limited (Lazarus 1961). Some studies have shown that with an increased number of sessions and a follow-up period, the differences in outcomes between the two approaches narrow and eventually disappear with chronic severe phobias (Gelder and Marks 1966, Gelder et al. 1967). As with the other reports reviewed in this section, these studies do not measure techniques or insight development.

Another relevant study reported by Lazarus (1966) concerned his treatment of patients with specific interpersonal problems (such as "lack of assertiveness") by means of one of three approaches: behavior rehearsal (a systematic role-playing technique in which patients practice desired behaviors), direct advice, and reflection-interpretation. The criterion of improvement was Lazarus' judgment that the patients were behaving "adaptively" in the area that had previously constituted the problem. Treatment lasted for only four thirty-minute sessions. Behavior rehearsal was judged significantly more effective in resolving specific interpersonal and social problems than either of the other approaches. The soundness and generalizability of this conclusion is limited by the fact that all therapy and evaluations were conducted by the same single therapist, raising the possibilities of experimenter bias and differential treatment skill. Further, the problems were extremely circumscribed, as was the treatment time. Finally, no detailed outlines of the various techniques (except for behavior rehearsal) are presented, and—pertinent to our current concerns—no measurement of insight or techniques occurred.

Sloane et al. (1975a,b) report a comparison of the outcomes

of short-term analytically oriented psychotherapy and behavior therapy in patients treated at a university outpatient clinic and diagnosed as either neurotic or personality disorder. The study is unusual not only in using "real" patients but also in using therapists experienced in the therapies being applied: experienced psychoanalysts and formerly trained behavior therapists. Definitions of the techniques permissible in each therapy were stipulated before treatment. A variety of questionnaire and rating scales verified that the insight-oriented therapists and the behaviorists were indeed using quite different techniques. Patients were randomly assigned to one of the two treatment groups or a waiting list control group. Assessments of the patients' initial status and progress were made by psychiatrist interviewers blind to the various study conditions.

Comparisons after four months of treatment (an average of only thirteen to fourteen sessions) revealed significant improvement in the target symptoms of all three groups. However, both treatment groups had improved equally and significantly more than patients on the waiting list. Behavior therapy patients were rated most improved on a global measure of improvement, while there were no differences among groups on scaled measures of work and social adjustment. One- and two-year follow-up measures were also taken, but meaningful comparisons are precluded by the fact that different amounts of further treatment were given in the three groups after the initial four-month study period. The authors conclude that there is no clear evidence for the superiority of either form of treatment to the other, although both are superior to no-treatment. Interestingly, no relationship was found between the "depth of intrapersonal exploration" and outcome. The relatively small number of treatment sessions and the fact that no formal measures of insight change are reported place limitations on the comparative generalizations that can be drawn from this study. Nonetheless, the general conclusion of parity in treatment results is quite similar to our previously discussed findings on the comparative effectiveness of "psychoanalysis" and other approaches.

A few comments appear in order. The studies reviewed thus far indicate that interpretive therapies do not produce significantly superior or even equivalent outcomes to behavioral approaches when the treatments and evaluation are limited to circumscribed difficulties. On the whole, behavioral approaches appear particularly strong and efficient when the problems are neither longstanding nor severely incapacitating. One should note, however, the straw-man quality and vagueness of many of the treatments given the interpretive label. This is not to demean the positive results obtained with behavioral approaches, but only to point out the looseness with which the term "insight" is usually bandied about. In fact, due to lack of measurement, there is nothing to indicate that the results of any of the studies reviewed above have anything to do with the attainment of insight. Additionally, there are no studies in the literature that even support the idea that interpretations by a therapist facilitate greater insight than other techniques. It is quite possible, for example, that greater insight might be produced by behavior change techniques than by interpretations. Some writers have even suggested that behavioral treatments often lead to patients becoming aware of etiological factors concerning their symptoms (for example, Cautela 1965, Hobbs 1962). Overall, the indefinite nature of interpretive therapies has allowed investigators to define any meeting in which there is speech between individuals designated "patients" and others designated "therapists" as insight-oriented. From our point of view such a definition is misleading and unjustifiable.

Therapy Studies Relating Measured Insight Changes to Adjustment

Our criticisms naturally lead to the following question: what are the results of therapy studies that do attempt, before measuring therapeutic changes, to independently assess that insight has occurred? We found only a handful of assorted reports bearing on this issue, and the definition of insight in almost all of them had little or nothing to do with Freud's notion of understanding the relationship between past and present. Again, the investigations centered mainly on hospitalized psychotic patients and recruited college students treated in groups. The fact that treatment duration in these studies typically lasted no more than three to six weeks implies that the investigators' anticipations were that insight attainment would require relatively little effort or time and that "working through" was not necessary for translating increased self-awareness into significant behavior change. From a psychoanalytic perspective such expectations, combined with the "patient" populations utilized, make it surprising that any positive results were found at all. The heterogeneity in the definition of insight can be noted in our brief descriptions of the studies.

Rashkis (1965) reports an investigation of the relationship

between the development of insight and prognosis in hospitalized psychotic patients. Insight development appears to be defined in terms of increasing patient awareness, as opposed to denial, of problems. Insight was measured by the increasing proportion of "insightful" as opposed to "denial" statements in response to questions over a period of months. No more explicit methodology for measurement of insight is reported and no treatment is described. The study found that hospitalized patients scoring higher on tests of perceptual organization, regardless of how disturbed they were at the beginning of treatment, moved toward answering questions about their hospitalization with either denial statements or insightful statements. Those initially scoring low on perceptual organization tended to remain non-insightful, showing an increase in unrelated and low-order explanatory type statements. Prognosis was measured in terms of the patients' hospitalization status two to four years after leaving the hospital. Data analysis revealed that all of the high perceptual organizers showing an increase in denial had been re-hospitalized at the same or another hospital at follow-up. All patients showing an increase in insight remained out of the hospital. No clear pattern emerged for the low-perceptual organizers, although as a group they tended to be re-hospitalized more often than the high-perceptual organizers. This study therefore provided evidence that psychotic patients with high perceptual organization tend to develop "insightful" responses more often than low-perceptual organizers, and that the development of insight for this group tends to bode well for prognosis. The types of treatment, patients, therapists, and measures utilized are left vague.

Roback (1972) in a methodologically careful study, investigated the comparative therapeutic effects of (1) group therapy stressing interpretations designed to foster insight and (2) a form of group therapy emphasizing member-to-member interactions without intentional insight facilitation. The patients were almost all diagnosed as schizophrenic and had been hospitalized continuously for an average of about eight years in their most current hospitalization. Insight was defined as the patient's "understanding and/or awareness of the relationship between current behavior (including feelings and attitudes) and past socio-psychological experiences" (p. 412). Patients were randomly assigned to one of four types of groups and seen three times per week for sixteen to thirty one-hour sessions. The groups were: insight group (interpretations and stress on member-to-therapist interactions), insight and interaction group (interpretations and stress on member-to-member interactions), interaction group (no interpretations, and reinforcement of member-to-member statements unrelated to personal problems), and control "audiovisual therapy" group (viewing films). Patient behaviors considered appropriate for the particular treatment conditions were "positively reinforced" by therapist verbal and nonverbal responses (such as approval statements, eye contact, head nodding); those patient behaviors considered inappropriate were "negatively reinforced (by responses such as therapist fidgeting and finger tapping). The fact that the treatment conditions differed in the designed ways was verified by blind judgments of transcripts for the techniques employed. In addition, the degree of insight produced was assessed both by blind ratings from transcripts and by patient scores on an insight rating scale measuring the ability to understand the underlying motivation of others.

Outcome—as measured by pre- to post-therapy changes on a wide array of behavioral, psychometric, and self-ratings—revealed no significant differences among groups on any one of the twenty-one measures of "personal functioning." However, the group combining insight with member-to-member interaction led to significantly more consistent indications of improvement over all the measures than any of the other groups. It might be conjectured that this finding is somewhat supportive of Freud's position, since the combined insight plus interaction group comes closest to exemplifying Freud's ideas concerning the necessity for working through attained insights. Yet, as Roback acknowledges, one must wonder whether therapeutic movement was hindered in the insight group or the interaction group by a therapist negatively reinforcing certain kinds of patient behavior, such as by frowning or fidgeting. One must also wonder how much therapeutic change could reasonably be expected from chronic psychotic patients seen for such a brief period of time. Roback himself reports data indicating that patients at the studied hospital that were not discharged or boarded out within three months of admission had a very small probability of leaving the hospital. As mentioned, this study's patients had been hospitalized continuously for approximately eight years.

A few investigations using recruited college students as patients have also attempted to independently assess insight development and relate it to measures of adjustment or therapeutic change. Mann and Mann (1959) compared the relative effectiveness of group discussion, task-oriented study group activity, and group-centered role playing in promoting insight. "Patients" for the twelve groups (three discussion, three study, and six role-playing) were ninety-six university students randomly selected from a graduate course. No description of the therapist(s) is provided, and no measures or descriptions of the therapy techniques are reported. Insight is defined as "the degree of congruence between an individual's view of himself and the view others have of him" (p. 91). Measures of insight were obtained at the beginning and near the end of each of the group experiences, which extended over a three-week period. The number of treatment hours or frequency of sessions is not presented. Results revealed that all groups significantly increased in measured insight, with no differences between groups in amount of insight gained. The authors go on to report no relationship between amount of insight and individual adjustment. However, no measure of adjustment is reported. In general, this sketchy, brief report of students, without any particular presenting problems, being seen for a few sessions by a nondescript therapist using nondefined techniques appears to offer little generalizable information concerning the relationship between insight and adjustment.

Abramowitz and Jackson (1974) compared the relative effectiveness of four group psychotherapy techniques differing in interpretive style: interpretive there-and-then, interpretive here-and-now, these treatments in combination, and problem discussion without interpretations (attention-placebo). The interpretive there-and-then group focused on the understanding of the causes of current feelings, attitudes, and behaviors with stress on the significance of childhood events. The interpretive here-and-now group focused on promoting self-awareness through an exploration of in-group feelings, behaviors, and attitudes without explicitly using group interactions as clues to understanding extratherapy behavior. The patients were college students recruited through announcements of the formation of groups "aimed at improving personal adjustment and interpersonal relation skills." All therapy groups met with the same "insight-oriented" therapist for ten ninety-minute sessions over a five-week period. The fact that the therapist's techniques differed in the prescribed ways was substantiated by blind judgments of tape-recorded therapy transcripts. Psychologist raters also blindly rated the there-and-then and combined groups as being characterized by an atmosphere significantly more "congenial" to the development of insight. Yet, while the trend was in the correct direction, members of the there-and-then and combined groups did not show significantly greater changes over therapy on an insight test measuring the ability to understand the underlying motivation of *others.*

Outcome was measured by eleven tests of psychosocial adjustment filled out by the patients immediately before and after therapy. No direct measures of behavior change or ratings by observers were used. Over all the groups, there was a significant reduction in self-reported seriousness of the core problem and a trend toward dissipation of generalized guilt feelings. There were no differences in favor of the insight-production groups on any one of the measures. The authors concluded that interpretations, regardless of temporal focus, were not necessary for movement on any of their outcome measures. Another analysis of the data, based on global benefit derived over all the measures, found that the combined treatment group produced consistently more positive outcomes than did the other groups. This is directly parallel to Roback's (1972) finding that the most consistent indications of improvement occurred in groups combining interpretations with interaction. Abramowitz and Jackson speculate that groups using combined approaches may produce greater success by facilitating greater freedom of expression, while providing more outlets for tension release and a greater number of ways in which problems can be "worked through." The results of this study are of course limited by the small number of sessions, the use of one therapist, the type of therapy (group), the questionable "patient" population, the definition of insight used, the failure to find significant differences on measured insight, and the confining of outcome measures to self-reports.

In looking back over the literature we have reviewed, we must conclude that Freud's ideas concerning the relationship between insight and change have not been adequately tested. The "insight therapy" described by most researchers appears to be a vague caricature of the approach outlined by Freud. Little attention is usually paid to the measurement of insight, the specification of techniques, the training of therapists, and the suitability of patients for the treatment. We feel that experimenters have not placed enough emphasis on the "working through" concept and have mistakenly read Freud's theory to mean that insights are directly and easily translated into change. Even granting the lack of detail in Freud's descriptions of technique, the majority of the studies appear naively out of touch with the nuances of the therapeutic process. It does not seem surprising that a few hours worth of interpretations cast at chronic psychotic patients or recruited college students produces little evidence of change. Perhaps the strongest impression drawn from a reading of the insight experimental literature relates to the diversity of ways in which the term is employed and the total lack of independent objective measurement of the insight concept in Freudian terms. Even defining insight as the ability to judge others is not the same as a definition emphasizing the understanding of one's own motivations. In fact, reviews of the experimental work dealing with person perception suggest that there is no clear relationship between accuracy in judging others and self-insight (Taft 1955, Shrauger and Altrocchi 1964). At the least, more direct tests of Freud's ideas would seem to require comparative studies using different operationalized levels of working through with chronic *neurotic* patients and experienced therapists in *individual* therapy. They would also require an independent measure of insight defined in terms of the patient's ability to conceptualize the relationship between his past and his present.

The Mythical Independence of Insight and Analyst Influence

Freud's early statements argue for the uniqueness and superiority of psychoanalysis as a therapy, due to its reliance on patient insight rather than therapist suggestion. He made it sound as though therapist influence played no part in promoting feelings of insight. The analyst was instructed not to directly suggest behavioral changes and not to use his personality to directly influence his patients' verbal productions or behavior. Descriptions of the analytic situation created the illusion of unsullied insights growing from a patient "freely" associating to a "blank screen" therapist. Yet as Freud moved his therapy from a focus on the recovery of repressed memories to the overcoming of patient *resistances* to certain ideas, it became increasingly difficult for him not to admit that persuasion and manipulation were taking place in his treatment. Freud's emphasis on the formation of a strong patient attachment to the analyst (transference) and the necessity for "working through" patient resistances fosters a view of the analyst as a convincer and a persuader. Despite the analyst's stated objective of non-interference with the patient's productions, a positive dependent relationship is purposefully established and explicitly used to prepare the patient to accept unacceptable ideas and agree with thoughts that would initially be denied. Freud's retreat from attributing change only to the nonsuggested recovery of childhood memories eventually led him to admit the possible role of suggestion and persuasion in his therapy. For example, in setting down his thoughts on interpreting the patient's relationship to the analyst (transference) he stated:

> . . . we readily admit that the results of psychoanalysis rest upon suggestion; by suggestion, however, we must understand, . . . the influencing of a person by means of the transference phenomena which are possible in his case. We take care of the patient's final independence by employing suggestion in order to get him to accomplish a piece of psychical work which has as its necessary result a permanent improvement in his physical functioning. (Freud, 1912b, p. 106)

Part of Freud's hesitation in admitting the possibility of suggestion was probably the result of a desire to have his method of treatment also accepted as an objective scientific way of learning "truths" about personality development. While therapist suggestion may lead to patient changes, therapist suggestion does not lead to data acceptable for validating hypotheses about personality. Freud never really came to terms with the differences involved in trying to learn about people as opposed to trying to change them. Psychoanalysis perpetuated the myth that patient insights and therapist influence had to be distinct and independent categories. Freud, in his attempt to create an illusion of a unique treatment, glossed over the possibility that analyst influence played a significant role in giving the patient the feeling that he was achieving self-understanding. A considerable amount of research supports the idea that, even in psychoanalysis, a patient's verbal productions and feelings of attained insight are not independent of therapist influence.

Shapiro (1971), in a review paper, skillfully documents the parallels between the analytic situation and research demonstrating the factors associated with increasing suggestibility and the placebo effect. Such parallels include situational ambiguity, sensory isolation, stimulus hunger, primitive fantasy, regression, marked anxiety, dependency, guilt, and depression. In addition, the placebo research literature suggests that psychoanalysis creates a placebogenic situation through its use of prestigious practitioners whose therapy requires considerable intellectual, emotional, and financial investment. Shapiro further comments that the method parallels conditions for obtaining the placebo effect: being detailed, elaborate, time-consuming, esoteric, fashionable, and sometimes dangerous. Other reviews of myriad empirical studies have strongly indicated that all therapists, including analysts, reinforce certain types of patient communications through verbal and nonverbal reactions, increasing the likelihood of their recurrence (for example, Frank 1961, Krasner 1962, 1971, Marmor 1964). Whether he is aware of it or not, the analyst, in selectively responding to patient statements, controls, shapes, and manipulates the direction of future patient behavior. In fact, Heller

(1971) points out that therapy systems emphasizing ambiguity and limited therapist responsiveness (such as analysis) create situations that are the most susceptible to the subtle interpersonal influence described in the studies of verbal conditioning.

From the standpoint of communications theory psychoanalysis must be considered an influence process, since all actions of the therapist influence the interaction with the patient. As Haley writes: "A basic rule of communication theory demonstrates the point that it is impossible for a person to avoid defining, or taking control of the definition of his relationship with another. According to this rule, all messages are not only reports but they also influence or command . . . Even if one tries not to influence another person by remaining silent, his silences become an influencing factor in the interchange" (Haley 1963, pp. 9–10).

At times Freud seems to dismiss the possibility of therapist influence by implying that insights in analytic therapy are based on "correct" rather than inaccurate interpretations. Presumably, insights based on correct hypotheses about the causal relationships between a patient's past and present are not to be considered "suggestion." It is implied that patient responses based on therapist suggestion can be differentiated from patient responses based on accurate interpretations ("insight"). But in fact it does not seem probable that such a differentiation can be made. Research evidence has consistently indicated that a patient's belief in interpretations and his consequent anxiety reduction do not depend on the accuracy of the interpretations. Investigators have found that individuals will enthusiastically accept bogus interpretations as accurate descriptions of their own personalities (Forer 1949, Dmitruk et al. 1973, O'Dell 1972, Mendell 1964, Stagner 1958, Sundberg 1955, Ulrich et al. 1963). Meehl (1956) labeled this phenomenon the "Barnum effect." Indeed, in some of the studies, vague general personality descriptions presented to subjects are accepted as being at least as accurate or even more accurate than results obtained from administered personality tests (O'Dell 1972, Sundberg 1955). While it has been reported that the prestige of the interpreter may influence the degree of acceptance of a bogus interpretation (Forer 1949), a handful of studies have found acceptance of the interpretations to be unrelated to the prestige of the person making the interpretations (Dmitruk et al. 1973, Ulrich et al. 1963). In addition, it has been found that subjects have been as likely to accept negative bogus personality evaluations as they are positive interpretations (Dmitruk et al. 1973). Gordon (1957), in detailing attempts to de-repress hypnotically induced conflicts, similarly concluded that accurate interpretations might not be necessary for anxiety reduction, since he had observed subjects experiencing a real sense of relief when they hit upon a plausible though incorrect explanation for their feelings.

Of special interest is a report by Mendell (1964), who argues that inaccurate interpretations can lead to positive changes in behavior. Mendell supports this position by citing two clinical examples of purposefully inexact interpretations influencing behavior. An inexact interpretation is defined as "one which does not follow from the dream, thought, fantasy, or behavior presented by the patient from the associations to such material" (p. 186). Mendell's first example concerns a case in which the therapist made an "inexact interpretation" of a disturbing dream. He writes:

> In response to this intervention, the patient moved from the pre-interpreted to the post-interpreted state. He suddenly appeared much relieved and stated that he was now no longer frightened by the dream since he understood it. He thought the material was quite clear. He gave some confirmatory evidence of lessening the anxiety by becoming relaxed, breathing more slowly, talking of the trip which was to begin the next day. (p. 187)

Mendell also describes a situation in which four patients in intensive psychotherapy were each presented with six inexact interpretations over a six-month period (approximately one a month).[2] Mendell reports that the patients responded to the random interpretations with significant anxiety reduction in twenty of the twenty-four interpretation presentations. Interpretations were rejected only twice and greeted with skepticism on only two occasions. While the clinical nature of Mendell's examples and methodology rules out the report as an empirical test of an hypothesis, the inferences drawn are nevertheless quite consistent with the results of more carefully controlled studies of interpretation accuracy.

In time even Freud acknowledged that patient responses could not be used as evidence for the correctness of interpretations. He wrote: "It appears, therefore, that the direct utterances of the patient after he has been offered a construction afford very little evidence upon the question whether we have been right or wrong" (Freud, 1937b, p. 263). He went on to indicate, though, that the course of an analysis in terms of future associations and other developments could aid in differentiating "insight" from therapist suggestion. Such a conclusion is not supported by the cited research literature. We would also like to underline the misleading and artificial distinction made between suggestion and insight. It is quite possible that analyst persuasion might be required to get a patient to believe an interpretation *even* if it is accurate.

The conclusion that a significant portion of the potential psychoanalytic therapeutic effect rests on persuasion and influence can be arrived at from a reading of Freud's own writings as well as a reading of the research literature in a number of areas (such as the work already mentioned on placebos, inexact interpretations, and verbal conditioning). For example, there is a considerable amount of evidence indicating that Freud influenced the productions of his patients in directions *he* chose and used strong suggestions in trying to convince patients of the correctness of his interpretations. In his early work on hysteria, Freud described how very difficult it was to extract the memories of seductions from his patients, how they protested and denied, and how they insisted that they had no feeling of remembering the traumatic scenes (Freud, 1896). In a later paper Freud stated:

> Having diagnosed a case of neurasthenic neurosis with certainty and having classified its symptoms correctly, we are in a position to translate the symptomatology into aetiology; and we may then boldly demand confirmation of our suspicions from the patient. We must not be led astray by initial denials. If we keep firmly to what we have inferred, we shall in the end conquer every resistance by emphasizing the unshakable nature of our convictions. (Freud, 1898, p. 269)

For four years Freud held to the hypothesis that neurosis in adulthood resulted from the child being seduced by a significant adult. Only reluctantly did he reformulate this hypothesis into the contention that adult neuroses result from a child having *fantasies* of seduction by an adult. We do not know how many patients in that interim period were convinced, on the strength of Freud's convictions, that they had been seduced. Other examples of Freud tenaciously clinging to his hypotheses regardless of the patient's response occur in Freud's description of the case of Dora and are well reviewed in a paper by Flowerman (1954). It is noted that when Dora answered "No" to an interpretation, Freud said:

> My expectations were by no means disappointed when this explanation of mine was met by Dora with a most emphatic negative. The 'no' uttered by a patient after a repressed thought has been presented to his conscious perception for the first time does no more than register the existence of a repression and its severity; it acts, as it were, as a gauge of the repression's strength. If this 'No,' instead of being regarded as the expression of an impartial judgment (of which, indeed, the patient is incapable), is ignored, and if work is continued the first evidence soon begins to appear that in such a case 'No' signifies the desired 'Yes.' (Freud 1905a, pp. 58–59)."

Flowerman goes on to document Freud's equating Dora's statements of "I don't know" with a confession of something repressed. In addition, Freud stated that patient exclamations such as "I didn't think that" or "I didn't think of that" could be translated "point blank" into: "Yes, I was unconscious of that." Freud also reported that Dora's statement of "I knew you would say that" is a very common way of laying aside knowledge that emerges from the unconscious (Flowerman 1954, pp. 427–428). In short, Freud indicated that any patient response to an interpretation (denial, agreement, or hesitation) could be taken as evidence of its validity. Stating that any patient response can be taken as evidence for the validity of an inference is equivalent to saying that patient responses may play little role in determining the direction of the analyst's interpretations. Wolpe and Rachman (1960), in a critique of Freud's formulation of the case of Little Hans, offer a host of similar examples of Freud validating his preconceptions on the basis of minimal and questionable data. Freud's advocacy of influencing patients is also implicitly acknowledged by his remark that Hans had to "be told many things he could not say himself, that he had to be presented with thoughts which he had so far shown no signs of possessing, and that his attention had to be turned in the direction that his father was expecting something to come" (Freud 1909a, p. 104).

The analyst's role as a persuader is also amplified by Freud's growing doubts about the possibility of patients ever recovering infantile memories. In one of his last papers he states: "Quite often we do not succeed in bringing the patient to recollect what has been repressed. Instead of that, if the analysis is carried out correctly, we produce in him an assured conviction of the truth of the construction which achieves the same therapeutic result as a recaptured memory" (Freud 1937b, pp. 265–266). The retreat from confidence in the analyst's ability to establish "what really happened" in childhood to a method emphasizing "this is what must have happened to you" is an open acknowledgement of suggestion occurring in the treatment. It also, of course, raises some serious questions about how a theory of infantile sexuality could be validated solely on the basis of information obtained from psychoanalytic therapy (Chodoff 1966).

Let us briefly review the points made in this section. It is our contention, based on the literature, that the analytic situation has a significant suggestive component. A patient's feeling of having gained insight cannot be separated from the analyst's manipulations within the session. Attempts to define psychoanalysis as a treatment uniquely independent of the therapist's influence do not appear justified. We also feel that this fact—that influence may occur—should not detract from psychoanalysis as a therapy. The concept of "therapy" presupposes that attempts will be made to help the patient change. If, however, one wishes to simultaneously hold out psychoanalysis as a method for validating scientific hypotheses, then the issue of suggestion becomes a tremendous obstacle. We do not wish to imply, by this, that psychoanalytic therapy sessions cannot generate useful hypotheses and information. We do mean that other, more objective methods are necessary to establish the validity of the hypotheses generated. Many writers on therapy have suggested that a part of what is therapeutic in psychoanalysis, behavior therapy, and other approaches may lie in making sense out of what seems senseless and providing the patient with a framework from which he feels that he can control what is happening to him (Greenberg 1973, Goldfried 1971, Hobbs 1962, Mendell 1964, Ezriel 1956). From this perspective, a patient's belief that he has insight might be of help in promoting change. We do not yet know whether the belief needs to be based on accurate interpretations.

Symptom Substitution: Are Insights Necessary?

Freud created the impression that interpretations leading to insights were *necessary* if one wished to achieve lasting symptom remission and behavior change. Other potentially more direct ways of dealing with symptoms were downgraded. Controversy has developed around the question of whether meaningful changes can be produced without patient insight. A good deal of the debate surrounding this issue has focused on the concept of symptom substitution. This concept is derived from the hydraulic-energy model of symptom formation proposed by psychoanalytic theory. According to this model, symptoms are the substitute expression of repressed impulses and underlying conflicts. Therefore, just removing a symptom without treating the underlying cause would theoretically result in either a reappearance of the original symptom or the formation of a new one. This possibility is certainly implied in Freud's writings (for example, Freud 1905b,c, 1910a, 1919b). Yet there are also a number of places where Freud indicates that symptoms may at times be ameliorated without antecedent insight and without the necessity of other subsequent significant problems arising.

Freud (1905b) pointed out that with "slighter episodic cases," where presumably the conflicts were less intense, recovery could be attained from many kinds of influences or even "spontaneously." Additionally, Freud (1915b) reported that it was not unusual for a patient to lose his symptoms (or pay no attention to them) as a result of developing very positive feelings for the analyst (transference cure). Of course, from a psychoanalytic position, a patient's giving up symptoms as he transfers feelings and conflicts into the relationship with the analyst can be interpreted as a form of substitute symptom in and of itself: transference neurosis (Freud, 1914c).

Another potential argument against the necessity for symptom substitution is raised by Weitzman (1967) and relates to Freud's conception that anxiety symptoms may serve as a signal that a dangerous instinctual demand is increasing in strength. The symptom of anxiety is, in this conception, substituted for the behavior demanded by the underlying instinctual arousal. The symptom prevents the behavioral expression of an impulse that might have been punished by parents in the past. Yet the symptom may presently be unnecessary in that the danger, which may actually have existed at the time of symptom formation, may no longer pose a real threat. The lack of danger would not be apparent to the individual however, because every time arousal occurs, the signal of anxiety fosters withdrawal and prevents him from discovering that the danger does not actually exist. Therefore, as Weitzman notes, having a patient face his fear while inhibiting flight may lead to the patient confronting the irrational nature of his conflict. In a sense, a behavioral treatment in this instance treats not only the symptom but the total "psychological matrix." This type of mechanism appears to be exemplified by Freud's (1920a) hypothesis that individuals suffering from post-traumatic reactions may at times master anxiety-arousing stimuli through repetitious dreams of catastrophic incidents.

The idea that symptom treatment can affect "underlying" causes is also consistent with reports of increased insights following behavior change (for example, Cautela 1965, Hobbs 1962). Kamil (1970) supports the position of symptom treatment affecting the total psychological picture with the finding that snake phobics decreased significantly on a projective test measure of castration anxiety after undergoing a systematic relaxation and desensitization procedure. Finally we might mention Rapaport's (1959) observation that even within Freud's theoretical postdictive system, there is no way of predicting the precise effects of energy redistribution between the various psychic systems when a symptom is removed. Various complex interactions could arise. Weitzman (1967) concludes that "from this vantage point it would appear that predictions of symptom substitution follow from a clinical rubric, and not with strict necessity from the analytic theory of the neuroses" (p. 308).

Thus it seems that, even for Freud, the removal of symptoms without insight attainment would not *necessarily* lead to a new incapacitating dysfunction. However, his writings certainly suggested that such a phenomenon could exist and would be a probable occurrence, particularly in chronic cases with severe underlying conflicts. Part of the problem in testing the symptom-substitution hypothesis lies in the fact that there is no overall agreement, especially between theoretical schools, as to what constitutes a "symptom" or an "underlying cause" (Bandura 1969, Cahoon 1968). The empirical designation of "substitutes" is determined by the broadness of the investigator's definition of symptom and the scope of his observations. Even with these definitional problems, papers and reviews of the research bearing on this issue are quite clear and consistent in concluding that new symptoms—generally defined as behaviors judged socially or personally maladaptive (Cahoon 1968)—do not necessarily arise when old ones are removed without attempts to promote insight. Since a wide variety of studies in addition to the major arguments are well reviewed in other papers, we will not repeat that detailed effort here (Bookbinder 1962, Cahoon 1968, Lazarus 1965, Mikulas 1972, Montgomery and Crowder 1972, Nurnberger and Hingtgen 1973, Weitzman 1967, Yates 1958). The evidence is consistent and solid that in many types of cases symptoms can be removed by behavioral treatments with no indication that the patient suffers any negative consequences. Specifically, studies have indicated little or no evidence of symptom substitution following behavioral treatments of tics, eneuresis[3] and various types of phobias and anxiety states. In fact, many of the investigations find signs of generalized improvement in functioning after the removal of an incapacitating symptom (for example, see the following reviews: Montgomery and Crowder 1972, Nurnberger and Hingtgen 1973).

On the other hand, behaviorists have conceded that symptom removal can at times lead to the development of new behaviors labeled symptoms or to a recurrence of the original symptom (Bandura 1969, Cahoon 1968, Lazarus 1965).[4] Yet the substitutes do not appear with the frequency Freud seemed to suggest, and behavior therapists typically state that they treat the new symptoms as maladaptive behaviors to be changed, just as they treated the old symptoms. On the basis of the evidence, advocates of symptom treatment do grant that in many cases the narrow application of techniques to change a specific behavior, without a broader conceptualization of the patient's problems, hinders the possibility of lasting change. For example, while emphasizing differences from psychoanalysis in his theoretical conceptions, Lazarus (1965) states: ". . . few experienced behavior therapists would disagree with the notion that treatment which leaves the neurotic roots untouched is likely to be short lived and unreliable" (p. 80).

A similar viewpoint is put forth by Nurnberger and Hingtgen (1973) after reviewing the experimental literature: "Treatment which is of insufficient duration, or which does not address itself to the disturbing emotional concomitants of the instrumental actions manipulated, or which is insufficiently sensitive to the necessity to prepare the patient for function in a genuine living milieu, rather than in the isolated laboratory condition, may indeed be unsuccessful, be associated with a high relapse rate, or even less likely, lead to emergence of new symptoms" (p. 233).

These statements are consistent with the fact that the symptom substitution hypothesis has received its greatest empirical support from studies of the surgical treatment of ulcers and investigations of the sudden removal of symptoms by persuasion or hypnotic techniques (for example, Badal et al. 1957, Browning and Houseworth 1953, Montgomery and Crowder 1972, Nurnberger and Hingtgen 1973, Seitz 1953, Spiegel 1967, Szasz 1949). The overriding message of these studies appears to be that quick removal of seriously incapacitating symptoms, without regard to the meaning or function of the symptom for the patient, increases the probability of a substitute symptom arising. This line of reasoning led Holland (1967) to conclude: "The way the symptom is removed is crucial. If the symptom is removed gently, if the patient is not coerced to give up the symptom, if the symptom can recur if the patient needs it, symptom removal may not be dangerous at all" (p. 1,283).

Another factor that appears to affect whether or not new symptoms will arise relates to the expectations of both patient and therapist. Spiegel (1967), in a vivid description of four cases, supports the contention that a patient's symptomatology can be significantly altered by feedback reflecting different physician expectancies. In a more experimental context, Gale (1971) has shown that the initial expectations of patients or the suggestions made by therapists can affect the probability of symptom substitution. This study focused on the reduction of the rate of smoking by behavioral techniques. Those subjects who initially expected new symptoms with reduction in smoking were more likely to get them than subjects who expected improved health. In addition, subjects were more likely to experience prolonged or enhanced substitute symptoms when they were led to expect symptom substitution by therapist suggestion.

In sum, the literature supports the observation that symptom substitution can occur but that it is a relatively rare event. Its occurrence appears determined by a number of factors, including the type and extent of symptomatology, the treatment conditions, and the patient-therapist expectations. While symptomatic treatments do at times result in low rates of symptom substitution (Crisp 1966), evidence also indicates that analytic therapy may be followed by new symptoms (Cremerius 1962). As yet there is no empirical basis for asserting that one approach to therapy is more preventative of future symptoms than another. In fact, Freud (1937a) himself concluded that there is no way of predicting what will happen to a patient after he has been analyzed. Although differing in many ways, both analysts and behaviorists seem to be in general agreement that if remission is to last, behavior change should not be brought about by the quick, insensitive application of treatment techniques that totally ignore the meaning and purposes served by the symptom in the patient's life. If this is so, the therapist's understanding of the symptom and the patient may be one of the crucial factors involved in producing lasting change.

Making blanket statements that would apply to all patients and all situations is plainly foolish. Are therapist interpretations the only means of securing lasting beneficial changes? Obviously not, since there is a wealth of evidence that many kinds of experiences and therapeutic techniques have led to meaningful and enduring changes. Is it necessary that a patient understand the relationship between his past and present in order to decrease his anxieties and change his behavior? Again, there are strong indications that there are many roads to change that may be differentially effective and efficient, depending upon the problem, the patient, and the therapist. Apparently, for many patients, self-understanding may follow making changes, while for others initial preparation and self-exploration may facilitate taking the risk of trying new solutions to old problems.

Insight as a Predictor of Outcome

Within the empirical literature, insight has also been viewed in terms of its prognostic value for therapeutic gain. Investigators have asked whether individuals with psychological sensitivity and openness to seeing intrapsychic causative factors are the most likely beneficiaries of treatment. With regard to psychotic patients, insight has often been specifically defined as an awareness by the individual that his emotional or intellectual functioning is impaired. These definitions of insight may be broadly linked to Freud's implication that those individuals most open to looking at themselves ("educable") would be the most suitable patients (Freud 1905b). Greater initial self-awareness would thus be predicted to lead more easily to better psychological adjustment.

The awareness of impairment definition has been used in investigations of the relationship between insight and prognosis in hospitalized patients. Eskey (1958) sorted psychotic hospitalized psychiatric patients into three groups depending upon the degree to which they verbalized recognition of their psychological difficulties (insight). Prognosis was evaluated by length of hospitalization in the three groups. There were no significant differences between the groups in time of hospitalization, and Eskey therefore concluded that prognosis was not related to intellectual recognition of existing problems. This study has been criticized by Roback (1974) for not reporting a standardized objective technique for assessing the degree of insight. In addition, it is obvious that other factors besides significant improvement may play an important role in determining the length of hospitalization (for example, whether relatives want the patient at home). Also, patients hospitalized for the same length of time might show different degrees of improvement. We might add that Karon and VandenBos (1972) have reported the finding that longer rather than shorter hospital treatment, consisting of psychoanalytic therapy with psychotic patients, was associated with greater improvement in thought disorder and a greater long-run ability to function outside of a hospital. Further adding to the confusion about the Eskey study is the fact that the treatment for almost all of the patients was shock or insulin therapy. There is little reason to expect that insight would mediate improvement with this kind of treatment. In fact, Kahn and Fink (1958, 1959) have shown better prognosis for shock therapy in patients premorbidly manifesting greater verbal denial. They also found verbal denial emerging as a result of electroconvulsive therapy. Roback notes it would probably have been of greater value if Eskey's patients had been placed in psychotherapy and improvement had been compared as a function of whether or not the patients had verbalized an awareness of impairment before therapy.

Linn (1965) did a study similar to Eskey's in design and outcome, investigating the relationship between insight and prognosis in psychotic patients hospitalized for the first time. Again, little relationship was found between insight (measured by the nature of the patient's initial statement that there was something wrong and willingness to seek voluntary hospitalization) and the course of the patient's symptoms and release from the hospital. Patients who willingly sought hospitalization following a doctor's advice did evidence a more positive prognosis. However, this might be explained by release from the hospital being determined by greater openness and acceptance of medical authority rather than objective change in psychological status. Linn did not describe any specific treatments given to the patients, and many of the general criticisms we have outlined for the Eskey study could be easily leveled at this investigation.

In contrast to the reports of no positive relationship between prognosis and initial insight in psychotic patients treated with shock or given no explicit treatment, a few studies have indicated that awareness of difficulties in psychotic patients is predictive of response to drug treatment or psychotherapy. Childers (1962) found that newly hospitalized, female, chronic undifferentiated schizophrenic patients improved more with phenothiazine treatment if they "accepted" the fact that they were ill than if they did not. There was no significant difference in response to medication by "accepters" and "deniers" who were diagnosed paranoid schizophrenic. The study offered no definition of "improvement" and no explicit methodology for differentiating accepters and deniers.

Hankoff et al. (1960) did a prognosis study of chronic male and female schizophrenic clinic outpatients who were initially rated on scales for acceptance or denial of mental illness. Prognosis was measured in terms of whether the patient prematurely dropped out of therapy or needed hospitalization within six months of the intake interview. Patients were treated in a double-blind fashion with either placebos or phenothiazines. Findings indicated that deniers treated with placebos had a higher hospitalization rate than accepters similarly treated (42 percent versus 19 percent). Outpatient treatment with drugs significantly reduced the hospitalization rate of deniers to the rate for accepters. The accepters did equally well with placebos or medication. The major effect shown was that treating denying patients with drugs rather than placebos significantly decreased the probability of either premature therapy termination or hospitalization. Outcome ratings by the treating psychiatrists after three months of treatment revealed that accepters did significantly better on measures of global improvement, change in anxiety level, and reduction in severity of thought disorder. There were no differences between the groups in a social behavior rating based on information obtained from relatives. Showing initial "insight" thus seemed to predict a rather positive prognosis independent of the treatment. On the other hand, denying patients appeared specifically benefited by drug treatment. Unfortunately, this study did not include a nontreated control group to verify the fact that treatment of any kind produced better results than nothing in the insightful patients. Direct comparisons with the Childers report are not possible because of the differences in the scope of diagnostic labels between studies and the differences in patient hospitalization status (inpatient versus outpatient). Further, the Childers study made use of only female patients, and a study by Greenberg et al. (1973) has suggested that the masculinity-femininity dimension may be related to the response to medication exhibited by psychiatric inpatients. In any event, both the Childers and Hankoff et al. reports sketch a relationship between initial awareness of difficulties and the outcome of therapy and drug treatments with schizophrenic inpatients and outpatients.

Parallel results have been reported by Rayner and Hahn (1964) who found that psychological test measures of a tendency to be reflective and self-analytic were predictive of success attained in psychoanalytically-oriented therapy by a sample of primarily nonpsychotic inpatients. Results with Rogerian client-centered psychotherapy, a treatment aimed at increasing self-awareness, have also been experimentally linked with variables analogous to patients' pre-therapy level of psychological-mindedness (Fiske et al. 1964, Kirtner and Cartwright 1958). Similarly, Luborsky et al. (1971), in their review of factors influencing the outcome of psychotherapy, report three out of five studies finding a significant association between psychotherapy outcome and initial self-awareness, insight, or sensitivity (Conrad 1952, Rosenberg 1954, Zolik and Hollon 1960, no relationship found in Raskin 1949, Rosenbaum et al. 1956).

Inconsistent with these conclusions is the finding of the Menninger Foundation's Psychotherapy Research Project (Kernberg et al. 1972) that initial psychological-mindedness, measured by the degree to which the patient felt his problems were environmentally determined (externalization), did not predict which patients would attain positive results with psychoanalysis or psychoanalytically oriented therapy. However, Greenson (1973) has questioned the broadness of definition used in this study in defining psychological-mindedness. He pointed out that patients beginning treatment for external reasons would not necessarily be low in psychological-mindedness, yet they would be included under such a categorization in the Menninger study definition of externalization of problems.

Two studies from the group psychotherapy literature are pertinent to this discussion. Yalom et al. (1967) obtained pretherapy scores on a psychological-mindedness scale from patients seen in five university outpatient groups. Therapist judgments of psychological-mindedness were also obtained after the first interview and after three months of therapy. The therapy technique used by the ten therapists was described as "dynamic, interactional." The test measure of psychological-mindedness predicted neither therapist ratings of improvement in three areas of psychosocial adjustment nor patient ratings in two out of these three areas. Therapist ratings were similarly not predictive of outcome on all measures. Abramowitz and Abramowitz (1974), in commenting on this study, have noted that the negative implications of these findings concerning the need for initial psychological-mindedness may not apply to insight-oriented groups. The conclusions are limited by the extent to which the "interactional" therapy implied a here-and-now problem-solving focus as opposed to a historical, there-and-then, insight-facilitating emphasis.

Abramowitz and Jackson (1974), in a study we have already reviewed, raised the possibility that interpretive techniques might be of special value when matched with specific patient variables such as high verbal intelligence, high psychological sophistication, or a favorable predisposition toward exploring childhood events. This general hypothesis was subsequently studied by Abramowitz and Abramowitz (1974) using the data obtained from the Abramowitz and Jackson investigation. Specifically, the authors asked whether the degree of patient psychological-mindedness before treatment would predict the outcome in insight- and noninsight-oriented group therapies. Pretherapy scores on an insight test measuring the ability to understand the underlying motivations of others served as the independent measure of psychological-mindedness. Findings, which fell just "shy" of conventional statistical significance, suggested that the insight-oriented groups led to more positive psychosocial changes, but only in patients having greater initial psychological sophistication. Psychological-mindedness was unrelated to change in the noninsight groups. Abramowitz and Abramowitz conclude that their findings indicate that the preference by analytically oriented therapists for psychologically sophisticated patients may be the result of such patients doing significantly better with an insight-oriented approach. At the least, this study suggests that patients' openness, sensitivity, and skill at conceptualizing problems within a psychological cause-and-effect framework may play a role in determining whether a patient will see himself as having benefited from a therapy based on historical interpretations. Our review of the literature has also tended to broadly support the prognostic usefulness of the concept of pre-therapy insight, defined either in terms of awareness of difficulties or of psychological-mindedness. However, the importance of this concept for outcome may vary significantly depending upon the method of measurement, the type of patient studied, and the type of treatment the patient subsequently receives. In general, if outcome is to be measured in terms of increased expressions of self-understanding, a patient's initial predisposition toward self-exploration would appear to have prognostic value.

The Therapist's Adjustment and Personal Therapy

The analytic position generally assumes that the therapist's self-insight and adjustment allows him to keep his personal needs from interfering with a patient's therapeutic progress. Freud's (1912a, 1937a) assumption was that a therapist's conflicts could lead to psychological blind spots, the distorting of patient material, and the using of patients to fulfill the therapist's own needs (countertransference). This would theoretically lead to less successful treatment outcomes. To combat the potential negative effects of the therapist's personality and distortions, Freud advocated analysis for the therapist with possible re-analyses at periodic intervals (Freud, 1937a). The bulk of the psychotherapy literature is certainly consistent with Freud's implication that the therapist's personality may play a significant role in determining outcome.[5] Also consistent with this implication are the numerous studies that have found that an individual's personality and level of adjustment may significantly affect his ability to make accurate inferences about the attitudes, behaviors, and personality characteristics of others (Bruner and Tagiuri 1954, Taft 1955, Shrauger and Altrocchi 1964). Seeman (1950), in a questionnaire survey of seventy prominent psychotherapists, found general agreement that at least some therapy should be provided for prospective therapists. In spite of this view, however, the prominent therapists were also in agreement that there was a lack of "real" evidence that the most effective therapists are also the best adjusted ones. Surprisingly, these issues have continued to receive relatively scant attention in the research literature. Are therapist insight and adjustment related to patient outcome? Does the therapist's personal analysis promote better results for his patients?

We were able to find relatively few investigations associating aspects of the therapist's level of adjustment and emotional state with patient outcome. All of these studies indicated that therapist disturbance is antitherapeutic. Bandura (1956) used a heterogeneous group of therapists from four different clinical settings in studying the relationships between therapist anxiety, self-insight, and therapeutic competence. Anxiety measures were derived from peer ratings, and insight was defined in terms of the correspondence between the therapist's self-ratings and the ratings of that therapist by his colleagues. Psychotherapeutic competence was determined from supervisor ratings. Results indicated that the more anxious therapists, whether they were insightful or not, were independently judged to be less competent. Garfield and Bergin (1971) similarly found, in a sample of graduate student therapists, that therapist personal adjustment as measured by psychological test scores, was positively related to patient psychotherapy outcomes. Outcome, in this study, was measured by both therapist ratings and patient changes on psychological test measures. The authors point out that their findings are consistent with evidence associating therapists' adjustment with their ability to empathize (Bergin and Solomon 1970, Bergin and Jasper 1969).

Karon and VandenBos, in a series of investigations of individual psychotherapy with schizophrenic patients, describe the variable of therapist "pathogenesis." This dimension, measured by projective test responses, describes the degree to which an individual unconsciously uses others who are dependent on him to meet his own needs, no matter what the cost to the dependent individual (Meyer and Karon, 1967). Student therapist pathogenic levels were correlated with outcome measures obtained on their schizophrenic patients. There was a strong relationship between therapist pathogenesis and outcome six months after therapy initiation. The more pathogenic the therapist, the poorer were the ratings of the patient's functioning, the greater was the patient's thought disorder, and the longer was the length of hospitalization. At later patient evaluations, as therapist experience increased, the relationship between initial therapist pathogenesis and outcome decreased to a nonsignificant level. There is no indication whether the therapists' pathogenesis levels decreased over time or whether they just learned to increasingly control this aspect of their personalities (Karon and VandenBos 1972, VandenBos and Karon 1971).

Other researchers, using mainly inexperienced therapists, have found that the therapist's conflicts and emotions can play a significant role in increasing specific distortions of patient material and determining therapist interventions. For example, Cutler (1958) measured therapist conflict areas by means of a rating scale and then compared therapist accounts of a series of therapy sessions with independent ratings of the same interviews. Therapists were shown to over- and underemphasize material related to their own conflict areas in their reports. In addition, therapist responses were judged less therapeutic and more defensive when they followed patient statements about areas previously rated conflictual for the therapist. Cutler concludes that a therapist's reports of his patients' or his own therapy behavior are not to be trusted as accurate. Similarly, Bandura et al. (1960) used ratings of therapists' personality characteristics and tape-recorded interviews to find a relationship between therapist personality and response to hostility. Those who typically expressed hostility directly and who evidenced a low need for approval were more likely to permit and encourage patient hostility than were therapists who customarily expressed little direct hostility and who showed a high need for approval. Overall, therapists were most likely to avoid hostility when it was directed toward them than toward other objects. Therapist avoidance as opposed to approach reactions usually had the effect of causing patients to drop the topic of hostility or to focus it on others. Relatedly, Yulis and Kiesler (1968) found that no matter what the topic of conversation, highly anxious, inexperienced therapists exhibited less personal involvement in their choice of interpretations than therapists with lower anxiety levels. Russell and Snyder (1963), using both verbal and physical measures, found that patient hostility led to therapist anxiety. While not replicating the Russell and Snyder findings, probably as a result of methodological differences, Heller et al. (1963) did demonstrate an association between patient response and therapist affective reaction. Employing actor patients in simulated therapy sessions, they demonstrated that dominant patient behavior evoked therapist dependency, in contrast to dependent patient behavior, which evoked therapist dominance. Patient friendliness and hostility led respectively to therapist friendliness and hostility.

Despite their limitations these studies unanimously suggest, as had Freud, that therapist adjustment and emotional response are related to aspects of therapeutic process and outcome. Thus it is natural to ask whether a therapist who has himself had therapy achieves results that are different from the outcomes produced by nontherapized therapists. Again, conclusions can only be based on a small number of scattered studies. There is also no way of comparing differences in the types of therapy the therapists had or even whether these therapies were deemed successful. Yet even with the heterogeneity and vagueness, a pattern does appear to emerge. The conclusion suggested by these studies is that the therapist's personal therapy plays a negligible or harmful role in the practice of inexperienced therapists who are in treatment. In contrast, personal therapy leads to the enhancement of therapeutic potential as the therapist becomes more experienced and distanced from his own treatment.

With regard to inexperienced therapists, Holt and Luborsky (1958) studied a large group of psychiatric residents in training at the Menninger Clinic. They found no relationship between change in supervisors' ratings of the residents' therapeutic competence and whether the resident had received therapy. There was also no relationship between changes in competence level and the duration of the residents' therapy. It should be noted that the vast majority of residents (about three quarters), irrespective of whether they had received treatment, were not judged to have improved in competence over the course of their training. One could question, as with other studies of this type, whether the supervisors' ratings really reflected therapeutic competence in terms of outcome for the patients.

A succession of investigations performed in Veterans Administration Mental Hygiene Clinics also looked at the factor of the therapist's personal therapy. Katz et al. (1958), in a study of thirteen clinics, found no relationship between therapist personal therapy and ratings of improvement on patients seen six months or longer. However, the patients' rated improvement was related to years of therapist experience. Similarly, McNair et al. (1963), in studying seven clinics, found no simple association between the premature termination of therapy by patients and whether their therapists had been treated, although therapist experience was related to duration. In contrast, McNair et al. (1964), using a sample drawn from three clinics, found that therapists with more personal therapy kept their patients longer. Relatedly, the number of treatment sessions correlated with positive outcome on measures of social change, psychological change, insight, and symptom reduction. The duration of the therapist's past analysis correlated with a standardized measure of patient ego strength three years after therapy was initiated. Yet this finding disappeared if the patient's initial level of ego strength was taken into account, suggesting that the therapists with more analysis had originally selected patients with higher ego strength for treatment. These few studies do not present data concerning the range of therapist experience levels at the various Mental Hygiene clinics, and one could raise questions concerning the possible interaction between outcome, the therapist's experience, and whether he himself had been treated. Specifically, does the therapist's having had therapy lead to different results, depending on his level of experience? A few studies suggest that it does indeed lead to different results.

Garfield and Bergin (1971) present a report on a group of relatively inexperienced graduate student therapists with varying levels of personal therapy. Patient change was measured on two psychological test measures of adjustment and the therapist's rating of patient disturbance. Due to the small numbers of therapists and patients involved and the nature of their distribution in the various groups, no statistical analyses were carried out. However, a descriptive look at the data consistently demonstrated that the therapists who had had the most personal therapy achieved the worst results while those with the least personal therapy achieved the best. Psychological test data on the therapists indicated that those who had received the most therapy were not more disturbed than those who had received the least. Thus the poor outcomes for the high-therapy therapists could not be attributed to their greater maladjustment. The authors propose that young therapists in therapy may be blocked in their therapeutic effectiveness by preoccupation with their own problems and the anxieties associated with being analyzed. Strupp's (1960) findings concerning the rated empathy levels of therapists who had or had not had personal therapy are consistent with this explanation. Experienced therapists who had been analyzed were rated as more empathic than experienced clinicians who had not had therapy, whereas, at lower levels of experience, therapist analysis appeared at best to have no effect on empathy and at worst to have a detrimental effect. Unlike the other therapist groups, analyzed therapists *with experience* were able to maintain higher levels of empathy no matter what their personal attitudes toward the patient. The implication of these findings is that the potential positive therapeutic effects of the therapist having had personal therapy would be most apparent when the therapist is experienced and finished with his own treatment.

Guild (1969), in a doctoral dissertation study of the therapeutic effectiveness of experienced analyzed and nonanalyzed therapists, lends support to the idea that personal therapy combined with experience facilitates effectiveness. The study focused on the therapist's ability to bring the conditions of empathy, warmth, and genuineness into his patient relationships. High levels of these therapist conditions have been shown to lead to increased patient self-exploration and constructive behavior change, while low levels have been associated with patient deterioration (Truax and Carkhuff 1967, Truax and Mitchell 1971). Ten analyzed and ten nonanalyzed therapists with an average of twelve and one half to fourteen years of experience served as subjects, along with three patients from each therapist matched for age, sex, education, hours in therapy, and income. Both therapists and patients filled out a standardized relationship questionnaire. Results were interpreted to mean that analyzed therapists and their patients had a more effective therapeutic relationship than nonanalyzed therapists and their patients. In general, the nonanalyzed clinicians and their patients were in much greater disagreement in their perception of the relationship. The patients tended to perceive the absence of the therapeutic conditions much more frequently than their nonanalyzed therapists. Contrastingly, analyzed therapists and their patients were in significantly greater agreement, particularly in perceiving and feeling the presence of warmth and empathy. These results are limited by the total reliance on questionnaire data, lack of controls or checks on the frequency with which patients were seen, and the possibility of significant initial differences in the personalities and motivation of those therapists who sought analysis as opposed to those who did not. Nonetheless, the findings are consistent with the other reports.

In sum, we are left with a relatively small number of studies examining the questions of therapist adjustment and personal therapy. The data that do exist are in agreement with Freud's general notion that therapist maladjustment and emotional response can make it more difficult to achieve therapeutic goals. In addition, the therapist's therapy does appear to have potential value in increasing his effectiveness. However, the therapist's years of experience and distance from his own treatment seem to be an important factor in determining whether his personal therapy will play a positive, neutral, or negative role in determining outcome. At the least, the results suggest that the therapist's personality and personal therapy history should be taken into account in studies of treatment outcome. Questions are also raised as to whether it is advisable for an individual to practice therapy and undergo a personal analysis at the same time (Garfield and Bergin 1971). Obviously this is a fertile area for future research. A determination of the role of personal therapy in the training of psychotherapists could be significantly aided by studies with more explicit measurements of the nature of the personal therapy, its outcome, and its effects on future therapeutic encounters.

Transference, Free Association, and the Couch

Before closing this chapter we would like to make a few comments about other areas of research that we examined. As other reviewers have found (Luborsky and Spence 1971, Luborsky et al. 1973, Meltzoff and Kornreich 1970), there has been relatively little quantitative research on the concept of transference even though this concept was introduced early in Freud's career (Breuer and Freud 1893–95) and plays a major role throughout his later writings on therapy. In general, for Freud, transference refers to a repetition of attitudes, feelings, and behavior derived from past early relationships and inappropriately expressed toward an individual in the patient's present life, particularly his analyst. In essence, there is an inappropriate transfer of reaction in which the person in the present is reacted to as if he were a significant person from the patient's past. Helping the patient come to see how his past is inappropriately affecting his present is taken as a goal of therapy.

Research in this area has primarily focused on whether judges can reliably rate the presence of transference and whether patients come to see their therapists as resembling their parents. Very little systematic work has been done associating changes in measured transference and outcome. Kernberg et al. (1972), in the Menninger study, did report that when the focus on the transference aspects of the relationship was high, patients diagnosed as borderline psychotic and treated by therapists with "high skill" improved significantly more. Malan (1963, 1973b), in his work on brief psychoanalytic psychotherapy at the Tavistock Clinic, has also reported some preliminary findings indicating that the most successful cases, in his treated samples, were those that emphasized interpretations linking transference reactions to the patients' parental relationships. While not all of the data have been published yet, Malan has stated that interpretations stressing the transference-parent link were the only type of interpretation that correlated significantly with therapy outcome ratings. Malan's findings are based on content analyses of the case records as dictated by the therapists. The possibility of the therapists' theoretical biases distorting the written case records must be taken into account in evaluating the significance of these results.

Crisp (1964a, 1964b, 1966), in a series of studies of behavior therapy, similarly addressed the question of whether outcome and transference are related. He developed a complex system of scoring transference from a comparison of ratings of father and therapist figures. A descriptive examination of the graphed data on symptom change and transference scores following a course of behavior therapy led to the conclusion that attitudes toward the therapist frequently change with or precede changes in symptomatology. This study, as with most others examining transference, does not clearly distinguish between attitudes toward the therapist and their appropriateness—a crucial distinction in Freud's conception. Also, there is no way of knowing whether the attitudes more regularly led to clinical change or resulted from it.

This group of investigations aimed at the transference-therapy outcome problem offers at least initial suggestive evidence that a focus on the transference aspects of the therapist-patient relationship may be one way of moving toward therapeutic gains. This does not, of course, detract from the possibility that different emphases in technique might be equally or more effective in attaining symptom remission. It also does not mean that the effects of transference interpretations can be separated from the therapist's influencing of the patient or the therapist's faith that such interpretations will work. Hopefully, future research will add greater clarity to the issue of how central a role transference interpretations play in achieving patient change in psychoanalytic psychotherapy and the mechanisms that mediate the change. Investigations shedding light on the precise conditions necessary for optimizing the effects of transference interpretations would also be of great value.

Attempts to reliably rate therapeutic transactions for transference have yielded mixed results. Strupp et al. (1966), using graduate student ratings of therapy sessions, found virtually no agreement among the four judges and the therapist in their ratings of transference. Conversely, Luborsky et al. (1973) were able to find some areas of agreement in ratings of transference by using experienced psychoanalysts, providing systematic definitions of the concepts to be rated, and limiting the samples to be rated to five-minute taped therapy segments. Even under these conditions, agreement among the four judges was quite variable, with no consensus on global transference ratings. Overall agreement was better when the focus was narrowed from a global rating to the amount of "transference present now" for each person or object being rated and the likelihood of transference being expressed in the future for each. Another study examining what led to the judges' rating agreements concluded that transference tended to be rated when the patient expressed strong feelings, particularly negative affect, toward the therapist (Lower et al. 1973). Despite the fact that inappropriateness in the patient's feelings is considered an outstanding trait of transference, judges made little reference in their responses to the patient's distortion of present attitudes due to the influence of past experience.

A series of other studies has used various rating methods to obtain indications of whether the patient's perceptions of his therapist come to coincide with his perceptions of his parents. Some studies have found evidence supportive of this idea (Chance 1952, Subotnik 1966a, 1966b), while others have not (Levin 1961, Sechrest 1962). The nonsupporting studies found the analyst was seen more like the patient's idealized self-image (Levin 1961) or like physicians, ministers, and teachers (Sechrest 1962) than parents. In general, these studies as a group do not provide strong evidence in either direction, and some writers have even questioned whether a classical transference reaction, theoretically outside the patient's awareness, could be determined solely from patient ratings of the therapist (Luborsky and Spence 1971).

An even more cogent issue is the fact that none of these studies addresses the question of whether the patients' perceptions of their therapists are, in each instance, inappropriate. Jackson and Haley (1963) argue that transference responses may be viewed as a logical result of the paradoxical nature of the relationship set up between analyst and patient. From this perspective, patient "transference responses" are not necessarily repetitive of early life history. The patient is seen as an adult being childlike due in part to the nature of the situation rather than as a result of an inappropriate regression into his childhood responses. Jackson and Haley outline a series of conflicting messages promoted by the nature of the analytic relationship:

> First, the situation is defined as one in which the patient will be benevolently helped to change. Second, the patient is encouraged to continue his usual behavior (and symptoms) because of the permissiveness of the analyst and in order that he will demonstrate his problems so they can be studied. Third, the patient is required to undergo a punishing ordeal as long as he continues his usual behavior. The patient is caught in an impossible paradox: to change, he must continue unchanged, while being benevolently helped to go through an ordeal until he changes. A patient must behave differently if he is to resolve the situation, but his different behavior will only be accepted if it occurs on the analyst's terms—otherwise, it is mere resistance. It does not seem surprising that a patient caught in this situation will exhibit 'irrational' behavior quite independent of his early infantile life and anachronistic forces that are also affecting his behavior. (p. 369)

The implication of this discussion is that a patient's behavior may take on a different meaning when viewed in the context of the therapy relationship. Indeed, the concept of transference requires that the patient's response must be inappropriate in the face of the therapist's behavior and emotional reactions. Most studies, in examining the transference question, do not focus on how the therapist is responding, and patient behavior is analyzed as if it occurred in a vacuum.[6] In the previous section we noted a number of studies which found that the therapist's emotions and conflicts can play a significant role in the therapeutic interaction. More specific to the present discussion is an investigation by Mueller (1969), who analyzed ratings of interpersonal behaviors from tape-recorded therapy (not psychoanalysis) sessions. Support was found for the idea that during psychotherapy a patient's behavior toward his therapist comes to increasingly resemble his behavior with parents and other significant figures. However, results also indicated that therapist behavior changed over time so that it actually became increasingly similar to the patient's recall of the behavior of parents and significant others. Thus the relationship was reciprocal, with both patient and therapist having effects on the other's behavior. Theoretically, the analyst's own therapy and neutrality should keep him from inappropriately reciprocating the behaviors of the patient's past. Yet this issue tends not to be directly addressed and evaluated in the transference research. It would be interesting to see how increasing levels of therapist neutrality and personal therapy would affect the occurrence of transference phenomena and eventual therapy outcome.[7] Such research would necessitate a focus on the therapist and his behaviors as well as the patient response.

As with the transference concept, research on the use of the couch and free association tends not to focus on how these technique possibilities affect therapy outcome. Freud originally began his use of the couch as an outgrowth of his work with hypnosis. It was used for two major reasons. The first was a "personal motive," in that he did not like being stared at for eight or more hours a day. The second was a technical motive evolving from his desire not to influence the course of the patient's verbalizations and associations through his own facial expressions. In the recumbent position the patient was asked to freely relate whatever went through his mind, no matter how trivial, illogical, or embarrassing, as though he was a traveler on a railway train describing the changing views he observed as he gazed out the window (Freud 1913a). Free association came to be regarded as the fundamental or basic rule of psychoanalysis. Its aim was to help bypass defensive resistances and reveal clues as to the unconscious determinants of the patient's difficulties. Thus the use of the couch and free association were primarily developed as information-gathering operations that would only indirectly lead to the attainment of insights.

Presumably, over the course of treatment, a patient's ability to associate freely should increase as his awareness expands and his defenses decrease. Yet as Luborsky and Spence (1971) note, there has not been any systematic study of whether clinical judges can reliably agree on free association ability or the extent to which it changes over treatment. Hall and Closson (1964) have found that experienced analysts judging seven and one half minute segments of audio-tape or typed transcripts could not discriminate psychotherapy sessions in which a patient was on the couch from those where he was sitting in a chair, even though they believed they had succeeded. However, since the therapist in the single case being studied was aware of the experimental situation, the possibility of experimenter bias must be considered. Further, the report does not make clear whether the procedure of free association was being used.

Other investigators using more standardized measuring techniques have found that aspects of the free association situation can be reliably studied. For example, Berdach and Bakan (1967) found some support for the idea that the lying-down position is more conducive to the recall of early memories than the sitting position. Subjects were male college students instructed to merely report memories that came to mind and the age at which the events occurred. Significant differences in the number of memories recalled appeared only for the zero to three year age interval. Weinstein (1966), using a similar method, also found that memories of anxiety for supine subjects were labeled as occurring chronologically earlier than those for upright subjects. No clear differences appeared between subjects more likely to use avoiding (repressors) as opposed to approaching defenses (sensitizers) when faced with threatening situations. There is of course no way of knowing in either of these studies whether the memories or the ages reported corresponded in any way to the reality of the subjects' lives. It is quite possible that subjects may have labeled events as occurring earlier when lying down due to the demand characteristics of the experimental situation and their expectations as to what kind of memories they should report when lying on a couch.

Additional studies using clinical judgments or standardized rating scales for adequacy of free association have found relationships between free association ability and tests of perceptual flexibility (Temerlin 1956, Bordin 1966a, 1966b), anxiety level (Kroth and Forrest 1969), psychiatric diagnosis (Mann 1967), and various psychological test indicators (Schneider 1953, Bordin 1966a, 1966b). Colby (1960b) reports that the presence of a male observer, in contrast to just a tape recorder, increased the number of references to people and to males in particular. Interpretations produced quantitative increases in free association and references to significant topics and people (Colby, 1961).

In sum, there is evidence that the study of free associations is a viable way for learning something about the personalities of the individuals being studied. However, as even Freud eventually acknowledged, free associations cannot be considered entirely free. The verbal conditioning studies indicate that patient response may be strongly influenced by the values and expectations of the analyst (Frank 1961, Krasner 1962, 1971; Marmor 1964, 1970). In contrast to the conclusions regarding the research potential of these procedures, there is no present evidence to either substantiate or deny that free associations and the couch play a significant role in achieving a *therapeutic* effect. In fact, some analysts, while acknowledging the research value of these techniques, have suggested that they might hinder therapeutic progress by diminishing the therapeutic effect of relationship variables and preventing the application of other potentially valuable approaches for achieving therapeutic changes (Marmor 1970, Robertiello 1967).

Overview

We would like to highlight a number of the points made in this chapter. Psychoanalytic therapy is generally seen as focused on the gaining of insight about the relationship between past and present feelings and behaviors. Freud's early work suggested that in addition to being educational, this would automatically lead to personality change and symptom remission. However, in Freud's later elaborations of his therapy and descriptions of his cases, he explicitly and implicitly moved away from directly linking insight with change. Research from a number of areas and also Freud's writings support the probability of the analytic situation having a significant suggestive component. In contrast to Freud's statements, we do not yet know whether insights based on accurate interpretations of the past lead to greater therapeutic effects than insights based on other types of interpretations. We also do not know whether interpretations are either the most efficient or effective means of providing patients with a feeling of self-understanding and control. Some have suggested that insights may result from behavior change as well as precede it. The data we reviewed are consistent in indicating that a therapy aimed at yielding insights is often not necessary for producing lasting symptom remission. Removing symptoms without patient insight does not tend to result in either new symptoms arising (symptom substitution) or shorter-lived remissions. It does appear, though, that the *therapist's* understanding of the meaning or purpose of the symptom for the patient may be helpful in effectively achieving symptom relief. The empirical literature also suggests that the most likely beneficiary of a treatment that is interpretive would be a patient who is psychologically minded and desirous of self-understanding.

Due in part to the lack of specificity in Freud's writings on therapy, researchers and clinicians have characterized a wide variety of vague short-term treatments using interpretations as "insight-oriented." For the most part there is little evidence that any of these treatments usually provide the patients with a sense of insight, let alone symptom relief. As a group, studies largely ignore Freud's concept of "working through" and his hesitations about using interpretive treatments for schizophrenic disorders or acute circumscribed problems. Even more distressing is the tendency for researchers to suggest that they are testing the efficacy of "the analytic therapeutic approach" when they are using relatively inexperienced untrained therapists performing amorphous treatments. More care is clearly needed both in defining treatments and selecting experienced skilled therapists to apply them. For the present we must conclude that researchers have not adequately tested Freud's idea that insight plus working through is of therapeutic benefit to patients.

Supportive of Freud is the research indicating that the therapist's personality and adjustment level have an effect on therapy process and outcome. On the basis of the available evidence, therapist maladjustment appears antitherapeutic and potentially harmful to patients. The effects of the therapist's personal therapy seem somewhat less clear. The evidence suggests that personal therapy has a neutral or harmful effect on the treatments performed by inexperienced therapists, while it potentiates better results for experienced analysts who are distanced from their own therapy. Questions are raised as to whether individuals who are in treatment should be doing therapy at the same time. This is an area with important implications for training, requiring significantly more attention and study.

Research on specific analytic concepts and techniques such as transference, free association, and the use of the couch is relatively scant. While there are some indications that Freud's general ideas about these matters may be useful in terms of learning about personality, there is no evidence that they are necessary factors in helping patients to overcome their symptoms. This conclusion does not contradict the idea that transference interpretations may be one of the keys to obtaining changes within a *psychoanalytic therapy.* It does, however, question the idea that a therapy utilizing transference interpretations must be uniquely superior in attaining symptom remissions to approaches not using transference interpretations. We commented, in our initial discussion of psychoanalytic therapy, that a direct relationship would have to be demonstrated between insight and symptom relief if the treatment, as orthodoxly formulated, is to be considered more than "educational." This relationship has not yet been demonstrated, and therefore the validity of the psychoanalytic explanation for symptom remission remains unsettled.

NOTES

1. Rennie and Fowler's (1941) description of 100 cases of recovered schizophrenics was as follows:

> In each case we chose to speak of recovery when we had evidence that the patient had been able to resume work or other productive activity, to present an appearance to family or friends that seemed in no way unusual or abnormal and to show adequate interest in his own appearance and status. In some cases the patient married and led a normal life, and in many others he reported that he was better than he had ever been previously. In some instances the family stated that the patient was keener and more mellow than before, that he had a new personality, etc. In no case have we considered the patient recovered if his behavior was in any way disturbing or obviously unsocial or if he expressed ideas that were psychotic or related to the acute phase of his illness. In each case the patient has been described as 'well,' 'as well as formerly' or 'better than formerly.' (p. 203)

2. The six inexact interpretations used by Mendell (1964) were:
    1. You seem to live your life as though you are apologizing all the time.
    2. Much of what you say now seems to be related to the difficulties you have with men.
    3. You seem hesitant in the exploration of your strong points.
    4. Apparently, you have always felt that you had to take on the burdens of all the family.
    5. You seem frightened of the effect your expression of feelings have on me and others.
    6. Much of what you say seems to be related to the difficulties you have with women.

3. Novick (1966) has found that there may be a difference in the probability of symptom substitution between enuretics who have always had their symptom (persistent) and those who acquired the symptom (acquired) after a history of at least six months completely free of any incidents of bed-wetting. While those who had acquired the symptom responded more favorably to a behavioral symptomatic treatment in terms of rate of improvement, they also had a higher relapse rate and greater deterioration in other areas of behavior following treatment. This study suggests that a knowledge of the patient's history may lead to predictably different treatments of choice for the same symptom.

4. Nurnberger and Hingtgen (1973) have summarized, from a behavioral perspective, the conditions outlined by others for maximizing the chances for new symptom forma-

tion. These include the following: (1) there is a failure to alter major reinforcing events controlling deviant behavior; (2) deviant target behavior is extinguished with no acceptable response put in its place; (3) deviant behavior is a response reinforced by avoidance of stimuli eliciting aversive emotional responses; (4) patient may possess a response hierarchy such that when the strongest deviant response is removed, the next in line replaces it; (5) when neurotic anxiety accompanies a response, the anxiety may have to be eliminated initially; and (6) spontaneous recovery of previously eliminated symptoms may occur after a long period with no treatments (p. 234).

5. Despite the fact that Freud and other theorists have similarly recognized the fact that the therapist's personality may play a significant role in the therapy process, there seems to be a divergence in the way this is handled. Freud tends to emphasize the potentially antitherapeutic aspects of the therapist's personality in advocating personal therapy and therapist neutrality. The emphasis appears to be on minimizing the effect of the therapist's personality. Contemporary writers have begun focusing on therapy more as an interpersonal than an intrapsychic process. Consequently, there is more talk of the therapist using certain personality attributes (such as warmth, empathy, and genuineness) and maximizing their effects in the therapy.

6. Similar examples of inattention to the potentially reciprocal nature of therapeutic transactions can be found in the research cited by Luborsky and Spence (1971) indicating the puzzling finding that judges can agree on the "goodness" of an analyst's interpretation or the empathy level of a therapist statement even if they have not heard what the patient said!

7. One study that suggested a relationship between therapist neutrality and transference behavior is reported by Baugh et al. (1970). They found that the interview behavior of "normal" female college students with a male interviewer could be predicted from a knowledge of the subjects' perceptions of the early relationship with their fathers. Those reporting relatively "poorer" early relationships exhibited significantly greater avoidance of eye contact and lower verbal productivity. Differences between the groups only appeared under a stress condition where the interviewer remained neutral and nonresponsive. Perceptions of the early relationship with mother did not predict the interview behavior with the male interviewer. We should note though that even in this situation the interviewers may have been actually recreating the nonresponsive behaviors some of the subjects had previously received from their fathers.

hapter 10

OVERVIEW
A Total Look at the Findings

WE HAVE completed a step-by-step, disciplined review of Freud's statements about a variety of major issues and tested them against the existing pool of scientific information. We have tried to appreciate the real complexity of his formulations and to subject them to tests neither softer nor more severe than those customarily applied to evaluating psychological theories. Rich findings have emerged, running the gamut from confirmation to contradiction, and at times revealing the totally unexpected. We will undertake in this chapter to provide a broad perspective on what we have uncovered. In the process we hope to clarify the strengths and weaknesses of Freud's work and, where possible, to propose revisions that will reconcile his ideas with contradictory scientific data.

There have been only a few previous large-scale attempts to judge whether Freud's theories are empirically tenable. An early appraisal by Sears (1943) is well known. However, it is by now quite outdated. Eysenck (1953b, 1965) has taken a strongly iconoclastic attitude toward psychoanalysis and has argued that it consists largely of untestable propositions. But his reviews of evidence bearing on Freud's ideas have either involved very narrow areas or been rather incomplete. A particularly dedicated effort to evaluate Freud's work was published by Kline in his book *Fact and Fantasy in Freudian Theory* (1972). He attempted to deal with almost every aspect of Freudian theory.

Conclusions from his book will be referred to, when appropriate, at various points in this chapter.

Scanning the spectrum of tests we have applied to Freud's theories, we are generally impressed with how often the results have borne out his expectations. Consider the following.

1. Important aspects of his developmentally based oral and anal personality typologies have emerged as reasonable propositions.[1] There are clusters of traits in children and adults corresponding to the core qualities associated with the oral and anal concepts. The oral character, as defined by his focus on oral body areas and activities, does seem to be unusually invested in establishing dependent ties with others that will ensure his security. The anal character, as defined by his preoccupation with anal functions and that which is dirty, does display a significant pattern of parsimony, compulsivity, and stubborn resistiveness in his behavior that seems to follow from Freud's account of the early conditions favoring the development of the anal defensive stance. It is true that little was found in the scientific literature to buttress Freud's view that the oral and anal patterns originate in crucial early oral and anal stages of development. However, this mainly reflects a paucity of data rather than the existence of negative evidence. The fact is that no investigator has yet made the large effort that would be required to observe children as they live through the so-called oral and anal phases and then to trace the impact of these experiences upon their later personalities. But it should be added that there are scattered bits of evidence in the literature, especially pertaining to the oral character, that tentatively point up the possibility of a tie between adult personality traits and early childhood experiences involving specific body areas, in a fashion consistent with Freud's framework of logic.

2. The etiology of homosexuality, phrased by Freud largely in developmental terms, has also stood up well to the known facts.[2] Convincing material can be cited which portrays the male homosexual's father as playing the hostile, rejecting role Freud assigned to him. To a lesser but still significant extent, there has been verification that the male homosexual's mother is "close" and "binding." This gives credence to Freud's view that male homosexuality arises in a context where the behavior of mother and father, by maximally intensifying Oedipal type rivalry, inhibits the taking of heterosexual love objects and presumably encourages a more defensive, regressive pattern of modeling self after mother. The empirical findings tend also to support Freud's explanation of female homosexuality insofar as they indicate that the fathers of female homosexuals display unusually hostile and frustrating

qualities that would render them disappointing to their daughters as love objects.

3. A key idea in Freud's formulation concerning the origin of the paranoid delusion has been moderately well validated.[3] A variety of ingenious laboratory techniques have been pressed into service to demonstrate that the paranoid schizophrenic is acutely sensitive to, and concerned about, homosexual themes. He does show heightened tuning to homosexual issues, as would be anticipated by Freud's notion that the paranoid delusion is a defensive projection of homosexual impulses.

4. Several aspects of the complex Oedipal theory, primarily as applied to the male, have been partially affirmed.[4] There is a line of experimental observation that fits the Oedipal notion that the male develops rivalry with father and fantasies of sexual closeness to mother. Further, as would be predicted from the Oedipal theory, there is solid evidence that erotic stimuli may arouse anxiety in the male and increase concern about body damage ("castration anxiety"). The construct validity of Freud's concept of castration anxiety has been reinforced by the fact that the literature bears out his prediction that such anxiety is higher in the male than the female. Relatedly, he was also right in his prediction that concern about loss of love, which he considered to be a significant factor in the female's coping with her Oedipal conflicts, would be higher in women than in men.

5. Although major components of Freud's dream theory did not come off well when empirically appraised, his idea that the dream can provide a vent or outlet for tension and disturbance was moderately supported.[5]

This brief sweep of what we have found to be supportive of Freud is intended to convey the wide-ranging sectors in which his thinking has proved to be scientifically sensible.

Where have we detected faults in his inventions?

1. His understanding of the nature of dreaming has been contradicted by many scientific observations. There is no empirical backing for his thesis that the dream is a camouflage wrapped around an inner concealed wish. Likewise, the accumulated research grossly contradicts his theory that the dream functions importantly to preserve sleep.

2. It has become clear, as we traced his thoughts concerning psychoanalytic therapy, that Freud never specified the necessary and sufficient conditions for achieving a therapeutic effect.[6] In addition, he moved farther and farther away from a concern with therapy outcome to a focus on the personality theory. Both Freud's writings and the experimental literature suggest that symptom

remission or behavior change does not necessarily follow solely from therapist interpretations or a feeling of insight attainment. Relatedly, studies have shown that psychoanalysts do differ considerably in their concept of psychoanalytic therapy, their therapeutic practices, and their modes of interpretation of the same clinical material. It is therefore difficult to view the therapy as a monolithic unified approach. Nonetheless, the outcome of a global entity labeled psychoanalytic therapy has been examined in a variety of studies. There are indications that the therapy performed by a number of analysts achieves better results than no treatment at all with chronic neurotic patients. However, granting the severe limitations in the available data, there is virtually no evidence that therapies labeled "psychoanalysis" result in longer-lasting or more profound positive changes than approaches that are given other labels and that are much less time-consuming and costly.

3. Particular segments of Freud's network of Oedipal concepts about the male seem to be untenable in the face of what we now know. Contrary to Freud's expectations, the male does not resolve his conflicts with father and identify with his masculinity primarily out of fear of him. Relatedly, the male probably does not accept father's superego standards and make them part of himself largely out of fear of father. The research findings suggest, in opposition, that the boy's masculine identification and development of moral standards are most facilitated by a positive, nurturant attitude on the part of father.[7]

4. A moderately negative picture can be derived from our analysis of Freud's formulations concerning women. We have not infrequently found (as he himself periodically acknowledged) that his theories specifically applicable to women are vague and so hazy they cannot be staked out as testable hypotheses. He seems to be definitely wrong in his assumption that a woman's attainment of psychosexual maturity is signaled by a shift of her erogenicity from the clitoris to the vagina. A number of his propositions concerning differences between women and men with regard to personality development and organization have either been empirically refuted or minimized. The research literature does not indicate that the process of achieving like-sex identity is more difficult or complex for the female than the male. It also does not indicate that the female has a more inferior concept of her body than the male. Further, it does not support Freud's notion that the male has a dramatically more severe set of superego standards than the female.

When we add up the totals resulting from our search, balancing the positive against the negative, we find that Freud has fared rather well. But like all theorists, he has proved in the long run to have far from a perfect score. He seems to have been right about a respectable number of issues, but he was also wrong about some important things. If one considers only his formulations concerning men and if, further, one considers only his theoretical propositions (as contrasted with his practical system of doing psychotherapy), his record of correct hits is excellent. Actually, an aim of this book was to be able to arrive at just such pinpointed distinctions concerning what is dependable and nondependable in Freud's total output.

One of the things we have most clearly verified is that it is possible to approach Freud's work in a scientific spirit. We have discovered that it is feasible to reduce his ideas to testable hypotheses. But more importantly, we have assembled an impressive array of empirical observations directly relevant to his hypotheses. Large masses of experimental information are available for testing psychoanalytic propositions. We have been amused by the fact that while there is the stereotyped conviction widely current that Freud's thinking is not amenable to scientific appraisal, the quantity of research data pertinent to it that has accumulated in the literature grossly exceeds that available for most other personality or developmental theories (for example, Piaget, Witkin, Allport, Eysenck). We have actually not been able to find a single systematic psychological theory that has been as frequently evaluated scientifically as have Freud's concepts! This is a real paradox. But why has the opposite impression become the common coinage? We can only guess. Perhaps the negative attitude of the psychoanalytic establishment toward experimental observations has persuaded those most interested in Freud's ideas to wear blinders that shut out the very existence of a vast literature. Where could one find a more dramatic example of "tunnel vision"?

Interestingly, the motivation to ignore the accumulated scientific facts has been reinforced by those at the opposite extreme, who are fervently hostile to Freud's views. They have been so deeply invested in the position that his views are mystical and untestable that they found it convenient to avoid the dissonance of confronting the real evidence. They have simply stuck with the refrain that Freud and science are incompatible. We would guess that another, but less important, reason for ignoring the wealth of empirical information pertinent to Freud's concepts is that so few attempts have been made to gather it together from the diverse places in which it is scattered. For example, as we have already shown, there is an amazing amount of information that has been buried for years in unpublished doctoral dissertations. We hope we have contributed significantly to the task of making all the information that is scientifically sound available for public scrutiny.

Let us turn now to the task of defining the full implications of the plus and minus observations we have assembled. Let us examine microscopically how they relate to each other. A series of topical discussions directed to this end will follow.

What Is Acceptable Validating Information?

We were puzzled, as we examined those studies supportive of Freud, to discover that they not infrequently involved sources of information alien to the Freudian model. For example, an important part of the scientific data giving substance to Freud's oral and anal personality typologies is based on conscious-self reports elicited by questionnaires. Most of the factor analytic studies that have shown that certain traits cluster together in accordance with Freud's typological schema (such as was found to be true of parsimony, neatness, and obstinacy in relation to the anal character) secured information from subjects by quite directly asking them whether they behaved in certain ways or entertained particular attitudes. There was no attempt made to tap into an unconscious sector of response. There are other striking examples of an analogous sort. Most of the studies concerned with testing Freud's theory concerning the role of parent behavior in the etiology of homosexuality have relied on simple questionnaires that asked persons to provide straightforward ratings of their parents or spontaneous descriptions of them. There have been few instances in which stratagems were employed to evade the subject's conscious defenses and to probe his "inner" feelings about his parents. Yet these "surface" reports have largely fitted Freud's hypotheses concerning the conditions likely to produce a homosexual orientation.

Still another somewhat paradoxical illustration of the matter we have under consideration is provided by our analysis of the dream literature. It will be recalled that Freud's theory (as we interpreted it) about the dream serving to vent impulses and tensions was supported by a series of studies that focused on the manifest rather than so-called latent content of dreams. That is, one could find proof of venting by looking at the immediate, obvious meanings of the words in which the dream was phrased. What Freud considered to be the superficial defensive aspect of the dream lent itself well to affirming a significant facet of his dream theory.

The examples just listed indicate that one need not necessarily rely on material extracted from unconscious sources in order to evaluate Freud's ideas. This is not to minimize the importance of data obtained from response levels that one can reasonably label as unconscious. We have seen the value of such data in the studies that used complex technologies to demonstrate that paranoid schizophrenics are unknowingly concerned, to a special degree, about homosexual themes. We have seen it, too, in studies that employed projective tests to show that castration anxiety increases in men exposed to erotic stimuli. But as Freud himself dramatized in his theory construction, everything is grist for the mill. He did not hesitate to incorporate into his skein of observations such diverse things as Schreber's autobiographical comments (apropos of the paranoia theory), his own perception (apropos of the dream theory) of the relation between having eaten olives that made him thirsty and the appearance of thirst imagery in his dreams, and (apropos of the Oedipal theory) the behavior of a character named Oedipus in a fictional drama.

It is at first sight strange that information derived from conscious levels of response and shaped by defensive biases should provide meaningful support for some of Freud's concepts. Incidentally, note that if one accepts the fact that such information can support Freud, the door is opened to the obverse possibility that it can be used to contradict him. What we would like to focus on are the factors affecting the appropriateness of evaluating Freud's ideas with information of this type. Is it appropriate, for example, for an investigator of Freud's homosexuality theory to ask a homosexual individual if his father generally treated him in a friendly or unfriendly manner and then expect the replies to represent sound scientific data? Our view would be that he would be justified in doing so if he considers this individual to have the required knowledge available to him and to have minimal reasons for biasing his reports of that knowledge (for example, on the basis of an awareness of the hypothesis being tested and a desire to affirm or not affirm it). It has previously been generally assumed that an individual's direct reports about a phenomenon such as how his parents treated him had negligible validity in a psychoanalytic framework. The fact that we have uncovered a number of instances in which such reports seem to be quite meaningful in relation to Freud's thinking suggests that it is time for a revision in perspective.

Unfortunately, despite some pertinent exploratory work (Baugh et al. 1970), there has been a lack of systematic exploration of the determinants of reports by individuals who are motivated to describe honestly their inner feelings or their recall of their relationships with significant figures such as their parents. We do not know, *on the average,* how defensively distorted such reports will be —how close they will come to real events. The exploration of this matter should have priority. It does not seem reasonable merely to differentiate grossly between so-called conscious and unconscious sources of information. There is probably a continuum of degrees to which an individual's direct reports about himself in a questionnaire or brief interview situation are relevant to Freud's constructs. There may be a great deal more pertinent information in presumably "surface" material than has been suspected or acknowledged. One may call to mind again the profitable outcome of dream analyses based on the direct meanings of the words comprising the dream. It may be that Freud far overestimated the extent to which the average individual's defensive needs render his direct reports about himself inappropriate for evaluating psychoanalytic propositions.

Reality of Developmental Vectors

Freud thought of personality as shaped by a succession of crucial experiences relating to mastery of impulses involving different areas of the body, all in the context of parental reactions toward the expression of such impulses. Some of his most basic concepts about this process are bracketed by the terms oral, anal, Oedipal, and genital. These terms frame a major segment of his vision concerning how people are psychologically put together. They are nodal points in his network of ideas. They integrate into a developmentally phrased framework the theoretical tools with which he most often worked to explain the construction of personality. A good part of the scientific material we have reviewed affirms the meaningfulness of this framework. While we have found little available evidence that would support Freud's idea that there are precise oral, anal, Oedipal, and genital phases in each individual's development, we have uncovered information indicating that fantasies and attitudes linked to the psychological meanings Freud assigned to these phases do exist and have consequences for behavior predictable from his definitions of them. There do seem to be important psychological phenomena paralleling the major dimensions in his developmental theories.

Consider the following sampling of facts we have compiled. There do seem to be constellations of traits corresponding to the processes Freud tied to learning to master oral and anal sensations. Oral and anal fantasies commonly occur, and they are correlated with patterns of behavior that fit the oral and anal personality typologies, respectively. Thus, persons unusually focused on the mouth and on themes of incorporation do display a special motivation to gain closeness and support from others. Similarly, persons focused on anal themes display traits such as obstinacy and neatness that Freud asserted were likely to develop if one were made anxious by parents about control of anal functions.

Unique perspectives are frequently provided by Freud's oral and anal concepts. We would remind you of Lerner's (1961) demonstration that stamp collectors are particularly concerned about anal matters. Recall, too, that Noblin (1962) was able to predict that anal characters would condition better than orals if rewarded by pennies, whereas oral characters would be more motivated by food rewards. In the instance of the prediction about the pennies, only Freud's formulation about the need to master anal impulses (considered in conjunction with his apparently far-out notion that feces and money are symbolically equated) made this possible. Our search of the literature has, in addition, affirmed certain aspects of the Oedipal concept, which is probably the most important segment in Freud's developmental explanatory scheme. There is fairly convincing proof that men do have differentiated attitudes about their parents that mirror a history of sexually tinged rivalry with father for mother as a love object. The male does, as Freud proposed, experience castration anxiety, and this anxiety is intensified by exposure to erotic stimuli. Special intimacy of the male child with mother does apparently set off defensive reactions in the sexual realm that conform to Freud's Oedipal model. It should be noted that our conclusion that there is empirical support for his theory of homosexuality also adds substantiality to his developmental explanatory system. He derived the homosexuality theory fairly directly from his Oedipal model. To find that it holds up to scrutiny, within the available research, adds another bit of construct validity to the core Oedipal formulation.

In short, we are impressed with the match between observed data and a paramount area of Freud's thinking. We do not, at this point, urge acceptance of his detailed developmental model. It remains to be seen whether his oral, anal, and other labeled stages occur when he says they do or in the sequence he proposes—or, indeed, whether they should even be called stages. But we do regard the forces he associated with the various developmental phases as entering significantly into the average person's life. Oral, anal, and Oedipal vectors are real and influential. We can meaningfully think of the average person as having to master a series of problems or conflicts paralleling those Freud ascribed to the developmental time periods. The psychological forces that are big in his system of thought do emerge in research reports as real and capable of explaining a range of interesting phenomena. On the basis of what we have learned, we would urge less skepticism about concepts such as orality and anality and Freud's notion about the Oedipal triangle. There is good reason to affirm his image of the child struggling his way to psychological equilibrium by trying to reconcile the erotogenicities of different body areas with the parental rules about what one may permissibly enjoy. While this is certainly only part of what shapes the child, we would judge there is a high probability that it accounts for a reasonably significant part of the variance.

What are some of the practical implications of accepting the reality of Freud's developmental vectors? First of all, there is a call to study them longitudinally. We badly need to follow samples of children over extended periods of time and to investigate how oral, anal, and Oedipal attitudes develop and change and also determine whether they predict adult attributes.[8] Secondly, we need to incorporate the developmental vectors routinely into our studies not only of personality but also of other areas such as vocational choice, behavior in educational settings, and social attitude formation. Masling et al. (1967, 1968) have provided us with an excellent example of the profit accruing from the systematic application of one of the developmental variables, namely orality, to a variety of research problems. As described earlier, they have shown that an objective orality index derived from inkblot responses is meaningfully related to such diverse phenomena as yielding behavior, obesity, alcoholism, and ability to utilize social cues. The way is obviously open for boldly looking at the role of the developmental vectors in a range of current research areas.

It would, by way of illustration, be reasonable to ask such questions as the following:

Is an individual's degree of external versus internal orientation or his degree of field independence linked to the nature of his oral fantasies?

To what extent is repression-sensitization a function of castration anxiety?

Would the nature of a man's Oedipal attitudes toward his father predict his hypnotizability?

Do feelings about self (for example, discrepancy between self and ideal self) relate to anal conflicts?

Do a man's views about the proper role for women mirror his Oedipal feelings about mother?

Many other reasonable inquiries of a similar order await exploration.

A third important and perhaps even more basic task is to turn our attention to devising better measures of the developmental variables. Good beginnings have been made in tapping attitudes relating to orality, anality, and even castration anxiety; but they are only beginnings. Further, we really have no tested, quantified methods for evaluating Oedipal feelings and fantasies. We need standardized ways of representing such things as how much erotic tension exists between a man and his mother, how competitive a man feels with his father, and the particular defense strategies being utilized by a man to cope with his Oedipal anxieties.

We are obviously proposing that the psychology establishment change its orientation toward Freud's developmental concepts. These concepts should no longer be treated as parochial to psychoanalysis, but rather as sound enough to be included in the everyday business of psychology. Of course, an important step in this direction will be taken when we begin systematically to inform students entering psychology concerning the existing rich pool of research data bearing on psychoanalytic propositions.

The Anal Constellation

Another cluster of findings that should be particularly considered concerns those pertinent to the anal character, homosexuality, and the paranoid delusion. In each of these areas the scientific evidence is somewhat substantiating of Freud's concepts. Those familiar with his thinking will recognize that he assumed a continuity among the mechanisms involved in anal character formulation, the etiology of homosexuality, and the incitement to paranoid defense. He explicitly proposed that the male homosexual has a disposition to being unusually sensitive to anal sensations and feelings; and, of course, he explained paranoid distortion as a means of coping with unacceptable homosexual fantasies (presumably having a significant anal-receptive component). The attributes he ascribed to the anal character, the homosexual, and the paranoid overlap significantly, even though the overlap may involve polar opposites and acceptance in one instance of anal impulses versus rejection in another. The unifying theme among the three categories is the idea that sensations and fantasies concerning the anal region of one's body (and the reactions of parents to such anal phenomena) play a noteworthy part in personality synthesis. There is persuasive construct validity in the fact that three different regions of Freud's thinking that are linked by an important common theoretical theme have held up moderately well to empirical probing. It is reassuring that three adjacent pieces in the jigsaw puzzle which are supposed to delineate an area all prove to have substance.

With such reassurance one can proceed to explore more forthrightly the implications of Freud's network of ideas about anality. It would be profitable to design studies that would deal with such questions as the following:

1. What factors determine whether an individual indulges his desires for anal stimulation (as is apparently true of many male homosexuals) as contrasted to controlling and shutting them out of awareness (as would typify these males with a paranoid potential)? For example, are there possibly, in line with Freud's assumption, "constitutional" differences in sensitivity to anal sensations that affect one's ability to control or deny such sensations? Valuable data concerning this issue might be obtained by observing individual differences in responsiveness of infants to the anal stimulation linked with defecation. Laboratory studies could also be done based on the effects of graded stimulation delivered to the infant's anal region. Or, by way of further example, and also in the spirit of some of Freud's views, is it possible that the male's need to deny anal sensations is a function of wanting to deny the existence of a body opening symbolizing for him repeated encounters with a father who sought to control and psychologically penetrate him, and in so doing to deny him masculinity?

2. How direct is the role of anal sensations in paranoid imagery? Does one find that increasing the paranoid schizophrenic's anal sensations intensifies his paranoid orientation? That is, does such an increase reinforce unacceptable homosexual fantasies which then need to be delusionally denied? This matter might, by way of illustration, be investigated by carefully evaluating shifts in the strength of paranoid ideation in paranoids who develop body symptoms that necessarily augment anal sensations (for example, constipation, hemorrhoids) and comparing them with the changes in paranoids who develop non-anal symptoms of analogous seriousness.

3. What are the differences between male and female homosexuals and also between male and female anal characters in the nature of their anal sensations and fantasies? These issues need to be explored simply because there are sex differences, implied by Freud, in these areas, but it would be stretching things to say that they are even vaguely understood, let alone empirically evaluated.

It bears repetition to say that fundamental to such experimental efforts is the availability of valid and reliable measures. We need to be able to capture the full complexity of how the individual experiences the anal phenomena linked to his existence. A beginning has been made in fashioning measures of this sort. There are scales available for evaluating attitudes toward dirt and fecal-like materials (for example, Rosenwald 1972b), anal traits such as neatness and stubbornness (Rosenwald 1972b, Segal 1961), reaction to quasi-symbolic anal themes (Blum 1949), and relative awareness of anal regions of one's body (Fisher 1970). But we do need to spell out the interrelationship of these measures and the major dimensions they embrace.

Male Identification and Superego Formation

An area of major defect we have discerned in Freud's theories relates to his description of how male identification and superego formation evolve in the course of resolving the Oedipal dilemma. As already outlined in an earlier chapter, Freud assumed that the driving force in the boy's giving up of the Oedipal struggle with father is his fear of being retaliatorily attacked (castrated) by him. He theorized, too, that it was this fear that *primarily* motivates the boy to identify with (rather than oppose) father and in the process not only to take on a male role but to make father's moral standards (superego) part of himself. After a detailed sifting of the empirical literature concerned with male identification and also that dealing with moral standards, we concluded that Freud was definitely incorrect in the emphasis he placed upon fear as a motivating force in the identification process and possibly wrong in the role he ascribed to fear in the formation of the superego. The scientific data suggest that it is father's warmth and nurturance that are particularly important in persuading his son to be masculine like him and perhaps also to accept his moral norms. The evidence opposing Freud is sufficiently strong to justify doubting his formulations in these areas and to place the burden of proof upon those who might wish to continue defending his identification and superego formulations.

The material we have uncovered suggests that the Oedipal struggle is resolved not primarily out of fear but rather on the basis of communications from father which might be paraphrased as follows: "You do not need to fear me. I want to be your friend. I want you to be like me. I will help and support you if you adopt my perspectives and style of behavior." If one accepts this idea, one can view the boy's castration anxiety (which presumably arises from Oedipal rivalry) not as a force motivating him to be like father but rather as a barrier between them that interferes with the identification process. A nurturant attitude on father's part would, within this framework, help to allay the boy's castration anxieties and convince him that closeness to father is safe and reasonable.

One of the immediate benefits of this revised theoretical perspective is that one need no longer take the awkward position that the core of the average boy's identity is something alien that has been stamped into him through fear.[9] The superego need no longer be portrayed as an entity that was imposed by psychological rape. This does not rule out the possibility that some males acquire identity primarily out of fear, but it argues that this is not what happens in the average or normal instance. Conceptualizing the superego as a series of standards accepted from father largely on a positive basis removes the need to treat it as a partitioned presence within the individual's personality system. It is not the equivalent of a miniature angry, judging father figure who has staked out a claim in the male child's interior and periodically sallies forth to witness transgressions. Rather, it can be treated theoretically as that which the male child has accepted as meaningful in the course of communicating with an important figure who has been supportive and whose closeness is valued.

Incidentally, the empirical data also indicate that Freud was probably wrong both in his assumption that the boy's superego is acquired largely at the time Oedipal tensions are resolved and that mother's standards contribute to it only in a minor degree. There is less and less justification for regarding the superego as a bundle which is almost exclusively delivered by one person during a specific point in time. The concept of the superego suggested by research findings, namely that it is positively assimilated and gradually integrated into self structures, is more capable than Freud's model of explaining the pervasive effects of moral standards on behavior. If Freud were correct in his portrayal of the superego as a relatively alien entity within the personality economy, one would expect its power to be much more susceptible to being isolated and minimized.

The revision in superego theory we have offered has implications, too, for psychoanalytic therapy as it is currently practiced and conceptualized. Surely interpretations related to superego issues would differ in relation to whether one pictures the superego as something imposed in contrast to something positively accepted. If an individual is told by a therapist that his guilt about certain issues is a derivative of an alien standard holding sway within him, he may be persuaded to use unrealistic coping mechanisms. One deals differently with a feeling one perceives as an approved part of self than as alien to self. The individual who tries to untangle guilt that he thinks is the end result of past hostile interaction with father, when it is, in fact, due to nurturant transactions with father, will be doing battle with a fiction. He will not be able to arrive at a genuine understanding of why his guilt is so powerful and difficult to jettison. In the same vein, a man will be misled who tries, in the psychotherapeutic setting, to trace back the nature of his difficulties with his father and who is constantly sensitized by therapist interpretations to focus on what is presumed to be the basically competitive nature of father-son interactions. He will significantly miss the role of father nurturance in the construction of his identity.

Freud's account of the male's relationship with his father is saturated with the language of antagonism. There now seems to be some reason to dispute the validity of such a schema as a context for exploring the history of a man's adventures with his father. If one assumes that any man who has been able to evolve a semblance of male identity and who shows some consistency in his moral attitudes had a father who delivered a reasonable minimal quantity of nurturant warmth, one might not so much emphasize rivalry in looking for the etiology of the average patient's difficulties with his father. There might be much more attention devoted to issues such as the seductive impact of father's warmth, the symbiotic consequences of father's closeness, the inadequate preparation that father's friendliness provides for the rivalry later encountered with other males, and the apparent contradiction between being a friendly son and fulfilling the cultural stereotype of an aggressive male. Fathers may, in general, be more friendly toward their sons than widely accepted role definitions of manhood would allow as acceptable. Perhaps fathers have to "sneak" their friendliness in forms that are confusing and conflict evoking. In any case, a new perspective on superego formation would necessarily raise questions about possible alterations in psychoanalytic therapeutic strategies.

Some Generalizations from the Dream Theory Analysis

We should like to trace certain ramifications of the fact that we could find little to confirm Freud's supposition that the dream is a secret vehicle for expressing an unconscious wish. We concluded from the available stock of scientific knowledge that dreams can serve to vent a diversity of feelings, tensions, and fantasies, both conscious and unconscious. They can no more be said to express one class of intents or tensions than does any other imaginative production. From this perspective, dream interpretation should not be a highly specialized search for The Wish. It becomes an enterprise that can explore at a number of levels what is occurring in an individual's psychological world. Each of his dreams, but even better a large sample of his dreams, affords the potential for exploring multidimensions of his feelings and attitudes. The potential seems to be the same as that afforded when examining a pool of responses to projective stimuli such as Roschach inkblots or Thematic Apperception pictures. We have already discussed in some detail how this change in conception concerning the meaning contained in dreams would affect its use in a psychotherapeutic setting.

At this point we would like to focus on the implications of the change for the interpretation of other kinds of imaginative productions that are considered important psychoanalytically. Freud regarded neurotic symptoms, daydreams, and delusions as fantasy creations. He also generally interpreted them as having wish-fulfilling functions. For example, Freud depicted neurotic symptoms as symbolic constructions, compromise formations that simultaneously express an unconscious wish (usually sexual) and a denial of the wish. The paralyzed arm of the conversion hysteric would presumably represent symbolically the acting out of a desired sexual fantasy. The concentration of attention upon it occasioned by its disablement would be viewed as providing a secret source of sexual satisfaction. But at the same time the paralysis in the arm would be regarded as preventing its use for any gratification and therefore signaling a state of inhibition.

In essence, Freud conceived of the neurotic symptom as a disguised expression of a forbidden wish. This sounds quite similar to his concept of what is contained in the dream. However, if the dream cannot empirically be reduced to an unconscious wish, we should ask whether the same might not turn out to be true for the symptom. Perhaps symptoms, like the dream, can serve as a means of expressing and coping with a spectrum of tensions, both conscious and unconscious. We actually have little dependable information bearing on this matter. But it is conceivable that neurotic symptoms might derive from (or, once established, vary as a function of) clearly apparent stresses (for example, traumatic accidents) in the environment, or a general need to experiment with a new approach to coping with radical changes in life role, or simply the pressure to vent great accumulations of tension. But perhaps more importantly, by analogy with what we discovered about the greater reality and perhaps even meaningfulness of manifest as compared to so-called latent dream content, we should consider the possibility that what is manifest in a symptom or a delusion is meaningful in its own right. The phobic patient who develops a fear of leaving the house may simply be indicating that he wants to stay home and not venture out into the world. There might not be a secret symbolic wish or intent concealed in his phobia, or the concealed intent may not be as important as the manifest one. The conversion hysteric who develops a paralyzed leg may be quite directly declaring that he wants to give up motility and become helplessly dependent. Even the paranoid schizophrenic who conjures up a world in which he is being endlessly persecuted may be announcing his sense of being overwhelmed by the hostility and cruelty impinging upon him. This may be just as important in the formation of his delusion as unconscious homosexual anxiety. Perhaps it requires the interaction of both variables to trigger the paranoid adaptation. We are proposing, in short, that the obvious, so-called surface qualities of neurotic and psychotic "productions" may contain just as much information about their nature and intent as do their presumed unconsciously based strata.

Freud's Ideas About Women

Freud's relative difficulty in decoding what he considered to be core psychological differences between the male and female is interesting to contemplate. In some instances his difficulty is betrayed by the blurred and nontestable structure of his statements. It will be recalled that it was not possible to evaluate his ideas about how superego formation occurs in the female specifically because they were too vague to pin down operationally. Furthermore, a number of his ideas about women that were testable proved not to be valid in terms of the existing scientific data. There is reasonably solid evidence that he was incorrect in his hypothesis that women have more complexities and difficulties than the male in arriving at identification with the like-sex parent. He was incorrect in his assumption that the feminine superego is dramatically less severe than that of the male. He was wrong, too, in his speculations about the need of the female to shift her erogenicity from the clitoris to the vagina in order to attain "mature" psychosexuality.

Actually, one discerns a trend for most of his documented errors and obscurities with respect to the psychology of women to concentrate around the dynamics of Oedipal relationships. Only one thing he had to say specifically about the Oedipal experiences of the female received empirical backing. This was his theory that she is more motivated than the male by fear of loss of love (and less by castration anxiety) in resolving her Oedipal conflicts and attachments. It should be added that, with a few minor exceptions, all of the scientific literature documenting the existence of the Oedipal encounter and the fact that erotic stimuli may, because of their association with Oedipal conflicts, arouse anxiety have used males as subjects. One is almost forced to conclude that Freud's Oedipal theories, as they apply to women, remain either largely untested or already contradicted in certain significant respects. Freud did, of course, declare that the Oedipal experiences of the female are less sharp and conclusive than those of the male. He may, however, have underestimated the degree to which this is true. His formulations about female Oedipal behavior need to be regarded with skepticism until more and better research evolves in this area. The researcher with psychoanalytic interests could pick no more strategic topic in which to invest his efforts.

In several areas where Freud did not postulate gross male-female differences, the application of his concepts to women has held up well. His concept of the anal character and Abraham's elaboration of the oral character have turned out to apply rather equivalently to females and males. Equally good confirmatory results have been obtained with male and female samples. There are hints that Freud's theory about paranoid delusions may hold up as well in female as male subjects. But there has been overwhelmingly more research with male paranoids than female paranoids; and we do need more projects that will look at the feminine side of the issue. In view of the increasing stockpile of research findings indicating that men and women really differ in personality organization, it would be fair to say that Freud was on the right track when he tried to conceptualize masculine and feminine personality development as involving divergent dynamics. However, it is in these sectors of divergence that he turned out to be least knowledgeable.

Psychopathology

Almost everything Freud wrote bears directly or indirectly on matters of psychopathology. He was devoted to clarifying how diverse psychological elements enter into the production of neurotic and psychotic symptoms. Many of his theories that we have explored deal with variables that are important to his models of psychopathology. The most obvious instance concerns his theory of paranoid delusion formation. In essence, he proposed that a paranoid distortion could represent a dramatic way of denying that one entertains bad or unacceptable wishes (with homosexual intent). Quite corroboratively, we did find that paranoid schizophrenics have shown in a number of studies that they are unusually sensitive about homosexual themes and act as if they want to deny or avoid them. They manifest just the sort of defensive sensitivity he postulated. It is a further, as yet unconfirmed step to assert, as Freud did, that the paranoid delusion represents a reversal and also a projection of the homosexual wish. But we do at least have a basis for accepting the foundational concept that the paranoid is someone struggling to master urges that are alien and anxiety-provoking. From this basis, too, Freud's general theory that most psychopathological symptoms are a means of coping with disturbing wishes and fantasies gains added credence.

The support we discerned for certain of the Oedipal formulations and the etiology of homosexuality adds reality to Oedipal and family dynamic variables that Freud often employed to explain the origins of psychological disturbance. He and other psychoanalysts have relied heavily on concepts such as Oedipal rivalry, castration anxiety, and fear of loss of love to make sense of patients' clinical histories. The fact that experiments demonstrate that normal men can be made anxious about heterosexual erotic stimuli in a fashion consistent with the Oedipal model makes it that much easier to accept the possibility that Oedipal anxieties play a part in the neurotic's disturbance. Note, too, that we have found affirmation for the reality of so-called pre-Oedipal forces such as oral and anal feelings that are employed explanatorily in Freud's clinical accounts. Overall, we can say that while the material we have reviewed only in small part *specifically* validates Freud's theories of symptom formation, it gives substance to the concepts and perspectives in which these theories are nestled.

Psychoanalytic Psychotherapy

Our review has stressed that psychoanalytic theory is a rich source for hypotheses about personality dynamics and that many of the hypotheses have proven to have substantial empirical support. Why then, we have asked ourselves, have the studies of psychoanalytic therapy not shown this approach to be uniquely superior to other treatments that emphasize different views of personality and different techniques? In posing this question we are defining treatment as a process with more than just an educational goal. We do not wish to dispute or demean the value of self-understanding and self-knowledge, yet it is our belief that most patients seek therapy for other reasons. Namely, they are uncomfortable and are experiencing disabling or incapacitating "symptoms" that are making it difficult for them to function interpersonally, heterosexually, or vocationally. They desire change, decreased depression, freedom from their own anxieties, and a feeling they can make choices on the basis of the realities of situations rather than on the basis of their own irrational fears.

Research on the outcome of psychotherapy has primarily focused on the idea that a patient will somehow "feel better" as a result of treatment and that the changes he experiences can be measured. While we recognize that some analysts do not see patient change as a necessary goal of therapy, Freud clearly implied that changes would come about as a result of "making the unconscious conscious" and providing patients with insights into their dynamics. Some may argue that the failure of research to demonstrate the superiority of the analytic approach is due to an anti-analytic bias. In answer to this we must point out that research has offered strong support for many of the psychoanalytic hypotheses about personality development. It is our speculation that the failure to find support for a uniquely superior psychoanalytic therapy cannot be attributed simply to bias and a lack of appropriate sensitive measures of behavioral and intrapsychic change.

In a sense, it is hard to imagine that psychoanalysis could, as a general entity, be found superior to other approaches, since the evidence indicates so clearly that there is no one conception of what psychoanalytic therapy is. The field is filled with vagueness, appeals to authority rather than evidence, lack of specificity in the definitions used, and unreliability in the application of techniques and dynamic conceptualizations. Consequently, what is psychoanalysis for one therapist may be designated heretical by another. Without the necessity for establishing empirical validity, all manner of claims and practices become equally validated once they are given the psychoanalytic blessing by an authoritative therapist. The vagueness and heterogeneity of clinical practice have translated into an amorphous research literature. Therapists, skilled and unskilled, experienced and inexperienced, are regularly given the mission of instilling insights and focusing on transference even though it is apparent that many have conflicting ideas about what they are doing and what it is that they hope to accomplish. Those recognized as knowledgeable often are not in agreement. It is our conclusion after reading through the literature that a single unified approach to the treatment of patients that can be labeled "psychoanalysis" does not exist.

It needs to be stressed that the failure to find psychoanalytic treatment superior to other approaches in therapeutic efficacy may derive from the fact that many analysts feel that promoting change, as such, is not a primary goal. They may feel supported in their position by Freud's statements that an analyst should not become too invested in patient change. Even here, there is often a simple underlying assumption that if a patient gains significant insights, he will automatically be altered, and no special efforts toward producing change need be made. Strupp (1973a,b) has called this the "Look, ma, no hands" phenomenon. The empirical literature has not yet given us an answer as to whether there is a direct link between insights and symptom relief. Actually, the process of change appears less directly derivable from insight than Freud initially suggested; and he did eventually move away from formulating a direct insight-change link. There are strong indications that many other components besides insight play a major role in achieving positive therapy outcomes.

Incidentally, we might add that the empirical validity of a number of the psychoanalytic hypotheses about personality may at times hinder the therapy by diverting analysts from a concern with observable patient change. For example, if an analyst assumes that change will automatically follow insights and continually finds evidence that his interpretations of the patient's dynamics are accurate, he may overlook or dismiss the observation that the patient is not feeling any better. In this instance, the validation of the personality theory may overshadow the ineffectiveness of the therapy. Research findings hint that the translation of even accurate insights into patient change may require significant analyst influence and suggestion. Indeed, it is impossible to conceive of a therapy that is independent of therapist influence. Freud's description of his own cases reveals that his approach was no exception.

Also potentially mediating against the possibility of psychoanalytic therapy producing uniquely significant patient change is the exhortation to analysts not to try to directly instigate behavioral changes and to remain "emotionally cold" and "opaque" (Freud 1912a,b). There is at present a voluminous empirical literature attesting to the fact that therapeutic changes with many kinds of "symptoms," from sexual dysfunctions to phobias, can be attained from the application of direct behavioral techniques without any attempts to promote insight. Changes produced in this manner do not usually appear to result in either substitute symptoms or shorter-lived cures. By explicitly devaluing the probability of obtaining changes directly and relatively quickly, many analysts may be unnecessarily constrained in their therapeutic expectations and techniques. Even within a psychoanalytic framework, research has not shown briefer psychoanalytic therapies to be less effective in decreasing symptoms than longer, more orthodox psychoanalyses. Freud's concern about the possible negative effects of the analyst's personality led to his emphasizing the necessity for analysts to remain emotionally distant from patients and to work through their conflicts in their own personal therapy. Analysts who have read these cautions as a need for completely removing the effects of the therapist's personality from the therapy may be hindering the probability of change in their patients.

A large body of research has indicated that the therapist's personality can have positive as well as negative effects. Specifically, the development and utilization of certain therapist attributes such as warmth, empathy, and genuineness have been demonstrated to promote patient self-exploration and change (Truax and Carkhuff 1967, Truax and Mitchell 1971). Analyst attempts, therefore, to completely eliminate therapist personality effects may remove positive along with negative influences on the course of treatment. If the aim is increased effectiveness, practitioners might do well to incorporate substantiated knowledge from all perspectives into their approach. This might mean, for some, using psychoanalytic theories as a framework for growth and development rather than as a set of blinders for automatically excluding the meaningfulness of other contributions. Since other approaches to therapy besides psychoanalysis have been found to lead to equally effective and sometimes more efficient symptom alleviation, one must speculate that there may be overlapping active ingredients in the treatments. The specification of these ingredients is a task worthy of all clinicians and researchers.

The advent of psychoanalytic psychotherapy held the promise of increasing understanding of personality and also providing more effective therapeutic strategies. To the extent that the theory is prematurely used to restrict and stifle new therapeutic perspectives, the promise shall remain unfulfilled. In some respects the clinician's observation that psychotherapy research is naive and insensitive is but a mirror of the researcher's perception of an ambiguous, nonintegrated therapy enterprise. If we are to have both better therapy and better therapy research, we will need fewer meaningless labels and a greater respect for clarity and precision in defining what we are doing.

Summary

By way of final summary, what are the major revisions and reservations with reference to Freud's ideas that we have proposed? Let us briefly enumerate them. 1. A new approach to dream interpretation based on the use of the manifest content. 2. The portrayal of the boy's acquisition of male identity and superego values as due more to father's nurturance than his threatening hostility. 3. The adoption of a skeptical attitude toward those formulations that aim specifically to define how Oedipal development in the female differs from that in the male. 4. A need to maintain a conservative and fundamentally questioning position concerning the effectiveness of psychoanalytic therapy and even whether the therapy exists as a clearly definable set of operations.

On the positive side, we have affirmed the basic soundness of Freud's thinking about the following: 1. The oral and anal character concepts as meaningful dimensions for understanding important aspects of behavior. 2. The Oedipal and castration factors in male personality development. 3. The relative importance of concern about loss of love in the woman's as compared to the man's personality economy. 4. The etiology of homosexuality. 5. The influence of anxiety about homosexual impulses upon paranoid delusion formation. 6. The soundness of the train of interlocking ideas about the anal character, homosexuality, and paranoid delusion formation. 7. The possible venting function of the dream.

We obviously have not made a total survey of Freud's theories. We have not looked at his elaborate accounts of how unconscious psychological processes are organized. We have not examined most of his ideas about the etiology of neurotic symptoms. We have not looked at his theories of humor, or his notions about the origins of forgetting and unintentional slips, or his views about the origins of schizophrenia. There are also out-of-fashion concepts such as the "death instinct" and the inheritance of racial memories that we have not appraised at all. These simply remain unfinished tasks to be completed. We would like to reiterate our initially stated assumption that a considerable scientific literature supports Freud's fundamental view that motives, feelings, and fantasies may exist in an individual without his awareness of them and that they may significantly influence his behavior. But this may, upon more formal testing, prove to be less true than we suppose. It is a measure of the span of Freud's thinking that so much remains to be done even after the large evaluative effort that constitutes this book.

NOTES

1. Kline (1972) concluded, in his evaluative review of the scientific data bearing on this issue, that oral and anal variables do enter significantly into behavior. However, he pointed out the absence of real evidence concerning the existence of distinct developmental phases that can be labeled as oral or anal.

2. Kline (1972) decided after his analysis of the scientific literature that Freud's theory concerning the etiology of homosexuality is not supported. However, his review was grossly incomplete and overlooked many positive findings.

3. Kline (1972) regarded the total available scientific evidence to be quite supportive of Freud's theory concerning paranoid delusions.

4. Kline (1972) concluded from his review of the scientific literature that important sectors of the Oedipal theory have promising validity.

5. Kline (1972) could not discern in the scientific literature any clear support for Freud's wish-fulfillment theory of dreaming. Overall, he was not able to arrive at any decisive plus or minus appraisals of Freud's concepts concerning the functions of dreaming.

6. Kline (1972), after sorting through the empirical literature concerned with psychoanalytic therapy, arrived at a rather skeptical position. He felt that the efficacy of the therapy had not been demonstrated. However, he also acknowledged the crudity of the methods available for investigating therapy outcome phenomena.

7. Kline (1972) argues, on the basis of his analysis of the empirical studies concerned with the determinants of superego severity, that they can generally be dismissed as irrelevant to Freud's concepts. He indicates that these studies have not dealt with the superego as the unconscious phenomenon that Freud envisioned it, and have falsely attributed superego significance to behaviors that relate more to the ego and to intellectual levels of response. However, we would differ with this view, which suggests that the empirical studies have dealt only with superficialities. We have reviewed numerous projects in which superego variables were measured not with questionnaires but with projective tests, intensive interviews, and observations of spontaneous behavior in situations where there were minimal reasons for putting on a socially desirable facade. In short, we would affirm the meaningfulness of the literature that contradicts Freud's theory that threat and fear are central in superego formation.

8. It is even possible that previous longitudinal studies (for example, Kagan and Moss 1962) could, with new perspectives, be reanalyzed to extract valuable information about the developmental vectors.

9. Freud did acknowledge that pre-Oedipal dependent relations with father contributed to the boy's sense of masculine identity, but his major emphasis was on the importance of what happened during the resolution of the Oedipal confrontation.

References

Aarons, L. "Diurnal Variations of Muscle Action Potentials and Word Associations Related to Psychological Orientation." *Psychophysiology*, 5 (1968), 77–91.

Aaronson, B. S., and Grumpelt, H. R. "Homosexuality and Some MMPI Measures of Masculinity-Femininity." *Journal of Clinical Psychology*, 17 (1961), 245–247.

Abel, H., and Sahinkaya, R. "Emergence of Sex and Race Friendship Preferences." *Child Development*, 33 (1962), 939–943.

Abel, T. M. "Idiosyncratic and Cultural Variations in the Resolution of Oral-Oedipal Motivational Patterns and Conflicts." *Journal of Psychology*, 57 (1964), 377–390.

Abelson, R. P., and Levine, J. "A Factor Analytic Study of Cartoon Humor among Psychiatric Patients." *Journal of Personality*, 26 (1958), 451–466.

Aberle, D. F. "Culture and Socialization." In F. L. K. Hsu, ed., *Psychological Anthropology*. Homewood, Ill.: Dorsey, 1961, pp. 381–399.

Abraham, K. "The Influence of Oral Erotism on Character Formation." In *Selected Papers*. London: Hogarth, 1927, pp. 383–406.

______. *Selected Papers on Psychoanalysis*. New York: Basic Books, 1968.

Abramowitz, S. I. "Locus of Control and Self-Reported Depression among College Students." *Psychological Reports*, 25 (1969), 149–150.

Abramowitz, S. I., and Abramowitz, C. V. "Psychological-Mindedness and Benefit from Insight-Oriented Group Therapy." *Archives of General Psychiatry*, 30 (1974), 610–615.

Abramowitz, S. I., and Jackson, C. "The Comparative Effectiveness of There-and-Then versus Here-and-Now Therapist Interventions in Group Psychotherapy." *Journal of Counseling Psychology*, 21 (1974), 288–293.

Abroms, G. M. "Persuasion in Psychotherapy." *American Journal of Psychiatry*, 124 (1968), 1212–1219.

Ackerman, N. W. "Paranoid State with Delusions of Injury by 'Black Magic.'" *Menninger Clinic Bulletin*, 2–3 (1938–39), 118–126.

Adams, A. B. "Choice of Infant Feeding Technique as a Function of Maternal Personality." *Journal of Consulting Psychology*, 23 (1959), 143–146.

Adams, H. E., Butler, J. R., and Noblin, C. D. "Effects of Psychoanalytically-Derived Interpretations: A Verbal Conditioning Paradigm?" *Psychological Reports*, 10 (1962), 691–694.

Adams, H. E., Noblin, C. D., Butler, J. R., and Timmons, E. O. "Differential Effect of Psychoanalytically-Derived Interpretations and Verbal Conditioning in Schizophrenics." *Psychological Reports*, 11 (1962), 195–198.

Adelson, J. "Creativity and the Dream." *Merrill-Palmer Quarterly*, 6 (1959–60), 92–97.

Adelson, J., and Redmond, J. "Personality Differences in the Capacity for Verbal Recall." *Journal of Abnormal and Social Psychology*, 57 (1958), 244–248.

Agnew, H. W., Jr., Webb, W. B., and Williams, R. L. "The First Night Effect: An EEG Study of Sleep." *Psychophysiology*, 2 (1966), 263–266.

______. "Comparison of Stage Four and 1-REM Sleep Deprivation." *Perceptual and Motor Skills*, 24 (1967), 851–858.

Agras, W. S., Chapin, H. N., and Oliveau, D. C. "The Natural History of Phobia." *Archives of General Psychiatry*, 26 (1972), 315–317.

Agras, S., Leitenberg, H., and Barlow, D. H. "Social Reinforcement in the Modification of Agoraphobia." *Archives of General Psychiatry*, 19 (1968), 423–427.

Ainsworth, M. D. S., Bell, S. M., and Stayton, D. J. "Individual Differences in the Development of Some Attachment Behaviors." *Merrill-Palmer Quarterly*, 18 (1972), 123–143.

References

Albino, R. C., and Thompson, V. J. "The Effects of Sudden Weaning on Zulu Children." *British Journal of Medical Psychology,* 29 (1956), 177–210.

Alexander, F. *Five Year Report of the Chicago Institute for Psychoanalysis.* 1932–1937.

———. "Psychoanalysis and Psychotherapy." *Journal of the American Psychoanalytic Association,* 2 (1954), 722–733.

———. *Psychoanalysis and Psychotherapy.* New York: Norton, 1956.

———. "Social Significance of Psychoanalysis and Psychotherapy." *Archives of General Psychiatry,* 11 (1964), 235–244.

Alexander, F., and Selesnick, S. T. "Freud-Bleuler Correspondence." *Archives of General Psychiatry,* 12 (1965), 1–9.

Alexander, I. E., and Blackman, S. "Castration, Circumcision, and Anti-Semitism." *Journal of Abnormal and Social Psychology,* 55 (1957), 143–144.

Allen, M. G. "Psychoanalytic Theory on Infant Gratification and Adult Personality." *Journal of Genetic Psychology,* 104 (1964), 265–274.

———. "Childhood Experience and Adult Personality: A Cross-Cultural Study Using the Concept of Ego Strength." *Journal of Social Psychology,* 71 (1967), 53–68.

Allen, Susan R., Oswald, I., Lewis, S., and Tagney, J. "The Effects of Distorted Visual Input on Sleep." *Psychophysiology,* 9 (1972), 498–504.

Allison, J. "Cognitive Structure and Receptivity to Low Intensity Stimulation." *Journal of Abnormal and Social Psychology,* 67 (1963), 132–138.

Alper, T. G., Blane, H. T., and Abrams, B. K. "Reactions of Middle and Lower Class Children to Finger Paints as a Function of Class Differences in Child-Training Practices." *Journal of Abnormal and Social Psychology,* 51 (1955), 439–448.

Althouse, R. H. "A Semantic Differential Investigation of Sexually Symbolic Concepts: Freud and Jung." *Journal of Projective Techniques and Personality Assessment,* 34 (1970), 507–512.

Altman, J. H. "Identification of Personality Traits Distinguishing Depression-Prone from Non-Depression-Prone Individuals." Unpublished doctoral dissertation, Rutgers University, The State University of New Jersey, 1971.

Altshuler, K. Z. "Comments on Recent Sleep Research Related to Psychoanalytic Theory." *Archives of General Psychiatry,* 15 (1966), 235–239.

Altucher, N. "Conflict in Sex Identification in Boys." Unpublished doctoral dissertation, University of Michigan, 1957.

Ammons, R. B., and Ammons, H. S. "Parent Preferences in Young Children's Doll-Play Interviews." *Journal of Abnormal and Social Psychology,* 44 (1949), 490–505.

Andersen, D. O., and Seitz, F. C. "Rorschach Diagnosis of Homosexuality: Schafer's Content Analysis." *Journal of Projective Techniques and Personality Assessment,* 33 (1969), 406–408.

Anderson, N. H. "Looking for Configurality in Clinical Judgment." *Psychological Bulletin,* 78 (1972), 93–102.

Andrews, J. D. W. "Psychotherapy of Phobias." *Psychological Bulletin,* 66 (1966), 455–480.

Angel, R. W. "The Concept of Psychic Determinism." *American Journal of Psychiatry,* 116 (1959), 405–408.

Angrilli, A. F. "The Psychosexual Identification of Pre-School Boys." *Journal of Genetic Psychology,* 97 (1960), 329–340.

Anker, J. M., and Walsh, R. P. "Group Psychotherapy, a Special Activity Program, and Group Structure in the Treatment of Chronic Schizophrenia." *Journal of Consulting Psychology,* 25 (1961), 476–481.

Ansbacher, H. L. "The Significance of the Socio-Economic Status of the Patients of Freud and of Adler." *American Journal of Psychotherapy,* 13 (1959), 376–382.

Antell, M. J. "The Effect of Priming and the Subliminal Presentation of Sexual and Aggressive Stimuli on Tests of Creativity." Unpublished doctoral dissertation, New York University, 1969.

Anthony, E. J. "An Experimental Approach to the Psychopathology of Childhood: Encopresis." *British Journal of Medical Psychology,* 30 (1957), 146–175.

Antrobus, J. S., and Antrobus, J. S. "Discrimination of Two Sleep Stages by Human Subjects." *Psychophysiology,* 4 (1967), 48–55.

Antrobus, J. S., Dement, W., and Fisher, C. "Patterns of Dreaming and Dream Recall: an EEG Study." *Journal of Abnormal and Social Psychology,* 69 (1964), 341–344.
Aoki, H. " 'Chopunnish' and 'Green Wood Indians': A note on Nez Perce Tribal Synonymy." *American Anthropologist,* 69 (1967), 505–506.
Appel, K., Myers, J. M., and Scheflen, A. E. "Prognosis in Psychiatry: Results of Psychiatric Treatment." *Archives of Neurology and Psychiatry,* 70 (1953), 459–468.
Appelbaum, S. A., Coyne, L., and Siegal, R. S. "Change in IQ During and After Long-Term Psychotherapy." *Journal of Projective Techniques and Personality Assessment,* 33 (1969), 290–297.
Apperson, L. B., and McAdoo, W. G., Jr. "Parental Factors in the Childhood of Homosexuals." *Journal of Abnormal Psychology,* 73 (1968), 201–206.
Archer, G. S., and Burgess, I. S. "A Further Investigation of Sexually Symbolic Concepts using the Semantic Differential Technique." *Journal of Projective Techniques and Personality Assessment,* 34 (1970), 369–372.
Arey, L. "Clinical State and Sleep-Dream Patterns of Reactive Schizophrenics." Paper presented at annual meeting of Association for Psychophysiological Study of Sleep, Palo Alto, California, 1964.
Arieti, S. "A Re-examination of the Phobic Symptom and of Symbolism in Psychopathology." *American Journal of Psychiatry,* 118 (1961), 106–110.
Armon, V. "Some Personality Variables in Overt Female Homosexuality." *Journal of Projective Techniques,* 24 (1960), 292–309.
Armstrong, R. G., and Hoyt, D. B. "Personality Structure of Male Alcoholics as Reflected in the IES Test." *Quarterly Journal of Studies on Alcohol,* 24 (1963), 239–248.
Aronfreed, J. "The Nature, Variety, and Social Patterning of Moral Responses to Transgression." *Journal of Abnormal and Social Psychology,* 63 (1961), 223–241.
______. "The Origin of Self-Criticism." *Psychological Review,* 71 (1964), 193–218.
______. *Conduct and Conscience.* New York: Academic, 1968.
Aronoff, J. "Freud's Conception of the Origin of Curiosity." *Journal of Psychology,* 54 (1962), 39–45.
Aronson, E. "The Effect of Effort on the Attractiveness of Rewarded and Unrewarded Stimuli." *Journal of Abnormal and Social Psychology,* 63 (1961), 375–380.
Aronson, E., and Mills, J. "The Effects of Severity of Initiation on Liking for a Group." *Journal of Abnormal and Social Psychology,* 59 (1959), 177–181.
Aronson, H., and Weintraub, W. "Social Background of the Patient in Classical Psychoanalysis." *Journal of Nervous and Mental Disease,* 146 (1968a), 91–97.
______. "Patient Changes during Classical Psychoanalysis as a Function of Initial Status and Duration of Treatment." *Psychiatry,* 31 (1968b), 369–379.
______. "Certain Initial Variables as Predictors of Change with Classical Psychoanalysis." *Journal of Abnormal Psychology,* 74 (1969), 490–497.
Aronson, M. L. "A Study of the Freudian Theory of Paranoia by Means of the Rorschach Test." *Journal of Projective Techniques,* 16 (1952), 397–411.
______. "A Study of the Freudian Theory of Paranoia by Means of the Blacky Pictures." *Journal of Projective Techniques,* 17 (1953), 3–19.
Arthur, A. Z. "Theories and Explanations of Delusions: a Review." *American Journal of Psychiatry,* 121 (1964), 105–115.
Arthur, B., and Schumann, S. "Family and Peer Relationships in Children with Paranoid Delusions." *Child Psychiatry and Human Development,* 1 (1970), 83–101.
Aserinsky, E., and Kleitman, N. "Regularly Occurring Periods of Eye Motility and Concomitant Phenomena during Sleep." *Science,* 118 (1953), 273–274.
Atkinson, R. M., and Ringuette, E. L. "A Survey of Biographical and Psychological Features in Extraordinary Fatness." *Psychosomatic Medicine,* 29 (1967), 121–133.
Auld, F., Goldenberg, G. M., and Weiss, J. V. "Measurement of Primary-Process Thinking in Dream Reports." *Journal of Personality and Social Psychology,* 8 (1968), 418–426.
Auld, F., Jr., and Murray, E. J. "Content-Analysis Studies of Psychotherapy." *Psychological Bulletin,* 52 (1955), 377–395.
Auld, F., Jr., and White, A. M. "Sequential Dependencies in Psychotherapy." *Journal of Abnormal and Social Psychology,* 58 (1959), 100–104.
Averill, J. R. "Grief: Its Nature and Significance." *Psychological Bulletin,* 70 (1968), 721–748.

References

Avnet, H. *Psychiatric Insurance.* New York: GHI, 1952.

Babcock, C. G. "The Manifest Content of the Dream." *Journal of the American Psychoanalytic Association,* 14 (1966), 154–171.

Bachrach, H. "Adaptive Regression, Empathy and Psychotherapy: Theory and Research Study." *Psychotherapy: Theory, Research and Practice,* 5 (1968), 203–209.

Bacon, M. K., Barry, H., and Child, I. L. "A Cross-Cultural Study of Correlates of Crime." *Journal of Abnormal and Social Psychology,* 66 (1963), 291–300.

———. "A Cross-Cultural Study of Drinking: II. Relations to Other Features of Culture." *Quarterly Journal of Studies on Alcohol* (1965), Supplement 3, 29–48.

Badal, D. W., Driscol, T. E., and Maultsby, M. "The Role of the Symptom in Psychosomatic Disease: Changes following Removal of a Symptom by Extrapsychic Means." *American Journal of Psychiatry,* 113 (1957), 1081–1088.

Baekeland, F. "Correlates of Home Dream Recall: Reported Home Sleep Characteristics and Home Dream Recall." *Comprehensive Psychiatry,* 10 (1969), 482–491.

Baekeland, F., Koulack, D., and Lasky, R. "Effects of a Stressful Presleep Experience on Electroencephalograph-Recorded Sleep." *Psychophysiology,* 4 (1968), 436–443.

Baekeland, F., and Lasky, R. "The Morning Recall of Rapid Eye Movement Period Reports Given Earlier in the Night." *Journal of Nervous and Mental Disease,* 147 (1968), 570–579.

Baekeland, F., Resch, R., and Katz, D. "Presleep Mentation and Dream Reports. I. Cognitive Style, Contiguity to Sleep, and Time of Night." *Archives of General Psychiatry,* 19 (1968), 300–311.

Bahn, A. K., Conwell, M., and Hurley, P. "Survey of Private Psychiatric Practice: Report on a Field Test." *Archives of General Psychiatry,* 12 (1965), 295–302.

Baker, B. L. "Symptom Treatment and Symptom Substitution in Enuresis." *Journal of Abnormal Psychology,* 74 (1969), 42–49.

Bales, R. F. *Interaction Process Analysis.* Cambridge, Mass.: Addison-Wesley, 1950.

Bandler, B. "The American Psychoanalytic Association and Community Psychiatry." *American Journal of Psychiatry,* 124 (1968), 1037–1042.

Bandura, A. "Psychotherapist's Anxiety Level, Self-Insight, and Psychotherapeutic Competence." *Journal of Abnormal and Social Psychology,* 52 (1956), 333–337.

———. *Principles of Behavior Modification.* New York: Holt, Rinehart and Winston, 1969.

Bandura, A., Lipsher, D. H., and Miller, P. E. "Psychotherapists' Approach-Avoidance Reactions to Patients' Expressions of Hostility." *Journal of Consulting Psychology,* 24 (1960), 1–8.

Bandura, A., Ross, D., and Ross, S. A. "A Comparative Test of the Status Envy, Social Power, and Secondary Reinforcement Theories of Identificatory Learning." *Journal of Abnormal and Social Psychology,* 67 (1963a), 527—534.

———. "Vicarious Reinforcement and Imitative Learning." *Journal of Abnormal and Social Psychology,* 67 (1963b), 601–607.

Bandura, A., and Walters, R. H. *Adolescent Aggression.* New York: Ronald, 1959.

Barad, M., Altshuler, K. Z., and Goldfarb, A. I. "A Survey of Dreams in Aged Persons." *Archives of General Psychiatry,* 4 (1961), 419–424.

Barber, T. X., Walker, P. C., and Hahn, K. W., Jr. "Effects of Hypnotic Induction and Suggestions on Nocturnal Dreaming and Thinking." *Journal of Abnormal Psychology,* 82 (1973), 414–427.

Barendregt, J. T., Bastiaans, J., and Vermeul-van Mullen, A. W. "A Psychological Study of the Effect of Psychoanalysis and Psychotherapy." In J. T. Barendregt, ed., *Research in Psychodiagnostics.* The Hague and Paris: Mouton, 1961, pp. 157–183.

Barnes, C. A. "A Statistical Study of the Freudian Theory of Levels of Psychosexual Development." *Genetic Psychology Monographs,* 45 (1952), 105–175.

Barron, F. "The Disposition toward Originality." *Journal of Abnormal and Social Psychology,* 51 (1955), 478–485.

Barron, F., and Leary, T. F. "Changes in Psychoneurotic Patients with and without Psychotherapy." *Journal of Consulting Psychology,* 19 (1955), 239–245.

Barry, H., III. "Cross-Cultural Research with Matched Pairs of Societies." *Journal of Social Psychology,* 79 (1969), 25–33.

Barry, H., III, Child, I. L., and Bacon, M. K. "Relation of Child Training to Subsistence Economy." *American Anthropologist,* 61 (1959), 51–63.

Bassos, C. A. "Affective Content and Contextual Constraint in Recall by Paranoid, Nonparanoid, and Nonpsychiatric Patients." *Journal of Consulting and Clinical Psychology,* 40 (1973), 126–132.

Baugh, J. R., Pascal, G. R., and Cottrell, T. B. "Relationship of Reported Memories of Early Experiences with Parents on Interview Behavior." *Journal of Consulting and Clinical Psychology,* 35 (1970), 23–29.

Baumrind, Diana. "Current Patterns of Parental Authority." *Developmental Psychology Monograph,* 4 (1971), 1–103.

Becher, B. A. "A Cross-Sectional and Longitudinal Study of the Effect of Education on Free Association Responses." *Journal of Genetic Psychology,* 97 (1960), 23–28.

Beck, A. T. "A Systematic Investigation of Depression." *Comprehensive Psychiatry,* 2 (1961), 163–170.

_____. "Thinking and Depression. I. Idiosyncratic Content and Cognitive Distortions." *Archives of General Psychiatry,* 9 (1963), 324–333.

_____. *Depression: Clinical, Experimental, and Theoretical Aspects.* New York: Hoeber Medical Division, Harper & Row, 1967.

Beck, A. T., and Hurvich, M. S. "Psychological Correlates of Depression. I. Frequency of 'Masochistic' Dream Content in a Private Practice Sample." *Psychosomatic Medicine,* 21 (1959), 50–55.

Beck, A. T., and Ward, C. H. "Dreams of Depressed Patients." *Archives of General Psychiatry,* 5 (1961), 462–467.

Becker, W. C., Peterson, D. R., Luria, Z., Shoemaker, D. J., and Hellmer, L. A. "Relations of Factors Derived from Parent-Interview Ratings to Behavior Problems of Five-Year-Olds." *Child Development,* 33 (1962), 509–535.

Behan, R. A., and Behan, F. L. "Comments on Seeman's Operational Analysis of the Freudian Theory of Daydreams." *Psychological Bulletin,* 51 (1954), 176–178.

Beier, E. G., and Ratzeburg, F. "The Parental Identification of Male and Female College Students." *Journal of Abnormal and Social Psychology,* 48 (1953), 569–572.

Beigel, H. G. "The influence of Body Position on Mental Processes." *Journal of Clinical Psychology,* 8 (1952), 193–199.

_____. "Mental Processes during the Production of Dreams." *Journal of Psychology,* 47 (1959), 171–187.

Beiser, H. R. "Self-Listening during Supervision of Psychotherapy." *Archives of General Psychiatry,* 15 (1966), 135–139.

Beitner, M. S. "Word Meaning and Sexual Identification in Paranoid Schizophrenics and Anxiety Neurotics." *Journal of Abnormal and Social Psychology,* 63 (1961), 289–293.

Belcher, M. M., and Bone, R. N. "The Relationship of Dream Report Ratings to Field Independence and Rigidity." Paper presented at annual meeting of Association for the Psychophysiological Study of Sleep, 1972.

_____. "Extraversion, Neuroticism, Field Independence and Reported Sleep and Dream Experiences." Paper presented at annual meeting of Association for the Psychophysiological Study of Sleep, 1972.

Belcher, M. M., Bone, R. N., and Montgomery, D. D. "Rigidity and Dream Recall." *Psychological Reports,* 30 (1972), 858.

Bellak, L. "Studying the Psychoanalytic Process by the Method of Short-Range Prediction and Judgment. *British Journal of Medical Psychology,* 31 (1958), 249–252.

_____. "The Treatment of Schizophrenia and Psychoanalytic Theory." *Journal of Nervous and Mental Disease,* 131 (1960), 39–46.

_____. "Research in Psychoanalysis." *Psychoanalytic Quarterly,* 30 (1961), 519–548.

_____. "The Role of Psychoanalysis in Contemporary Psychiatry." *American Journal of Psychotherapy,* 24 (1970), 470–476.

Bellak, L., and Smith, M. "An Experimental Exploration of the Psychoanalytic Process. Exemplification of a Method." *Psychoanalytic Quarterly,* 25 (1956), 385–414.

Beller, E. K. "Dependency and Autonomous Achievement Striving Related to Orality and Anality in Early Childhood." *Child Development,* 28 (1957), 287–315.

Belmont, L., and Birch, H. G. "Re-individualizing the Repression Hypothesis." *Journal of Abnormal and Social Psychology,* 46 (1951), 226–235.

Beloff, H. "The Structure and Origin of the Anal Character." *Genetic Psychology Monographs*, 55 (1957), 141–172.
Bene, Eva. "On the Genesis of Female Homosexuality." *British Journal of Psychiatry*, 111 (1965a), 815–821.
———. "On the Genesis of Male Homosexuality: an Attempt at Clarifying the Role of the Parents." *British Journal of Psychiatry*, 111 (1965b), 803–813.
Benfari, R. C. "Relationship between Early Dependence Training and Patient-Therapist Dyad." *Psychological Reports*, 25 (1969), 552–554.
Benjamin, J. D. "Approaches to a Dynamic Theory of Development. Round Table, 1949. 2. Methodological Considerations in the Validation and Elaboration of Psychoanalytical Personality Theory." *American Journal of Orthopsychiatry*, 20 (1950), 139–156.
———. "Prediction and Psychopathological Theory." In Jessner, L., and Pavenstedt E., eds., *Dynamic Psychopathology in Childhood*. New York: Grune and Stratton, 1959, pp. 6–77.
Bennett, E. M., and Cohen, L. R. "Men and Women: Personality Patterns and Contrasts." *Genetic Psychology Monographs*, 59 (1959), 101–155.
Bentler, P. M., and Prince, C. "Personality Characteristics of Male Transvestites: III." *Journal of Abnormal Psychology*, 74 (1969), 140–143.
Berdach, E., and Bakan, P. "Body Position and the Free Recall of Early Memories." *Psychotherapy: Theory, Research and Practice*, 4 (1967), 101–102.
Berezin, M. A. "The Theory of Genital Primacy in the Light of Ego Psychology." *Journal of the American Psychoanalytic Association*, 17 (1969), 968–987.
Berg, C. "The Problem of Homosexuality. Part I." *American Journal of Psychotherapy*, 10 (1956), 696–708.
———. "The Problem of Homosexuality. Part II." *American Journal of Psychotherapy*, 11 (1957), 65–79.
Berger, P. L. "Investigation of Two Theories of Neurotic Anxiety: Freud vs. Mowrer." Unpublished doctoral dissertation, University of Missouri, 1962.
Berger, R. J. "Experimental Modification of Dream Content by Meaningful Verbal Stimuli." *British Journal of Psychiatry*, 109 (1963), 722–740.
———. "Oculomotor Control: a Possible Function of REM Sleep." *Psychological Review*, 76 (1969), 144–164.
Berger, R. J., and Oswald, I. "Effects of Sleep Deprivation on Behaviour, Subsequent Sleep, and Dreaming." *Journal of Mental Science*, 108 (1962), 457–465.
Bergin, A. E. "The Evaluation of Therapeutic Outcomes." In Bergin, A. E., and Garfield S. L., eds., *Handbook of Psychotherapy and Behavior Change*. New York: Wiley, 1971, pp. 217–270.
Bergin, A. E., and Jasper, L. G. "Correlates of Empathy in Psychotherapy: a Replication." *Journal of Abnormal Psychology*, 74 (1969), 477–481.
Bergin, A. E., and Solomon, S. "Personality and Performance Correlates of Empathic Understanding in Psychotherapy." In Hart, I. T., and Tomlinson, T., eds., *New Directions in Client-Centered Therapy*. Boston: Houghton Mifflin, 1970, pp. 223–236.
Bergman, P., Malasky, C., and Zahn, T. P. "Relation of Sucking Strength to Personality Variables." *Journal of Consulting Psychology*, 31 (1967), 426–428.
———. "Oral Functions in Schizophrenia." *Journal of Nervous and Mental Disease*, 146 (1968), 351–359.
Bergmann, M. S. "Homosexuality on the Rorschach Test." *Menninger Clinic Bulletin*, 9 (1945), 78–83.
Berkowitz, L. "Experimental Investigations of Hostility Catharsis." *Journal of Consulting and Clinical Psychology*, 35 (1970), 1–7.
Bernick, N. "The Development of Children's Sexual Attitudes as Determined by the Pupil-Dilation Response." Unpublished doctoral dissertation, University of Chicago, 1966.
Bernstein, A. "Some Relations between Techniques of Feeding and Training during Infancy and Certain Behavior in Childhood." *Genetic Psychology Monographs*, 51 (1955), 3–44.
Bernstein, L., and Chase, P. H. "The Discriminative Ability of the Blacky Pictures with Ulcer Patients." *Journal of Consulting Psychology*, 19 (1955), 377–380.
Bertrand, S., and Masling, J. "Oral Imagery and Alcoholism." *Journal of Abnormal Psychology*, 74 (1969), 50–53.

Betz, B. J. "Bases of Therapeutic Leadership in Psychotherapy with the Schizophrenic Patient." *American Journal of Psychotherapy,* 17 (1963), 196–212.

______. "The Problem-Solving Approach and Therapeutic Effectiveness." *American Journal of Psychotherapy,* 20 (1966), 45–56.

______. "Studies of the Therapist's Role in the Treatment of the Schizophrenic Patient." *American Journal of Psychiatry,* 123 (1967), 963–971.

Beutler, L. E., Johnson, D. T., Neville, C. W., Jr., and Workman, S. N. "Effort Expended in Seeking Treatment as a Determiner of Treatment Evaluation and Outcome: the Honor of a Prophet in His Own Country." *Journal of Consulting and Clinical Psychology,* 39 (1972), 495–500.

Bevan, W. "Subliminal Stimulation: a Pervasive Problem for Psychology." *Psychological Bulletin,* 61 (1964), 81–99.

Biddle, W. E. "Investigation of the Oedipus Phantasy by Hypnosis." *American Journal of Psychiatry,* 114 (1957), 175.

______. "Images." *Archives of General Psychiatry,* 9 (1963), 464–470.

Bieber, L., Dain, H. J., Dince, P. R., Drellich, M. G., Grand, H. G., Gundlach, R. H., Kremer, M. W., Rifkin, A. H., Wilbur, C. B., and Bieber, T. B. *Homosexuality: A Psychoanalytic Study of Male Homosexuals.* New York: Basic Books, 1962.

Bieliauskas, V. J. "Recent Advances in the Psychology of Masculinity and Femininity." *Journal of Psychology,* 60 (1965), 255–263.

Bieri, J., Lobeck, R., and Galinsky, M. D. "A Comparison of Direct, Indirect, and Fantasy Measures of Identification." *Journal of Abnormal and Social Psychology,* 58 (1959), 253–258.

Bierman, R. "Dimensions of Interpersonal Facilitation in Psychotherapy and Child Development." *Psychological Bulletin,* 72 (1969), 338–352.

Biles, D. "Birth Order and Delinquency." *Australian Psychologist,* 6 (1971), 189–193.

Biller, H. B. "Father Dominance and Sex-Role Development in Kindergarten-Age Boys." *Developmental Psychology,* 1 (1969), 87–94.

______. *Father, Child, and Sex Role.* Lexington, Mass.: Heath, 1971.

Biller, H. B., and Barry, W. "Sex-Role Patterns, Paternal Similarity, and Personality Adjustment in College Males." *Developmental Psychology,* 4 (1971), 107.

Biller, H. B., and Borstelmann, L. J. "Masculine Development: an Integrative Review." *Merrill-Palmer Quarterly,* 13 (1967), 253–294.

Binder, J. L. "The Relative Proneness to Shame or Guilt as a Dimension of Character Style." Unpublished doctoral dissertation, University of Michigan, 1970.

Bird, C., and Monachesi, E. D. "Prejudice and Discontent." *Journal of Abnormal and Social Psychology,* 49 (1954), 29–35.

Bishop, F. V. "Anality, Privation, and Dissonance." Unpublished doctoral dissertation, New York University, 1965.

______. "The Anal Character: a Rebel in the Dissonance Family." *Journal of Personality and Social Psychology,* 6 (1967), 23–36.

Blatt, S. J. "An Attempt to Define Mental Health." *Journal of Consulting Psychology,* 28 (1964), 146–153.

Blau, T. H., and Blau, L. R. "The Sucking Reflex: The Effects of Long Feeding vs. Short Feeding on the Behavior of a Human Infant." *Journal of Abnormal and Social Psychology,* 51 (1955), 123–125.

Bliss, E. L., Clark, L. D., and West, C. D. "Studies of Sleep Deprivation—Relationship to Schizophrenia." *Archives of Neurology and Psychiatry,* 81 (1959), 348–359.

Bloch, E. L., and Goodstein, L. D. "Body-Product Attitudes as a Function of Repression-Sensitization." *Perceptual and Motor Skills,* 28 (1969), 476–478.

Block, W. E., and Ventur, P. A. "A Study of the Psychoanalytic Concept of Castration Anxiety in Symbolically Castrated Amputees." *Psychiatric Quarterly,* 37 (1963), 518–526.

Blondel, G. "An Investigation into the Relationship Between the Rorschach Test and the First Dream in Therapy." Unpublished doctoral dissertation, New York University, 1958.

Blum, E. M. "The Young Rebel: Self-Regard and Ego-Ideal." *Journal of Consulting Psychology,* 23 (1959), 44–50.

______. "Psychoanalytic Views on Alcoholism: A Review." *Quarterly Journal of Studies on Alcohol,* 27 (1966), 259–299.

Blum, G. S. "A Study of the Psychoanalytic Theory of Psychosexual Development." *Genetic Psychology Monographs,* 39 (1949), 3–99.
———. "A Reply to Seward's Psychoanalysis, Deductive Method, and the Blacky Test." *Journal of Abnormal and Social Psychology,* 45 (1950), 536–537.
———. "An Experimental Reunion of Psychoanalytic Theory with Perceptual Vigilance and Defense." *Journal of Abnormal and Social Psychology,* 49 (1954), 94–98.
———. "Perceptual Defense Revisited." *Journal of Abnormal and Social Psychology,* 51 (1955), 24–29.
———. "Defense Preferences among University Students in Denmark, France, Germany, and Israel." *Journal of Projective Techniques and Personality Assessment,* 28 (1964), 13–19.
Blum, G. S., and Hunt, H. F. "The Validity of the Blacky Pictures." *Psychological Bulletin,* 49 (1952), 238–250.
Blum, G. S., and Kaufman, J. B. "Two Patterns of Personality Dynamics in Male Peptic Ulcer Patients as Suggested by Responses to the Blacky Pictures." *Journal of Clinical Psychology,* 8 (1952), 273–278.
Blum, G. S., and Miller, D. R. "Exploring the Psychoanalytic Theory of the 'Oral Character.'" *Journal of Personality,* 20 (1952), 287–304.
Blumberg, S., and Maher, B. A. "Trait Attribution as a Study of Freudian Projection." *Journal of Social Psychology,* 65 (1965), 311–316.
Bobbitt, Ruth A. "The Repression Hypothesis Studied in a Situation of Hypnotically Induced Conflict." *Journal of Abnormal and Social Psychology,* 56 (1958), 204–212.
Bodin, A. M., and Geer, J. H. "Association Responses of Depressed and Non-Depressed Patients to Words of Three Hostility Levels." *Journal of Personality,* 33 (1965), 392–408.
Bohn, M. J., Jr. "Therapist Responses to Hostility and Dependency as a Function of Training." *Journal of Consulting Psychology,* 31 (1967), 195–198.
Bokert, E. G. "The Effects of Thirst and a Related Verbal Stimulus on Dream Reports." *Dissertation Abstracts,* 28 (1968), 4753b.
Bolgar, H. "Consistency of Affect and Symbolic Expression: a Comparison between Dreams and Rorschach Responses." *American Journal of Orthopsychiatry,* 24 (1954), 538–545.
Bolin, B. J. "An Investigation of Relationship between Birth-Duration and Childhood Anxieties." *Journal of Mental Science,* 105 (1959), 1045–1052.
Bombard, J. A. "An Experimental Examination of Penis Envy." Unpublished doctoral dissertation, Wayne State University, 1969.
Bone, R. N. "Extraversion, Neuroticism and Dream Recall." *Psychological Reports,* 23 (1968), 922.
Bone, R. N., and Belcher, M. M. "The Differential Relationship of Questionnaire and Diary Dream Recall to the Sixteen Personality Factor Inventory." Presented at West Virginia Academy of Sciences, April, 1972.
———. "Dream Report Ratings and Pearson's Novelty Experiencing Scale." Presented at annual meeting of Association for the Psychophysiological Study of Sleep, 1972.
Bone, R. N., Belcher, M. M., Thomas, W., and Calef, R. S. "Extraversion, Neuroticism, Psychoticism and Recurrent Dream Ratings." Presented at annual meeting of the Association for the Psychophysiological Study of Sleep, 1972.
Bone, R. N., Betts, R. R., Calef, R. S., Cowling, L. W., and Ivey, E. "Personality Correlates of Nighmare Frequency." Presented at annual meeting of Association for the Psychophysiological Study of Sleep, 1973.
———. "Personality Correlates and the Recurrent Dreamer." Presented at annual meeting of the Association for the Psychophysiological Study of Sleep, 1973.
Bone, R. N., Bottis, R. A., Maraffi, C. K., Conner, H., Jr., and Calef, R. S. "Extraversion, Neuroticism, Psychoticism and Dimensions of Dreaming." Presented at annual meeting of the Association for the Psychophysiological Study of Sleep, 1971.
Bone, R. N., Carlson, R. J., and Johnson, C. "The Relationship of Sex Differences in Dream Recall to the Sixteen Personality Factor Questionnaire." Presented at annual meeting of the Association for the Psychophysiological Study of Sleep, 1970.
Bone, R. N., Choban, M. C., and McAllister, D. S. "The Relationship of Stroop Color Word Interference to Dream Recall." Presented at annual meeting of the Association for the Psychophysiological Study of Sleep, 1971.

Bone, R. N., Cogan, R. T., Bettis, R. A., Ptaszkiewicz, J., and Calef, R. S. "Introversion, Extraversion, Dreams and Jung." Presented at annual meeting of the Association for the Psychophysiological Study of Sleep, 1973.

Bone, R. N., Cogan, R. T., Nawara, D. D., and Calef, R. S. "Tolerance for Ambiguity and Two Measures of Dream Recall." Presented at annual meeting of the Association for the Psychophysiological Study of Sleep, 1972.

Bone, R. N., and Corlett, F. "Brief Report: Frequency of Dream Recall, Creativity, and a Control for Anxiety." *Psychological Reports,* 22 (1968), 1355–1356.

Bone, R. N., Gogates, A., Jr., and Calef, R. S. "The Differential Relationship of Novelty Seeking to Dream Recall." Presented at annual meeting of the Association for the Psychophysiological Study of Sleep, 1971.

Bone, R. N., Hopkins, D. C., Calef, R. S., and Cowling, L. W. "Dream Recall and Openness to Experience." Presented at annual meeting of the Association for the Psychophysiological Study of Sleep, 1973.

Bone, R. N., Kesecker, Mary P., and Calef, R. S. "Recurrent Dreaming and the Sixteen Personality Factor Questionnaire." Presented at annual meeting of the Association for the Psychophysiological Study of Sleep, 1973.

Bone, R. N., McIntyre, C. L., Buttermore, G., Jr., and Calef, R. S. "Volunteering for Sleep and Dream Research and Dream Recall." Presented at annual meeting of Association for the Psychophysiological Study of Sleep, 1973.

Bone, R. N., Murray, D. W., Jr., Rancy, R. W., and Calef, R. S. "Recurrent Dreams, Sex Differences and Dimensions of Dreaming." Presented at annual meeting of Association for the Psychophysiological Study of Sleep, 1973.

Bone, R. N., Nelson, A. E., and McAllister, D. S. "Dream Recall and Repression-Sensitization. *Psychological Reports,* 27 (1970), 766.

Bone, R. N., Thomas, T. A., and Kinsolving, D. L. "Relationship of Rod-and-Frame Scores to Dream Recall." *Psychological Reports,* 30 (1972), 58.

Bonner, H. "The Problem of Diagnosis in Paranoic Disorder." *American Journal of Psychiatry,* 107 (1951), 677–683.

Bookbinder, L. J. "Simple Conditioning versus the Dynamic Approach to Symptoms and Symptom Substitution: a Reply to Yates." *Psychological Reports,* 10 (1962), 71–77.

Bookhammer, R. S., Meyers, R. W., Schober, C. C., and Piotrowski, Z. A. "A Five-Year Clinical Follow-up Study of Schizophrenics Treated by Rosen's 'Direct Analysis' Compared with Controls." *American Journal of Psychiatry,* 123 (1966), 602–604.

Bordin, E. S. "Free Association: an Experimental Analogue of the Psychoanalytic Situation." In Gottschalk, L. A., and Auerbach, A., eds., *Methods of Research in Psychotherapy.* New York: Appleton-Century-Crofts, 1966a, pp. 189–208.

______. "Personality and Free Association." *Journal of Consulting Psychology,* 30 (1966b), 30–38.

Bourguignon, E. E. "Dreams and Dream Interpretation in Haiti." *American Anthropologist,* 56 (1954), 262–268.

Braaten, L. J., and Darling, C. D. "Overt and Covert Homosexual Problems among Male College Students." *Genetic Psychology Monographs,* 71 (1965), 269–310.

Bradford, J. L. "Sex Differences in Anxiety." Unpublished doctoral dissertation, University of Minnesota, 1968.

Brady, J. P. "Psychotherapy, Learning Theory, and Insight." *Archives of General Psychiatry,* 16 (1967), 304–311.

Bramel, D. "A Dissonance Theory Approach to Defensive Projection." *Journal of Abnormal and Social Psychology,* 64 (1962), 121–129.

Brandt, L. W. "Studies of 'Dropout' Patients in Psychotherapy: a Review of Findings." *Psychotherapy: Theory, Research and Practice,* 2 (1965), 6–12.

Brar, H. S. "Semantic Differential Investigation of Sexually Symbolic Concepts Using a Psychiatric Population." *Journal of Personality Assessment,* 37 (1973), 260–262.

Breger, L., Hunter, I., and Lane, R. W. "The Effect of Stress on Dreams." *Psychological Issues,* 7 (1971), Monograph 27.

Brender, W. J., and Kramer, E. "A Comparative Need Analysis of Immediately-Recalled Dreams and TAT Responses." *Journal of Projective Techniques and Personality Assessment,* 31 (1967), 74–77.

Brener, E. M. "Castration Anxiety, Sexual Fantasy, and Sexual Adjustment." Unpublished doctoral dissertation, Boston University Graduate School, 1969.

Brenneis, C. B. "Male and Female Ego Modalities in Manifest Dream Content." *Journal of Abnormal Psychology,* 76 (1970), 434–442.

———. "Factors Affecting Diagnostic Judgments of Manifest Dream Content in Schizophrenia." *Psychological Reports,* 29 (1971), 811–818.

Brenner, C. "Psychoanalysis and Science." *Journal of the American Psychoanalytic Association,* 16 (1968), 675–696.

Breuer, J., and Freud, S. *Studies on Hysteria (1893–1895).* In J. Strachey, ed. (in collaboration with A. Freud), *The Standard Edition of the Complete Psychological Works of Sigmund Freud.* London: Hogarth, 1955, Vol. 2, pp. 1–311.

Brickman, H. R., Schwartz, D. A., and Doran, S. M. "The Psychoanalyst as a Community Psychiatrist." *American Journal of Psychiatry,* 122 (1966), 1081–1087.

Brill, N. Q., Koegler, R. R., Epstein, L. J., and Forgy, E. W. "Controlled Study of Psychiatric Outpatient Treatment." *Archives of General Psychiatry,* 10 (1964), 581–595.

Briskin, G. J. "Identification in Group Therapy." *Journal of Abnormal and Social Psychology,* 56 (1958), 195–198.

Brodbeck, A. J. "Learning Theory and Identification: IV. Oedipal Motivation as a Determinant of Conscious Development." *Journal of Genetic Psychology,* 84 (1954), 219–227.

Brody, B. "Freud's Case-Load." *Psychotherapy: Theory, Research and Practice,* 7 (1970), 8–12.

Brody, E. B. "Continuing Problems in the Relationship between Training in Psychiatry and in Psychoanalysis in the U.S.A." *Journal of Nervous and Mental Disease,* 136 (1963), 58–67.

Bromberg, P. M. "The Effects of Fear and Two Modes of Anxiety on Social Affiliation and Phobic Ideation." Unpublished doctoral dissertation, New York University, 1967.

Bronfenbrenner, U. "Freudian Theories of Identification and their Derivatives." *Child Development,* 31 (1960), 15–40.

Bronson, Wanda C. "Dimensions of Ego and Infantile Identification." *Journal of Personality,* 27 (1959), 532–545.

Brooks, J. "The Insecure Personality: a Factor Analytic Study." *British Journal of Medical Psychology,* 42 (1969), 395–403.

Brosin, H. W. "Validation of Psychoanalytic Theory." *Journal of the American Psychoanalytic Association,* 3 (1955), 489–495.

Brown, D. G. "Sex-Role Preference in Young Children." *Psychological Monographs,* 70 (1956), No. 421.

———. "The Development of Sex-Role Inversion and Homosexuality." *Journal of Pediatrics,* 50 (1957), 613–619.

———. "Sex-Role Development in a Changing Culture." *Psychological Bulletin,* 55 (1958), 232–242.

———. "Homosexuality and Family Dynamics." *Bulletin of the Menninger Clinic,* 27 (1963), 227–232.

Brown, D. G., and Tolor, A. "Human Figure Drawings as Indicators of Sexual Identification and Inversion." *Perceptual and Motor Skills,* 7 (1957), 199–211.

Brown, J. S., and Kosterlitz, N. "Selection and Treatment of Psychiatric Outpatients." *Archives of General Psychiatry,* 11 (1964), 425–438.

Browning, J. S., and Houseworth, J. H. "Development of New Symptoms Following Medical and Surgical Treatment of Duodenal Ulcer." *Psychosomatic Medicine,* 15 (1953), 328–336.

Bruner, J. S., and Tagiuri, R. "The Perception of People." In G. Lindzey, ed., *Handbook of Social Psychology,* Vol. 2. Cambridge, Mass.: Addison-Wesley, 1954, pp. 634–654.

Brunkan, R. J. "Perceived Parental Attitudes and Parental Identification in Relation to Field of Vocational Choice." *Journal of Counseling Psychology,* 12 (1965), 39–47.

Brush, F. R., Bush, R. R., Jenkins, W. O., John, W. F., and Whiting, J. W. M. "Stimulus Generalization after Extinction and Punishment: an Experimental Study of Displacement." *Journal of Abnormal and Social Psychology,* 47 (1952), 633–640.

Burdock, E. I., Cheek, F., and Zubin, J. "Predicting Success in Psychoanalytic Training. In Hoch, P. H., and Zubin, J., eds., *Current Approaches to Psychoanalysis. Proceedings of the 48th Annual Meeting of the American Psychopathological Association.* New York: Grune and Stratton, 1960, pp. 176–191.

Burgess, M. M., Reivich, R. S., and Silverman, J. J. "Effects of Frustration and Aggression on Physiological Arousal Level in Depressed Subjects." *Perceptual and Motor Skills,* 27 (1968), 743–749.
Burnell, G. M., and Solomon, G. F. "Early Memories and Ego Function." *Archives of General Psychiatry,* 11 (1964), 556–567.
Burnham, R. K. "The Relationship of Personality to Oral Conditions in Children: an Evaluation by Means of the Rorschach and the Blacky Test." Unpublished doctoral dissertation, New York University, 1957.
Burns, B. P. "The Activation of Posthypnotic Conflict via Free Imagery: a Study of Repression and Psychopathology." Unpublished doctoral dissertation, Michigan State University, 1972.
Burton, R. V., Maccoby, E. E., and Allinsmith, W. "Antecedents of Resistance to Temptation in Four-Year-Old Children." *Child Development,* 32 (1961), 689–710.
Busch, F. "Transference in Psychological Testing." *Journal of Projective Techniques and Personality Assessment,* 32 (1968), 509–512.
Bush, R. R., and Whiting, J. W. M. "On the Theory of Psychoanalytic Displacement." *Journal of Abnormal and Social Psychology,* 48 (1953), 261–272.
Buss, A. H., and Brock, T. C. "Repression and Guilt in Relation to Aggression." *Journal of Abnormal and Social Psychology,* 66 (1963), 345–350.
Butler, J. R. "Behavioral Analysis of Psychoanalytically Derived Interpretations Presented on Operant Schedules of Reinforcement." Unpublished doctoral dissertation, Louisiana State University, 1962.
Butler, R. P., and Bieliauskas, V. J. "Performance of Paranoid Schizophrenics and Passive-Aggressives on Two Masculinity-Femininity Tests." *Psychological Reports,* 31 (1972), 251–254.
Butterfield, E. C. "The Interruption of Tasks: Methodological, Factual, and Theoretical Issues." *Psychological Bulletin,* 62 (1964), 309–322.
Bychowski, G. "Psychosis Precipitated by Psychoanalysis." *Psychoanalytic Quarterly,* 35 (1966), 327–339.
Byrne, D. "The Relationship between Humor and the Expression of Hostility." *Journal of Abnormal and Social Psychology,* 53 (1956), 84–89.
______. "Drive Level, Response to Humor, and the Cartoon Sequence Effect." *Psychological Reports,* 4 (1958), 439–442.
______. "Repression-Sensitization as a Dimension of Personality." *Progress in Experimental Personality Research,* 1 (1964), 169–220.
______. "Parental Antecedents of Authoritarianism." *Journal of Personality and Social Psychology,* 1 (1965), 369–373.
Byrne, D., and Sheffield, J. "Response to Sexually Arousing Stimuli as a Function of Repressing and Sensitizing Defenses." *Journal of Abnormal Psychology,* 70 (1965), 114–118.
Byrne, D., Steinberg, M. A., and Schwartz, M. S. "Relationship between Repression-Sensitization and Physical Illness." *Journal of Abnormal Psychology,* 73 (1968), 154–155.
Cahoon, D. D. "Symptom Substitution and the Behavior Therapies: a Reappraisal." *Psychological Bulletin,* 69 (1968), 149–156.
Caine, T. M. "The Expression of Hostility and Guilt in Melancholic and Paranoid Women." *Journal of Consulting Psychology,* 24 (1960), 18–22.
Cairns, R. B., and Lewis, M. "Dependency and the Reinforcement Value of a Verbal Stimulus." *Journal of Consulting Psychology,* 26 (1962), 1–8.
Caldwell, B. M. "The Effects of Infant Care." In Hoffman, M. L., and Hoffman, L. W., eds., *Review of Child Development.* New York: Russell Sage Foundation, 1964, pp. 9–87.
Cameron, P. "Confirmation of the Freudian Psychosexual Stages Utilizing Sexual Symbolism." *Psychological Reports,* 21 (1967), 33–39.
Campbell, E. H. "The Social-Sex Development of Children." *Genetic Psychology Monographs,* 21 (1939), 461–552.
Campos, L. P. "Relationship between Time Estimation and Retentive Personality Traits." *Perceptual and Motor Skills,* 23 (1966), 59–62.
Canestrari, R. E., Jr. "Spatial Stimulus Generalization Gradients and Id, Ego, and Superego Strength. *Perceptual and Motor Skills,* 19 (1964), 51–55.

Cansever, G. "Psychological Effects of Circumcision." *British Journal of Medical Psychology,* 38 (1965), 321–331.

Cantor, J. R., and Zillmann, D. "Resentment toward Victimized Protagonists and Severity of Misfortunes They Suffer as Factors in Humor Appreciation." *Journal of Experimental Research in Personality,* 6 (1973), 321–329.

Cappon, D. "Morphology and Other Parameters of Phantasy in the Schizophrenias." *Archives of General Psychiatry,* 1 (1959), 33–50.

———. "Results of Psychotherapy." *British Journal of Psychiatry,* 110 (1964), 35–45.

Carden, N. L., and Schramel, D. J. "Observations of Conversion Reactions Seen in Troops Involved in the Viet Nam Conflict." *American Journal of Psychiatry,* 123 (1966), 21–31.

Caron, A. J., and Wallach, M. A. "Recall of Interrupted Tasks under Stress: a Phenomenon of Memory or of Learning?" *Journal of Abnormal and Social Psychology,* 55 (1957), 372–381.

Carp, F. M. "Psychosexual Development of Stutterers." *Journal of Projective Techniques,* 26 (1962), 388–391.

Carpenter, S. I. S. "Psychosexual Conflict, Defense, and Abstraction." Unpublished doctoral dissertation, University of Michigan, 1965.

Carr, J. E. "Differentiation Similarity of Patient and Therapist and the Outcome of Psychotherapy." *Journal of Abnormal Psychology,* 76 (1970), 361–369.

Carrington, P. "Dreams and Schizophrenia." *Archives of General Psychiatry,* 26 (1972), 343–350.

Carroll, D., Lewis, S. A., and Oswald, I. "Effect of Barbiturates on Dream Content." *Nature,* 223 (1969), 865–866.

Carstairs, G. M., and Grygier, T. G. "Anthropological, Psychometric, and Psychotherapeutic Aspects of Homosexuality." *Bulletin of British Psychological Society,* 32 (1957), 46–47.

Cartwright, D. S. "Effectiveness of Psychotherapy: a Critique of the Spontaneous Remission Argument." *Journal of Counseling Psychology,* 2 (1955a), 290–296.

———. "Success in Psychotherapy as a Function of Certain Actuarial Variables." *Journal of Consulting Psychology,* 19 (1955b), 357–363.

———. "Note on 'Changes in Psychoneurotic Patients with and without Psychotherapy.' " *Journal of Consulting Psychology,* 20 (1956), 403–404.

Cartwright, D. S., Robertson, R. J., Fiske, D. W., and Kirtner, W. L. "Length of Therapy in Relation to Outcome and Change in Personal Integration." *Journal of Consulting Psychology,* 25 (1961), 84–88.

Cartwright, R. D. "A Comparison of the Response to Psychoanalytic and Client-Centered Psychotherapy." In Gottschalk, L. A., and Auerbach, A. A., eds., *Methods of Research in Psychotherapy.* New York: Appleton-Century-Crofts, 1966a, pp. 517–529.

———. "Dream and Drug-Induced Fantasy Behavior." *Archives of General Psychiatry,* 15 (1966b), 7–15.

———. "Sleep Fantasy in Normal and Schizophrenic Persons." *Journal of Abnormal Psychology,* 80 (1972), 275–279.

———. "The Influence of a Conscious Wish on Dreams: a Methodological Study of Dream Meaning and Function." *Journal of Abnormal Psychology,* 83 (1974), 387–393.

Cartwright, R. D., Bernick, N., Borowitz, G., and Kling, A. "Effect of an Erotic Movie on the Sleep and Dreams of Young Men." *Archives of General Psychiatry,* 20 (1969), 262–271.

Cartwright, R. D., and Monroe, L. J. "Relation of Dreaming and REM Sleep: the Effects of REM Deprivation under Two Conditions." *Journal of Personality and Social Psychology,* 10 (1968), 69–74.

Cartwright, R. D., Monroe, L. J., and Palmer, C. "Individual Differences in Response to REM Deprivation." *Archives of General Psychiatry,* 16 (1967), 297–303.

Cartwright, R. D., and Ratzel, R. "Light and Deep Sleeper Differences: Fantasy Scores from REM, Stage 2 and REM Deprivation Awakenings." *Psychophysiology,* 7 (1971), 331.

———. "Effects of Dream Loss on Waking Behaviors." *Archives of General Psychiatry,* 27 (1972), 277–280.

Castaldo, V., and Holzman, P. S. "The Effects of Hearing One's Own Voice on Sleep Mentation." *Journal of Nervous and Mental Disease,* 144 (1967), 2–13.

Cattell, R. B. *Personality and Motivation Structure and Measurement.* Yonkers: New World, 1957.

Cattell, R. B., and Luborsky, L. B. "Personality Factors in Response to Humor." *Journal of Abnormal and Social Psychology,* 42 (1947), 402–421.

Cattell, R. B., and Morony, J. H. "The Use of the 16 PF in Distinguishing Homosexuals, Normals, and General Criminals." *Journal of Consulting Psychology,* 26 (1962), 531–540.

Cattell, R. B., and Warburton, F. W. *Objective Personality and Motivation Tests.* Urbana: University of Illinois, 1967.

Cautela, J. H. "Desensitization and Insight." *Behavior Research and Therapy,* 3 (1965), 59–64.

Cava, Esther L., and Raush, H. L. "Identification and the Adolescent Boy's Perception of His Father." *Journal of Abnormal and Social Psychology,* 47 (1952), 855–856.

Cazavelan, J., and Epstein, S. "Daydreams of Female Paranoid Schizophrenics." *Journal of Clinical Psychology,* 22 (1966), 27–32.

Centers, R. "The Anal Character and Social Severity in Attitudes." *Journal of Projective Techniques and Personality Assessment,* 33 (1969), 501–506.

Chamandy, V. "The Differentiation of Paranoid and Nonparanoid Schizophrenia on the Basis of Interpersonal Style and Level of Premorbid Adjustment." Unpublished doctoral dissertation, Catholic University of America, 1972.

Chambers, J. L., and Broussard, L. J. "Need-Attitudes of Normal and Paranoid Schizophrenic Males." *Journal of Clinical Psychology,* 16 (1960), 233–237.

Chance, E. "A Study of Transference in Group Psychotherapy." *International Journal of Group Psychotherapy,* 2 (1952), 40–53.

Chang, J., and Block, J. "A Study of Identification in Male Homosexuals." *Journal of Consulting Psychology,* 24 (1960), 307–310.

Chang, S. C. "Dream-Recall and Themes of Hospitalized Schizophrenics." *Archives of General Psychiatry,* 10 (1964), 119–122.

Chapman, L. J., Burstein, A. G., Day, D., and Verdone, P. "Regression and Disorders of Thought." *Journal of Abnormal and Social Psychology,* 63 (1961), 540–545.

Chapman, L. J., and Chapman, J. P. "Genesis of Popular but Erroneous Psychodiagnostic Observations." *Journal of Abnormal Psychology,* 72 (1967), 193–204.

______. "Illusory Correlation as an Obstacle to the Use of Valid Psychodiagnostic Signs." *Journal of Abnormal Psychology,* 74 (1969), 271–280.

Chase, P. H. "A Note on Projection." *Psychological Bulletin,* 57 (1960), 289–290.

Chertok, L. "Tensions among Psychotherapists." *American Journal of Psychiatry,* 121 (1965), 1106–1108.

Chess, S., Thomas, A., Birch, H. G., and Hertzig, M. "Implications of a Longitudinal Study of Child Development for Child Psychiatry." *American Journal of Psychiatry,* 117 (1960), 434–441.

Chessick, R. D. "Use of the Couch in the Psychotherapy of Borderline Patients." *Archives of General Psychiatry,* 25 (1971), 306–313.

Child, I. L., Cooperman, M., and Wolowitz, H. M. "Esthetic Preference and other Correlates of Active versus Passive Food Preference." *Journal of Personality and Social Psychology,* 11 (1969), 75–84.

Childers, A. T., and Hamil, B. M. "Emotional Problems in Children as Related to the Duration of Breast Feeding in Infancy." *American Journal of Orthopsychiatry,* 2 (1932), 134–142.

Childers, R. T., Jr. "Prognostic Significance of Insight in Schizophrenia." *American Journal of Psychiatry,* 119 (1962), 361–362.

Chodoff, P. "A Critique of Freud's Theory of Infantile Sexuality." *American Journal of Psychiatry,* 123 (1966), 507–518.

Chodoff, P., and Lyons, H. "Hysteria, the Hysterical Personality and 'Hysterical' Conversion." *American Journal of Psychiatry,* 114 (1958), 734–740.

Chodorkoff, B., and Cooke, G. "Development of an Inventory to Measure Psychosexual Development." *Psychological Reports,* 27 (1970), 186.

Clark, D. R. "The Treatment of Monosymptomatic Phobia by Systematic Desensitization." *Behaviour Research and Therapy,* 1 (1963), 63–68.

Clark, R. A., and Sensibar, M. R. "The Relationship between Symbolic and Manifest Projections of Sexuality with some Incidental Correlates." *Journal of Abnormal and Social Psychology,* 50 (1955), 327–334.

Clark, T. R., and Epstein, R. "Self-Concept and Expectancy for Social Reinforcement in Noninstitutionalized Male Homosexuals." *Journal of Consulting and Clinical Psychology,* 38 (1972), 174–180.

Clemes, S. "Repression and Hypnotic Amnesia." *Journal of Abnormal and Social Psychology,* 69 (1964), 62–69.

Clemes, S. R., and Dement, W. C. "Effect of REM Sleep Deprivation on Psychological Functioning." *Journal of Nervous and Mental Disease,* 144 (1967), 485–491.

Clum, G. A., and Clum, J. "Choice of Defense Mechanisms and Their Relationship to Mood Level." *Psychological Reports,* 32 (1973a), 507–510.

———. "Mood Variability and Defense Mechanism Preference." *Psychological Reports,* 32 (1973b), 910.

Cochrane, C. T. "Effects of Diagnostic Information on Empathic Understanding by the Therapist in a Psychotherapy Analogue." *Journal of Consulting and Clinical Psychology,* 38 (1972), 359–365.

Cofer, D. H. "Identification of the Depressive Personality as a Function of Perception of Parental Attitudes, Feelings, and Reactions." Unpublished doctoral dissertation, Rutgers University, The State University of New Jersey, 1972.

Cohen, A. R. "Experimental Effects of Ego-Defense Preference on Interpersonal Relations." *Journal of Abnormal and Social Psychology,* 52 (1956), 19–29.

Cohen, D. B. "Frequency of Dream Recall Estimated by Three Methods and Related to Defense Preference and Anxiety." *Journal of Consulting and Clinical Psychology,* 33 (1969), 661–667.

———. "Current Research on the Frequency of Dream Recall." *Psychological Bulletin,* 73 (1970), 433–440.

———. "Dream Recall and Short-Term Memory." *Perceptual and Motor Skills,* 33 (1971), 867–871.

———. "Presleep Experience and Home Dream Reporting: an Exploratory Study." *Journal of Consulting and Clinical Psychology,* 38 (1972), 122–128.

———. "Sex Role Orientation and Dream Recall." *Journal of Abnormal Psychology,* 82 (1973), 246–252.

Colby, K. M. *An Introduction to Psychoanalytic Research.* New York: Basic Books, 1960a.

———. "Experiment on the Effects of an Observer's Presence on the Image System during Psychoanalytic Free-Association." *Behavioral Science,* 5 (1960b), 216–232.

———. "On the Greater Amplifying Power of Causal-Correlative over Interrogative Inputs on Free Association in an Experimental Psychoanalytic Situation." *Journal of Nervous and Mental Disease,* 133 (1961), 233–239.

———. "Sex Differences in Dreams of Primitive Tribes." *American Anthropologist,* 65 (1963), 1116–1122.

Cole, N. J. "Psychiatrists, Employers, and Information Exchange." *Archives of General Psychiatry,* 25 (1971), 381–384.

Cole, N. J., Branch, C. H., and Allison, R. B. "Some Relationships between Social Class and the Practice of Dynamic Psychotherapy." *American Journal of Psychiatry,* 118 (1962), 1004–1012.

Collier, R. M. "A Scale for Rating the Responses of the Psychotherapist." *Journal of Consulting Psychology,* 17 (1953), 321–326.

———. "Consciousness as a Regulatory Field: a Theory of Psychotherapy." *Journal of Abnormal and Social Psychology,* 55 (1957), 275–282.

Collins, G. W. "Dreaming and Adaptation to Stress." Unpublished doctoral dissertation, University of Oregon, 1966.

Collins, L. G. "Pain Sensitivity and Ratings of Childhood Experience." *Perceptual and Motor Skills,* 21 (1965), 349–350.

Compton, A. "A Study of the Psychoanalytic Theory of Anxiety. I. The Development of Freud's Theory of Anxiety." *Journal of the American Psychoanalytic Association,* 20 (1972), 3–44.

Comrey, A. L. "Factored Homogeneous Item Dimensions in Personality Research." *Educational and Psychological Measurement,* 21 (1961), 419–431.

———. "A Study of 35 Personality Dimensions." *Educational and Psychological Measurement,* 22 (1962), 543–552.

______. "Scales for Measuring Compulsion, Hostility, Neuroticism and Shyness." *Psychological Reports,* 16 (1965), 697–700.

______. "Comparison of Personality and Attitude Variables." *Educational and Psychological Measurement,* 26 (1966), 853–860.

Comrey, A. L., and Jamison, K. "Verification of Six Personality Factors." *Educational and Psychological Measurement,* 26 (1966), 945–953.

Condon, W. S. "The Freudian Model of Human Nature." Unpublished doctoral dissertation, University of Pittsburgh, 1962.

Conrad, D. C. "An Empirical Study of the Concept of Psychotherapeutic Success." *Journal of Consulting Psychology,* 16 (1952), 92–97.

Conrad, E. H. "Psychogenic Obesity: the Effects of Social Rejection upon Hunger, Food Craving, Food Consumption, and the Drive-Reduction Value of Eating for Obese versus Normal Individuals." Unpublished doctoral dissertation, New York University, 1969.

Cooke, G., and Chodorkoff, B. "Reliability of Classification of Behaviors within Psychosexual Stages." *Psychological Reports,* 26 (1970), 751–754.

Coons, W. H. "Interaction and Insight in Group Psychotherapy." *Canadian Journal of Psychology,* 11 (1957), 1–8.

Cooper, A. M., Karush, A., Easser, B. R., and Swerdloff, B. "The Adaptive Balance Profile and Prediction of Early Treatment Behavior." In Goldman, G., and Shapiro, S., eds., *Developments in Psychoanalysis at Columbia University.* New York: Hafner, 1966, pp. 183–214.

Cooperman, M., and Child, I. L. "Relation of Esthetic Sensitivity to Psychoanalytic Character Traits." Presented at annual meeting of American Psychological Association, San Francisco, 1968.

______. "Differential Effects of Positive and Negative Reinforcement on Two Psychoanalytic Character Types." *Journal of Consulting and Clinical Psychology,* 37 (1971), 57–59.

Coriat, I. H. "Some Statistical Results of the Psychoanalytic Treatment of the Psychoneuroses." *Psychoanalytic Review,* 4 (1917), 209–216.

Corman, H. H., Escalona, S. K., and Reiser, M. F. "Visual Imagery and Preconscious Thought Processes." *Archives of General Psychiatry,* 10 (1964), 160–172.

Coslett, S. B. "The WAIS Masculinity-Femininity Index in a Paranoid Schizophrenic Population." *Journal of Clinical Psychology,* 21 (1965), 62.

Couch, A., and Kenniston, K. "Yeasayers and Naysayers: Agreeing Response Set as a Personality Variable." *Journal of Abnormal and Social Psychology,* 60 (1960), 151–174.

Cox, F. N. "An Assessment of Children's Attitudes towards Parent Figures." *Child Development,* 33 (1962), 821–830.

Coyle, F. A., Jr. "Knee and Arm Joints in Human Figure Drawings as Indicants of Paranoid Trends: Replication and Extension." *Perceptual and Motor Skills,* 22 (1966), 317–318.

Coyne, L., and Holzman, P. S. "Three Equivalent Forms of a Semantic Differential Inventory." *Educational and Psychological Measurement,* 26 (1966), 665–674.

Cremerius, J. *Die Beurteilung des Behandlungserfolges in der Psychotherapie.* Berlin, Gottingen, Heidelberg: Springer-Verlag, 1962.

Crisp, A. H. "An Attempt to Measure an Aspect of transference." *British Journal of Medical Psychology,* 37 (1964a), 17–30.

______. "Development and Application of a Measure of 'Transference.' " *Journal of Psychosomatic Research,* 8 (1964b), 327–335.

______. " 'Transference,' 'Symptom Emergence' and 'Social Repercussion' in Behaviour Therapy. A Study of Fifty-Four Treated Patients." *British Journal of Medical Psychology,* 39 (1966), 179–196.

Cutler, R. L. "Countertransference Effects in Psychotherapy." *Journal of Consulting Psychology,* 22 (1958), 349–356.

Cutler, R. L., Bordin, E. S., Williams, J., and Rigler, D. "Psychoanalysts as Expert Observers of the Therapy Process." *Journal of Consulting Psychology,* 22 (1958), 335–340.

Dahlstrom, W. G., and Prange, A. J., Jr. "Characteristics of Depressive and Paranoid Schizophrenic Reactions on the Minnesota Multiphasic Personality Inventory." *Journal of Nervous and Mental Disease,* 131 (1960), 513–522.

Dallett, J. "Theories of Dream Function." *Psychological Bulletin,* 79 (1973), 408–416.

Dana, R. H., and Hopewell, E. "Repression and Psychopathology: a Cross-Validation Failure." *Psychological Reports,* 19 (1966), 626.
Daston, P. G. "Perception of Homosexual Words in Paranoid Schizophrenia." *Perceptual and Motor Skills,* 6 (1956), 45–55.
Davidman, H. "Evaluation of Psychoanalysis. A Clinician's View." In Hoch, P. H., and Zubin, J., eds., *The Evaluation of Psychiatric Treatment. The Proceedings of the 52nd Annual Meeting of the American Psychopathological Association.* New York: Grune and Stratton, 1964, pp. 32–44.
Davids, A. "Ego Functions in Disturbed and Normal Children: Aspiration, Inhibition, Time Estimation, and Delayed Gratification." *Journal of Consulting and Clinical Psychology,* 33 (1969), 61–70.
Davids, A., Joelson, M., and McArthur, C. "Rorschach and TAT Indices of Homosexuality in Overt Homosexuals, Neurotics, and Normal Males." *Journal of Abnormal and Social Psychology,* 53 (1956), 161–172.
Davis, H. V., Sears, R. R., Miller, H. C., and Brodbeck, A. J. "Effects of Cup, Bottle and Breast Feeding on Oral Activities of Newborn Infants." *Pediatrics,* 2 (1948), 549–558.
Davis, R. E., and Ruiz, R. A. "Infant Feeding Method and Adolescent Personality." *American Journal of Psychiatry,* 122 (1965), 673–678.
Davison, G. C. "Counter-Control in Behavior Modification." In Hamerlynck, L. A., Handy, L., and Mash, E., eds., *Critical Issues in Behavior Modification.* Champaign, Ill.: Research, 1973, pp.
Davison, G. C., and Taffel, S. J. "Effects of Behavior Therapy." Presented at annual meeting of American Psychological Association, Honolulu, 1972.
Dawson, J. G., Noblin, C. D., and Timmons, E. O. "Dynamic and Behavioral Predictors of Hypnotizability." *Journal of Consulting Psychology,* 29 (1965), 76–78.
Day, D. "Dream Interpretation as a Projective Technique." *Journal of Consulting Psychology,* 13 (1949), 416–420.
Dean, R. B., and Richardson, H. "Analysis of MMPI Profiles of Forty College-Educated Overt Male Homosexuals." *Journal of Consulting Psychology,* 28 (1964), 483–486.
DeCharms, R., Levy, J., and Wertheimer, M. "A Note on Attempted Evolutions of Psychotherapy." *Journal of Clinical Psychology,* 10 (1954), 233–235.
DeLuca, J. N. "The Structure of Homosexuality." *Journal of Projective Techniques and Personality Assessment,* 30 (1966), 187–191.
———. "Performance of Overt Male Homosexuals and Controls on the Blacky Test." *Journal of Clinical Psychology,* 23 (1967), 497.
———. "Psychosexual Conflict in Adolescent Enuretics." *Journal of Psychology,* 68 (1968), 145–149.
———. "Some Determinants of Sex-Role Identification in Young Children." Unpublished master's thesis, Brown University, 1960.
DeMartino, M. F., ed., *Dreams and Personality Dynamics.* Springfield, Ill.: Charles C. Thomas, 1959.
Dement, W. C. "Dream Recall and Eye Movements during Sleep in Schizophrenics and Normals." *Journal of Nervous and Mental Disease,* 122 (1955), 263–269.
———. "The Effect of Dream Deprivation." *Science,* 131 (1960), 1705–1707.
———. "Experimental Dream Studies." In J. H. Masserman, ed., *Science and Psychoanalysis. Scientific Proceedings of the Academy of Psychoanalysis.* New York: Grune and Stratton, 1964, pp. 129–162.
———. "Studies of the Function of Rapid Eye Movement (Paradoxical Sleep in Human Subjects)." In M. Jouvet, ed., *Aspects Anatomo-Fonctionals de la Physiologie du Sommeil.* Paris: Center National de la Recherche Scientifique, 1965.
Dement, W. C., and Fisher, C. "Experimental Interference with the Sleep Cycle." *Canadian Psychiatric Association Journal,* 8 (1963), 400–405.
Dement, W. C., Kahn, E., and Roffwarg, H. P. "The Influence of the Laboratory Situation on the Dreams of the Experimental Subject." *Journal of Nervous and Mental Disease,* 140 (1965), 119–131.
Dement, W., and Wolpert, E. A. "The Relation of Eye Movements, Body Motility, and External Stimuli to Dream Content." *Journal of Experimental Psychology,* 55 (1958a), 543–553.

———. "Relationships in the Manifest Content of Dreams Occurring on the Same Night." *Journal of Nervous and Mental Disease,* 126 (1958b), 568–578.

DeMichele, J. H. "The Interpretations of Anxiety by Various Psychotherapeutic Schools." *Journal of Consulting Psychology,* 18 (1954), 47–52.

Denker, P. G. "Results of Treatment of Psychoneuroses by the General Practitioner: a Follow-Up Study of 500 Patients." *Archives of Neurology and Psychiatry,* 57 (1947), 504–505.

Desroches, H. F., and Kaiman, B. D. "The Relationship between Dream Recall and Symptoms of Emotional Instability." *Journal of Clinical Psychology,* 20 (1964), 350–352.

Deutsch, H. "Psychoanalytic Therapy in the Light of Follow-Up." *Journal of the American Psychoanalytic Association,* 7 (1959), 445–458.

DeWolfe, A. S. "Identification and Fear Decrease." *Journal of Consulting Psychology,* 31 (1967), 259–263.

DeWolfe, A. S., and Davis, W. E. "Pattern Analysis and Deviation Scores in Clinical Research: Mean Scatter Revisited." *Journal of Personality Assessment,* 36 (1972), 307–313.

Dickey, B. A. "Attitudes toward Sex Roles and Feelings of Adequacy in Homosexual Males." *Journal of Consulting Psychology,* 25 (1961), 116–122.

DiGiovanni, P. "A Comparison between Orthodox Group Psychotherapy and Activity Group Therapy in the Treatment of Chronic Hospitalized Schizophrenics." Unpublished doctoral dissertation, University of Illinois, 1958.

DiMascio, A., and Brooks, G. W. "Free Association to a Fantasied Psychotherapist." *Archives of General Psychiatry,* 4 (1961), 513–516.

Dinoff, M., Rickard, H. C., Salzberg, H., and Sipprelle, C. N. "An Experimental Analogue of Three Psychotherapeutic Approaches." *Journal of Clinical Psychology,* 16 (1960), 70–73.

Distler, L. S. "Patterns of Parental Identification: an Examination of Three Theories." Unpublished doctoral dissertation, University of California, Berkeley, 1964.

Distler, L. S., May, P. R. A., and Tuma, A. H. "Anxiety and Ego Strength as Predictors of Response to Treatment in Schizophrenic Patients." *Journal of Consulting Psychology,* 28 (1964), 170–177.

Dittman, A. T. "The Interpersonal Process in Psychotherapy: Development of a Research Method." *Journal of Abnormal and Social Psychology,* 47 (1952), 236–244.

Dmitruk, V. M., Collins, R. W., and Clinger, D. L. "The 'Barnum Effect' and Acceptance of Negative Personal Evaluation." *Journal of Consulting and Clinical Psychology,* 41 (1973), 192–194.

Doidge, W. T., and Holtzman, W. H. "Implications of Homosexuality among Air Force Trainees." *Journal of Consulting Psychology,* 24 (1960), 9–13.

Dombrose, L. A., and Slobin, M. S. "The IES Test." *Perceptual and Motor Skills,* 8 (1958), 347–389.

Domhoff, B., and Gerson, A. "Replication and Critique of Three Studies on Personality Correlates of Dream Recall." *Journal of Consulting Psychology,* 31 (1967), 431.

Domhoff, B., and Kamiya, J. "Problems in Dream Content Study with Objective Indicators." *Archives of General Psychiatry,* 11 (1964), 525–532.

Doris, J., and Fierman, E. "Humor and Anxiety." *Journal of Abnormal and Social Psychology,* 53 (1956), 59–62.

Dorus, E., Dorus, W., and Rechtschaffen, A. "The Incidence of Novelty in Dreams." *Archives of General Psychiatry,* 25 (1971), 364–368.

Douvan, E., and Adelson, J. *The Adolescent Experience.* New York: Wiley, 1966.

Draper, E., Meyer, G. G., Parzen, Z., and Samuelson, G. "On the Diagnostic Value of Religious Ideation." *Archives of General Psychiatry,* 13 (1965), 202–207.

Dreger, R. M., and Barnert, M. "Measurement of the Custom and Conscience Functions of the Superego." *Journal of Social Psychology,* 77 (1969), 269–280.

Dudek, S. Z. "Effects of Different Types of Therapy on the Personality as a Whole." *Journal of Nervous and Mental Disease,* 150 (1970), 329–345.

———. "A Longitudinal Study of Piaget's Developmental Stages and the Concept of Regression. II. *Journal of Personality Assessment,* 36 (1972), 468–478.

Dudycha, G. J., and Dudycha, M. M. "Childhood Memories: a Review of the Literature." *Psychological Bulletin,* 38 (1941), 668–682.

Due, F. O., and Wright, M. E. "The Use of Content Analysis in Rorschach Interpretation: 1. Differential Characteristics of Male Homosexuals." *Journal of Projective Techniques,* 9 (1945), 169–177.

Duhrssen, A., and Jorswieck, E. "Ein empirisch-statistische Untersuchung zur Leistungsfähigkeit psychoanalytischer Behandlung (An empirical-statistical Investigation into the Efficacy of Psychoanalytic Therapy)." *Nervenarzt,* 36 (1965), 166–169.

Dundes, A. "Earth-Diver: Creation of the Mythopoeic Male." *American Anthropologist,* 64 (1962), 1032–1051.

Dunn, S., Bliss, J., and Sippola, E. "Effects of Impulsivity, Introversion, and Individual Values upon Association under Free Conditions." *Journal of Personality,* 26 (1958), 61–76.

Dupont, R. L., Jr., and Grunebaum, H. "Willing Victims: the Husbands of Paranoid Women." *American Journal of Psychiatry,* 125 (1968), 151–159.

Durrett, Mary E. "The Relationship of Early Infant Regulation and Later Behavior in Play Interviews." *Child Development,* 30 (1959), 211–216.

Dyrud, J. "Treatment of Anxiety States." *Archives of General Psychiatry,* 25 (1971), 298–305.

Edwards, H. E. "The Relationship between Reported Early Life Experiences with Parents and Adult Male Homosexuality." Unpublished doctoral dissertation, University of Tennessee, 1963.

Eggan, D. "The General Problem of Hopi Adjustment." *American Anthropologist,* 45 (1943), 357–373.

———. "The Manifest Content of Dreams: a Challenge to Social Science." *American Anthropologist,* 54 (1952), 469–485.

Eichler, J. M. "A Developmental Study of Action, Fantasy and Language Aggression in Latency Aged Boys." Unpublished doctoral dissertation, Boston University Graduate School, 1972.

Eiduson, Bernice T. "Structural Analysis of Dreams: Clues to Perceptual Style." *Journal of Abnormal and Social Psychology,* 58 (1959), 335–339.

Eisenthal, S. "Suicide and Aggression." *Psychological Reports,* 21 (1967), 745–751.

Elenewski, J. J. "A study of Insomnia: the Relationship of Psychopathology to Sleep Disturbance." Unpublished doctoral dissertation, University of Miami, 1971.

Ellenberger, H. F. *The Discovery of the Unconscious.* New York: Basic Books, 1970.

Ellis, A. "The Blacky Test Used with a Psychoanalytic Patient." *Journal of Clinical Psychology,* 9 (1953), 167–172.

———. "The Effectiveness of Psychotherapy with Individuals Who Have Severe Homosexual Problems." *Journal of Consulting Psychology,* 20 (1956), 191–195.

———. "Outcome of Employing Three Techniques of Psychotherapy." *Journal of Clinical Psychology,* 13 (1957), 344–350.

Ellman, C. S. "An Experimental Study of the Female Castration Complex." Unpublished doctoral dissertation, New York University, 1970.

Emery, M. P. "The Differential Assimilation of Dream Content into Waking Consciousness." Unpublished doctoral dissertation, Columbia University, 1971.

Emmerich, W. "Parental Identification in Young Children." *Genetic Psychology Monographs,* 60 (1959), 257–308.

Endicott, N. A., and Endicott, J. "Improvement in Untreated Psychiatric Patients." *Archives of General Psychiatry,* 9 (1963), 575–585.

Ends, E. J., and Page, C. W. "A Study of Three Types of Group Psychotherapy with Hospitalized Male Inebriates." *Quarterly Journal of Studies on Alcohol,* 18 (1957), 263–277.

Engel, G. L. "Some Obstacles to the Development of Research in Psychoanalysis." *Journal of the American Psychoanalytic Association,* 16 (1968), 195–229.

Epstein, A. W. "Recurrent Dreams." *Archives of General Psychiatry,* 10 (1964), 25–30.

Erdelyi, M. H. "Role of Fantasy in the Poetzl (Emergence) Phenomenon." *Journal of Personality and Social Psychology,* 24 (1972), 186–190.

Eriksen, C. W. "Perceptual Defense as a Function of Unacceptable Needs." *Journal of Abnormal and Social Psychology,* 46 (1951), 557–564.

———. "Defense against Ego-Threat in Memory and Perception." *Journal of Abnormal and Social Psychology,* 47 (1952), 230–235.

Eriksen, C. W., and Kuethe, J. L. "Avoidance Conditioning of Verbal Behavior without Awareness: a Paradigm of Repression." *Journal of Abnormal and Social Psychology,* 53 (1956), 203–209.

Erikson, E. H. "Growth and Crises of the Healthy Personality." In M. Senn, ed., *Symposium on the Healthy Personality.* New York: Josiah Macy, Jr. Foundation, 1950, pp. 91–46.

______. "The Dream Specimen of Psychoanalysis." *Journal of the American Psychoanalytic Association,* 2 (1954), 5–56.

Erikson, R. V., and Roberts, A. H. "Some Ego Functions Associated with Delay of Gratification in Male Delinquents." *Journal of Consulting and Clinical Psychology,* 36 (1971), 378–382.

Errera, P., McKee, B., Smith, C., and Gruber, R. "Length of Psychotherapy. Studies Done in a University Community Psychiatric Clinic." *Archives of General Psychiatry,* 17 (1967), 454–458.

Escalona, S. "Problems in Psycho-Analytic Research." *International Journal of Psycho-Analysis,* 33 (1952), 11–21.

______. "The Impact of Psychoanalysis upon Child Psychology. *Journal of Nervous and Mental Disease,* 126 (1958), 429–440.

Eskey, A. "Insight and Prognosis." *Journal of Clinical Psychology,* 14 (1958), 426–429.

Evans, R. B. "Childhood Parental Relationships of Homosexual Men." *Journal of Consulting and Clinical Psychology,* 33 (1969), 129–135.

______. "Sixteen Personality Factor Questionnaire Scores of Homosexual Men." *Journal of Consulting and Clinical Psychology,* 34 (1970), 212–215.

______. "Physical and Biochemical Characteristics of Homosexual Men." *Journal of Consulting and Clinical Psychology,* 39 (1972), 140–147.

Exner, J. E., Jr. "Rorschach Responses as an Index of Narcissism." *Journal of Projective Techniques and Personality Assessment,* 33 (1969), 324–330.

Eylon, Y. "Birth Events, Appendicitis, and Appendectomy." *British Journal of Medical Psychology,* 40 (1967), 317–332.

Eysenck, H. J. "The Effects of Psychotherapy: an Evaluation." *Journal of Consulting Psychology,* 16 (1952), 319–324.

______. *The Structure of Human Personality.* London: Methuen, 1953a.

______. *Uses and Abuses of Psychology.* Harmondsworth, England: Penguin, 1953b.

______. "A Reply to Luborsky's Note." *British Journal of Psychology,* 45 (1954), 132–133.

______. "The Effects of Psychotherapy: a Reply." *Journal of Abnormal and Social Psychology,* 50 (1955), 147–148.

______. *Handbook of Abnormal Psychology.* New York: Basic Books, 1961a.

______. "A Note on 'Impulse Repression and Emotional Adjustment.' " *Journal of Consulting Psychology,* 25 (1961b), 362–363.

______. "Behaviour Therapy, Spontaneous Remission and Transference in Neurotics." *American Journal of Psychiatry,* 119 (1963), 867–871.

______. "The Outcome Problem in Psychotherapy: a Reply." *Psychotherapy: Theory, Research and Practice,* 1 (1964), 97–100.

______. *Fact and Fiction in Psychology.* Harmondsworth, England: Penguin, 1965.

______. *The Effects of Psychotherapy.* New York: International Science, 1966.

______. "Relapse and Symptom Substitution after Different Types of Psychotherapy." *Behavior Research and Therapy,* 7 (1969), 283–287.

______. "The Experimental Study of Freudian Concepts." *Bulletin of British Psychological Society,* 25 (1972a), 261–267.

______. "Note on 'Factors Influencing the Outcome of Psychotherapy.' " *Psychological Bulletin,* 78 (1972b), 403–405.

Eysenck, H. J., and Soueif, M. "An Empirical Test of the Theory of Sexual Symbolism." *Perceptual and Motor Skills,* 35 (1972), 945–946.

Eysenck, H. J., and Wilson, G. D. *The Experimental Study of Freudian Theories.* London: Methuen, 1973.

Ezriel, H. "Experimentation within the Psychoanalytic Session." *British Journal of Philosophical Science,* 7 (1956), 25.

Fahs, H., Hogan. T. P., and Fullerton. D. T. "An Emotional Profile of Depression." *Psychological Reports,* 25 (1969), 18.

Fancher. R. E., and Strahan, R. F. "Galvanic Skin Response and the Secondary Revision of Dreams: a Partial Disconfirmation of Freud's Dream Theory." *Journal of Abnormal Psychology,* 77 (1971), 308–312.
Farber. M. L. "The Anal Character and Political Aggression." *Journal of Abnormal and Social Psychology,* 51 (1955), 486–489.
———. "Anality, Political Aggression, Acquiescence, and Questionnaire Construction." *Journal of Abnormal and Social Psychology,* 56 (1958), 278–279.
Farley, J., Woodruff, R. A., Jr., and Guze, S. B. "The Prevalence of Hysteria and Conversion Symptoms." *British Journal of Psychiatry,* 114 (1968), 1121–1125.
Farrell, B. A. "The Scientific Testing of Psycho-Analytic Findings and Theory. III." *British Journal of Medical Psychology,* 24 (1951), 35–41.
Fauls, L. B., and Smith, W. D. "Sex-Role Learning of Five-Year-Olds." *Journal of Genetic Psychology,* 89 (1956), 105–117.
Feather, B. W., and Rhoads, J. M. "Psychodynamic Behavior Therapy." *Archives of General Psychiatry,* 26 (1972), 503–511.
Feder, Carol Z. "Relationship between Self-Acceptance and Adjustment, Repression-Sensitization and Social Competence." *Journal of Abnormal Psychology,* 73 (1968), 317–322.
Feifel, H., and Eells, J. "Patients and Therapists Assess the Same Psychotherapy." *Journal of Consulting Psychology,* 27 (1963), 310–318.
Feinberg, I. "Recent Sleep Research: Findings in Schizophrenia and Some Possible Implications for the Mechanism of Action of Chlorpromazine and for the Neurophysiology of Delirium." In D. V. Siva Sankar, ed., *Schizophrenia: Current Concepts of Research.* Hicksville, N.Y.: PJD Publications, 1969, pp. 739–750.
Feinberg, I., Koresko, R. L., and Gottlieb, F. "Further Observations on Electrophysiological Sleep Patterns in Schizophrenia." *Comprehensive Psychiatry,* 6 (1965), 21.
Feinberg, I., Koresko, R. L., Gottlieb, F., and Wender, P. H. "Sleep Electroencephalographic and Eye-Movement Patterns in Schizophrenic Patients." *Comprehensive Psychiatry,* 5 (1964), 44–53.
Feinsilver, D. B., and Gunderson, J. G. "Psychotherapy for Schizophrenics—Is It Indicated? a Review of the Relevant Literature." *Schizophrenia Bulletin,* 6 (1972), 11–23.
Feirstein, A. "Personality Correlates of Tolerance for Unrealistic Experiences." *Journal of Consulting Psychology,* 31 (1967), 387–395.
Feldman, F. "Results of Psychoanalysis in Clinic Case Assignments." *Journal of American Psychoanalytic Association,* 16 (1968), 274–300.
Feldman, J. "Attitudinal Relationships of Paranoid Schizophrenic and Nonpsychotic Patients toward Recognized Needs in Themselves and in Others." Unpublished doctoral dissertation, University of Miami, 1965.
Feldstein, S. "REM Deprivation: the Effects on Ink Blot Perception and Fantasy Processes." Unpublished doctoral dissertation, City University of New York, 1972.
Fenichel, O. *Ten years of the Berlin Psychoanalytic Institute,* 1920–1930.
———. *The Psychoanalytic Theory of Neurosis.* New York: Norton, 1945.
Feshbach, S. "The Drive-Reducing Function of Fantasy Behavior." *Journal of Abnormal and Social Psychology,* 50 (1955), 3–11.
———. "The Effects of Emotional Restraint upon the Projection of Positive Affect." *Journal of Personality,* 31 (1963), 471–481.
Feshbach, S., and Singer, R. D. "The Effects of Fear Arousal and Suppression of Fear upon Social Perception." *Journal of Abnormal and Social Psychology,* 55 (1957), 283–288.
Fey, W. F. "Doctrine and Experience: Their Influence upon the Psychotherapist." *Journal of Consulting Psychology,* 22 (1958), 403–409.
Fiedler, F. E. "A Comparison of Therapeutic Relationships in Psychoanalytic, Nondirective and Adlerian Therapy." *Journal of Consulting Psychology,* 14 (1950a), 436–445.
———. "The Concept of an Ideal Therapeutic Relationship." *Journal of Consulting Psychology,* 14 (1950b), 239–245.
———. "Factor Analyses of Psychoanalytic, Non-Directive, and Adlerian Therapeutic Relationships." *Journal of Consulting Psychology,* 15 (1951), 32–38.
Fiedler, F. E., and Senior, K. "An Exploratory Study of Unconscious Feeling Reactions in Fifteen Patient-Therapist Pairs." *Journal of Abnormal and Social Psychology,* 47 (1952), 446–453.

Fierman, L. B. "Myths in the Practice of Psychotherapy." *Archives of General Psychiatry,* 12 (1965), 408–414.

Fink, P. J. "Correlations between 'Actual' Neurosis and the Work of Masters and Johnson." *Psychoanalytic Quarterly,* 39 (1970), 38–51.

Finney, J. C. "The MMPI as a Measure of Character Structure as Revealed by Factor Analysis." *Journal of Consulting Psychology,* 25 (1961a), 327–336.

______. "Some Maternal Influences on Children's Personality and Character." *Genetic Psychology Monographs,* 63 (1961b), 199–278.

______. "Maternal Influences on Anal or Compulsive Character in Children." *Journal of Genetic Psychology,* 103 (1963), 351–367.

Finney, J. C. "Relation and Meaning of the New MMPI Scales." *Psychological Reports,* 18 (1966), 459–70.

Fiorentino, Diane, Sheppard, C., and Merlis, S. "Emotions Profile Index (EPI) Pattern for Paranoid Personality Types: Cross-Validation and Extension." *Psychological Reports,* 26 (1970), 303–308.

Firestein, S. K. "Problems of Termination in the Analysis of Adults." *Journal of American Psychoanalytic Association,* 17 (1969), 222–237.

Fisher, C. "Subliminal and Supraliminal Influences on Dreams." *American Journal of Psychiatry,* 116 (1960), 1009–1017.

______. "Psychoanalytic Implications of Recent Research on Sleep and Dreaming. Part I: Empirical findings." *Journal of American Psychoanalytic Association,* 13 (1965a), 197–270.

______. "Psychoanalytic Implications of Recent Research on Sleep and Dreaming. Part II: Implications for Psychoanalytic Theory." *Journal of American Psychoanalytic Association,* 13 (1965b), 271–303.

______. "Psychological Significance of the Dream-Sleep Cycle." In H. A. Witkin and H. B. Lewis, eds., *Experimental Studies of Dreaming.* New York: Random House, 1967, pp. 76–127.

Fisher, C., and Dement, W. C. "Studies on the Psychopathology of Sleep and Dreams." *American Journal of Psychiatry,* 119 (1963), 1160–1168.

Fisher, C., and Paul, I. H. "The Effect of Subliminal Visual Stimulation on Images and Dreams: a Validation Study." *Journal of American Psychoanalytic Association,* 7 (1959), 35–83.

Fisher, D. F., and Keen, S. L. "Verbal Recall as a Function of Personality Characteristic." *Journal of Genetic Psychology,* 120 (1972), 83–92.

Fisher, J., and Breger, L., eds. *The Meaning of Dreams: Recent Insights from the Laboratory.* State of California: Department of Mental Hygiene, Research Symposium No. 3, 1969.

Fisher, S. "Plausibility and Depth of Interpretation." *Journal of Consulting Psychology,* 20 (1956), 249–256.

______. "Projective Methodologies." In P. Farnsworth, O. McNemar, and Q. McNemar, eds., *Annual Review of Psychology.* Palo Alto, California: Annual Reviews, 1967, pp. 165–190.

______. *Body Experience in Fantasy and Behavior.* New York: Appleton-Century-Crofts, 1970.

______. *The Female Orgasm.* New York: Basic Books, 1973.

Fisher, S., and Osofsky, H. "Sexual Responsiveness in Women: Psychological Correlates." *Archives of General Psychiatry,* 17 (1967), 214–226.

______. "Sexual Responsiveness in Women: Physiological Correlates." *Psychological Reports,* 22 (1968), 214–226.

Fiske, D. W. "Multivariate Psycho-Analysis." Review of *Psychotherapy and Psychoanalysis: Final Report of the Menninger Foundation's Psychotherapy Research Project* by O. F. Kernberg, E. D. Burstein, L. Coyne, A. Appelbaum, L. Horwitz, and H. Voth. *Contemporary Psychology,* 19 (1974), 12–13.

Fiske, D. W., Cartwright, D. S., and Kirtner, W. L. "Are Psychotherapeutic Changes Predictable?" *Journal of Abnormal and Social Psychology,* 69 (1964), 418–426.

Fiss, H., Klein, G. S., and Bokert, E. "Waking Fantasies Following Interruption of Two Types of Sleep." *Archives of General Psychiatry,* 14 (1966), 543–551.

Fiss, H., Klein, G. S., Shollar, E., and Levine, B. E. "Changes in Dream Content as a Function of Prolonged REM Sleep Interruption." *Psychophysiology,* 5 (1968), 217.

Flavell, J. H. "Repression and the 'Return of the Repressed.' " *Journal of Consulting Psychology,* 19 (1955), 441–443.

Fleischl, M. F. "The Problem of Sucking." *American Journal of Psychotherapy,* 11 (1957), 86–97.

Fletcher, M. B. "A Study of the Relationship between Aggression in the Verbally Reported Content of Dreams and Some Conceptually Related Measures of Personality." Unpublished doctoral dissertation, University of Tennessee, 1970.

Flowerman, S. H. "Psychoanalytic Theory and Science." *American Journal of Psychotherapy,* 8 (1954), 415–441.

Forer, B. R. "The Fallacy of Personal Validation: a Classroom Demonstration of Gullibility." *Journal of Abnormal and Social Psychology,* 44 (1949), 118–123.

Forer, B. R., Farberow, N. L., Feifel, H., Meyer, M. M., Sommers, V. S., and Tolman, R. C. "Clinical Perception of the Therapeutic Transaction." *Journal of Consulting Psychology,* 25 (1961), 93–101.

Foulds, G. A. " 'Psychic: Somatic' Symptoms and Hostility." *British Journal of Social and Clinical Psychology,* 5 (1966), 185–189.

Foulds, G. A., Caine, T. M., and Creasy, M. A. "Aspects of Extra- and Intro-Punitive Expression in Mental Illness." *Journal of Mental Science,* 106 (1960), 599–610.

Foulkes, D. "Dream Reports from Different Stages of Sleep." *Journal of Abnormal and Social Psychology,* 65 (1962), 14–25.

———. "Theories of Dream Formation and Recent Studies of Sleep Consciousness." *Psychological Bulletin,* 62 (1964), 236–247.

———. *The Psychology of Sleep.* New York: Scribner's, 1966.

———. "Nonrapid Eye Movement Mentation." *Experimental Neurology,* 1967, Supplement 4, 28–38.

———. "Drug Research and the Meaning of Dreams." *Experimental Medicine and Surgery,* 27 (1969), 39–52.

———. "Dream-Like Fantasy Scale: A Rating Manual." *Psychophysiology,* 7 (1971), 335–336.

Foulkes, D., Pivik, T., Ahrens, J. B., and Swanson, E. M. "Effects of Dream Deprivation on Dream Content: an Attempted Cross-Night Replication." *Journal of Abnormal Psychology,* 73 (1968), 403–415.

Foulkes, D., Pivik, T., Steadman, H. S., Spear, P. S., and Symonds, J. D. "Dreams of the Male Child: an EEG Study." *Journal of Abnormal Psychology,* 72 (1967), 457–467.

Foulkes, D., and Rechtschaffen, A. "Presleep Determinants of Dream Content: Effects of Two Films." *Perceptual and Motor Skills,* 19 (1964), 983–1005.

Foulkes, D., and Vogel, G. "Mental Activity at Sleep Onset." *Journal of Abnormal Psychology,* 70 (1965), 231–243.

Fox, H. M., Daniels, E. M., and Wermer, H. "Applicants Rejected for Psychoanalytic Training." *Journal of American Psychoanalytic Association,* 12 (1964), 692–716.

Framo, J. L., Osterweil, J., and Boszormenyi-Nagi, I. "A Relationship between Threat in the Manifest Content of Dreams and Active-Passive Behavior in Psychotics." *Journal of Abnormal and Social Psychology,* 65 (1962), 41–47.

Franck, K., and Rosen, E. "A Projective Test of Masculinity-Femininity." *Journal of Consulting Psychology,* 13 (1949), 247–256.

Frank, G. H. "The Role of the Family in the Development of Psychopathology." *Psychological Bulletin,* 64 (1965), 191–205.

Frank, J. D. *Persuasion and Healing.* Baltimore, Md.: Johns Hopkins University, 1961.

———. *Persuasion and Healing: A Comparative Study of Psychotherapy.* New York: Schocken, 1965.

Frank, J. D., Gliedman, L. H., Imber, S. D., Nash, E. H., and Stone, A. R. "Why Patients Leave Psychotherapy." *Archives of Neurology and Psychiatry,* 77 (1957), 283–299.

Frank, J. D., Gliedman, L. H., Imber, S. D., Stone, A. R., and Nash, E. H. "Patients' Expectancies and Relearning as Factors Determining Improvement in Psychotherapy." *American Journal of Psychiatry,* 115 (1959), 961–968.

Frank, J. D., Nash, E. H., Stone, A. R., and Imber, S. D. "Immediate and Long-Term Symptomatic Course of Psychiatric Outpatients." *American Journal of Psychiatry,* 120 (1963), 429–439.

Franz, A., and Wilson, G. W. "Quantitative Dream Studies: A Methodological Attempt at a Quantitative Evaluation of Psychoanalytic Material." *Psychoanalytic Quarterly,* 4 (1935), 371–407.

Fredericson, E. "Competition: The Effects of Infantile Experience upon Adult Behavior." *Journal of Abnormal and Social Psychology,* 46 (1951), 406–409.

Freedman, A., Luborsky, L., and Harvey, R. B. "Dream Time (REM) and Psychotherapy: Correlates of REM Time with a Patient's Behavior in Psychotherapy." *Archives of General Psychiatry,* 22 (1970), 33–39.

Freedman, D. A. "On the Limits of the Effectiveness of Psychoanalysis: Early Ego and Somatic Disturbances." *International Journal of Psycho-Analysis,* 53 (1972), 363–370.

Freedman, M. *Homosexuality and Psychological Functioning.* Belmont, Ca.: Brooks/Cole, 1971.

Freedman, N., Grand, D., and Karacan, I. "An Approach to the Study of Dreaming and Changes in Psychopathological States." *Journal of Nervous and Mental Disease,* 143 (1966), 399–405.

Freeman, T. "Psycho-Analytical Psychotherapy in the National Health Service." *British Journal of Psychiatry,* 113 (1967), 321–327.

French, T. *The Integration of Behavior. II. The Integrative Process in Dreams.* Chicago, Ill.: University of Chicago, 1954.

Frenkel-Brunswik, E. "Meaning of Psychoanalytic Concepts and Confirmation of Psychoanalytic Theories." *Scientific Monthly,* 79 (1954), 293–300.

Freud, A., and Burlingham, D. T. *War and Children.* New York: International Universities, 1943.

Freud, S. "The Aetiology of Hysteria." (1896) In J. Strachey, ed. (in collaboration with A. Freud), *The Standard Edition of the Complete Psychological Works of Sigmund Freud.* London: Hogarth, 1962, Vol. 3, pp. 187–221.

______ "Sexuality in the Aetiology of the Neurosis." (1898) In J. Strachey, ed. (in collaboration with A. Freud), *The Standard Edition of the Complete Psychological Works of Sigmund Freud.* London: Hogarth, 1962, Vol. 3, pp. 259–285.

______. "The Interpretation of Dreams." (1900) In J. Strachey, ed. (in collaboration with A. Freud), *The Standard Edition of the Complete Psychological Works of Sigmund Freud.* London: Hogarth, 1953, Vols. 4 and 5, pp.

______. "Freud's Psycho-Analytic Procedure." (1904[1903]) In J. Strachey, ed. (in collaboration with A. Freud), *The Standard Edition of the Complete Psychological Works of Sigmund Freud.* London: Hogarth, 1953, Vol. 7, pp. 247–254.

______. "Fragment of an Analysis of a Case of Hysteria." (1905a) In J. Strachey, ed. (in collaboration with A. Freud), *The Standard Edition of the Complete Psychological Works of Sigmund Freud.* London: Hogarth, 1955, Vol. 7, pp. 7–134.

______. "On Psychotherapy." (1905b [1904]) In J. Strachey, ed. (in collaboration with A. Freud), *The Standard Edition of the Complete Psychological Works of Sigmund Freud.* London: Hogarth, 1953, Vol. 7, pp. 255–268.

______. "Psychical (or Mental) Treatment." (1905c) In J. Strachey, ed. (in collaboration with A. Freud), *The Standard Edition of the Complete Psychological Works of Sigmund Freud.* London: Hogarth, 1953, Vol. 7, pp. 281–302.

______. "Three Essays on Sexuality." (1950) In J. Strachey, ed. (in collaboration with A. Freud), *The Standard Edition of the Complete Psychological Works of Sigmund Freud.* London: Hogarth, 1961, Vol. 7, pp. 135–243.

______. "Character and Anal Erotism." (1908) In J. Strachey, ed. (in collaboration with A. Freud), *The Standard Edition of the Complete Psychological Works of Sigmund Freud.* London: Hogarth, 1959, Vol. 9, pp. 169–175.

______. "Analysis of a Phobia in a Five-Year-Old Boy." (1909b) In J. Strachey, ed. (in collaboration with A. Freud), *The Standard Edition of the Complete Psychological Works of Sigmund Freud.* London: Hogarth, 1955, Vol. 10, pp. 3–149.

______. "Notes upon a Case of Obsessional Neurosis." (1909b) In J. Strachey, ed. (in collaboration with A. Freud), *The Standard Edition of the Complete Psychological Works of Sigmund Freud.* London: Hogarth, 1955, Vol. 10, pp. 151–320.

______. "Five Lectures on Psycho-Analysis." (1910a [1909]) Second Lecture. In J. Strachey, ed. (in collaboration with A. Freud), *The Standard Edition of the Complete Psychological Works of Sigmund Freud.* London: Hogarth, 1957, Vol. 11, pp. 21–28.

______. *Leonardo da Vinci and a Memory of his Childhood.* (1910b) New York: Norton, 1964.

______. "The Future Prospects of Psycho-Analytic Therapy." (1910c) In J. Strachey, ed. (in collaboration with A. Freud), *The Standard Edition of the Complete Psychological Works of Sigmund Freud.* London: Hogarth, 1957, Vol. 11, pp. 139–151.

———. " 'Wild' Psycho-Analysis." (1910d) In J. Strachey, ed. (in collaboration with A. Freud), *The Standard Edition of the Complete Psychological Works of Sigmund Freud.* London: Hogarth, 1957, Vol. 11, pp. 219–227.

———. "Psychoanalytic Notes on an Autobiographical Account of a Case of Paranoia (Dementia Paranoides)." (1911a) In J. Strachey, ed. (in collaboration with A. Freud), *The Standard Edition of the Complete Psychological Works of Sigmund Freud.* London: Hogarth, 1958, Vol. 12, pp. 1–82.

———. "The Handling of Dream-Interpretation in Psycho-Analysis." (1911b) In J. Strachey, ed. (in collaboration with A. Freud), *The Standard Edition of the Complete Psychological Works of Sigmund Freud.* London: Hogarth, 1958, Vol. 12, pp. 89–96.

———. "Recommendations to Physicians Practicing Psycho-Analysis." (1912a) In J. Strachey, ed. (in collaboration with A. Freud), *The Standard Edition of the Complete Psychological Works of Sigmund Freud.* London: Hogarth, 1958, Vol. 12, pp. 109–120.

———. "The Dynamics of Transference." (1912b) In J. Strachey, ed. (in collaboration with A. Freud), *The Standard Edition of the Complete Psychological Works of Sigmund Freud.* London: Hogarth, 1958, Vol. 12, pp. 97–108.

———. "On Beginning the Treatment. (Further Recommendations on the Technique of Psycho-Analysis I.)" (1913a) In J. Strachey, ed. (in collaboration with A. Freud), *The Standard Edition of the Complete Psychological Works of Sigmund Freud.* London: Hogarth, 1958, Vol. 12, pp. 121–144.

———. "The Disposition to Obsessional Neurosis. A Contribution to the Problem of Choice of Neurosis." (1913b) In J. Strachey, ed. (in collaboration with A. Freud), *The Standard Edition of the Complete Psychological Works of Sigmund Freud.* London: Hogarth, 1958, Vol. 12, pp. 311–326.

———. "On Narcissism: An Introduction." (1914a) In J. Strachey, ed. (in collaboration with A. Freud), *The Standard Edition of the Complete Psychological Works of Sigmund Freud.* London: Hogarth, 1957, Vol. 14, pp. 67–102.

———. "On the History of the Psycho-Analytic Movement." (1914b) In J. Strachey, ed. (in collaboration with A. Freud), *The Standard Edition of the Complete Psychological Works of Sigmund Freud.* London: Hogarth, 1957, Vol. 14, pp. 3–66.

———. "Remembering, Repeating, and Working Through." (1914c) In J. Strachey, ed. (in collaboration with A. Freud), *The Standard Edition of the Complete Psychological Works of Sigmund Freud.* London: Hogarth, 1958, Vol. 12, pp. 145–156.

———. "A Case of Paranoia Running Counter to the Psycho-Analytic Theory of the Disease." (1915a) In J. Strachey, ed. (in collaboration with A. Freud), *The Standard Edition of the Complete Psychological Works of Sigmund Freud.* London: Hogarth, 1957, Vol. 14, pp. 261–272.

——— "Observations on Transference-Love. (Other Recommendations on the Technique of Psycho-Analysis III.)" (1915b [1914]) In J. Strachey, ed. (in collaboration with A. Freud), *The Standard Edition of the Complete Psychological Works of Sigmund Freud.* London: Hogarth, 1958, Vol. 12, pp. 157–171.

———. "Some Character Types Met with in Psychoanalytic Work." (1916) In J. Strachey, ed. (in collaboration with A. Freud), *The Standard Edition of the Complete Psychological Works of Sigmund Freud.* London: Hogarth, 1957, Vol. 14, pp. 309–333.

———. "A Metapsychological Supplement to the Theory of Dreams." (1917a) In J. Strachey, ed. (in collaboration with A. Freud), *The Standard Edition of the Complete Psychological Works of Sigmund Freud.* London: Hogarth, 1957, Vol. 14, pp. 217–235.

———. "On Transformations of Instinct as Exemplified in Anal Erotism." (1917b) In J. Strachey, ed. (in collaboration with A. Freud), *The Standard Edition of the Complete Psychological Works of Sigmund Freud.* London: Hogarth, 1955, Vol. 17, pp. 125–133.

———. "The Analytic Therapy." (1917c) In J. Strachey, ed. (in collaboration with A. Freud), *The Standard Edition of the Complete Psychological Works of Sigmund Freud.* London: Hogarth, 1961, Vol. 16, pp. 448–477.

———. "From the History of an Infantile Neurosis." (1918 [1914]) In J. Strachey, ed. (in collaboration with A. Freud), *The Standard Edition of the Complete Psychological Works of Sigmund Freud.* London: Hogarth, 1955, Vol. 17, pp. 7–122.

———. " 'A Child Is Being Beaten.' A Contribution to the Study of the Origin of Sexual

Perversions." (1919a) In J. Strachey, ed. (in collaboration with A. Freud), *The Standard Edition of the Complete Psychological Works of Sigmund Freud.* London: Hogarth, 1955, Vol. 17, pp. 179–204.
______. "Lines of Advance of Psycho-Analytic Therapy." (1919b [1918]) In J. Strachey, ed. (in collaboration with A. Freud), *The Standard Edition of the Complete Psychological Works of Sigmund Freud.* London: Hogarth, 1955, Vol. 17, pp. 157–168.
______. "Beyond the Pleasure Principle." (1920a) In J. Strachey, ed. (in collaboration with A. Freud), *The Standard Edition of the Complete Psychological Works of Sigmund Freud.* London: Hogarth, 1955, Vol. 18, pp. 3–64.
______. "The Psychogenesis of a Case of Homosexuality in a Woman." (1920b) In J. Strachey, ed. (in collaboration with A. Freud), *The Standard Edition of the Complete Psychological Works of Sigmund Freud.* London: Hogarth, 1955, Vol. 18, pp. 145–172.
______. "Dreams and Telepathy." (1922a) In J. Strachey, ed. (in collaboration with A. Freud), *The Standard Edition of the Complete Psychological Works of Sigmund Freud.* London: Hogarth, 1955, Vol. 18, pp. 195–220.
______. "Some Neurotic Mechanisms in Jealousy, Paranoia and Homosexuality." (1922b) In J. Strachey, ed. (in collaboration with A. Freud), *The Standard Edition of the Complete Psychological Works of Sigmund Freud.* London: Hogarth, 1955, Vol. 18, pp. 221–232.
______. "A Seventeenth-Century Demonological Neurosis." (1923a [1922]) In J. Strachey, ed. (in collaboration with A. Freud), *The Standard Edition of the Complete Psychological Works of Sigmund Freud.* London: Hogarth, 1961, Vol. 19, pp. 69–105.
______. "The Ego and the Id." (1923b) In J. Strachey, ed. (in collaboration with A. Freud), *The Standard Edition of the Complete Psychological Works of Sigmund Freud.* London: Hogarth, 1961, Vol. 19, p. 3–66.
______. "The Infantile Genital Organization. An Interpolation into the Theory of Sexuality." (1923c) In J. Strachey, ed. (in collaboration with A. Freud), *The Standard Edition of the Complete Psychological Works of Sigmund Freud.* London: Hogarth, 1951, Vol. 19, pp. 141–145.
______. "Two Encyclopedia Articles." (1923d [1922]) In J. Strachey, ed. (in collaboration with A. Freud), *The Standard Edition of the Complete Psychological Works of Sigmund Freud.* London: Hogarth, 1961, Vol. 18, p. 235–259.
______. "The Dissolution of the Oedipus Complex." (1924) In J. Strachey, ed. (in collaboration with A. Freud), *The Standard Edition of the Complete Psychological Works of Sigmund Freud.* London: Hogarth, 1961, Vol. 19, pp. 173–179.
______. "Some Psychical Consequences of the Anatomical Distinction between the Sexes." (1925) In J. Strachey, ed. (in collaboration with A. Freud), *The Standard Edition of the Complete Psychological Works of Sigmund Freud.* London: Hogarth, 1961, Vol. 19, pp. 243–258.
______. "The Future of an Illusion." (1927) In J. Strachey, ed. (in collaboration with A. Freud), *The Standard Edition of the Complete Psychological Works of Sigmund Freud.* London: Hogarth, 1961, Vol. 21, pp. 3–56.
______. "Dostoevsky and Parricide." (1928 [1927]) In J. Strachey, ed. (in collaboration with A. Freud), *The Standard Edition of the Complete Psychological Works of Sigmund Freud.* London: Hogarth, 1961, Vol. 21, pp. 173–196.
______. "Female Sexuality." (1931) In J. Strachey, ed. (in collaboration with A. Freud), *The Standard Edition of the Complete Psychological Works of Sigmund Freud.* London: Hogarth, 1961, Vol. 21, pp. 221–243.
______. "Explanation, Applications and Orientations." (1933a) In J. Strachey, ed. (in collaboration with A. Freud), *The Standard Edition of the Complete Psychological Works of Sigmund Freud.* London: Hogarth, 1964, Vol. 22, pp. 136–157.
______. "Femininity." (1933b) In J. Strachey, ed. (in collaboration with A. Freud), *The Standard Edition of the Complete Psychological Works of Sigmund Freud.* London: Hogarth, 1964, Vol. 22, pp. 112–135.
______. "New Introductory Lectures on Psychoanalysis." (1933c) In J. Strachey, ed. (in collaboration with A. Freud), *The Standard Edition of the Complete Psychological Works of Sigmund Freud.* London: Hogarth, 1964, Vol. 22, pp. 3–182.
______. *The Problem of Anxiety.* New York: Norton, 1936.

———. "Analysis Terminable and Interminable." (1937a) In J. Strachey, ed. (in collaboration with A. Freud), *The Standard Edition of the Complete Psychological Works of Sigmund Freud.* London: Hogarth, 1964, Vol. 23, pp. 209–253.
———. "Construction in analysis." (1937b) In J. Strachey, ed. (in collaboration with A. Freud), *The Standard Edition of the Complete Psychological Works of Sigmund Freud.* London: Hogarth, 1964, Vol. 23, pp. 255–269.
———. "The Interpretation of Dreams." In A. A. Brill, ed., *The Basic Writings of Sigmund Freud.* New York: The Modern Library, 1938, pp. 181–468.
Freund, K. "Some problems in the Treatment of Homosexuality." In H. J. Eysenck, ed., *Behavior Therapy and the Neuroses.* New York: Pergamon, 1960, pp. 312–326.
———. *Die Homosexualitat beim Mann.* Leipzig: S. Hirgel, 1963.
Freund, K., Langevin, R., Zajac, Y., Steiner, B., and Zajec, A. "Parent-Child Relations in Transsexual and Non-Transsexual Homosexual Males." *British Journal of Psychiatry,* 124 (1974), 22–23.
Friberg, R. R. "A Study of Homosexuality and Related Characteristics in Paranoid Schizophrenia." Unpublished doctoral dissertation, University of Minnesota, 1965.
Friedman, J. "Weight Problems and Psychological Factors." *Journal of Consulting Psychology,* 23 (1959), 524–527.
Friedman, S. "Oral Activity Cycles in Mild Chronic Schizophrenia." *American Journal of Psychiatry,* 125 (1968), 743–751.
Friedman, S. M. "An Empirical Study of the Castration and Oedipus Complexes." *Genetic Psychology Monographs,* 46 (1952), 61–130.
Friend, M. R., Schiddel, L., Klein, B., and Dunaeff, D. "Observations on the Development of Transvestitism in Boys." *American Journal of Orthopsychiatry,* 24 (1954), 563–575.
Friess, C., and Nelson, M. J. "Psychoneurotics Five Years Later." *American Journal of Mental Science,* 203 (1942), 539–558.
Furer, M. "Psychic Development and the Prevention of Mental Illness." *Journal of the American Psychoanalytic Association,* 10 (1962), 606–616.
Gadpaille, W. J. "Research into the Physiology of Maleness and Femaleness." *Archives of General Psychiatry,* 26 (1972), 193–206.
Galbraith, G. G., and Lieberman, H. "Associative Responses to Double Entendre Words as a Function of Repression-Sensitization and Sexual Stimulation." *Journal of Consulting and Clinical Psychology,* 39 (1972), 322–327.
Galdston, I. "A Midcentury Assessment of the Residuum of Freud's Psychoanalytic Theory." *American Journal of Psychotherapy,* 11 (1957), 548–559.
Gale, J. "The Effects of Expectation and Suggestion upon Symptom Substitution." Unpublished doctoral dissertation, University of Tennessee, 1971.
Galinsky, M. D. "Relationships among Personality, Defense, and Academic Failure." *Journal of Personality Assessment,* 35 (1971), 359–363.
Gardner, G. E. "Evidences of Homosexuality in One Hundred and Twenty Unanalyzed Cases with Paranoid Content." *Psychoanalytic Review,* 18 (1931), 57–62.
———. "Problems of Early Infancy." *Journal of the American Psychoanalytic Association,* 3 (1955), 506–514.
Garduk, E. L., and Haggard, E. A. "Immediate Effects on Patients of Psychoanalytic Interpretations." *Psychological Issues,* 7 (1972), Monograph 28.
Garetz, F. K. "A Statistical Study of Treatment Oriented Behavior." *Archives of General Psychiatry,* 10 (1964), 306–309.
Garfield, S. L., and Bergin, A. E. "Personal Therapy, Outcome and Some Therapist Variables." *Psychotherapy: Theory, Research and Practice,* 8 (1971), 251–253.
Garfield, S. L., Helper, M. M., Wilcott, R. C., and Muffly, R. "Effects of Chlorpromazine on Behavior in Emotionally Disturbed Children." *Journal of Nervous and Mental Disease,* 135 (1962), 147–154.
Garner, H. H. "Passivity and Activity in Psychotherapy." *Archives of General Psychiatry,* 5 (1961), 411–417.
Geer, J. H., and Silverman, I. "Treatment of a Recurrent Nightmare by Behavior-Modification Procedures: A Case Study." *Journal of Abnormal Psychology,* 72 (1967), 188–190.
Gelder, M. G. "Verbal Conditioning as a Measure of Interpersonal Influence in Psychiatric Interviews." *British Journal of Social and Clinical Psychology,* 7 (1968), 194–209.

Gelder, M. G., and Marks, I. M. "Severe Agoraphobia: A Controlled Prospective Trial of Behaviour Therapy." *British Journal of Psychiatry,* 112 (1966), 309–319.
Gelder, M. G., Marks, I. M., and Wolff, H. H. "Desensitization and Psychotherapy in the Treatment of Phobic States: A Controlled Inquiry." *British Journal of Psychiatry,* 113 (1967), 53–73.
Gelfman, M. "A Post-Freudian Comment on Sexuality." *American Journal of Psychiatry,* 126 (1969), 651–657.
Gerz, H. O. "Experience with the Logotherapeutic Technique of Paradoxical Intention in the Treatment of Phobic and Obsessive-Compulsive Patients." *American Journal of Psychiatry,* 123 (1966), 548–553.
Gibbins, R. J., and Walters, R. H. "Three Preliminary Studies of a Psychoanalytic Theory of Alcohol Addiction." *Quarterly Journal of Studies on Alcohol,* 21 (1960), 618–641.
Gibby, R. G., Stotsky, B. A., Miller, D. R., and Hiler, E. "Prediction of Duration of Therapy from the Rorschach Test." *Journal of Consulting Psychology,* 17 (1953), 348–354.
Giedt, F. H. "Comparison of Visual, Content, and Auditory Cues in Interviewing." *Journal of Consulting Psychology,* 19 (1955), 407–416.
Gigi, J. L. "The Overt Male Homosexual: A Primary Description of a Self-Selected Population." Unpublished doctoral dissertation, University of Oregon, 1970.
Gill, M. M., Simon, J., Fink, G., Endicott, N. A., and Paul, I. H. "Studies in Audio-Recorded Psychoanalysis. I. General Considerations." *Journal of the American Psychoanalytic Association,* 16 (1968), 230–244.
Gillespie, W. H. "The General Theory of Sexual Perversion." *International Journal of Psycho-Analysis,* 37 (1956), 396–403.
Gillin, J. C., Buchsbaum, M. S., Jacobs, L. S., Fram, D. H., Williams, R. B., Jr., Vaughan, T. B., Jr., Mellon, E., Snyder, F., Wyatt, R. J. "Partial REM Sleep Deprivation, Schizophrenia and Field Articulation." *Archives of General Psychiatry,* 30 (1974), 653–662.
Gillin, J., Jacobs, L., Fram, D., Williams, R., and Snyder, F. "Partial REM Deprivation in Unmedicated Psychiatric Patients." *Psychophysiology,* 9 (1972), 139.
Gillman, R. D. "Brief Psychotherapy: A Psychoanalytic View." *American Journal of Psychiatry,* 122 (1965), 601–611.
______. "The Dreams of Pregnant Women and Maternal Adaptation." *American Journal of Orthopsychiatry,* 38 (1968), 688–692.
Ginott, H., and Lebo, D. "Play Therapy Limits and Theoretical Orientation." *Journal of Consulting Psychology,* 25 (1961), 337–340.
Giora, Z. "The Function of the Dream: A Reappraisal." *American Journal of Psychiatry,* 128 (1972), 1067–1073.
______. "Dream Recall: Facts and Perspectives." *Comprehensive Psychiatry,* 14 (1973), 159–167.
Giovacchini, P. L. "Dreams and the Creative Process." *British Journal of Medical Psychology,* 39 (1966), 105–115.
Glassman, B. M., and Siegel, A. "Personality Correlates of Survival in a Long-Term Hemodialysis Program." *Archives of General Psychiatry,* 22 (1970), 566–574.
Glatt, C. T. "Some Rorschach Correlates of Change in Clinical Status: An Investigation of Ego Repression in Schizophrenia." Unpublished doctoral dissertation, Michigan State University, 1971.
Glatter, A. N., and Hauck, P. "A Comparison between Normals and Mental Patients of the Perception of Sexual Symbols." *Journal of Clinical Psychology,* 14 (1958), 204–206.
Glatter, A. N., and Reece, M. M. "Tactility and Sexual Symbolism." *Perceptual and Motor Skills,* 14 (1962), 302.
Gleser, G. C., Gottschalk, L. A., and Springer, K. J. "An Anxiety Scale Applicable to Verbal Samples." *Archives of General Psychiatry,* 5 (1961), 593–605.
Gleser, G. C., and Ihilevich, D. "An Objective Instrument for Measuring Defense Mechanisms." *Journal of Consulting and Clinical Psychology,* 33 (1969), 51–60.
Gleser, G. C., and Sacks, M. "Ego Defenses and Reaction to Stress: A Validation Study of the Defense Mechanisms Inventory." *Journal of Consulting and Clinical Psychology,* 40 (1973), 181–187.
Glick, B. S. "Freud's Dream Theory and Modern Dream Research." *American Journal of Psychotherapy,* 21 (1967), 630–643.

———. "Conditioning Therapy with Phobic Patients: Success and Failure." *American Journal of Psychotherapy,* 24 (1970), 92–101.

Glixman, A. F. "An Analysis of the Use of the Interruption-Technique in Experimental Studies of Repression." *Psychological Bulletin,* 45 (1948), 491–506.

Globus, G. G. "Rapid Eye Movement Cycle in Real Time." *Archives of General Psychiatry,* 15 (1966), 654–659.

Glover, E. "Research Methods in Psycho-Analysis." *International Journal of Psycho-Analysis,* 33 (1952), 403–409.

———. *On the Early Development of Mind.* New York: International Universities, 1956.

———. *The Technique of Psycho-Analysis.* New York: International Universities, 1958.

———. "Remarks on Success and Failure in Psychoanalysis and Psychotherapy." In B. B. Wolman, ed, *Success and Failure in Psychoanalysis and Psychotherapy.* New York: Macmillan, 1972, pp. 131–152.

Goddard, K. E., Broder, G., and Wenar, C. "Special article—Reliability of Pediatric Histories, a Preliminary Study." *Pediatrics,* 28 (1961), 1011–1018.

Goethals, G. W. "Symbiosis and the Life Cycle." *British Journal of Medical Psychology,* 46 (1973), 91–96.

Goin, M. K., Yamamoto, J., and Silverman, J. "Therapy Congruent with Class-Linked Expectations." *Archives of General Psychiatry,* 13 (1965), 133–137.

Goldberg, L. R. "Simple Models or Simple Processes? Some Research on Clinical Judgments." *American Psychologist,* 23 (1968), 483–496.

———. "Man versus Model of Man: A Rationale, Plus Some Evidence, for a Method of Improving on Clinical Inferences." *Psychological Bulletin,* 73 (1970), 422–432.

Goldberg, P. A., and Milstein, J. T. "Perceptual Investigation of Psychoanalytic Theory Concerning Latent Homosexuality in Women." *Perceptual and Motor Skills,* 21 (1965), 645–646.

Goldenberg, G. M. "An Investigation of Primary-Process Thinking in the Manifest Dream Report." Unpublished doctoral dissertation, Wayne State University, 1963.

Goldfried, M. R., Stricker, G., and Weiner, I. B. *Rorschach Handbook of Clinical and Research Applications.* Englewood Cliffs, N. J.: Prentice-Hall, 1971.

Goldhirsh, M. I. "Manifest Content of Dreams of Convicted Sex Offenders." *Journal of Abnormal and Social Psychology,* 63 (1961), 643–645.

Goldin, P. C. "Experimental Investigation of Selective Memory and the Concept of Repression and Defense." *Journal of Abnormal Psychology,* 69 (1964), 365–380.

Goldman, F. "Breastfeeding and Character-Formation." *Journal of Personality,* 17 (1948), 83–103.

———. "Breastfeeding and Character Formation. II. The Etiology of the Oral Character in Psychoanalytic Theory." *Journal of Personality,* 19 (1950/51), 189–196.

Goldman-Eisler, F. "The Problem of 'Orality' and of its Origin in Early Childhood." *Journal of Mental Science,* 97 (1951), 765–782.

Goldmann, T. S. "Projection, Paranoia, and Cognitive Dissonance." Unpublished doctoral dissertation, Pennsylvania State University, 1971.

Goldstein, A. P. *Therapist-Patient Expectancies in Psychotherapy.* New York: Pergamon, 1962.

———. *Structured Learning Therapy.* New York: Academic, 1973.

Goldstein, G., Neuringer, C., Reiff, C., and Shelly, C. H., "Generalizability of Field Dependency in Alcoholics." *Journal of Consulting and Clinical Psychology,* 32 (1968), 560–564.

Goldstein, S. "A Projective Study of Psychoanalytic Mechanisms of Defense." Unpublished doctoral dissertation, University of Michigan, 1952.

Goodenough, D. R., Lewis, H. B., Shapiro, A., Jaret, L., and Sleser, I. "Dream Reporting Following Abrupt and Gradual Awakenings from Different Types of Sleep." *Journal of Personality and Social Psychology,* 2 (1965), 170–179.

Goodenough, D. R., Lewis, H. B., Shapiro, A., and Sleser, I. "Some Correlates of Dream Reporting Following Laboratory Awakenings." *Journal of Nervous and Mental Disease,* 140 (1965), 365–373.

Goodenough, D. R., Shapiro, A., Holden, M., and Steinschriber, L. "A Comparison of 'Dreamers' and 'Nondreamers': Eye Movement, Electroencephalograms, and the Recall of Dreams." *Journal of Abnormal and Social Psychology,* 59 (1959), 295–302.

Goodman, I. Z. "Influence of Parental Figures on Schizophrenic Patients." *Journal of Abnormal Psychology,* 73 (1968), 503–512.

Goodwin, D. W., Guze, S. B., and Robins, E. "Follow-Up Studies in Obsessional Neurosis." *Archives of General Psychiatry,* 20 (1969), 182–187.

Gordon, C. M. "Some Effects of Information, Situation, and Personality on Decision Making in a Clinical Setting." *Journal of Consulting Psychology,* 30 (1966), 219–224.

______. "Some Effects of Clinician and Patient Personality on Decision Making in a Clinical Setting." *Journal of Consulting Psychology,* 31 (1967), 477–480.

Gordon, H. L. "A Comparative Study of Dreams and Responses to the Thematic Apperception Test: I. A Need-Press Analysis." *Journal of Personality,* 22 (1953–54), 234–253.

Gordon, J. E. "Leading and Following Psychotherapeutic Techniques with Hypnotically Induced Repression and Hostility." *Journal of Abnormal and Social Psychology,* 54 (1957), 405–410.

Gordon, J. E., Martin, B., and Lundy, R. M. "GSR's During Repression, Suppression, and Verbalization in Psychotherapeutic Interviews." *Journal of Consulting Psychology,* 23 (1959), 243–251.

Goshen, C. E. "The Original Case Material of Psychoanalysis." *American Journal of Psychiatry,* 108 (1952), 829–834.

Gottheil, E. "Conceptions of Orality and Anality." *Journal of Nervous and Mental Disease,* 141 (1965a), 155–160.

______. "An Empirical Analysis of Orality and Anality." *Journal of Nervous and Mental Disease,* 141 (1965b), 308–317.

Gottheil, E., and Stone, G. C. "Factor Analytic Study of Orality and Anality." *Journal of Nervous and Mental Disease,* 146 (1968), 1–17.

Gottschalk, L. A. "Some Applications of the Psychoanalytic Concept of Object Relatedness: Preliminary Studies on a Human Relations Content Analysis Scale Applicable to Verbal Samples." *Comprehensive Psychiatry,* 9 (1968), 608–620.

Gottschalk, L. A., Gleser, G. C., and Springer, K. J. "Three Hostility Scales Applicable to Verbal Samples." *Archives of General Psychiatry,* 9 (1963), 254–279.

Graham, S. R. "Patient Evaluation of the Effectiveness of Limited Psychoanalytically Oriented Psychotherapy." *Psychological Reports,* 4 (1958), 231–234.

______. "The Effects of Psychoanalytically Oriented Psychotherapy on Levels of Frequency and Satisfaction in Sexual Activity." *Journal of Clinical Psychology,* 16 (1960), 94–95.

Grand, S., Freedman, N., and Jortner, S. "Variations in REM Dreaming and the Effectiveness of Behavior in Group Therapy." *American Journal of Psychotherapy,* 23 (1969), 667–680.

Granzberg, G. "Hopi Initiation Rites—A Case Study of the Validity of the Freudian Theory of Culture." *Journal of Social Psychology,* 87 (1972), 189–195.

Grauer, D. "Homosexuality in Paranoid Schizophrenia as Revealed by the Rorschach Test." *Journal of Consulting Psychology,* 18 (1954), 459–462.

Gray, J. J. "The Effect of Productivity on Primary Process and Creativity." *Journal of Projective Techniques and Personality Assessment,* 33 (1969), 213–218.

Gray, P. "Limitations of Psychoanalysis." *Journal of the American Psychoanalytic Association,* 13 (1965), 181–190.

Gray, S. W., and Klaus, R. "The Assessment of Parental Identification." *Genetic Psychology Monographs,* 54 (1956), 87–114.

Grayson, H. T., Jr. "Psychosexual Conflict in Adolescent Girls Who Experienced Early Parental Loss by Death." Unpublished doctoral dissertation, Boston University Graduate School, 1967.

Greenberg, R. "Dream Interruption Insomnia." *Journal of Nervous and Mental Disease,* 144 (1967), 18–21.

Greenberg, R., and Leiderman, P. H. "Perceptions, the Dream Process and Memory: An Up-to-Date Version of Notes on a Mystic Writing Pad." *Comprehensive Psychiatry,* 7 (1966), 517–523.

Greenberg, R., and Pearlman, C. "Delirium Tremens and Dreaming." *American Journal of Psychiatry,* 124 (1967), 133–142.

Greenberg, R., Pearlman, C., Fingar, R., Kantrowitz, J., and Kawliche, S. "The Effects of Dream Deprivation: Implications for a Theory of the Psychological Function of Dreaming." *British Journal of Medical Psychology,* 43 (1970), 1–11.

Greenberg, R., Pearlman, D. A., and Gampel, D. "War Neuroses and the Adaptive Function of REM Sleep." *British Journal of Medical Psychology,* 45 (1972), 27–33.

Greenberg, R., Pillard, R., and Pearlman, C. "The Effect of Dream (Stage REM) Deprivation on Adaptation to Stress." *Psychosomatic Medicine,* 34 (1972), 257–262.

Greenberg, R. P. "Effects of Presession Information on Perception of the Therapist and Receptivity to Influence in a Psychotherapy Analogue." *Journal of Consulting and Clinical Psychology,* 33 (1969), 425–429.

———. "The Influence of Referral Information Upon the Psychotherapeutic Relationship." *Psychotherapy: Theory, Research, and Practice,* 2 (1972), 213–215.

———. "Anti-Expectation Techniques in Psychotherapy: The Power of Negative Thinking." *Psychotherapy: Theory, Research, and Practice,* 10 (1973), 145–148.

Greenberg, R. P., Fisher, S., and Shapiro, J. "Sex-Role Development and Response to Medication by Psychiatric In-Patients." *Psychological Reports,* 33 (1973), 675–677.

Greenberger, E. "Fantasies of Women Confronting Death." *Journal of Consulting Psychology,* 29 (1965), 252–260.

Greenblatt, D. "Semantic Differential Analysis of the 'Triangular System' Hypothesis in 'Adjusted' Overt Male Homosexuals." Unpublished doctoral dissertation, University of California, Los Angeles, 1966.

Greenfield, N. S., and Lewis, W. C., eds. *Psychoanalysis and Current Biological Thought.* Madison and Milwaukee: University of Wisconsin, 1965.

Greenleaf, E. "The Schreber Case: Remarks on Psychoanalytic Explanation." *Psychotherapy: Theory, Research and Practice,* 6 (1969), 16–20.

Greenson, R. R. "The Selection of Candidates for Psychoanalytic Training." *Journal of the American Psychoanalytic Association,* 9 (1961), 135–145.

———. "A Critique of Kernberg's 'Summary and Conclusions.' " *International Journal of Psychiatry,* 11 (1973), 91–94.

Greenspan, J. "Sex of the Persecutor in Female Paranoid Patients." *Archives of General Psychiatry,* 9 (1963), 217–223.

Greenspan, J., and Myers, J. M., Jr. "A Review of the Theoretical Concepts of Paranoid Delusions with Special Reference to Women." *Pennsylvania Psychiatric Quarterly,* 1 (1961), 11–28.

Greenstein, J. M. "Father Characteristics and Sex Typing." *Journal of Personality and Social Psychology,* 3 (1966), 271–277.

Greenwald, A. G. "Behavior Change Following a Persuasive Communication." *Journal of Personality,* 33 (1965), 370–391.

Grey, A., and Kalsched, D. "Oedipus East and West: An Exploration via Manifest Dream Content." *Journal of Cross-Cultural Psychology,* 2 (1971), 337–352.

Grieser, C. "The Adaptive Function of Stage REM Sleep: The Effect of Dreaming on the Recall of Threatening Stimuli." Unpublished doctoral dissertation, Boston University, 1971.

Grieser, C., Greenberg, R., and Harrison, R. H. "The Adaptive Function of Sleep: The Differential Effects of Sleep and Dreaming on Recall." *Journal of Abnormal Psychology,* 80 (1972), 280–286.

Griffith, R. M., Miyagi, O., and Tago, A. "The Universality of Typical Dreams: Japanese vs. Americans." *American Anthropologist,* 60 (1958), 1173–1179.

Grimshaw, L. "The Outcome of Obsessional Disorder. A Follow-Up Study of 100 Cases." *British Journal of Psychiatry,* 111 (1965), 1051–1056.

Grinder, R. E. "Parental Childrearing Practices, Conscience, and Resistance to Temptation of Sixth-Grade Children." *Child Development,* 33 (1962), 803–820.

Grinker, R. "Identity or Regression in American Psychoanalysis?" *Archives of General Psychiatry,* 12 (1965), 113–125.

———. "Two of His Analysands Recall the 'Real' Freud: Report on a Meeting of the American Academy of Psychoanalysis." *Roche Report: Frontiers of Psychiatry,* 4 (1974), 3.

Grinspoon, L., Ewalt, J. R., and Shader, R. "Psychotherapy and Pharmacotherapy in Chronic Schizophrenia." *American Journal of Psychiatry,* 124 (1968), 1645–1652.

Groen, J. J. "The Psychosomatic Specificity Hypothesis for the Etiology of Peptic Ulcer." *Psychotherapy and Psychosomatics,* 19 (1971), 295–309.

Grossman, D. "An Experimental Investigation of a Psychotherapeutic Technique." *Journal of Consulting Psychology,* 16 (1952), 325–331.

Grosz, H. J., and Grossman, K. G. "Clinician's Response Style: A Source of Variation and Bias in Clinical Judgments." *Journal of Abnormal Psychology,* 73 (1968), 207–214.

Gruen, A. "Two Views on the Use of the Couch: The Couch?—Or the Man?" *Psychoanalytic Review,* 54 (1967), 72–80.
Gruver, G. G. "College Students as Therapeutic Agents." *Psychological Bulletin,* 76 (1971), 111–127.
Grygier, T. G. "Psychometric Aspects of Homosexuality." *Journal of Mental Science,* 103 (1957), 514–526.
______. "Homosexuality, Neurosis, and Normality." *British Journal of Delinquency,* 4 (1958), 59–61.
______. *The Dynamic Personality Inventory.* London: N.F.E.R., 1961.
Guerney, B., Jr., and Stollak, G. E. "Problems in Living, Psychotherapy Process Research, and an Autoanalytic Method." *Journal of Consulting Psychology,* 29 (1965), 581–585.
Guertin, W. H. "A Transposed Analysis of Paranoid Schizophrenics." *Psychological Reports,* 4 (1958), 591–594.
Guild, M. "Therapeutic Effectiveness of Analyzed and Non-Analyzed Therapists." Unpublished doctoral dissertation, St. John's University, 1969.
Guilford, J. P. *Psychometric Methods,* 2d ed. New York: McGraw-Hill, 1956.
______. *Fundamental Statistics in Psychology and Education.* London: McGraw-Hill, 1958.
______. *Personality.* New York: McGraw-Hill, 1959.
Guilford, J. P., and Zimmerman, W. S. *The Guilford-Zimmerman Temperament Survey: Manual of Instructions and Interpretations.* Beverly Hills, Calif.: Sheridan, 1949.
Gulevich, G., Dement, W., and Johnson, L. "Psychiatric and EEG Observations on a Case of Prolonged (264 Hours) Wakefulness." *Archives of General Psychiatry,* 15 (1966), 29–35.
Gundlach, R. H. "Childhood Parental Relationships and the Establishment of Gender Roles of Homosexuals." *Journal of Consulting and Clinical Psychology,* 33 (1969), 136–139.
Gundlach, R. H., and Riess, B. F. "Birth Order and Sex of Siblings in a Sample of Lesbians and Non-Lesbians." *Psychological Review,* 20 (1967), 61–62.
Gurin, G., Veroff, J., and Feld, S. *Americans View their Mental Health: A Nationwide Interview Survey.* New York: Basic Books, 1960.
Gutheil, E. "Reply to a Letter to the Editor." *American Journal of Psychotherapy,* 12 (1958), 627–629.
Guthrie, G. M. "Structure of Maternal Attitudes in Two Cultures." *Journal of Psychology,* 62 (1966), 155–165.
Guttman, S. A. "Criteria for Analyzability." *Journal of the American Psychoanalytic Association,* 8 (1960), 141–151.
______. "Some Aspects of Scientific Theory Construction and Psycho-Analysis." *International Journal of Psycho-analysis,* 46 (1965), 129–136.
Guze, S. B. "Conversion Symptoms in Criminals." *American Journal of Psychiatry,* 121 (1964), 580–583.
______. "The Diagnosis of Hysteria: What Are We Trying To Do? *American Journal of Psychiatry,* 124 (1967), 491–498.
Guze, S. B., and Perley, M. J. "Observations on the Natural History of Hysteria." *American Journal of Psychiatry,* 119, 1963, 960–965.
Guze, S. B., Woodruff, R. A., and Clayton, P. J. "A study of Conversion Symptoms in Psychiatric Outpatients." *American Journal of Psychiatry* 128 (1971), 643–646.
Haas, K. "Direction of Hostility and Psychiatric Symptoms." *Psychological Reports,* 16 (1965), 555–556.
Haggard, E. A., Brekstad, A., and Skard, A. G. "On the Reliability of the Anamnestic Interview." *Journal of Abnormal and Social Psychology,* 61 (1960), 311–318.
Hagman, E. R. "A Study of Fears of Children of Preschool Age." *Journal of Experimental Education,* 1 (1932), 110–130.
Haley, J. *Strategies of Psychotherapy.* New York: Grune and Stratton, 1963.
Hall, C. S. "Diagnosing Personality by the Analysis of Dreams." *Journal of Abnormal and Social Psychology,* 42 (1947), 68–79.
______. "A Cognitive Theory of Dream Symbols." *Journal of General Psychology,* 48 (1953a), 169–186.
______. "A Cognitive Theory of Dreams." *Journal of General Psychology,* 49 (1953b), 273–282.
______. "The Significance of the Dream of Being Attacked." *Journal of Personality,* 24 (1955), 168–180.

———. "Strangers in Dreams: An Empirical Confirmation of the Oedipus Complex." *Journal of Personality* (1963), 336–345.
———. "A Modest Confirmation of Freud's Theory of a Distinction Between the Superego of Men and Women." *Journal of Abnormal Psychology,* 69 (1964), 440–442.
———. "A Comparison of the Dreams of Four Groups of Hospitalized Mental Patients with Each Other and with a Normal Population." *Journal of Nervous and Mental Disease,* 143 (1966), 135–139.
———. "Representation of the Laboratory Setting in Dreams." *Journal of Nervous and Mental Disease,* 144 (1967), 198–206.
Hall, C. S. and Domhoff, B. "Friendliness in Dreams." *Journal of Social Psychology,* 62 (1964), 309–314.
Hall, C. S., and Van de Castle, R. L. "An Empirical Investigation of the Castration Complex in Dreams." *Journal of Personality* 33 (1965), 20–29.
———. "*The Content Analysis of Dreams.* New York: Appleton-Century-Crofts" 1966.
Hall, M. D. "Parent-Child Interactions in Latency-Age Boys with Learning Inhibitions." Unpublished doctoral dissertation, University of Minnesota, 1963.
Hall, M., and Keith, R. A. "Sex-Role Preference among Children of Upper and Lower Social Class." *Journal of Social Psychology,* 62 (1964), 101–110.
Hall, R. A., and Closson, W. G., Jr. "An Experimental Study of the Couch." *Journal of Nervous and Mental Disease,* 138 (1964), 474–480.
Hamburg, D. A., Bibring, G. L., Fisher, C., Stanton, A. H., Wallerstein, R. S., Weinstock, H. I., and Haggard, E. "Report of Ad Hoc Committee on Central Fact-Gathering Data of the American Psychoanalytic Association." *Journal of the American Psychoanalytic Association,* 15 (1967), 841–861.
Hamilton, V. "Conflict Avoidance in Obsessionals and Hysterics, and the Validity of the Concept of Dysthymia." *Journal of Mental Science,* 103 (1957), 666–676.
Hammer, E. F. "A Psychoanalytic Hypothesis concerning Sex Offenders: A Study by Clinical Psychologic Techniques." *Journal of Clinical and Experimental Psychopathology,* 18 (1957), 177–184.
Hammett, V. B. "A Consideration of Psychoanalysis in Relation to Psychiatry Generally, circa 1965." *American Journal of Psychiatry,* 122 (1965), 42–54.
Handal, P. J., and Rychlak, J. F. "Curvilinearity between Dream Content and Death Anxiety and the Relationship of Death Anxiety to Repression-Sensitization." *Journal of Abnormal Psychology,* 77 (1971), 11–16.
Haney, J. N. "A Multistage Model of Repression." Unpublished doctoral dissertation, Ohio University, 1971.
Hankoff, L. D., Engelhardt, D. M.; Freedman, N.; Mann, D.; and Margolis, R. "Denial of Illness in Schizophrenic Outpatients: Effects of Psychopharmacological Treatment." *Archives of General Psychiatry,* 3 (1960), 105–112.
Harms, E. *Problems of Sleep and Dream in Children.* New York: Macmillan, 1964.
Harris, A. "A Comparative Study of Results in Neurotic Patients Treated by Two Different Methods." *Journal of Mental Science,* 100 (1954), 718–721.
Harrison, S. I. "Is psychoanalysis 'Our Science'? Reflections on the Scientific Status of Psychoanalysis." *Journal of the American Psychoanalytic Association,* 18 (1970), 125–149.
Hartlage, L. C. "Subprofessional Therapists' Use of Reinforcement Versus Traditional Psychotherapeutic Techniques with Schizophrenics." *Journal of Consulting and Clinical Psychology,* 34 (1970) 181–183.
Hartley, R. E. "Sex-Role Identification: A Symposium. A Developmental View of Female Sex-Role Definition and Identification." *Merrill-Palmer Quarterly,* 10 (1964), 3–16.
Hartley, Ruth E., Hardesty, F. P., and Gorfein, D. S. "Children's Perceptions and Expressions of Sex Preference." *Child Development,* 33 (1962), 221–227.
Hartmann, E. "Dreaming Sleep (the D-State) and the Menstrual Cycle." *Journal of Nervous and Mental Disease,* 143 (1966), 406–416.
———. "The 90-Minute Sleep-Dream Cycle." *Archives of General Psychiatry,* 18 (1968a), 280–286.
———. "Longitudinal Studies of Sleep and Dream Patterns in Manic-Depressive Patients." *Archives of General Psychiatry,* 19 (1968b), 312–329.
Hartmann, E., Baekeland, F., and Zwilling, G. R. "Psychological Differences between Long and Short Sleepers." *Archives of General Psychiatry,* 26 (1972), 463–468.

Hartmann, E., Verdone, P., and Snyder, F. "Longitudinal Studies of Sleep and Dreaming Patterns in Psychiatric Patients." *Journal of Nervous and Mental Disease,* 142 (1966), 117–126.

Hartshorne, H., and May, M. A. *Studies in the Nature of Character. Vol. II. Studies in Service and Self Control.* New York: Macmillan, 1929.

Hartup, W. W. "Some Correlates of Parental Imitation in Young Children." *Child Development,* 33 (1962), 85–96.

Hartup, W. W., and Zook, E. A. "Sex-Role Preferences in Three- and Four-Year-Old Children." *Journal of Consulting Psychology,* 24 (1960), 420–426.

Harway, N. I., Dittmann, A. T., Raush, H. L., Bordin, E. S., and Rigler, D. "The Measurement of Depth of Interpretation." *Journal of Consulting Psychology,* 19 (1955), 247–253.

Harway, N. I., and Iker, H. P. "Content Analysis and Psychotherapy." *Psychotherapy: Theory, Research and Practice,* 6 (1969), 97–104.

Haskell, D., Pugatch, D., and McNair, D. M. "Time-Limited Psychotherapy for Whom." *Archives of General Psychiatry,* 21 (1969), 546–552.

Hastings, D. W. "Follow-Up Results in Psychiatric Illness." *American Journal of Psychiatry,* 114 (1958), 1057–1066.

Hauri, P. "Effects of Evening Activity on Subsequent Sleep and Dreams." Unpublished doctoral dissertation, University of Chicago, 1967.

Hauri, P., and Hawkins, D. R. "Phasic REM, Depression, and the Relationship between Sleeping and Waking." *Archives of General Psychiatry,* 25 (1971), 56–63.

Hauri, P., Sawyer, J., and Rechtschaffen, A. "Dimensions of Dreaming: A Factored Scale for Rating Dream Reports." *Journal of Abnormal Psychology,* 72 (1967), 16–22.

Hauser, S. T., and Shapiro, R. L. "Differentiation of Adolescent Self-Images." *Archives of General Psychiatry,* 29 (1973), 63–68.

Havener, P. H., and Izard, C. E. "Unrealistic Self-Enhancement in Paranoid Schizophrenics." *Journal of Consulting Psychology,* 26 (1962), 65–68.

Hawkins, D. R. "A Review of Psychoanalytic Dream Theory in the Light of Recent Psycho-Physiological Studies of Sleep and Dreaming." *British Journal of Medical Psychology,* 39 (1966), 85–104.

Hayman, M. "Drugs—and the Psychoanalyst." *American Journal of Psychotherapy,* 21 (1967), 644–654.

Heap, R. F., and Sipprelle, C. N. "Extinction as a Function of Insight." *Psychotherapy: Theory, Research and Practice,* 3 (1966), 81–84.

Heilbrun, A. B., Jr. "The Measurement of Identification." *Child Development,* 36 (1965), 111–127.

______. "Sex-Role Identity in Adolescent Females: A Theoretical Paradox." *Adolescence,* 3 (1968), 79–88.

______. "Effects of Briefing upon Client Satisfaction with the Initial Counseling Contact." *Journal of Consulting and Clinical Psychology,* 38 (1972), 50–56.

Heilbrun, A. B., Jr., and Norbert, N. "Sensitivity to Maternal Censure in Paranoid and Non-Paranoid Schizophrenics." *Journal of Nervous and Mental Disease,* 152 (1971), 45–49.

______. "Style of Adaptation to Aversive Maternal Control and Paranoid Behavior." *Journal of Genetic Psychology,* 120 (1972), 145–153.

Heilbrunn, G. "Psychoanalysis of Yesterday, Today, and Tomorrow." *Archives of General Psychiatry,* 4 (1961), 321–330.

______. "Results with Psychoanalytic Therapy: Report of 241 Cases." *American Journal of Psychotherapy,* 17 (1963), 427–435.

______. "Results with Psychoanalytic Therapy and Professional Commitment." *American Journal of Psychotherapy,* 20 (1966), 89–99.

Heine, R. W. "A Comparison of Patients' Reports on Psychotherapeutic Experience with Psychoanalytic, Nondirective and Adlerian Therapists." *American Journal of Psychotherapy,* 7 (1953), 16–23.

Heinicke, C. M. "Some Antecedent and Correlates of Guilt-Fear in Young Boys." Unpublished doctoral dissertation, Harvard University, 1953.

______. "Frequency of Psychotherapeutic Session as a Factor Affecting Outcome: Analysis of Clinical Ratings and Test Results." *Journal of Abnormal Psychology,* 74 (1969), 533–560.

Heinstein, M. I. "Behavioral Correlates of Breast–Bottle Regimes under Varying Parent–

Infant Relationships." *Monographs of the Society for Research in Child Development,* 28 (1963), No. 88.

Heller, K. "Laboratory Interview Research as an Analogue to Treatment." In A. E. Bergin and S. L. Garfield, eds., *Handbook of Psychotherapy and Behavior Change.* New York: Wiley, 1971.

Heller, K., Myers, R., and Kline, L. V. "Interviewer Behavior as a Function of Standardized Client Roles." *Journal of Consulting Psychology,* 27 (1963), 117–122.

Henry, W., Sims, J. H., and Spray, S. L. "Mental Health Professionals in Chicago: Some Preliminary Observations on Origins and Practice." In J. M. Shlien, ed., *Research in Psychotherapy.* Washington, D. C.: American Psychological Association, 1968, pp. 547–571.

———. *The Fifth Profession (Becoming a Psychotherapist).* San Francisco: Jossey-Bass, 1971.

Herron, W. G. "The Evidence for the Unconscious." *Psychoanalysis and the Psychoanalytic Review,* 49 (1962), 70–92.

Hersen, M. "Case Report: The Use of Behavior Modification Techniques within a Traditional Psychotherapeutic Context." *American Journal of Psychotherapy,* 24 (1970), 308–313.

———. "Nightmare Behavior: A Review." *Psychological Bulletin,* 78 (1972), 37–48.

Hes, J. P. "Depression and Dreams." *American Journal of Psychiatry,* 122 (1965/66), 1067.

Hess, E. H., Seltzer, A. L., and Shlien, J. M. "Pupil Response of Hetero- and Homosexual Males to Pictures of Men and Women: A Pilot Study." *Journal of Abnormal Psychology,* 70 (1965), 165–168.

Hetherington, E. M. "The Effects of Familial Variables on Sex Typing, on Parent-Child Similarity, and on Imitation in Children." In J. P. Hill, ed., *Minnesota Symposia on Child Psychology. Vol. 1.* Minneapolis: University of Minnesota, 1967, pp. 82–107.

Hetherington, E. M., and Brackbill, Y. "Etiology and Covariation of Obstinacy, Orderliness, and Parsimony in Young Children." *Child Development,* 34 (1963), 919–943.

Higdon, J. "Power and Sexual Dynamics in Female Paranoids and Nonparanoids." Unpublished doctoral dissertation, Southern Illinois University, 1972.

Hiler, E. W. "An Analysis of Patient-Therapist Compatibility.' *Journal of Consulting Psychology,* 22 (1958), 341–347.

Hilgard, E. R. "Impulsive versus Realistic Thinking: An Examination of the Distinction between Primary and Secondary Processes in Thought." *Psychological Bulletin,* 59 (1962), 477–488.

Hirt, M., Ross, W. D., Kurtz, R., and Gleser, G. C. "Attitudes to Body Products among Normal Subjects." *Journal of Abnormal Psychology,* 74 (1969), 486–489.

Hitson, H. M., and Funkenstein, D. H. "Family Patterns and Paranoidal Personality Structure in Boston and Burma." *International Journal of Social Psychiatry,* 5 (1959–60), 182–190.

Hobbs, N. "Sources of Gain in Psychotherapy." *American Psychologist,* 17 (1962), 741–747.

Hobson, J. A., Goldfrank, F., and Snyder, F. "Respiration and Mental Activity in Sleep." *Journal of Psychiatric Research,* 3 (1965), 79–90.

Hoedemaker, F., Kales, A., Jacobson, A., and Lichtenstein, E. "Dream Deprivation: An Experimental Reappraisal." Presented at annual meeting of the Association for the Psychophysiological Study of Sleep, 1963.

Hoffman, M. L. "Childrearing Practices and Moral Development: Generalizations from Empirical Research." *Child Development,* 34 (1963), 295–318.

———. "Father Absence and Conscience Development." *Developmental Psychology,* 4 (1971), 400–406.

Hoffman, M. L., and Hoffman, L. W. *Review of Child Development Research.* New York: Russell Sage Foundation, 1964.

Hoffman, M. L., and Saltzstein, H. D. "Parent Discipline and the Child's Moral Development." *Journal of Personality and Social Psychology,* 5 (1967), 45–57.

Hofling, C. K., and Meyers, R. W. "Recent Discoveries in Psychoanalysis." *Archives of General Psychiatry,* 26 (1972), 518–523.

Hogan, R. A. "Implosive Therapy in the Short Term Treatment of Psychotics." *Psychotherapy: Theory, Research and Practice,* 3 (1966), 25–32.

Holland, B. C. "Discussion." Appended to H. Spiegel, "Is Symptom Removal Dangerous?" *American Journal of Psychiatry,* 123 (1967), 1282–1283.

Hollender, M. H. "Is the Wish to Sleep a Universal Motive for Dreaming?" *Journal of the American Psychoanalytic Association,* 10 (1962), 323–328.
Hollingshead, A. B., and Redlich, F. C. *Social Class and Mental Illness.* New York: Wiley, 1958.
Hollon, T. H., and Zolik, E. S. "Self-Esteem and Symptomatic Complaints in the Initial Phase of Psychoanalytically Oriented Psychotherapy." *American Journal of Psychotherapy,* 16 (1962), 83–93.
Holmes, D. S. "Security Feelings and Affective Tones of Early Recollections: A Re-evaluation." *Journal of Projective Techniques and Personality Assessment,* 29 (1965), 314–318.
______. "Repression or Interference? A Further Investigation." *Journal of Personality and Social Psychology,* 22 (1972), 163–170.
Holmes, D. S., and Watson, R. I. "Early Recollection and Vocational Choice." *Journal of Consulting Psychology,* 29 (1965), 486–488.
Holt, H., and Winick, C. "Group Psychotherapy with Obese Women." *Archives of General Psychiatry,* 5 (1961), 156–168.
Holt, R. R. "Personality Growth in Psychiatric Residents." *Archives of Neurology and Psychiatry,* 81 (1959), 203–215.
______. "Measuring Libidinal and Aggressive Motives and their Control by Means of the Rorschach Test." In D. Levine, ed., *Nebraska Symposium on Motivation.* Lincoln, Nebraska: University of Nebraska, 1966, pp. 1–47.
Holt, R. R., and Luborsky, L. "The Selection of Candidates for Psychoanalytic Training: On the Use of Interviews and Psychological Tests." *Journal of the American Psychoanalytic Association,* 3 (1955), 666–681.
______. *Personality Patterns of Psychiatrists, Vol. II.* Ann Arbor, Mich.: Edwards Brothers, 1958.
Holt, R. R., and Peterfreund, E., eds. *Psychoanalysis and Contemporary Science. Vol. 1. An Annual of Integrative and Interdisciplinary Studies.* New York: Macmillan, 1972.
Holway, A. R. "Early Self-Regulation of Infants and Later Behavior in Play Interviews." *American Journal of Orthopsychiatry,* 19 (1949), 612–623.
Holzman, P. S., and Gardner, R. W. "Leveling and Repression." *Journal of Abnormal and Social Psychology,* 59 (1959), 151–155.
Hook, S., ed. *Psychoanalysis, Scientific Method, and Philosophy.* New York: New York University, 1959.
Hooker, E. "Parental Relations and Male Homosexuality in Patient and Nonpatient Samples." *Journal of Consulting and Clinical Psychology,* 33 (1969), 140–142.
Horowitz, M. J. "Psychic Trauma: Return of Images after a Stress Film." *Archives of General Psychiatry,* 20 (1969), 552–559.
Horowitz, M. J., and Becker, S. S. "Cognitive Response to Stressful Stimuli." *Archives of General Psychiatry,* 25 (1971), 419–428.
Horton, P. C., and Coppolillo, H. P. "Unconscious Causality and the Pyramid of Science." *Archives of General Psychiatry,* 26 (1972), 512–517.
Horwitz, W. A., Polatin, P., Kolb, L. C., and Hoch, P. H. "A Study of Cases of Schizophrenia Treated by Direct Analysis." *American Journal of Psychiatry,* 114 (1958), 780–783.
Howard, G., Signori, E. I., and Rempel, H. "Further Research on the Picture Titles Subtest of the IES Test." *Perceptual and Motor Skills,* 22 (1966), 119–122.
Howard, K. I., and Orlinsky, D. E. "Psychotherapeutic Processes." *Annual Review of Psychology,* 23 (1972), 615–668.
Howarth, E. "Extroversion and Dream Symbolism: An Empirical Study." *Psychological Reports,* 10 (1962), 211–214.
Howe, E. S. "Effects of Grammatical Qualifications on Judgments of the Depth and of the Anxiety Arousal Potential of Interpretive Statements." *Journal of Consulting and Clinical Psychology,* 34 (1970), 159–163.
Howe, E. S., and Pope, B. "The Dimensionality of Ratings of Therapist Verbal Responses." *Journal of Consulting Psychology,* 25 (1961), 296–303.
Hubbard, B. L. "An Attempt to Identify, by Psychometric and Peer Rating Techniques, Three Oral Character Types Described in Psychoanalytic Literature." Unpublished doctoral dissertation, University of North Carolina at Chapel Hill, 1967.
Hunter, R. A., and MacAlpine, I. "Follow-Up Study of a Case Treated in 1910 by 'The Freud Psycho-Analytic Method.' " *British Journal of Medical Psychology,* 26 (1953), 64–67.
Husband, R. W. "Sex Differences in Dream Contents." *Journal of Abnormal and Social Psychology,* 28–30 (1933–36), 513–521.

Huschka, M. "The Child's Response to Coercive Bowel Training." *Psychosomatic Medicine,* 4 (1942), 301–328.
Hyman, H. T. "The Value of Psychoanalysis as a Therapeutic Procedure." *Journal of the American Medical Association,* 107 (1936), 326–329.
Imber, R. "An Experimental Study of the Oedipus Complex." Unpublished doctoral dissertation, Rutgers, The State University, 1969.
Imber, S. D., Frank, J. D., Nash, E. H., Stone, A. R., and Gliedman, L. H. "Improvement and Amount of Therapeutic Contact: An Alternative to the Use of No-Treatment Controls in Psychotherapy." *Journal of Consulting Psychology,* 21 (1957), 309–315.
Ingram, I. M. "Obsessional Personality and Anal-Erotic Character." *Journal of Mental Science,* 107 (1961), 1035–1042.
Irwin, T. C. "A Contribution to the Construct Validation of the Oral Scales of the Blacky Pictures Test." Unpublished doctoral dissertation, University of Rochester, 1963.
Isaacs, K. S., and Haggard, E. A. "Some Methods Used in the Study of Affect in Psychotherapy." In L. Gottschalk and A. H. Auerbach, eds., *Methods of Research in Psychotherapy.* New York: Appleton-Century-Crofts, 1966, pp. 226–239.
Iscoe, I., and Stevenson, H. W. *Personality Development in Children.* Austin, Texas: University of Texas, 1960.
Ivey, E. "Significance of the Sex of the Psychiatrist." *Archives of General Psychiatry,* 2 (1960), 622–631.
Jackson, D. D., and Haley, J. "Transference Revisited." *Journal of Nervous and Mental Disease,* 137 (1963), 363–371.
Jackson, S. W. "The History of Freud's Concepts of Regression." *Journal of the American Psychoanalytic Association,* 17 (1969), 743–784.
Jacobs, A. "Responses of Normals and Mental Hospital Patients to Freudian Sexual Symbols." *Journal of Consulting Psychology,* 18 (1954), 454.
Jacobs, M. A. "The Addictive Personality: Prediction of Success in a Smoking Withdrawal Program." *Psychosomatic Medicine,* 34 (1972), 30–38.
Jacobs, M. A., Anderson, L. S., Champagne, E., Karush, N., Richman, S. J., and Knapp, P. H. "Orality, Impulsivity and Cigarette Smoking in Men: Further Findings in Support of a Theory." *Journal of Nervous and Mental Disease,* 143 (1966), 207–219.
Jacobs, M. A., Knapp, P. H., Anderson, L. S., Karush, N., Meissner, R., and Richman, S. J. "Relationship of Oral Frustration Factors with Heavy Cigarette Smoking in Males." *Journal of Nervous and Mental Disease,* 141, (1965), 161–171.
Jacobs, M. A., and Spilken, A. Z. "Personality Patterns Associated with Heavy Cigarette Smoking in Male College Students." *Journal of Consulting and Clinical Psychology,* 37 (1971), 428–432.
Jacobs, M. A., Spilken, A. Z., Norman, M. M., Anderson, L., and Rosenheim, E. "Perceptions of Faulty Parent-Child Relationships and Illness Behavior." *Journal of Consulting and Clinical Psychology,* 39 (1972), 49–55.
Jacobs, M. O. "A Validation Study of the Oral Erotic Scale of the Blacky Pictures Test." Unpublished doctoral dissertation, University of Oklahoma, 1957.
Jacobson, G., and Ryder, R. G. "Parental Loss and Some Characteristics of the Early Marriage Relationship." *American Journal of Orthopsychiatry,* 39 (1969), 779–787.
Jersild, A. T., Lazar, E. A., and Brodkin, A. M. *The Meaning of Psychotherapy in the Teacher's Life and Work.* New York: Teachers College, Columbia University, 1962.
Johnson, C. P. "Oral Dependence and Its Relationship to Field Dependence and Dependent Behavior in Same and Mixed Sex Pairs." Unpublished doctoral dissertation, State University of New York at Buffalo, 1973.
Johnson, G. B. "Penis-Envy? Or Pencil-Needing?" *Psychological Reports,* 19 (1966), 758.
Johnson, H. "Psychoanalysis: Some Critical Comments." *American Journal of Psychiatry,* 113 (1956), 36–40.
Johnson, H., and Eriksen, C. W. "Preconscious Perception: A Re-examination of the Poetzl Phenomenon." *Journal of Abnormal and Social Psychology,* 62 (1961), 497–503.
Johnson, L. C. "Body Cathexis as a Factor in Somatic Complaints." *Journal of Consulting Psychology,* 20 (1956), 145–149.
Jonas, C. H. "An Objective Approach to the Personality and Environment in Homosexuality." *Psychiatric Quarterly,* 18 (1944), 626–647.

Jones, A. "Sexual Symbolism and the Variables of Sex and Personality Integration." *Journal of Abnormal and Social Psychology,* 53 (1956), 187–190.

______. "Sexual Symbolic Response in Prepubescent and Pubescent Children." *Journal of Consulting Psychology,* 25 (1961), 363–387.

Jones, A., and Lepson, D. S. "Mediated and Primary Stimulus-Generalization Bases of Sexual Symbolism." *Journal of Consulting Psychology,* 31 (1967), 79–82.

Jones, E. "Report of the Clinic Work" (London Clinic of Psychoanalysis): 1926–1936.

______. *The Life and Work of Sigmund Freud,* Vols. 1, 2, and 3. New York: Basic Books, 1953, 1955, 1957.

______, ed. *Sigmund Freud: Collected Papers,* Vol. 1. New York: Basic Books, 1959.

Jones, R. M. *Ego Synthesis in Dreams.* Cambridge, Mass.: Schenkman, 1962.

______. "The Problem of 'Depth' in the Psychology of Dreaming." *Journal of Nervous and Mental Disease,* 139 (1964a), 507–515.

______. "Psychosexuality in Speech Development." *Perceptual and Motor Skills,* 19 (1964b), 390.

______. "Dream Interpretation and the Psychology of Dreaming." *Journal of the American Psychoanalytic Association,* 13 (1965), 304–319.

______. "The Psychoanalytic Theory of Dreaming—1968." *Journal of Nervous and Mental Disease,* 147 (1968), 587–604.

______. *The New Psychology of Dreaming.* New York: Grune and Stratton, 1970.

Jordan, B. T., and Butler, J. R. "GSR as a Measure of the Sexual Component in Hysteria." *Journal of Psychology,* 67 (1967), 211–219.

Jordan, B. T., and Kempler, B. "Hysterical Personality: An Experimental Investigation of Sex-Role Conflict." *Journal of Abnormal Psychology,* 75 (1970), 172–176.

Jorgensen, E. C., and Howell, R. J. "Changes in Self, Ideal-Self Correlations from Ages 8 through 18." *Journal of Social Psychology,* 79 (1969), 63–67.

Jourard, S. M. "Identification, Parent-Cathexis, and Self-Esteem." *Journal of Consulting Psychology,* 21 (1957), 375–380.

Kadushin, C. *Why People go to Psychiatrists.* New York: Atherton, 1969.

Kagan, J. "The Child's Perception of the Parent." *Journal of Abnormal and Social Psychology,* 53 (1956), 257–258.

Kagan, J., and Lemkin, J. "The Child's Differential Perception of Parental Attributes." *Journal of Abnormal and Social Psychology,* 61 (1960), 440–447.

Kagan, J., and Moss, H. A. "The Stability of Passive and Dependent Behavior from Childhood through Adulthood." *Child Development,* 31 (1960), 577–591.

______. *Birth to Maturity: A study in Psychological Development.* New York: Wiley, 1962.

Kagan, J., and Mussen, P. H. "Dependency Themes on the TAT and Group Conformity." *Journal of Consulting Psychology,* 20 (1956), 29–32.

Kahn, M., Baker, B. L., and Weiss, J. M. "Treatment of Insomnia by Relaxation Training." *Journal of Abnormal Psychology,* 73 (1968), 556–558.

Kahn, R. L., and Fink, M. "Changes in Language during Electroshock Therapy." In P. H. Hoch and J. Zubin, eds., *Psychopathology of Communication.* New York: Grune and Stratton, 1958, pp. 126–139.

______. "Personality Factors in Behavioral Response to Electroshock Therapy." *Journal of Neuropsychiatry,* 1 (1959), 45–49.

Kales, A., Hoedemaker, F. S., Jacobson, A., and Lichtenstein, E. L. "Dream Deprivation: An Experimental Reappraisal." *Nature,* 204 (1964), 1337–1338.

Kales, J., Allen, C., Preston, T. A., Tan, T., and Kales, A. "Changes in REM Sleep and Dreaming with Cigarette Smoking and Following Withdrawal." *Psychophysiology,* 7 (1970), 347–348.

Kaley, H. W. "The Effects of Subliminal Stimuli and Drive on Verbal Responses and Dreams." Unpublished doctoral dissertation, New York University, 1969.

Kalsched, D. E. "Adaptive Regression and Primary Process in Dream Reports." Unpublished doctoral dissertation, Fordham University, 1972.

Kamil, L. J. "Psychodynamic Changes through Systematic Desensitization." *Journal of Abnormal Psychology,* 76 (1970), 199–205.

Kant, O. "Dreams of Schizophrenic Patients." *Journal of Nervous and Mental Disease,* 95 (1942), 335–347.

Kanter, V. B., and Hazelton, J. E. "An Attempt to Measure Some Aspects of Personality in Young Men with Duodenal Ulcer by Means of Questionnaires and a Projective Test." *Journal of Psychosomatic Research,* 8 (1964), 297–309.
Kaplan, H. I., and Kaplan, H. S. "A Psychosomatic Concept." *American Journal of Psychotherapy,* 11 (1957), 16–38.
———. "Current Theoretical Concepts in Psychosomatic Medicine." *American Journal of Psychiatry,* 115 (1959), 1091–1096.
Kapotas, C. N. "An Investigation of the Psychoanalytic Theory of Psychosexual Genesis of Paranoid Schizophrenia." Unpublished doctoral dissertation, New York University, 1955.
Karacan, I., Goodenough, D. R., Shapiro, A., and Starker, S. "Erection Cycle during Sleep in Relation to Dream Anxiety." *Archives of General Psychiatry,* 15 (1966), 183–189.
Kardiner, A., Karush, A., and Ovesey, L. "A Methodological Study of Freudian Theory: I. Basic Concepts." *Journal of Nervous and Mental Disease,* 129 (1959a), 11–19.
——— "A Methodological Study of Freudian Theory: II. The Libido Theory." *Journal of Nervous and Mental Disease,* 129 (1959b), 133–143.
———. "A Methodological Study of Freudian Theory: III. Narcissism, Bisexuality and the Dual Instinct Theory." *Journal of Nervous and Mental Disease,* 129 (1959c), 207–221.
Karno, M. "Communication, Reinforcement and 'Insight'—the Problem of Psychotherapeutic Effect." *American Journal of Psychotherapy,* 19 (1965), 467–479.
Karon, B. P. "The Resolution of Acute Schizophrenic Reactions: A Contribution to the Development of Non-Classical Psychotherapeutic Techniques." *Psychotherapy: Theory, Research and Practice,* 1 (1963), 27–43.
———. "An Experimental Study of Parental Castration Phantasies in Schizophrenia." *British Journal of Psychiatry,* 110 (1964), 67–73.
Karon, B. P., and O'Grady, P. "Intellectual Test Changes in Schizophrenic Patients in the First Six Months of Treatment." *Psychotherapy: Theory, Research, and Practice,* 6 (1969), 88–96.
Karon, B. P., and Vandenbos, G. R. "Experience, Meditation, and the Effectiveness of Psychotherapy with Schizophrenics." *British Journal of Psychiatry,* 116 (1970), 427–428.
———. "The Consequences of Psychotherapy for Schizophrenic Patients." *Psychotherapy: Theory, Research, and Practice,* 9 (1972), 111–119.
———. "Medication and/or Psychotherapy with Schizophrenics: Which Part of the Elephant Have You Touched? " Michigan State University Psychotherapy Project, Bulletin No. 15, 1973.
Karr, B. "Freudian Aggression Theory: Two Hypotheses." *Psychotherapy: Theory, Research and Practice,* 8 (1971), 259–263.
Karush, A., Daniels, G., O'Connor, J., and Stern, L. O. "The Response to Psychotherapy in Chronic Ulcerative Colitis. I. Pretreatment Factors." *Psychosomatic Medicine,* 30 (1968), 255–276.
———. "The Response to Psychotherapy in Chronic Ulcerative Colitis. II. Factors Arising from the Therapeutic Situation." *Psychosomatic Medicine,* 31 (1969), 201–226.
Katcher, A. "The Discrimination of Sex Differences by Young Children." *Journal of Genetic Psychology,* 87 (1955), 131–143.
Katcher, A., and Levin, M. "Children's Conceptions of Body Size." *Child Development,* 26 (1955), 103–110.
Katz, M. M., Cole, J. O., and Lowery, H. A. "Nonspecificity of Diagnosis of Paranoid Schizophrenia." *Archives of General Psychiatry,* 11 (1964), 197–202.
Katz, M. M., Lorr, M., and Rubinstein, E. A. "Remainer Patient Attributes and their Relation to Subsequent Improvement in Psychotherapy." *Journal of Consulting Psychology,* 22 (1958), 411–414.
Kaufmann, H. "Definitions and Methodology in the Study of Aggression." *Psychological Bulletin,* 64 (1965), 351–364.
Kausler, D. H. "A World Series for Learning Psychologists." Review of G. H. Bower, ed., *The Psychology of Learning and Motivation: Advances in Research and Theory, Contemporary Psychology,* 19 (1974), 13–14.
Kaye, H. E., Berl, S., Clare, J., Eleston, M., Gershwin, B. S., Gershwin, P., Kogan, L. S.,

Torda, C., and Wilbur, C. B. "Homosexuality in Women." *Archives of General Psychiatry,* 17 (1967), 626–634.
Kayton, R., and Biller, H. B. "Perception of Parental Sex-Role Behavior and Psychopathology in Adult Males." *Journal of Consulting and Clinical Psychology,* 36 (1971), 235–237.
______. "Sex-Role Development and Psychopathology in Adult Males." *Journal of Consulting and Clinical Psychology,* 38 (1972), 208–210.
Kazamias, N. G. "Sex Difference in the Incidence of Grandiose Delusions in Paranoid Patients in Greece." *International Journal of Social Psychiatry,* 16 (1970), 228–231.
Kehoe, M. J. "Facial Pain: Hypnotic Suggestion as a Method of Treatment." *American Journal of Psychiatry,* 123 (1967), 1577–1581.
Keiser, S. "Psychoanalysis—Taught, Learned, and Experienced." *Journal of the American Psychoanalytic Association,* 17 (1969), 238–267.
Keller, P. A., and Murray, E. J. "Imitative Aggression with Adult Male and Female Models in Father Absent and Father Present Negro Boys." *Journal of Genetic Psychology,* 122 (1973), 217–221.
Kelman, H. "How Does Psychoanalysis Fit into the Total Concept of Care?" *American Journal of Psychotherapy,* 26 (1972), 195–206.
Kemp, D. E. "The AB Scale and Attitudes toward Patients: Studies of a Disappearing Phenomenon." *Psychotherapy: Theory, Research and Practice,* 6 (1969), 223–228.
Kendrick, D. C., and Clarke, R. V. G. "Attitudinal Differences between Heterosexually and Homosexually Oriented Males." *British Journal of Psychiatry,* 113 (1967), 95–99.
Kenyon, F. E. "Studies in Female Homosexuality. IV. Social and Psychiatric Aspects." *British Journal of Psychiatry,* 114 (1968a), 1137–1350.
______. "Studies in Female Homosexuality—Psychological Test Results." *Journal of Consulting and Clinical Psychology,* 32 (1968b), 510–513.
Kepecs, J. G. "Some Patterns of Somatic Displacement." *Psychosomatic Medicine,* 25 (1953), 425–432.
______. "Theories of Transference Neurosis." *Psychoanalytic Quarterly,* 35 (1966), 497–521.
______. "Psychoanalysis Today. A Rather Lonely Island." *Archives of General Psychiatry,* 18 (1968), 161–167.
Kepecs, J. G., and Wolman, R. "Preconscious Perception of the Transference." *Psychoanalytic Quarterly,* 41 (1972), 172–194.
Kernberg, O. F. "Summary and Conclusions of 'Psychotherapy and Psychoanalysis, Final Report of the Menninger Foundation's Psychotherapy Research Project.' " *International Journal of Psychiatry,* 11 (1973a), 62–77.
______. "Author's Reply." *International Journal of Psychiatry,* (1973b), 95–103.
Kernberg, O. F., Burstein, E. D., Coyne, L., Appelbaum, A., Horwitz, L., and Voth, H. "Psychotherapy and Psychoanalysis." *Bulletin of the Menninger Clinic,* 36 (1972), Nos. 1, 2, 1–178.
Kessel, L., and Hyman, H. T. "The Value of Psychoanalysis as a Therapeutic Procedure." *Journal of the American Medical Association,* 101 (1933), 1612–1615.
Kessel, P., and McBrearty, J. F. "Values and Psychotherapy: A Review of the Literature." *Perceptual and Motor Skills,* 25 (1967), 669–690.
Khajavi, F., and Hekmat, H. "A Comparative Study of Empathy. The Effects of Psychiatric Training." *Archives of General Psychiatry,* 25 (1971), 490–493.
Kiesler, C. A., and Singer, R. D. "The Effects of Similarity and Guilt on the Projection of Hostility." *Journal of Clinical Psychology,* 19 (1963), 157–162.
Kiesler, D. J. "Some Myths of Psychotherapy Research and the Search for a Paradigm." *Psychological Bulletin,* 65 (1966), 110–136.
Kimeldorf, C., and Geiwitz, P. J. "Smoking and the Blacky Orality Factors." *Journal of Projective Techniques and Personality Assessment,* 30 (1966), 167–168.
King, B. D. "Learning and Orality: The Relationship between Oral Receptivity and Serial Learning, Verbal Recall and Grade-Point Average in College Women." Unpublished doctoral dissertation, Boston University School of Education, 1970.
King, G. F., and Schiller, M. "Ego Strength and Type of Defensive Behavior." *Journal of Consulting Psychology,* 24 (1960), 215–217.
King, H. H. "An Investigation of Relationships between Hypnotic Susceptibility, Manifest

Dream Content and Personality Characteristics." Unpublished doctoral dissertation, Louisiana State University, 1971.
Kirtner, W. L., and Cartwright, D. S. "Success and Failure in Client-Centered Therapy as a Function of Initial In-Therapy Behavior." *Journal of Consulting Psychology,* 22 (1958), 329–333.
Kish, G. B. "Correlates of Active-Passive Food Preferences: Failure to Confirm a Relationship with Alcoholism." *Perceptual and Motor Skills,* 31 (1970), 839–847.
Kissinger, R. D., and Tolor, A. "The Attitudes of Psychotherapists toward Psychotherapeutic Knowledge: A Study in Differences among the Professions." *Journal of Nervous and Mental Disease,* 140 (1965), 71–79.
Klackenberg, G. "Thumbsucking: Frequency and Etiology." *Pediatrics,* 4 (1949), 418–424.
Klaf, F.S. "Female Homosexuality and Paranoid Schizophrenia: A Survey of 75 Cases and Controls." *Archives of General Psychiatry,* 4 (1961), 84–86.
Klaf, F. S., and Davis, C. A. "Homosexuality and Paranoid Schizophrenia: A Survey of 150 Cases and Controls." *American Journal of Psychiatry,* 116 (1960), 1070–1075.
Klee, G. D., and Warthen, J. "Report on a Survey of Baltimore Analysts." *Psychiatric News,* 17 (1968).
Klein, H. R. "A Study of Changes Occurring in Patients during and after Psychoanalytic Treatment." In P. H. Hoch and J. Zubin, eds., *Current Approaches to Psychoanalysis. Proceedings of the 48th Annual Meeting of the American Psychopathological Association.* New York: Grune and Stratton, 1960, pp. 151–175.
———. *Psychoanalysts in Training: Selection and Evaluation.* Psychoanalytic Clinic for Training and Research, Department of Psychiatry, Columbia University, College of Physicians and Surgeons, 1965.
Klein, H. R., and Horwitz, W. A. "Psychosexual Factors in the Paranoid Phenomena. *American Journal of Psychiatry,* 105 (1949), 697–701.
Klein, R. H., and Iker, H. P. "The Lack of Differentiation between Male and Female in Schreber's Autobiography." *Journal of Abnormal Psychology,* 83 (1974), 234–239.
Kline, P. "An Investigation into the Freudian Concept of the Anal Character." Unpublished doctoral dissertation, University of Manchester, 1967a.
———. "Obsessional Traits and Emotional Instability in a Normal Population." *British Journal of Medical Psychology,* 40 (1967b), 153–157.
———. "The Use of Cattell's 16 PF Test and Eysenck's EPI with a Literate Population in Ghana." *British Journal of Social and Clinical Psychology,* 6 (1967c), 97–107.
———. "Obsessional Traits, Obsessional Symptoms and Anal Erotism." *British Journal of Medical Psychology,* 41 (1968a), 299–305.
———. "The Validity of the Dynamic Personality Inventory." *British Journal of Medical Psychology,* 41 (1968b), 307–313.
———. "The Anal Character: A Cross-Cultural Study in Ghana." *British Journal of Social and Clinical Psychology,* 8 (1969a), 201–210.
———. "A Study of the Oedipus Complex and Neurotic Symptoms in a Non-Psychiatric Population." (Letter to the editor.) *British Journal of Medical Psychology,* 42 (1969b), 291–292.
———. *A Projective and Psychometric Study of the Oral Character.* Proceedings of the VII International Conference for the Society of Rorschach and Projective Techniques. Vienna: Hans Huber, 1970.
———. *Fact and Fantasy in Freudian Theory.* London: Methuen, 1972.
———. "The Validity of Gottheil's Oral Trait Scale in Great Britain." *Journal of Personality Assessment,* 37 (1973), 551–554.
Klinger, E. "Development of Imaginative Behavior: Implications of Play for a Theory of Fantasy." *Psychological Bulletin,* 72 (1969), 277–298.
Klorman, R., and Chapman, L. J. "Regression in Schizophrenic Thought Disorder." *Journal of Abnormal Psychology,* 74 (1969), 199–204.
Klugman, S. F. "Retention of Affectively Toned Verbal Material by Normals and Neurotics." *Journal of Abnormal and Social Psychology,* 53 (1956), 321–327.
Knapp, P. H. "Short-Term Psychoanalytic and Psychosomatic Predictions." *Journal of the American Psychoanalytic Association,* 11 (1963), 245–280.
———. "Libido: A Latter-Day Look." *Journal of Nervous and Mental Disease,* 142 (1966), 395–417.

Knapp, P. H., Levin, S., McCarter, R. H., Wermer, H., and Zetzel, E. "Suitability for Psychoanalysis: A Review of 100 Supervised Analytic Cases." *Psychoanalytic Quarterly*, 29 (1960), 459–477.

Knapp, P. H., Mushatt, C., Nemetz, S. J., Constantine, H., and Friedman, S. "The Context of Reported Asthma during Psychoanalysis." *Psychosomatic Medicine*, 32 (1970), 167–188.

Knight, R. P. "The Relationship of Latent Homosexuality to the Mechanism of Paranoid Delusions." *Bulletin of the Menninger Clinic*, 4 (1940), 149–159.

______. "Evaluation of the Results of Psychoanalytic Therapy." *American Journal of Psychotherapy*, 98 (1941), 434–446.

Knott, P. D., and Drost, B. A. "Sex-Role Identification, Interpersonal Aggression, and Anger." *Psychological Reports*, 27 (1970), 154.

Koegler, R., and Brill, Q. *Treatment of Psychiatric Outpatients.* New York: Appleton-Century-Crofts, 1967.

Koegler, R. R., and Kline, L. Y. "Psychotherapy Research: An Approach Utilizing Autonomic Response Measurements." *American Journal of Psychotherapy*, 19 (1965), 268–279.

Kogan, N. "Authoritarianism and Repression." *Journal of Abnormal and Social Psychology*, 53 (1956), 34–37.

Kohlberg, L. "Moral Development and Identification." In H. W. Stevenson, ed., *Child Psychology.* Chicago: University of Chicago, 1963, pp. 277–332.

______. "A Cognitive-Developmental Analysis of Children's Sex-Role Concepts and Attitudes." In Eleanor Maccoby, ed., *The Development of Sex Differences.* Stanford: Stanford University, 1966, pp. 82–173.

Kohlberg, L., and Zigler, E. "The Impact of Cognitive Maturity on the Development of Sex-Role Attitudes in the Years 4 to 8." *Genetic Psychology Monographs*, 75 (1966), 89–165.

Kokonis, N. D. "Sex-Role Identification in Schizophrenia: Psychoanalytic and Role-Theory Predictions Compared." Unpublished doctoral dissertation, Illinois Institute of Technology, 1971.

______. "Sex-Role Identification in Neurosis: Psychoanalytic-Developmental and Role Theory Predictions Compared." *Journal of Abnormal Psychology*, 80 (1972), 52–57.

Kolb, L. C., and Montgomery, J. "An Explanation for Transference Cure: Its Occurrence in Psychoanalysis and Psychotherapy." *American Journal of Psychiatry*, 115 (1958), 414–421.

Koresko, R. L., Snyder, F., and Feinberg, I. " 'Dream Time' in Hallucinating and Non-Hallucinating Schizophrenic Patients." *Nature*, 199 (1963), 1118.

Korner, I. N. "The Mechanics of Suppression: An Experimental Investigation." *Journal of Consulting Psychology*, 30 (1966), 269–272.

Korner, I. N., and Buckwalter, M. M. "Effects of Age and Intelligence on the Operation of Suppression." *Journal of Consulting Psychology*, 31 (1967) 637–639.

Kott, M. G. "Learning and Retention of Words of Sexual and Nonsexual Meaning." *Journal of Abnormal and Social Psychology*, 50 (1955), 378–382.

Koulack, D. "Effects of Somatosensory Stimulation on Dream Content." *Archives of General Psychiatry*, 20 (1969), 718–725.

______. "Effects of Thirst on the Sleep Cycle." *Journal of Nervous and Mental Disease*, 151 (1970), 143–145.

______. "Rapid Eye Movements and Visual Imagery during Sleep." *Psychological Bulletin*, 78 (1972), 155–158.

Kovar, L. "A Reconsideration of Paranoia." *Psychiatry*, 29 (1966), 289–305.

Kracke, W. H. "The Maintenance of the Ego: Implications of Sensory Deprivation Research for Psychoanalytic Ego Psychology." *British Journal of Medical Psychology*, 40 (1967), 17–28.

Kraft, T. "Psychoanalysis and Behaviorism: A False Antithesis." *American Journal of Psychotherapy*, 23 (1969), 482–487.

Kramer, M., ed. *Dream Psychology and the New Biology of Dreaming.* Springfield, Ill.: Charles C. Thomas, 1969.

______. "Manifest Dream Content in Normal and Psychopathologic States." *Archives of General Psychiatry*, 22 (1970), 149–159.

Kramer, M., Baldridge, B. J., Whitman, R. M., Ornstein, P. H., and Smith, P. C. "An

Exploration of the Manifest Dream in Schizophrenic and Depressed Patients." *Diseases of the Nervous System,* 30 (1969), 126–130.
Kramer, M., Whitman, R. M., Baldridge, B., and Lansky, L. "Depression: Dreams and Defenses." *American Journal of Psychiatry,* 122 (1965), 411–419.
Kramer, M., Whitman, R. M., Baldridge, B., and Ornstein, P. H. "Drugs and Dreams. III: The Effects of Impramine on the Dreams of Depressed Patients." *American Journal of Psychiatry,* 124 (1968), 1385–1392.
Kramer, M., Whitman, R. M., and Winget, C. "A Survey Approach to Normative Dream Content: Sex, Age, Marital Status, Race and Educational Differences." *Psychophysiology,* 7 (1970), 325.
Krasner, L. "The Therapist as a Social Reinforcement Machine." In H. H. Strupp and L. Luborsky, eds., *Research in Psychotherapy.* Vol. 2. Washington, D.C.: American Psychological Association, 1962, pp. 61–94.
———. "The Operant Approach in Behavior Therapy." In A. E. Bergin and S. L. Garfield, eds., *Handbook of Psychotherapy and Behavior Change.* New York: Wiley, 1971, pp. 612–652.
Kreitler, H. and Shulamith, K. "Children's Concepts of Sexuality and Birth." *Child Development,* 37 (1966), 363–378.
Kremer, M. W., and Rifkin, A. "The Early Development of Homosexuality: A Study of Adolescent Lesbians." *American Journal of Psychiatry,* 126 (1969), 91–96.
Krieger, M. H., and Worchel, P. "A Quantitative Study of the Psychoanalytic Hypotheses of Identification." *Psychological Reports,* 5 (1959), 448.
Kringlen, E. "Obsessional Neurotics: A Long-Term Follow-Up." *British Journal of Psychiatry,* 111 (1965), 709–722.
Krohn, A. S. "Level of Object Representation in the Manifest Dream and Projective Tests: A Construct Validation Study." Unpublished doctoral dissertation, University of Michigan, 1972.
Kroth, J. A. "The Analytic Couch and Response to Free Association." *Psychotherapy: Theory, Research and Practice,* 7 (1970), 206–208.
———. "An Experimental Investigation of Free Association Effectiveness as a Function of Posture: Implications for Counseling." Unpublished doctoral dissertation, Florida State University, 1969.
Kroth, J. A., and Forrest, M. S. "Effects of Posture and Anxiety Level on Effectiveness of Free Association." *Psychological Reports,* 25 (1969), 725–726.
Krout, M. H., and Tabin, J. K. "Measuring Personality in Developmental Terms: The Personal Preference Scale." *Genetic Psychology Monographs,* 50 (1954), 289–335.
Kubie, L. S. "A Pilot Study of Psychoanalytic Practice in the United States." *Psychiatry,* 13 (1950), 227–245.
———. "Psychoanalysis and Scientific Method." *Journal of Nervous and Mental Disease,* 131 (1960), 495–512.
———. "The Concept of Dream Deprivation: A Critical Analysis." *Psychosomatic Medicine,* 24 (1962), 62–65.
Kurland, M. L. "Oneiromancy: An Historic View of Dream Interpretation." *American Journal of Psychotherapy,* 26 (1972), 408–416.
Kurland, S. H. "The Lack of Generality in Defense Mechanisms as Indicated in Auditory Perception." *Journal of Abnormal and Social Psychology,* 49 (1954), 173–177.
Kurtz, R. M. "Sex Differences and Variations in Body Attitudes." *Journal of Consulting and Clinical Psychology,* 33 (1969), 625–629.
Kurtz, R. R., and Grummon, D. L. "Different Approaches to the Measurement of Therapist Empathy and their Relationship to Therapy Outcomes." *Journal of Consulting and Clinical Psychology,* 39 (1972), 106–115.
Kwawer, J. S. "An Experimental Study of Psychoanalytic Theories of Overt Male Homosexuality." Unpublished doctoral dissertation, New York University, 1971.
LaBarre, W. "The Influence of Freud on Anthropology." *American Imago,* 15–16 (1958–59), 275–328.
Lachmann, F. M., Lapkin, B., and Handelman, N. S. "The Recall of Dreams: Its Relation to Repression and Cognitive Control." *Journal of Abnormal and Social Psychology,* 64 (1962), 160–162.

Laffal, J. "The Learning and Retention of Words with Association Disturbances." *Journal of Abnormal and Social Psychology,* 47 (1952), 454–462.
Lakin, M., and Lebovits, B. "Bias in Psychotherapists of Different Orientations." *American Journal of Psychotherapy,* 12 (1958), 79–86.
Lambert, W. W., Triandis, L. M., and Wolf, M. "Some Correlates of Beliefs in the Malevolence and Benevolence of Supernatural Beings: A Cross-Cultural Study." *Journal of Abnormal and Social Psychology,* 58 (1959), 162–169.
Landis, C. "Statistical Evaluation of Psychotherapeutic Methods." In L. E. Hinsie, ed., *Concepts and Problems of Psychotherapy.* New York: Columbia University, 1937, pp. 155–169.
Landy, E. E. "Sex Differences in Some Aspects of Smoking Behavior." *Psychological Reports,* 20 (1967), 575–580.
Lane, R. C., and Singer, J. L. "Familial Attitudes in Paranoid Schizophrenics and Normals from Two Socioeconomic Classes." *Journal of Abnormal and Social Psychology,* 59 (1959), 328–339.
Lane, R. W. "The Effect of Preoperative Stress on Dreams." Unpublished doctoral dissertation, University of Oregon, 1966.
Lang, P. J., and Lazovik, A. D. "Experimental Desensitization of a Phobia." *Journal of Abnormal and Social Psychology,* 66 (1963), 519–525.
Langer, E. J., and Abelson, R. P. "A Patient By Any Other Name . . . : Clinician Group Difference in Labeling Bias." *Journal of Consulting and Clinical Psychology,* 42 (1974), 4–9.
Langs, R. J. "Earliest Memories and Personality: A Predictive Study." *Archives of General Psychiatry,* 12 (1965), 379–390.
______. "Manifest Dreams from Three Clinical Groups." *Archives of General Psychiatry,* 14 (1966), 634–643.
______. "Stability of Earliest Memories under LSD-25 and Placebo." *Journal of Nervous and Mental Disease,* 144 (1967a), 171–184.
______. "Manifest Dreams in Adolescents: A Controlled Pilot Study." *Journal of Nervous and Mental Disease,* 145 (1967b), 43–52.
Langs, R. J., Rothenberg, M. B., Fishman, J. R., and Reiser, M. F. "A Method for Clinical and Theoretical Study of the Earliest Memory." *Archives of General Psychiatry,* 3 (1960), 523–534.
Lansky, L. M., Crandall, V. J., Kagan, J., and Baker, C. T. "Sex Differences in Aggression and its Correlates in Middle-Class Adolescents." *Child Development,* 32 (1961), 45–58.
Lanyon, R. I. "Verbal Conditioning: Transfer of Training in a Therapy-Like Situation." *Journal of Abnormal Psychology,* 72 (1967), 30–34.
LaVoie, J. C. "Punishment and Adolescent Self Control: A Study of the Effects of Aversive Stimulation, Reasoning, and Sex of Parent." Unpublished doctoral dissertation, University of Wisconsin, 1970.
LaVoie, J. C., and Looft, W. R. "Parental Antecedents of Resistance-to-Temptation Behavior in Adolescent Males." *Merrill-Palmer Quarterly of Behavior and Development,* 19 (1973), 107–116.
Lazare, A. "The Hysterical Character in Psychoanalytic Theory: Evolution and Confusion." *Archives of General Psychiatry,* 25 (1971), 131–137.
Lazare, A., Klerman, G. L., and Armor, D. J. "Oral, Obsessive, and Hysterical Personality Patterns." *Archives of General Psychiatry,* 14 (1966), 624–630.
______. "Oral, Obsessive and Hysterical Personality Patterns: Replication of Factor Analysis in an Independent Sample." *Journal of Psychiatric Research,* 7 (1970), 275–290.
Lazarus, A. A. "Group Therapy of Phobic Disorders by Systematic Desensitization." *Journal of Abnormal and Social Psychology,* 63 (1961), 504–510.
______. "The Results of Behavior Therapy in 126 Cases of Severe Neurosis." *Behaviour Research and Therapy,* 1 (1963), 69–79.
______. "Behavior Therapy, Incomplete Treatment, and Symptom Substitution." *Journal of Nervous and Mental Disease,* 140 (1965), 80–86.
______. "Behaviour Rehearsal vs. Non-Directive Therapy vs. Advice in Effecting Behavior Change." *Behaviour Research and Therapy,* 4 (1966), 209–212.
Lazarus, R. S., and Alfert, E. "Short-Circuiting of Threat by Experimentally Altering Cognitive Appraisal." *Journal of Abnormal Psychology,* 69 (1964), 195–205.

Lazowick, L. M. "On the Nature of Identification." *Journal of Abnormal and Social Psychology,* 51 (1955), 175–183.
Lee, S. G. "Social Influences in Zulu Dreaming." *Journal of Social Psychology,* 47 (1958), 265–283.
Lefley, H. P. "Masculinity-Femininity in Obese Women." *Journal of Consulting and Clinical Psychology,* 37 (1971), 180–186.
Lehrman, N. S. "Precision in Psychoanalysis." *American Journal of Psychiatry,* 116 (1960), 1097–1103.
Lehrman, S. R. "Psychoanalytic Orientation in Psychotherapy." *Archives of Neurology and Psychiatry,* 81 (1958), 351–361.
Leichty, M. M. "The Effect of Father-Absence During Early Childhood upon the Oedipal Situation as Reflected in Young Adults." *Merrill-Palmer Quarterly,* 6 (1959–60), 212–217.
Lerner, B. "Rorschach Movement and Dreams: a Validation Study Using Drug-Induced Dream Deprivation." *Journal of Abnormal Psychology,* 71 (1966), 75–86.
———. "Dream Function Reconsidered." *Journal of Abnormal Psychology,* 72 (1967), 85–100.
Lerner, B. "Auditory and Visual Thresholds for the Perception of Words of Anal Connotation: An Evaluation of the 'Sublimation Hypothesis' on Philatelists." Unpublished doctoral dissertation, Yeshiva University, 1961.
Lerner, J., and Shanan, J. "Coping Style of Psychiatric Patients with Somatic Complaints." *Journal of Personality Assessment,* 36 (1972), 28–32.
Lesse, S. "Experimental Studies on the Relationship between Anxiety, Dreams and Dream-Like States." *American Journal of Psychotherapy,* 13 (1959), 440–455.
———. "Placebo Reactions and Spontaneous Rhythms in Psychotherapy." *Archives of General Psychiatry,* 10 (1964), 497–505.
———. "Hypochondriasis and Psychosomatic Disorders Masking Depression." *American Journal of Psychotherapy,* 21 (1967), 607–620.
Lessler, K. "Cultural and Freudian Dimensions of Sexual Symbols." *Journal of Consulting Psychology,* 28 (1964), 46–53.
Lessler, K., and Erickson, M. T. "Response to Sexual Symbols by Elementary School Children." *Journal of Consulting and Clinical Psychology,* 32 (1968), 473–477.
Lessler, K., and Strupp, H. H. "Outcome Evaluations and Affective Response of Psychotherapists to Patients in Treatment." *Psychotherapy: Theory, Research and Practice,* 4 (1967), 103–106.
Lester, D. "Antecedents of the Fear of the Dead." *Psychological Reports,* 19 (1966), 741–742.
Levin, R. B. "An Empirical Test of the Female Castration Complex." *Journal of Abnormal Psychology,* 71 (1966), 181–188.
Levin, T. "The Function of the Idealized Self-Image in Transference Formation: A Study of Eight Psychoanalytic Patients to Determine the Function of the Projected Idealized Self-Image in the Evaluation of the Analyst, Using Q-Methodology." Unpublished doctoral dissertation, New York University, 1961.
Levinger, G., and Clark, J. "Emotional Factors in the Forgetting of Word Associations." *Journal of Abnormal and Social Psychology,* 62 (1961), 99–105.
Levison, P. K., Zax, M., and Cowen, E. L. "An Experimental Analogue of Psychotherapy for Anxiety Reduction." *Psychological Reports,* 8 (1961), 171–178.
Levy, D. M. "Fingersucking and Accessory Movements in Early Infancy: An Etiologic Study." *American Journal of Psychiatry,* 7 (1927–28), 881–918.
———. " 'Controlled Situation' Studies of Children's Responses to the Differences in Genitalia." *American Journal of Orthopsychiatry,* 10 (1940), 755–762.
———. *Maternal Overprotection.* New York: Columbia University, 1943.
Levy, J. "Regression in the Service of the Ego Cognitive Control, and Sexual Identification." Unpublished doctoral dissertation, Michigan State University, 1961.
———. "Early Memories: Theoretical Aspects and Application." *Journal of Projective Techniques and Personality Assessment,* 29 (1965), 281–291.
Levy, J., and Grigg, K. A. "Early Memories." *Archives of General Psychiatry,* 7 (1962), 57–69.
Levy, L. H. "Sexual Symbolism: A Validity Study." *Journal of Consulting Psychology,* 18 (1954), 43–46.
Lewis, H. B., Goodenough, D. R., Shapiro, A., and Sleser, I. "Individual Differences in Dream Recall." *Journal of Abnormal Psychology,* 71 (1966), 52–59.

Lewis, J. M., Griffith, E. C., Riedel, A. F., and Simmons, B. A. "Studies in Abstraction: Schizophrenia and Orality: Preliminary Results." *Journal of Nervous and Mental Disease,* 129 (1959), 564–567.

Lewis, M. A. and Schoenfeldt, L. F. "Developmental-Interest Factors Associated with Homosexuality." *Journal of Consulting and Clinical Psychology,* 41 (1973), 291–293.

Lewis, N. D. C., and Hoch, P. H. "Clinical Psychiatry and Psychotherapy." *American Journal of Psychiatry,* 120 (1964), 637–643.

Lewis, S. A. "Experimental Induction of Castration Anxiety and Anxiety over Loss of Love." Unpublished doctoral dissertation, Yeshiva University, 1969.

Lewis, W. C., and Berman, M. "Studies of Conversion Hysteria. I. Operational Study of Diagnosis." *Archives of General Psychiatry,* 13 (1965), 275–282.

Lewit, D. W., Brayer, A. R., and Leiman, A. H. "Externalization in Perceptual Defense." *Journal of Abnormal and Social Psychology,* 65 (1962), 6–13.

Liberman, R. P. "Behavioral Modification of Schizophrenia: A Review." *Schizophrenia Bulletin,* 6 (1972), 37–48.

Lichtenstein, H. "Changing Implications of the Concept of Psychosexual Development." *Journal of the American Psychoanalytic Association,* 18 (1970), 300–318.

Liddicoat, R. "Homosexuality." *British Medical Journal,* 2 (1957), 1110–1111.

Lidz, T. "The Relevance of Family Studies to Psychoanalytic Theory." *Journal of Nervous and Mental Disease,* 135 (1962), 105–112.

Lief, H. I., Lief, V. F., Warren, C. O., and Heath, R. G. "Low Dropout Rate in a Psychiatric Clinic: Special Reference to Psychotherapy and Social Class." *Archives of General Psychiatry,* 5 (1961), 200–211.

Limentani, A. "The Assessment of Analysability: A Major Hazard in Selection for Psychoanalysis." *International Journal of Psycho-Analysis,* 53 (1972), 351–361.

Lindner, H. "The Blacky Pictures Test: A Study of Sexual and Non-Sexual Offenders." *Journal of Projective Techniques,* 17 (1953), 79–84.

Linn, E. L. "Relevance of Psychotic Patients' 'Insight' to Their Prognosis." *Archives of General Psychiatry,* 13 (1965), 424–428.

Linn, L. "Psychoanalytic Contributions to Psychosomatic Research." *Psychosomatic Medicine,* 20 (1958), 88–98.

Lipp, L., Kolstoe, R., James, W., and Randall, H. "Denial of Disability and Internal Control of Reinforcement: A Study Using a Perceptual Defense Paradigm." *Journal of Consulting and Clinical Psychology,* 32 (1968), 72–75.

Lipton, S. D. "Freud's Position on Problem Solving in Dreams." *British Journal of Medical Psychology,* 40 (1967), 147–149.

Lish, J. A. "The Influence of Oral Dependency, Failure, and Social Exposure upon Self-Esteem and Depression." Unpublished doctoral dissertation, New York University, 1969.

Littman, R. A., Nidorf, L. J., and Sundberg, N. D. "Characteristics of a Psychosexual Scale: The Krout Personal Preference Scale." *Journal of Genetic Psychology,* 98 (1961), 19–27.

Livson, N., and Peskin, H. "Prediction of Adult Psychological Health in a Longitudinal Study." *Journal of Abnormal Psychology,* 72 (1967), 509–518.

Locke, E. A. "Is Behavior Therapy Behavioristic? (An Analysis of Wolpe's Psychotherapeutic Methods.)" *Psychological Bulletin,* 76 (1971), 318–327.

Loesch, J. G., and Greenberg, N. H. "Some Specific Areas of Conflicts Observed During Pregnancy: A Comparative Study of Married and Unmarried Pregnant Women." *American Journal of Orthopsychiatry,* 32 (1962), 624–636.

London, P. *The Modes and Morals of Psychotherapy.* New York: Holt, Rinehart and Winston, 1964.

Loney, J. "An MMPI Measure of Maladjustment in a Sample of 'Normal' Homosexual Men." *Journal of Clinical Psychology,* 27 (1971), 486–488.

______. "Background Factors, Sexual Experiences, and Attitudes Toward Treatment in Two 'Normal' Homosexual Samples." *Journal of Consulting and Clinical Psychology,* 38 (1972), 57–65.

______. "Family Dynamics in Homosexual Women." *Archives of Sexual Behavior,* 2 (1973), 343–350.

Loper, R. G., Kammeier, Sister M. L., and Hoffman, H. "MMPI Characteristics of College

Freshman Males Who Later Became Alcoholics." *Journal of Abnormal Psychology,* 82 (1973), 159–162.

Lorand, S., and Console, W. A. "Therapeutic Results in Psycho-Analytic Treatment without Fee (Observation on Therapeutic Results)." *International Journal of Psycho-Analysis,* 39 (1958), 59–64.

Lord, M. M. "Activity and Affect in Early Memories of Adolescent Boys." *Journal of Personality Assessment,* 35 (1971), 448–456.

Lorr, M., and McNair, D. M. "Correlates of Length of Psychotherapy." *Journal of Clinical Psychology,* 20 (1964), 497–504.

———. "Methods Relating to Evaluation of Therapeutic Outcome." In L. A. Gottschalk and A. A. Auerbach, eds., *Methods of Research in Psychotherapy.* New York: Appleton-Century-Crofts, 1966, pp. 573–594.

Lorr, M., McNair, D. M., Michaux, W. W., and Raskin, A. "Frequency of Treatment and Change in Psychotherapy." *Journal of Abnormal and Social Psychology,* 64 (1962), 281–292.

Lower, R. B., Escoll, P. J., and Huxster, H. K. "Bases for Judgments of Analyzability." *Journal of the American Psychoanalytic Association,* 20 (1972), 610–621.

Lower, R. B., Escoll, P. J., Little, R. B., and Ottenberg, P. "An Experimental Examination of Transference." *Archives of General Psychiatry,* 29 (1973), 738–741.

Lowery, R. J. "Male-Female Differences in Attitudes toward Death." Unpublished doctoral dissertation, Brandeis University, 1965.

Lowinger, P. L., and Dobie, S. "Attitudes and Emotions of the Psychiatrist in the Initial Interview." *American Journal of Psychotherapy,* 20 (1966), 17–34.

Luborsky, L. "A Note on Eysenck's Article 'The Effects of Psychotherapy: An Evaluation.' " *British Journal of Psychology,* 45 (1954), 129–131.

———. "Clinicians' Judgments of Mental Health: A Proposed Scale." *Archives of General Psychiatry,* 7 (1962), 407–417.

———. "Another Reply to Eysenck." *Psychological Bulletin,* 78 (1972), 406–408.

Luborsky, L., and Auerbach, A. H. "The Symptom-Context Method: Quantitative Studies of Symptom Formation in Psychotherapy." *Journal of the American Psychoanalytic Association,* 17 (1969), 68–99.

Luborsky, L., Blinder, B., and Schimek, J. "Looking, Recalling, and GSR as a Function of Defense." *Journal of Abnormal Psychology,* 70 (1965), 270–280.

Luborsky, L., Chandler, M., Auerbach, A. H., and Cohen, J. "Factors Influencing the Outcome of Psychotherapy: A Review of Quantitative Research." *Psychological Bulletin,* 75 (1971), 145–185.

Luborsky, L., Graff, H., Pulver, S., and Curtis, H. "A Clinical-Quantitative Examination of Consensus on the Concept of Transference." *Archives of General Psychiatry,* 29 (1973), 69–75.

Luborsky, L., and Schimek, J. "Psychoanalytic Theories of Therapeutic and Developmental Change: Implications for Assessment." In P. Worchel and D. Byrne, eds., *Personality Change.* New York: Wiley, 1964, pp. 73–99.

Luborsky, L., and Shevrin, H. "Forgetting of Tachistoscopic Exposures as a Function of Repression." *Perceptual and Motor Skills,* 14 (1962), 189–190.

Luborsky, L., and Spence, D. P. "Quantitative Research on Psychoanalytic Therapy. In A. E. Bergin and S. L. Garfield, eds., *Handbook of Psychotherapy and Behavior Change.* New York: Wiley, 1971, pp. 408–438.

Lustman, S. L. "Some Issues in Contemporary Psychoanalytic Research." *Psychoanalytic Study of the Child,* 18 (1963), 51–74.

Lynn, D. B. "Divergent Feedback and Sex-Role Identification in Boys and Men." *Merrill-Palmer Quarterly,* 10 (1964), 17–23.

———. *Parental and Sex Role Identification.* Berkeley, Calif.: McCutchan, 1969.

MacAlpine, I., and Hunter, R. A. "Observations on the Psychoanalytic Theory of Psychosis: Freud's 'A Neurosis of Demoniacal Possession in the Seventeenth Century.' " *British Journal of Medical Psychology,* 27 (1954), 175–192.

MacDonald, W. S., Blochberger, C. W., and Maynard, H. M. "Group Therapy: A Comparison of Patient-Led and Staff-Led Groups on an Open Hospital Ward." *Psychiatric Quarterly Supplement,* 38 (1964), 290–303.

Mack, J. E. "Dreams and Psychosis." *Journal of the American Psychoanalytic Association,* 17 (1969), 206–221.

Mackinnon, D. W., and Dukes, W. F. "Repression." In L. Postman, ed., *Psychology in the Making.* New York: Knopf, 1962, pp. 662–744.
MacNeilage, P. F., Cohen, D. B., and MacNeilage, L. A. "Subject's Estimation of Sleep-Talking Propensity and Dream-Recall Frequency." *Journal of Consulting and Clinical Psychology,* 39 (1972), 341.
Madow, L., and Snow, L. H., Eds. *The Psychodynamic Implications of the Physiological Studies on Dreams.* Springfield, Ill.: Charles C. Thomas, 1970.
Maes, J. L. "Identification of Male College Students with Their Fathers and Some Related Indices of Affect Expression and Psychosexual Adjustment." Unpublished doctoral dissertation, Michigan State University, 1963.
Malan, D. H. *A Study of Brief Psychotherapy.* Springfield, Ill.: Charles C. Thomas, 1963.
______. "Science and Psychotherapy." *International Journal of Psychiatry,* 11 (1973a), 87–90.
______. "The Problem of Relevant Variables in Psychotherapy Research." *International Journal of Psychiatry,* 11 (1973b), 336–346.
Malan, D. H., Bacal, H. A., Heath, E. S., and Balfour, F. H. G. "A Study of Psychodynamic Changes in Untreated Neurotic Patients: I. Improvements That Are Questionable on Dynamic Criteria." *British Journal of Psychiatry,* 114 (1968), 525–551.
Malan, D. H., Heath, E. S., Bacal, H. A., and Balfour, F. H. G. "Psychodynamic Changes in Untreated Neurotic Patients: II. Apparently Genuine Improvements." *Archives of General Psychiatry,* 32 (1975), 110–126.
Mandel, H. "A Q-Methodology Investigation of the Oral and Anal Character as Described by Psychoanalytic Theory." Unpublished doctoral dissertation, New York University, 1958.
Mandler, G. "Parent and Child in the Development of the Oedipus Complex." *Journal of Nervous and Mental Disease,* 136 (1963), 227–235.
Mann, J. H., and Mann. C. H. "Insight as a Measure of Adjustment in Three Kinds of Group Experience." *Journal of Consulting Psychology,* 23 (1959), 91.
Mann, L., "The Relation of Rorschach Indices of Extraversion-Introversion to Certain Dream Dimensions." *Journal of Clinical Psychology,* 11 (1955), 80–81.
Mann, N. A. "The Relationship between Defense Preference and Response to Free Association." *Journal of Projective Techniques and Personality Assessment,* 31 (1967), 54–61.
Manosevitz, M. "Early Sexual Behavior in Adult Homosexual and Heterosexual Males." *Journal of Abnormal Psychology,* 76 (1970), 396–402.
______. "The Development of Male Homosexuality." *Journal of Sex Research,* 8 (1972), 31–40.
Manosevitz, M., and Lanyon, R. I. "Fear Survey Schedule: A Normative Study." *Psychological Reports,* 17 (1965), 699–703.
Marcus, D. S. "Cognitive Correlates of Oral Fixation." Unpublished doctoral dissertation, New York University, 1965.
Marcus, I. M. *Currents in Psychoanalysis.* New York: International Universities, 1971.
Marcus, M. M. "The Relation of Personality Structure to the Capacity for Memory Retention." Unpublished doctoral dissertation, University of Pittsburgh, 1963.
Markowitz, A., and Ford, L. H., Jr. "Defensive Denial and Selection of a Target for Projection." *Journal of Experimental Research in Personality,* 2 (1967), 272–277.
Markowitz, I., Mark, J. C., and Seiderman, S. "An Investigation of Parental Recognition of Children's Dreams: A Preliminary Report." *Science and Psychoanalysis,* 6 (1963), 135–151.
Marks, I. M. "The Origins of Phobic States." *American Journal of Psychotherapy,* 24 (1970), 652–676.
Marks, I. M., and Gelder, M. G. "A Controlled Retrospective Study of Behaviour Therapy in Phobic Patients." *British Journal of Psychiatry,* 111 (1965), 561–573.
Marmor, J. "Validation of Psychoanalytic Techniques." *Journal of the American Psychoanalytic Association,* 3 (1955), 496–505.
______. "The Reintegration of Psychoanalysis into Psychiatric Practice." *Archives of General Psychiatry,* 3 (1960), 569–574.
______. "Psychoanalytic Therapy and Theories of Learning." *Science and Psychoanalysis,* 7 (1964), 265–279.
______. "The Current Status of Psychoanalysis in American Psychiatry." *American Journal of Psychiatry,* 125 (1968), 679–680.
______. "Limitations of Free Association." *Archives of General Psychiatry,* 22 (1970), 160–165.

Marquis, D. P., Sinnett, E. R., and Winter, W. D. "A Psychological Study of Peptic Ulcer Patients." *Journal of Clinical Psychology,* 8 (1952), 266–272.

Marshall, J. R. "The Expression of Feelings." *Archives of General Psychiatry,* 27 (1972), 786–790.

Masling, J., Johnson, C., and Saturansky, C. "Oral Imagery, Accuracy of Perceiving Others, and Performance in Peace Corps Training." *Journal of Personality and Social Psychology,* 30 (1974), 414–419.

Masling, J., Rabie, L., and Blondheim, S. H. "Obesity, Level of Aspiration, and Rorschach and TAT Measures of Oral Dependence." *Journal of Consulting Psychology,* 31 (1967), 233–239.

Masling, J., Weiss, L., and Rothschild, B. "Relationships of Oral Imagery to Yielding Behavior and Birth Order." *Journal of Consulting and Clinical Psychology,* 32 (1968), 89–91.

Maslow, A. H., and Szilagyi-Kessler, I. "Security and Breast-Feeding." *Journal of Abnormal and Social Psychology,* 41 (1946), 83–85.

Masserman, J. H. "Psychotherapy as the Mitigation of Uncertainties." *Archives of General Psychiatry,* 26 (1972), 186–188.

Matarazzo, R. G. "Research on the Teaching and Learning of Psychotherapeutic Skills." In A. E. Bergin and S. L. Garfield, eds., *Handbook of Psychotherapy and Behavior Change.* New York: Wiley, 1971, pp. 895–924.

Materson, J. F., "The Symptomatic Adolescent Five Years Later: He Didn't Grow Out of It." *American Journal of Psychiatry,* 123 (1967), 1338–1345.

May, P. R. A. "Research in Psychotherapy and Psychoanalysis." *International Journal of Psychiatry,* 11 (1973), 78–86.

May, P. R. A., and Tuma, A. H. "Treatment of Schizophrenia: An Experimental Study of Five Treatment Methods." *British Journal of Psychiatry,* 111 (1965), 503–510.

May, R. "Paranoia and Power Anxiety." *Journal of Projective Techniques and Personality Assessment,* 34 (1970), 412–418.

Mayman, M. "Early Memories and Character Structure." *Journal of Projective Techniques and Personality Assessment,* 32 (1968), 303–316.

———, "Psychoanalytic Research: Three Approaches to the Experimental Study of Subliminal Processes." *Psychological Issues,* 8 (1973), No. 30.

Mayo, P. R. "Some Psychological Changes Associated with Improvement in Depression." *British Journal of Social and Clinical Psychology,* 6 (1967), 63–68.

———. "Women with Neurotic Symptoms Who Do Not Seek Treatment." *British Journal of Medical Psychology,* 42 (1969), 165–169.

McArthur, C., Waldron, E., and Dickinson, J. "The Psychology of Smoking." *Journal of Abnormal and Social Psychology,* 56 (1958), 267–275.

McCawley, A. "Paranoia and Homosexuality." *New York State Journal of Medicine,* 71 (1971), 1506–1513.

McCord, J., McCord, W., and Thurber, E. "Some Effects of Paternal Absence on Male Children." *Journal of Abnormal and Social Psychology,* 64 (1962), 361–369.

McCord, W., McCord, J., and Howard, A. "Familial Correlates of Aggression in Nondelinquent Male Children." *Journal of Abnormal and Social Psychology,* 62 (1961), 79–93.

McCord, W., McCord, J., and Verden, P. "Family Relationships and Sexual Deviance in Lower-Class Adolescents." *International Journal of Social Psychiatry,* 8 (1961–62), 165–179.

McCully, R. S., Glucksman, M. L., and Hirsch, J. "Nutrition Imagery in the Rorschach Materials of Food-Deprived, Obese Patients." *Journal of Projective Techniques and Personality Assessment,* 32 (1968), 375–382.

McDonagh, J. M. "The Relationship between Familial Characteristics and Two Measures of Dependency." Unpublished doctoral dissertation, University of Oklahoma, 1970.

McElroy, W. A. "Methods of Testing the Oedipus Complex Hypothesis." *Quarterly Bulletin of the British Psychological Association,* 1 (1950), 364–365.

McGuire, M. T. *Reconstructions in Psychoanalysis.* New York: Appleton-Century-Crofts, 1971.

McKegney, F. "The Incidence and Characteristics of Patients with Conversion Reactions: I. A General Hospital Consultation Service Sample." *American Journal of Psychiatry,* 124 (1967), 542–545.

McLaughlin, F. "Problems of Reanalysis." *Journal of the American Psychoanalytic Association,* 7 (1959), 537–547.
McLaughlin, T. J. "Visual Attention as a Function of Stimulus Content in Paranoid and Non-Paranoid Schizophrenics." Unpublished doctoral dissertation, Boston University Graduate School, 1972.
McNair, D. M., and Lorr, M. "Therapists' Judgments of Appropriateness of Psychotherapy Frequency Schedules." *Journal of Consulting Psychology,* 24 (1960), 500–506.
———. "An Analysis of Professed Psychotherapeutic Techniques." *Journal of Consulting Psychology,* 28 (1964), 265–271.
McNair, D. M., Lorr, M., and Callahan, D. M. "Patient and Therapist Influences on Quitting Psychotherapy," *Journal of Consulting Psychology,* 27 (1963), 10–17.
McNair, D. M., Lorr, M., Young, H. H., Roth, I., and Boyd, R. W. "A Three-Year Follow-Up of Psychotherapy Patients." *Journal of Clinical Psychology,* 20 (1964), 258–264.
McNeil, E. B., and Blum, G. S. "Handwriting and Psychosexual Dimensions of Personality." *Journal of Projective Techniques,* 16 (1952), 476–484.
McPherson, M. W., Popplestone, J. A., and Evans, K. A. "Perceptual Carelessness, Drawing Precision, and Oral Activity Among Normal Six-Year-Olds." *Perceptual and Motor Skills,* 22 (1966), 327–330.
McReynolds, P., Landes, J., and Acker, M. "Dream Content as a Function of Personality Incongruency and Unsettledness." *Journal of General Psychology,* 74 (1966), 313–317.
Meehl, P. E. "Wanted—A Good Cookbook." *American Psychologist,* 11 (1956), 262–272.
Meer, S. J. "Authoritarian Attitudes and Dreams." *Journal of Abnormal and Social Psychology,* 51 (1955), 74–78.
Megargee, E. I., ed. *Research in Clinical Assessment.* New York: Harper & Row, 1966.
Mehrabian, A. "Significance of Posture and Position in the Communication of Attitude and Status Relationships." *Psychological Bulletin,* 71 (1969), 359–372.
Meichenbaum, D. H., Gilmore, J. B., and Fedoravicius, A. "Group Insight versus Group Desensitization in Treating Speech Anxiety." *Journal of Consulting and Clinical Psychology,* 36 (1971), 410–421.
Meier, C. A., Ruef, H., and Ziegler, A. "Forgetting of Dreams in the Laboratory." *Perceptual and Motor Skills,* 26 (1968), 551–557.
Meissner, W. W. "Affective Response to Psychoanalytic Death Symbols." *Journal of Abnormal and Social Psychology,* 56 (1958), 295–299.
———. "Dreaming as Process." *International Journal of Psycho-Analysis,* 49 (1968), 63–79.
Meketon, B. W., Griffith, R. M., Taylor, V. H., and Wiedeman, J. S. "Rorschach Homosexual Signs in Paranoid Schizophrenics." *Journal of Abnormal and Social Psychology,* 65 (1962), 280–284.
Melnick, B. "Patient-Therapist Identification in Relation to Both Patient and Therapist Variables and Therapy Outcome." *Journal of Consulting and Clinical Psychology,* 38 (1972), 97–104.
Meltzoff, J., and Kornreich, M. *Research in Psychotherapy.* New York: Atherton, 1970.
Mendell, W. "The Phenomenon of Interpretation." *American Journal of Psychoanalysis,* 24 (1964), 184–189.
Mendelsohn, G. A., and Geller, M. H. "Structure of Client Attitudes toward Counseling and Their Relation to Client-Counselor Similarity." *Journal of Consulting Psychology,* 29 (1965), 63–72.
Menninger, K. *Theory of Psychoanalytic Technique.* New York: Basic Books, 1958.
Messer, A. A. "The 'Phaedra Complex.' " *Archives of General Psychiatry,* 21 (1969), 213–218.
Meyer, A. E. "Psychoanalytic versus Behavior Therapy of Male Homosexuals: A Statistical Evaluation of Clinical Outcome." *Comprehensive Psychiatry,* 7 (1966), 110–117.
Meyer, R. G., and Karon, B. P. "The Schizophrenogenic Mother Concept and the TAT." *Psychiatry,* 30 (1967), 173–179.
Migdole, S. M. "An Investigation of Orality, Depression, and Denial in Obese and Non-Obese Adolescent Females." Unpublished doctoral dissertation, Boston University School of Education, 1967.
Mikulas, W. L. "Criticisms of Behavior Therapy." *Canadian Psychologist,* 13 (1972), 83–104.
Miles, D. W. "The Import for Clinical Psychology of the Use of Tests Derived from Theories

about Infantile Sexuality and Adult Character." *Genetic Psychology Monographs,* 50 (1954), 227–288.

Miles, H. W., Barrabee, E. L., and Finesinger, J. E. "The Problem of Evaluation of Psychotherapy: With a Follow-Up Study of 62 Cases of Anxiety Neurosis." *Journal of Nervous and Mental Disease,* 114 (1951), 359–365.

Miller, A. R. "Analysis of the Oedipal Complex." *Psychological Reports,* 24 (1969), 781–782.

Miller, C. W. "The Paranoid Syndrome." *Archives of Neurology and Psychiatry,* 45 (1941), 953–963.

Miller, D. R., and Stine, M. E. "The Prediction of Social Acceptance by Means of Psychoanalytic Concepts." *Journal of Personality,* 20 (1951), 162–174.

Miller, D. R., and Swanson, G. E. *Inner Conflict and Defense.* New York: Schocken, 1966.

Miller, J. B. "Dreams During Varying Stages of Depression." *Archives of General Psychiatry,* 20 (1969), 560–565.

Miller, J. O., and Gross, S. J. "Curvilinear Trends in Outcome Research." *Journal of Consulting and Clinical Psychology,* 41 (1974), 242–244.

Miller, P. M., Bradley, J. B., Gross, R. S., and Wood, G. "Review of Homosexuality Research (1960–1966) and Some Implications for Treatment." *Psychotherapy: Theory, Research and Practice,* 5 (1968), 3–6.

Miller, P. R. "The Effeminate Passive Obligatory Homosexual." *Archives of Neurology and Psychiatry,* 80 (1958), 612–618.

Miller, W. G., and Hannum, T. E. "Characteristics of Homosexuality Involved Incarcerated Females." *Journal of Consulting Psychology,* 27 (1963), 277.

Milner, E. "Effects of Sex Role and Social Status on the Early Adolescent Personality." *Genetic Psychology Monographs,* 40 (1949), 231–325.

Minkowich, A. "Correlates of Superego Functions." Unpublished doctoral dissertation, University of Michigan, 1959.

Minkowich, A., Weingarten, L. L., and Blum, G. S. "Empirical Contributions to a Theory of Ambivalence." *Journal of Abnormal Psychology,* 71 (1966), 30–41.

Mintz, E. E. "Transference in Co-Therapy Groups." *Journal of Consulting Psychology,* 27 (1963), 34–39.

Mintz, J., Luborsky, L., and Auerbach, A. H. "Dimensions of Psychotherapy: A Factor-Analytic Study of Ratings of Psychotherapy Sessions." *Journal of Consulting and Clinical Psychology,* 36 (1971), 106–120.

Mintz, N. L. "Patient Fees and Psychotherapeutic Transactions." *Journal of Consulting and Clinical Psychology,* 36 (1971), 1–8.

Minuchin, P. "Sex-Role Concepts and Sex Typing in Childhood as a Function of School and Home Environments." *Child Development,* 36 (1965), 1033–1048.

Modlin, H. C. "Psychodynamics and Management of Paranoid States in Women." *Archives of General Psychiatry,* 8 (1963), 263–268.

Molish, B. H. "Projective Methodologies." In P. H. Mussen and M. R. Rosenzweig, eds., *Annual Review of Psychology.* Palo Alto, Calif.: Annual Reviews, 1972, pp. 577–614.

Monge, R. H. "Developmental Trends in Factors of Adolescent Self-Concept." *Developmental Psychology,* 8 (1973), 382–393.

Monroe, L. J. "Psychological and Physiological Differences between Good and Poor Sleepers." *Journal of Abnormal Psychology,* 72 (1967), 255–264.

Monroe, L. J., Rechtschaffen, A., Foulkes, D., and Jensen, J. "Discriminability of REM and NREM Reports." *Journal of Personality and Social Psychology,* 2 (1965), 456–460.

Montgomery, D. D., and Bone, R. N. "Dream Recall and Cognitive Style." *Perceptual and Motor Skills,* 31 (1970), 386.

Montgomery, G. T., and Crowder, J. E. "The Symptom Substitution Hypothesis and the Evidence." *Psychotherapy: Theory, Research and Practice,* 9 (1972), 98–102.

Moore, R. A., and Selzer, M. L. "Male Homosexuality, Paranoia, and the Schizophrenias." *American Journal of Psychiatry,* 119 (1963), 743–747.

Moos, R. H. "The Retention and Generalization of Operant Conditioning Effects in an Interview Situation." *Journal of Abnormal and Social Psychology,* 66 (1963), 52–58.

Moos, R. H., and Mussen, P. "Sexual Symbolism, Personality Integration, and Intellectual Functioning." *Journal of Consulting Psychology,* 23 (1959), 521–523.

Morris, C. *Variations of Human Values.* Chicago: University of Chicago, 1956.

Morris, G. O., Williams, H. L., and Lubin, A. "Misperception and Disorientation during Sleep Deprivation." *Archives of General Psychiatry,* 2 (1960), 247–254.
Moskowitz, A. E. "A Clinical and Experimental Approach to the Evaluation and Treatment of a Conversion Reaction with Hypnosis." *International Journal of Clinical and Experimental Hypnosis,* 12 (1964), 218–227.
Moulton, R. "A Survey and Re-evaluation of the Concept of Penis Envy." *Contemporary Psychoanalysis,* 7 (1970), 84–104.
Moulton, R. W., Burnstein, E., Liberty, P. G., Jr., and Altucher, N. "Patterning of Parental Affection and Disciplinary Dominance as a Determinant of Guilt and Sex Typing." *Journal of Personality and Social Psychology,* 4 (1966), 356–363.
Mowrer, O. H. "Identification: A Link between Learning Theory and Psychotherapy." In O. H. Mowrer, ed., *Learning Theory and Personality Dynamics.* New York: Ronald, 1950, pp. 573–616.
Mucha, T. F., and Reinhardt, R. F. "Conversion Reactions in Student Aviators." *American Journal of Psychiatry,* 127 (1970), 493–497.
Mueller, W. J. "Patterns of Behavior and Their Reciprocal Impact in the Family and in Psychotherapy." *Journal of Counseling Psychology,* 16 (1969), No. 2, Part 2.
Mullen, F. G., Jr. "Estimation of the University of Freudian and Jungian Sexual Symbols." *Perceptual and Motor Skills,* 26 (1969), 1041–1042.
Murphy, L. B. *The Widening World of Childhood.* New York: Basic Books, 1962.
Murphy, W. F. "A Comparison of Psychoanalysis with the Dynamic Psychotherapies." *Journal of Nervous and Mental Disease,* 126 (1958), 441–450.
Murray, E. J. "Case Report: A Case Study in a Behavioral Analysis of Psychotherapy." *Journal of Abnormal and Social Psychology,* 49 (1954), 305–310.
______. "Conflict and Repression during Sleep Deprivation." *Journal of Abnormal and Social Psychology,* 59 (1959), 95–101.
______. "Verbal Reinforcement in Psychotherapy." *Journal of Consulting and Clinical Psychology,* 32 (1968), 243–246.
Murray, E. J., and Berkun, M. M. "Displacement as a Function of Conflict." *Journal of Abnormal and Social Psychology,* 51 (1955), 47–56.
Murray, J. B. "Learning in Homosexuality." *Psychological Reports,* 23 (1968), 659–662.
Murstein, B. I. "The Effect of Amount of Possession of the Trait of Hostility on Accuracy of Perception of Hostility in Others." *Journal of Abnormal and Social Psychology,* 62 (1961), 216–220.
Murstein, B. I., and Pryer, R. S. "The Concept of Projection: A Review." *Psychological Bulletin,* 56 (1959), 353–374.
Musiker, H. R. "Sex Identification and Other Aspects of the Personality of the Male Paranoid Schizophrenic." Unpublished doctoral dissertation, Boston University Graduate School, 1952.
Muslin, H. L., Burstein, A. G., Gedo, J. E., and Sadow, L. "Research on the Supervisory Process: I. Supervisor's Appraisal of the Interview Data." *Archives of General Psychiatry,* 16 (1967), 427–431.
Mussen, P. "Some Antecedents and Consequents of Masculine Sex-Typing in Adolescent Boys." *Psychological Monographs,* 75 (1961), No. 506.
Mussen, P., and Distler, L. "Child-Rearing Antecedents of Masculine Identification in Kindergarten Boys." *Child Development,* 31 (1960), 89–100.
Mussen, P., and Rutherford, E. "Parent-Child Relations and Parental Personality in Relation to Young Children's Sex Role Preferences." *Child Development,* 34 (1963), 589–607.
Mussen, P., Young, H. B., Gaddini, R., and Morante, L. "The Influence of Father-Son Relationships on Adolescent Personality and Attitudes." "*Journal of Child Psychology and Psychiatry,* 4 (1963), 3–16.
Nagel, E. "Methodological Issues in Psychoanalytic Theory." In S. Hook, ed., *Psychoanalysis, Scientific Method, and Philosophy.* New York: New York University, 1959, pp. 38–56.
Nahin, B. "Psychosexuality and Memory." Unpublished thesis, Bennington College, 1953.
Namnum, A. "The Problem of Analyzability and the Autonomous Ego." *International Journal of Psycho-Analysis,* 49 (1968), 271–275.
Naroll, R. "What Have We Learned from Cross-Cultural Surveys?" *American Anthropologist,* 72 (1970), 1227–1288.

National Society for the Study of Education. *Child Psychology.* The sixty-second yearbook of the National Society for the Study of Education. Edited by H. W. Stevenson, with assistance of J. Kagan and C. Spiker. Chicago: University of Chicago, 1963.

Natsoulas, T. "Converging Operations for Perceptual Defense." *Psychological Bulletin,* 64 (1965), 393–401.

Nelson, S. E. "Psychosexual Conflicts and Defenses in Visual Perception." *Journal of Abnormal and Social Psychology,* 51 (1955), 427–433.

Neuman, G. G., and Salvatore, J. C. "The Blacky Test and Psychoanalytic Theory: A Factor-Analytic Approach to Validity." *Journal of Projective Techniques,* 22 (1958), 427–431.

Newton, N. R. "The Relationship between Infant Feeding Experience and Later Behavior." *Journal of Pediatrics,* 38 (1951), 28–40.

Newton, P. M. "Recalled Dream Content and the Maintenance of Body Image." *Journal of Abnormal Psychology,* 76 (1970), 134–139.

Nickols, J. "Effects of Group Projective Testing on Rorschach Scores." *Journal of Clinical Psychology,* 23 (1967), 497.

Noble, D. "A Study of Dreams in Schizophrenia and Allied States." *American Journal of Psychiatry,* 107 (1951), 612–616.

Noblin, C. D. "Experimental Analysis of Psychoanalytic Character Types through the Operant Conditioning of Verbal Responses." Unpublished doctoral dissertation, Louisiana State University, 1962.

Noblin, C. D., Timmons, E. O., and Kael, H. C. "Differential Effects of Positive and Negative Verbal Reinforcement on Psychoanalytic Character Types." *Journal of Personality and Social Psychology,* 4 (1966), 224–228.

Noblin, C. D., Timmons, E. O., and Reynard, Marian C. "Psychoanalytic Interpretations as Verbal Reinforcers: Importance of Interpretation Content." *Journal of Clinical Psychology,* 19 (1963), 479–481.

Nolan, J. D., Mattis, P. R., and Holliday, W. C. "Long-Term Effects of Behavior Therapy: A 12-month Follow-Up." *Journal of Abnormal Psychology,* 76 (1970), 88–92.

Norman, J. P. "Evidence and Clinical Significance of Homosexuality in 100 Unanalyzed Cases of Dementia Praecox." *Journal of Nervous and Mental Disease,* 107 (1948), 484–489.

Normington, C. J. "Some Aspects of Psychosexual Development in Process-Reactive Schizophrenia." Unpublished doctoral dissertation, Michigan State University, 1964.

Novey, S. "The Principle of 'Working Through' in Psychoanalysis." *Journal of the American Psychoanalytic Association,* 10 (1962), 658–676.

———. "The Significance of the Actual Historical Event in Psychiatry and Psychoanalysis." *British Journal of Medical Psychology,* 37 (1964), 279–290.

Novick, J. "Symptomatic Treatment of Acquired and Persistent Enuresis." *Journal of Abnormal Psychology,* 71 (1966), 363–368.

Nunberg, H. "Evaluation of the Results of Psycho-Analytic Treatment." *International Journal of Psycho-Analysis,* 35 (1954), 2–7.

Nunberg, N. "Symposium on the Theory of the Therapeutic Results of Psycho-Analysis." *International Journal of Psycho-Analysis,* 18 (1937), 161–169.

Nurnberger, J. I., and Hingtgen, J. N. "Is Symptom Substitution an Important Issue in Behavior Therapy?" *Biological Psychiatry,* 7 (1973), 221–236.

Oberndorf, C. P. "Unsatisfactory Results of Psychoanalytic Therapy." *Psychoanalytic Quarterly,* 19 (1950), 393–407.

Oberndorf, C. P., Greenacre, P., and Kubie, L. "Symposium on the Evaluation of Therapeutic Results." *Yearbook of Psychoanalysis,* 5 (1949), 9–34.

O'Connor, J. F., Daniels, G., Karush, A., Moses, L., Flood, C., and Stern, Lenore O. "The Effects of Psychotherapy on the Course of Ulcerative Colitis: a Preliminary Report." *American Journal of Psychiatry,* 20 (1964), 738–742.

O'Connor, J. F., and Stern, L. O. "Symptom Alteration: An Evaluation of the Theory." *Archives of General Psychiatry,* 16 (1967), 432–436.

O'Connor, P. J. "Aetiological Factors in Homosexuality as Seen in Royal Air Force Psychiatric Practice." *British Journal of Psychiatry,* 110 (1964), 381–391.

O'Dell, J. W. "P. T. Barnum Explores the Computer." *Journal of Consulting and Clinical Psychology,* 38 (1972), 270–273.

Offenkrantz, W., and Rechtschaffen, A. "Clinical Studies of Sequential Dreams." 1. A Patient in Psychotherapy." *Archives of General Psychiatry,* 8 (1963), 497–508.

Offenkrantz, W., and Tobin, A. "Psychoanalytic Psychotherapy." *Archives of General Psychiatry,* 30 (1974), 593–606.

Olinick, S. L. "Negative Therapeutic Reaction." *Journal of the American Psychoanalytic Association,* 18 (1970), 655–672.

Oliver, W. A., and Mosher, D. L. "Psychopathology and Guilt in Heterosexual and Subgroups of Homosexual Reformatory Inmates." *Journal of Abnormal Psychology,* 73 (1968), 323–329.

O'Neill, M., and Kempler, B. "Approach and Avoidance Responses of the Hysterical Personality to Sexual Stimuli." *Journal of Abnormal Psychology,* 74 (1969), 300–305.

O'Nell, C. W. "A Cross-Cultural Study of Hunger and Thirst Motivation Manifested in Dreams." *Human Development,* 8 (1965), 181–193.

Onheiber, P., White, P. T., DeMyer, M. K., and Ottinger, D. R. "Sleep and Dream Patterns of Child Schizophrenics." *Archives of General Psychiatry,* 12 (1965), 568–571.

Orbach, C. H. "Perceptual Defense and Somatization: A Comparison of the Perceptual Thresholds of Obese and Peptic Ulcer Patients." Unpublished doctoral dissertation, University of Southern California, 1960.

Orgel, S. Z. "Effect of Psychoanalysis on the Course of Peptic Ulcer." *Psychosomatic Medicine,* 20 (1958), 117–123.

Orlansky, H. "Infant Care and Personality." *Psychological Bulletin,* 46 (1949), 1–48.

Orlinsky, D. E. "Rorschach Test Correlates of Dreaming and Dream Recall." *Journal of Projective Techniques and Personality Assessment,* 30 (1966), 250–253.

Orne, M. T. "Implications for Psychotherapy Derived from Current Research on the Nature of Hypnosis." *American Journal of Psychiatry,* 118 (1962), 1097–1103.

Orne, M. T., and Wender, P. H. "Anticipatory Socialization for Psychotherapy: Method and Rationale." *American Journal of Psychiatry,* 124 (1969), 1202–1212.

Ornitz, E. M., Ritvo, E. R., and Walter, R. D. "Dreaming Sleep in Autistic and Schizophrenic Children." *American Journal of Psychiatry,* 122 (1965–66), 419–424.

Orr, W. F., Dozier, J. E., Green, L., and Cromwell, R. L. "Self-Induced Waking: Changes in Dreams and Sleep Patterns." *Comprehensive Psychiatry,* 9 (1968), 499–506.

Osgood, C. E., Suci, G. J., and Tannenbaum, P. H. *The Measurement of Meaning.* Urbana: Ill.: University of Illinois, 1957.

Othmer, E., Hayden, M. P., and Segelbaum, R. "Encephalic Cycles during Sleep and Wakefulness in Humans: A 24-Hour Pattern." *Science,* 164 (1969), 447–449.

Ovesey, L., and Person, E. "Gender Identity and Sexual Psychopathology in Men: A Psychodynamic Analysis of Homosexuality, Transsexualism, and Transvestism." *Journal of the American Academy of Psychoanalysis,* 1 (1973), 53–72.

Page, J., and Warkentin, J. "Masculinity and Paranoia." *Journal of Abnormal and Social Psychology,* 33 (1938), 527–531.

Paitich, D. "Attitudes toward Parents in Male Homosexuals and Exhibitionists." Unpublished doctoral dissertation, University of Toronto, 1964.

Palm, R. "The Psychodynamics of Enuresis." *American Imago,* 9–10 (1952–53), 167–180.

Palmer, R. D. "Patterns of Defensive Response to Threatening Stimuli: Antecedents and Consistency." *Journal of Abnormal Psychology,* 73 (1968), 30–36.

Paolino, A. F. "Dreams: Sex Differences in Aggressive Content." *Journal of Projective Techniques and Personality Assessment,* 28 (1964), 219–226.

Parloff, M. B., Goldstein, N., and Iflund, B. "Communication of Values and Therapeutic Change." *Archives of General Psychiatry,* 2 (1960), 300–304.

Patterson, C. H. "Divergence and Convergence in Psychotherapy." *American Journal of Psychotherapy,* 21 (1967), 4–17.

Patterson, G. R. "Parents as Dispensers of Aversive Stimuli." *Journal of Personality and Social Psychology,* 2 (1965), 844–851.

Patterson, V., Levene, H., and Breger, L. "Treatment and Training Outcomes with Two Time-Limited Therapies." *Archives of General Psychiatry,* 25, (1971), 161–167.

Pattison, E. M. "The Patient after Psychotherapy." *American Journal of Psychotherapy,* 24 (1970), 194–215.

Paul, G. L. *Insight vs. Desensitization in Psychotherapy.* Stanford, Calif.: Stanford University Press, 1966.

———. "Insight versus Desensitization in Psychotherapy Two Years after Termination." *Journal of Consulting Psychology,* 31 (1967), 333–348.

Paul, G. L., and Shannon, D. T. "Treatment of Anxiety through Systematic Desensitization in Therapy Groups." *Journal of Abnormal Psychology,* 71 (1966), 124–135.

Paul, I. H., and Fisher, C. "Subliminal Visual Stimulation: A Study of Its Influence on Subsequent Images and Dreams." *Journal of Nervous and Mental Disease,* 129 (1959), 315–340.

Payne, C. R., "Some Freudian Contributions to the Paranoia Problem." *Psychoanalytic Review,* 1 (1913–14), 76–93; 187–202; 308–321; 445–451.

———. "Some Freudian Contributions to the Paranoia Problem." *Psychoanalytic Review,* 2 (1915), 93–101; 200–202.

Payne, D., and Mussen, P. "Parent-Child Relations and Father Identification among Adolescent Boys." *Journal of Abnormal and Social Psychology,* 52 (1956), 358–362.

Pearlman, C. A. "Latent Learning Impaired by REM Sleep Deprivation." *Psychonomic Science,* 25 (1971), 135–136.

Pearson, G. H. J. "Some Early Factors in the Formation of Personality." *American Journal of Orthopsychiatry,* 1 (1930–31), 284–291.

Pedersen, F., and Marlowe, D. "Capacity and Motivational Differences in Verbal Recall." *Journal of Clinical Psychology,* 16 (1950), 219–222.

Persons, R. W. "The Mosher Guilt Scale: Theoretical Formulation, Research Review and Normative Data." *Journal of Projective Techniques and Personality Assessment,* 34 (1970), 266–270.

Persons, R. W., and Marks, P. A. "Self-Disclosure with Recidivists: Optimum Interviewer-Interviewee Matching." *Journal of Abnormal Psychology,* 76 (1970), 387–391.

Peskin, H. "Pubertal Onset and Ego Functioning." *Journal of Abnormal Psychology,* 72 (1967),. 1–15.

———. "Multiple Prediction of Adult Psychological Health from Preadolescent and Adolescent Behavior." *Journal of Consulting and Clinical Psychology,* 38 (1972), 155–160.

———. "Influence of the Developmental Schedule of Puberty on Learning and Ego Functioning." *Journal of Youth and Adolescence,* 2 (1973), 273–290.

Peterfreund, E. *Information, Systems and Psychoanalysis: An evolutionary Biological Approach to Psychoanalytic Theory.* New York: International Universities, 1971.

Peterson, C. H., and Spano, F. L. "Breast Feeding, Maternal Rejection and Child Personality." *Character and Personality,* 10 (1941), 62–66.

Pettit, T. F. "Anality and Time." *Journal of Consulting and Clinical Psychology,* 33 (1969), 170–174.

Pfeffer, A. Z. "A Procedure for Evaluating the Results of Psychoanalysis: A Preliminary Report." *Journal of the American Psychoanalytic Association,* 7 (1959), 418–444.

———. "Follow-Up Study of a Satisfactory Analysis." *Journal of the American Psychoanalytic Association,* 9 (1961), 698–718.

———. "Analysis Terminable and Interminable—Twenty-Five Years Later." *Journal of the American Psychoanalytic Association,* 11 (1963a), 131–142.

———. "The Meaning of the Analyst after Analysis." *Journal of the American Psychoanalytic Association,* 11 (1963b), 229–244.

Pierce, C. M., Mathis, J. L., Lester, B. K., and Nixon, O. L. "Dreams of Food during Sleep Experiments." *Psychosomatics,* 5 (1964), 374–377.

Pierce, C. M., Whitman, R. M., Maas, J. W., and Gay, M. L. "Enuresis and Dreaming." *Archives of General Psychiatry,* 4 (1961), 166–170.

Pierce, R. M., and Schauble, P. G. "Graduate Training of Facilitative Counselors: The Effects of Individual Supervision." *Journal of Counseling Psychology,* 17 (1970), 210–215.

Pinckney, G. A. "Relative Strengths of Impulse, Ego, and Superego in Female College Students." *Perceptual and Motor Skills,* 17 (1963), 340.

Pine, F. "Incidental Stimulation: a Study of Preconscious Transformations." *Journal of Abnormal and Social Psychology,* 60 (1960), 68–75.

———. "Incidental versus Focal Presentation of Drive Related Stimuli." *Journal of Abnormal and Social Psychology,* 62 (1961), 482–490.

______. "Creativity and Primary Process: Sample Variations." *Journal of Nervous and Mental Disease,* 134 (1962), 506–511.

______. "The Bearing of Psychoanalytic Theory on Selected Issues in Research on Marginal Stimuli." *Journal of Nervous and Mental Disease,* 138 (1964), 205–222.

______. "On the Structuralization of Drive-Defense Relationships." *Psychoanalytic Quarterly,* 39 (1970), 17–37.

Pine, F., and Holt, R. R. "Creativity and Primary Process: A Study of Adaptive Regression." *Journal of Abnormal and Social Psychology,* 61 (1960), 370–379.

Pintler, M. H., Phillips, R., and Sears, R. R. "Sex Differences in the Projective Doll Play of Preschool Children." *Journal of Psychology,* 21 (1946), 73–80.

Piorkowski, G. K. "Anxiety-Reducing Efficacy of Distraction, Catharsis, and Rationalization in Two Personality Types." *Journal of Consulting Psychology,* 31 (1967), 279–285.

Pishkin, V. "Psychosexual Development in Terms of Object and Role Preferences." *Journal of Clinical Psychology,* 16 (1960), 238–240.

Pitcher, E. G., and Prelinger, E. *Children Tell Stories: An Analysis of Fantasy.* New York: International Universities, 1963.

Pittel, S. M. "Superego Functions and the Antecedents of Guilt." Unpublished doctoral dissertation, University of California, Berkeley, 1964.

Pittel, S. M., and Mendelsohn, G. A. "Measurement of Moral Values: A Review and Critique. *Psychological Bulletin,* 66 (1966), 22–35.

Pivik, T., and Foulkes, D. " 'Dream Deprivation': Effects on Dream Content." *Science,* 153 (1966), 1282–1284.

Planansky, K., and Johnston, R. "The Incidence and Relationship of Homosexual and Paranoid Features in Schizophrenia." *Journal of Mental Science,* 108 (1962), 604–615.

Podolnick, E. E., and Field, P. B. "Emotional Involvement, Oral Anxiety, and Hypnosis." *International Journal of Clinical and Experimental Hypnosis,* 18 (1970), 194–210.

Pollock, G. H. "Transference Neurosis." *Archives of General Psychiatry,* 6 (1962a), 294–306.

______. "Childhood Parent and Sibling Loss in Adult Patients." *Archives of General Psychiatry,* 7 (1962b), 295–305.

Pollock, G. H., and Muslin, H. L. "Dreams during Surgical Procedures." *Psychoanalytic Quarterly,* 31 (1962), 175–202.

Pope, B., and Siegman, A. W. "Interviewer-Interviewee Relationship and Verbal Behavior of Interviewee in the Initial Interview." *Psychotherapy: Theory, Research and Practice,* 3 (1966), 149–152.

______. "Interviewer Warmth in Relation to Interviewer Verbal Behavior." *Journal of Consulting and Clinical Psychology,* 32 (1968), 588–595.

Pope, B., Siegman, A. W., Blass, T., and Cheek, J. "Some Effects of Discrepant Role Expectations on Interviewee Verbal Behavior in the Initial Interview." *Journal of Consulting and Clinical Psychology,* 39 (1972), 501–507.

Porach, L. B. "The Relationship of Masculine and Feminine Identification to Dream Scores, and to Menstrual Cycle Reactions." Unpublished doctoral dissertation, University of Virginia, 1970.

Portnoff, G., Baekeland, F., Goodenough, D. R., Karacan, I., and Shapiro, A. "Retention of Verbal Materials Perceived Immediately Prior to Onset of Non-REM Sleep." *Perceptual and Motor Skills,* 22 (1966), 751–758.

Potter, H. W., and Klein, H. R. "Toward Unification of Training in Psychiatry and Psychoanalysis." *American Journal of Psychiatry,* 108 (1951), 193–197.

Powell, W. J., Jr. "Differential Effectiveness of Interviewer Interventions in an Experimental Interview." *Journal of Consulting and Clinical Psychology,* 32 (1968), 210–215.

Preston, G. A. "Parental Role Perceptions and Identification in Adolescent Girls." Unpublished doctoral dissertation, University of Michigan, 1965.

Pritt, T. E. "A Comparative Study between Male Homosexuals' and Heterosexuals' Perceived Parental Acceptance-Rejection, Self-Concepts and Self-Evaluation Tendencies." Unpublished doctoral dissertation, University of Utah, 1971.

Proctor, J. T., and Briggs, A. G. "The Utility of Dreams in the Diagnostic Interview with Children." In E. Harms, ed., *Problems of Sleep and Dream in Children.* New York: Macmillan, 1964, pp. 92–101.

Prosen, H. "Sexuality in Females with Hysteria." *American Journal of Psychiatry,* 124 (1967), 687–692.
Prothro, E. T. "Patterns of Permissiveness among Preliterate Peoples." *Journal of Abnormal and Social Psychology,* 61 (1960), 151–154.
Prugh, D. G. "Part II. Etiology of Colonic Disorders: Childhood Experience and Colonic Disorders." *Annals of New York Academy of Sciences,* 58 (1953–54), 355–376.
Pryor, D. B. "Regression in the Service of the Ego: Psychosexual Development and Ego Functions." Unpublished doctoral dissertation, Michigan State University, 1962.
———. "A Comparison of the Occurrences of Oral and Anal Content on the Rorschach." *Journal of Projective Techniques and Personality Assessment,* 31 (1967), 26–28.
Pulver, S. E. "Narcissism: The Term and the Concept." *Journal of the American Psychoanalytic Association,* 18 (1970), 319–341.
Pumpian-Mindlin, E. "Considerations in the Selection of Patients for Short-Term Therapy." *American Journal of Psychotherapy,* 7 (1953), 641–652.
Purcell, K. "Memory and Psychological Security." *Journal of Abnormal and Social Psychology,* 47 (1952), 433–440.
Pustell, T. E. "The Experimental Induction of Perceptual Vigilance and Defense." *Journal of Personality,* 25 (1957), 425–438.
Pyles, M. K., Stolz, H. R., and MacFarlane, J. W. "The Accuracy of Mothers' Reports on Birth and Development Data." *Child Development,* 6 (1935), 165–176.
Pytkowicz, A. R., Wagner, N. N., and Sarason, I. G., "An Experimental Study of the Reduction of Hostility through Fantasy." *Journal of Personality and Social Psychology,* 5 (1967), 295–303.
Quay, H. "The Effect of Verbal Reinforcement on the Recall of Early Memories." *Journal of Abnormal and Social Psychology,* 59 (1959), 254–257.
Rabban, M. "Sex-Role Identification in Young Children in Two Diverse Social Groups." *Genetic Psychology Monographs,* 42 (1959), 81–158.
Rabin, A. I. "The Israeli Kibbutz (Collective Settlement) as a Laboratory for Testing Psychodynamic Hypotheses." *Psychological Record,* 7 (1957), 111–115.
———. "Some Psychosexual Differences between Kibbutz and Non-Kibbutz Israeli Boys." *Journal of Projective Techniques,* 22 (1958), 328–332.
Rabiner, E. L., Reiser, M. F., Barr, H. L., and Gralnick, A. "Therapists' Attitudes and Patients' Clinical Status: A Study of 100 Psychotherapy Pairs." *Archives of General Psychiatry,* 25 (1971), 555–569.
Rabinowitz, W. "Anality, Aggression, and Acquiescence." *Journal of Abnormal and Social Psychology,* 54 (1957), 140–142.
Rabkin, R. "Is the Unconscious Necessary?" *American Journal of Psychiatry,* 125 (1968), 313–319.
Rachman, S. *The Effects of Psychotherapy.* Oxford: Pergamon, 1971.
Ramsey, G. V. "Studies of Dreaming." *Psychological Bulletin,* 50 (1953), 432–455.
Ramzy, I. "Research in Psycho-Analysis: Contribution to Discussion." *International Journal of Psycho-Analysis,* 43 (1962), 292–296.
———. "Research Aspects of Psycho-Analysis." *Psychoanalytic Quarterly,* 32 (1963), 58–76.
Rand, G., and Wapner, S. "Postural Status as a Factor in Memory." *Journal of Verbal Learning and Verbal Behavior,* 6 (1967), 268–271.
Rangell, L. "Similarities and Differences between Psychoanalysis and Dynamic Psychotherapy." *Journal of the American Psychoanalytic Association,* 2 (1954), 734–744.
———. "The Dream in the Practice of Psychoanalysis." *Journal of the American Psychoanalytic Association,* 4 (1956), 122–137.
———. "Psychoanalysis and Neuropsychiatry: A Look at their Interface." *American Journal of Psychiatry,* 127 (1970), 125–131.
Rapaport, C. "Character, Anxiety and Social Affiliation." Unpublished doctoral dissertation, New York University, 1963.
Rapaport, D. *Emotions and Memory.* New York: International Universities, 1950.
———. "The Structure of Psychoanalytic Theory: A Systematizing Attempt." In S. Koch, ed., *Psychology: A Study of a Science.* Vol. 1. New York: McGraw-Hill, 1959, pp. 55–183.
———. "The Structure of Psychoanalytic Theory." *Psychological Issues,* 2 (1960), No. 6.
Rapaport, G. M. "A Study of the Psychoanalytic Theory of the Anal Character." Unpublished doctoral dissertation, Northwestern University, 1955.

Rashkis, H. A. "Insight, Denial, and Prognosis." *Archives of General Psychiatry,* 12 (1965), 96–98.

Raskin, A., Schulterbrandt, J., Reatig, N., and Rice, C. E. "Factors of Psychopathology in Interview, Ward Behavior, and Self-Report Ratings of Hospitalized Depressives." *Journal of Consulting Psychology,* 31 (1967), 270–278.

Raskin, N. J. "An Analysis of Six Parallel Studies of the Therapeutic Process." *Journal of Consulting Psychology,* 13 (1949), 206–220.

______. "The Psychotherapy Research Project of the American Academy of Psychotherapists." *Proceedings of the 73rd Annual Convention of APA* (1965), 253–254.

Raush, H. L., Sperber, Z., Rigler, D., Williams, J., Harway, N. I., Bordin, E. S., Dittmann, A. T., and Hays, W. L. "A Dimensional Analysis of Depth of Interpretation." *Journal of Consulting Psychology,* 20 (1956), 43–48.

Rawn, M. L. "An Experimental Study of Transference and Resistance Phenomena in Psychoanalytically Oriented Psychotherapy." *Journal of Clinical Psychology,* 14 (1958), 418–425.

Rayner, E. H., and Hahn, H. "Assessment for Psychotherapy: A Pilot Study of Psychological Test Indicators of Success and Failure in Treatment." *British Journal of Medical Psychology,* 27 (1964), 331–342.

Rechtschaffen, A., and Foulkes, D. "Effect of Visual Stimuli on Dream Content." *Perceptual and Motor Skills,* 20 (1965), 1149–1160.

Rechtschaffen, A., and Maron, L. "The Effect of Amphetamine on the Sleep Cycle." *Electroencephalography and Clinical Neurophysiology,* 16 (1964), 438–445.

Rechtschaffen, A., Schulsinger, F., and Mednick, S. A. "Schizophrenia and Physiological Indices of Dreaming." *Archives of General Psychiatry,* 10 (1964), 89–93.

Rechtschaffen, A., and Verdone, P. "Amount of Dreaming: Effect of Incentive, Adaptation to Laboratory, and Individual Differences." *Perceptual and Motor Skills,* 19 (1964), 947–958.

Rechtschaffen, A., Verdone, P., and Wheaton, J. "Reports of Mental Activity during Sleep." *Canadian Psychiatric Association Journal,* 8 (1963), 409–414.

Rechtschaffen, A., Vogel, G., and Shaikun, G. "Interrelatedness of Mental Activity during Sleep." *Archives of General Psychiatry,* 9 (1963), 536–547.

Reid, J. R., and Finesinger, J. E. "Inference Testing in Psychotherapy." *American Journal of Psychiatry,* 107 (1951), 894–900.

______. "The Role of Insight in Psychotherapy." *American Journal of Psychiatry,* 108 (1952), 726–734.

Reis, W. "A Comparison of the Interpretation of Dream Series with and without Free Association." Unpublished doctoral dissertation, Western Reserve University, 1951.

Reitzell, Jeanne M. "A Comparative Study of Hysterics, Homosexuals and Alcoholics Using Content Analysis of Rorschach Responses." *Journal of Projective Techniques,* 13 (1949), 127–141.

Rempel, H., and Signori, E. I. "Further Research on the IES Photo-Analysis Subtest with Special Reference to Sex Differences." *Perceptual and Motor Skills,* 17 (1963), 295–298.

______. "Sex Differences in Self-Rating of Conscience as a Determinant of Behavior." *Psychological Reports,* 15 (1964), 277–278.

Rennie, T. A. C., and Fowler, J. B. "Analysis of One Hundred Cases of Schizophrenia with Recovery." *Archives of Neurology and Psychiatry,* 46 (1941), 197–229.

Reuter, M.W., and Biller, H.B. "Perceived Paternal Nurturance—Availability and Personality Adjustment among College Males." *Journal of Consulting and Clinical Psychology,* 40 (1973), 339–342.

Reyher, J. "Comment on Artificial Induction of Post-Hypnotic Conflict." *Journal of Abnormal Psychology,* 74, (1969), 420–422.

Reyher, J., and Basch, J. A., "Degree of Repression and Frequency of Psychosomatic Symptoms." *Perceptual and Motor Skills,* 30 (1970), 559–562.

Reyher, J., and Smeltzer, W. "Uncovering Properties of Visual Imagery and Verbal Association: A Comparative Study." *Journal of Abnormal Psychology,* 73 (1968), 218–222.

Ribner, S., "A Test of the Masculine Protest Theory of Anti-Social Behavior." Unpublished doctoral dissertation, New York University, 1972.

Rice, D. G., and Thurrell, R. J. "Teaching Psychological Evaluation to Psychiatric Residents." *Archives of General Psychiatry,* 19 (1968), 737–742.

Richardson, G. A., and Moore, R. A. "On the Manifest Dream in Schizophrenia." *Journal of the American Psychoanalytic Association,* 11 (1963), 281–302.
Riese, W. "Freudian Concepts of Brain Function and Brain Disease." *Journal of Nervous and Mental Disease,* 127 (1958), 287–307.
Riesman, D. *Individualism Reconsidered.* New York: Doubleday Anchor, 1955.
Riess, B. F. "Changes in Patient Income Concomitant with Psychotherapy." *Journal of Consulting Psychology,* 31 (1967), 430.
Riess, B. F., Gundlach, R., and Sager, C. J. "The Uses and Interpretations of a Follow-Up Study of Patients in Psychoanalytic Psychotherapy." *Journal of Psychology,* 53 (1962), 219–232.
Ritter, W. P. "Verbal Conditioning and the Recalled Content of Dreams." Unpublished doctoral dissertation, Columbia University, 1963.
———. "The Susceptibility of Dream Recall to Indirect Suggestion Patterned after Verbal Conditioning." *American Journal of Psychotherapy,* 19 (1965), 87–98.
Ritz, M. D. "The Relationship between Oedipal Conflicts and Pre-Operational Functioning in Aggressive Boys during the Latency Period." Unpublished doctoral dissertation, Case Western Reserve University, 1969.
Roback, H. B. "The Comparative Influence of Insight and Non-Insight Psychotherapies on Therapeutic Outcome: A Review of the Experimental Literature." *Psychotherapy: Theory, Research and Practice,* 8 (1971), 23–25.
———. "Experimental Comparison of Outcomes in Insight- and Non-Insight-Oriented Therapy Groups." *Journal of Consulting and Clinical Psychology,* 38 (1972), 411–417.
———. "Insight: A Bridging of the Theoretical and Research Literatures." *Canadian Psychologist,* 15 (1974), 61–88.
Robbins, L. L., and Wallerstein, R. S. "The Research Strategy and Tactics of the Psychotherapy Research Project of the Menninger Foundation and the Problem of Controls." In E. A. Rubinstein and M. B. Parloff, eds., *Research in Psychotherapy.* Washington, D.C.: American Psychological Association, 1962, pp. 27–43.
Robbins, P. R. "An Approach to Measuring Psychological Tensions by Means of Dream Associations." *Psychological Reports,* 18 (1966), 959–971.
Robbins, P. R., and Tanck, R. H. "Community Violence and Aggression in Dreams: An Observation. *Perceptual and Motor Skills,* 29 (1969), 41–42.
———. "The Repression-Sensitization Scale, Dreams, and Dream Associations." *Journal of Clinical Psychology,* 26 (1970), 219–221.
Robertiello, R. C. "Two Views on the Use of the Couch: The Couch." *Psychoanalytic Review,* 54 (1967), 69–71.
Roberts, E. "Thumb and Finger Sucking in Relation to Feeding in Early Infancy." *American Journal of Diseases of Children,* 68 (1944), 7–8.
Robertson, R. J. "Experience as a Factor in Length of Therapy." *Psychotherapy: Theory, Research and Practice,* 2 (1965), 112–113.
Robin, A. M. "An Investigation of Certain Assertions of Psychoanalysis in Reference to Symbols for Masculinity and Femininity." Unpublished doctoral dissertation, Temple University, 1962.
Robinson, S. A., and Hendrix, V. L. "The Blacky Test and Psychoanalytic Theory: Another Factor-Analytic Approach to Validity." *Journal of Projective Techniques and Personality Assessment,* 30 (1966), 597–603.
Rodgers, D. A., and Ziegler, F. J. "Cognitive Process and Conversion Reactions." *Journal of Nervous and Mental Disease,* 144 (1967), 155–170.
Rogers, A. H. "The Self Concept in Paranoid Schizophrenia." *Journal of Clinical Psychology,* 14 (1958), 365–366.
Rogers, J. M. "Operant Conditioning in a Quasi-Therapy Setting." *Journal of Abnormal and Social Psychology,* 60 (1960), 247–252.
Rogerson, B. C. F., and Rogerson, C. H. "Feeding in Infancy and Subsequent Psychological Difficulties." *Journal of Mental Science,* 85 (1939), 1163–1182.
Rosen, M. S. "Trust, Orality and Openness to Sensory Experience: A Study of Some Personality Correlates of Creativity." Unpublished doctoral dissertation, New York University, 1971.
Rosenbaum, M. "Dreams in Which the Analyst Appears Undisguised—a Clinical and Statistical Study." *International Journal of Psycho-analysis,* 46 (1965), 429–437.

Rosenbaum, M., Friedlander, J., and Kaplan, S. M. "Evaluation of Results of Psychotherapy." *Psychosomatic Medicine,* 18 (1956), 113–132.
Rosenberg, B. G. "Compulsiveness as a Determinant in Selected Cognitive-Perceptual Performances." *Journal of Personality,* 21 (1953), 506–516.
Rosenberg, S. "The Relationship of Certain Personality Factors to Prognosis in Psychotherapy." *Journal of Clinical Psychology,* 10 (1954), 341–345.
Rosenblatt, P. C. "A Cross-Cultural Study of Child Rearing and Romantic Love." *Journal of Personality and Social Psychology,* 4 (1966), 336–338.
Rosenfeld, H. "Remarks on the Relation of Male Homosexuality to Paranoia, Paranoid Anxiety and Narcissism." *International Journal of Psycho-Analysis,* 30 (1949), 36–47.
Rosenstock, I. M. "Perceptual Aspects of Repression." *Journal of Abnormal and Social Psychology,* 46 (1951), 304–315.
Rosenthal, D. "Changes in Some Moral Values Following Psychotherapy." *Journal of Consulting Psychology,* 19 (1955), 431–436.
Rosenthal, D., and Frank, J. D. "Psychotherapy and the Placebo Effect." *Psychological Bulletin,* 53 (1956), 294–302.
Rosenthal, I. "Reliability of Retrospective Reports of Adolescence." *Journal of Consulting Psychology,* 27 (1963), 189–198.
Rosenthal, M. J., Ni, E., Finkelstein, M. and Berkwits, G. K. "Father-Child Relationships and Children's Problems." *Archives of General Psychiatry,* 7 (1962), 360–373.
Rosenthal, R. *Experimenter Effects in Behavioral Research.* New York: Appleton-Century-Crofts, 1966.
Rosenwald, G. C. "The Relation of Drive Discharge to the Enjoyment of Humor." *Journal of Personality,* 32 (1964), 682–698.
______. "Conflict, Functional Disruption, and Defense-Effectiveness." *Journal of Personality Assessment,* 36 (1972a), 218–229.
______. "Effectiveness of Defenses Against Anal Impulse Arousal." *Journal of Consulting and Clinical Psychology,* 39 (1972b), 292–298.
Rosenwald, G. C., Mendelsohn, G. A., Fontana, A., and Portz, A. T. "An Action Test of Hypotheses Concerning the Anal Personality." *Journal of Abnormal Psychology,* 71 (1966), 304–309.
Rosenzweig, S. "A Transvaluation of Psychotherapy: A Reply to Hans Eysenck." *Journal of Abnormal and Social Psychology,* 49 (1954), 298–304.
Ross, H. D. "Use of Obscene Words in Psychotherapy." *Archives of General Psychiatry,* 6 (1962), 123–131.
Ross, R. P. "Separation Fear and the Fear of Death in Children." Unpublished doctoral dissertation, New York University, 1966.
Ross, S., Fisher, A. E., and King, D. "Sucking Behavior: A Review of the Literature." *Journal of Genetic Psychology,* 91 (1957), 63–81.
Ross, W. D. "Persisting Transference after Interrupted Psychoanalyses and Other Therapeutic Relationships." *Comprehensive Psychiatry,* 9 (1968), 327–343.
Ross, W. D., Hirt, M., and Kurtz, R. "The Fantasy of Dirt and Attitudes toward Body Products." *Journal of Nervous and Mental Disease,* 146 (1968), 303–309.
Roth, N. "Dream Data on the Relation of Perception and Motility." *Perceptual and Motor Skills,* 14 (1962a), 427–430.
______. "Ego Defenses and Perception." *Perceptual and Motor Skills,* 15 (1962b), 117–118.
Rubinstein, B. B., *Psychoanalysis and Contemporary Science.* An annual of integrative and interdisciplinary studies. Vol. II. New York: Macmillan, 1973.
Ruch, J. C., and Morgan, A. H. "Subject Posture and Hypnotic Susceptibility: A Comparison of Standing, Sitting, and Lying-Down Subjects. *International Journal of Clinical and Experimental Hypnosis,* 19 (1971), 100–108.
Ruebush, B. K., Byrum, M., and Farnham, L. J. "Problem Solving as a Function of Children's Defensiveness and Parental Behavior." *Journal of Abnormal and Social Psychology,* 67 (1963), 355–362.
Ruebush, B. K., and Waite, R. R. "Oral Dependency in Anxious and Defensive Children." *Merrill-Palmer Quarterly of Behavior and Development,* 7 (1961), 181–190.
Russell, P. D., and Snyder, W. U. "Counselor Anxiety in Relation to Amount of Clinical Experience and Quality of Affect Demonstrated by Clients." *Journal of Consulting Psychology,* 27 (1963), 358–363.

Rutstein, E. H. "The Effects of Aggressive Stimulation on Suicidal Patients: An Experimental Study of the Psychoanalytic Theory of Suicide." Unpublished doctoral dissertation, New York University, 1970.

Rychlak, J. F. "Recalled Dream Themes and Personality." *Journal of Abnormal and Social Psychology,* 60 (1960), 140–143.

Rychlak, J. F., and Brams, J. M. "Personality Dimensions in Recalled Dream Content." *Journal of Projective Techniques,* 27 (1963), 226–234.

Rycroft, C. "The Analysis of a Paranoid Personality." *International Journal of Psycho-Analysis,* 41 (1960), 59–69.

Ryle, A., and Lunghi, M. "Parental and Sex-Role Identification of Students Measured with a Repertory Grid Technique." *British Journal of Social and Clinical Psychology,* 11 (1972), 149–161.

Sadow, L., Gedo, J. E., Miller, J., Pollock, G., Sabshin, M., and Schlessinger, N. "The Process of Hypothesis Change in Three Early Psychoanalytic Concepts." *Journal of the American Psychoanalytic Association,* 16 (1968), 245–273.

Sager, C. J., Gundlach, R., Kremer, M., Lenz, R., and Royce, J. R. "The Married in Treatment: Effects of Psychoanalysis on the Marital State." *Archives of General Psychiatry,* 19 (1968), 205–217.

Sager, C. J., Riess, B. F., and Gundlach, R. "Follow-Up Study of the Results of Extra-Mural Analytic Psychotherapy." *American Journal of Psychotherapy,* 18 (1964), 161–173.

Saghir, M. T., and Robins, E. "Homosexuality: I. Sexual Behavior of the Female Homosexual." *Archives of General Psychiatry,* 20 (1969), 192–201.

———. "Male and Female Homosexuality: Natural History." *Comprehensive Psychiatry,* 12 (1971), 503–510.

Salamy, J., and Williams, H. L. "Instrumental Responding to an Internal State of Consciousness during Sleep." Paper presented at Southwestern Psychological Association Convention, Austin, Texas, 1969.

Saltzstein, S. W. "Relationship between Oedipal Conflict and Castration Anxiety as a Function of Repressive and Sensitizing Defenses." Unpublished doctoral dissertation, New York University, 1971.

Salzman, L. "Paranoid State: Theory and Therapy." *Archives of General Psychiatry,* 2 (1960), 679–693.

———. "Memory and Psychoanalysis." *British Journal of Medical Psychology,* 39 (1966), 197–206.

Sampson, H. "Deprivation of Dreaming Sleep by Two Methods: I. Compensatory REM Time." *Archives of General Psychiatry,* 13 (1965), 79–86.

———. "Psychological Effects of Deprivation of Dreaming Sleep." *Journal of Nervous and Mental Disease,* 143 (1966), 305–317.

Sampson, H., Weiss, J., Mlodnosky, L., and Hause, E. "Defense Analysis and the Emergence of Warded-Off Mental Contents." *Archives of General Psychiatry,* 26 (1972), 524–532.

Sandler, J. "Studies in Psychopathology Using a Self-Assessment Inventory: I. The Development and Construction of the Inventory." *British Journal of Medical Psychology,* 27 (1954), 142–145.

———. "On the Concept of Superego." *Psychoanalytic Study of the Child,* 15 (1960), 128–162.

Sandler, J., and Dare, C. "The Psychoanalytic Concept of Orality." *Journal of Psychosomatic Research,* 14 (1970), 211–222.

Sandler, J., Dare, D., and Holder, A. "Basic Psychoanalytic Concepts: VII. Special Forms of Transference." *British Journal of Psychiatry,* 117 (1970a), 561–568.

———. "Basic Psychoanalytic Concepts: IX. Working Through." *British Journal of Psychiatry,* 117 (1970b), 617–621.

Sandler, J., and Hazari, A. "The 'Obsessional': On the Psychological Classification of Obsessional Character Traits and Symptoms." *British Journal of Medical Psychology,* 33 (1960), 113–122.

Sandler, J., Holder, A., and Dare, C. "Basic Psychoanalytic Concepts: II. The Treatment of Alliance." *British Journal of Psychiatry,* 116 (1970), 555–558.

Sandler, J., and Pollock, A. B. "Studies in Psychopathology Using a Self-Assessment Inventory: IV. Some Neurotic Gastrointestinal Symptoms: Defaecatory Difficulty in Men and Women." *British Journal of Medical Psychology,* 27 (1954), 241–246.

Sanford, N. "The Dynamics of Identification." *Psychological Review,* 62 (1955), 106–118.
Sankar, D. V., ed. *Schizophrenia: Current Concepts and Research.* Hicksville, N. Y.: PJD, 1969.
Sappenfield, B. R. "Repression and the Dynamics of Conflict." *Journal of Consulting Psychology,* 29 (1965), 266–270.
______. "The Primacy of Narcissism." *Psychological Reports,* 25 (1969), 428–430.
Sarason, S. B. "Dreams and Thematic Apperception Test Stories." *Journal of Abnormal and Social Psychology,* 39 (1944), 486–492.
Sargent, H. D., Coyne, L., Wallerstein, R. S., and Holtzman, W. H. "An Approach to the Quantitative Problems of Psychoanalytic Research." *Journal of Clinical Psychology,* 23 (1967), 243–291.
Sarlin, C. N. "The Current Status of the Concept of Genital Primacy." *Journal of the American Psychoanalytic Association,* 18 (1970), 285–299.
Sarnoff, I. "Identification with the Aggressor: Some Personality Correlates of Anti-Semitism among Jews." *Journal of Personality,* 20 (1951–52), 199–218.
______. "Reaction Formation and Cynicism." *Journal of Personality,* 28 (1960), 129–143.
______. *Testing Freudian Concepts: An Experimental Social Approach.* New York: Springer, 1971.
Sarnoff, I., and Corwin, S. M. "Castration Anxiety and the Fear of Death." *Journal of Personality,* 27 (1959), 374–385.
Sarnoff, I., and Zimbardo, P. G. "Anxiety, Fear and Social Affiliation." *Journal of Abnormal and Social Psychology,* 62 (1961), 356–363.
Sarwer-Foner, G. J. "Psychoanalytic Theories of Activity-Passivity Conflicts and of the Continuum of Ego Defenses." *Archives of Neurology and Psychiatry,* 78 (1957), 413–418.
Saul, L., and Sheppard, E. "An Attempt to Quantify Emotional Forces Using Manifest Dreams: a Preliminary Study." *Journal of the American Psychoanalytic Association,* 4 (1956), 486–502.
Saul, S., Sheppard, E., Selby, D., Lhamon, W., Sachs, D., and Master, R. "The Quantification of Hostility in Dreams with Reference to Essential Hypertension." *Science,* 119 (1954), 382–383.
Scagnelli, J. M. "A Study of the Etiology and Symptomatology of the Paranoid Syndrome." Unpublished doctoral dissertation, University of North Carolina at Chapel Hill, 1971.
Schaefer, C. E. "Primary Process Elements in the Draw-A-Person Protocols of Creative Young Women." *Perceptual and Motor Skills,* 35 (1972), 245–246.
Schafer, R. "Contributions of Longitudinal Studies to Psychoanalytic Theory." *Journal of the American Psychoanalytic Association,* 13 (1965), 605–618.
Schaffer, H. R., and Emerson, P. R. "The Development of Social Attachments in Infancy." *Child Development Monographs,* 29 (1964), No. 2.
Schechter, N., Schmeidler, G. R., and Staal, M. "Dream Reports and Creative Tendencies in Students of the Arts, Sciences, and Engineering." *Journal of Consulting Psychology,* 29 (1965), 415–421.
Scheffler, R. Z. "From Five to Six: A Longitudinal Study of Psychodynamic Change." Unpublished doctoral dissertation, Harvard University, 1971.
Schiffer, D. "Relation of Inhibition of Curiosity to Homosexuality." *Psychological Reports,* 27 (1970), 771–776.
Schill, T. "Sex Differences in Identification of the Castrating Agent on the Blacky Test." *Journal of Clinical Psychology,* 22 (1966), 324–325.
Schjelderup, H. "Lasting Effects of Psychoanalytic Treatment." *Psychiatry,* 18 (1955), 103–133.
Schlesinger, V. J. "Anal Personality Traits and Occupational Choice: A Study of Accountants, Chemical Engineers and Educational Psychologists." Unpublished doctoral dissertation. University of Michigan, 1963.
Schlessinger, N. "Supervision of Psychotherapy: A Critical Review of the Literature." *Archives of General Psychiatry,* 15 (1966), 129–134.
Schmeidler, G. R. "Visual Imagery Correlated to a Measure of Creativity." *Journal of Consulting Psychology,* 29 (1965), 78–80.
Schmidl, F. "Psychoanalysis as Science." *Journal of the American Psychoanalytic Association,* 7 (1959), 127–145.
Schmidt, E., and Brown, P. "Experimental Testing of Two Psychoanalytic Hypotheses." *British Journal of Medical Psychology,* 38 (1965), 177–180.

Schneider, S. C. S. "An Analysis of Presurgical Anxiety in Boys and Girls." Unpublished doctoral dissertation, University of Michigan, 1960.
Schneider, S. F. "Prediction of Psychotherapeutic Relationship from Rorschach's Test." Unpublished doctoral dissertation, University of Michigan, 1953.
Schofield, W. *Psychotherapy: The Purchase of Friendship.* Englewood Cliffs, N. J.: Prentice-Hall, 1964.
Schonbar, R. A. "Temporal and Emotional Factors in the Selective Recall of Dreams." *Journal of Consulting Psychology,* 25 (1961), 67–73.
———. "Differential Dream Recall Frequency as a Component of Life Style.' " *Journal of Consulting Psychology,* 29 (1965a), 468–474.
———. "Interpretation and Insight in Psychotherapy." *Psychotherapy: Theory, Research and Practice,* 2 (1965), 78–83.
———. "The Fee as a Focus for Transference and Countertransference." *American Journal of Psychotherapy,* 21 (1967), 275–285.
Schonbar, R. A., and Davitz, J. R. "The Connotative Meaning of Sexual Symbols." *Journal of Consulting Psychology,* 24 (1960), 483–487.
Schorer, E., E., Lowinger, P., Sullivan, T., and Hartlaub, G. H. "Improvement Without Treatment." *Diseases of the Nervous System,* 29 (1968), 100–104.
Schucman, H., and Thetford, W. N. "Expressed Symptoms and Personality Traits in Conversion Hysteria." *Psychological Reports,* 23 (1968), 231–243.
Schwartz, B. J. "The Measurement of Castration Anxiety and Anxiety over Loss of Love." *Journal of Personality,* 24 (1955), 204–219.
———. "An Empirical Test of Two Freudian Hypotheses Concerning Castration Anxiety." *Journal of Personality,* 24 (1956), 318–327.
Schwartz, D. A. "A Re-view of the 'Paranoid' Concept." *Archives of General Psychiatry,* 8 (1963), 349–361.
Schwartz, F., and Rouse, R. O. "The Activation and Recovery of Associations." *Psychological Issues,* 3 (1961), Monograph 9.
Schwartz, F., and Schiller, P. H. "A Psychoanalytic Model of Attention and Learning." *Psychological Issues,* 6 (1968–70), Monograph 23.
Schwartz, G. E., and Johnson, H. J. "Effects of Preference on Displacement in Approach-Avoidance Conflict." *Journal of Abnormal Psychology,* 73 (1968), 487–491.
Schwartz, S. "The Effects of Sexual Arousal, Sex Guilt and Expectancy for Censure on Appreciation for Varying Degrees of Sex Relevant Humor." Unpublished doctoral dissertation, Syracuse University, 1971.
Scott, E. M. "Psychosexuality of the Alcoholic." *Psychological Reports,* 4 (1958), 599–602.
Scott, M. B., and Lyman, S. M. "Paranoia, Homosexuality and Game Theory." *Journal of Health and Social Behavior,* 9 (1968), 179–187.
Sears, P. S. "Child-Rearing Factors Related to Playing of Sex-Typed Roles." *American Psychologist,* 8 (1953), 431.
Sears, R. R. "Experimental Studies of Projection: I. Attribution of Traits." *Journal of Social Psychology,* 7 (1936), 151–163.
———. *Survey of Objective Studies of Psychoanalytic Concepts.* Bulletin 51. New York: Social Science Research Council, 1943.
———. *Survey of Objective Studies of Psychoanalytic Concepts.* Ann Arbor, Mich.: Edwards Brothers, 1951.
———. "The Growth of Conscience." In I. Iscoe and H. W. Stevenson, eds., *Personality Development in Children.* Austin, Tex.: University of Texas, 1960, pp. 92–111.
Sears, R. R., Maccoby, E. E., and Levin, H. *Patterns of Child Rearing.* Evanston, Ill.: Row, Peterson and Co., 1957.
Sears, R. R., Rau, L., and Alpert, R. *Identification and Child Rearing.* Stanford, Calif.: Stanford University, 1965.
Sears, R. R., Whiting, J. W. M., Nowlis, V., and Sears, P. S. "Some Child-Rearing Antecedents of Aggression and Dependency in Young Children." *Genetic Psychology Monographs,* 47 (1953), 135–234.
Sears, R. R., and Wise, G. W. "Approaches to a Dynamic Theory of Development. Round Table, 1949. 1. Relation of Cup Feeding in Infancy to Thumb-Sucking and the Oral Drive." *American Journal of Orthopsychiatry,* 20 (1950), 123–138.

Sechrest, L. "Stimulus Equivalents of the Psychotherapist." *Journal of Individual Psychology,* 18 (1962), 172–176.

Seeman, W. "Clinical Opinion on the Role of Therapist Adjustment in Psychotherapy." *Journal of Consulting Psychology,* 14 (1950), 49–52,.

Segal, B. "Illustrations of Therapeutic Intervention of A and B Therapists." *Psychotherapy: Theory, Research and Practice,* 8 (1971), 273–275.

Segal, S. J. "A Psychoanalytic Analysis of Personality Factors in Vocational Choice." *Journal of Counseling Psychology,* 8 (1961), 202–210.

Seiden, R. H. "The Psychoanalytic Significance of Onset Age in Bronchial Asthma." *Journal of Asthma Research,* 3 (1966), 285–289.

Seitz, P. F. D. "Experiments in the Substitution of Symptoms by Hypnosis: II. *Psychosomatic Medicine,* 25 (1953), 405–424.

______. "The Consensus Problem in Psychoanalytic Research." In L. A. Gottschalk and A. H. Auerbach, eds., *Methods of Research in Psychotherapy.* New York: Appleton-Century-Crofts, 1966.

Semon, R. G., and Goldstein, N. "The Effectiveness of Group Psychotherapy with Chronic Schizophrenic Patients and an Evaluation of Different Therapeutic Methods." *Journal of Consulting Psychology,* 21 (1957), 317–322.

Serban, G. "Freudian Man versus Existential Man: The Spirit of the Age in the Formulation of the Concept of Man in Modern Psychiatry." *Archives of General Psychiatry,* 17 (1967), 598–607.

Seward, G. H. "The Relation between Psychoanalytic School and Value Problems in Therapy." *American Journal of Psychoanalysis,* 22–23 (1962–63), 138–152.

Seward, J. P. "Psychoanalysis, Deductive Method, and the Blacky Test." *Journal of Abnormal and Social Psychology,* 45 (1950), 529–535.

Sewell, W. H. "Infant Training and the Personality of the Child." *American Journal of Sociology,* 58 (1952–53), 150–159.

Sewell, W. H., and Mussen, P. H. "The Effects of Feeding, Weaning, and Scheduling Procedures on Childhood Adjustment and the Formation of Oral Symptoms." *Child Development,* 23 (1952), 185–191.

Shafar, S., and Jaffe, J. R. "Behaviour Therapy in the Treatment of Psychoneurosis." *British Journal of Psychiatry,* 111 (1965), 1199–1203.

Shakow, D. "The Recorded Psychoanalytic Interview as an Objective Approach to Research in Psychoanalysis." *Psychoanalytic Quarterly,* 29 (1960), 82–97.

Shapiro, A. K. "Placebo Effects in Medicine, Psychotherapy, and Psychoanalysis." In A. E. Bergin and S. L. Garfield, eds., *Handbook of Psychotherapy and Behavior Change.* New York: Wiley, 1971, pp. 439–473.

Shapiro, A., Goodenough, D. R., and Gryler, R. B. "Dream Recall as a Function of Method of Awakening." *Psychosomatic Medicine,* 25 (1963), 174–180.

Shapiro, J. G. "Agreement between Channels of Communication in Interviews." *Journal of Consulting Psychology,* 30 (1966), 535–538.

Sheehan, P. W. "Artificial Induction of Posthypnotic Conflict." *Journal of Abnormal Psychology,* 74 (1969), 16–25.

Sheflin, J. "An Application of Hess' Pupillometric Procedure to a Psychiatric Population. An Approach Utilizing Sexual Stimuli." Unpublished doctoral dissertation, Purdue University, 1969.

Shepherd, R. T. "The Role of Personality Variables in Determining Perceptual Defense and Vigilance." Unpublished doctoral dissertation, University of Georgia, 1963.

Sheppard, E. "Systematic Dream Studies: Clinical Judgment and Objective Measurements of Ego Strength." *Comprehensive Psychiatry,* 4 (1963), 263–270.

Sheppard, E., and Karon, B. "Systematic Studies of Dreams: Relationship between the Manifest Dream and Associations to the Dream Elements." *Comprehensive Psychiatry,* 5 (1964), 335–344.

Sheppard, E., and Rosenhan, D. "Thematic Analysis of Dreams: Inter-Scorer Reliabilities." *Perceptual and Motor Skills,* 21 (1965), 375–384.

Sherman, M. H. "Peripheral Cues and the Invisible Countertransference." *American Journal of Psychotherapy,* 19 (1965), 280–292.

Sherwood, M. *The Logic of Explanation in Psychoanalysis.* New York: Academic, 1969.

Shevrin, H., and Fisher, C. "Changes in the Effects of a Waking Subliminal Stimulus as a Function of Dreaming and Nondreaming Sleep." *Journal of Abnormal Psychology,* 72 (1967), 362–368.

Shevrin, H., and Luborsky, L. "The Measurement of Preconscious Perception in Dreams and Images: An Investigation of the Poetzl Phenomenon." *Journal of Abnormal and Social Psychology,* 56 (1958), 285–294.

Shevrin, H., Smith, W. H., and Fitzler, D. E. "Average Evoked Response and Verbal Correlates of Unconscious Mental Processes." *Psychophysiology,* 3 (1971), 149–162.

Shirley, A. W. "The Scientific Status of Psychoanalytic Dream Theory." *British Journal of Medical Psychology,* 43 (1970), 13–17.

Shirley, R. W., and Romney, A. K. "Love Magic and Socialization: A Cross-Cultural Study." *American Anthropologist,* 64 (1962), 1028–1031.

Shlien, J. M., ed. *Research in Psychotherapy.* Vol. III. Washington, D. C.: American Psychological Association, 1968.

Shockley, F. M. "The Role of Homosexuality in the Genesis of Paranoid Conditions." *Psychoanalytic Review,* 1 (1913–14), 431–438.

Shore, M. F., and Massimo, J. L. "Comprehensive Vocationally Oriented Psychotherapy for Adolescent Delinquent Boys: A Follow-Up Study." *American Journal of Orthopsychiatry,* 36 (1966), 609–615.

Shorr, M. "Trust, Orality and Openness to Sensory Experience: A study of Some Personality Correlates of Creativity." Unpublished doctoral dissertation, New York University, 1971.

Shrauger, S., and Altrocchi, J. "The Personality of the Perceiver as a Factor in Person Perception." *Psychological Bulletin,* 62 (1964), 289–303.

Siegel, N. H. "Characteristics of Patients in Psychoanalysis." *Journal of Nervous and Mental Disease,* 135 (1962), 155–158.

Siegelman, M. "Adjustment of Male Homosexuals and Heterosexuals." *Archives of Sexual Behavior,* 2 (1972), 9–25.

Siegelman, M. "Birth Order and Family Size of Homosexual Men and Women." *Journal of Consulting and Clinical Psychology,* 41 (1973), 164.

———. "Parental Background of Male Homosexuals and Heterosexuals." *Archives of Sexual Behavior,* 3 (1974), 3–18.

Signori, E. I., and Rempel, H. "Research on the Modified Picture Titles Subtest of the IES Test." *Perceptual and Motor Skills,* 24 (1967), 1255–1258.

Signori, E. I., and Schwartzentruber, A. M. "Development of Items for Assessment of Id, Ego, and Superego Tendencies in a Variety of Moral Situations." *Perceptual and Motor Skills,* 28 (1969), 551–555.

Sillman, L. R. "Femininity and Paranoidism." *Journal of Nervous and Mental Disease,* 143 (1966), 163–170.

Silverman, L. H. "A Technique for the Study of Psychodynamic Relationships: The Effects of Subliminally Presented Aggressive Stimuli on the Production of Pathological Thinking in a Schizophrenic Population." *Journal of Consulting Psychology,* 30 (1966), 103–111.

Silverman, L. H., Kwawer, J. S., Wolitzky, C., and Coron, M. "An Experimental Study of Aspects of the Psychoanalytic Theory of Male Homosexuality." *Journal of Abnormal Psychology,* 82 (1973), 178–188.

Silverman, L. H., and Spiro, R. H. "Further Investigation of the Effects of Subliminal Aggressive Stimulation on the Ego Functioning of Schizophrenics." *Journal of Consulting Psychology,* 31 (1967), 225–232.

Simon, J. "Research in Psychoanalysis: Experimental Studies." *Journal of the American Psychoanalytic Association,* 18 (1970), 644–654.

Simpson, M. *Parent Preferences of Young Children.* New York: Teachers College, Columbia University, 1935.

Simsarian, D. P. "Case Histories of Five Thumb Sucking Children Breast Fed on Unscheduled Regimes, without Limitation of Nursing Time." *Child Development,* 18 (1947), 180–184.

Singer, M. I. "Comparison of Indicators of Homosexuality on the MMPI." *Journal of Consulting and Clinical Psychology,* 34 (1970), 15–18.

Sirota, L. M. "A Factor Analysis of Selected Personality Domains." Unpublished doctoral dissertation, University of Michigan, 1957.
Sklansky, M. A., Isaacs, K. S., Levitov, E. S., and Haggard, E. A. "Verbal Interaction and Levels of Meaning in Psychotherapy." *Archives of General Psychiatry,* 14 (1966), 158–170.
Slater, M. K. "Ecological Factors in the Origin of Incest." *American Anthropologist,* 61 (1959), 1042–1059.
Slater, P. E., and Slater, D. A. "Maternal Ambivalence and Narcissism: A Cross-Cultural Study." *Merrill-Palmer Quarterly,* 11 (1965), 241–259.
Slavin, J. H. "The Role of Power Conflicts in the Psychodynamics of Paranoid Women." Unpublished doctoral dissertation, University of Michigan, 1970.
Sloane, R. B. "Behavior Therapy and Psychotherapy: Integration or Disintegration." *American Journal of Psychotherapy,* 23 (1969a), 473–481.
______. "The Converging Paths of Behavior Therapy and Psychotherapy." *American Journal of Psychiatry,* 125 (1969b), 877–885.
Sloane, R. B., Staples, F. R., Cristol, A. H., Yorkston, N. J., and Whipple, K. "Short-Term Analytically Oriented Psychotherapy versus Behavior Therapy." *American Journal of Psychiatry,* 132 (1975a), 373–377.
______. *Psychotherapy vs. Behavior Therapy.* Cambridge, Mass.: Harvard University Press, 1975b.
Slote, G. M. "Feminine Character and Patterns of Interpersonal Perception." Unpublished doctoral dissertation, New York University, 1962.
Smith, M. E., and Hall, C. "An Investigation of Regression in a Long Dream Series." *Journal of Gerontology,* 19 (1964), 66–71.
Smock, C. D. "Replication and Comments: An Experimental Reunion of Psychoanalytic Theory with Perceptual Vigilance and Defense." *Journal of Abnormal and Social Psychology,* 53 (1956), 68–73.
Smock, C. D., and Thompson, G. G. "An Inferred Relationship between Early Childhood Conflicts and Anxiety Responses in Adult Life." *Journal of Personality,* 23 (1954), 88–98.
Snortum, J. R., Gillespie, J. F., Marshall, J. E., McLaughlin, J. P., and Mosberg, L. "Family Dynamics and Homosexuality." *Psychological Reports,* 24 (1969), 763–770.
Snyder, F. "The New Biology of Dreaming." *Archives of General Psychiatry,* 28 (1963), 381–391.
______. "In Quest of Dreaming." In H. A. Witkin and H. B. Lewis, eds., *Experimental Studies of Dreaming.* New York: Random House, 1967, pp. 3–75.
Snyder, W. U. "The Present Status of Psychotherapeutic Counseling." *Psychological Bulletin,* 44 (1947), 322–333; 378–381.
Sobel, R. "Role Conflict or Resistance: A New Look at Certain Phases of Psychotherapy." *American Journal of Psychotherapy,* 18 (1964), 25–34.
Sobel, R., and Ingalls, A. "Resistance to Treatment: Explorations of the Patient's Sick Role." *American Journal of Psychotherapy,* 18 (1964), 562–573.
Socarides, C. W. "Theoretical and Clinical Aspects of Overt Male Homosexuality." *Journal of the American Psychoanalytic Association,* 8 (1960), 552–566.
______. "The Historical Development of Theoretical and Clinical Concepts of Overt Female Homosexuality." *Journal of the American Psychoanalytic Association,* 11 (1963), 386–414.
Solley, C. M., and Murphy, G. *Development of the Perceptual World.* New York: Basic Books, 1960.
Solway, K. S. "Freudian and Cultural Symbolism." *Journal of Clinical Psychology,* 27 (1971), 516–518.
Sopchak, A. L. "Parental Identification and Tendency toward Disorders as Measured by the Minnesota Multiphasic Personality Inventory." *Journal of Abnormal and Social Psychology,* 47 (1952), 159–165.
Spanjaard, J. "The Manifest Dream Content and Its Significance for the Interpretation of Dreams." *International Journal of Psycho-Analysis,* 50 (1969), 221–235.
Speisman, J. C. "Depth of Interpretation and Verbal Resistance in Psychotherapy." *Journal of Consulting Psychology,* 23 (1959), 93–99.
Speisman, J. C., Lazarus, R. S., Mordkoff, A., and Davison, L. "Experimental Reduction of Stress Based on Ego-Defense Theory." *Journal of Abnormal Psychology,* 68 (1964), 367–380.

Spence, D. P. "Conscious and Preconscious Influences on Recall: Another Example of the Restricting Effects of Awareness." *Journal of Abnormal Psychology,* 68 (1964), 92–99.
Spence, D. P., and Ehrenberg, B. "Effects of Oral Deprivation on Responses to Subliminal and Supraliminal Verbal Food Stimuli." *Journal of Abnormal Psychology,* 69 (1964), 10–18.
Spence, D. P., Gordon, Carol M., and Rabkin, J. "Effects of Rejection on Psychogenic Hunger." *Psychosomatic Medicine,* 28 (1966), 27–33.
Spiegel, D., Brodkin, S. G., and Keith-Spiegel, P. "Unacceptable Impulses, Anxiety and the Appreciation of Cartoons." *Journal of Projective Techniques and Personality Assessment,* 33 (1969), 154–159.
Spiegel, H. "Is Symptom Removal Dangerous?" *American Journal of Psychiatry,* 123 (1967), 1279–1283.
Spiegel, H., and Linn, L. "The 'Ripple Effect' Following Adjunct Hypnosis in Analytic Psychotherapy." *American Journal of Psychiatry,* 126 (1969), 53–58.
Spiegel, R. "Anger and Acting Out: Masks of Depression." *American Journal of Psychotherapy,* 21 (1967), 597–606.
Spilken, A. Z., Jacobs, M. A., Muller, J. J., and Knitzer, J. "Personality Characteristics of Therapists: Description of Relevant Variables and Examination of Conscious Preferences." *Journal of Consulting and Clinical Psychology,* 33 (1969), 317–326.
Spiro, M. E. *Children of the Kibbutz.* Cambridge, Mass.: Harvard University, 1958.
Srole, L., Langner, T. S., Michael, S. T., Opler, M. K., and Rennie, T. A. C. *Mental Health in the Metropolis: The Midtown Manhattan Study.* New York: McGraw-Hill, 1962.
Stagner, R. "The Gullibility of Personnel Managers." *Personnel Psychology,* 11 (1958), 203–208.
Stagner, R., Lawson, E. D., and Moffitt, J. W. "The Krout Personal Preference Scale: A Factor-Analytic Study." *Journal of Clinical Psychology,* 11 (1955), 103–113.
Stagner, R., and Moffitt, J. W. "A Statistical Study of Freud's Theory of Personality Types." *Journal of Clinical Psychology,* 12 (1956), 72–74.
Starer, E. "Cultural Symbolism: A Validity Study." *Journal of Consulting Psychology,* 19 (1955), 453–454.
Starer, E., and Tanner, H. "An Analysis of Responses of Male Schizophrenic Patients to Freudian-Type Stimuli." *Journal of Clinical Psychology,* 18 (1962), 58–61.
Starer, E., Weinberger, J., and Ahbel, G, "An Analysis of Polygraphic Responses of Chronic Regressed Male Schizophrenic Patients to Freudian-Type Stimuli." *Journal of Clinical Psychology,* 19 (1963), 43–44.
Stark, S. "Rorschach Movement, Fantastic Daydreaming, and Freud's Concept of Primary Process: Interpretive Commentary." *Perceptual and Motor Skills,* 22 (1966), 523–532.
Starker, S., and Goodenough, D. R. "Effects of Sleep State and Method of Awakening upon Thematic Appreception Test Productions at Arousal." *Journal of Nervous and Mental Disease,* 150 (1970), 188–194.
Stein, A. "Guilt as a Composite Emotion: The relationship of Child-Rearing Variables to Superego Response." Unpublished doctoral dissertation, University of Michigan, 1958.
Stendler, Celia B. "Possible Causes of Overdependency in Young Children." *Child Development,* 25 (1954), 125–146.
Stengel, E. "The Scientific Testing of Psycho-Analytic Findings and Theory. I." *British Journal of Medical Psychology,* 24 (1951), 26–29.
Stennett, R. G., and Thurlow, M. "Cultural Symbolism: The Age Variables." *Journal of Consulting Psychology,* 22 (1958), 496.
Stephan, W. G. "Parental Relationships and Early Social Experiences of Activist Male Homosexuals and Male Heterosexuals." *Journal of Abnormal Psychology,* 82 (1973), 506–513.
Stephens, W. N. *The Oedipus Complex: Cross-Cultural Evidence.* New York: Free Press of Glencoe, 1962.
Sternlof, R. E. "Differential Perception in Paranoid Schizophrenia and Depression as a Function of Structure and Content." Unpublished doctoral dissertation, University of Oklahoma, 1964.
Stevens, H. A., and Reitz, W. E. "An Experimental Investigation of Projection as a Defense Mechanism." *Journal of Clinical Psychology,* 26 (1970), 152–154.

_____. "The Challenge of Results in Psychotherapy." *American Journal of Psychiatry,* 116 (1959a), 120–123.
_____. "Direct Instigation of Behavioral Changes in Psychotherapy." *Archives of General Psychiatry,* 1 (1959b), 99–107.
_____. "Processes of Spontaneous Recovery from the Psychoneuroses." *American Journal of Psychiatry,* 117 (1961), 1057–1064.
Stewart, H. F., Jr. "Repression: Experimental Studies Since 1943." *Psychoanalysis and the Psychoanalytic Review,* 49 (1962), 93–99.
Stieper, D. R., and Wiener, D. N. "The Problem of Interminability in Out-Patient Psychotherapy." *Journal of Consulting Psychology,* 23 (1959), 237–242.
Stoler, N. "Client Likability: A Variable in the Study of Psychotherapy." *Journal of Consulting Psychology,* 27 (1963), 175–178.
Stoller, R. J. "The Bedrock of Masculinity and Femininity: Bisexuality." *Archives of General Psychiatry,* 26 (1972), 207–212.
_____. "Overview: The Impact of New Advances in Sex Research on Psychoanalytic Theory." *American Journal of Psychiatry,* 130 (1973), 241–251.
Stolorow, R. D. "Causality-Interpretation and the Precipitation of Distress." *Journal of Personality Assessment,* 35 (1971), 122–127.
Story, R. I. "The Relationship between the Effects of Conflict Arousal and Oral Fixation on Thinking." Unpublished doctoral dissertation, University of Michigan, 1963.
_____. "Effects on Thinking of Relationships between Conflict Arousal and Oral Fixation." *Journal of Abnormal Psychology,* 73 (1968), 440–448.
Stoyva, J. M. "Posthypnotically Suggested Dreams and the Sleep Cycle." *Archives of General Psychiatry,* 12 (1965), 287–294.
Stoyva, J., and Kamiya, J. "Electrophysiological Studies of Dreaming as the Prototype of a New Strategy in the Study of Consciousness." *Psychological Review,* 75 (1968), 192–205.
Strachey, J. "Papers on Technique (1911–1915[1914]): Editor's Introduction." In J. Strachey, ed. (in collaboration with A. Freud), *The Standard Edition of the Complete Psychological Works of Sigmund Freud.* London: Hogarth, 1958, Vol. 12, pp. 85–88.
Straus, M. A. "Anal and Oral Frustration in Relation to Sinhalese Personality." *Sociometry,* 20 (1957), 21–31.
Strickland, B. R., and Crowne, D. P. "Need for Approval and the Premature Termination of Psychotherapy." *Journal of Consulting Psychology,* 27 (1963), 95–101.
Stringer, P. "A Note on the Factorial Structure of the Dynamic Personality Inventory." *British Journal of Medical Psychology,* 43 (1970), 95–103.
Strong, E. K., Jr. *Vocational Interests of Men and Women.* Stanford, Calif.: Stanford University Press, 1943.
Stross, L., and Shevrin, H. "Hypnosis as a Method for Investigating Unconscious Thought Processes: A Review of Research." *Journal of the American Psychoanalytic Association,* 17 (1969), 100–135.
Strupp, H. H. "The Effect of the Psychotherapist's Personal Analysis upon his Techniques." *Journal of Consulting Psychology,* 19 (1955a), 197–204.
_____. "An Objective Comparison of Rogerian and Psychoanalytic Techniques." *Journal of Consulting Psychology,* 19 (1955b), 1–7.
_____. "Psychotherapeutic Technique, Professional Affiliation, and Experience Level." *Journal of Consulting Psychology,* 19 (1955c), 97–102.
_____. "A Multidimensional Comparison of Therapist Activity in Analytic and Client-Centered Therapy." *Journal of Consulting Psychology,* 21 (1957), 301–308.
_____. "The Performance of Psychiatrists and Psychologists in a Therapeutic Interview." *Journal of Clinical Psychology,* 14 (1958a), 219–226.
_____. "The Performance of Psychoanalytic and Client-Centered Therapists in an Initial Interview." *Journal of Consulting Psychology,* 22 (1958b), 265–274.
_____. "Nature of Psychotherapists' Contribution to Treatment Process." *Archives of General Psychiatry,* 3 (1960), 219–231.
_____. "The Outcome Problem in Psychotherapy Revisited." *Psychotherapy: Theory, Research and Practice,* 1 (1963–64a), 1–13.
_____. "The Outcome Problem in Psychotherapy: A Rejoinder." *Psychotherapy: Theory, Research and Practice,* 1 (1963–64b), 101.

———. "Who Needs Intrapsychic Factors in Clinical Psychology?" *Psychotherapy: Theory, Research and Practice,* 4 (1967), 145–150.
———. "Toward a Specification of Teaching and Learning in Psychotherapy." *Archives of General Psychiatry,* 21 (1969), 203–212.
———. "Ferment in Psychoanalysis and Psychoanalytic Psychotherapy." In B. B. Wolman, ed., *Success and Failure in Psychoanalysis and Psychotherapy.* New York: Macmillan, 1972a, pp. 71–103.
———. "On the Technology of Psychotherapy." *Archives of General Psychiatry,* 26 (1972b), 270–278.
———. *Psychotherapy: Clinical, Research, and Theoretical Issues.* New York: Jason Aronson, 1973a.
———. "Toward a Reformulation of the Psychotherapeutic Influence." *International Journal of Psychiatry,* 11 (1973b), 263–327.
Strupp, H. H., and Bergin, A. E. "Some Empirical and Conceptual Bases for Coordinated Research in Psychotherapy: A Critical Review of Issues, Trends, and Evidence. *International Journal of Psychiatry,* 7 (1969), 18–90.
Strupp, H. H., and Bloxom, A. L. "Preparing Lower-Class Patients for Group Psychotherapy: Development and Evaluation of a Role-Induction Film." *Journal of Consulting and Clinical Psychology,* 41 (1973), 373–384.
Strupp, H. H., Chassan, J., and Ewing, J. "Toward the Longitudinal Study of the Psychoanalytic Process." In L. Gottschalk and A. Auerbach, eds., *Methods of Research in Psychotherapy.* New York: Appleton-Century-Crofts, 1966, pp. 361–400.
Strupp, H. H., Wallach, M. S., and Wogan, M. "Psychotherapy Experience in Retrospect: Questionnaire Survey of Former Patients and Their Therapists." *Psychological Monographs,* 78 (1964), 1–45.
Strupp, H. H., and Williams, J. V. "Some Determinants of Clinical Evaluations of Different Psychiatrists." *Archives of General Psychiatry,* 2 (1960), 434–400.
Subotnik, L. "Transference in Client-Centered Play Therapy." *Psychology,* 3 (1966a), 2–17.
———. "Transference in Child Therapy: A Third Replication. *Psychology Record,* 16 (1966b), 265–277.
———. "Spontaneous Remission of Emotional Disturbance in a General Medical Practice." Presented at annual convention of the Western Psychological Association, Vancouver, 1969.
———. "Spontaneous Remission of Deviant MMPI Profiles among College Students." *Journal of Consulting and Clinical Psychology,* 38 (1972a), 191–201.
———. "Spontaneous Remission: Fact or Artifact?" *Psychological Bulletin,* 77 (1972b), 32–48.
Suckman, E. A. "Sociocultural Variations in Illness and Medical Care." *American Journal of Sociology,* 70 (1964), 319–331.
Sullivan, R. W., and Bone, R. N. "The Relationship of Sensation Seeking and Dream Recall." Presented at meeting for the Association for the Psychophysiological Study of Sleep, 1971.
Sundberg, N. D. "The Acceptability of 'Fake' versus Bona Fide Personality Test Interpretations." *Journal of Abnormal and Social Psychology,* 50 (1955), 145–147.
Sundland, D. M., and Barker, E. N. "The Orientation of Psychotherapists." *Journal of Consulting Psychology,* 26 (1962), 201–212.
Swanson, E. M., and Foulkes, D. "Dream Content and the Menstrual Cycle." *Psychophysiology,* 4 (1967), 373–374.
———. "Dream Content and the Menstrual Cycle." *Journal of Nervous and Mental Disease,* 145 (1968), 358–363.
Swanson, G. E. "Some Effects of Member Object-Relationships on Small Groups." *Human Relations,* 4 (1951), 355–380.
Swensen, C. H. "Commitment and the Personality of the Successful Therapist." *Psychotherapy: Theory, Research and Practice,* 8 (1971), 31–36.
Swerdloff, B. "The Predictive Value of the Admissions Interview: A Search for the Psychodynamic Factors Related to Changes in the Patient and his Situation." Unpublished doctoral dissertation, Columbia University, 1960.
Szasz, T. S. "Psychiatric Aspects of Vagotomy II: A Psychiatric Study of Vagotomized Ulcer Patients with Comments on Prognosis." *Psychosomatic Medicine,* 11 (1949), 187–199.

______. "Three Problems in Contemporary Psychoanalytic Training." *Archives of General Psychiatry,* 3 (1960), 82–94.

______. "The Problem of Privacy in Training Analysis: Selections from a Questionnaire Study of Psychoanalytic Practices." *Journal for the Study of Interpersonal Processes,* 25 (1962), 195–207.

______. "Psychoanalytic Treatment as Education." *Archives of General Psychiatry,* 9 (1963), 46–52.

Szasz, T. S., and Nemiroff, R. A. "A Questionnaire Study of Psychoanalytic Practices and Opinions." *Journal of Nervous and Mental Disease,* 137 (1963), 209–221.

Taft, R. "The Ability to Judge People." *Psychological Bulletin,* 52 (1955), 1–23.

Tanck, R. H., and Robbins, P. R. "Pupillary Reactions to Sexual, Aggressive, and Other Stimuli as a Function of Personality." *Journal of Projective Techniques and Personality Assessment,* 34 (1970), 277–282.

Tanner, C. E., Pasewark, R. A., and Fitzgerald, B. J. "Use of the Edwards Personal Preference Schedule with Paranoid Schizophrenics." *Psychological Reports,* 24 (1969), 988.

Tarachow, S., Korin, H., and Friedman, S. "Perception Experiments in a Study of Ambivalence." *Archives of Neurology and Psychiatry,* 78 (1957), 167–176.

Tart, C. T. "Toward the Experimental Control of Dreaming: A Review of the Literature." *Psychological Bulletin,* 64 (1965), 81–91.

______. "Approaches to the Study of Hypnotic Dreams." *Perceptual and Motor Skills,* 28 (1969), 864.

Tauber, E. S., and Green, M. R. "Color in Dreams." *American Journal of Psychotherapy,* 16 (1962), 221–229.

Taulbee, E. S., and Stenmark, D. E. "The Blacky Pictures Test: A Comprehensive Annotated and Indexed Bibliography (1949–1967)." *Journal of Projective Techniques and Personality Assessment,* 32 (1968), 105–137.

Taylor, J. W. "Relationship of Success and Length in Psychotherapy." *Journal of Consulting Psychology,* 20 (1956), 332.

Teevan, R. C. "Personality Correlates of Undergraduate Field of Specialization." *Journal of Consulting Psychology,* 18 (1954), 212–214.

Temerlin, M. K. "One Determinant of the Capacity to Free-Associate in Psychotherapy." *Journal of Abnormal and Social Psychology,* 53 (1956), 16–18.

Tenzer, A. "Differential Learning and Differential Forgetting: An Investigation of the Repression Hypothesis." Unpublished doctoral dissertation, Columbia University, 1962.

Terman, L. M., and Miles, C. *Sex and Personality.* New York: McGraw-Hill, 1936.

Terwilliger, R. F. "Free Association Patterns as a Factor Relating to Semantic Differential Responses." *Journal of Abnormal and Social Psychology,* 65 (1962), 87–94.

Thelen, M. H. "Similarities of Defense Preferences within Families and within Sex Groups." *Journal of Projective Techniques and Personality Assessment,* 29 (1965), 461–464.

Thetford, W. N., and Schucman, H. "Conversion Reactions and Personality Traits." *Psychological Reports,* 27 (1970), 1005–1006.

Thomas, A. "Purpose versus Consequence in the Analysis of Behavior." *American Journal of Psychotherapy,* 24 (1970), 49–64.

Thomas, R. W. "An Investigation of the Psychoanalytic Theory of Homosexuality." Unpublished doctoral dissertation, University of Kentucky, 1951.

Thompson, N. L., Jr. "Family Background and Sexual Identity in Male and Female Homosexuals." Unpublished doctoral dissertation, Emory University, 1971.

Thompson, N. L., Jr., McCandless, B. R., and Strickland, B. R. "Personal Adjustment of Male and Female Homosexuals and Heterosexuals." *Journal of Abnormal Psychology,* 78 (1971), 237–240.

Thompson, N. L., Jr., Schwartz, D. M., McCandless, B. R., and Edwards, D. A. "Parent-Child Relationships and Sexual Identity in Male and Female Homosexuals and Heterosexuals." *Journal of Consulting and Clinical Psychology,* 41 (1973), 120–127.

Thurston, J. R., and Mussen, P. H. "Infant Feeding Gratification and Adult Personality." *Journal of Personality,* 19 (1951), 449–458.

Timmons, E. O., and Noblin, C. D. "The Differential Performance of Orals and Anals in a Verbal Conditioning Paradigm." *Journal of Consulting Psychology,* 27 (1963), 383–386.

Tippett, J. S., and Silber, E. "Autonomy of Self-Esteem." *Archives of General Psychiatry,* 14 (1966), 372–385.

Tobin, S. S., and Etigson, E. "Effect of Stress on Earliest Memory." *Archives of General Psychiatry,* 1968, 19, 435–444.

Tokar, J. T., and Steffire, V. "Language Patterns of Associations to Key Words from Dream Symbols." *Diseases of the Nervous System,* 33 (1972), 367–371.

Tolor, A., and Reznikoff, M. "A New Approach to Insight: A Preliminary Report." *Journal of Nervous and Mental Disease,* 130 (1960), 286–296.

Toman, W. "Pause Analysis as a Short Interviewing Technique." *Journal of Consulting Psychology,* 17 (1953), 1–7.

Torda, C. "Dreams of Subjects with Loss of Memory for Recent Events." *Psychophysiology,* 6 (1969), 358–365.

Traisman, A. S., and Traisman, H. S. "Thumb and Finger-Sucking: A Study of 2,650 Infants and Children." *Journal of Pediatrics,* 52 (1958), 566–572.

Tribich, D., and Messer, S. "Psychoanalytic Type and Status of Authority as Determiners of Suggestibility." *Journal of Consulting and Clinical Psychology,* 42 (1974), 842–848.

Trinder, J., and Kramer, M. "Dream Recall." *American Journal of Psychiatry,* 128 (1971), 296–301.

Trosman, H. "Dream Research and the Psychoanalytic Theory of Dreams." *Archives of General Psychiatry,* 9 (1963), 9–18.

Trosman, H., Rechtschaffen, A., Offenkrantz, W., and Wolpert, E. "Studies in Psychophysiology of Dreams: IV. Relations among Dreams in Sequence." *Archives of General Psychiatry,* 3 (1960), 602–607.

Truax, C. B. "The Repression Response to Implied Failure as a Function of the Hysteria-Psychasthenia Index." *Journal of Abnormal and Social Psychology,* 55 (1957), 188–193.

Truax, C. B., and Carkhuff, R. R. *Toward Effective Counseling and Psychotherapy.* Chicago: Aldine, 1967.

Truax, C. B., and Mitchell, K. M. "Research on Certain Therapist Interpersonal Skills in Relation to Process and Outcome." In A. E. Bergin and S. L. Garfield, eds., *Handbook of Psychotherapy and Behavior Change.* New York: Wiley, 1971, pp. 299–344.

Tryon, M. C. "Evaluation of Adolescent Personality by Adolescents." *Monograph of the Society for Research in Child Development,* 1939, No. 4.

Tuckman, A. J. "Brief Psychotherapy and Hemodialysis." *Archives of General Psychiatry,* 23 (1970), 65–69.

Uhr, L., and Miller, J. G., eds. *Drugs and Behavior.* New York: Wiley, 1960.

Ullman, M. "Dreams and Arousal." *American Journal of Psychotherapy,* 12 (1958a), 222–228.

———. "The Dream Process." *American Journal of Psychotherapy,* 12 (1958b), 671–690.

Ullman, P. "Parental Participation in Child-Rearing as Evaluated by Male Social Deviates." Unpublished doctoral dissertation, University of Oregon, 1959.

———. "Parental Participation in Child-Rearing as Evaluated by Male Social Deviates." *Pacific Sociological Review,* 3 (1960), 89–95.

Ulrich, R. E., Stachnik, T. J., and Stainton, N. R. "Student Acceptance of Generalized Personality Interpretations." *Psychological Reports,* 13 (1963), 831–834.

Unger, S. M. "Antecedents of Personality Differences in Guilt Responsivity." *Psychological Reports,* 10 (1962), 357–358.

Urbina, S. P. "Cultural and Sex Differences in Affiliation and Achievement Drives as Expressed in Reported Dream Content and a Projective Technique." Unpublished doctoral dissertation, Fordham University, 1972.

Van De Castle, R. L. "Dreams and Menstruation." *Psychophysiology,* 4 (1967), 374–375.

Van De Castle, R. L., and Kinder, P. "Dream Content During Pregnancy." *Psychophysiology,* 4 (1968), 373–377.

Van Den Aardweg, G. J. M. "A Brief Theory of Homosexuality. "*American Journal of Psychotherapy,* 26 (1972), 52–68.

VandenBos, G. R., and Karon, B. P. "Pathogenesis: A New Therapist Dimension Related to Therapeutic Effectiveness. " *Journal of Personality Assessment,* 35 (1971), 252–260.

Vaughan, J. A., Jr., and Knapp, R. H. "A Study in Pessimism." *Journal of Social Psychology,* 59 (1963), 77–92.

Veldman, D. J., and Bown, O. H. "Personality and Performance Characteristics Associated with Cigarette Smoking among College Freshmen." *Journal of Consulting and Clinical Psychology,* 33 (1969), 109–119.

Verdone, P. "Temporal Reference of Manifest Dream Content." *Perceptual and Motor Skills,* 20 (1965), 1253–1268.

Verinis, J. S. "Inhibition of Humor Enjoyment: Effects of Sexual Content and Introversion-Extraversion." *Psychological Reports,* 26 (1970), 167–170.

Vestre, N. D., and Watson, C. G. "Behavioral Correlates of the MMPI Paranoia Scale." *Psychological Reports,* 31 (1972), 851–854.

Vitanza, A. A., and Rawn, M. L. "An Objective Investigation of Psychosexual Development in Dreams." *Psychological Reports,* 4 (1958), 647–648.

Vogel, G. W. "REM Deprivation: III. Dreaming and Psychosis." *Archives of General Psychiatry,* 18 (1968), 312–329.

______. "Dreaming and Schizophrenia." *Psychiatric Annals,* 4 (1974), 63–77.

Vogel, G. W., Barrowclough, B., and Giesler, D. D. "Limited Discriminability of REM and Sleep Onset Reports and Its Psychiatric Implications." *Archives of General Psychiatry,* 26 (1972), 449–455.

Von Holt, H. W., Jr. "A Slip of the Tongue." *Journal of Abnormal Psychology,* 72 (1967), 213–220.

Von Holt, H. W., Sengstake, C. B., Sanada, B. C., and Draper, W. A. "Orality, Image Fusion, and Concept Formation." *Journal of Projective Techniques,* 24 (1960), 194–198.

Vorster, D. "Psychotherapy and the Results of Psychotherapy." *South African Medical Journal,* 40 (1966), 934–936.

Voth, H. M. "Some Effects of Freud's Personality on Psychoanalytic Theory and Technique." *International Journal of Psychiatry,* 4 (1972), 48–61.

Voth, H. M., Cancro, R., and Kissen, M. "Choice of Defense." *Archives of General Psychiatry,* 18 (1968), 36–41.

Wachtel, P. L. "Psychology, Metapsychology, and Psychoanalysis." *Journal of Abnormal Psychology,* 74 (1969), 651–660.

Wake, M. B. "Unconscious Response to Sexual Symbols." Unpublished doctoral dissertation, Wayne State University, 1966.

Wallace, H. E., and Whyte, M. B. "Natural History of the Psychoneuroses." *British Medical Journal,* 1 (1959), 144–148.

Wallach, M. A. "Two Correlates of Symbolic Sexual Arousal: Level of Anxiety and Liking for Esthetic Material." *Journal of Abnormal and Social Psychology,* 61 (1960), 396–401.

Wallach, M. S. "Dream Report and Some Psychological Concomitants." *Journal of Consulting Psychology,* 27 (1963), 549.

Wallach, M. S., and Strupp, H. H. "Psychotherapists' Clinical Judgments and Attitudes towards Patients." *Journal of Consulting Psychology,* 24 (1960), 316–323.

______. "Dimensions of Psychotherapists' Activity." *Journal of Consulting Psychology,* 28 (1964), 120–125.

Wallerstein, R. S. "The Problem of the Assessment of Change in Psychotherapy." *International Journal of Psycho-Analysis,* 44 (1963), 31–41.

______. "The Goals of Psychoanalysis: A Survey of Analytic Viewpoints." *Journal of the American Psychoanalytic Association,* 13 (1965), 748–770.

______. "The Current State of Psychotherapy: Theory, Practice, Research." *Journal of the American Psychoanalytic Association,* 14 (1966), 183–225.

______. "The Challenge of the Community Mental Health Movement to Psychoanalysis." *American Journal of Psychiatry* 124 (1968a), 1049–1056.

______. "The Psychotherapy Research Project of the Menninger Foundation: A Semifinal View." In J. M. Shlien, ed., *Research in Psychotherapy.* Washington, D. C.: American Psychological Association, 1968b, pp. 584–605.

Wallerstein, R. S., and Sampson, H. "Issues in Research in the Psychoanalytic Process." *International Journal of Psycho-Analysis,* 52 (1971), 11–50.

Walters, A. "Psychogenic Regional Sensory and Motor Disorders Alias Hysteria." *Canadian Psychiatric Association Journal,* 14 (1969), 573–590.

Walters, O. S. "A Methodological Critique of Freud's Schreber Analysis." *Psychoanalytic Review,* 42 (1955), 321–342.

Wangh, M. "Psychoanalytic Thought on Phobia: Its Evolution and Its Relevance for Therapy." *American Journal of Psychiatry,* 123 (1967), 1075–1080.

Ward, C. H. "Psychotherapy Research: Dilemmas and Directions." *Archives of General Psychiatry,* 10 (1964), 596–622.

Ward, C. H., Beck, A. T., and Rascoe, E. "Typical dreams: Incidence among Psychiatric Patients." *Archives of General Psychiatry,* 5 (1961), 606–615.
Ward, W. D. "Process of Sex-Role Development." *Developmental Psychology,* 1 (1969), 163–8.
Wassermann, I. "A Letter to the Editor—Polish Review." *American Journal of Psychotherapy,* 12 (1958), 623–630.
Watson, C. G. "A Test of the Relationship between Repressed Homosexuality and Paranoid Mechanisms." *Journal of Clinical Psychology,* 21 (1965), 380–384.
Watson, D. J. "Some Social Psychological Correlates of Personality: A Study of the Usefulness of Psychoanalytic Theory in Predicting to Social Behavior." Unpublished doctoral dissertation, University of Michigan, 1952.
Watts, G. P. "The Carkhuff Discrimination Scale as a Predictor of Accurate Perception of Others." *Journal of Consulting and Clinical Psychology,* 41 (1973), 202–206.
Waxenberg, S. E. "Psychosomatic Patients and Other Physically Ill Persons: A Comparative Study." *Journal of Consulting Psychology,* 19 (1955), 163–169.
Waxenberg, S. E., Dickes, R., and Gottesfeld, H. "The Poetzl Phenomenon Re-examined Experimentally." *Journal of Nervous and Mental Disease,* 135 (1962), 387–398.
Weber, J. J., Elinson, J., and Moss, L. M. "The Application of Ego Strength Scales to Psychoanalytic Clinic Records." In G. Goldman and S. Shapiro, eds., *Developments in Psychoanalysis at Columbia University.* New York: Hafner, 1966, pp. 215–281.
———. "Psychoanalysis and Change: A Study of Psychoanalytic Clinic Records Utilizing Electronic Data-Processing Techniques." *Archives of General Psychiatry,* 17 (1967), 687–709.
Wechsler, D. *The Measurement and Appraisal of Adult Intelligence.* Baltimore, Md: Waverly Press, 1958.
Weems, L. B., Jr. "The Effects of Race and Paranoia on Power Involvements." Unpublished doctoral dissertation, University of Michigan, 1970.
Weiland, H., and Steisel, I. M. "An Analysis of Manifest Content of the Earliest Memories of Children." *Journal of Genetic Psychology,* 92 (1958), 41–52.
Weingarden, A. M. "Persistence of Cathexis: A requisite Condition for the Incorporation of Recent Experiences into Dreams." Unpublished doctoral dissertation, Wayne State University, 1972.
Weingold, H. P., Adams, H. E., and Wittman, F. "Sexual Symbolism, Abstract Designs, and the PRT." *Psychological Reports,* 13 (1963), 90.
Weinstein, I. P. "The Recall of Memories as a Function of Repressing and Sensitizing Defenses and Body Position." Unpublished doctoral dissertation, Michigan State University, 1966.
Weinstock, A. R. "Family Environment and the Development of Defense and Coping Mechanisms." *Journal of Personality and Social Psychology,* 5 (1967), 67–75.
Weintraub, W., and Aronson, H. "The Application of Verbal Behavior Analysis to the Study of Psychological Defense Mechanisms: Methodology and Preliminary Report." *Journal of Nervous and Mental Disease,* 134 (1962), 169–181.
———. "The Application of Verbal Behavior Analysis to the Study of Psychological Defense Mechanisms: IV: Speech Pattern Associated with Depressive Behavior."
———. *Journal of Nervous and Mental Disease,* 144 (1967), 22–28.
———. "A Survey of Patients in Classical Psychoanalysis: Some Vital Statistics." *Journal of Nervous and Mental Disease,* 146 (1968), 98–102.
———. "Application of Verbal Behavior Analysis to the Study of Psychological Defense Mechanisms: V. Speech Pattern Associated with Overeating." *Archives of General Psychiatry,* 21 (1969) 739–744.
———. "Is Classical Psychoanalysis a Dangerous Procedure?" *Journal of Nervous and Mental Disease,* 149 (1969b), 224–228.
Weiss, L. "Effects of Subject, Experimenter and Task Variables on Compliance with the Experimenter's Expectations." *Journal of Projective Techniques and Personality Assessment,* 33 (1969), 247–256.
Weiss, L., and Masling, J. "Further Validation of a Rorschach Measure of Oral Imagery: A Study of Six Clinical Groups." *Journal of Abnormal Psychology,* 76 (1970), 83–87.
Weiss, S. L. "Perceived Effectiveness of Psychotherapy: a Function of Suggestion?" *Journal of Consulting and Clinical Psychology,* 39 (1972), 156–159.
Weissman, H. N., Goldschmid, M. L., and Stein, D. D. "Psychotherapeutic Orientation and

Training: Their Relation to the Practices of Clinical Psychologists." *Journal of Consulting and Clinical Psychology,* 37 (1971), 31–37.

Weitzman, B. "Behavior Therapy and Psychotherapy." *Psychological Review,* 74 (1967), 300–317.

Welkowitz, J., Cohenm, J., and Ortmeyer, D. "Value System Similarity: Investigation of Patient-Therapist Dyads." *Journal of Consulting Psychology,* 31 (1967), 48–55.

Wells, W. D., and Goldstein, R. L. "Sears' Study of Projection: Replications and Critique." *Journal of Social Psychology,* 64 (1964), 169–179.

Wernimont, P. F., and Fitzpatrick, S. "The Meaning of Money." *Journal of Applied Psychology,* 56 (1972), 218–226.

Werry, J. S. "The Conditioning Treatment of Enuresis." *American Journal of Psychiatry,* 123 (1966), 226–229.

West, D. J. "Parental Figures in the Genesis of Male Homosexuality." *International Journal of Social Psychiatry,* 5 (1959–60), 85–97.

Wheeler, W. M. "An Analysis of Rorschach Indices of Male Homosexuality." *Journal of Projective Techniques and Rorschach Research Exchange,* 13 (1949), 97–126.

Whitaker, L., Jr. "The Use of an Extended Draw-a-Person Test to Identify Homosexual and Effeminate Men." *Journal of Consulting Psychology,* 25 (1961), 482–485.

Whitehorn, J. C., and Betz, B. J. "A Study of Psychotherapeutic Relationships between Physicians and Schizophrenic Patients." *American Journal of Psychiatry,* 111 (1954), 321–331.

______. "A Comparison of Psychotherapeutic Relationships between Physicians and Schizophrenic Patients when Insulin is Combined with Psychotherapy and When Psychotherapy Is Used Alone." *American Journal of Psychiatry,* 113 (1957), 901–910.

______. "Further Studies of the Doctor as a Crucial Variable in the Outcome of Treatment with Schizophrenic Patients." *American Journal of Psychiatry,* 117 (1960), 215–223.

Whitener, R. W., and Nikelly, A. "Sexual Deviation in College Students." *American Journal of Orthopsychiatry,* 34 (1964), 486–492.

Whiting, B. B. "Sex Identity Conflict and Physical Violence: A Comparative Study." *American Anthropologist,* 67 (1965), 123–140.

Whiting, J. W. "Sorcery, Sin, and the Superego: A Cross-Cultural Study of Some Mechanisms of Social Control." In M. R. Jones, ed., *Nebraska Symposium on Motivation.* Lincoln, Nebr.: University of Nebraska, 1959, pp. 174–195.

______. "Socialization Process and Personality." In F. L. Hsu, ed., *Psychological Anthropology.* Homewood, Illinois: Dorsey, 1961, pp. 355–380.

Whiting, J. W., and Child, I. L. *Child Training and Personality: A Cross-Cultural Study.* New Haven: Yale University, 1953.

Whiting, J. W., Child, I. L., Lambert, W. W., Fischer, A. M., Fischer, J. L., Nydegger, C., Hydegger, W., Maretzki, H., Maretzki, T., Minturn, L., Romney, A. K., and Romney, R. *Field Guide for a Study of Socialization.* New York: Wiley, 1966.

Whitman, R. M. "Remembering and Forgetting Dreams in Psychoanalysis." *Journal of the American Psychoanalytic Association,* 11 (1963), 752–774.

Whitman, R. M., Kramer, M., and Baldridge, A. B. "Which Dream Does the Patient Tell?" *Archives of General Psychiatry,* 8 (1963), 277–282.

______. "Experimental Study of Supervision of Psychotherapy." *Archives of General Psychiatry,* 9 (1963), 529–535.

Whitman, R. M., Kramer, M., Ornstein, P. H., and Baldridge, B. J. "The Physiology, Psychology and Utilization of Dreams." *American Journal of Psychiatry,* 124 (1967), 287–302.

Whitman, R., Ornstein, P. H., and Baldridge, B. J. "An Experimental Approach to the Psychoanalytic Theory of Dreams and Conflicts." *Comprehensive Psychiatry,* 5 (1964), 349–363.

Whitman, R. M., Pierce, C. M., and Maas, J. W. "Drugs and Dreams." In L. Uhr and J. G. Miller, eds., *Drugs and Behavior.* New York: Wiley, 1960, pp. 591–595.

Whitman, R. M., Pierce, C. M., Maas, J. W., and Baldridge, B. J. "Drugs and Dreams: II. Imipramine and Prochlorperazine." *Comprehensive Psychiatry,* 2 (1961), 219–226.

______. "The Dreams of the Experimental Subject." *Journal of Nervous and Mental Disease,* 134 (1962), 431–439.

Wideman, G. H. "Survey of Psychoanalytic Literature on Overt Male Homosexuality." *Journal of the American Psychoanalytic Association,* 10 (1962), 386–409.
Wiener, D. N. "The Effect of Arbitrary Termination on Return to Psychotherapy." *Journal of Clinical Psychology,* 15 (1959), 335–338.
Wiener, G. "Neurotic Depressives and Alcoholics: Oral Rorschach Percepts." *Journal of Projective Techniques,* 20 (1956), 435–455.
Wild, C. "Creativity and Adaptive Regression." *Journal of Personality and Social Psychology,* 2 (1965), 161–169.
Wilkins, W. "Desensitization: Social and Cognitive Factors Underlying the Effectiveness of Wolpe's Procedure." *Psychological Bulletin,* 76 (1971), 311–317.
———. "Psychoanalytic and Behavioristic Approaches toward Depression: A Synthesis?" *American Journal of Psychiatry,* 128 (1971), 358–359.
Wilkinson, F. R., and Cargill, D. W. "Repression Elicited by Story Material Based on the Oedipus Complex." *Journal of Social Psychology,* 42 (1955), 209–214.
Willis, J. H., and Bannister, D. "The Diagnosis and Treatment of Schizophrenia: A Questionnaire Study of Psychiatric Opinion." *British Journal of Psychiatry,* 111 (1965), 1165–1171.
Wilson, A., and Smith, F. J. "Counterconditioning Therapy Using Free Association: A Pilot Study." *Journal of Abnormal Psychology,* 73 (1968), 474–478.
Wilson, G. D., ed. *The Psychology of Conservatism.* New York: Academic, 1973.
Wilson, W. P., and Zung, W. W. "Attention, Discrimination, and Arousal during Sleep. *Archives of General Psychiatry,* 15 (1966), 523–528.
Winch, R. F. "The Relation between Courtship Behavior and Attitudes towards Parents among College Men." *American Sociological Review,* 8 (1943), 164–174.
———. "Interrelations between Certain Social Background and Parent-Son Factors in a Study of Courtship among College Men." *American Sociological Review,* 11 (1946), 333–343.
———. "Primary Factors in a Study of Courtship." *American Sociological Review,* 12 (1947), 658–666.
———. "The Relation between the Loss of a Parent and Progress in Courtship." *Journal of Social Psychology,* 29 (1949), 51–56.
———. "Courtship in College Women." *American Journal of Sociology,* 55 (1949–50), 269–278.
———. "Some Data Bearing on the Oedipus Hypothesis." *Journal of Abnormal and Social Psychology,* 45 (1950), 481–489.
———. "Further Data and Observations on the Oedipus Hypothesis: The Consequence of an Inadequate Hypothesis." *American Sociological Review,* 16 (1951), 784–795.
Winget, C., and Kapp, F. T. "The Relationship of the Manifest Content of Dreams to Duration of Childbirth in Primiparae." *Psychosomatic Medicine,* 34 (1972), 313–320.
Winget, C., Kramer, M., and Whitman, R. "The Relationship of Socio-economic Status and Race to Dream Content." Sleep Study Abstracts. *Psychophysiology,* 7 (1970), 325–326.
Winokur, G., Guze, S. B., and Pfeiffer, E. "Developmental and Sexual Factors in Women: A Comparison between Control, Neurotic and Psychotic Groups." *American Journal of Psychiatry,* 115 (1959), 1097–1100.
Winter, S. K. "Characteristics of Fantasy While Nursing." *Journal of Personality,* 37 (1969), 58–72.
Winter, W. D., and Prescott, J. W. "A Cross Validation of Starer's Test of Cultural Symbolism." *Journal of Consulting Psychology,* 21 (1957), 22.
Wiseman, R. J., and Reyher, J. "Hypnotically Induced Dreams Using the Rorschach Inkblots as Stimuli: A Test of Freud's Theory of Dreams." *Journal of Personality and Social Psychology,* 27 (1973), 329–336.
Wispe, L. G., and Parloff, M. B. "Impact of Psychotherapy on the Productivity of Psychologists." *Journal of Abnormal Psychology,* 70 (1965), 188–193.
Witkin, H. A. "Influencing Dream Content." In M. Kramer, ed., *Dream Psychology and the New Biology of Dreaming.* Springfield, Ill.: Charles C. Thomas (1969), pp. 285–343.
Witkin, H. A., Dyk, A. B., Faterson, H. F., Goodenough, D. R., and Karp, S. A. *Psychological Differentiation.* New York: Wiley, 1962.
Witkin, H. A., Lewis, H. B., Hertzman, M., Meissner, P., Machover, K., and Wapner, S. *Personality Through Perception.* New York: Harper and Brothers, 1954.

Wittenborn, J. R. "A Study of Adoptive Children." *Psychological Monographs,* 70 (1956), No. 408.

Wittkower, E. D., and Naiman, J. "Psychoanalysis in International Perspective." *British Journal of Medical Psychology,* 46 (1973), 97–103.

Wolf, A. P. "Childhood Association, Sexual Attraction, and the Incest Taboo: A Chinese Case." *American Anthropologist,* 68 (1966), 883–898.

Wolf, E. "Learning Theory and Psychoanalysis." *British Journal of Medical Psychology,* 39 (1966), 1–10.

Wolff, W. "Fact and Value in Psychotherapy." *American Journal of Psychotherapy,* 8 (1954), 466–486.

Wolfman, C., and Friedman, J. "A Symptom and Its Symbolic Representation in Earliest Memories." *Journal of Clinical Psychology,* 20 (1964), 442–444.

Wolman, B. B. "Evidence in Psychoanalytic Research." *Journal of the American Psychoanalytic Association,* 12 (1964), 717–733.

______. "Interactional Psychotherapy with Schizophrenics." *Psychotherapy: Theory, Research and Practice,* 3 (1966), 61–70.

Wolman, R. N. "Early Recollections and the Preception of Others: A Study of Delinquent Adolescents." *Journal of Genetic Psychology,* 116 (1970), 157–163.

Wolowitz, H. M. "Food Preferences as an Index of Orality." *Journal of Abnormal Psychology,* 69 (1964), 650–654.

______. "Attraction and Aversion to Power: A Psychoanalytic Conflict Theory of Homosexuality in Male Paranoids." *Journal of Abnormal Psychology,* 70 (1965), 360–370.

______. "Oral Involvement in Peptic Ulcer." *Journal of Consulting Psychology,* 31 (1967), 418–419.

Wolowitz, H. M., and Barker, M. J. "Alcoholism and Oral Passivity." *Quarterly Journal of Studies on Alcohol,* 29 (1968), 592–597.

Wolowitz, H. M., and Shorkey, C. "Power Themes in the TAT Stories of Paranoid Schizophrenic Males." *Journal of Projective Techniques and Personality Assessment,* 30 (1966), 591–596.

______. "Power Motivation in Male Paranoid Children." *Psychiatry: Journal for the Study of Interpersonal Processes,* 32 (1969), 459–466.

Wolowitz, H. M., and Wagonfeld, S. "Oral Derivatives in the Food Preferences of Peptic Ulcer Patients: An Experimental Test of Alexander's Psychoanalytic Hypothesis." *Journal of Nervous and Mental Disease,* 146 (1968), 18–23.

Wolpe, J. "The Prognosis in Unpsychoanalysed Recovery from Neurosis." *American Journal of Psychiatry,* 118 (1961), 35–39.

______. "Discussion of Experimental Studies in Desensitization." In J. Wolpe, A. Salter, and L. J. Reyna, eds., *The Conditioning Therapies.* New York: Holt, Rinehart and Winston, 1964, pp. 50–53.

Wolpe, J., and Rachman, S. "Psychoanalytic 'Evidence': A Critique Based on Freud's Case of Little Hans." *Journal of Nervous and Mental Disease,* 130 (1960), 135–148.

Wolpert, E. A. "Studies in Psychophysiology of Dreams: II. An Electromyographic Study of Dreaming." *Archives of General Psychiatry,* 2 (1960), 231–241.

______. "Two Classes of Factors Affecting Dream Recall." *Journal of the American Psychoanalytic Association,* 20 (1972), 45–58.

Wood, A. B. "Transference in Client Centered Therapy and in Psychoanalysis." *Journal of Consulting Psychology,* 15 (1951), 72–75.

Woodmansey, A. C. "Emotion and the Motions: An Inquiry into the Causes and Prevention of Functional Disorders of Defection." *British Journal of Medical Psychology,* 40 (1967), 207–223.

Worchel, P. "Anxiety and Repression." *Journal of Abnormal and Social Psychology,* 50 (1955), 201–205.

______. "Catharsis and the Relief of Hostility." *Journal of Abnormal and Social Psychology,* 55 (1957), 238–243.

Worell, L. "The Ring of Punishment: A Theoretical and Experimental Analogue of Repression-Suppression." *Journal of Abnormal Psychology,* 70 (1965), 201–209.

Worthy, M., and Craddick, R. A. "Semantic Differential Investigation of Sexually Symbolic Concepts." *Journal of Projective Techniques and Personality Assessment,* 33 (1969), 78–80.

Yalom, I. D., Houts, P. S., Zinberg, S. M., and Rand, K. H. "Prediction of Improvement in

Group Psychotherapy: An Exploratory Study." *Archives of General Psychiatry,* 17 (1967), 159–168.

Yamahiro, R. S., and Griffith, R. M. "Validity of Two Indices of Sexual Deviancy." *Journal of Clinical Psychology,* 16 (1960), 21–24.

Yamamoto, J., and Goin, M. K. "On the Treatment of the Poor." *American Journal of Psychiatry,* 122 (1965), 267–271.

Yarrow, L. J. "The Relationship between Nutritive Sucking Experiences in Infancy and Non-nutritive Sucking in Childhood." *Journal of Genetic Psychology,* 84 (1954), 149–162.

———. "Maternal Deprivation: Toward an Empirical and Conceptual Re-evaluation." *Psychological Bulletin,* 58 (1961), 459–490.

Yarrow, M. R., Campbell, J. D., and Burton, R. V. *Child Rearing.* San Francisco: Jossey-Bass, 1968.

Yates, A. J. "Symptoms and Symptom Substitution." *Psychological Review,* 65 (1958), 371–374.

Yorke, C. "A Critical Review of Some Psychoanalytic Literature on Drug Addiction." *British Journal of Medical Psychology,* 43 (1970), 141–153.

Young, F. W. "The Function of Male Initiation Ceremonies: A Cross-Cultural Test of an Alternative Hypothesis." *American Journal of Sociology,* 67 (1961–62), 379–391.

———. "Incest Taboos and Social Solidarity." *American Journal of Sociology,* 72 (1966–67), 589–600.

Yulis, S., and Kiesler, D. J. "Countertransference Response as a Function of Therapist Anxiety and Content of Patient Talk." *Journal of Consulting and Clinical Psychology,* 32 (1968), 413–319.

Zacher, A., Greenberg, M. S., and Buckhout, R. "Reactions of Normal and Passive-Depressed Subjects to Injustice in Social Exchange Situations." *Journal of Experimental Research in Personality,* 4 (1970), 228–232.

Zamansky, H. S. "An Investigation of the Psychoanalytic Theory of Paranoid Delusions." *Journal of Personality,* 26 (1958), 410–425.

Zechowy, A. C. "The Influence of Social Class on the Psychodynamics of Obesity." Unpublished doctoral dissertation, State University of New York at Buffalo, 1969.

Zeichner, A. M. "Psychosexual Identification in Paranoid Schizophrenia." *Journal of Projective Techniques,* 19 (1955), 67–77.

Zeigler, H. P. "Displacement Activity and Motivational Theory: A Case Study in the History of Ethology." *Psychological Bulletin,* 61 (1964), 362–376.

Zeller, A. F. "An Experimental Analogue of Repression: I. Historical Summary." *Psychological Bulletin,* 47 (1950), 39–51.

Zetel, E. R. "The Effects of Psychotherapy." *International Journal of Psychiatry,* 1 (1965), 144–150.

Ziegler, F. J., and Imboden, J. B. "Contemporary Conversion Reactions: II. A Conceptual Model." *Archives of General Psychiatry,* 6 (1962), 279–287.

Ziegler, F. J., Imboden, J. B., and Meyer, E. "Contemporary Conversion Reactions: A Clinical Study." *American Journal of Psychiatry,* 116 (1960), 901–910.

Zimet, C. N., and Fine, H. J. "Primary and Secondary Process Thinking in Two Types of Schizophrenia." *Journal of Projective Techniques and Personality Assessment,* 29 (1965), 93–99.

Zimmer, H. "The Roles of Conflict and Internalized Demands in Projection." *Journal of Abnormal and Social Psychology,* 50 (1955), 188–192.

Zimmerman, W. B. "Sleep Mentation and Auditory Awakening Thresholds." *Psychophysiology,* 6 (1970), 540–549.

Zolik, E. S., and Hollon, T. N. "Factors Characteristic of Patients Responsive to Brief Psychotherapy." *American Psychologist,* 15 (1960), 287.

Zubek, J. P., and MacNeil, M. "Perceptual Deprivation Phenomena: Role of the Recumbent Position." *Journal of Abnormal Psychology,* 72 (1967), 147–150.

Zuckerman, M. "Save the Pieces! A Note on 'The Role of the Family in the Development of Psychopathology.' " *Psychological Bulletin,* 66 (1966), 78–80.

Zuk, G. H. "Sex-Appropriate Behavior in Adolescence." *Journal of Genetic Psychology,* 93 (1958), 15–32.

Zung, W. W., Wilson, W. P., and Dodson, W. E. "Effect of Depressive Disorders on Sleep EEG Responses." *Archives of General Psychiatry,* 10 (1964), 439–445.

Name Index

Subject Index

CANISIUS COLLEGE LIBRARY
3 5084 00263 6010

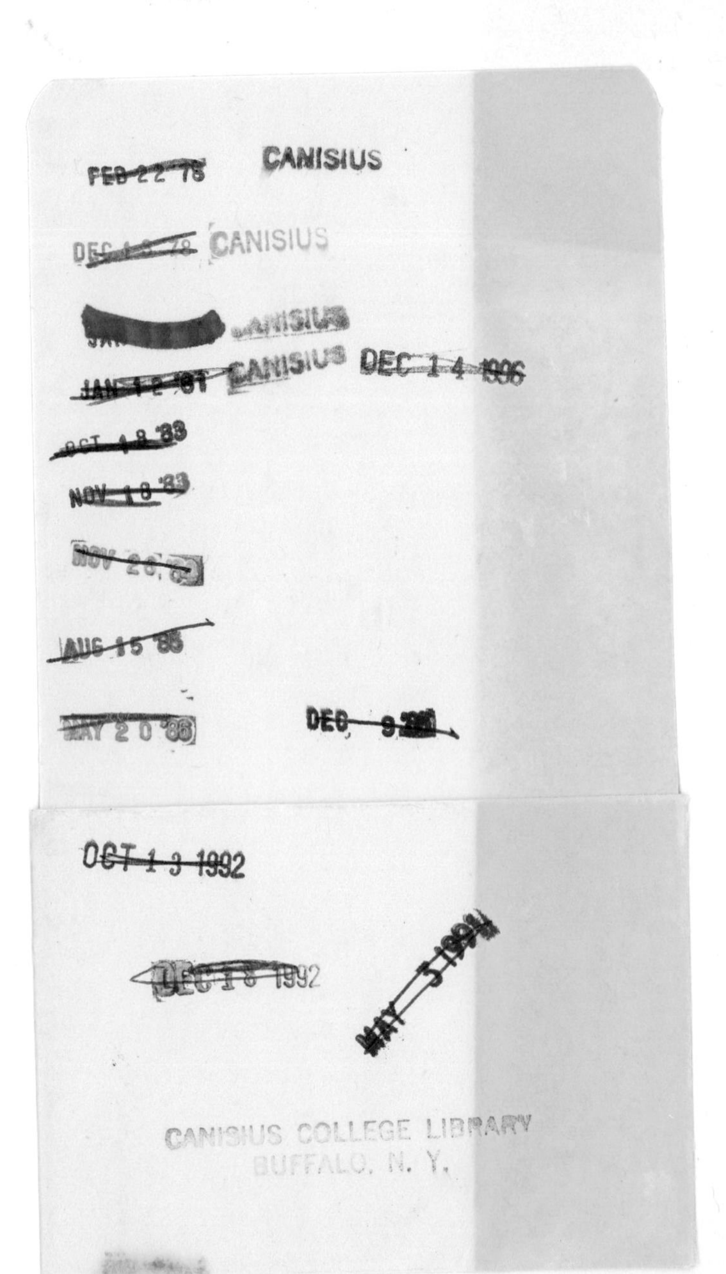
CANISIUS
CANISIUS
CANISIUS
CANISIUS
CANISIUS COLLEGE LIBRARY
BUFFALO, N. Y.